RUSSIA'S EMPIRES

RUSSIA'S EMPIRES

VALERIE A. KIVELSON
AND RONALD GRIGOR SUNY

New York   Oxford
OXFORD UNIVERSITY PRESS

Oxford University Press is a department of the University of Oxford.
It furthers the University's objective of excellence in research, scholarship,
and education by publishing worldwide. Oxford is a registered trade mark
of Oxford University Press in the UK and certain other countries.

Published in the United States of America by
Oxford University Press
198 Madison Avenue, New York, NY 10016,
United States of America.

For titles covered by Section 112 of the US Higher Education
Opportunity Act, please visit www.oup.com/us/he for the
latest information about pricing and alternate formats.

Library of Congress Cataloging-in-Publication Data

Names: Kivelson, Valerie A. (Valerie Ann), author. | Suny, Ronald Grigor,
    author.
Title: Russia's empires / Valerie A. Kivelson and Ronald Suny.
Description: New York, NY : Oxford University Press, 2016. | Includes
    bibliographical references and index.
Identifiers: LCCN 2016039305 (print) | LCCN 2016042966 (ebook) | ISBN
    9780199924394 (pbk. : alk. paper) | ISBN 9780190647629 ()
Subjects: LCSH: Russia--Colonies--History. | Russia--Territorial
    expansion--History. | Russia--Foreign relations. | Imperialism--History.
Classification: LCC DK43 .K53 2016 (print) | LCC DK43 (ebook) | DDC
    327.47--dc23
LC record available at https://lccn.loc.gov/2016039305

9 8 7 6 5 4 3 2 1

Printed by R.R. Donnelley, United States of America

To our daughters, who inspire us and keep us young
Sevan and Anoush
Rebecca, Leila, and Tamar

CONTENTS

List of Maps xi
Preface xiii
Spelling and Dating xvii
About the Authors xviii
Timeline xix

INTRODUCTION   THINKING ABOUT EMPIRE   1
                  Empires   2
                  Russia's Imperial Formations   6

CHAPTER ONE   BEFORE EMPIRE: EARLY RUS
                  VISIONS OF DIVERSITY OF LANDS
                  AND PEOPLES   17
                  Before the State: The Peoples of Rus   18
                  New Models for Understanding Kievan Rus:
                      Stateless Head or Galactic Polity   27
                  Appanage Rus and Further Fragmentation   32
                  Mongol Khans and the Aura of Empire   38

CHAPTER TWO   IMPERIAL BEGINNINGS: MUSCOVY   44
                  Building a State; Claiming an Empire   44
                  Ivan the Terrible: Imperial Principles in Practice   47
                  Muscovite Autocracy: Power and Obligation   52
                  Who Were the Muscovites? What Was Russia?   54
                  The People Speak: The Time of Troubles   57
                  Imperial Conquest and Control   61

CHAPTER THREE   DISRUPTING THE EASY ROAD
                  FROM EMPIRE TO NATION-STATE:
                  A THEORETICAL INTERLUDE   75

Nation, Nationalism, and the Discourse of the
    Nation 78

CHAPTER FOUR   RESPONSIVE RULE AND ITS LIMITS:
                    FORCE AND SENTIMENT IN THE
                    EIGHTEENTH CENTURY 89
                    Succession, Consultation, and the Politics
                        of Affirmation 91
                    The Petrine Revolution and the Imperial State 93
                    Peter's Successors: A Century of Women
                        (and Children) on Top 98

CHAPTER FIVE   RUSSIANS' IDENTITIES IN THE
                    EIGHTEENTH CENTURY: A MULTITUDE
                    OF POSSIBILITIES 116
                    What Does *Russian* Mean? Thinking About Nations in
                        the Eighteenth Century 116
                    A Multiplicity of Nations: The Peoples and Divisions
                        of Empire 121
                    Imperial Expansion in the Eighteenth Century 134

CHAPTER SIX   IMPERIAL RUSSIA IN THE MOMENT
                    OF THE NATION, 1801–1855 140
                    A Kind of Constitution 141
                    Clash of Empires 145
                    Imperial Conservatism 153
                    The Decembrists 154
                    Official Nationality 157
                    The Intelligentsia 161
                    Expansion, Conquest, and Rebellion 166
                    Imagining the Russian "Nation": Between West
                        and East 177

CHAPTER SEVEN   WAR, REFORMS, REVOLT,
                    AND REACTION 183
                    A Foolish War 184
                    The Great Reforms: Nations, Subjects,
                        and Citizens 185
                    Participatory Politics and Categories
                        of Difference 192

Who Are We? More Questions of National
    Identity   194
Russification, Diversity, and Empire   199
"Pacifying" the Peripheries   203
Conquering Central Asia   210
Counter-Reforms and Political
    Polarization   215
Empire and the Revolutionary Movement   220

CHAPTER EIGHT   IMPERIAL ANXIETIES: 1905–1914   227
The Fate of Empires in the Twentieth Century   228
The Modernizing Empire and Its Discontents   234
Imperial Overreach: Tsarist Modernization
    and Expansion   236
The First Revolution, 1905   240
When Nationalism Goes Public: Reimagining
    Empire   249

CHAPTER NINE   CLASH AND COLLAPSE OF EMPIRES:
                    1914–1921   255
The Great War   255
Nationality and Class Across the Revolutionary
    Divide   266
Soviet Power   275
Soviet Nationality Policies   280

CHAPTER TEN   MAKING NATIONS, SOVIET-STYLE:
                    1921–1953   290
The Stalin Years, 1928–1953   295
Beating Peasants into Submission   299
Empire-State and State of Nations   301
Building National Bolshevism   309
From Hot War to Cold War: External Empire as
    Defensive Expansion   311
Cold War at Home: The Internal Empire   317
Soviet Discursive Power   323

CHAPTER ELEVEN   IMPERIAL IMPASSES: REFORM,
                    REACTION, REVOLUTION   329
Policy and Experience: Friendship
    of the Peoples   334
A Strange Empire   337

The Soviet Union in the World   340
Stagnation   344
Gorbachev and the Test of Perestroika   349

CHAPTER TWELVE   THE END OF EMPIRE, 1991–2016 . . .
                      OR NOT?   364
                      Vladimir Putin and the Rebuilding
                          of the State   368
                      Democratic Recession in the Post-Soviet
                          States   376
                      Post-Superpower Russia and NATO
                          Expansion   381
                      Red Lines in the Near Abroad: Georgia
                          and Ukraine   385

                      CONCLUSION   394
                      Credits   403
                      Index   405

LIST OF MAPS

Map 1.1   Early Rus

Map 1.2   Rus principalities

Map 1.3   The Mongol Empire

Map 1.4   Tatar khanates

Map 2.1   The expansion of the Russian Empire

Map 5.1   Partitions of Poland

Map 6.1   Napoleonic Europe

Map 6.2   Russian expansion in the Caucasus

Map 7.1   Crimean War, 1853–1856

Map 7.2   Ethnic groups in the Russian Empire

Map 7.3   Territorial changes after the Russo-Turkish War
of 1877–1878

Map 7.4   Pogroms against Jews, 1871–1906

Map 7.5   Russian imperial expansion in Central Asia, 1795–1914

Map 8.1   Europe, North Africa, and the Middle East in 1914 and 1919

Map 8.2   Decolonization, 1945–2016

Map 8.3   Demonstrations, strikes, disturbances, 1905–1907

Map 9.1   The Eastern Front and losses from the Treaty
of Brest-Litovsk

Map 9.2   Transcaucasia, 1918–1921

Map 9.3   The Russian Civil War, 1917–1922

Map 10.1   Ethnic groups of the South Caucasus

Map 10.2   Deportations and resettlements in the Soviet Union,
1941–1953

Map 10.3   Europe during the Cold War, 1945–1991

Map 11.1   The Nagorno-Karabakh War

Map 11.2   Results of the March 17, 1991 Referendum on the Future of
           the Soviet Union
Map 11.3   The breakup of the Soviet Union
Map 12.1   NATO expansion and Russia's Near Abroad
Map 12.2   The Russo-Georgian War of 2008
Map 12.3   The struggle for Ukraine

PREFACE

Russia's Empires is the product of twenty-six years of conversation and debate about interpretations of history across the modern/premodern divide. Our shared love of Russia and its often depressing, endlessly fascinating history has provided a focus for ongoing discussions of big, theoretical questions. The central puzzle that we have confronted together has to do with understanding the meaning of political mobilization and engagement in non-democratic polities. The concept of "the nation" lies at the heart of our investigation. In the last decades of the twentieth century, theorists of the nation, Ronald Suny among them, demonstrated that the idea of a "nation" as a group of people conceived of as homogeneous, equal, and sovereign, was a modern and Western one. Not a timeless, organic fact, the idea of the nation as bearer of political sovereignty was instead symptomatic of a particular historical moment. Whatever political solidarities preexisted that late-eighteenth/early-nineteenth-century development, they were not the same as this modern Nation. As an early modernist, Valerie Kivelson has been concerned with figuring out precisely what came before or how to understand the many alternative forms of political affiliation and mobilization that might antedate, rival, or coexist with the national. Sometimes, premodern alternatives look a good deal like modern national solutions, and can defy neat categorization. These were the places where the two of us often disagreed in our interpretations and where our liveliest discussions ensued. We came to understand that some theorists who brought us their insights about the nation as a modern construct often threw the baby out with the bathwater, failing to notice earlier "national" formations, collective identifications of ethnic and religious peoples, and insisting that such constructions could only happen in the wake of the French Revolution or in an era of Romantic fervor.

Entertaining as our two-sided debates were, we realized that these questions demanded more rigorous investigation. In efforts to work through these issues, we taught several courses together over the years. No doubt we confused our students with our divergent opinions, but we learned greatly from them, and we build on many of their insights in the pages that follow. We are convinced that even though they and we might still be somewhat confused, we are now confused on a much higher level.

The classroom conversations helped us realize that the framework of the nation, although our initial point of departure, would not suffice to cover the dimensions of Russian history of most interest to us. Empire, instead, served far better to illuminate the long history of Russia. With the framework of empire, we were able to escape the endlessly looping debate over whether Russians did or did not develop a sense of themselves as part of a nation, and if so, when. Instead, using the concept of empire, we were able to study precisely the issues most interesting to us: the ways that ordinary people imagined their position within a non-democratic polity—whether the Muscovite tsardom or the Soviet Union—and what concessions the rulers had to make, or appear to make, in order to establish their authority and preserve their rule.

We are not the first to apply the concept of empire to the study of Russian history, but we believe that our story does something unique. First, our book tackles the long stretch of the history of the region, from the murkiest beginnings to its most recent yesterday, and follows the vicissitudes of empire, the absence, the coalescence, the setbacks of imperial aspirations, across the centuries. We do not impose the category, but find it a productive lens for tracking developments over time. Second, the framework of empire allows us to address pressing questions of how various forms of non-democratic governance managed to succeed and survive, or, alternatively, what caused them to collapse and disappear. Studying Russia's long history in an imperial guise pressures us to attend to forms of inclusion, displays of reciprocity, and manifestations of ideology that might otherwise go unnoted, overlooked under the bleak record of coercion and oppression that so often characterizes ideas about Russia.

People have often asked us how we managed the business of coauthoring this book. The natural assumption would be that Valerie Kivelson wrote the early chapters and Ronald Suny the later ones. That assumption would be wrong. In fact, Ron wrote the first draft of the entire book, on the basis of our conversations and lecture notes. (Thank you, Ron!) Working from that draft, Valerie critically questioned, reworked, and revised, introducing new sections and removing others. (Thank you, Val!) Together we rethought the argument and rewrote just about every word. We have exchanged so many versions that we have completely lost track of who wrote what and can confidently claim that every chapter is completely coauthored.

We have greatly enjoyed the process of writing this book together, and we hope that readers will enjoy it as well. We offer it as what we call a "non-textbook," that is, an interpretive essay or an analytical survey rather than a comprehensive compendium of important people and events. Our hope is that the argument will engage readers regardless of their level of familiarity with the material, while accessible writing and definitions of terms will remove barriers for those new to the field. We have aimed throughout for intellectual coherence over coverage, and we have kept our questions about empire, diversity, reciprocity, and solidarity constantly in view.

Along the way, our students and colleagues have inspired and taught us. They pushed us to explore new angles, to read more widely, to consider alternative possibilities. We would like to thank them each individually, but given the two and a half decades of gestation of this work, our debts of gratitude have surpassed the listing capacity of a brief preface. Since this is in many ways a book about collectivities, we will fall back on collective thanks to the students in our co-taught classes: Absolutism and Dictatorship; Empires in History; Russia's Empires; and Russia Under the Tsars. We need to acknowledge the generosity of the History Department at the University of Michigan in indulging our wish to teach together so many times. We thank countless Michigan colleagues for their help and ideas, among others: Victor Lieberman, Olga Maiorova, Douglas Northrop, Jeffrey Veidlinger, Geoff Eley, Susan Juster, and, outside the University of Michigan: Lewis Siegelbaum, Jane Burbank, Frederick Cooper, Aleksandr Semyonov, Donald Ostrowski, Nancy Shields Kollmann, Paul Bushkovitch, Ernest Zitser, Louise McReynolds, and Serhii Plokhy.

Charles Cavaliere at Oxford University Press has been a marvel of enthusiasm, encouragement, and generosity in shepherding this book through to completion. The impressive and capable team at the Press has been a joy to work with. Sara Birmingham, Francelle Carapetyan, and Roxanne Klaas have generously devoted their time to this project, and their efforts have improved the clarity and secured the illustrations for the book. Charles rounded up a daunting list of reviewers for the project, first at the initial stage as a proposal and then again as readers for the final manuscript. Our sincere thanks to all the reviewers of *Russia's Empires:*

Jane Burbank, New York University
Andrew Jenks, California State University, Long Beach
Austin Jersild, Old Dominion University
Shoshana Keller, Hamilton College
Michael Khodarkovsky, Loyola University
Charles King, Georgetown University
Edward J. Lazzerini, Indiana University
Eric Lohr, American University
Elaine MacKinnon, University of West Georgia
Alexander Stephen Morrison, Nazarbayev University
Stephen Norris, Miami University
Matthew Payne, Emory University
David G. Rowley, University of Wisconsin–Platteville
Willard Sunderland, University of Cincinnati
Glennys Young, University of Washington

We especially appreciate the smart, careful, informed readings and substantive suggestions offered by the readers in the final round. Our thanks go to Shoshana Keller, Eric Lohr, Alexander Morrison, and Willard Sunderland. Their generosity with their expertise and their ideas, as well as their time, made this a better book.

We also owe a special thanks to Stephen Norris, whose knowledge of *lubki* proved invaluable in tracking down a few hard to find photographs. We thank Alexi Ehrlich for his smart and insightful reading of the full manuscript. His suggestions contributed greatly to the book. Remaining errors and stubborn clinging to interpretations of course remain our own responsibility.

We also want to thank our families and friends for putting up with our obsessive preoccupation with Russia's empires, a preoccupation that is unlikely to go away any time in the foreseeable future. And we want to assure our readers that even after writing this book together and debating every idea, every word, and every punctuation mark, we remain the best of friends.

SPELLING AND DATING

We have used the Library of Congress transliteration system for Russian and other languages with a few modifications. Familiar names like Trotsky or Dostoevsky have been left in their usual English forms, but most Russian names have been given a Russian form, e.g., Mikhailovskii. Names from other languages have been rendered as close to the original as possible. The soft sign in Russian, usually shown as ', has been left off in words like *Rus* but may appear in footnotes or quotations.

Tsarist Russia and early Soviet Russia used the Julian calendar up to February 1918, which was thirteen days behind the Western Gregorian calendar in the twentieth century, twelve days behind in the nineteenth century. We have used the Russian dating (Julian) but have indicated where Western dating is used before 1918.

ABOUT THE AUTHORS

VALERIE A. KIVELSON (PhD Stanford University) teaches at the University of Michigan, where she is Thomas N. Tentler Collegiate Professor and Arthur F. Thurnau Professor of History. Her publications include *Desperate Magic: The Moral Economy of Witchcraft in Seventeenth-Century Russia; Cartographies of Tsardom: The Land and Its Meanings in Seventeenth-Century Russia*; and *Autocracy in the Provinces: Russian Political Culture and the Gentry in the Seventeenth Century.* She is the editor of *Witchcraft Casebook: Magic in Russia, Poland, and Ukraine, 15th–21st Centuries* [*Russian History/Histoire russe* 40, nos. 3–4 (2013)]; coeditor, with Joan Neuberger, of *Picturing Russia: Explorations in Visual Culture*; and with Robert H. Greene, coeditor of *Orthodox Russia: Studies in Belief and Practice.*

RONALD GRIGOR SUNY is Wiliam H. Sewell Distinguished University Professor of History at the University of Michigan; Emeritus Professor of Political Science and History at the University of Chicago; and Senior Researcher at the National Research University—Higher School of Economics, St. Petersburg, Russia. He is author of *The Baku Commune, 1917–1918; The Making of the Georgian Nation; Looking Toward Ararat: Armenia in Modern History; The Revenge of the Past: Nationalism, Revolution, and the Collapse of the Soviet Union; The Soviet Experiment: Russia, the USSR, and the Successor States; "They Can Live in the Desert But Nowhere Else": A History of the Armenian Genocide*; and coeditor of *A Question of Genocide: Armenians and Turks at the End of the Ottoman Empire.*

TIMELINE

862	Legendary date for founding of Rus state
c. 988	Grand Prince Vladimir of Kiev converts to Christianity
1015	Death of Vladimir
1169	Sack of Kiev by Andrei Bogoliubskii, prince of Vladimir-Suzdal'
1223	Mongol forces appear at River Kalka; Russians defeated
1237–1242	Mongol conquest
1240– c. 1450	Appanage Period
1325	Metropolitan of Kiev and All Rus transfers to Moscow
1380	Battle of Kulikovo Field
1386	Founding of Polish-Lithuanian Union
1437–1439	Greek Orthodox and Roman Catholic churches negotiate a short-lived union
1453	Constantinople falls to Ottoman Turks
1462–1505	Reign of Ivan III
1478	Muscovy defeats Novgorod
1480	Conventional date for end of Tatar domination
1497	Law code Sudebnik issued; updated in 1550

1500

1533–1584	Reign of Ivan IV (the Terrible)
1547	Coronation of Ivan (the Terrible) as tsar
1552	Kazan captured
1556	Asktrakhan defeated
1565–1572	Ivan the Terrible's reign of terror: the Oprichnina
1581–1582	Yermak defeats the khanate of Siberia

1598	Riurikid line dies out with death of Fedor
1598–1605	Boris Gudonov is appointed non-dynastic tsar
1598–1613	Time of Troubles

1600

1605-1606	Reign of the First False Dmitrii
1613	Michael Romanov chosen as new tsar by an Assembly of the Land (Zemskii Sobor)
1648	Uprisings in Moscow and other towns
1654	Annexation of Ukraine ("Little Russia'); beginning of Old Believer schism
1655	Annexation of Vilno ("White Russia")
1667	Patriarch Nikon deposed
1670–1671	Razin Rebellion
1682	Peter assumes throne, with Sophia as regent; First revolt of the streltsy
1685	Founding of Slavo-Greco-Latin Academy in Moscow
1689	Treaty of Nerchinsk with China
1696	Defeat of Azov
1697	Atlasov explores Kamchatka
1697–1698	Peter's visit to the West; revolt of streltsy crushed

1700

1703	Founding of St. Petersburg
1707–1708	Bulavin Rebellion
1700–1721	Great Northern War; defeat of Swedes
1721	Peter assumes title of emperor
1722	Table of Ranks introduced
1725	Death of Peter the Great
1725–1727	Reign of Catherine I
1727–1730	Regin of Peter II
1730	Constitutional Crisis; struggle over terms of succession
1730–1740	Reign of Anna Ivanovna
1740	Succession struggle: Ivan VI; Coup installs Elizabeth Petrovna

1740–1761	Reign of Elizabeth Petrovna
1762	Reign of Peter III; Coup installs Catherine II
1762–1796	Reign of Catherine II (the Great)
1764–1767	Founding of German colonies along the Lower Volga
1767	Peasants forbidden to submit complaints against their landowners
1769–1794	Catherine publishes satirical journals
1772	First Partition of Poland
1773–1775	Pugachev's Rebellion
1774	Treaty of Kuchuk-Kainardji
1785	Catherine issues Charter to the Nobility and Charter to the Towns
1791	Pale of Settlement established
1793	Second Partition of Poland
1795	Third Partition of Poland
1796	Accession of Paul I to the throne

1800

1801	Murder of Paul, accession of Alexander I; eastern Georgia absorbed into the empire
1801–1825	Reign of Alexander I
1803	Free Agriculturalist Law gives serfs the right to purchase their freedom
1806	Conquest of Daghestan and Baku
1807	Treaty of Tilsit between Russia and Napoleon
1808	Invasion of Finland
1809	Annexation of Finland
1812	Napoleon invades Russia
1813–1814	Alexander I pursues Napoleon
1815	Poland fully absorbed into Russia
1816	First military colonies established
1825	Decembrist Revolt
1825–1855	Reign of Nicholas I
1828	Former khanate of Erevan incorporated into the empire
1830–1831	Polish rebellion

1832	Codification of Fundamental Laws; Poland put under military rule
1835	Jews designated as inorodtsy
1853–1856	Crimean War
1855–1881	Reign of Alexander II
1857	Establishment of Secret Committee on the Peasant Question
1859	Surrender of Shamil; conquest of Caucasus completed
1860	Founding of Vladivostok
1861	Tsar issues decree emancipating the serfs
1861–1874	The Great Reforms
1863	Polish rebellion
1864	Trial by jury introduced
1864–1885	Conquest of Central Asia
1867	Alaska sold to the United States
1870	"Ilminskii system" establishes network of missionary schools
1874	Reform of draft makes almost all young males eligible to be called
1877	Congress of Berlin begins
1877–1878	Russo-Turkish War; Treaty of San Stefano imposes harsh terms on Ottomans
1881–1894	Reign of Alexander III
1881	Widespread anti-Jewish pogroms
1894–1917	Reign of Nicholas II
1897	First census

1900

1904–1905	Russo-Japanese War
1905	Revolution and uprisings throughout the empire; "Bloody Sunday" massacre; October Manifesto, establishment of Duma
1907	Nicholas II changes electoral laws to reassert control over Duma
1914–1918	First World War
1914	General Strike in St. Petersburg
1917	February–March: Nicholas II abdicates, Provisional Government set up. October–November: Bolsheviks under V. I. Lenin seize power.
1918	Treaty of Brest-Litovsk

1918–1921	Russian Civil War
1921–1928	New Economic Policy
1922	Union of Soviet Socialist Republics (USSR) founded
1923	Bolsheviks ban all other political parties
1924	Lenin dies
1928–1932	First Five-Year Plan
1928	Stalin consolidates power; rapid industrialization gets under way
1929	Collectivization begins
1932–1933	Massive famine in Ukraine
1933–1937	Second Five-Year Plan
1936–1938	Stalin's Purges; Terror exercised against "enemies of the people"
August 1939	Stalin and Hitler sign a non-aggression pact
September 1939	Stalin and Hitler both invade Poland to begin World War II
June 1941	Germany invades the Soviet Union. September 1941–January 1944: Blockade of Leningrad
August 1942–February 1943	Battle of Stalingrad
July 1943	Battle of Kursk
February 1945	"Big Three," Churchill, Roosevelt and Stalin, meet at Yalta
May 1945	Berlin captured; victory over Germany
1946	Cold War begins
February 1946	Stalin's Supreme Soviet election speech
1946–1947	Re-collectivization of agriculture leads to widespread famine
1948	Communist Party "coup" in Czechoslovakia
March 1953	Stalin dies
September 1953	Nikita Khrushchev becomes First Secretary of the Communist Party of the Soviet Union
1954	Virgin Lands Campaign gets under way
1956	Khrushchev gives "Secret Speech" at the 20th Party Congress, denounces "cult of personality" and begins de-Stalinization

November 1956	Hungarian Revolt crushed by Red Army
June 1957	Khrushchev defeats attempted coup by "Anti-Party Group"
October 1957	Sputnik spacecraft launched
April 1961	Yuri Gagarin becomes the first person in space
August 1961	Berlin Wall erected
October 1962	Cuban Missile Crisis
October 1964	Khrushchev is peacefully removed from power and replaced by Leonid Brezhnev
August 1968	Invasion of Soviet troops ends reformist "Prague Spring" in Czechoslovakia
1975	Soyuz-Apollo space mission; height of détente
1979	Soviet invasion of Afghanistan
Summer 1980	United States boycotts Moscow Summer Olympics
November 1982	Brezhnev dies
1985	Mikhail Gorbachev becomes Soviet leader
February–March 1986	Gorbachev introduces perestroika at the 27th Party Congress
April 1986	Chernobyl nuclear accident
February 1989	Soviet troops fully withdrawn from Afghanistan
March–April 1989	First democratic elections since 1917 held for newly established Congress of People's Deputies
1989	Berlin Wall falls
1990	Lithuania is the first Soviet Republic to declare independence from Moscow
June 1991	Boris Yeltsin elected president of the Russian SFSR
July 1991	Strategic Arms Reduction Treaty (START 1) signed
August 1991	Coup attempt against Gorbachev by Communist hard-liners thwarted
December 1991	Soviet Union dissolved and Gorbachev resigns
1992	Economic Shock Therapy and privatization begins

October 1993	Yeltsin's dissolution of the Russian Supreme Soviet leads to violent clashes
December 1994–August 1996	First Chechen War
August 1999–April 2009	Second Chechen War
August 1999	Vladimir Putin named prime minister
December 1999	Yeltsin resigns and Putin becomes president

2000

March 2000	Putin wins presidential elections
2003	Energy oligarch Mikhail Khodorkovsky arrested for alleged fraud
September 2004	Beslan school seized by Chechen terrorists, killing over 300 people.
October 2006	Dissident reporter Anna Politkovskaya murdered
March 2008	Dmitry Medvedev elected president for a four-year term
August 2008	Russo-Georgian War
April 2010	New START Nuclear Arms Reduction Treaty signed by Russia and the United States
March 2012	Vladimir Putin elected president for a six-year term
February 2014	Russia hosts 2014 Winter Olympics in Sochi
February–May 2014	Russia annexes Crimea, seizing it from Ukraine; Russian forces support pro-Russian separatists in Eastern Ukraine
September 2015	Russian intervention into Syrian civil war begins

RUSSIA'S EMPIRES

THINKING ABOUT EMPIRE

For centuries, Russia has loomed in the imagination of Western observers as an imperial power, an empire ruled by a powerful and autocratic sovereign who holds absolute dominion over subjugated populations. Not long before we completed this book, a popular writer on Russia wrote that "Mr. Putin . . . sees himself in an unbroken tradition of Russian personal leadership and imperial-national power from the czars to today."[1] Journalists and politicians, as well as historians, are often driven by a powerful urge to search the past for enduring patterns that tell us something about our own times and the near future. Historians, in turn, read particular political formations backward and forward through time, discovering roots of later formations in earlier precursors. The shape of the present appears already and always evident in the past, waiting impatiently to be released. In *Russia's Empires,* we are trying something different even though some of the story might sound familiar. The past, we believe, never speaks to the present directly, in unmediated ways. Thinking about the history of Russia in its broad sweep, our interest is to appreciate the otherness of the past and to seek new understandings suggested by the evidence of worlds long gone.

Our book began in conversations between two friends, developed when we taught three courses together, and evolved, ever changing, while jointly writing this text. In *Russia's Empires,* we adopt the analytical framework of "empire," so central to ideas and stereotypes about Russia, to guide our investigation. Our goal is not to presume imperial practices of domination, but rather to test the concept of empire as applied to the long history of the lands that will at various times compose a Russian polity. We aim to see how that heuristic (a fancy word for a teaching device or method) can make us understand Russia in new ways. Reciprocally, those new insights into the complex history of the region pressure us to rethink and carefully define the concept of "empire" itself. This exercise helps us situate historical anomalies, for instance, the destructive reign of Ivan

---

[1]Simon Sebag Montefiore, "Putin's Imperial Adventure in Syria," *New York Times*, October 9, 2015.

the Terrible or the nation-forming enthusiasm of the early Bolsheviks, in meaningful and comparative contexts.

   In *Russia's Empires*, our intention is not to impose categories, whether imperial or other, on the recalcitrant and multifarious past. Rather, the book proposes
that various formations flash on the scene at different times. By looking at their
meanings in context, we appreciate them for what they were at the time rather
than as antecedents or imperfect drafts of things to come. Even the ostensible
object of our study, an elusive entity called Russia, did not appear all at once. The
imperial rubric urges us to question the utility of positing a singular "Russian"
history for the many lands and peoples at times subject to, at times independent
of, and at times, predating, a state called Russia. While acknowledging continuity
across historical periods, we also pay attention to what institutions, discourses
(ways of thinking and speaking), and practices did not survive. The imperial
framework allows us to attend to diffuse modes of political organization and fissiparous forms of power that would not qualify by any rigorous standards as
constituting a state, or even as an empire.

EMPIRES

Empire as a category is unavoidable in thinking about Russian history, yet it has
often been deployed without much serious engagement with the concept's range of
possible meanings. How are we to understand empire? What is the nature of imperialism and imperial rule? Empire is an extraordinarily durable form of government,
running back into the ancient Middle East and Mediterranean worlds, Chinese antiquity, and other state formations in Asia and Eurasia. In our definition we follow
historian Anthony Pagden, who has traced the various meanings attached to empire
in European discourses. In its original meaning in classical times, *imperium*
described the executive authority of Roman magistrates and eventually came to
refer to "non-subordinate power." By the sixteenth century, empire took on the
meaning of a state, the political relationships that held groups of people together in
an extended system, but from Roman times on it already possessed one of the
modern senses of empire as a state exercising control on an immense geographical
scale, an "extended territorial dominion." From Augustus' time, "to claim to be an
imperator was to claim a degree, and eventually a kind of power, denied to mere
kings." Absolute or autocratic rule was identified with empire, along with the idea
that an empire referred to "a diversity of territories under a single authority." These
three meanings—supreme power of the ruler; a vast domain; and diversity of lands
and peoples—clung fast to the idea of empire and survived into modern times. To
Pagden's trifold definition, we add two more: dominion over distinctive, separately
constituted (or imagined to be separate) lands and people; and an unequal distribution of power between center, or metropole, and periphery or colony.
   Emperors were more than kings. Whereas a king ruled a single land or people
(even though the population might be diverse), an emperor ruled over many peoples and lands, often over many princes and even kings, and their power was

supreme, in most cases understood as subordinate only to the divine.[2] Between kings and their people there was some degree of commonality. Kings of England, though they might be descendants of Danes or Germans, were the kings of the English (later of the Britons), a group eventually imagined as a singular entity. The country was made up of what Victor Lieberman calls a "political ethnicity," a people with some shared sense of community, religion, or connection to the dynasty or state.[3] Empire is far more than that—a vast realm of many diverse peoples, perhaps even principalities and kingdoms, emirates and grand duchies. In such a mosaic of countries, peoples, and political forms, solving the problem of shared identity was far more difficult.

While the model of empire in the minds of many European thinkers, from ancient times through the present day, has been the Roman Empire, for Russians in medieval times the most proximate models were the Eastern Roman Empire (Byzantium) and the Mongol Empire established first by Chingis Khan. Eventually Russia became a vast, contiguous, continental empire, like the Chinese, Ottoman, and Austro-Hungarian Empires, and unlike the overseas empires of Britain, the Netherlands, Spain, France, and Portugal. As an "ideal type," that is, an abstract conceptual model, empire can be seen as a kind of state or as a particular form of domination or control that is exercised inequitably and with different forms of domination and different relations of power in each of its multiple constituent subordinated regions. Empires do not aspire to homogeneous rule over integrated populations, but rather to rule through deliberate construction and maintenance of difference and distinction.

Keeping in mind that ideal types are valuable for heuristic purposes but do not exist in their pure form in nature or history, the ideal type of empire, then, is useful as a way of distinguishing different forms of states and ways of governing. Empire is fundamentally different from what eventually emerged as the ideal type of the nation-state. While empire implies inequitable rule over something different, nation-state rule is, at least in theory if not in practice, the same for all members of the nation. In empire, unlike nations, the distance and difference of the rulers was often part of the ideological justification for the superordination of the ruling bodies. The right to rule in empire resides with the ruling people or institutions, not in the consent of the governed. Neither tsarist Russia nor the Soviet Union was an ethnically "Russian Empire" with the metropole completely identified with a ruling Russian nationality. Instead, the ruling institution—tsar and nobility in one case, the Communist Party elite in the other—was multinational, though primarily Russian, and exerted imperial sway over Russian and non-Russian subjects alike.

---

[2] Anthony Pagden, *Lords of All the World: Ideologies of Empire in Spain, Britain, and France, c. 1500–c. 1800* (New Haven and London: Yale University Press, 1995), pp. 12, 15, 16, 27–28. Also fundamental in thinking about empire is Jane Burbank and Frederick Cooper, *Empires in World History: Power and the Politics of Difference* (Princeton, NJ: Princeton University Press, 2010).

[3] Victor B. Lieberman, *Why Was Nationalism European? Political Ethnicity in Southeast Asia and Europe, c. 1400–1850* (Cambridge, MA: Harvard University Press, forthcoming).

Empires by definition face the problem of ruling variegated populations, and are forced to find effective techniques for securing some degree of passivity if not acquiescence from their assorted lands and peoples. They have deployed various approaches. Occasionally they aimed for *assimilation and acculturation*. In the early modern period, this generally took the form of conversion. In more recent times, empires offered often false promises of egalitarian incorporation of the colonized as citizens, raising what Frederick Cooper and Anne Stoler call "the tensions of empire." More often, empires utilized *rule through difference* (that is, cobbling together different regions and peoples, each subject to their own relations with the center), or *delegation* (that is, indirect rule through regional authorities). In extremis, empires have ordered *eradication* (through genocide or deportation). Most empires, Russia among them, resort to all these techniques in various combinations and ratios, but for the Russian Empire, it was differentiation that dominated throughout its history.

The problem of maintaining empire through tolerance of diversity and the production of difference was accompanied by policies and practices that seem to contradict differentiation, that is, the construction of cultural homogeneities that held the disparate elements of empire together. Cultural homogeneities could involve discourses of loyalty to the monarch or state, patriotism or love of the land, affection for the particular landscape, language, or customs of a place. Affection for people and practices close to oneself was not the same as a full-blown commitment to nation, in the sense of a cultural political community that had ambitions of self-rule, autonomy, or statehood. If an empress dressed in an elaborate costume based on peasant wear, that gesture might connote a link with the simple folk but hardly a concession to allow them to rule themselves.

To sum up, in our view empire is a structure of governance that manifests some or all of the following four characteristics: First, it is a polity ruled by a sovereign claiming absolute sovereignty, an autocrat answering to no earthly power. Empires are ruled by a sovereign who often reigns above other rulers and kings, a king of kings. In most cases, second, empire is a polity ruling a vast domain composed of a collection of disparate lands and peoples, generally subjugated through conquest. Third, empire is based on inequitable, hierarchical relations of power between a privileged metropole, that is, the center, and disadvantaged, subordinated peripheries. This, in turn, means that, fourth and, most fundamental, its form of rule is exercised through difference rather than through integration or assimilation. Empire was a polity based on conquest and maintained through the difference between the ruling institution and its subjects, as well as the subordination of periphery to the imperial center. Through conquest and force, the self-rule and/or sovereignty of subjects, peoples, and polities were usurped by imperial centers, and inequitable relationships of superiors ruling over designated inferiors were established.

From its first glimmers in the princedoms of the medieval period through the fall of the Soviet Union, power in its various iterations was built on relations of difference, whether of tribe or language, faith or region, estate, rank, class, gender, or dynasty. Through most of their history, Russian rulers and those they ruled understood membership in the polity as particularized, manifested in different modes, allowing different claims and different obligations according to hierarchies of difference. Only in the final decades of the Old Regime and again in the Soviet era did another, almost contradictory aspect of imperial rule, the supreme, unitary, central command of a sovereign ruler, contest the primacy of rule through difference. In those eras, the centralizing state began to push toward more unified forms of governance and a more homogeneous demographic vision. Even then, however, during periods of conscious if inconsistent Russification, assertions of uniform central power never eclipsed the default presumptions and strategies of differentiation. Through the course of Russian history, we see these very different strands of imperial governance weaving in and around each other, in perpetual motion, sometimes one variant rising to the fore, sometimes another. War and violence both made the Russian Empire and brought it to an end in 1917, when it was replaced by a new state formation with both imperial and national characteristics, the Soviet Union, itself the product of economic and military collapse and revolutionary violence. When one considers square acreage and continuity over time, the Russian Empire was the largest land empire and the most durable in history.

It is hard today to imagine any legitimate polity other than the nation-state. Entities without national bases, such as ISIS, the Islamic State of Iraq and Syria, with its claims to a supranational status as a religiously based "Caliphate," or international cartels and multinational corporations, have no legitimate place in the modern political imagination. Although it still attracts much support, a multi-national organization such as the European Union provokes resistance and hostility precisely on the grounds of its challenge to the autonomy of its constituent nation-states. An aspiring "empire" would seem entirely illegitimate today, and even anachronistic, a throwback in time. In the past, however, as Benedict Anderson reminds us, kingdoms and empires "appeared for most men [*sic*] the only imaginable 'political' system." Old regime states were marked by royal or imperial "high centres" and porous boundaries; "sovereignties faded imperceptibly into one another."[4] Historians have often been in a hurry to brush empires into the dustbin of history, but most states well into the twentieth century remained dynastic realms even as they adopted attributes and attitudes of nation-states. Only gradually and later than many suppose did institutionalized hierarchies and distinctions, codified in the law, give way to the aspirational fiction of equality and homogeneity, also sanctified by law no matter how many differences and gradations remained in the real life of the citizenry.

Rather than see empires as doomed to collapse and inevitably to be replaced by nation-states—a too-familiar trajectory in scholarly and popular literature—or seek the roots of the Russian nation, our book respects the longevity, durability, and flexibility of empires as they met new challenges in a modernizing world. We also consider empire not simply as a descriptive term but one that reveals

---

[4]Benedict Anderson, *Imagined Communities: Reflections on the Origin and Spread of Nationalism* (London: Verso, 1983), p. 19.

basic dynamics of particular polities. Empires are able to do some things precisely because they are empires—inequitable states with relatively porous borders
that incorporate others without assimilating them—but they are constrained
from easily doing other things, like homogenizing and equalizing their diverse
populations, precisely because it is the differences between ruler and ruled, the
superiority of the former and the inferiority of the latter, that justifies and legitimizes the right of the former to rule over the latter.

As we test the utility of the concept of empire, throughout the book we also investigate how empires maintained themselves, how they survived. What kept these
vast states together? And very important, how, if at all, did its rulers maintain an
essential degree of cohesion? For the answers we look not only to institutions and
practices but also to the emotional ties and claims of reciprocity that bound people
to their rulers and to one another. Though empires most often come into being
through war, violence, and conquest, few states in history have ruled exclusively or
for very long through the raw exercise of coercive power alone. Raw force was
never enough to keep and rule the empire. Besides coercive power there is also
what we call discursive power—the theater of power, the symbolics that represent
and legitimize the rule of the few over the many. Over time, governments have
sought to gain legitimacy and authority by convincing subordinated populations
that the rulers have the right to rule and that those being ruled gain some benefits
from the relationship with their imperial overlords. The people ruled had to feel
that they too benefited from the inequitable, often repressive, imperial arrangement, and that the oppressive arrangements were both right and natural. We refer
to this two-way street of paternalistic government and obedience to authority as
"reciprocity," a give-and-take between the powerful and their subjects.

Ordinary people as well as elites had the possibility of opting out of the system,
difficult as that might have been, by rebelling or migrating. But, in spite of the
often brutal subjugation of colonized peoples, many subjects of empires tacitly
accepted that their association with the empire was more beneficial than exploit-
ative. Perception, and often acceptance, of inequitable treatment is an important
part of the imperial relationship. Distinctions, hierarchies, and subordination
were far more frequently the norm through history than were equality and popular empowerment, and these gradations of status and privilege appeared to all
concerned natural, inevitable, and even right. Being colonized might be imposed
externally, but it is often maintained by the internalization of a sense of superiority and inferiority. These kinds of beliefs and emotions leave few concrete traces
in the historical record, but they can make or break an empire, and hence, we
attempt to attend to their faint imprints in the sources.

RUSSIA'S IMPERIAL FORMATIONS

In this book, we offer a brief survey of Russia's history through the lens of empire.
But unlike a conventional textbook that aspires to cover as much as possible all
aspects and events of a national history, this work is an extended historical essay,

an attempt, to tell a particular story of the ways an empire makes itself, rules its peoples, and survives the treacherous threats to its existence. We start with the medieval era, generally known as the period of Kievan Rus, a murky phase of history when none of our standard categories of state, nation, or empire captures the looseness or complexity of people's affiliations or of power relationships. Even appending this history to a narrative of Russia's development proves nettlesome, as Kiev, the center of medieval Rus's political aspirations, is now the capital of Ukraine, a resolutely and distinctly non-Russian state. The terms *Russia* and *Russian* did not yet exist, and the history of the Rus lands links only tenuously with that of the later people and state that we study in this book. When Russians talk about ancient Rus as their historical point of origin, they make a kind of imperial claim on the past and future of lands and people with distinctive histories and, since 1991, independent states: Ukraine, Belarus, and Lithuania. It is a charged act, therefore to begin "Russian history" with the history of medieval Rus. We are fully cognizant of the way that Rus history is rightfully claimed by several present-day nations and of the dangers of retrospective continuity inherent in our decision to begin our study with this contentious past. It was in the medieval era, however, that some of the key defining patterns that would be creatively repurposed in later centuries evolved, and Rus came to figure critically in later Russian historical mythology and memory. Dynastic lineage, religious affiliation, law, architectural models, interactions with the nomads of the steppe, and, most important to our purpose, power relations negotiated and defined through collective distinction, explicit hierarchies, and reciprocity all trace their origins to medieval Rus.

The Kievan period came to an abrupt halt with the Mongol-Tatar invasions of 1237–1240. As a peripheral outpost at the margins of the Chingissids' great continental dominion, Rus came to know and understand the practices of empire.[5] Princes of each of the small Rus principalities negotiated special deals with their steppe overlords, and the hierarchs of the Orthodox Church did the same, winning special legal immunities, fiscal privileges, tax-collection junkets, and military support. Acknowledging the suzerainty of their Tatar emperors or "khans," whom they titled "tsars," the Rus accommodated to imperial structures of rule. After more than two centuries of Tatar domination, the great steppe empires crumbled in the fifteenth century. In the absence of an imperial overlord, the grand princes of Moscow emerged as the functional rulers of the lands of North-East Rus. Their default mode of rule drew on long-familiar patterns and structures. They ruled through differentiated and hierarchically unequal collectivities.

In Muscovy—the Russian state that emerged gradually in the second half of the fifteenth century—grand princes and, later, tsars, consciously took up the imperial mantle. But in addition to touting their own supreme and increasingly sacralized status, they played up their responsiveness to popular desires for order

---

[5]The Chingissids were the ruling dynasty of the Mongol-Tatar empire, and were descendants of Genghis Khan, now usually transliterated as Chingis Khan. In the Russian context, the steppe conquerors are usually called Tatars instead of Mongols.

and justice, for a stern and merciful paternal ruler. Reciprocity among unequals figured in political ideology alongside more predictable concepts of divinely endowed sovereign authority. By the Time of Troubles, the period of breakdown that ushered in the seventeenth century and the Romanov dynasty, this language of reciprocity had been adopted by the tsar's subjects as a mode of confronting the collective inequities of imperial rule. Inflected with this newly empowering notion of reciprocity, popular movements advanced claims based on membership in particular groups. As members of a stratified, differentiated society, they demanded the protections due to their particular status groups. This profound sense of particularism, and stratification as the basis for inclusion in the polity, resonated and harmonized with an essentially imperial form of rule. Russian governance for much of its history (and even today) can be characterized by the wonderfully counterintuitive label of "authoritarianism with the consent of the governed" or "responsive authoritarianism."[6] The consent, of course, was seldom given in free elections but was manifested in cooperation with the authorities or acquiescence in their dominion.

Once it emerged as the most powerful of the Russian principalities, Muscovy made its neighbors nervous and was perceived to be a threat to others. Yet, paradoxically, such a vast state was uniquely vulnerable, from nomads in East and Central Asia and Crimea, and from aspiring rivals to its west. Lithuania posed a particular challenge in the early decades of Muscovite consolidation, and effectively militarized powers such as Poland, Sweden, the Tatars, or the Ottoman or Hapsburg Empires posed ongoing threats in later centuries. Russia was neither consistently aggressive and expansive nor always capable of repulsing assaults from bellicose neighbors. Moreover, its very vastness presented immense problems for governance, communication, and the formation of a sense of shared history and fate. For most of its political existence Russia—and even the Soviet Union—can be thought of, not as a security state, but as an "insecurity state," reacting to multiple exposures, foreign threats, and domestic instabilities.

Under Peter the Great imperial Russia reached the Baltic Sea, founded a new capital, St. Petersburg, on the Finnish Gulf, and became a major force in European diplomacy. With Peter's radical reforms imposed from above, practices of consent and reciprocity within the realm temporarily faded from view in the first quarter of the eighteenth century. In his full-bore drive to recast the political and cultural landscape of Russia, Peter brooked no opposition, and sought no approbation. He

---

[6]We take the first phrase from Maria Lipman et al., "Russia on the Move," Carnegie Endowment for International Peace *Policy Outlook* (June 2012), http://carnegieendowment.org/files/russia_on_ the_move.pdf; and the second from Robert P. Weller, "Responsive Authoritarianism and Blind-Eye Governance in China," in *Socialism Vanquished, Socialism Challenged*, ed. N. Bandelj and D. J. Solinger (Oxford: Oxford University Press, 2012), pp. 83–98. Some attribute the phrase to Francis Fukayama. See also Mary E. Gallagher and Jonathan K. Hanson, "Power Tool or Dull Blade? Resilient Autocracy and the Selectorate Theory," in *Why Communism Did Not Collapse: Understanding Authoritarian Resilience in Asia and Europe*, ed. Martin Dimitrov (Cambridge: Cambridge University Press, 2013), pp. 185–204.

sought no "consent of the governed." After the emperor's death in 1725, however, and throughout the rest of the eighteenth century, the reciprocity imagined by seventeenth-century Muscovites resurfaced, now in a more sentimental guise, among court elites. Notions of the natural condition of difference and differential rights, privileges, and obligations continued to hold sway. In the late eighteenth century, though, in an important and ultimately risky intellectual move, the affective sense of reciprocity that bound elites to their "little mother" ruler, Catherine the Great, was extended downward as well, resulting in a honeyed vision of love and obligation binding elites to their serfs.

This move bore dangerous fruit for the regime in the nineteenth century, when Western ideas of nation turned the saccharine vision of affective bonds between masters and serfs and between Russian overlords and colonial subjects into a new obligation of reciprocity that required not only merciful condescension but liberation. The age-old sense of rule through natural hierarchy was challenged by an emerging sense of equality and sameness. New forms of claim-making, based in growing notions of popular sovereignty, intensified the new understandings of reciprocity. Ideas began to circulate about "nations" as entities legitimated by the sovereign right of their people, rather than by royal dynastic claims or imperial might. Russians and non-Russians alike fiercely contested rival notions of what kind of state Russia was, how Russia was like or not like Western nation-states, and how the imperial form could be reconciled with the national. Intellectual elites debated how to reach the people, how they might teach them or learn from them.

These mobilizing ideas sparked the revolutions of 1905 and 1917, which at least notionally were based on ideas of universal equality and popular participation. Society and state together were to bring prosperity and empowerment to a newly liberated people. Yet concepts of difference—who was to be included in the socialist community and who was to be excluded—reappeared almost immediately after the revolution and continued with devastating effects throughout the Soviet era. Ascribed class status and designated national identities determined people's possibilities in the Soviet Union, and familiar patterns of petitioning to authority for merciful intervention continued. As implausible as it might seem to outside observers, even Stalin and his subjects understood that they stood in a relation of reciprocity, a rough social contract between state and people. Loyalty, obedience, and hard work were expected to be rewarded with favors and privileges, anticipated material well-being, and security; perceived disloyalty or dissent, which could be manufactured against anyone at any time, was brutally punished.

Although we can continue to trace patterns of differential rights and rites of reciprocity in the era of Stalin and beyond, we also detect increasing tendencies toward the centralized sovereignty of our first definition of empire. With the mobility, both voluntary and involuntary, of populations came intermixing, and regions designated by nationality came increasingly to look and speak and interact with institutions of State and Party in much the same ways as those in any other part of the country. Russian became the uniform language of public life, and

Kremlin decrees and Party dictates increasingly applied to all Soviets, not just to some. While inequality of center and periphery undoubtedly continued and the republics and regions retained their status as ethnonational enclaves, both the differentiation and the privilege of the center took on new coloration. We see a rising emphasis on Soviet "imperial" rulers as absolute sovereigns over their lands and peoples, with an ability or at least a claim to command all alike, and the generation of a shared identity of belonging to a common *sovetskii narod* (Soviet people). Class distinctions were declared no longer relevant, and in time removed from the internal passports that all Soviet citizens carried. The multiple strands of our definition of empire here begin not only to compete for preeminence but to contradict one another. Individuals were pulled between their ethnonational identifications, which remained on the passports, and their amalgamation into a generic *sovetskii chelovek* (Soviet person).

The imperious quality of rule—with imperious defined as "domineering, dictatorial, overbearing"—in many ways overshadowed the characteristic of differentiation and rule through lateral distinction. The principal power and privilege differentiations were the vertical ones between the *nomenklatura* (higher party officials), rank-and-file party members, and the rest of the population. Under Stalin and late Soviet regimes, the formal administrative differentiation of republics on

A Soviet passport issued in 1954 in Soviet Ukraine to Vera Eremenko, a forty-eight-year-old woman living in Nikolayev. In response to question 3 on the form, her nationality is listed as "Ukrainian." Under question 5, the passport indicates her social class as "Collective Farm Worker."

ethno-cultural grounds was retained, but with little distinction in modes of governance. What had been envisioned as an egalitarian multinational state in the early Soviet years evolved rapidly into a more centralized imperial formation that we define as "pseudo-federalism." This solution to the problem of governance retained imperial proclivities in its presumption of unquestioned and untrammeled power concentrated in the metropole but steadily set aside rule by distinction in favor of imperious centralization and homogenous enforcement. The more phony the federalism, the more the state appears imperial; the more real the shared distribution of power among legally protected and equal federal units, the more national it appears. The imperial lens here allows us to foreground and interpret particular changes in forms of governance and ways of imagining populations.

The end of the Soviet Union at first replaced a regime based on officially-proclaimed notions of the common good, social equality, and shared obligations with a capitalist society of individual enterprise and differentiated rewards. The social safety net that the Soviets had incompletely erected was shredded, and a free-for-all economy led to general impoverishment cast into sharp relief by the visibility of obscenely rich oligarchs favored by the government. Yet in popular attitudes and even state policies, the idea of reciprocal obligations of the state and the people remained. Society expected aid from the state, and ultimately the state renewed some of the protections that had been embedded in Russian political practices of the past. ↑ generational support of Putin/Rus nationalism

Entering the twenty-first century, the Russian state, as well as the other former Soviet states, now newly independent, looked much more like nation-states than at almost any time in their histories. Empire as a political form seemed historically moribund. Yet the image of Russia as empire, now conceived in the language of *velikaia derzhava* (Great Power), remained a phantom in the imagination of both Russian politicians and many in neighboring states, wary of the behemoth next door. The Russian Federation, we argue, is today an authoritarian multinational state but one with imperial characteristics, a state, like many others in the world, that defies easy categorization.

From Muscovite times Russia exhibited aspects of a "national" community—in the sense of a country and people with a thin coherence and some shared popular and elite ideas about the polity, the realm, and the roles and identities of the people within it—without the connotations and cluster of meanings that would be attached to a modern notion of nation from the late eighteenth century on. We shall elaborate in this book the various senses of collective identity that people in Russia expressed. At the same time, Russia operated within an imperial paradigm of governance—rule by a sovereign and a group of people (the ruling dynasty, the nobility) having the right to rule, sanctioned by reciprocal duties, by service, by God, nature, and physical force. Soviet Russia perpetuated this paradigm of rightful consolidation of power: the Communist vanguard was required to master a singular form of political knowledge. It is precisely these kinds of imperial tendencies, which hindered an easy transition to more democratic forms of governance, that we intend to highlight in this work.

Nation and empire are often defined as antithetical political formations, and Ronald Suny among others has explored the tensions between the two, the ways in which each prevented and undercut the full articulation of the other. These distinctions are clearer when one restricts examination to ideal types than in rough-and-tumble realities that care nothing for the labels of political science. In historical experience, we see the practices of empire working in polities that we would usually characterize as nation-states, and nation-making practices working in polities that look, walk, and smell like empire. Differentiation occurs at times in nation-states, just as homogenization, e.g., Russification, can happen in empires. Should forced assimilation of a minority population into the dominant ethnicity be considered a nationalizing practice, or because force, even violence, is deployed during homogenization, does it not look imperial in its involuntary imposition? Here our layered definition of empire allows us to work within an imperial rubric while understanding the nuances and complexities and without forcing historical messiness into overly neat boxes. Both practices of differentiation and coercive assimilation carry imperial valences, and both have unintentionally produced ethnonational grievances and powerful identification with fellow ethnonationals. In Russia, as in other multinational empires, the nation/empire dichotomy is much more difficult to maintain than in more homogeneously integrated nations of Europe or in transoceanic empires.

Furthermore, we argue that imperial practices constituted the fundamental practices of Russian rule both internally, within what is generally understood as the Russian, potentially "national," core, as well as in the more conventional "colonial" holdings of the ethnically and religiously distinct peripheries. Hierarchical subordination, division, and governance through categories of difference defined the experience of all Russian subjects without exception. Studies of the "colonized," the non-Russian regions of the empire, have tended to focus on particular areas in isolation, set apart from what Ian Campbell calls the "master narrative of Russian history."[7] Textbooks and syllabi reproduce this thematic segregation, recounting the dramatic story of Imperial Russian history as a tale of rise and fall centered on Moscow and St. Petersburg, perhaps with an admixture of Russian provincial life and a bit of Ukraine thrown in, but the rest of the empire is generally addressed in special set-asides, with dedicated chapters on imperial expansion and colonial rule. With this book, we follow a handful of important scholars in taking up the challenge of truly integrating the history of the peripheries with the mainstream history of Russia itself and arguing that in fundamental ways, their histories are indivisible.

As we examine Russia's history through the conceptual framework of empire, we engage frequently with the ideas of other scholars, that is, with the historiography of the field. For students of history, much of the excitement of studying the past comes from the interplay of ideas, the creative rethinking that allows us to

---

[7]Ian Campbell, *Knowledge and the Ends of Empire: Kazak Intermediaries and Russian Rule on the Steppe, 1800-1917* (Ithaca, NY: Cornell University Press, forthcoming).

view the historical record in new and different ways. History does not speak to us in a self-evident way; its lessons are always ambiguous and dependent on the reader's perceptions and reconstructions of the past. We have deliberately made our conversations with other scholars explicit in the pages that follow. We necessarily rely on the work of our colleagues in this synthetic work. We advance our own arguments about Russia's inherently imperial development and we signal when we draw on the work of others and where we wish to differ from their views, whether to disagree, to add to them, or modify them.

Looming large in the landscape of historical scholarship on Russian empire are the synthetic analyses of Andreas Kappeler, Geoffrey Hosking, and Alexander Etkind, along with the comprehensive study of empires by Jane Burbank and Frederick Cooper.[8] In his book, translated from German as *The Russian Empire: A Multi-Ethnic History*, Kappeler emphasizes Russia's reliance on the technique of cooptation of elites into its imperial system by preserving their privileged status. We fully accept the importance of this strategy, and we see it as compatible with the forms of imperial rule that we discuss here, but as only one of several modes of imperial governance used by various Russian regimes. In *Russia: People and Empire, 1552–1917*, Hosking makes a quite different argument. Working from different premises, he is particularly interested in the tensions between empire and nation, that is, between autocratic rule from on high and a more collective form of governance based on the people of the nation, a group united by a shared sense of collective belonging. Hosking highlights the regime's consistent hostility to any form of spontaneous collective action, organization, or demands from below. He underscores the ways that the imperial regime systematically crushed the expression of national solidarity or civic engagement, and viewed the population not as the basis of sovereignty but as resources to be exploited and expended as necessary. We find his picture compelling, and our study confirms many of his findings. Our argument differs from his, however, in several ways. We make the case that the people as a whole always played a more significant role than Hosking allows, and that in many circumstances the regime tacitly or overtly acknowledged that role. More specifically, we emphasize the importance of reciprocity between ruler and ruled that not only added an important veneer of legitimacy to imperial rule but also tied subjects and rulers together in meaningful ways. Furthermore, we find less of a polarized conflict between nation and empire than Hosking and many other scholars describe. Instead, we see a suppler interweaving of the two. The imperial center alternately or even simultaneously fostered, suppressed, and ignored national impulses among its people, and those same people explored modes of assertion, identification, and affiliation that

[8]Andreas Kappeler, *Rußland als Vielvölkerreich. Entstehung, Geschichte, Zerfall* (Munich: Verlag C. H. Beck, 1992); translated into English as *The Russian Empire: A Multi-Ethnic History*, trans. Alfred Clayton (New York: Routledge, 2001); Geoffrey Hosking, *Russia: People and Empire, 1552–1917* (Cambridge, MA: Harvard University Press, 1997); Jane Burbank and Frederick Cooper, *Empires in World History: Power and the Politics of Difference* (Princeton, NJ: Princeton University Press, 2011).

moved in the productive spaces between imperial grandeur and national particularism. Finally, we differ from these two important predecessors in that our study
continually works to braid together the "colonial" pieces of the story, that is, the
study of the imperial peripheries, the focus of Kappeler's book, with the metropolitan story, that is, the study of the centers of power, the subject of Hosking's
work. These, we insist, cannot be told as separate stories, but form a single, mul-
tifaceted narrative.

The cultural and intellectual historian Alexander Etkind has recently characterized Russian imperial practices as a form of "internal colonization."[9] He underscores the parallels between the "internal colonization" of Russia by the
imperial state and of Russian peasants by literate elites and the "external colonization" of the non-Russian regions. We find his formulation thought-provoking,
but again our take is somewhat different. We stress not the parallels or simultane-
ity of two separate imperial arenas but the fundamentally constitutive role of
imperial modes of governance. For most of its history Russian rule was structured imperially. As a differentiated rights regime, it extended its "national" imperial practices to a broad imperial canvas. It had no other form of rule on offer.
Finally, Burbank and Cooper have written a sweeping survey of empires that
emphasizes difference and diversity and how it has been managed in diverse ways
over time. They provide a capacious and useful definition of empire: "Empires are
large political units, expansionist or with a memory of power extended over
space, polities that maintain distinction and hierarchy as they incorporate new
people." The "empire-state declares the non-equivalence of multiple populations."[10]
The book is deliberately iconoclastic and begins by pushing aside the conventional directional narrative of imperial decline and the rise of the nation-state. In
their discussions of the trajectories of various empires, they show that imperial
actors did not give in to what looks to some historians as the inevitable triumph
of the nation-form and the nation-state over archaic imperial forms. Even as late
as the 1940s and 1950s, the British and French Empires were flexibly adjusting to
new pressures and formulating new, more inclusive ideas of federation and confederation, even citizenship. Only when they came to appreciate the costly implications of extending national citizenship in the modern age—the requirement of
providing for the welfare of their populations most particularly—did these
twentieth-century empires dispose of their colonies, even though somewhat reluctantly and with resistance. The costs of holding on, in the face of anti-colonial
movements and the new obligations of citizenship, were too much to bear, and
the age of empires came to an end—or so it seemed.

In their exploration of "repertoires of rule" in the context of "politics of difference," Burbank and Cooper luxuriate in the varieties of empire, yet they explicitly abjure an explanatory theory of empire beyond the management of difference.

---

[9]Alexander Etkind, *Internal Colonization: Russia's Imperial Experience* (Cambridge and Malden,
MA: Polity, 2011).
[10]Burbank and Cooper, *Empires*, p. 8.

We concur with their idea of the centrality of difference, but we aim to add to their description an explanation of the dynamics of empire. We explore what imperial structures and discourses allow empires to do and make them likely to do, and what, because they are empires, they are constrained from doing or even unable to do.

In Russia, as well as in the metropoles of overseas empires like France and England, ideas and practices of imperial rule coincided and often reinforced the sense of national identity. From the sixteenth or seventeenth century on, Russia, England, and France can be said to have been "imperial nations," that is, polities in which the collective identity of rulers and ruled was infused with imperial aims and ambitions. In later centuries, even though nation and empire moved in different directions, one toward homogenization, the other toward differentiation, paradoxically the two processes—nation-making and empire-building—often went on simultaneously, producing tensions, contradictions, and problems of governance along the way.[11] For much of Russia's history Russian political self-identity was tightly tied to its empire, vast in scope, diverse and differentiated in composition, with an emphasis on the need for strong and authoritative rule from above. But many of those in charge also thought seriously about the advantages of a more homogenized population, a more nationalized realm that could be mobilized more easily in times of war as Western European peoples appeared to be. When challenged by the dynamism of nation-states emerging in Western Europe, imperial rulers in the east, Ottoman and Russian among them, attempted to "modernize" their empires through nationalization of the population. Far from accepting the judgment of nationalists that they were anachronisms, these empires worked creatively and persistently to reshape themselves in order to survive and prosper in the modern world. In these "modernizing empires" vulnerable and insecure tsars and Communists envisioned their subjects as constituting a unique, potentially unitary community that even in its diversity might be moved by a singular inspiration. Vladimir Putin responds to and continues much of this legacy, promoting Russia as a Great Power with a strong mixture of exclusivist Russian nationalism and selective and convenient references to history.

Empire has multiple manifestations but it is not a loose, amorphous term that can apply to any and all political formations. We take seriously the interwoven strands that define imperial regimes: supreme power of the ruler; sovereignty over subordinated lesser rulers; a vast domain encompassing a diversity of lands and peoples; unequal distribution of power between center and periphery; and rule through difference. By following these threads, the chapters that follow illuminate the ways that one strand or another comes to the fore at different times, lending its color and texture to the particular cloth of empire. By pulling on these threads individually, we expose both the elasticity of Russia's imperial formations

---

[11]For a fruitful discussion of the mutual constitution of empires and nations, see Krishan Kumar, "Nation-States as Empires, Empires as Nation-States: Two Principles, One Practice?," *Theory and Society* 39, no. 2 (March 2010): 119–43.

and the limits beyond which the fiber of empire would not stretch. It must never be forgotten that imperial, Russian rule clothes itself in widely varying garments: sometimes it is characterized by differentiation and division, sometimes by high-handed centralization and uniformity. No matter what the clothing, it has almost always been worn under an imperial mantle and with traces of the other elements of imperial rule partly visible. With this rigorous and layered definition always in play, this study, we believe, offers new ways of understanding Russia's long and storied history.

BRIEF BIBLIOGRAPHY

Anderson, Benedict. *Imagined Communities: Reflections on the Origin and Spread of Nationalism.* London and New York: Verso, 1983.

Burbank, Jane, and Frederick Cooper. *Empires in World History: Power and the Politics of Difference.* Princeton, NJ: Princeton University Press, 2010.

Burbank, Jane, Mark von Hagen, and Anatolyi Remnev, eds. *Russian Empire: Space, People, Power 1700–1930.* Bloomington: Indiana University Press, 2007.

Etkind, Alexander. *Internal Colonization: Russia's Imperial Experience.* Cambridge and Malden, MA: Polity, 2011.

Gerasimov, Il'ya, Marina Mogil'ner, and Aleksandr Semonov, eds. *Imperiia i natsiia v zerkale istoricheskoi pamiati.* Moscow: Novoe Izdatel'stvo, 2011.

Hosking, Geoffrey A. *Russia: People and Empire, 1552–1917.* Cambridge, MA: Harvard University Press, 1997.

Kappeler, Andreas. *The Russian Empire: A Multi-Ethnic History.* Translated by Alfred Clayton. New York: Routledge, 2001.

Lieven, D. C. B. *Empire: The Russian Empire and Its Rivals.* New Haven, CT: Yale University Press, 2001.

Miller, Alexei, and Alfred J. Rieber, eds. *Imperial Rule.* Budapest: Central European University Press, 2004.

Pagden, Anthony. *Lords of All the World: Ideologies of Empire in Spain, Britain, and France, c. 1500–c. 1800.* New Haven, CT: Yale University Press, 1995.

ONE

Before Empire
Early Rus Visions of Diversity
of Lands and Peoples

The polities of the eastern Slavic lands in their earliest existence were loose networks of leaders, warriors, peasants, tradesmen, and slaves, and only much later, in Muscovite times, could one speak of a state in the classical sense, first formulated by the German sociologist Max Weber, of an institution able to monopolize legitimate violence over a given territory.[1] The earliest histories of the region are legends about the founding of the princely dynasty and tales of the deeds of the ruling princes. Known by the collective name of the Rus, the princely dynasty and the ruling elite eventually came to be identified with the realm and gave their name to the land. Rus was not at first a unified polity but a mafia-like network of merchants and warlords, primarily engaged in capturing the pagan populations of the region for sale in the slave markets of Baghdad and Constantinople and profiting from the other riches of the forests: honey, wax, timber, and, above all, fur. They ranged through territory extending from the Baltic to the Black Sea, and from the lands occupied by Polish and Germanic peoples in the west to the Urals in the east.

Occupying the distant fringes of a world defined by the political might and religious stature of the Byzantine Empire, the Rus did not aspire to rival that shining center or to claim imperial status for themselves. Instead, they gradually built a weak polity based on the same premise that would later constitute the basic building block of empire: the fundamental and rightful differences between

---

[1] Weber wrote: "a state is a human community that (successfully) claims the monopoly of the legitimate use of physical force within a given territory. Note that 'territory' is one of the characteristics of the state. Specifically, at the present time, the right to use physical force is ascribed to other institutions or to individuals only to the extent to which the state permits it. The state is considered the sole source of the 'right' to use violence. Hence, 'politics' for us means striving to share power or striving to influence the distribution of power, either among states or among groups within a state. This corresponds essentially to ordinary usage." Max Weber, "Politics as a Vocation," in *From Max Weber: Essays in Sociology*, trans., ed., and with intro. by H. H. Gerth and C. Wright Mills and new preface by Bryan S. Turner (New York: Routledge, 1948; 1991), p. 78.

..istinct groups of people occupying their own separate lands, differences that could not and should not be erased.

BEFORE THE STATE: THE PEOPLES OF RUS

Archeologists have confirmed descriptions found in medieval historical chronicle accounts of this period of a heterogeneous population scattered throughout the lands of Rus: Baltic and Finno-Ugric peoples, Turkic peoples, and various tribes and assortments of Slavs. Scandinavians entered from the northwest, following the great river routes in search of silver coins from the cosmopolitan centers of Baghdad and then Constantinople. Some of these Scandinavian Vikings, called Varangians in the Rus context, settled in northern Rus, as is evident from the thunderbolt amulets and Norse burial sites that they left behind. The chronicles, the medieval accounts that record the history and prehistory of the Rus, claim that they were invited in to rule the country in the year 862, to bring order to it. The discordant tribes—the Chuds, the Slavs, the Krivichians, and the Ves—purportedly gathered together and "said to themselves, 'Let us seek a prince who may rule over us and judge us according to the Law.' They accordingly went overseas to the Varangian Russes, and appealed to the great Varangian prince Riurik, saying: 'Our land is great and rich, but there is no order in it. Come and rule and reign over us.'"[2]

This story records an event that may well never have happened. It is important, therefore, not for its historical accuracy but for the way it crystalizes the chronicler's sense of the way the world was ordered. The calling of a particular subset of Varangians ("known as Russes, just as some are called Swedes, and others Normans, English, and Gotlanders, for they were thus named"[3]) by the joint decision of other groups of people identified as Chuds, Slavs, Krivichians, and Ves suggests that the chronicle's authors entertained a general picture of the world as a collection of identifiable peoples (in Russian *iazytsi*, literally, tongues, languages). In fact, the primary surviving chronicle, known as the *Tale of Bygone Years* or *The Primary Chronicle*, tips us off to the centrality of this vision of the world in the mental universe of its authors from its opening lines: "After the flood, the sons of Noah divided the earth among them. To the lot of Shem fell the Orient. . . ."[4] Subsequent pages catalog the peoples of the earth and their locations. The world is seen as a collection of naturally distinct human communities, each with its own proper territory. "Certain Slavs settled also on the Dnieper, and were likewise called Polyanians (People of the Field). Still others were named Derevlians (Forest People) because they lived in the forests."[5] Division of the

---

[2]*The Russian Primary Chronicle, Laurentian Text*, translated and edited by Samuel Hazzard Cross and Olgerd P. Sherbowitz-Wetzor (Cambridge, MA: Mediaeval Academy of America, 1973), p. 59; Donald Ostrowski, ed., *Povest' vremenykh let*, http://hudce7.harvard.edu/~ostrowski/pvl/index .html, last consulted February 14, 2016.
[3]*Russian Primary Chronicle*, p. 59.
[4]Ibid., p. 51.
[5]Ibid., p. 53.

world into separate human collectives, each with its own character, habits, and piece of the globe, was a fundamental element in the chroniclers', and maybe their audiences', view of the world. Yet little evidence survives to suggest that these peoples understood themselves as constituting political units or saw any particular connection with a broader realm.[6]

Despite the chronicles' claim about Riurik, there was no founding moment in 862, and no Rus state—and certainly no *Russian* state—was created in that year. The tale highlights and assigns an individual name for the presence of Scandinavians, who had already been coming for over a century to the upper reaches of the Volga River, where they had lived among Slavs and Balts, some passing through en route to Baghdad, others settling, raising families, and cremating their dead in boats in the Viking fashion, leaving telltale signs such as Thor's hammerlets for archeologists to unearth. But they did not found a state. Centuries would pass before a state took shape or an entity called Russia would emerge. The chronicle itself describes a process by which "the Rus land came to be (*otkudu rus'kaia zemlia stala est'*)."[7] Princes and tribes fought among themselves and with their neighbors. They killed some, looted others, and moved on to seek further spoils. They developed productive trade routes and at times made beneficial arrangements with local hunters and farmers to buy, or perhaps to seize, their goods and to transport and sell them.

The tenth-century Byzantine emperor Constantine Porphyrogenitus left a description of their relations with what he labeled their "Slav tributaries," members of tribal groups within the "Slavonic regions," that show these trading relations in a peaceable light. All winter long, he says, the "chiefs together with all the Rus . . . go off on the *poliudie*, which means 'rounds,' that is, to . . . the Slavs who are tributaries of the Rus." Doing the rounds involved collecting furs and other forest products from these tributaries and taking them off for sale or trade in distant markets. On what terms, precisely, the Rus extracted goods from the people of the forest—whether by force, intimidation, or sale—is left unstated, but Porphyrogenitus informs us that these tributaries maintained their overlords through the winter, suggesting that relations were cordial enough that the Rus felt safe wintering among them. Further supporting the idea that there was some kind of sale or exchange involved, the emperor reports that other Slavic tribes carved out single-hulled boats from the trunks of the huge trees that filled the forests, and floated them down the river to the city of Kiev, where they sold them to the Russes.[8] Force was surely also a factor in the surrender of furs and forest

---

[6]See the discussions in Yulia Mikhailova, "Power and Property Relations in Rus and Latin Europe: A Comparative Analysis" (Ph.D. dissertation, University of New Mexico, Albuquerque, 2013), pp. 73, 79–80; and P. S. Stefanovich, *Boiare, otroki, druzhiny: Voenno-politicheskaia elita Rusi v X–XI vv.* (Moscow: Indrik, 2012).

[7]*The Russian Primary Chronicle, 1*; Donald Ostrowski, ed., *Povest' vremenykh let*, p. 1: http://hudce7 .harvard.edu/~ostrowski/pvl/index.html, last consulted February 14, 2016.

[8]Constantine Porphyrogenitus, *De administrando imperio*, ed. Gyula Moravcsik, trans. R. J. H. Jenkins, rev. ed. (Washington, DC: Dumbarton Oaks, 2012), pp. 62–63.

products to the armed warriors of Rus. The chronicle tells of tribute in fur that was imposed on the tribes of the region.

As Porphyrogenitus's descriptions show, there was neither infrastructure nor claim to territory. Rulers built their authority on their personal charisma, armed power, and the loyalty of their retinue (*druzhina*) secured through the generous distribution of plundered goods, attained, in turn, by raids carried out with their retainers. Gradually, however, out of the separate groups and tribes, a few small centers of wealth and power arose, places situated on river routes where they could profit from trade and tribute as well as campaigns of pillage. Of these, Novgorod, situated on the Volkhov River in the northwest, was one of the earliest and wealthiest, and, somewhat later, Kiev was built on the Dnieper River in the south. The two came to form part of a chain of fortified outposts along the rivers of Rus, loosely connected in a dynastic union that looked to Kiev as its nominal center and its prince as the first among equals, the "grand prince." Well positioned to profit from trade with the Muslim east and with Christian Byzantium in the south, with Poles and Hungarians to the west, and through Novgorod, with the Baltic and Central Europe, Kiev and the other Rus towns flourished in the ninth, tenth, and eleventh centuries. Retrospectively, Kiev lent its name to this period in East Slavic history, known as the age of Kievan Rus.

When Grand Prince Vladimir of Kiev converted to Orthodox Christianity around 988, religious ideas quickly suffused notions of legitimate authority. As a newly minted Christian prince, according to the chronicles, Vladimir wrestled with weighty questions about the distribution of authority between him and his Lord. Confused about how all this would work out, he hesitated before punishing evildoers, assuming that they would face divine justice after death. Only when his wise advisers assured him that it was his duty to maintain earthly order did he accept this responsibility. The chronicles tell us further that he took seriously his Christian obligation to feed and care for the poor and defenseless and to uphold the autonomy of the Church in matters spiritual. He won the privilege of marrying into the Byzantine imperial line, rare and perhaps unprecedented for a newly converted pagan, and he used Christianity to consolidate his princely power. Yet Vladimir was not so arrogant as to equate himself with the Byzantine emperor and remained a *Velikii kniaz'* (Grand Prince). Neither he nor his heirs adopted "regalia in the sense of divinely charged instruments of sovereignty bestowed on a ruler in an ecclesiastical inauguration ritual definitively and irrevocably transforming his status."[9] Their rule was princely, validated by the assent of their military retinues, their fellow princes, and the townspeople of their urban centers, and backed by force.

---

[9]Jonathan Shepard, "Rus'," in *Christianization and the Rise of Christian Monarchy: Scandinavia, Central Europe and Rus' c. 900–1200,* edited by Nora Berend (Cambridge: Cambridge University Press, 2006), pp. 394–95. Christian Raffensperger argues that the word *kniaz',* here translated as "prince" in accord with common practice, would be more accurately translated as "king." "The Lost Kingdom of Rus': A Challenge to the Traditional Translation of *Kniaz',*" talk presented at the Association for Slavic, East European, and Eurasian Studies, Boston, November 21–24, 2013.

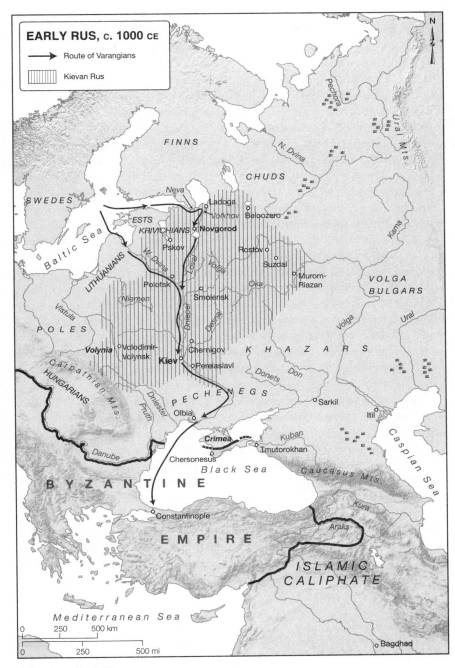

EARLY RUS, c. 1000 CE

→ Route of Varangians

|||||| Kievan Rus

N

FINNS

CHUDS

Pechora

Ural Mts.

N. Dvina

SWEDES

Neva

Ladoga

Volkhov

Beloozero

Kama

ESTS

KRIVICHIANS

Novgorod

Baltic Sea

Pskov

Rostov

Lovat

Volga

Suzdal

Murom-
Riazan

VOLGA
BULGARS

LITHUANIANS

W. Dvina

Polotsk

Niemen

Smolensk

Oka

Ural

Vistula

Dnieper

Desna

Volga

POLES

Volynia

Volodimir-
Volynsk

Kiev

Chernigov

K H A Z A R S

Pereiaslavl

Donets

Don

Carpathian Mts.

HUNGARIANS

Dniester

PECHENEGS

Sarkil

Pruth

Olbia

Itil

Danube

Crimea

Kuban

Tmutorokhan

Caspian Sea

Chersonesus

Black Sea

Caucasus Mts.

B Y Z A N T I N E

Kura

Constantinople

Araks

E M P I R E

ISLAMIC
CALIPHATE

Mediterranean Sea

0   250   500 km

0   250   500 mi

Bagdhad

Map 1.1. Early Rus.

21

When Vladimir died in 1015, no clear custom or system dictated who should succeed him. Rus observed no tradition of primogeniture (the practice of having the eldest son succeed his father), and in any case, no clear age sequence was evident among his many sons by many simultaneous and overlapping (pre-Christian) wives. In the absence of clarity, his sons fought for his crown. That the prize should go to one of his sons seems to have been little disputed. By this time, political legitimacy was based largely on dynastic claims. The chronicle presumes the importance of dynastic ties, and projects it back into the earliest centuries of Rus. In its account of the legendary conquest of Kiev by Rus warriors in the early 880s, it describes how Oleg, a kinsman of Riurik, came to the city and deposed the local leaders, saying dismissively, "You are not princes nor even of princely stock, but I am of princely birth."[10] "Princely stock," then, was understood by the chroniclers as a prerequisite for rulership.

Within the dynastic clan, however, primacy was often determined by murder, fratricide, and the support (or duplicity) of warrior-retainers. The chroniclers relate that Vladimir's twelve sons by his many wives initiated a pattern of bloodshed as one after another raised armies and called on foreign allies to engage each other's troops in combat, or, more duplicitously, had their brothers murdered. As time went by and Christian monogamy helped establish a clearer genealogical order, a general commitment to dynastic seniority also came into play. A loose pattern of lateral succession gradually took shape, according to which the grand princely title would pass not from father to son but horizontally, across a generation of brothers and male cousins, before passing to a senior son or nephew of the next generation. But this lateral sequence never assumed any explicit formulation, and the particular constellations of surviving contestants shaped each successive round of competition. At each transition, princes had to win followers and make strategic alliances with foreigners (Poles, Varangians, nomadic Pechenegs, and others).[11] When townspeople grew restive and asserted themselves politically, they too had to be cajoled and appeased. Until the twelfth century, Kiev and its constituent principalities had neither an administrative infrastructure (bureaucracy) except for the developing Church hierarchy, nor any hope of a monopoly over legitimate violence. It had no fixed boundaries nor a cohesive "national" myth.[12] Early Rus was a nonterritorial, quite mobile system of tribute-collection and constant warfare based on gift-giving, pillage, and a certain degree of dynastic charisma.

With conversion to Christianity, imposed from the top by Vladimir and then energetically fostered by his son Iaroslav, institutions began to develop—an ecclesiastical hierarchy and apparatus, monasteries, militarized monastic outposts

---

[10]*Russian Primary Chronicle*, p. 146. Donald Ostrowski notes that Kievan sources do not refer to the eponymous founder of the dynasty in legitimizing princely succession. The idea of a Riurikid dynasty was retrospectively invented much later. Donald Ostrowski, "Systems of Succession in Rus' and Steppe Societies," *Ruthenica* 11 (2012), 58.

[11]Stefanovich, *Boiare, otroki, druzhiny*, esp. 480–503.

[12]Charles Halperin, "The Concept of the *Russkaia Zemlia* and Medieval National Consciousness from the Tenth to the Fifteenth Centuries," *Nationalities Papers* 8 (1980): 75–86.

in the forests—and a literary culture among a small elite. The process of Christianization in the general population took centuries, but where the institutional church had a presence, local communities experienced profound effects. For instance, even something as meaningful as funerary practices tracked the presence or absence of diocesan institutions. Simon Franklin and Jonathan Shephard write: "By a pleasing coincidence, a tour through the graveyards of the late tenth to late eleventh centuries broadly confirms the ecclesiastical topography: where there were bishops there was a Christian flock; where there were no bishops the land was largely pagan."[13] This is a striking example of the way that even small, probably understaffed outposts of an institutionalized church could effect seismic changes in practice and belief in short order. Of course, equally striking illustrations of the glacial pace of conversion can also be found: pagan burial (barrow graves) continued in parts of Rus, particularly in rural areas, far from the ecclesiastical eyes, and Christian inhumation caught on slowly outside urban and monastic circles. Chronicles continue to report pagan practices such as bear-worship and the eating of horse and bear meat through the eleventh century.[14] Although Christianity spread slowly, Kievan Rus nonetheless produced a rich religious and secular culture, a heritage of chronicle-writing, hagiography, architecture, and iconography of great beauty, based on wealth accumulated through successful raiding and trading. Literacy caught on in surprising ways in non-elite lay circles and left its mark in the humble production of craftspeople who inscribed their names on the pots they made or the spindle whorls they carved from slate, of townspeople who scrawled casual notes to one another, and in the various individuals who scratched graffiti messages on the stone walls of churches.[15] It was this range of cultural production, along with the prominence of Rus princes and princesses in the broad dynastic world of medieval Europe, that gave rise, in later centuries, to a nostalgic image of a Kievan Golden Age.

What kind of early identity, or identities, formed among the people of the lands of Rus? From the earliest records the peoples of the region were culturally and linguistically diverse.[16] *The Tale of Bygone Years* notes that Slavs, Balts, Turkic and Finnic peoples lived in the region and that the Slavs were divided into distinct groups. Scholars generally point to the adoption and spread of Orthodox Christianity in 988 (traditional date) and through the next few centuries as the critical juncture at which indigenous populations and their Rus rulers came to

---

[13]Simon Franklin and Jonathan Shepard, *The Emergence of Rus: 750–1200* (London and New York: Longman, 1996), p. 228.
[14]Ibid., p. 352; and I. V. Dubov, "Spornye voprosy etnicheskoi istorii Severo-Vostochnoi Rusi IX–XIII vekov," *Voprosy istorii* (1990), no. 5: 15–27.
[15]Simon Franklin, *Writing, Society, and Culture in Early Rus, c. 950–1300* (Cambridge and New York: Cambridge University Press, 2002), pp. 47–82.
[16]This is a point well made by Andreas Kappeler, *Russland als Vielvolkerreich: Entstehung, Geschichte, Zerfall* (Munich: C. H. Beck'sche Verlagsbuchhandlung, 1992), now available in English: *The Russian Empire: A Multinational History* (Harlow, England: Pearson Education Limited, 2001).

Archangel Gabriel, or *Angel with Golden Hair*, Novgorod, twelfth century.

Church of the Intercession on the Nerl, Bogoliubovo, twelfth century.

constitute a community that fused the notions of Orthodoxy and Rus identity. This position seems to us to exaggerate the degree to which the diverse population saw itself as a unified whole or even cared much one way or another in these early centuries. Still, archeology confirms that Christian motifs proliferated throughout the region and crosses surface alongside pagan amulets and in time displace Thor's hammers in excavation sites. Orthodoxy and dynastic rule provided strands of identification and affiliation that could be mobilized in times of crisis, particularly at the margins of Rus where populations came into contact and sometimes clashed with people they saw as distinct from themselves: the Catholics of Poland, the pagans (later Catholics) of Lithuania, and the non-Christian nomadic peoples of the steppe, the vast grasslands that stretched eastward into Siberia and Central Asia.[17]

Even at these putative boundaries where self can come into sharp focus against the contrasting other, distinctions may have been less clear-cut than we like to imagine. The understanding of the world as a collection of diverse human collectivities was fundamental in a Rus geopolitical and moral imaginary. A Southern Rus chronicle, the Hypatian Codex, includes a lovely meditation on an early-twelfth-century battle between the Rus and the Polovtsians, a fierce nomadic group from the steppe, illustrating the extent to which division of peoples was seen as fully right and in accord with divine plan. Meditating on the incursion, the author of this passage in the Codex explained, "an angel is appointed to each creation: to clouds, and fogs, and snow, and hail, and frost. There are angels for sounds and for thunders, angels of winter, of heat, of autumn, spring, and summer. . . . Angels are appointed to all creation." Turning to the human sphere, he extended his overview: "In the same way, an angel is appointed to every given land in order to take care of each land, even if the land is pagan." Not only were "lands," with their assigned peoples, the natural constitutive elements of human diversity, but each had a God-given title to that land and even a guardian angel assigned to go with it.

Applying the lesson to the current moment of conflict between the Christian Rus and their pagan neighbors, the chronicler continued, "In case of God's anger at a land, God commands that angel to wage a war against the [guilty] land. . . . Likewise, it occurred that God sent pagan aliens against us on account of our sins, and they won by God's command, for they were being led by an angel by God's command."[18] As analyzed by Yulia Mikhailova, this passage tells us a great deal about the attitudes of the Southern Rus toward the pagan raiders against whom they battled and with whom their world was so deeply intermeshed. Sometimes one side wins, sometimes the other. It all follows God's plan. Without demonizing the Polovtsians across religious or ethnic lines, the chronicler

---

[17]Nicholas V. Riasanovsky, "Historical Consciousness and National Identity: Some Considerations on the History of Russian Nationalism" (New Orleans: The Graduate School of Tulane University, 1991), pp. 2–3; Omeljan Pritsak, "The Origin of Rus'," *Russian Review* 36, no. 3 (July 1977): 249–73.
[18]*Ipat'evskaia letopis'* (g. 1111), pp. 262–63.

acknowledges Christian and pagan alike as part of God's creation, each assigned an angel, each entitled to a land, and each playing a rightful part.[19] The tale reveals a view of the world that is premised on human diversity with no ambition to transcend it.

A sense that divisions among mankind were natural did not mean that those distinctions were insurmountable. Looking to the east, we find that however strong a sense of belonging to the Rus dynasty may have been, it did not create barriers to marrying outside the clan. In the late twelfth century, for instance, the unfortunate refugee Prince Yuri, son of the murdered Andrei Bogoliubskii of Vladimir-Suzdal, wed the powerful Queen Tamar of Georgia. Tamar was an Orthodox monarch, but the chronicles drop hints of equally intimate interactions between the Rus and the pagan and Muslim nomads with whom they nominally battled. Princes married into the families of Pecheneg (Turkic nomadic) leaders, and could call on the services of subjects who had fully mastered steppe languages. The mutual involvement was deep enough that in one particular tale, Charles Halperin observes, "familiarity with Pecheneg ways is taken for granted."[20] To the west, where sectarian divides increasingly split the Christian world, sharpening into the Great Schism between the Orthodox East and Catholic West, we again find as much or even more indifference to these divisions as awareness of them. Along these lines, historian Christian Raffensperger has recently challenged scholars to reimagine Rus history and to recognize that it was a full participant in the general currents of medieval Europe. Through the twelfth century, Rus princes intermarried with all the reigning dynasties of Northern and Western Europe, and were part of a European dynastic order. Connected by trade through the Baltic and more southerly routes, participating in the formal trade alliance of the Hanseatic League, and sharing with other European elites an appreciation of Byzantium as the living embodiment of imperial grandeur, Rus was no isolated outlier. Only when religious divisions grew sharper, as Byzantium went into temporary decline and Rus identity began to spread beyond the dynasty itself and to encompass a broader swath of the population, did Rus back out of its European networks. European dynastic marriages became a thing of the past, until they were once again adopted in the early eighteenth century, when Peter the Great came along

---

[19]Yulia Mikhailova, "Angels for Pagans: The Discourse of Angels in the Hypatian Codex as a Conceptualization of the Cooperation Between Christian Slavs and Pagan Turks in Southern Rus'," talk presented at the American Society for Eurasian and East European Studies, Philadelphia, Nov. 2015. Mikhailova points out that Christians are granted individual angels, while pagans receive theirs collectively, like forces of nature. See also Donald Ostrowski, "Pagan Past and Christian Identity in the Primary Chronicle," in *Historical Narratives and Christian Identity on a European Periphery: Early History Writing in Northern, East-Central, and Eastern Europe (c. 1070–1200)*, ed. Ildar H. Garipzanov (Turnhout, Belgium: Brepols, 2011), pp. 229–53.
[20]Charles Halperin, *Russia and the Golden Horde: The Mongol Impact on Medieval Russian History* (Bloomington: Indiana University Press, 1987), p. 13.

to shake things up. [21] Overall, given the shortage of grass-roots sources, assessing the degree to which common folk recognized an abstract common identity is difficult, but it seems safe to say that the Orthodox Church and with the reigning princes offered the two most promising loci around which such identification could develop.

NEW MODELS FOR UNDERSTANDING KIEVAN RUS: STATELESS HEAD OR GALACTIC POLITY

Scholarship from the mid-twentieth century, heavily influenced by the Great Power politics and Cold War divisions of the world, often overstated the extent both of state-building and of the imperial ambitions of Rus warrior princes. For instance, Russian émigré historian George Vernadsky constructed a detailed (and largely fanciful) outline of complex Kievan political institutions and practices from fragmentary hints in surviving sources, fueled by a good deal of wishful thinking. Similarly, his assessment of medieval Kiev's glorious "Imperial Plan and Its Failure, 878–972," while a gripping tale, suffers from being wildly overstated and grandiose, an exercise in reading modern political ambitions into the disorderly past. He writes:

> The political history of Kievan Russia opens with a century of bold adventure: with an attempt on the part of the Norse rulers of Kiev to build up a vast empire stretching from the Baltic to the Black Sea and from the Carpathian Mountains to the Caspian Sea. A series of daring campaigns was undertaken, both by sea and by land, with Constantinople and Transcaucasia as the two main objectives; at one time the mouths of both Volga and Danube were controlled by the Russians.[22]

The vision is grand and bold, but the picture of ambitious long-range planning, the dream of a stable empire (even if doomed to failure, as conceded by Vernadsky's chapter title), the clearly delineated territorial span, and even the misleading word "control" are all figments of historical imagination rather than reflections of historical evidence.

Vernadsky's swashbuckling Varangian heroes did indeed smash the mighty Khazars (a largely nomadic Turkic people based at the mouth of the Volga, remarkable for the fact that its elite converted to Judaism) and break their control of the Volga trade. They also swept west to the Danube, where they settled for a short stay and enjoyed the local produce and wine, but lasting control of territory was not at issue in either case. Their campaigns were launched in response to the demands of their hungry warriors, who reminded them that other warlords' men were clad in

---

[21]Christian Raffensperger, *Reimagining Europe: Rus' in the Medieval World* (Cambridge, MA: Harvard University Press, 2012). On royal marriages in later centuries, see Russell E. Martin, *A Bride for the Tsar: Bride Shows and Marriage Politics in Early Modern Russia* (DeKalb: Northern Illinois University Press, 2012).

[22]Vernadsky, *Kievan Russia*, p. 19.

fine raiment, the spoils of war, whereas they would go naked if their leaders did not find new lands to pillage. An inherent logic of mutual reliance and mutual enrichment dictated that princes build their political power and military success on the loyalty and service of their retinue, and that loyalty in turn relied on successful raiding and distribution of loot. If warrior princes failed to lead successful raids, if princes aspiring to the grand princely title failed to distribute adequate largess, their hopes might be easily dashed when their retinues melted away and their erstwhile supporters lent allegiance to other contenders. These were not the first steps in empire-building, but rather the motivations of what Georges Duby calls a medieval "economy of gift, pillage, and largess," which pushed Kiev's warrior princes to respond to the urging of their supporters and to engage in endless warfare.[23]

Kievan Rus was not an empire or even a fully constituted state. Even at their height, the Rus principalities enjoyed no real political unity. They were only loosely sutured together by ideas of dynastic solidarity and by the symbolic claims to seniority held by the grand prince of Kiev. Within various solidarity groups—of kin, region, or religion—affective bonds were celebrated in song and story. In the absence of more structural or institutional reinforcement, the language of paternal, filial, fraternal, and Christian love served as an alternative social glue. These symbolic and narrative bonds were reinforced sporadically through exercise of coercive power and perhaps more effectively through discursive, cultural power manifested through images, icons, churches, and the teachings of the Church. For the warrior elite and residents of towns, affiliation with one or another dynastic prince was important, but this should not be confused with loyalty to an abstraction like a state. Indeed, the word "realm" might be preferred instead of "state," for the grand princes of Kiev seem to have had little or no conception of a state as a bounded territorial unit governed by a single sovereign entity, aspiring to administer, tax, and control its people. Instead, their conception of the Kievan polity and its territorial parameters remained amorphous and shifting.

The concept and title of "grand prince" of a unitary Kievan realm entered Kievan vocabulary and political consciousness slowly, as an import from Byzantium, vying for some time with other titles derived from other intermingled political cultures. The polity itself (if there was one) was constituted imprecisely around a loosely defined people (the Rus) and was ruled piecemeal by interconnected competing and conflicting branches of the princely line. Grand princely deathbed testaments demonstrate that the goal of princely politics remained personal and familial. They did not encompass any broader aspirations toward unified sovereignty or territorial rule. After battling brothers and cousins for the grand princely seat, dying titleholders would divide hard-won holdings among their sons, bestowing bits and pieces as appanages (largely autonomous holdings) to each of their male offspring. With these bequests, grand princes subjected the dynastic holdings to successive rounds of fragmentation, and within each appanage, his sons might subdivide still further

[23]Georges Duby, *The Early Growth of the European Economy: Warriors and Peasants from the Seventh to the Twelfth Century* (Ithaca, NY: Cornell University Press, 1974), p. 57.

among his own sons in the following generation. Rather than consolidating a realm, an idea in which they showed little interest, they divided.

One might say that Kiev was like the sun in what Victor Lieberman has called a "solar polity," a radiant center that extends a force field out from the center, but that force diminishes the farther it goes from the center. Perhaps a more accurate fit, given Kiev's tendency toward reiterative cycles of fragmentation, is S. J. Tambiah's idea of a "galactic polity" with multiple gravitational centers, such as, in various periods of Rus history, Kiev, Novgorod, Volynia, Chernigov, and Tmutorokhan. Scholars of Southeast Asia use the term to describe a loose political formation with multiple powerful nodes, each exerting its progressively attenuating force with ever-diminishing efficacy, in expanding concentric circles, and with a possibility of new stars coalescing and forming new solar systems.[24]

The galactic model resonates with recent scholarship that casts doubt on the entire premise of a "Kievan Rus,'" and posits instead a loosely affiliated set of successive, rival, and overlapping centers that predated the Kievan claim to centrality. Simon Franklin and Jonathan Shephard document the relatively late entry of Kiev on to the Rus stage, and the rival efforts of other centers—Chernigov, Tmutorokhan, Novgorod—to build themselves into imposing citadels of Christian rule. Attentive to the power of the retinues and the very loose configuration that held the princes together under the nominal leadership of the grand prince in Kiev, Donald Ostrowski proposes that we set aside the whole idea of a unified Kievan state and adopt instead David Sneath's model of a "headless state," "a decentralized and distributed power found in aristocratic orders." Ostrowski writes: "The entity that is usually called 'Kievan Rus' was an aristocratic state, with horizontal power relations and virtually no vertical subordination to the center."[25] That polity "did have a capital (Kiev), and insofar as someone occupied the capital seat it focused the attention of and was competed for by, those princes who were in the line (or lines) of succession and by a few who were not. Yet there was no central government. Instead there were several local governments—in Chernigov, Smolensk, Murom-Riazan', Novgorod, Pereiaslavl', Polotsk, Rostov-Suzdal, Volodimir-Volynsk, Tmutorokhan, and Kiev itself."[26] "Princes did rule localities, but without a central or unifying authorization or

---

[24]Victor Lieberman, *Strange Parallels: Southeast Asia in Global Context, c. 800–1830, Volume 1: Integration on the Mainland* (Cambridge: Cambridge University Press, 2003), p. 33. Stanley Jeyaraja Tambiah, "The Galactic Polity in Southeast Asia," in *Culture, Thought, and Social Action* (Cambridge, MA: Harvard University Press, 1973), pp. 3–31; O. W. Wolters, *History, Culture, and Region in Southeast Asian Perspectives*, rev. ed., Studies on Southeast Asia 26 (Ithaca, NY: Southeast Asia Publications, Southeast Asia Program, Cornell University, 1999), 27, http://hdl.handle.net/2027/heb.02480.

[25]Ostrowski, "Systems of Succession in Rus' and Steppe Societies," pp. 30, 58. Also, David Sneath, *The Headless State: Aristocratic Orders, Kinship Society, and Misrepresentations of Nomadic Inner Asia* (New York: Columbia University Press, 2007), p. 1. Sneath's concept has proven both suggestive and controversial and has been critically reviewed by Sergei Abashin, Devin DeWeese, Adrienne Edgar, Peter Golden, and Valerie Kivelson, among others. See, for example, the discussion in *Ab Imperio* 4 (2009).

[26]Ostrowski, "Systems of Succession in Rus' and Steppe Societies," p. 30.

affiliation. Instead, what legitimized a prince's claim to be able to rule in a city or town was (1) eligibility—whether his father had ruled there, (2) aristocratic self-regulation—whether the other princes accepted his claim, and (3) external regulation—whether the townsmen accepted the prince as their prince."[27]

Playing with the Ostrowski/Sneath "headless state" model, we suggest that we should invert the phrase: the grand prince, with his numinous title and his seat in the coveted symbolic center, was rather a "stateless head." Kiev and its reigning grand prince occupied the pinnacle of the political imagination for several centuries. From the time of Vladimir on, grand princes, though lacking much actual power, worked energetically to broadcast an image of themselves as authoritative rulers, as "heads." With grandiose gestures they began to express an ambition to rule, rather than simply to loot and dominate. Their aspirations translated into reality only gradually. Coins were minted but not widely circulated, and probably used more as talismans of power than as exchangeable currency. Borrowing from the Byzantine tradition, princes began to present themselves as lawgivers, even though little evidence survives to suggest that their laws were ever enforced. Law-giving remained a mostly symbolic act. In the eleventh century a law code, the *Russkaia Pravda*, was written up, but even here there is no mention of anything like a state apparatus. The law codes mainly recorded ways to protect people in the prince's service or to resolve disputes between two contending parties without much discernable interference by authorities. No mention of record-keeping enters the code, suggesting that even when the prince sent authorized agents to oversee a case, no formal leger preserved the judgment or registered enforcement.

Responding to a world of aggregated difference rather than unified state control, laws and treaties, such as they were, presumed categories of distinction and maintained legal distinction through hierarchies of value and penalties. Assaults on agents of the prince were treated separately from attacks on other people, and payments for killing or violations of honor were set according to graded scales, according to ethnic identity (Varangians, Greek), regional origin (Novgorodian, Kievan), occupational status (merchant, sheriff, agent of prince, peasant, or slave), confessional affiliation, and gender (the monetary compensation for killing a woman was half that for a man of the same standing). Even different body parts were carefully listed along with the compensation to be awarded in case of injury or disfigurement. Manly beards and mustaches rated a lofty 12-grivna repayment; fingers only three. Legal thinking took shape as a catalogue of differentiated types and groups, rights, and payments, and was projected as an emanation of a grand prince at the helm.

At the same time that grand princes strove to project an image of themselves as solemn and pious rulers, they commanded little actual power. They lacked a central government, administrative institutions or, in fact, a *state*. Enhancing the case for viewing Kievan Rus as stateless, another inventive Russian historian, A. A. Gorskii, argues that there is no evidence at all of any centralization or unification prior to the Mongol invasions. He points out that our own deeply

---

[27]Ibid., p. 58.

Map 1.2. Rus principalities.

entrenched assumptions lead us to believe that a system of independent lands would necessarily be unstable or that the rise of a centralized state power is inevitable.[28] In other words, the very notion of a Kievan "state" is a later imposition. Without bureaucracy, administrative institutions, or enforcement of law, there was no state to be governed or ruled. Collectively, these radical revisions

---

[28]A. A. Gorskii, "Territorial'no-politicheskie izmeniniia na Rusi v XIV–XV vv.—ob"edinenie ili peredel?" in *The Book of Royal Degrees and the Genesis of Russian Historical Consciousness*, ed. Gail Lenhoff and Ann Kleimola (Bloomington, IN: Slavica, 2011), pp. 201–15.

upend the myth of a golden age of Kiev and offer a welcome and overdue reassessment of the shifting, contentious, and shapeless constellation of princedoms that constituted Kievan Rus.

APPANAGE RUS AND FURTHER FRAGMENTATION

The Rus lands fragmented even further, if such a thing is imaginable, in the twelfth and thirteenth centuries. This dissipation of an already fissiparous Rus was partly due to the infinite subdivision caused by the practice of partible inheritance (dividing property among the eligible heirs). It was also a result of constant warfare between branches of the princely families and practices of "predatory kinship," whereby competing lineages sought to expand their resource bases in order to support their growing numbers of sons, sometimes by swallowing the holdings of their more distant kin.[29] Economically this fragmentation may have been exacerbated by the surprising success of local economies, which developed rapidly in the eleventh and twelfth centuries and lost much of the impetus that had previously forced them to look to Kiev and its rich markets, full of imports from Byzantium and the Muslim world. With the dissemination of technologies that had once been imported from abroad or known only in Kiev, such as glassblowing and brickmaking, the development of local markets strengthened regional economies at the expense of any central or integrated economy over a broader area.

During this period, Rus princes seem to have turned their attention inward, to the politics and profits of their own principalities. They set aside whatever tenuous ties had previously oriented them toward Kiev and subordinated them nominally to the aura, if not the actual person, of the Kievan grand prince. Even the chroniclers who had constantly lamented the costs of princely fratricide and chided their princes for allowing the nomads of the steppe to enslave and slaughter Orthodox men and women, turned their attention to celebrating the accomplishments of their local patrons and the glories of their particular princely branch. The population seems to have developed a shared identity more through the inchoate commonalities of personal ornamentation, such as the glass beads and bangles worn by women throughout Rus, than through identification with a unified polity. This is an intriguing instance of a tenuous unification from below, through craft production, exchange, and fashion choices of ordinary people, rather than from above, through the efforts of statesmen or ideologues.

While princes continued to fight over the title of grand prince, they increasingly based their operations in their own appanage holdings, territories they held by dint of patrimonial legacy. Famously, one ambitious and power-hungry prince, Andrei Bogoliubskii, fought fiercely against his cousins to attain the title of grand prince of Kiev and then promptly burned the city to the ground and abandoned it, returning to his own stronghold in the northeast. By Bogoliubskii's time, the

---

[29]The concept of predatory kinship comes from Eleanor Searle, *Predatory Kinship and the Creation of Norman Power, 840–1066* (Berkeley: University of California Press, 1988).

Fragments of glass bracelets from Riazan, twelfth–thirteenth century. Though shown here in black and white, the fragments are vividly colored. Similar bracelets are found all over the Rus lands.

centrifugal pull of regionalism was outweighing the communal force of dynastic unity, such as it was. The title of grand prince of Kiev had become unmoored from an actual place. From a "galactic state," Rus had fallen into what we might call "cosmic confusion." This period of division is known as the Appanage Period or, in the lexicon of Soviet historical writing, the "period of feudal fragmentation." Headless and stateless to begin with, Rus had become a miscellany of separate lands, the component pieces that an imperial ruler might assemble.

In this period of dissolution, various branches of the Rus came to distinguish themselves from the others as they oriented themselves differently in a world of cultural fluidity. Identities—ethnic, religious, and linguistic—were constantly in flux, and would be for centuries to come. Out of the confusion, half a millennium later, emerged peoples who would fiercely defend how different they were from their neighbors. Geographic location contributed to this process of differentiation as each subset of the Rus took inspiration from or resisted the incursions of its immediate neighbors. In the north, the urban mercantile hub of Novgorod developed its own unique political-cultural mix as it entered the lucrative trading network of the Hanseatic League, a vibrant medieval union of merchants engaged in Baltic and North Sea trade. Novgorod derived its enormous wealth from trade in the products of the huge territories it controlled in the northeast, territories rich in fur-bearing animals, whose thick pelts sold well on the European market.

Novgorod's close engagement with the Hanseatic League fueled cultural as well as political and economic experimentation. The churchmen of "Lord Novgorod the Great," as the city immodestly styled itself, produced a corpus of unique works of art, architecture, and writing of great sophistication and beauty. Novgorod remained loosely in the orbit of the Kievan Rus but with an independence of approach and orientation that left it perennially distinct.

A number of centers competed for dominance in the Rus lands. The principalities of Galicia and Volynia in the southwest enjoyed a number of successes in winning and holding the grand princely title over All Rus, but by the mid-twelfth century the Galician-Volynian chronicle makes clear they were increasingly oriented toward their non-Rus neighbors—Poles, Lithuanians, and Hungarians. The reigning princes forged marriages with these proximate dynasties, and, even more dramatically, in the mid-twelfth century one of their most successful rulers, Danylo Romanovych, received a crown from the pope. He did not, however, convert to Catholicism from Orthodoxy. In urban development and population policy, Danylo also followed a Polish template. Sharing a medieval discourse that attributed particular behaviors and characteristics to entire groups of people, he invited Armenian and Jewish merchants and German artisans to settle in his urban centers, convinced they would spur economic development.

After the brief period of flourishing, in the fourteenth century the region was absorbed by Poland (Galicia and western Volynia) and the Grand Duchy of Lithuania (the rest of Volynia). The regions were incorporated in imperial fashion, as distinctive units. Retaining its separate standing under Polish rule, Galicia called itself the Kingdom of Rus. Only gradually did a deeper assimilation into Poland and Lithuania, respectively, take place. Firmly within the Polish and Lithuanian political communities, the southwestern regions' interactions with a broader Rus grew even more tenuous.[30]

---

[30]This discussion of Galicia-Volynia and the section on Lithuania that follows draws on Nancy Shields Kollmann, "The Principalities of Rus' in the Fourteenth Century," in *The New Cambridge Medieval History*, vol. 6, *c. 1300–c. 1415*, ed. Michael Jones (Cambridge: Cambridge University Press, 2000), pp. 764–94; and S. C. Rowell, *Lithuania Ascending: A Pagan Empire in East-Central Europe, 1295–1345* (Cambridge: Cambridge University Press, 1994).

The powerful new state formation of the Grand Duchy of Lithuania also drew some of the Rus principalities, including Kiev itself, into its ambit. A Baltic people, Lithuanians remained pagan long after the rest of Eastern Europe had adopted one form of Christianity or another. In the fourteenth century the Lithuanian nobility that ruled former Rus lands followed their subjects and converted to Orthodoxy. The Duchy's East Slavic Orthodox populations came to be known as Ruthenians. The presence of Ruthenian populations in what would become contested borderlands would give fodder to centuries of disputes in the future.

In 1386 through a canny maneuver, the Lithuanian king agreed to convert to Catholicism in order to marry the daughter of the Polish king and achieve a personal union, soon to become permanent, between the Kingdom of Poland and the Grand Duchy of Lithuania. Each piece of this huge and unwieldy state retained significant autonomy and each held on to its own signature political, cultural, and linguistic identity. In imperial fashion, the Polish-Lithuanian Commonwealth glued its holdings together as a patchwork of constituent elements: former kingdoms and grand duchies, urban centers with their own rules and rights, religious communities with their own courts and customs. Aside from assigning a hereditary prince to each region, they tended to leave governance to local elites. The combined kingdoms offered a potent model of imperial agglomeration to the aspiring princes of northeast Rus, once they began thinking of consolidating their power.

It was in the northeast that yet another stub of the Kievan dynasty settled into localized rule within several competing principalities, eventually acknowledging a new nominal center in the city of Vladimir and ultimately, Moscow. The Orthodox Church provided the only sense of unity to these fractured territories, but with Orthodox populations dispersed among the various polities of the region, control over Church administration was contested. In 1299 the Metropolitan of Kiev and All Rus moved physically to Vladimir, in the northeast, and in 1325 to Moscow, signaling (at least to somewhat later Moscow propagandists) a transfer of religious authority and a concomitant rise of a new regional power.

Like the rulers of the other heirs of Kiev, the princes of northeast Rus also participated in a polyglot and multicultural world and in the peripheries of three empires: Byzantium, Lithuania, and the Horde. Alternately allying and competing with the Lithuanians, enriching themselves through and struggling with Novgorod, and confronting ethnically, religiously, and religiously diverse populations nearer to home, northeast Rus drew on some of the models embodied by its neighbors east and west and rejected others. After 1237, the Mongol empire imposed yet another, more forcible, imperial inspiration. Under the Golden Horde, the Rus principalities gradually stabilized and developed their own political and religious culture in the region west of the Urals.

An important school of thought maintains that this period represented such a sharp rupture with the Kievan past that it makes no sense to claim a historical connection between Kievan Rus and the state of Muscovy that would emerge centuries later in the Russian northeast. Not only did numerous different traditions grow out of, mix with, and subsume the remains of Rus, but the princely successors in the northeast themselves seemed sublimely uninterested in preserving or claiming a Kievan heritage. Chronicle accounts and other textual sources from the thirteenth and fourteenth centuries make few explicit references to the early Kievan past. Appanage Period naming practices indicate little reverence for or even memory of earlier greatness. The names that circulated within the ruling dynasty in the ninth through eleventh centuries—Riurik, Sviatoslav, Iaropolk, Vseslav—faded from use, and the princes of the northeast began to baptize their sons with a whole new assortment of names: Andrei, Vasilii, Daniil, Iuri. As we have seen, instead of basing claims to legitimacy on a story of deep historical lineage, the chronicles explained princely succession through immediate descent from a ruling father or elder brother. Only in the fifteenth century, when Moscow was on the rise, did Kiev come to be seen as a hub for historical memory and self-congratulation, a sacral site for a myth of state formation.[31] Since Kiev had formed no solid state, and certainly not a centralized one, the fabulists needed to do some serious historical revision. The reigning princes of Moscow patronized artists who emblazoned images of saintly Kievan-era princes in frescoes on the walls and arches of the Kremlin churches. Newly ascendant families tried to legitimize their status by inventing creative lines of descent, whether from Riurikid princes, foreign royalty, or ancient loyal servitors at the princely courts. The chronicles of Kiev were copied and recopied as testaments to the grandeur of the Orthodox past of Rus, and ancient law codes were reproduced and circulated.

This imaginative recuperation of Kiev creates a significant, though largely post-hoc, bridge between the pre- and post-Mongol polities and societies of Rus. Whether or not the medieval experience belongs as part of an account of "Russia's Empires" depends to some extent on how much weight one gives to the stories that Russians told themselves from the fifteenth century forward. It certainly cannot be claimed exclusively by Russian history, since its complicated trajectory places it also in the histories of the nations that would emerge as Poland, Lithuania, and, of course, Ukraine. Like the histories of those countries, which themselves would take shape centuries later, the story of Russia cannot be told without its originary moment, which coalesced around Kiev and the Rus principalities.

We think a case can be made for important continuities between medieval Rus and Muscovy, on the basis of religious tradition, linguistic and cultural, architectural and iconographic legacies, and even dynastic heritage. Certainly the built environments and physical spaces of the city centers of Rus, the fortified kremlins, domed churches, and bell towers stood as markers of continuity. Chronicles and law codes were copied and preserved, signaling ongoing interest and some degree of historical memory. Andrei Bogoliubskii, the prince who blithely burned the city of Kiev to the ground in 1169, built the city of Vladimir, his own northern capital, as a "new Kiev," suggesting that these transfers and references were self-conscious, and the continuities more significant than the "Rupture School" would allow. Regardless of how explicitly these legacies were

---

[31]Ostrowski, "Systems of Succession in Rus' and Steppe Societies," p. 30.

appreciated in the intervening centuries, it is hard to discount the through-lines in the development of religion, culture, and princely rule. More to the point of our analysis, we would stress that while Kievan Rus cannot under any definition be understood as an imperial power, it occupied a place in a world constituted of diverse peoples and collectivities, each with its own rites and customs, and its own distinctive privileges and obligations. Already in the Kievan era, Orthodox Slavs participated in a polyglot world characterized by encounters and interactions across collective groups defined by difference and differentiated by collective understandings. In this way, the galaxy of Rus principalities anticipated and set the groundwork for the imperial regimes to follow.

By the late eleventh century, as is evident in the chronicle *Tale of Bygone Years*, the clerical authors defined Rus as the land ruled by the princely line. By the twelfth century, members of the dynasty too expressed a sense that they were Rus princes and ruled over the land of the Rus. Yet we can trace no shared collective identity beyond the elite. Churchmen attempted to instill a sense of commitment to a common Orthodox Rus and filled the chronicles with laments at the destruction of Rus lands and the suffering of the Rus people due to the internal battles among the princes, but their words appear to have had little effect.

Occasionally a ruler took the lessons of the Church to heart and attempted, vainly, to halt the bloodshed within Rus and among relatives. Movingly, in 1096 Prince Vladimir Monomakh wrote to implore his princely first cousin, Oleg, son of Sviatoslav, to stop the killing after both had lost sons to the ongoing war. He reminded his cousin that the Lord instructs men to live in harmony with their brethren, to love them and forgive them. "Behold how good and how pleasant it is for brethren to dwell together in unity! (Ps. 133:1)." But Monomakh acknowledges that such bonds have never sufficed to stop senseless warfare: "There were wars in the days of our wise grandsires and our righteous and blessed sires. For the devil, who desires no good to the race of man, continues to incite us." The letter conveys the raw pain of the father's loss: "When my son was slain, and you beheld his blood and his mutilated corpse as he lay like a withered flower or a slaughtered lamb, you might have stood over him and said, as you read the secret thoughts of your soul, 'Alas, what have I done?'" Instead, Oleg expressed no remorse. Even so, Monomakh declares himself willing to make peace with his son's killer, in order to stop the intra-familial bloodshed for the general good, "for I wish no ill, but I desire rather the good of my kinsmen and of the land of Rus'." He urges his kinsman to "make peace and be reconciled. . . . Let us not set ourselves up as avengers, but rather trust in God. . . . Let us not bring ruin upon the land of Rus'."[32] Still, the internecine strife continued, punctuated by occasional paroxysms of shared suffering in the face of incursions of Turkic steppe nomads—Pechenegs, Cumans, or Polovtsians, and ultimately, the Mongols—from the south and east.

---

[32]"Letter of Vladimir Monomakh to Oleg, Son of Svyatoslav," Appendix II, in *The Russian Primary Chronicle, Laurentian Text*, pp. 216–18.

MONGOL KHANS AND THE AURA OF EMPIRE

By the time the Mongol forces appeared suddenly at the River Kalka in 1223, Kievan Rus as a unified entity, if such it had ever been, was in shambles. Internal divisions had grown so sharp, and, on the other hand, regional economies had grown so prosperous, that whatever symbolic lure the city had once enjoyed had evaporated. With the arrival of the Mongols, a new, fully imperial overlord came to dominate the Rus lands. But the Mongols, more commonly known as Tatars in the Russian context, did not settle in central Russia. They were interested in building broad trade networks and using Russia as a source of tribute. After the initial period of ruthless conquest and a brief experiment with direct rule, they developed a system of indirect rule, employing the local Rus authorities as their intermediaries. As imperial rulers, the Mongol khans were accustomed to working with different peoples. Though essentially a nomadic society, they delineated their metropolitan center from their colonial peripheries, of which frozen, forested Rus was perhaps the most peripheral of all. They demanded that their subject princes journey across the icy tundra to pay homage to the khans in Karakorum (Qaraqorum), their capital in distant Mongolia and then later, after the westernmost piece of the empire, the Golden Horde, split from the greater Mongol Empire, to the camp/city of Sarai on the Volga. When their Christian agents refused to participate in the requisite rituals at the Mongol court, they were schooled in blood. According to Giovanni di Plano Carpini, an envoy to the Mongol court from the pope in 1245–1246,

> [. . .] when Michael [of Chernigov], one of the princes of Russia, came to submit to Bati, the Tartars first tried to make him pass between two fires. After this they said that he should bow south to Chingis Khan, but he replied that he would gladly bow to Bati and his servants but not to the image of a dead man because this is improper for a Christian. When he was repeatedly told through his son Yaroslav that he must bow, and yet he refused, Bati ordered Prince Michael killed if he would not bow. The prince replied that he preferred to die rather than do what was wrong. Bati sent Michael to one of his followers who trampled on his chest with his boots until the prince died. Meanwhile the prince comforted one of his soldiers who stood near by him by saying: "Be strong because your punishment will not last long and then at once eternal joy will follow." After this his head was cut off quickly with a knife. The soldier, to tell the truth, also had his head cut off with a knife.[33]

Michael came to be venerated as a martyr to the cause of Christian struggle, but resistance was the exception rather than the norm. No unified "Russia" had congealed at this point, and religious and ethnic battle lines were not much in evidence. In fact, ecclesiastical and princely wealth and institutional strength increased greatly thanks to the Tatar policy of supporting the religious institutions

---

[33]Giovanni DiPlano Carpini, *The Story of the Mongols Whom We Call the Tartars: Friar Giovanni di Plano Carpini's Account of His Embassy to the Court of the Mongol Khan*, trans. Erik Hildinger (Boston: Branden, 1996), pp. 44–45.

and powerful elites in their subject territories. Through a profusion of deals and privileges, immunities and protections, the Tatars won support from the leaders of Rus. Issuing protective charters (*iarliki*), backed by the imposing force of Tatar warriors, the Tatar rulers doled out tax exemptions and exclusive jurisdictional rights to the Church. They won the loyalty of princes by handing them the lucrative privilege of collecting taxes for the khan. In the process of gathering the required funds, the princes were able to squeeze their dependents a bit harder and to skim the extra off the top. Cozy deals with their imperial "oppressors" allowed both religious and secular elites to secure their positions and to enrich themselves.

The princes of Moscow, who sprang from a junior branch of the dynastic line, proved to be particularly loyal and cooperative agents . . . for a while. But as time passed, the princes of Moscow also began to manipulate the Tatars, playing their hand well, using the power of the khans' authority and military might against their domestic rivals. Recent decades of scholarship have dramatically revised the older picture of heroic resistance by the "Russian Land" against a hated infidel foe. Rather than rallying Orthodox Russia and throwing the oppressors out, the Rus princes competed for their favor and generally acknowledged the legitimacy of Chingissid imperial rule, that is, of the line of Chingis (Genghis) Khan. The great battles that Russian patriotic legend later came to celebrate as grand turning points, moments when Orthodox Russia rose up to defeat the Tatars, turn out to reflect instead the deep interweaving of Russia into the political culture of the steppe. The storied battle of Kulikovo Field (1380) allowed for a short-lived Russian victory, but the heroic prince Dmitrii Donskoi fought not against the forces of a legitimate Chingissid khan but against an upstart leader, a pretender, Mamai. When Mamai was crushed a few years later and order reestablished in the Golden Horde, Donskoi reconfirmed his loyalty to his steppe suzerain and resumed collecting (and skimming) the khan's taxes.

Assessments of the effects of the Tatar "Yoke," that is, the period during which Rus paid tribute to their steppe overlords, range widely. Traditional views attributed all that was negative in Russia's later historical development to the Tatars. In this vision, Rus was destroyed and impoverished, first by the attacks, and then by the onerous taxes imposed by the Tatars, and its political forms were shaped by centuries of subservience. The Tatars were even held accountable for Russia's failure to participate in Europe's Renaissance. Surviving sources from the period and later fueled these grim calculations. And indeed, the initial attacks and occasional punitive raids during the centuries of domination were brutal and bloody. A medieval chronicle reports on the conquest of the city of Suzdal' in 1238 in graphic terms:

> On Sunday, February 8, . . . early in the morning the Tatars approached the city from all sides and began to hit the city [walls] with rams, and began to pour great stones into the center of the city from far away, as if by God's will, as if it rained inside the city; many people were killed inside the city and all were greatly frightened and trembled. . . . The Tatars . . . began to search after the princes and their mother, and found that they were inside the church. . . . [They]

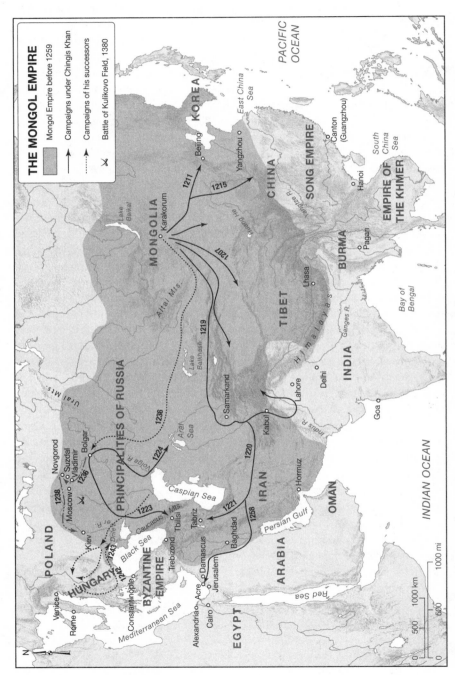

Map 1.3. The Mongol Empire.

THE MONGOL EMPIRE

Mongol Empire before 1259

→ Campaigns under Chingis Khan

⇢ Campaigns of his successors

✈ Battle of Kulikovo Field, 1380

broke the gates of the church and slaughtered those who were inside and resisted. . . . The Tatars then brought many fire logs inside the church and set it on fire. Those present in the choir loft, praying gave their souls to God; they were burned and joined the list of martyrs.[34]

Newer reexaminations of the impact of the Mongols on Russia, however, lead to very different conclusions. The initial attacks and consequent bloodshed were undeniably horrific, but the subsequent centuries allowed Rus the benefits of participation in a great Tatar empire. The Mongols drew Rus into the lucrative transcontinental markets that formed the source of their own riches. The Rus economy bounced back quickly after the initial devastation. The new turn in scholarship recasts the Mongols' so-called economic oppression of Rus as economic integration into the lucrative trade routes protected by the Pax Mongolica. Archeological finds support the supposition that Rus benefited from its integration into the Mongols' vast Eurasian trade network. For instance, excavations in Novgorod have uncovered walnuts and glazed pottery from the emporia of the Middle East and the Black Sea region.

In previous centuries, the Byzantine Empire offered the Rus a model of imperial grandeur and welcomed them into a kind of tutelary status as a newly converted Orthodox princedom under the religious authority of the Patriarch (head of the Orthodox Church) of Constantinople. Under the Mongols, Rus gained its first direct experience of being part of a great empire. Recent research also confirms that Rus princes drew on this experience in developing their own models of rule. From Mongol-Tatar practices they derived their understandings of how best to manage populations and benefit from the arrangements. Reversing the standard historiographic polarities, Ostrowski argues that the Mongol government itself was not despotically structured; therefore it could not have served as the model for any putative Muscovite despotism. On the contrary, Ostrowski argues, the "steppe principle" in Muscovite politics dictated the active participation of a boyar (noble) council and of wise advisers.[35] The primary lessons the Rus seem to have drawn from their sojourn in the Mongol Empire were clever and low-cost ways to enrich the center through taxation while leaving diverse populations to manage their own affairs with significant autonomy. This commitment to rule through diversity, whether bolstering and coopting elites or maneuvering populations to police and tax themselves, as well as a long-standing practice of consultation with elites, would provide a crucial component in Russia's own experience of creating and maintaining an empire.

---

[34]Dmytryshyn, *Medieval Russia: A Source Book, 850–1700* (Gulf Breeze, FL: Academic International Press, 2000), p. 148; *Polnoe sobranie russkikh* letopisei, Vol. 10, (Moscow: Nauka, 1965), pp. 108–19.
[35]Halperin, *Russia and the Golden Horde*, pp. 83–85; Donald Ostrowski, *Muscovy and the Mongols: Cross-Cultural Influences on the Steppe Frontier, 1304–1589* (Cambridge: Cambridge University Press, 2002), 108–32.

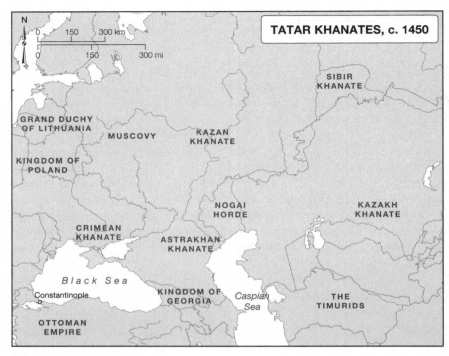

Map 1.4. Tatar khanates.

The Mongol-Tatar mode of indirect rule through already existing power structures and institutions layered onto a deep history of similar interactions within Rus. Power relations had long been negotiated, whether collaboratively or coercively, among collectives and territories understood as inherently distinct, with their own customs and their own standing. Our survey has shown the strength and persistence of this mode of thinking, of categorizing, naturalizing, and operating through difference. Starting with the division of earth among the sons of Noah after the Flood, Rus sources continue to present the world as a collection of collectives, people to be understood by their distinction as separate tribes, peoples, religious communities, social groups, or principalities.

Eventually, the monumental achievement of the Mongol Empire collapsed, a consequence of its own astonishing logistical successes in subduing most of a continent. The western-most piece, the Golden Horde, which held Rus in its orbit, split from the Mongol hub by the early fourteenth century, and by the mid-fifteenth century the Horde in turn weakened and splintered into smaller khanates: Kazan, Astrakhan, Uzbek, Qazaq, and Nogai Hordes, Crimea, and Siberia. In the same period, Constantinople fell to the Ottoman Turks (1453), and the Byzantine Empire, after more than a thousand years, was extinguished. In this space of fragmentation and realignment, the upstart Muscovite dynasty sought to succeed the

Mongols, inserting themselves in the political upheavals of the steppe and gradually taking on the aura of both the Great Khan and the Basileus (the Byzantine Emperor). Moscow emerged as one of the key players in the violent steppe politics of the era.

BRIEF BIBLIOGRAPHY

Franklin, Simon, and Jonathan Shepard. *The Emergence of Rus: 750–1200*. London; New York: Longman, 1996.

Halperin, Charles J. *Russia and the Golden Horde: The Mongol Impact on Medieval Russian History*. Bloomington: Indiana University Press, 1987.

Kaiser, Daniel H. *The Growth of the Law in Medieval Russia*. Princeton, NJ: Princeton University Press, 1980.

Kollmann, Nancy Shields. "The Principalities of Rus' in the Fourteenth Century." In *The New Cambridge Medieval History*, Vol. 6, *c. 1300–c. 1415*. Edited by Michael Jones. Cambridge: Cambridge University Press, 2000, pp. 764–94.

Martin, Janet. *Medieval Russia, 950–1584*. Cambridge: Cambridge University Press, 2007.

Ostrowski, Donald G. *Muscovy and the Mongols: Cross-Cultural Influences on the Steppe Frontier, 1304–1589*. Cambridge: Cambridge University Press, 2002.

————. "Systems of Succession in Rus' and Steppe Societies." *Ruthenica* 11 (2012): 29–58.

Plokhy, Serhii. *The Origins of the Slavic Nations: Premodern Identities in Russia, Ukraine, and Belarus*. Cambridge: Cambridge University Press, 2006.

Raffensperger, Christian. *Reimagining Europe: Kievan Rus' in the Medieval World*. Cambridge, MA: Harvard University Press, 2012.

Sneath, David. *The Headless State: Aristocratic Orders, Kinship Society, and Misrepresentations of Nomadic Inner Asia*. New York: Columbia University Press, 2007.

TWO

Imperial Beginnings
Muscovy

Russia can be said to have acquired a recognizable state structure beginning with the reign of Ivan III (b. 1440, r. 1462–1505). During the fourteenth and fifteenth centuries, by hook or by crook, through dynastic marriage, conquest, or ostensibly voluntary "donation," the princes of Moscow incorporated one independent principality after another, until they controlled a sizable assemblage of territories, including the vast northern Novgorodian lands after their definitive defeat in 1478. The regnant city of Moscow is the root of the English name usually used to designate the realm that it shaped, Muscovy. The city itself took on the architectural and symbolic grandeur due it as the center of a rapidly expanding enterprise. Under Ivan III and his son Vasilii III, the Moscow Kremlin (fortress and center of princely and religious power) was surrounded by the imposing red brick walls and filled with the beautiful gold-domed cathedrals that stand to this day.

BUILDING A STATE; CLAIMING AN EMPIRE

Muscovy started to develop some of the characteristic legal, administrative, and institutional functions and trappings of a state. No longer able to run the operation of the realm out of his chambers with the aid of his retinue, the ruler gradually accumulated a small administrative staff. From the last quarter of the fifteenth century, official business began to be conducted by designated clerks and scribes working in particular administrative units, chancelleries, dedicated to conducting diplomatic affairs, or later, to supervising the military, land distribution, and so forth. A new law code issued in 1497, the *Sudebnik,* standardized judicial procedure and built in penalties for corruption, favoritism, or abuse of judicial office. In the 1470s, Ivan III referred to himself on his official seal as "by God's grace sovereign of all Rus." gesturing to a single Orthodox political entity encompassing the entire population and polity.

In the same period, Muscovy began to constitute itself as an imperial state. The obverse of the same seal proclaims Ivan sovereign not only of "All Rus," but

Kremlin walls and cathedrals. The tall "Ivan the Great" bell tower stands at the right of the photograph. The Archangel Michael Cathedral, where all grand princes and tsars were buried, is recognizable with its scalloped arches and pointy central dome in the middle of the picture.

also of all of its component parts, still understood and listed individually, as the divisible elements of empire. In a textual outer ring, it names him "grand prince of Vladimir, and Moscow, and Novgorod, and Pskov, and Tver, and Iugorsk, Viatka, Perm, and Bolgar." With this seal, Ivan III adopted the Byzantine double-headed eagle (symbolizing Rome/Byzantium and likely borrowed from the Holy Roman Empire) as a royal symbol.

This same ruler experimented with claiming the title of "tsar," the title traditionally reserved for acknowledged imperial rulers: Byzantine, Roman, Mongol-Tatar. Ivan III played with the title, sometimes styling himself "White Tsar," in deference to steppe traditions of associating cardinal directions with color and "white" with the west. His grandson, Ivan IV (the Terrible), was the first to take the title as a stable, official designation, following his coronation as "tsar" in 1547. From the sixteenth century, Muscovite princes made reference to the Roman Empire, and they even concocted a fantastic family tree that inserted the Riurikid clan, now consolidated in historical retrospect as a meaningful dynastic heritage, into the genealogical line of Prus', a mythical son of Emperor Augustus. The crucial message conveyed in this fictive heritage was not the foreignness of the lineage, but rather its imperial quality. Pictorially, in the vivid images of the great *Litsevoi letopisnyi svod* (Illustrated Chronicle Compendium), an enormous history of Russia and the world compiled in the 1570s, the Russian tsar wears the recognizable insignia of imperial power, just like his Byzantine, Mongol, Roman, or Pharaonic counterparts. In the more than 16,000 miniatures that illustrate the *Litsevoi letopisnyi*

The seal of Grand Prince Ivan III of Moscow announces Muscovy's imperial ambitions. The front shows St. George slaying the dragon and enumerates Ivan's various titles. The obverse side features the imperial double-headed eagle, and the encircling text lists all the component lands subjugated to Muscovite rule, each listed separately.

оудрѣжлонегоцрптпоьлгооугоднѣм
митпаоритпцеегдатповоюепшдовен:
воіѧ ньодвехъ егопрьодꙋ. имнѫже
стпаомнра. дллптихостпнеготпихонье
змолможнтіепожнпе. попеꙗкомь
слгочестіи. нчтотпьл. ьзгла. тлыво
ѥсичрьмнроан нсивдшлмньнлшнмъ
нтпевъеслапоꙋ аосылꙗешꙋꙋсирꙋнстп.

Coronation of Ivan Vasilevich as Tsar, 1547. Illustration from the *Illustrated Historical Chronicle* (*Litsevoi letopisnyi svod*), 1570s. Ivan is crowned with a crown with crenellations or peaks, signifying his new imperial status.

svod, all these mighty rulers share the common trait of a crown with raised points or crenellations. Together, all these visual and symbolic markers trumpeted the Muscovite aspiration to be recognized as legitimately *imperial* rulers.

IVAN THE TERRIBLE: IMPERIAL PRINCIPLES IN PRACTICE

Ivan the Terrible (b. 1530, r. 1533–1584) presents an interesting and challenging case study. The first Russian ruler consistently to claim the title of tsar/emperor, Ivan set many of the patterns that would characterize later Muscovite governance, but he also flagrantly and dramatically flaunted other norms. Historians often divide Ivan's reign into two parts, roughly the "good," reforming early years, up to around 1564, and the "terrible," chaotic later years, 1564 until 1572 in some tellings, and right through Ivan's death in others. While this chronology oversimplifies the story and papers over the violence of the early period, it does reflect something of the overall condition of the state in these periods.[1]

The beginning of his reign ushered in a number of important institutional and cultural programs. Under the leadership of Metropolitan Makarii (1542–1563), the head of the Russian Orthodox Church, scribes and scholars assembled vast compilations of religious and historical writings, amassing thousands of manuscript pages. Makarii oversaw the development of important programs of fresco paintings that adorned the walls of important churches and royal chambers inside the Kremlin and beyond. Together, much of this cultural production was designed to convey the essentials of a newly evolving political-theological theory about the role of the tsar in an eschatological narrative of Russia's role in divine history. The tsar was envisioned as divinely selected emissary, entrusted with the weighty responsibility of ruling with sternness and mercy and leading his Orthodox Christian people to salvation at the End Times, the fateful day of the Last Judgment. This was a triumphant vision that celebrated the certainty of divine approbation, not one that dwelled on terror and despair in the face of a coming apocalypse. Given a pious, righteous ruler, Orthodox Russians could rest easy in their destined march toward salvation and heavenly rewards.

The early years of Ivan IV's reign built on and escalated precedents already evident under his recent predecessors. A number of institutional reforms created new structures and administrative-judicial practices. The *Sudebnik* (law code) of 1550 updated and greatly expanded on Ivan III's *Sudebnik* of 1497. The earlier code pertained primarily to the fair and impartial conduct of trials. The 1550 code, by contrast, extended its ambition. It aimed to regulate not just the behavior of state officials but of the population more broadly. It touched upon both criminal and what we would call civil affairs, such as property rights and

---

[1]On Ivan's minority, see Mikhail Krom. "The 'Widowed Kingdom'," *Russian Studies in History* 53, no. 1 (2014), 13–27; and his *"Vdovstvuiushchee tsarstvo": Politicheskii krizis v Rossii 30–40-kh godov XVI veka* (Moscow: Novoe Literaturnoe Obozrenie, 2010), pp. 120–28, 407–10.

inheritance. It enumerated fines to be assessed in cases when members of society were dishonored by the words or actions of others. Monetary compensation varied according to the gender, social rank, and standing of the offended party, thus continuing the long-standing commitment to viewing society as composed of different collectives with different allocations of privileges and obligations.

Reforms of local administration, tax-collection, and policing delegated those functions to locally selected officials. Previously, taxes and policing had fallen to designated *namestniki* (often translated as vicegerents), members of the elite who were granted regional jurisdictions as their "feeding" zones (*kormlenie*), areas and populations from which they were free to squeeze as many resources as they could over and above what they owed to the grand princely treasury. In the formal decrees introducing the reforms, Ivan or his advisers acting in his name (since he was only three years old when he took the throne) declared that the ruler granted this devolution of administrative functions in response to local requests. It is noteworthy that a regime that would go down in history as the zenith (or nadir) of arbitrary, cruel despotism went out of its way to advertise its responsiveness to the desires of local communities. The delegation of function proved a cagey move on the part of the regime: in one sweep the reforms freed communities from the exploitation and arbitrary exactions of the *namestniki* and obligated them to take on those responsibilities free of charge. By granting a degree of self-administration, the regime coopted the population as a whole into the business of running the state, and made the local representatives answerable with their lives and fortunes for the success of their operations. If the locally appointed tax officials (known as *starosty* or elders) failed to collect the mandated tax money or the locally chosen police elder allowed criminals to run free, they were, by oath, sworn to accept "whatever penalty you, Sovereign, decree." The consequences for these local agents could be harsh: whipping, imprisonment, confiscation of property, or enduring prolonged beatings on the shins. Election to these posts was, understandably, viewed as a mixed blessing.

Ivan's reign also saw the first summoning of an "assembly of the land (*zemskii sobor*)," an ad hoc gathering of church hierarchs, secular elites, and free ranks of townspeople and servitors who convened in the capital, usually at the initiative of the tsar and his council, to consult with them on pressing issues of the day. Similar assemblies continued to meet at the tsar's initiative, or, in the absence of a tsar, at the initiative of concerned groups of people, well into the seventeenth century. An assembly of the land should not be confused with a legislative body. It was not a parliament with decisive or binding powers, nor was it elective in a modern sense of the word. There was no ongoing institutional structure in place, and no commitment to or expectation of regular convocations. It did, however, embody the same impulse that we have seen in the decrees on local administration: an imperative to demonstrate the regime's interest in broader opinion and its concern with obtaining public acquiescence. Historical scholarship has invested enormous ideological meaning in the *zemskii sobor*, which has become a touchstone for the political values of its interpreters at any given moment. It has been interpreted as everything from an expression of the soulful unity of tsar and people (a romanticized vision) to a genuine "estate-representative" democratic body (a rosy-tinted vision) to a crass, meaningless sham (an interpretation that prompts the question of why anyone bothered to call such meetings repeatedly, if they had no meaning). In assessing the phenomenon of the *zemskii sobor*, it is important to set aside expectations and judgments based on western European norms. "Democracy" was not an available or even remotely desirable goal for Muscovites: in fact, in one of his querulous letters to Queen Elizabeth of England, Ivan derided her for letting lowly merchants guide her policy decisions instead of imperiously making them herself. What the *zemskii sobor* tradition allowed was a channel of communication between tsar and people, a way to gauge the climate of opinion, their willingness, for instance, to subsidize a war, and a way to involve a relatively broad cross-section of the population in the processes of decision-making and governance. It pulled common people, townspeople, and merchants from provincial towns and petty gentry landholders from their provincial estates, as well as high-ranking nobles and church hierarchs, into a shared public experience. While we have no letters or reports to document the reactions of participants, when they returned to their homes, they could say and feel that they had been part of great events, they had witnessed historic decisions in the making. Whether or not they had an actual voice in the proceedings, its deliberate theatricality coopted participants, turning spectators into actors. It functioned as one of many "strategies of integration," as historian Nancy Shields Kollmann describes them.[2] As we will see, shortly after Ivan's reign, when the tsarist line died out and Muscovy languished without a ruler, the *zemskii sobor* tradition offered a means for the Russian people to gather and work out a solution to the dangerous vacuum that faced them. These various mechanisms exemplify the ways that Russia's imperial regime consciously and demonstratively showcased its duties of reciprocity, of listening, involving, and responding to the supplications of its people.

Ivan the Terrible did not earn his historical epithet by just and merciful reform, however, and it seems appropriate to spend a few moments on the other side, the strange and violent aspect of his reign. Even his "good" early period was punctuated with outbreaks of violence and intimations of things to come, but the true horrors began in December 1564, when the monarch abruptly abandoned his post and withdrew from Moscow. This understandably threw his people into great confusion, as the chronicles report. Hereditary rulers simply do not quit. Great processions of Muscovites trudged out to Alexandrov, the monastic enclave where he had taken refuge, and begged him to return to his people. The tsar agreed, on condition that he be given a free hand to punish the high nobles, known as boyars, and the less-exalted bureaucrats who, he asserted, had been robbing the treasury and generally taking advantage of their posts. His anger, he added, did not extend to the common people. With this irascible outburst began

---

[2]Nancy Shields Kollmann, *By Honor Bound: State and Society in Early Modern Russia* (Ithaca, NY: Cornell University Press, 1999), pp. 169–202.

Ivan's *Oprichnina*, a painful time in Russia's history when Ivan's henchmen, called *oprichniki*, rode about the country in black robes, with severed dogs' heads and brooms attached to their saddles (ostensibly to sniff out treachery and sweep it away), with free rein to rob, extort, rape, and kill the rest of the population, the so-called *Zemshchina* or "the Land."

The source base for this episode is riddled with problems: surviving Russian documents either keep cautiously silent or suffer from questions about their authenticity, and foreign accounts tend toward the sensational. Like today, blood and gore sold well in sixteenth-century Europe, so it is hard to assess the truth of the outrageous tales of villainous Ivan playing cat-and-mouse games with his foes, ordering his victims served up with apples in their mouths, or whooping it up (shouting "Hoyda! Hoyda!") with his son and his gang of thugs while slaughtering people in the street.

Given the questions that shroud the sources, historians have been unable to reach a consensus concerning the *Oprichnina*. It has been interpreted as everything from an enlightened strategy by a strong, centralizing ruler to the insane paranoia of a madman. In the arc of Russian history, it has been described as perfectly epitomizing the despotism of a tyrannical system or, alternatively, as an aberrant moment, a violent exception to a far more restrained norm. A recent monograph by Nancy Shields Kollmann on crime and punishment in Muscovy lends weight to the argument that the *Oprichnina* was seen at the time as a shocking state of exception to the rule of law and standards of justice that were already well established by the mid sixteenth century.[3] Moreover, the fact that Ivan felt compelled to break free of the limits that constrained his retribution against the boyars suggests that such limits indeed existed prior to his creation of the *Oprichnina*, or at least that he thought they did. No formal institutional checks and balances were in place to restrain his actions, but well-placed people expected the tsar to consider their interests. Ivan may well have felt the weight of the inclusive, consultative, and consensual mode of decision-making that had been standard practice for centuries. Perhaps even the common people shared the expectation of merciful protection, as suggested by the tsar's (untrustworthy) reassurance that they would be spared his wrath. Judging by the fleeting hints in the carefully worded Russian chronicles of the time, the tsar's willful actions seem to have been viewed by his bewildered people with consternation and alarm.

Nonetheless, in some ways even this exceptional moment of tyrannical excess conforms to and confirms the central pattern we have identified in Russia's imperial rule, that is, rule through division and distinction. Consider the strategy adopted by the erratic ruler when he decided to discipline perceived traitors. Instead of concentrating power, he divided it. He invented his *Oprichnina*, a separate, special realm for himself and his inner circle, where the rules that applied to the rest of society no longer obtained. The choice of the name is significant: *oprich'*

---

[3]Nancy Shields Kollmann, *Crime and Punishment in Early Modern Russia* (Cambridge and New York: Cambridge University Press, 2012), pp. 314–21.

means "except," and the term *oprichnina* was used to designate a widow's portion, a share of land or wealth set aside, apart, separate from an estate. His *Oprichnina* operated literally as a state of exception. In a system based on different rules for different collectives of people by status, religion, type, or location, Ivan acted logically and in accord with the fundamental inegalitarian and particularistic premises of his time. To find a space for innovation, he had to create a new subdivision and decree the specific laws and rules by which its members would be governed. In this case, the newly prescribed law was lawlessness.

Elements of the same strategy of imperial differentiation may have been in play in later episodes when Ivan abdicated the throne and installed others—first his sons, then, in 1575, a Chingissid convert, Simeon Bekbulatovich—in his place, carving out a humbler appanage for himself as "Prince Ivan Vasil'evich of Moscow." To guarantee the staffing of his "lesser" court, Ivan petitioned his new sovereign that he should have the pick of men, who would be assigned to him without penalty. Again, the rationale for this action remains murky, but the resort to a strategy of division and separation is clear and consistent. After briefly entertaining the "rule" of Bekbulatovich, Ivan resumed his tsarist station but continued his course of subdivision: he named Bekbulatovich "Grand Prince of Tver," one of the formerly independent princely appanages, a title he held for a decade.[4] Subdividing and differentiating the realm into distinct units, slicing it up into component parts with unique concatenations of rights and obligations, came as easily to Ivan and was as much a part of his political culture as was dividing his world into allies and traitors and chopping the latter into their component parts.

The Muscovite state took the interests of the elite as its primary concern. But the state also had its own interests that sometimes differed from those of the noble elite. Moreover, the state considered the interests of its lowly subjects as well. We cannot tell to what extent tsarist concern with the common folk was motivated by fear of resistance and rebellion, by a tradition of reciprocity between ruler and ruled, or by conviction that the ruler was obligated to protect his people and give them justice, but the obligation to care for the humble flock figured prominently in Muscovite discourse. At least from the mid-sixteenth century, Muscovite political rhetoric maintained that the tsar was supposed to rule "with sternness and mercy," to live up to God's standards of justice. Metropolitan Makarii was responsible for surrounding the young Ivan with a wealth of didactic imagery intended to inculcate in him a sense of his obligation to rule piously according to the mandate of his divine overlord.

Over time the message seems to have spread beyond the elite circles that crafted them, to be internalized and insistently expressed by the tsar's subjects. In petitions to the tsar, in trials, and in times of riot and rebellion, the populace

---

[4]Most recently on Bekbulatovich: Donald Ostrowski, "Simeon Bekbulatovich's Remarkable Career as Tatar Khan, Grand Prince of Rus', and Monastic Elder," *Russian History* 39, no. 3 (2012): 269–99; and discussion by Aleksandr Filiushkin, Charles J. Halperin, and Janet Martin, 301–338; response by Ostrowski, 339–45.

reminded the ruler of his responsibility to serve their interests and the interests of God on high. During a major urban revolt in 1648, gentry petitioners emphasized this point, writing: "Remember that you, Sovereign, were called to the tsardom by God himself, not by your own wish." When necessary, the ruler was considered justified in using force to maintain order, or even obligated to do so. The same gentry petitioners in 1648 complained that the tsar was overly merciful and had failed in his duty to punish wrongdoers. "God chose your Sovereign father of blessed memory and you, Great Sovereign, . . . and entrusted to you, Sovereigns, the tsarist sword for the punishment of evildoers and the praise of the virtuous." Because he failed to use that sword, and "as a consequence of the fact that your tsarist highness is so patient, evil people . . . accrue all sorts of advantages and riches from serving on state business, regardless of the fact that through them destruction overtakes the entire people." "Everyone is weeping to the sovereign," they reported, "that the sovereign, they say, does not stand up for us poor people, for the lowborn and the defenseless, handing over his realm to thievery."[5]

One might call this appeal for punitive action "consensual violence," that is, the legitimate and accepted use of force justified within the conventions and values of the social order. Ivan IV was described as "awesome" (*groznyi*), which has been translated as "terrible" but actually meant fearsome or awesome, characteristics which the seventeenth-century petitioners saw as positive attributes in a sovereign ruler. But Ivan went further than other tsars in his unsanctioned use of violence, provoking murmurs of dismay and perhaps muffled efforts at conspiracy (though not actual revolt) within his realm. When his son and heir died suddenly, probably from a blow dealt by the tsar himself, the Riurikid dynasty sputtered to a halt, leaving the throne vacant, Moscow "widowed," and ushering in the *Smutnoe vremia* (Time of Troubles).

MUSCOVITE AUTOCRACY: POWER AND OBLIGATION

Russian autocrats (*samoderzhtsy*, pl.; *samoderzhets,* sing.) claimed that their power stemmed from a combination of inheritance and divine selection (through the Church). The term *samoderzhets* had from the sixteenth century meant a sovereign ruler free of foreign overlordship, not one having unlimited autocratic power.[6] Russia remained a country in which politics were about "the competition between boyar clans and the personal relations of those clans and individuals within them with the tsar . . . The tsar ruled by balancing boyar factions among

---

[5]"Nakaz Vladimirtsev vybrannomu imi iz svoei sredy dvorianinu . . ." (June 28, 1648), *Sankt-Peterburgskii Institut istorii RAN (SPbII)* [St. Petersburg Institute of History], *sobranie A. M. Artem'eva,* no. 2.
[6]Paul Bushkovitch, "Succession, Election, Autocracy, and 'Absolutism' in Early Modern Russia," unpublished paper delivered at the Russian History Workshop, University of Michigan, October 25, 2012, p. 5.

each other and balancing all the boyars with his personal favorites."[7] The autocrats were obligated both by ideology and practical constraints to receive the consent of an inner circle of boyars. At moments of crisis in the late sixteenth and first half of the century, they consulted with and were acclaimed by a broad cross-section of stakeholders interested in the outcome of the political chaos, gathered at assemblies of "all the land."

For all the attention paid to the obligations of the monarch to the will of the "land," the actual policies of the regime aimed to extract maximal resources from the land with minimal expenditure. The reform of local administration, discussed above, exemplified this mode of governance: casting the reform as a generous response to popular supplication, the new forms of local administration facilitated tax collection and policing on the cheap by dumping them onto local communities. In similar fashion, the state rewarded its armies with land rather than salaries and expected military men to support themselves from their estates. From the late sixteenth century, the regime bolstered its elite servitors' position by guaranteeing them a pool of free labor. A series of decrees legally fixed people to the land, enserfing the mass of the peasantry. Tying the peasants to the land served multiple interests at once. Not only did it satisfy the landholders and permit the state to maintain an unsalaried army, but it also shifted much of the burden of maintaining law and order onto the landlords, facilitated the task of keeping track of taxpayers (now locked in place), and preserved the viability of taxpaying collectives by keeping their members accountable and on the spot.

It is worth noting that some benefit accrued to the peasants themselves in the initial phases of enserfment, although later generations faced harsher strictures. Peasants were tied to the land, restricted in their movements, but at the same time they were guaranteed land to work and with which to provide for their families and pay what was due to their lords. Moreover, since taxes and dues were assessed collectively, it served the interest of peasant farmers to make sure their neighbors stuck around and shouldered their share of the payments. Otherwise, the entire burden would fall on those who remained. While some peasants clearly chafed under the restrictions of enserfment legislation, as demonstrated by the large number of runaways reported by irate landholders, others may have appreciated the security that they gained. In the parallel case of townspeople, active support for an equivalent restriction of movement is clear: petitions survive in which townspeople plead for a ban on residents' leaving the town and shirking the collective obligation to pay taxes. It is also illuminating to recall that the binding of peasants to the land in Russia occurred at roughly the same time that English peasants were being deprived of land through the so-called enclosure movement, which legislated the privatization of common lands, forced hundreds

---

[7]Ibid., p. 7; Nancy Kollmann, *Kinship and Politics: The Making of the Muscovite Political System, 1345–1547* (Stanford, CA: Stanford University Press, 1987); Robert Crummey, *Aristocrats and Servitors: The Boyar Elite in Russia, 1613–1689* (Princeton, NJ: Princeton University Press, 1983).

of thousands of people off their lands, and increased "free labor" and production for the market, thus laying the foundations for capitalism in England.

In attempting to stabilize the population, the regime also stimulated certain kinds of mobility—desertion, flight to the frontiers and beyond, posting, migration, or exile to Siberia and Ukraine. The Muscovite state was coercive and relatively weak. It could come down hard on transgressors, but only on selective occasions and only when it was informed and could find the malefactors. Moreover, it was ambitious, and its expansive agendas led to ambivalent policies. Legal decrees mandated that the population stay put: peasants on their landlords' estates, townspeople in their towns. Yet the need to build and man the fortresses along the frontier and to farm or hunt in newly conquered lands impelled policymakers to hedge their bets. Movement was prohibited and flight was proscribed, except to the frontiers, where the influx of men was welcomed. Even the leaden weight of serfdom, thus, proved conditional, situational, variable, depending on the time, place, and circumstances.

WHO WERE THE MUSCOVITES? WHAT WAS RUSSIA?

By the fifteenth and sixteenth centuries, Moscow emerged as the single dominant power in the lands of Northeast Rus, and began to articulate a commitment to a specifically Russian Orthodoxy, premised on the sovereign independence of the Orthodox ruler. Although Russia may not yet have been an empire in the full sense of the word, by the late fifteenth century Russian sources express a sense of satisfaction in the grand prince's supreme sovereignty and Orthodox mandate.

Residents of the northeast Slavic lands gradually came to express elements of a sense of internal solidarity cultivated through shared experiences, through the consolidation of religion, the institutional growth of the Church, linguistic differentiation, and eventually by the overarching presence of a single Muscovite state (from roughly the fifteenth century). At the frontiers, identification with a sense of Russian distinctiveness was sharpened in the struggles with peoples seen to be different. Religion served in those pre- and early modern times much as ethnicity does today, as one available vocabulary of identity, but even something as seemingly straightforward as a religious divide proved difficult to recognize and maintain. The Greek Orthodox Church, for instance, brought Christianity to the shores of the Dnieper in the ninth century, and provided direction for the Russian Church for centuries thereafter. But after 1437, when the Greeks attempted to unite with their Catholic rivals in a fruitless bid to stave off Ottoman assaults, Greek Orthodoxy became corrupted in Russian eyes, and after the fall of Constantinople to the Turks sixteen years later, the Greek Church was further tainted by its "captivity," its subordination to the rule of the Sultan. After the Ottoman conquest, when Greek scholars, clerics, and theologians fled their homeland and took refuge in the seminaries and universities of Europe, their "Greek" Orthodoxy took on shades of the Jesuit-inspired Orthodox institutions that sheltered them. Historian Nikolaos Chrissidis demonstrates that when Muscovy in the seventeenth century turned to these erudite "Greeks" for religious guidance and instruction, the theology, curricula, textbooks, and science that they brought with them were already as much Jesuit as Greek.[8] As a people, Greeks, despite being Russia's enlighteners and co-religionists, carried a social stigma in Muscovy. Russians frequently described them as cunning, devious, and scheming, in contrast to Muscovites' self-designation as simple, honest, and straightforward. Religion alone, or religion simply defined, could not offer an unambiguous litmus test for membership or exclusion, for belonging or foreignness.

For all its isolation and supposed xenophobia, Russia was surprisingly ecumenical in its attitudes toward foreigners. Vasilii III (r. 1505–1525), for instance, took as his second wife Elena Glinskaia (who would become mother to Ivan the Terrible), whose father and uncles were relatively recent immigrants from the Grand Duchy of Lithuania. As Paul Bushkovitch writes of her uncle, who became influential at the Muscovite court, he was "an Orthodox prince of Tatar origin (the official genealogy made him a descendent of Mamai and in the female line from Chingis Khan) from the Grand Duchy of Lithuania."[9] Her complex background posed no obstacle to marriage at the highest level.

In the later sixteenth and seventeenth centuries, within the ethnically and religiously heterogeneous realm, the "test" for advancing in Muscovy, in most situations, was profession of Russian Orthodoxy. In most instances, conversion to Orthodoxy would suffice to allow foreigners or non-Slavic subjects to move laterally into Russian society, maintaining whatever rank in the social hierarchy they had enjoyed previously within their own community. Even at the most elite level, converted nobles and royals could slot right into the Muscovite court hierarchy. Conversion smoothed the way for Ivan the Terrible's second wife, Kuchenei Temriukovna Cherkasskaia, the daughter of a Muslim prince from Kabardia in the North Caucasus. She converted to Orthodoxy, taking the baptismal name Maria, and her brothers rode her coattails to success in the court elite. However, conversion was neither fully sufficient nor absolutely essential to integration in Muscovite society.[10] Newcomers not infrequently managed to slip into the Muscovite elite without undergoing conversion, and, on the other hand, the sacramental cleansing of baptism did not remove all traces of difference from "new converts." Favorably disposed Chingissid princes left the world of the steppe khanates to enter Muscovite service in the mid-fifteenth century and were rewarded by Grand Prince Vasilii II with their own dependent khanate in the southeasterly region of Kasimov, where they were able to administer their own

---

[8]Nikolaos Chrissidis, *An Academy at the Courts of the Tsars: Greek Scholars and Jesuit Education in Early Modern Russia* (DeKalb: Northern Illinois University Press, 2016).

[9]Paul Bushkovitch, "Princes Cherkasskii or Circassian Murzas: The Kabardians in the Russian Boyar Elite 1560–1700," *Cahiers du monde russe* 45, no. 1–2 (2004): 9–30; quote on p. 11.

[10]Janet Martin, "Multiethnicity in Muscovy: A Consideration of the Christian and Muslim Tatars in the 1550s–1580s," *Journal of Early Modern History* 5, no. 1 (2001): 1–23. Charles Halperin, "A Chingissid Saint of Russian Orthodox Church: The Life of Peter, Tsarevich of the Horde," *Canadian-American Slavic Studies* (1975): 324–35.

people within and apart from the Muscovites, their quasi-independence delegated in an imperial fashion.[11]

Historian Charles Halperin analyzes the historical path of "Peter, Tsarevich of the Horde," a scion of the Chingissid line who converted to Orthodoxy and entered the Russian landholding elite in the fourteenth century. His conversion and piety earned him the status of saint by the fifteenth century when his "Life" was composed. But despite his easy passage from Muslim Tatar to Russian landholder and Orthodox saint, when it came time to choose him a bride, his new sovereign found him a suitable Tatar convert. Janet Martin finds that low-level military servitors too continued to seek spouses among their own kind and to follow different agrarian patterns, with more emphasis on animal husbandry than agriculture, than their ethnically Russian counterparts. These different patterns persisted even after converts settled in historically Russian areas and continued several generations after conversion. While conversion could ease horizontal movement, it did not entirely erase heritage. Still, as a general principle, Yuri Slezkine's elegant summation holds true: "In seventeenth-century Muscovy, 'Russian' had been equal to 'Orthodox' (although not the other way around), and baptism had dispelled foreignness along with darkness."[12]

If not from the very beginning, then in the next few centuries, Russian identity, to the extent that we can detect it, became closely tied with religion, a shifting, expanding territory, and the state. The identification with Orthodoxy was both a link to something larger and more ecumenical than Russia, with Orthodox Christendom, but at the same time a link to a particularly Russian religion, services and rites performed in Slavonic rather than Greek. In the East, unlike Western Europe where a universal church speaking Latin dominated, various peoples took the universalism of Christianity and particularized it, made it their own "national" church. Armenians, Georgians, Bulgarians, as well as Russians transformed the message of Christ directed at all into a special message directed to their own. One of the leading scholars to emphasize the subjective side of ethnicity, Anthony D. Smith, adds yet another component that reinforces group solidarity: the idea of ethnic election, a belief that one's own group is a chosen people with a specific relationship to the land and to God.[13] Most if not all early modern societies in the Muslim and Judeo-Christian world developed some variant of a Chosen People mythology, but for Muscovy it bore special weight because of the Russians' awareness of being the sole

[11]Michael Khodarkovsky, *Russia's Steppe Frontier: The Making of a Colonial Empire, 1500–1800* (Bloomington: Indiana University Press, 2004), p. 203.

[12]Yuri Slezkine, "Naturalists Versus Nations: Eighteenth-Century Russian Scholars Confront Ethnic Diversity," in *Russia's Orient: Imperial Borderlands and Peoples, 1700–1917,* edited by Daniel R. Brower and Edward J. Lazzerini (Bloomington and Indianapolis: Indiana University Press, 1997), p. 32.

[13]Anthony D. Smith, "Ethnic Election and National Destiny: Some Religious Origins of Nationalist Ideals," *Nations and Nationalism* 5, no. 3 (July 1999): 331–55; see also his *Myths and Memories of the Nation* (Oxford and New York: Oxford University Press, 1999). On the New Israel idea in the Muscovite context, see Daniel Rowland, "Third Rome or the New Israel?" *Russian Review* 55 (1996): 591–614.

surviving independent Orthodox state in a world where all other Orthodox societies had fallen to the Ottomans or the Safavids. For this reason, when Ivan the Terrible's son died without an heir in 1598, and when one pretender after another scrambled onto the throne, the mythos of Russia as New Israel lent added bite to the struggle to define and protect Orthodoxy: if the battle were lost, divine wrath might sentence Russia to the banishment and dispersal that had been the fate of the Jews.

THE PEOPLE SPEAK: THE TIME OF TROUBLES

The Time of Troubles is another period in Russian history that has generated fierce debate among historians, and has generated as many explanations as monographs. A recent study by Isaiah Gruber offers a satisfying, multitiered interpretation. He argues that after the Riurikid line died out with the death of Ivan the Terrible's son Fedor in 1598, and in the absence of a clear heir to the throne, the inner circles in the Kremlin, and particularly Patriarch Iov, the head of the Russian Church, manufactured an innovative set of criteria for justifying the choice of a non-dynastic successor. The candidate they settled on was the last tsar's brother-in-law, Boris Godunov. Along with the familiar elements of divine will and clerical affirmation but without the usual ironclad support of genealogical descent, Iov developed and disseminated an expanded list of qualifications for rule. Godunov, he declared, had been selected by what Gruber labels "*vox populi*," popular acclamation, and "*vox feminina*," that is, he was blessed with the crown by his sister, widow of the late tsar. Neither of these elements of legitimation was a complete break with the past, which would have made them difficult to sell to the population at large. They both built on long ingrained traditions. The *vox populi*, for instance, had been tacitly acknowledged in Ivan the Terrible's decrees on local administration and in the living tradition of the Assembly of the Land, while the *vox feminina*, the specially blessed role of the wives and mothers of the rulers, had a similarly long and recognized place in Russia's religiously informed political theory. The tsaritsa's womb, as Isolde Thyrêt demonstrates, was understood as a blessed site, and her maternal sufferings gave her direct and immediate access to the blessings of another suffering mother, the Mother of God, heavenly paladin and protector of the realm.[14] Nonetheless, the patriarch took the bold step of featuring these two elements as key supports for Godunov's legitimacy, thereby unintentionally loosing an explosive force in Russia's history.

When Godunov fell dead in 1605 and a popular pretender who claimed to be the long-dead Tsarevich Dmitrii, youngest son of Ivan the Terrible, occupied Moscow, the same handy criteria of *vox feminina* and *vox populi* could be trotted out in support of his coronation, along with the old arguments about lineage, divine

---

[14]Isaiah Gruber, *Orthodox Russia in Crisis: Church and Nation in the Time of Troubles* (DeKalb: Northern Illinois University Press, 2012); Isolde Thyrêt, "'Blessed Is the Tsaritsa's Womb': The Myth of Miraculous Birth and Royal Motherhood in Muscovite Russia," *Russian Review* 53, no. 4 (1994): 479–96.

selection, and clerical acclamation. Conveniently for the pretender, the dead boy's mother attested to his miraculous return, and animated crowds affirmed his legitimacy. When this Dmitrii fell victim to the knives of his opponents, new ideological combinations and configurations of these planks intertwined in support of a rapid array of claimants to the throne, including a series of copycat False Dmitriis returned from beyond the grave, and other fabricated long-lost heirs. Each successful claimant to the throne installed his own patriarch, so church leaders rose and fell as quickly as their secular counterparts. Gruber argues that as religious leaders and their particular visions of Orthodoxy rose and toppled in rapid sequence, any sense of a monolithic Orthodoxy shattered, and the definition of Truth itself was up for grabs, to be defined by the victors or by the people.

For the sake of narrative and interpretive clarity, S. F. Platonov, who wrote a magisterial work on the Time of Troubles at the beginning of the last century, divided the Troubles into three phases: first, the dynastic crisis precipitated by the death of the last tsar without an heir; second, the social upheaval caused by Cossack rebellions and a mass movement in support of the first False Dmitrii; and third, a period of foreign invasions, when Polish and Swedish forces charged in to take advantage of the chaos in Muscovy. The Swedes occupied much of the northern territories, while the Poles marched all the way to Moscow and occupied the Kremlin. This dismal fate understandably called forth a strong response from Russians of all ranks and regions. Influential segments of the population mobilized in defense of their "widowed Moscow," to defend her from the onslaughts of Catholic Poles. Kuzma Minin, a merchant from the trading town of Nizhnii Novgorod, joined forces with Prince Dmitrii Pozharskii, who, despite his princely title was a petty landholder from the provinces. The two called upon their countrymen to make the two ultimate sacrifices, of money and lives, to save the tsardom from foreign domination. Platonov exults at the formation of a voluntary army, the "National Militia," that these ordinary Russians cobbled together at great cost in wealth and blood.[15]

During times of foreign invasion and resistance to occupation, people develop a reactive commitment to defend their way of life and their threatened political community. It is often in the face of foreigners that the legitimacy of one's own polity is affirmed.[16] In more recent centuries this came to be called patriotism or nationalism. In seventeenth century Russia, a sense of existential danger, allegiance to life as it had been known, and antipathy to foreigners—Catholic Poles, Lutheran

---

[15]S. F. Platonov, *The Time of Troubles: A Historical Study of the Internal Crises and Social Struggle in the Sixteenth- and Seventeenth-Century Muscovy*, trans. John T. Alexander (Lawrence: University of Kansas Press, 1970).

[16]The sociologist Randall Collins writes: "The power-prestige of the state . . . in the external arena, above all the experience of mobilization for war, is the most overwhelming of all social experiences. . . . The legitimacy of state rulers comes in considerable part from their people's sense of geopolitics as it affects their own state." (*Macrohistory: Essays in the Sociology of the Long Run* [Stanford, CA: Stanford University Press, 1999], pp. 8, 89.) Although, as we have seen in the previous chapter, some substratum of identification has to be in place before interactions with foreigners can even be perceived as such.

Swedes—motivated key leaders who in turn were able to mobilize ordinary people to come to the defense of Russia. At such moments of vulnerability and peril a more cohesive sense of a threatened collective arises. These movements, arising without a mandate from any constituted authorities, suggest that their leaders had reconceived of Russia not simply as the possession of the Muscovite tsar but as a pious community ruled by the tsar but, in his absence, constituted by the people.

The experience of mobilization must have been a heady one for the armed regiments, Cossacks, and merchants who took part. When finally the battles came to a halt and the throne still stood vacant, an Assembly of the Land gathered all the stakeholders outside Moscow in 1613. Through horse-trading and wheeling and dealing, they chose a new tsar, the young Michael Romanov, to ascend the throne. The *vox populi* had had its moment in the sun, and had chosen a sovereign that would cast the popular assembly back into shadow. To call this fleeting manifestation of collective awareness and mobilization a "national awakening," as Platonov did, would be premature. Nonetheless, this eventful fifteen-year period of the Troubles fostered a new popular collective consciousness and reinforced a sense of inclusion in the tsarist polity. What is more, the newly chosen Romanov dynasty acknowledged this new conception after 1613, emphasizing the fact that the coronation of Michael Romanov was triply determined: Tsar Michael's publicists celebrated the fact that he was chosen by the will of God, by dynastic connections to the defunct Riurikid line, and by the voice of the people, who, in turn were depicted as bearers of divine inspiration, the true repository of the will of God.[17]

Claims about who precisely had the authority to speak God's truth and what form that truth should take became bones of ferocious contention later in the century. Massive rebellions shook the realm repeatedly, picking up on familiar themes and practices, like pretendership and popular identification of the true, righteous tsar that had been introduced during the Troubles. Claudio Sergio Nun-Ingerflom describes a rising sense among the people that they constituted a collective repository of political legitimacy, beginning with the supporters of the False Dmitriis and maturing during the Razin Rebellion of 1670–1671. Led by the Cossack Stenka Razin and drawing most of its support from disgruntled Cossacks from Ukraine and from non-Russians in the Volga region, the rebellion moved toward Moscow and brought radical political ideas in its wake. Reflecting or generating a new, abstract sense of popular sovereignty, the rebel leader claimed to have the support of the (dead) son of the reigning tsar, but rather than trot out his pet impostor for all to see, he kept him invisible, intangible, thereby (according to Nun-Ingerflom's provocative argument) allowing his authority to disseminate into an abstraction, a shared sense of popular sovereignty.[18] Most contemporary

---

[17]Daniel Rowland, "The Problem of Advice in Muscovite Tales About the Time of Troubles," *Russian Review* 6, no. 1 (1979): 259–83.
[18]Claudio Sergio Nun-Ingerflom, "How Old Magic Does the Trick for Modern Politics," in *Witchcraft Casebook: Magic in Russia, Poland, and Ukraine, 15th–21st Centuries*, ed. Valerie Kivelson, *Russian History/Histoire russe* 40, no. 3–4 (2013): 428–50; and his forthcoming monograph, *Le Tsar c'est moi, ou L'Imposture permanente: une autre histoire politique de la russie, XVe–XXie siècles*.

historians are reluctant to read such a politicized national consciousness back into the seventeenth century, but as Gruber and Nun-Ingerflom's contributions demonstrate, a vocal movement in scholarship is pushing us to explore the kinds of collective affiliations and mobilizations that could coalesce, however temporarily, in the early modern period, well before the French Revolution put its modern stamp on the concept of the nation and of popular sovereignty.[19]

Some later reverberations of this dawning sense of popular Russianness can be felt in the ruptures within the Russian Orthodox Church in the 1660s. At that time, the religious unity that Russian Orthodoxy had enjoyed more or less unbroken to that point was riven by the first major Church schism, or rather, as historian Georg Michels would have it, by a series of schisms caused by widespread disaffection with the institutional church. Inchoate initially, these eruptions would later congeal into the Old Believer Movement, an effort to retain and recover older, supposedly more authentic forms of prayer and ritual. Conventional accounts maintain that the Schism grew out of a group of influential clerics and their even more influential patron, Tsar Aleksei Mikhailovich (b. 1629, r. 1645–1676), who were dedicated to the reform and purification of religious practice. What began amicably soon shattered into irreconcilable factions, divided primarily over issues of personalities and institutional hierarchies, but gradually crystallizing their disagreements over points of translation and ritual. The irascible Patriarch Nikon, who sponsored new translations of religious texts and took an idealized vision of originary Greek Orthodoxy as his template, clashed with the intransigent Archpriest Avvakum, a fiery preacher intolerant of the foibles of his parishioners and an intemperate critic of innovation. In 1667, both men were censured and demoted at a Church Council staffed by visiting Eastern Patriarchs and the Russian church hierarchy. The tsar stood back while the Council took action, but he supported the effort to guide the Church back to a more middle road.

The feuding parties framed the debates in eerily modern terms, and the texts of the Schism have served to fuel historical discussions of tensions between Church and State. Attempts, however, to see the Schism as a clash between the secular and the sacred or to cast it as Russia's answer to Europe's Reformations or to the Investiture Controversy—which in the eleventh and twelfth centuries pitted popes against monarchs—prove misguided. More to the point here, the debates over the relative merits of Greek as opposed to Russian practices raise the question of what "Russia" meant to these combatants. Avvakum's blistering attacks on Nikon's grecophilia and his insistent conviction that simple, pure, unadorned "Russian ways" marked the path to virtue, contain seeds of a far later, nineteenth-century, cultural nationalism and even foreshadow the rise of the Slavophile movement. But Avvakum's invective must be placed in the context of the seventeenth century,

---

[19]Valerie Kivelson suggests "enfranchised subjecthood" as a modified framework for understanding Muscovite political engagement and the kinds of entitlements that membership in the polity conferred on ordinary people. "Muscovite 'Citizenship': Rights without Freedom," *Journal of Modern History* 74:3 (2002): 465–89.

where the yardstick of cultural value had more to do with avoiding divine wrath than with justifying popular sovereignty.

Avvakum eventually met his death by fire, condemned for his stubborn heresy, and Nikon was stripped of his patriarchal title and confined in a monastery for his arrogant conduct, but the official Orthodox Church continued to endorse his position and to condemn the heterodox practices of sectarians, defrocked priests, and self-proclaimed prophets. With the help of highly educated Greek, Ruthenian (Orthodox Slavs from the Polish-Lithuanian Commonwealth), and Ukrainian clerics, the hierarchy continued Nikon's drive to improve the textual and educational standards of the Russian clergy. The involvement of "scheming Greeks" drew negative commentary from supporters of Avvakum, who wished to defend what they were coming to understand as ancient Russian traditions, regardless of their actual antiquity, from corrupting assault. Fueled by narratives of persecution and martyrdom, the Old Belief consolidated a position as defenders of the true Russian way, and the full unity of the Church was never to be restored.

IMPERIAL CONQUEST AND CONTROL

Ivan III, called the Great, set Moscow on an imperial course by conquering and incorporating previously independent polities, particularly Novgorod, which had evolved an altogether different political, cultural, and economic profile from Moscow, and which chafed against its incorporation for almost a century. With the incorporation of the enormous, fur-rich Novgorodian lands in the north in the last quarter of the fifteenth century, Muscovy's territories expanded many-fold. Importantly, the grand prince followed his victory with a massive deportation of leading landholders, deemed traitors not only to Moscow but to Orthodoxy because of their suspected attempts to ally with the Catholic Casimir IV, king of Poland and grand prince of Lithuania. Vying directly with neighboring Lithuania for territories in the west, Ivan III and his son, Vasilii III, enacted further relocations of populations, deliberately reshaping allegiances in contested border regions.[20] An imperial vision led to forced appropriation of property, removals of local elites, and the conferring of title to land to Russians considered more loyal to the regime. This action of collective branding of a group as traitors and their forced relocation en masse set an unhappy precedent. It would be adopted again in Novgorod and elsewhere by Ivan's grandson, Ivan IV, still suspicious of Novgorodians as a distinctive and inherently suspect category of people nearly a century after their initial subjugation. It would recur as a defining strategy of imperial rule throughout the centuries.

---

[20]M. M Krom, *Mezh Rus'iu i Litvoi: zapadnorusskie zemli v sisteme russko-litovskikh otnoshenii kontsa XV–pervoi treti XVI v.* Issledovaniia po Russkoi Istorii 4 (Moscow: Arkheograficheskii Tsentr', 1995), pp. 199–232. For an English translation of several chapters, see M. M. Krom, "Excerpts from Between Rus' and Lithuania: The West Russian Lands in the System of Russo-Lithuanian Relations at the End of the Fifteenth and in the First Third of the Sixteenth Centuries," *Russian Studies in History* 40, no. 4 (2002): 9–93.

Conventionally subsumed under the gentle turn of phrase "the gathering of the Russian lands," the extension of Muscovite sovereignty has sometimes been cast as the natural reuniting of an organic unity, the happy fusion of a people awaiting a strong leader to bring them together. But the violence of incorporation, the enduring distinctiveness of the cultures, and the collective punishment of the population, not to mention the imperious manner of the deportation and resettlement, reveal the growth of Moscow as a recognizably imperial process.

The further military victories of Ivan III's grandson, Ivan IV, initiated a new chapter in Muscovy's imperial history, recognized even at the time. With the conquest of Kazan and Astrakhan in the mid-sixteenth century, the Muscovite state incorporated ethnically compact non-Russian territories, indeed alien polities. It also transformed a largely Orthodox Slavic Russia, in which the non-Russian population lived scattered among Orthodox Slavs, into a recognizably multinational empire, with distinctive subordinated lands and peoples. These conquests differed from earlier incursions in the Lithuanian border regions and in Novgorodian lands. There the populations were predominantly Orthodox and spoke a form of Russian readily comprehensible by Muscovites. Both territories had long been contested and claimed by Moscow. The two Tatar khanates, Kazan and Astrakhan, were a different matter. They were freestanding, independent Muslim states, fragments remaining after the collapse of the Golden Horde. They were ruled by legitimate steppe rulers and populated by religiously, linguistically, and culturally foreign peoples. Muscovite control in its newly conquered holdings remained weak, even nominal, for decades after the conquest, but that did not diminish Russia's triumphant claims. Ivan immediately added "Tsar of Kazan" to his official title. Gail Lenhoff notes that "By January of 1553, diplomats were being instructed to reference the conquest as evidence of Ivan's imperial status," and to use this status to leverage further imperial claims in the former Kievan lands.[21]

The tsars adopted the designation *Rusiia* for their realm instead of *Rus*. Unlike the Byzantine emperor or the Mongol khan, the Russian tsar presented himself not as ruler of the whole world or universe, but only as the absolute and sovereign ruler of all of Russia (*gosudar', tsar' i velikii kniaz' vseia Rusii, samoderzhets*, that is, sovereign, tsar, and grand prince of all Russia, autocrat).[22] Yet as conqueror of Kazan and Astrakhan, the Muscovite tsar deliberately assumed the mantle of legitimacy of the Mongol khans, and as he pushed further south and east he sought the allegiance and subordination of the lesser rulers of Siberia and the North Caucasus.

Historians have formulated a variety of more or less satisfying explanations for the Muscovites' eastward drive, and probably some mixture of them was at

---

[21]Gail Lenhoff, "Politics and Form in the *Stepennaia Kniga*," in *The Book of Royal Degrees and the Genesis of Russian Historical Consciousness*, ed. Gail Lenhoff and Ann Kleimola (Bloomington, IN: Slavica, 2011), p. 162.

[22]Paul Bushkovitch, "The Formation of a National Consciousness in Early Modern Russia," *Harvard Ukrainian Studies* 10, nos. 3/4, *Concepts of Nationhood in Early Modern Eastern Europe* (1986), p. 363.

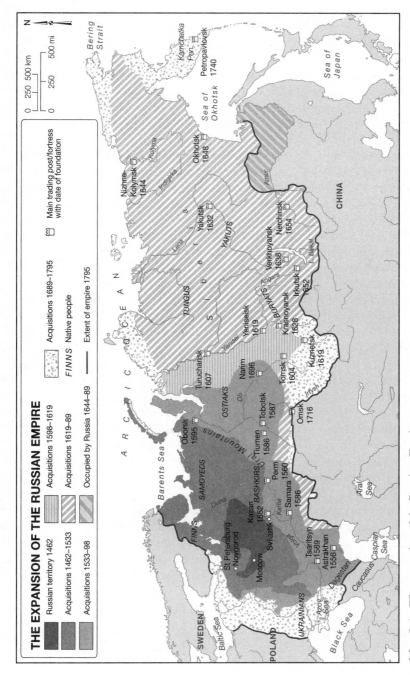

Map 2.1. The expansion of the Russian Empire.

THE EXPANSION OF THE RUSSIAN EMPIRE

- Russian territory 1462
- Acquisitions 1462–1533
- Acquisitions 1533–98
- Acquisitions 1598–1619
- Acquisitions 1619–89
- Occupied by Russia 1644–89
- Acquisitions 1689–1795
- *FINNS* Native people
- Extent of empire 1795
- ⊡ Main trading post/fortress with date of foundation

0   250   500 km
0   250   500 mi

Bering Strait

Kamchatka Pen.

Petropavlovsk 1740

Sea of Japan

Sea of Okhotsk

Okhotsk 1648

Amur

Nerchinsk 1654

CHINA

Kolyma

Nizhne Kolymsk 1644

Indigirka

Lena

Yakutsk 1632

YAKUTS

Verkhoyansk 1638

L. Baikal

Irkutsk 1652

Angara

BURYATS

ARCTIC OCEAN

TUNGUS

S I B E R I A

Yenisei

Yeniseisk 1619

Krasnoyarsk 1628

Turuchansk 1607

Ob

Narim 1696

Tomsk 1604

Kuznetsk 1619

OSTIAKS

Tobolsk 1587

Irtysh

Omsk 1716

Barents Sea

Oborsk 1595

Ural Mountains

Tiumen 1586

SAMOYEDS

FINNS

Dvina

Perm

Kama

BASHKIRS

Volga

St Petersburg

Novgorod

Moscow

Kazan 1552

Sviazhk

Samara 1586

Tsaritsyn 1589

Astrakhan 1556

SWEDEN

Baltic Sea

POLAND

UKRAINIANS

Azov Sea

Black Sea

Caucasus

Dagestan

Caspian Sea

Aral Sea

N

work. Some of these explanations can be dismissed as mystical ("the urge to the sea"), or political-polemical (inherent Russian aggression), products of the same kind of specious reasoning that gave American history the idea of "Manifest Destiny." Some variant on historical vengeance for centuries of Tatar domination is equally unfounded. More compelling is the argument that the Muscovite regime deliberately and systematically strategized to subdue the steppe. Prior to the conquest of Kazan, the Muscovites had already made several forays in that direction, and, having recognized the logistical difficulties of campaigning so far from home, they erected a fortress outpost at Sviiazhk as a staging post for their attack.

This vision of a premeditated plan for aggrandizement is complicated, however, by studies that illuminate the degree to which Moscow and Kazan were enmeshed in each other's politics prior to the conquest. Since the time of the Golden Horde and to some extent even before, Rus had been a full participant in the diplomacy and trade of the steppe. The era of Tatar domination had exposed them to the benefits of connecting with Eurasian trade routes. With constant exchanges of diplomats and princely hostages, Kazan and Moscow each had a long history of attempts to meddle in the other's internal affairs and external orientation without challenging the other's essential right to exist. It was only with the collapse of a scheme to install a friendly faction on the throne in Kazan that Moscow took the ultimate decision to besiege the city and incorporate the khanate. The distinction between manipulation of a puppet khanate, which may be considered a policy limited to hegemony, and outright imperial conquest may seem small in hindsight, but the shift in 1552 from equal participation in steppe politics to conquest and control actually signaled a sharp break in the tsardom's foreign policy and presaged the course ahead.[23]

In general, Muscovite diplomatic sources display little religious animus against their neighbors and partners to the east. As Brian Boeck notes, "until the last decades of the seventeenth century, relations between the Muscovite and Ottoman empires were couched in terms of 'love' and 'friendship'."[24] Even in clerical writings, polemical representations of a struggle with steppe powers as a war between Orthodoxy and Islam take on a divisive animus only from the mid-fifteenth century and developed more emphatically in the mid-sixteenth century with the conquest of Kazan. Metropolitan Makarii blessed those who fell in the Kazan campaign with "martyrs crowns," and a great icon, *Blessed Is the Host of the Heavenly Tsar*, painted to commemorate the battle, illustrates this promise. The icon depicts flights of angels delivering crowns straight from the hands of

---

[23]For more on the conquest of Kazan, see Jaroslaw Pelenski, *Russia and Kazan: Conquest and Imperial Ideology (1438–1560s)* (The Hague: Mouton, 1974).

[24]Brian J. Boeck, *Imperial Boundaries: Cossack Communities and Empire-Building in the Age of Peter the Great* (Cambridge and New York: Cambridge University Press, 2009), p. 41.

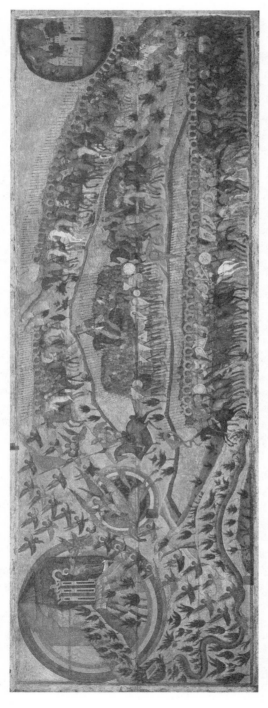

Blessed is the Host of the Heavenly Tsar, painted icon from the Dormition Cathedral of the Kremlin, 1550s. The icon depicts three layers of time simultaneously: biblical time, earthly-historical time, and the End Times. The city in flames on the right represents Sodom and Gomorrah, Kazan at the time of the conquest (1552), and the cities of the coming End Times. The walled city on the left represents Jerusalem, Moscow, and the New Jerusalem predicted in the Book of Revelation. The Mother of God and Baby Jesus hand out martyrs' crowns to the fallen soldiers.

Mary and Jesus to the fallen heroes returning from their victorious campaign to Moscow, depicted as the New Jerusalem of the Book of Revelation.[25]

Still, this "clash of civilizations" conception never fully replaced a more pragmatic approach to interaction with the steppe and its peoples. As Muscovite troops pushed farther into Muslim, shamanic, and ultimately Buddhist territories, they maintained a practice of having each of the parties involved in an agreement swear according to their own gods or their own customs, showing a willingness to accept and work with difference, to enforce compliance through a variety of forms of the sacred. For this purpose, a copy of the Koran was kept in the Kremlin, to facilitate mutually binding oaths with Muslim subjects and polities. As Michael Khodarkovsky has shown, once the goal of Muscovite policy had shifted away from joint participation to conquest and domination, the authorities were able to use their intimate knowledge of steppe practices to manipulate the outcomes. When the Shamkhal of Daghestan or the Kabardinian princes made an agreement with the tsar, Khodarkovsky explains, they believed they had concluded a treaty between equals, as Russian-Tatar agreements had traditionally been, but the Russians uniformly chose to translate and interpret the agreements as the supplications of inferiors to the mighty Russian sovereign.[26]

Not all Russian expansion can be so easily attributed to deliberate Kremlin policy. Some interpretations in fact posit the opposite explanation and claim that the initiative came from below, from free-spirited Cossacks, trappers, and explorers motivated by an inherent restlessness and a spirit of adventure. The state, in this scenario, followed willy-nilly after this ungovernable advance guard, doing its best to shore up unexpected gains and to protect its unruly subjects. A telling example, the famous Yermak, a Cossack leader who made the first inroads into Siberia, crossed the Ural Mountains without the permission of the tsar. In fact, Yermak and his men were outlaws, wanted for piracy along the Volga and Black Sea coasts, and they pushed into Siberia against the explicit (though ambivalent) orders of the tsar. Ivan IV ostensibly warned them not to rile up tribal people across the mountains. If they provoked attacks against Russians, they would suffer his wrath. If, however, they managed to subdue the Siberians, Ivan— speaking like a good businessman—said he might reconsider. As it happened, Yermak and his Cossack band defeated the Tatars of the Khanate of Siberia in 1581–1582 and drove the reigning khan out of his stronghold. They built a Russian outpost, Tobolsk, and soon received the tsar's blessing and support.

These two examples, Kazan and Tobolsk, indicate a joint initiative from above and below: Muscovite advance was a product of the combined efforts of state

[25]Daniel Rowland, "Two Cultures, One Throne Room: Secular Courtiers and Orthodox Culture in the Golden Hall of the Moscow Kremlin," in *Orthodox Russia: Studies in Belief and Practice*, ed. Valerie A. Kivelson and Robert H. Green (University Park, PA: Penn State University Press, 2003), pp. 33–57.
[26]Michael Khodarkovsky, "From Frontier to Empire: The Concept of the Frontier in Russia, Sixteenth-Eighteenth Centuries," *Russian History* 19, nos. 1–4 (1992): 115–28; *Where Two Worlds Met: The Russian State and the Kalmyk Nomads, 1600–1771* (Ithaca, NY: Cornell University Press, 1992).

planners and self-motivated adventurers, with an admixture of accident and luck. Following on the heels of these conquests, settlers flowed in from the Russian lands, again through a mélange of private ambition and state mandate. Peasants fled the increasingly constrained circumstances of serfdom to find freer opportunities in wide-open Siberia. At the same time, convicts found themselves exiled to Siberia by state authorities who, from the beginning of the seventeenth century, recognized that they could kill two birds with one stone: they could rid themselves of criminals and, at the same time, augment the Russian population of their new holdings. Just as foreigners had slotted into their equivalent positions in Muscovite society, so exiles were dispatched to Siberia and immediately enrolled in state service in some function parallel to what they had done at home. Exiles filled the ranks of the military; staffed the governors' offices; built the towns, churches, and fortifications; and farmed whatever land proved viable for agriculture. Siberia came to signify both freedom and exile.

Two other motivations behind Russian expansion demand serious consideration: profit and proselytizing. Profit is the more straightforward of the two, and unquestionably spurred on Russian conquest. Siberia, though cold and inhospitable, held dual allure: its wealth of natural resources and its possibilities as a conduit to the emporia of China and Central Asia. First on the Muscovites' agenda was securing the luxuriant pelts of Siberian martens, foxes, and especially valuable sables. Much of Russian expansion to the east into Siberia was motivated by a search for small, fuzzy animals.[27] Meditating on Siberia's long history as a source of natural resources, Alexander Etkind makes the interesting point that the fur trade is analogous to the exploitation of gas and oil in Siberia: "The state's dependence on them makes the population superfluous. Extracting, storing, and delivering these resources makes security more important than liberty. Reliance on these resources destroys the environment, natural and cultural. And as fur was centuries ago, so oil too is counted in barrels."[28] In the sixteenth and seventeenth century, however, Muscovite authorities worked according to a very different calculation. The subdued population was indispensible to Russian goals. Tsarist decrees are very explicit that the task entrusted to the servitors of the empire was to quell the indigenous people and to subject them to the *iasak*, the annual tribute collected in furs. Instructions from Moscow consistently insisted on the imperative to "bring the *iasak* people under the tsar's mighty hand," to administer an oath that they would serve him loyally, and then, to "protect the *iasak* people" and "treat them tenderly."

Treating the indigenous hunters and trappers of Siberia well, protecting them in their native ways, and guaranteeing them justice and mercy under the tsar's shielding hand were important, well-publicized elements of Moscow's strategy and vision for imperial control. In 1599, for instance, the newly crowned tsar Boris

---

[27]Erika Monahan demonstrates that fur was not the only, or necessarily even the most important, commodity traded in and through Siberia, but it certainly was a major one: *The Merchants of Siberia: Trade in Early Modern Eurasia* (Ithaca, NY: Cornell University Press, 2016).

[28]Etkind, *Internal Colonization*, p. 89.

Godunov specified that his Siberian officials should assemble the Siberian locals to assure them of his good wishes, his earnest protection, and his desire that they should suffer no need or oppression. The tsar promised, "that they should live in peace, without fees, in towns or yurts, in provinces and districts." He insisted that his goal was that "they should live in peace and quiet . . . and joyously, their fields will bring profit to us."[29] Fifty years later, the explorer Petr Beketev understood that his mission was to approach to indigenous people "with good, and not with war or violence," and "to bring the lands of unpacified indigenous peoples under the sovereign's great tsarist hand and to call them to him and rule them tenderly, and to collect *iasak* from them for the sovereign with great joy as the merciful God allows." Further, he should assure them they could remain securely in the land to which they belonged: "they would live within their landmarks, along the Selenga River and on Lake Baikal and along the Kilka River, without fear."[30]

Of course this benign plan did not reflect the full reality. In an earlier effort to collect furs from native Siberians, the same Beketev reported that various groups of Buriats, Tungus, and Iakuts "did not wish to come under the Sovereign's mighty hand," and so he and his men opened fire, indiscriminately killing the insubordinate resisters. He recorded forty dead in one skirmish, ninety in another. When a group of Iakuts refused to hand over the requisite tribute, "with God's mercy and the luck of the sovereign [Beketev's men] managed to take one of the fortifications, and killed 20 leaders in it." When they failed to take the rest of the fortified strongholds by direct assault, "they set fire to them with all the Iakut people inside."[31] Reports of massacre and carnage abound, and Russian imperial advance entailed all the hideous consequences, intended and unintended, that tend to accompany conquest and colonization. Disease devastated native communities, fur-bearing animal populations were overhunted and rapidly driven to extinction, and settlers expropriated land, disrupted animal and human migration patterns, and robbed indigenous peoples of their livelihoods. Native people were enslaved, and women were abducted or purchased as "wives" for the largely male Russian settlers. The picture was not pretty.

Yet precisely by the logic raised by Etkind, the population was *not* superfluous. The tsar needed the indigenous people as trappers, guides, translators, and laborers, and, what is more, needed them to maintain their non-Russian ways, their non-Russian identity. By a procedural quirk, only non-Christian natives were subject to the *iasak*; once converted, they were required to leave their natal communities (where the possibility of religious "backsliding" was considered too great a risk) and to move into Russian settlements. Within the fortified walls,

---

[29]G. F. Miller, *Istoriia Sibiri*, vol. 1 (Moscow and Leningrad: Nauka, 1937), 383–84 (no. 33); 381–82 (no. 31); 390–92 (no. 39).
[30]Petr Beketev in *Zapiski russkikh puteshestvennikov XVI–XVII vv.*, comp. and ed. N. I. Prokof'ev and L. I. Alekhina (Moscow: Sovetskaia Rossiia, 1988), pp. 361, 364–65.
[31]Basil Dmytryshyn, E. A. P. Crownhart-Vaughn, and Thomas Vaughan, eds., *Russia's Conquest of Siberia: A Documentary Record, 1558–1700*, Vol. 1 (Portland: Oregon Historical Society Press, 1990), pp. 136–48.

baptized with Christian names, these converts were folded into the Russian population and subject to the standard tax in money rather than *iasak* in fur. They were no longer useful as providers of furs once they converted and assimilated. So when the officials ordered, cajoled, and threatened their frontier representatives to treat the natives well, they had real reason to do so. They also had good reason, both practical and ideological, to preserve the natives in their traditional environments, protected in their distinctive ways and encouraged to exercise their skills as hunters and trappers.

Thinking back to the four-part schema of imperial approaches to conquered populations that we established in the Introduction, we see that Muscovite authorities had no incentive to *eradicate* their new subjects. Nor did they have an interest in *assimilating* them, another one of our four options, because assimilation diminished collection of *iasak*. This important finding returns us to the question of religious mission, or proselytism, the remaining prong of our exploration of motivations for Russia's imperial advance. Empire and evangelical mission so often marched hand-in-hand that historians have tended to presume this was the case in Russia as well. And certainly Muscovite records of conquest and expansion are filled with invocations of Orthodoxy, divine will, and illumination of the darkness. But these sources require careful reading to make sure that we can see what they meant, rather than what we *expect* them to mean.

Religious and secular authors alike extolled their imperial adventures as campaigns to spread the glory of God and tsar to the ends of the earth. For instance, Savva Esipov, a cleric in the service of the archbishop of Tobolsk, wrote the Esipov Chronicle in 1636. The hero of Esipov's account is the brave commoner and man of the people, the Cossack Yermak Timofeev, introduced above. In Esipov's telling, Yermak boldly fulfills the will of God:

> God sent his chosen one to purify the land and to conquer the infidel Khan Kuchium and to destroy the abominable gods and their unholy temples. . . . God chose a leader not from famous men, the Tsar's commanding generals and leaders, but the ataman Yermak son of Timofey. . . . [He and his men] gave their heads no rest and their eyes no sleep, until by the help of God they won victory over the accursed infidels.

Esipov insists that Siberia was conquered "by the will of God" and "by a Russian army, assembled and led by the *ataman* Yermak son of Timofey and his valiant, excellent company of like-minded thinkers."[32]

Yet, strikingly rare in this and other formulations from the time are references to actual conversion. The goal throughout was quite clearly "to purify the land" through the subjugation of the "accursed infidels," to have them bow to the superior might and glory of God and tsar. Their allegiance to the Orthodox tsar was

---

[32]*Yermak's Campaign in Siberia: A Selection of Documents Translated from the Russian Chronicles by Tatiana Minorsky and David Wileman*, ed. Terence Armstrong (London: Hakluyt Society, 1975), p. 62.

to be manifested by their taking a formal oath of submission and by payment of *iasak*, not by conversion. Orthodox enlightenment would spread across the land, but not primarily through amassing flocks of converts. Rather it would occur as a natural by-product of Russian colonization and rule. Esipov continued his description of the Christianization of Siberia: "the Russian Cossacks established cities there, and God's holy churches were erected."[33] Russian cities, churches, and settlers sufficed to Christianize the land. No conversion was required.

Writing about sixty years later, Semyon Remezov, another Siberian chronicler, proclaimed that "all Siberia has been glorified by God and affirmed in God's truths, and adorned with churches, and filled with towns and settlements in eternal glory." The same author imagined that Yermak's arrival in Siberia brought a "light of inexpressible joy" to the land, so "it was as though an eagle had covered his nest, Siberia, with his fledglings and had given each city a feather of his glory."[34] In a pointillist vision of Christianization, these Muscovite chroniclers took satisfaction in the Christianization not of the whole Siberian land and its indigenous population but rather of *points in space*. Each of these points was a Russian outpost or settlement. Each was sanctified by the presence of Russian Orthodox colonists. The sacrality of these Russian bastions was cemented by the erection of Orthodox "churches, . . . towns and settlements in eternal glory." This granular, non-homogeneous model of Christian empire is visually represented in Remezov's illustration of his vision of the eagle feathers of Christian glory, radiating out from a divine center to particular, isolated cities across Siberia.[35]

Missionary zeal was not a primary motivation in Muscovite expansion, though after conquest missionaries sometimes followed, in desultory fashion. Muscovites conceived of empire as a terrain on which their political and religious superiority could be established through a scattering of outposts that announced and enforced their dominance. The presence of people of other tribes, faiths, and customs on the rest of that land served to emphasize the greatness of the Christian sovereign who could coerce or inspire loyal servitude from such a variety of people. A Bashkir clan leader recalled that in the very year of the conquest of Kazan, the "White Prince," that is, the tsar, decreed: "Let no one run away, let all remain true to their faith and customs." In return for the leader's sworn oath (*shert*) and promise to pay tribute in marten pelts, the tsar bestowed on him "a "patent [*iarlyk*], gifts of food and satin cloth," and granted him "the rank of noble."[36] The variegated population and terrain underscored Muscovy's imperial standing and built the wealth of Orthodox Russia.

Muscovite power spread across Eurasia all the way to the Pacific by the 1630s. In the seventeenth century, they also became increasingly embroiled in the messy

---

[33]*Ibid.*, p. 70.

[34]*Ibid.*, p. 248.

[35]Valerie Kivelson, *Cartographies of Tsardom: The Land and Its Meanings in Seventeenth-Century Russia* (Ithaca, NY: Cornell University Press, 2006), pp. 149–70.

[36]Quoted in Willard Sunderland, *Taming the Wild Field: Colonization and Empire on the Russian Steppe* (Ithaca, NY: Cornell University Press, 2004), p. 22.

An illustration from Semyon Remezov's chronicle of Russian conquest of Siberia. The text announces that Yermak's arrival in Siberia brought a "light of inexpressible joy" to the land. The haloed eagle sends rays of Christian enlightenment to illuminate the land, but its rays reach only selected points in the Siberian landscape, that is, Russian cities and outposts. The rest of the land is untouched by the light. The big city at the bottom of the page is Tobolsk, capital of Russian Siberia.

politics of the Polish-Lithuanian Commonwealth and of the Ukrainian lands to the south and west. The incorporation of the Cossack-controlled territories of the Ukrainian frontier provides a useful complement to our investigation of Muscovite eastward advances. *Ukraina* means borderland or frontier zone, and it functioned throughout the Muscovite period as a buffer, an indeterminate gray area between regional powers.

The Cossacks, who have flickered in and out of our discussion, were a population of mixed ethnic origins, part Tatar, part Slavic, who formed bands in the loosely governed borderlands between Russia, Poland, and Crimea, land nominally governed by the Polish-Lithuanian Commonwealth in the sixteenth and first half of the seventeenth centuries. They operated as free agents, often signing on as mercenary or adjunct forces fighting for one or another of the rival states in the area. "Early Cossack identity was not defined by common language or common origins but by common interest," writes historian Brian Boeck, by their commitment "to an anti-bureaucratic and egalitarian political system." They defined their way of life through their commitment to *volia*, freedom, which they interpreted as freedom from regulation and registration, from conscription and serfdom, freedom to elect their own leaders and judge themselves in all matters.

Their fundamental values were in many ways the polar opposite of all that constituted Muscovy. And yet, in an insightful study, Boeck finds that the Muscovite state in many ways created the Cossacks and maintained them in their freedom.

Beginning in the sixteenth century, the Muscovites (like their Polish rivals) contracted with Cossack hosts to fight for them against their regional competitors, but as much as possible left their commitments undocumented. Conducting business off the books allowed the regime, as Boeck puts it, "plausible deniability" for any ensuing violence. By flying under the radar, Cossacks proved valuable weapons in Russia's contests with the Poles, Crimeans, and Ottomans. To preserve this arrangement, desirable to both parties, the state accepted the Cossacks' anomalous status and the Cossacks milked the situation. "By the mercy of the Great Sovereigns our Host is comprised of free people, and they live in cooperation with one another."[37] Boeck notes that although "the precise parameters of the deal would shift over time, and the contours of Cossack identity would also change dramatically, . . . the distinction between Cossacks and ordinary subjects of the tsar would persist into the twentieth century." We might depart from Boeck's assessment slightly, only to endorse his position more forcefully. The Cossacks, we would add, *were* "ordinary subjects of the tsar," in that they persisted as a distinctive collective, defined by their own culture and by the "separate deal" that they enjoyed within the empire. Some groups benefited more than others from these deals—for instance, Russian peasants, comprising about 90 percent of the population, suffered under the harsh conditions of serfdom, certainly a raw deal—but all were part and parcel of a heterogeneous agglomeration, an empire of separate deals.[38] More than three hundred years later, as we will see in Chapter 12, a weak post-Soviet Russian state under President Boris Yeltsin would in a similar pattern pay off regional governors with particular privileges and special arrangements in order to gain their support.

Muscovite leadership found in their covert deals with the Cossacks an inexpensive and safe alternative to open warfare with powerful neighbors. As Boeck writes, "the Muscovite state generally pursued a risk averse policy toward the steppe," with "cautious consolidation," rather than "unlimited expansion," as the "prevailing objective in the south." (Boeck proffers this reasoned reading as an alternative to the "one-size-fits-all" explanations often invoked by more polemical scholars. Norman Davies, for instance, described Russia's "addiction" to territorial conquest as "an extreme case of *bulimia politica*, of the so-called 'canine hunger,' of gross territorial obesity in an organism that could only survive by consuming more and more of its neighbors flesh and blood." Boeck strongly counters such a reckless and ahistorical characterization.)[39] Moscow's careful

[37]Brian Boeck, *Imperial Boundaries*, pp. 22, 27, 29.

[38]Ibid., p. 30.

[39]Norman Davies, *Europe: A History* (Oxford, 1996), p. 655; quoted in Brian Boeck, "Containment vs. Colonization: Muscovite Approaches to Settling the Steppe," in *Peopling the Periphery: Slavic Settlement in Eurasia from Muscovite to Soviet Times*, ed. Nicholas Breyfogle, Abby Schrader, and Willard Sunderland (London: Routledge, 2007), pp. 41–60; quote on p. 44.

avoidance of confrontation was hard to maintain, however, and through a complex chain of events in which Moscow weighed its risk-averse tendencies (already seen in Ivan IV's reluctance to inflame Siberian Tatars) against opportunity for expansion, by the mid-1650s the eastern Ukrainian lands came into the imperial orbit of the Orthodox tsar.

The decades that followed witnessed a curious twist in the cultural history of imperial annexation. While Moscow extended its dominion to areas previously under the sway of Catholic Poland-Lithuania, Ukrainian clerics flooded north, bringing with them sophisticated baroque forms, ideas, and educational models that swiftly came to define Russian culture. Articulating categories of Russianness and Orthodoxy, making explicit their overlaps, their inclusions and exclusions, these scholarly clerics played a critical role in developing an idea of a Russian nation. As historian Serhii Plokhy writes, "The entanglement of the concepts of nationality and imperial statehood that took place during the encounter between Kyivan [Kievan] and Muscovite elites appears to have been crucial for the formation of Russian imperial identity, and, additionally, for the "invention of Russia."[40] Appending their Ukrainian "Little Russia" to the broad category of "All-Russia," writers coming out of the Kievan-Mohyla Academy tradition advocated an inclusive Russian identity. They traced a seamless continuity stretching from Prince Volodymyr (or Vladimir, the medieval ruler) through "the successors of his pious Ruthenian state (*rossiskiia derzhava*), even unto our most illustrious and pious sovereign Tsar and Grand Prince Aleksei Mikhailovich, autocrat of all Great, Little, and White Russia."[41] While Moscow participated in the creation of the independent Cossacks, then, Ukrainian clerics advanced and profoundly influenced the creation of an idea of Russia.

With the annexation of Ukraine ("Little Russia") in 1654 and Vilnius ("White Russia") in 1655, the imperial claims were bolstered, and the monarch, Tsar Aleksei Mikhailovich, was proclaimed "tsar of all Great, Little, and White Russia."[42] He reveled in listing all the many lands that he ruled. Extending on the rather brief list we have seen on the seal of Ivan III, Aleksei was adulated as "sovereign tsar and grand prince, by grace of God, of all Russia, Vladimir, Moscow, Novgorod, tsar of Kazan, tsar of Astrakhan, sovereign of Pskov, and grand prince of Smolensk, Tver, Iurgorsk, Perm, Viatka, Bolgar, and others, sovereign and grand prince of the Nizhnii Novgorodian lands, of Chernigov, Riazan, Polotsk, Rostov, Iaroslavl, Belozero, Liefland, Udorsk, Obdorsk, Kondinsk, and ruler of all the Siberian lands and of the great river Ob, and ruler of the Northern lands and

---

[40]Serhii Plokhy, *The Origins of the Slavic Nations: Premodern Identities in Russia, Ukraine, and Belarus* (New York: Cambridge University Press, 2006), pp. 250–51.

[41]From the *Synopsis*, quoted in Plokhy, *Origins of the Slavic Nations*, p. 260.

[42]James Cracraft, "Empire Versus Nation: Russian Political Theory Under Peter I," *Harvard Ukrainian Studies* 10, nos. 3/4 (December 1986): 524–40; reprinted in Cracraft, ed., *Major Problems in the History of Imperial Russia* (Lexington and Toronto: D. C. Heath, 1994), pp. 224–34. Citations hereafter are from the former publication.

sovereign of many other lands."[43] The state seal of Aleksei Mikhailovich, adopted in 1667, depicted an eagle with raised wings, topped with three crowns symbolizing Kazan, Astrakhan, and Siberia, and bordered by three sets of columns, representing Great, Little, and White Russia.[44] In this late-seventeenth-century vision, state, Orthodoxy, autocratic tsar, and empire, with all its distinct constituent parts, were combined in an elaborate system of reinforcing legitimations. With a multiplicity of separate deals, diverse administrative formulas, tax and tribute arrangements, local exemptions and immunities, concessions and demands, the empire drew in its varied lands and peoples through responsive, locally specific policies of governance through distinction.

BRIEF BIBLIOGRAPHY

Boeck, Brian J. *Imperial Boundaries: Cossack Communities and Empire-Building in the Age of Peter the Great.* Cambridge; New York: Cambridge University Press, 2009.

Gruber, Isaiah. *Orthodox Russia in Crisis: Church and Nation in the Time of Troubles.* DeKalb: Northern Illinois University Press, 2012.

Khodarkovsky, Michael. *Russia's Steppe Frontier: The Making of a Colonial Empire, 1500–1800.* Bloomington: Indiana University Press, 2002.

Kivelson, Valerie A. *Cartographies of Tsardom: The Land and Its Meanings in Seventeenth-Century Russia.* Ithaca, NY: Cornell University Press, 2006.

Kollmann, Nancy Shields. *Crime and Punishment in Early Modern Russia.* Cambridge; New York: Cambridge University Press, 2012.

———. *Kinship and Politics: The Making of the Muscovite Political System, 1345–1547.* Stanford, CA: Stanford University Press, 1987.

Monahan, Erika. *The Merchants of Siberia: Trade in Early Modern Eurasia.* Ithaca, NY: Cornell University Press, 2016.

Plokhy, Serhii. *The Origins of the Slavic Nations: Premodern Identities in Russia, Ukraine, and Belarus.* Cambridge and New York: Cambridge University Press, 2006.

Romaniello, Matthew P. *The Elusive Empire: Kazan and the Creation of Russia, 1552–1671.* Madison: University of Wisconsin Press, 2012.

Rowland, Daniel. "The Problem of Advice in Muscovite Tales About the Time of Troubles," *Russian Review* 6, no. 1 (1979): 259–83.

---

[43]The great seal is reproduced in *Zapiski russkikh puteshestvennikov XVI–XVII vv.*, p. 351. Massa includes in the tsar's titles sovereignty over the Nogais, Severia, Livonia, and the Samoyeds: see Isaac Massa, *A Short History of the Beginnings and Origins of These Present Wars in Moscow Under the Reign of Various Sovereigns Down to the Year 1610*, trans. and ed. by G. Edward Orchard (Toronto: University of Toronto Press, 1982), p. 23. Dmytryshyn provides a slightly different version in Basil Dmytryshyn, E. A. P. Crownhart-Vaughan, and Thomas Vaughn, eds., *Russia's Conquest of Siberia, 1558–1700: To Siberia and Russian America: Three Centuries of Russian Eastward Expansion*, Vol. 1, *A Documentary Record* (Portland: Oregon Historical Press, 1985), p. 400.

[44]Richard S. Wortman, *Scenarios of Power: Myth and Monarchy from to Peter the Great to the Abdication of Nicholas II.* New abridged one-vol. paperback edition (Princeton and Oxford: Princeton University Press, 2006), p. 14.

THREE

Disrupting the Easy Road
from Empire to Nation-State
A Theoretical Interlude

Although imperialism carries a distinctly malodorous taint in the contemporary world, signaling intrusive and overbearing rule by outside, alien powers, its perfume smelled far sweeter in the eighteenth and nineteenth centuries. In fact, as we have seen in the previous chapter and will become even clearer in the following chapters, Russia worked hard to cast itself as an empire so it could keep up with its stylish neighbors, and worked overtime to convince those neighbors that they should take it seriously as such. Empire had set the bar high for sovereign power across Eurasia for millennia and persisted as a glorious model until the early twentieth century, but the newly emerging concept of "nation" began to give it a run for its money in the late eighteenth and early nineteenth centuries.[1]

Empire and nation are far from the only forms of power relations that are possible in a world of possibilities.[2] In our discussion of medieval Rus, for instance, we've seen a variety of other alternatives: "headless state," "galactic polity," tribal conglomerate, or symbolic union. A "city-state" model may also be usefully invoked for the period of Appanage Rus, although the state might still be hard to discern. In Muscovite times, we have noted a tactical reliance on "non-state entities," such as the Cossack hosts along the southern border, which allowed the tsarist regime to invoke a useful "plausible deniability" concerning cross-border violence inflicted by the Cossacks against Ottoman and Crimean Tatars. Political scientist Charles King explains that similar utility prolongs the unresolved status of unrecognized states such as South Ossetia, Abkhazia, and Transnistria

---

[1]Mark Beissinger, "The Persisting Ambiguity of Empire," *Post-Soviet Affairs* 11, no. 2 (1995): 149–84.
[2]Jane Burbank and Frederick Cooper, *Empires in World History: Power and the Politics of Difference* (Princeton, NJ: Princeton University Press, 2010), p. 10.

in the post-Soviet spaces of the twenty-first century.[3] Other non-national/ non-imperial actors proliferate when one adopts a wide-angle lens and looks beyond conventional state borders. Pirates, crime syndicates, mobilized diasporic or religious transnational movements, multi-state unions (such as the European Union and the United Nations), and multinational corporations all command people and resources, shape policy, and, to varying degrees, control violence in political formations that conform to neither of these two models. But in the late-eighteenth and early-nineteenth-century European context, political thinkers and actors were preoccupied with nation-states and empires as the most powerful and effective state formations, and they have dominated political thinking since that time.

In this chapter we jump ahead in our chronological narrative and anticipate developments yet to come for Russia as it moves into the eighteenth century. We pause for this digressive interlude in order to provide a theoretical road map of terms and concepts that will begin to come into play in the chapters that follow.

When we talk about nations, we might be referring to two quite different ways of thinking. The first and most common is to think of nations as real entities, objectively existing groups of people who are relatively homogeneous, bounded in some way by shared culture, conventions, and values, and who feel a common identity. This is certainly the way nationalists think about nations, and at times groups of people do experience such "nationness." The other way—and this is more common among scholars today—is to see the nation as far more subjective, as a creation of discourse, a way of imagining community, inventing traditions, and mobilizing people around the idea that they collectively constitute a continuous, organic whole with a historical past and a shared destiny. Here one would look at how various intellectuals, politicians, journalists, writers, artists, and ordinary people represent the nation, what they write, say, think, and feel about their common belonging and affiliation (and affection) for one another and sense of distance from and perhaps hostility toward those outside the nation.

All groups work out over time a sense of who they are and who they are not, and peoples and ethnic groups do the same. But it is precisely the style and language with which they describe and understand who they are, and predict what they are likely to need, that is key to what kind of group we are describing. Their shared identities give rise to convictions about their common interests. Stereotypes about national character may develop. Sometime, somewhere in early modern Russia, a holy fool (*iurodivyi*) ostensibly said, "We Russians do not need bread. We eat one another, and this is enough to satisfy us to the full."[4] In our understanding, we look at the various, changing ways Russians and others defined Russia and Russians, and we find the concepts of a people (*narod*) and a

[3] Charles King, "The Benefits of Ethnic War: Understanding Eurasia's Unrecognized States," *World Politics* 53, no. 4 (July 2001): 524–52.

[4] John Le Donne, "Ruling Families in the Russian Political Order, 1689–1825," *Cahiers du monde russe et soviétique* 28, nos. 3–4 (July–December 1987): 307.

nation are neither given nor fixed, but rather developing, changing, contested processes that are never completely made, and are constantly evolving.[5]

One might think of nation-state and empire as two state formations on a continuum, each one representing an ideal type that never exists in that pure state in the real world. Rather than fixed and stable, they may flow into one another, transforming over time into the other. One or the other form may dominate in a polity's mode of governance or a population's sense of collective affiliation, but those moments may dissipate and one mode may yield to the other. Empire—or imperialism, the activities of empires—is not a thing but a way of governing a state, a political practice that involves initially conquest and subordination of another and later maintaining, even producing or reproducing, difference and overlordship.

When a state apparatus attaches to the nation or makes its claim to legitimacy on the basis of the will of the people conceived as a nation, the result is a hyphenated concept, a nation-state. A nation-state as well is a way of governing by creating equal citizens under the law and eliminating distinctions and hierarchies as much as possible: one might call this process "nationalizing." A nation-state may appear stable, homogeneous, coherent, and yet with the rise of ethnic, sub-ethnic, religious, cultural, or regionalist movements may be perceived by subaltern populations as imperial. For those identifying with the dominant population in Belgium, it is a nation-state, perhaps a multinational state, but for a Flemish militant who feels the oppression of the Walloon majority, Belgium is a kind of mini-empire. The term *empire* has been used polemically for small states like Belgium, Georgia, and Estonia, and it may seem anomalous to refer to such nationalizing states as empires. But it is precisely with the assimilating, homogenizing, or discriminating practices of the nationalizing state that relationships of difference and subordination—here considered the ingredients of an imperial relationship—are exposed.

The more a state institutionalizes difference and maintains a hierarchy among its people between the ruling group or institution and the rest of the people, the more it approaches the ideal type of empire. The more a state attempts to homogenize its population, reduce difference and hierarchy, and bring the rulers in line with the people, the more it approaches the ideal type of a nation-state. Whether a state is in the process of nation-state building or empire-building can only be determined after the fact. If the core has been successful in integrating the population of its expanding territory into accepting the legitimacy of the central authority, then (nation)-state-building has occurred, but if much of the population is kept apart and distinct or rejects or resists that authority, then that state can be

---

[5]Here and throughout, we build on the work of many scholars in the field. On Russia's experience of empire in a comparative view, see, among others, Alexei Miller and Alfred J. Rieber, *Imperial Rule* (Budapest: Central European University, 2005); Jane Burbank, Mark von Hagen, and Anatolyi Remnev, eds., *Russian Empire: Space, People, Power, 1700–1930* (Bloomington: Indiana University Press, 2007); and Jane Burbank and Frederick Cooper, *Empires in World History: Power and the Politics of Difference* (Princeton, NJ: Princeton University Press, 2010).

considered an empire.[6] Many, if not most, of the oldest nation-states of our own time began their historic evolution as heterogeneous dynastic conglomerates. In many ways they were much more like empires than the nation-states they would become. Only after the hard work of nationalizing homogenization by state authorities were hierarchical and differentiated imperial relationships between metropole and periphery transformed into relatively egalitarian nation-states based on a horizontal notion of equal citizenship. Interestingly enough, even long after a nation-state has been consolidated, fissures and divisions can appear that make the state look imperial to minority populations. England united the British Isles, created a Great Britain, a United Kingdom, only to come up against Irish resistance to colonial connections, Welsh insistence on their distinctiveness, and a Scottish nationalist movement determined to achieve independence.

States before the nineteenth century, particularly before the French Revolution, are often referred to as *anciens régimes*, old regimes that had varied populations, local laws in effect, different weights and measures, inscribed customs and traditions. *Anciens régimes* combined elements of empire and nation-state. Even after the French Revolution, in what has been called "the age of nationalism," the very process of nation-making stimulated not only the sense of nationhood of the dominant people but often the ethnonational consciousness of subordinate populations. As Czechs, Slovaks, Poles, Armenians, Georgians, and others distinguished themselves (perhaps in part because they had been told they were different by others), nationalizing states found it difficult to completely assimilate the whole population of their state into the dominant nationality. Those who then resisted assimilation into the ruling nationality became defined as "minorities" and ended up in colonial relationships with the metropolitan nation. In these cases "nation-making" laid bare the underlying imperialism of the state. Indeed, the so-called age of nationalism, given the persistence of great landed empires, the "New Imperialism" and the "Scramble for Africa" after 1870, might more accurately be called "the age of empires."

NATION, NATIONALISM, AND THE DISCOURSE OF THE NATION

There could not be anything like a nation-state until people had the idea of a nation and until they thought they already possessed or could make themselves into a nation. While empire and nation-state are kinds of states and ways of governing, a *nation* is a community of people with shared understandings of who they are and what they want. It is a political practice with its own vocabulary, ways of behaving, conventions of belonging, and shared feelings, its own affective dispositions. Often the idea of a nation in the minds of various thinkers or political leaders came before ordinary people imagined themselves to be members of a particular nation.

---

[6]Michael Hechter, *Internal Colonialism: The Celtic Fringe in British National Development, 1536–1966* (Berkeley: University of California Press, 1975), pp. 60–64.

The term *nation* was used in a variety of meanings long before the full conception of a modern nation as it is generally understood today came into being.

Nation as a word was derived from the Latin *natio* (from the verb *nasci*, meaning to be born). The early meanings of nation included a group of people born in the same place or having common genetic ancestry, but also one's place of birth, or a society of university students from the same region or speaking the same language. The word came into English in the fourteenth century from the Old French *nacion*, and by the sixteenth century was loosely related to "group" or "class," as in Edmund Spenser's "nation" of birds in *The Faerie Queene*. Foreign or strange people were referred to as "nations," though in the seventeenth and eighteenth centuries nobilities like the Polish *szlachta* and the Hungarian magnates also designated themselves the nation. The French king in the eighteenth century considered himself to be *la nation* and was disturbed by those intellectuals who were arguing that the nation was separate from the king and was to be identified with the people. (His concern proved to be prescient. The French nation would sever itself from the monarchy while severing the king from his head in 1793.) Philosophers, politicians, monarchs, and revolutionaries fought over the meaning of this contested and increasingly powerful political concept.[7]

When mobilized, the concept of nation engenders a particular kind of political practice. The idea of nation creates a community that believes it is empowered to grant political legitimacy to the state, which then represents the people constituted as a nation. The question then arises, What do we call the various political communities that existed before the full emergence of the modern nation? Such political communities, whether in medieval Western Europe or Muscovy, had nominally defined boundaries, with their members recognized (at least to some degree) from above, by each other, and by themselves, as members, with obligations and claims, and often with some sense of the people as a site of ideological (if not practical) sovereignty. But in such ancient, medieval, and early modern political communities there were hardly ever any aspirations to homogenization of the population, social equality, or political horizontality. Rather, inequality and hierarchy based on birth and achievement were accepted as part of the social order, sanctioned by God and nature. While there was no social equality between peasants and nobles, men and women, rulers and ruled, nevertheless there were understandings that various groups in society had both obligations and privileges. Such political communities, with their own values, notions of the political, affective ties, and sense of the entitlements associated with membership in the polity, operated long before the appearance of the modern concept and discourse of the nation in the late eighteenth and early nineteenth centuries. Scholars have referred to these earlier political formations variously as "proto-nations," "ethnies," or "political ethnicities." However one refers to them, they should not be

---

[7]A brilliant account of this contest over the idea of nation in eighteenth-century France is given in David Bell, *The Cult of the Nation in France: Inventing Nationalism, 1680–1800* (Cambridge, MA: Harvard University Press, 2003).

conflated with those cultural and political communities in modern times that sought to rule themselves.

Among the meanings attached to the word *nation* in early modern Europe one sense was an ethno-territorial one. In Russia this sense of territorialized people already existed in the Muscovite period, though the words used would not have been *natsiia* (the Russian calque on the French *la nation*) but *zemlia* (land). Maps from the seventeenth century depict the empire as a collection of "lands," each belonging to a particular people: "the land of the pacified Samoyeds"; "the land of the Iakuts"; "the land of [the principality of] Vladimir"; "the land of Great Muscovy."

A map drawn by the Siberian cartographer Semyon Remezov at the very end of the seventeenth century naturalizes the relationship between each "people" and their "land." In his representation of Siberia, each territory is attributed to a group of people. Each "land" is depicted as a sharply delineated and differently colored patch, visually keeping the right people in their designated places. The map emphasizes the diversity of lands and peoples while ignoring the extent and limit of the tsar's control. Lands beyond the reach of the tsar, notably China (the orange blob in the top left corner) and the Khanate of Bukhara (the orange blob in the top right), appear as yet more instances of the given order, the divine distribution of particular lands to the various peoples of the earth. This territorialized vision of naturally occurring human communities anticipates elements of the more modern national discourse discussed below.

With the explosive break of European colonies with their motherlands, beginning with the American Revolution, the idea of nations as new polities endowed with rights of self-governance entered the language of politics.[8] The full-blown modern concept of nation that emerged with the French Revolution in 1789 took on a quite radical political coloration.[9] Nation came to mean a group of people who imagine themselves to be a political community distinct from the rest of mankind and on that basis deserving of self-determination, which usually entails self-rule, control of its own territory (the "homeland"), and perhaps a state of its own.

Along with the widespread use of nation, another word—*nationalism*—appeared to describe the love of the nation or the claim that the nation deserved one's highest loyalty, above family or friend. Coined by the German philosopher Johann Gottfried von Herder (1744–1803), "nationalism" came into wider circulation after 1830, particularly in the writings of the Italian radical Giuseppe

---

[8]The rhetoric of popular sovereignty was invoked earlier in England's Glorious Revolution of 1688. See Stephen Pincus, "Nationalism, Universal Monarchy, and the Glorious Revolution," in *State/Culture: State-Formation after the Cultural Turn*, ed. George Steinmetz (Ithaca, NY, and London: Cornell University Press, 1999), pp. 182–210.

[9]William H. Sewell, Jr., "The French Revolution and the Emergence of the Nation Form," in *Revolutionary Currents: Transatlantic Ideology and Nation Building, 1688–1821*, ed. Michael Morrison and Melinda Zook (Lanham, MD: Rowman and Littlefield, 2004), pp. 91–125; and Lynn Hunt, *Politics, Culture, and Class in the French Revolution* (Berkeley and Los Angeles: University of California Press, 1984), pp. 123–25.

This spectacular "ethnographic map" was created by the Siberian servitor/ cartographer Semyon Ulianovich Remezov between 1699 and 1701 by order of Peter the Great. It depicts Eurasian space as divided into clearly delineated "lands," each belonging to a particular people. In the hand-drawn original, the constituent units are brightly painted in yellows, browns, and oranges. Some units are labeled as subject to the Russian Empire, while others are designated as "unpacified." The map displays in graphic form the way the empire is conceptualized as an aggregation of lands and peoples, with distinction clearly created and maintained, each people placed in its appropriate color swatch and firmly outlined in black. The map illustrates the impulse to maintain distinction rather than homogenize imperial conquests, and to affirm the connection of each people with its proper territory. Around the margins appear other realms, such as the "Tsardom of the Chinese land," in the top left. Remezov placed north at the bottom and south at the top of this map, making it confusing for modern viewers, accustomed to a northern orientation.

Mazzini (1805–1872), who used it to mean "the exaggeration, the pervasion, of the legitimate *sentiment de nationalité* (feeling of nationality)."[10] The word went on to mean whatever a particular writer wished it to mean. Here we might think of "nationalism" as the sentiment or doctrine that expresses primary or ultimate loyalty to and affection for a particular nation and dedication to its promotion and advancement. We distinguish nationalism from patriotism, which refers to a primary loyalty and love for a particular state, dynasty, or ruler—a noble sentiment often found among, well, nobles.

---

[10]G. de Bertier de Sauvigny, "Liberalism, Nationalism, Socialism: The Birth of Three Words," *The Review of Politics* 32, no. 2 (April 1970): 160.

By the nineteenth century both nation and nationalism took on a whole cluster of associations and understandings, which we call "the discourse of the nation." The term *discourse* has multiple meanings—from polite conversation to the dominant ways in which given people think, speak, and act. By discourse we are referring here to the universe of possible meanings in a specific historical time and place, the imaginable understandings of what is true, real, and possible.

The meanings that came to surround the signifier *nation* in modern times (roughly post-1750) allowed for the power of nations and nationalism to constitute collective loyalties, legitimize governments, and mobilize and inspire people to fight, kill, and die for their country. Once unleashed, the discourse of the nation had extraordinary power and durability, continuing as a principal ingredient in the political languages of our globalized age. This cluster of ideas includes the conviction that humanity is naturally divided into separate and distinct nationalities or nations (a vision already evident in the Muscovite map above). Members of a nation reach full freedom and fulfillment of their essence by developing their national identity and culture, and their identity with the nation is superior to all other forms of identity—class, gender, individual, familial, tribal, regional, imperial, dynastic, religious, or even patriotic devotion to a state or government.

Though the nation may be divided or gradated along several axes, it is politically and civilly (under the law) made up of equals. As in the plot of a romantic novel in which hero and heroine of different classes find harmony and happiness in a love that transcends their social distinctions, so in the ideal of nation, class and region are to be effaced in a national homogenization. The analogy with a romantic novel is not an arbitrary choice: the idea of the nation blossomed in the Romantic Age, and from its inception shared the idealization of passionate, selfless, unstinting commitment to an elevated object of attachment. Again paralleling romantic, novelistic conventions, the discourse of the nation acknowledges that each nation is unique, with its own separate past, present, and destiny, and that all national members share common origins, historical experiences, interests, and culture, which may include language and religion. Yet at the same time it presumes the developmental process of the nation to be universal: all people go through this development, though unevenly and at different rates.

Within the discourse of the nation, in contrast to earlier political discourses, lies the powerful (and presently hegemonic) political claim that nations, rather than military conquerors, divinely ordained monarchs, theistic leaders, or dynasties, have unique rights to sovereignty and political representation. A fundamental tenet of national discourse is that the people of a nation possess a right to self-rule. This right may have been realized only occasionally in the past but ought to exist fully in the present. The moral-political claim is that nations ought to constitute sovereign states if they desire, and all legitimate states ought to represent a nation. As the Swiss constitutional scholar Johann Kaspar Bluntschli (1808–1881) put it in 1866: "Every nation has the vocation and right to form a state. Just as mankind is divided into a number of nations, so the world should be divided into the same number of states. Every nation is a state, every state a nation."[11]

Nations in the modern sense exist within this discourse of the nation. They are political communities that imagine themselves in a particular way that became possible only with the coincidence of the idea that cultural communities ought to become political communities and that the ordinary people within those communities ought to be able to rule themselves or at least choose those who govern them. This moral imperative to self-rule often pairs with ideas of citizenship, of the people as bearers of political rights and ultimately as an electorate or site of political choice. Finally, the modern sense of nation articulates a community of people, citizens, that is separate from and grants legitimacy to the state but is not to be conflated with the state. The nation is the imagined political community, while the modern state is the set of institutions legitimized by the nation. The nation's destiny, as prophesied by the discourse of the nation, is to form a state, or take over an existing state, and become a nation-state.

Flowing from the discourse of the nation is a narrative of human history that claims that the nation is always present, though often concealed, to be realized fully over time in a world of states in which the highest form is a world of nation-states. The nation in this vision is understood as primordial, always with us, organic, and continuous. The national may be present in people's unconscious and may need to be brought forth or willed into consciousness. Ernest Gellner has called this the "Sleeping Beauty" view of the nation; the nation is asleep for centuries but awakened in modern times. In this "primordialist" discourse, however, the nation is never completely subjective, never simply about the way people think and feel about their political community, but always has an objective and inherent (hence, primordial) base in the real world. The national history is one of continuity, antiquity of origins, heroism and past greatness, martyrdom and sacrifice, victimization, and overcoming of trauma.

In contrast to the primordialist view of nations as naturally occurring social, even genetic, phenomena, scholars in recent decades have emphasized the modern and constructed aspects of nation-making. In this "constructivist" view, which has been referred to as the "Bride of Frankenstein" view of the nation, nations are neither natural nor primordial but the result of hard constitutive intellectual and political work of elites and masses.[12] In this book we track the

---

[11]J. K. Bluntschli, *Allgemeine Staatslehre* (6th ed., 1866); cited in Michael Hughes, *Nationalism and Society: Germany 1800–1945* (London and New York: Edward Arnold, 1988), p. 17.
[12]Ernest Gellner, *Nations and Nationalism*, p. 48; for "Sleeping Beauty" and "Bride of Frankenstein," see Ronald Grigor Suny, *The Revenge of the Past: Nationalism, Revolution, and the Collapse of the Soviet Union* (Stanford, CA: Stanford University Press, 1993), pp. 3–4. See also Etienne Balibar, "The Nation Form: History and Ideology," from Etienne Balibar and Immanuel Wallerstein, *Race, Nation, Class: Ambiguous Identities* (London: Verso, 1991), pp. 86–106; Benedict Anderson, *Imagined Communities: Reflections on the Origin and Spread of Nationalism* (London: Verso, 1983).

processes of mental construction that went into shaping, reshaping, and unraveling ideas about Russia as empire and nation.

Nations are social and cultural constructions (what else could they be, given that they are made by human beings, not by nature?), but they are made over time from available resources (language communities, religious allegiances, existing polities, and geography), as well as mass hostilities and elite interests. Identification with one's nation, then, begins with empathetic attachments to those included within the group and distance and difference from those without. Shared narratives link the members of the nation together in a constructed community that—given the discourse of the nation—legitimizes the people's right to rule themselves through their chosen leaders. The political community is often based on prior cultural, linguistic, religious, or ethnic grounds, and such nations are referred to as "ethnic nations." In contrast, other nations, like the United States, Switzerland, or France at the time of the revolution, are based on commitment to shared political concepts. Such nations are referred to as "civic nations."

Whether ethnic or civic, the nation is an affective community, as are families and ethnic groups, that believes that it shares sentiments, interests, and a common fate. Threats to the group are threats to the individuals identified with that group; anxieties, resentments, fears, and hatreds may be attached to that collective identity and make up the emotional disposition of the group out of which more specific emotional responses emerge when the requisite stimuli are experienced. From these dispositions and emotions predictable action tendencies occur. When nations experience threats, or feel humiliated or discriminated against, the unfortunate result can be conflict or violence.

Though the discourse of the nation began as an expression of state patriotism, through the nineteenth century it increasingly became ethnicized until the "national community" was understood to be a cultural community of shared language, religion, and/or other characteristics with a durable, antique past, shared kinship, common origins, and narratives of progress through time. The Herderian idea of the nation as a cultural collective, an ethnicity, in many cases overwhelmed the political sense of nation proposed by the French revolutionaries, that is, a commitment to the inclusion of any and all (male) members of the political community, a civic, non-ethnic conception of citizenship.

The term *ethnicity* raises its own complications, and introducing it into our examination of the nation and nationality requires further definition. In our view, ethnicity is primarily about shared kinship, culture, cultural rights, and perhaps some limited political recognition. As with many ordinary language usages of "nation," many references to ethnicity treat it as if it were an essential, ancient, primordial, continuous, and organic identity. In our understanding, ethnicity is like nation a constructed identity but one that starts more specifically from notions of shared kinship, real or fictional. While the discourse of the nation is more often about popular sovereignty, state power, and control of a territorial homeland based on a shared culture, which might be ethnic or political, ethnicity is not particularly grounded in territory. For those who base nations on ethnicity or shared biology, the ways in which notions of shared pasts and common origins have been constructed and reimagined, how primary languages themselves were selected from dialects and elevated to dominance through print and schooling, and how history itself was employed to justify claims to the world's real estate, in other words, all the ways in which concerted effort and hard work went into forging a nation, are forgotten or deliberately suppressed. Ethnic nationalists have strived to make the nation and the state congruent, an almost utopian goal since identities are fluid and people are mobile. It is not a great stretch to argue that much of modern history and its sanguinary violence have been about making nations and states fit together in a world where the two almost never match.

From roughly the late eighteenth century to the present, the state merged with the "nation," and almost all modern states claimed to be nation-states, in either an ethnic or civic sense, with governments asserting that they derived power from and exercised it in the interest of the nation. For such a proposition to work effectively, modern states, even absolutist ones, had to foster some degree of popular allegiance, and the identification offered by nationalism provided that essential collective cohesion between the governors and the governed. After years of destructive civil and religious warfare across Europe in the fifteenth through the seventeenth centuries, both masses and elites had an interest in supporting the centralization of state power and the ideological (usually religious) homogenization of the political community.

States, in the sense of institutionalized centralizing political authorities, arose before the nation, the politically conscious body of subjects or citizens. Both in the run-up to state formation and in the moments when states vigorously make nations, nationalism brought individuals together with a shared sense of large-scale political solidarity. The dynamic potential of nationalist mobilization made anti-imperial and anti-colonial movements possible, and supplied rulers with the potential basis of popular legitimacy. Nationalism, in other words, as Ernest Gellner, Eric J. Hobsbawm, and other theorists of nationalism have demonstrated, may precede the nation. Historically, we find that preexisting nations are not a prerequisite to state formation; rather, it is nationalizing states or movements that very often create nations.

Looking at the early history of nations and states, political scientist Anthony Marx, like Georg Simmel and Frederic Barth before him, has shown that the first steps toward national unity in early modern Europe were taken by exclusion rather than inclusion—by persecuting Muslims and Jews in Spain, Catholics in England, and Huguenots in France. In its first phase, legitimated state rule was established in Western European states where bloody religious and civil wars were fought in order to determine which religion would dominate in a particular state, and what form of political structure would prevail.

Countering liberal arguments that Western civic nationalisms were inclusive, while Eastern nationalisms were ethnic and exclusive, Anthony Marx contends that all nationalisms begin with exclusions. Those advocates of civic nationalism who condescendingly hold that their formulation is more pacific should recognize their common moments of origin with ethnic nationalisms. The passions of the masses combined with the pragmatic interests of elites in the sixteenth and seventeenth centuries to establish the exclusionary political community on which later generations were able to build more tolerant liberal societies and democracies.[13] Later ideals of inclusion would be built on the original base of definition by exclusion.

By the twentieth century, imagined national communities had become the most legitimate basis for the constitution of states, displacing dynastic, religious, and class discourses—and posing a serious challenge to alternative formulas for political legitimation, like those underpinning empires. Once-viable imperial states became increasingly vulnerable to nationalist movements that in turn gained strength from the new understanding that states ought to represent, if not coincide, with nations. The simultaneous rise of notions of democratic representation of subaltern interests accentuated the fundamental tension between inequitable imperial relationships and horizontal conceptions of national citizenship. Liberal states with representative institutions—Great Britain, France, Belgium, and the Netherlands—could be (and were) effective imperial powers until their rhetoric of equality took root among their colonial subjects. The pervasive rhetoric about the altruistic and emancipatory aims of empire encouraged subjects of "liberal" overseas empires to seek fulfillment of democratic promises. Bids for colonial citizenship in North and South America, Asia, and Africa took place first within imperial structures and then, when those promises proved hollow, through struggles for independence.[14]

Wary of just such dangers, the great contiguous empires of the Romanovs, the Ottomans, and the Habsburgs resisted democratization that would have undermined the right to rule of the dominant imperial elite and the hierarchical and inequitable relationship between metropole and periphery in the empire. While empires were among the most ubiquitous and long-lived polities in history, they were progressively subverted in modern times by the powerful combination of nationalism and democracy.

The French Revolution has been considered the fount from which flowed modern radicalism, liberalism, conservatism, and nationalism. Many historians consider it to be the principal turning point into modernity—as if an abrupt break with the past and tradition, as imagined by the revolutionaries, were possible. In 1789 the French revolutionaries proclaimed the radical principle of popular sovereignty and linked it to the concept of the nation. As stated in Article 3 of the Declaration of the Rights of Man, "The principle of all sovereignty rests

---

[13]Anthony W. Marx, *Faith in Nation: Exclusionary Origins of Nationalism* (Oxford and New York: Oxford University Press, 2003).
[14]Mrinalini Sinha, "Suffragism and Internationalism: The Enfranchisement of British and Indian Women Under an Imperial State," *The Indian Economic and Social History Review* 36, no. 4 (1999): 461–84.

essentially in the nation. No body and no individual may exercise authority that does not emanate from the nation expressly."

For Russia, however, and much of monarchical Europe, this principle was a kind of time bomb at the foundation of empires and absolute monarchies. As Europe reeled before the popular force of 1789, Russia stood as a seawall against the waves of radicalism. When nationalists talked about the unity of shared spirit and blood within the nation, Russia represented "the most imperial of nations," comprising more different peoples than any other. There was pride in diversity. The academician Heinrich Storch boasted in 1797, commenting that "no other state on earth contains such a variety of inhabitants."[15] In its own imagery Russia was the Roman Empire reborn. Like many multiethnic countries, the Russian Empire was a potential candidate for a civic national identity inclusive of all the various peoples ruled by the tsar. Yet such patriotic affiliation to the state was challenged by both the emerging ethnonationalisms of myriad different minorities within the empire and, as we shall see, by the end of the nineteenth century, by the chauvinistic, assimilationist, Russifying nationalism of key Russian public figures.

As the discourse of the nation took shape in and after the French Revolution and the Napoleonic wars, as concepts of "the people" and popular sovereignty spread through Europe, the traditional monarchical concepts of the divinely ordained tsar held at bay any concession to the new national populism. Russian resistance to Napoleon, as well as the expansion of the empire into the Caucasus and Finland, accentuated the imperial image of irresistible power, displayed physically on both battlefield and parade ground by the martinet tsars of the early nineteenth century.[16] Challenged by the novel notions of popular sovereignty, democracy, and nationalism, Imperial Russia was prepared to adapt, however reluctantly at times, to a changing and threatening world, but it was not about to give in or give up to nation-states. What looks in retrospect to have been the inevitable rise of nations and the age of nationalism was for the Russian tsars an age of imperial increase and celebration of its own unique autocratic answer to how peoples ought to be governed.

BRIEF BIBLIOGRAPHY

Anderson, Benedict R. O'G. *Imagined Communities: Reflections on the Origin and Spread of Nationalism*. London and New York: Verso, 1983.

Balibar, Étienne, and Immanuel Maurice Wallerstein. *Race, Nation, Class: Ambiguous Identities*. London and New York: Verso, 1991.

Bell, David Avrom. *The Cult of the Nation in France: Inventing Nationalism, 1680–1800*. Cambridge, MA: Harvard University Press, 2003.

---

[15]Quoted in Andreas Kappeler, *Rußland als Vielvölkerreich. Entstehung, Geschichte, Zerfall* (Munich: Verlag C. H. Beck, 1992), p. 121; Richard Wortman, *Scenarios of Power: Myth and Ceremony in Russian Monarchy, Vol. I, From Peter the Great to the Death of Nicholas* (Princeton: Princeton University Press, 1995), pp. 136–37.

[16]Wortman, *Scenarios of Power*, I, p. 170.

Burbank, Jane, and Frederick Cooper. *Empires in World History: Power and the Politics of Difference*. Princeton, NJ: Princeton University Press, 2010.

Eley, Geoff, and Ronald Grigor Suny, eds. *Becoming National: A Reader*. New York: Oxford University Press, 1996.

Gellner, Ernest. *Nations and Nationalism*. Ithaca, NY: Cornell University Press, 1983.

Lieberman, Victor. *Why Was Nationalism European? Political Ethnicity in Southeast Asia and Europe, c. 1400–1850*. Cambridge, MA: Harvard University Press, forthcoming.

Marx, Anthony W. *Faith in Nation: Exclusionary Origins of Nationalism*. Oxford and New York: Oxford University Press, 2003.

Smith, Anthony D. *The Ethnic Origins of Nations*. Oxford and New York: Basil Blackwell, 1987.

Suny, Ronald Grigor. *The Revenge of the Past: Nationalism, Revolution, and the Collapse of the Soviet Union*. Stanford, CA: Stanford University Press, 1993.

FOUR

RESPONSIVE RULE AND ITS LIMITS
Force and Sentiment
in the Eighteenth Century

"Two autocrats can be held directly responsible for instilling the idea of the nation in the Russian elite and awakening it to the potent and stimulating sense of national pride: these were Peter I and Catherine II." So writes political scientist Liah Greenfeld in her study of the rise of nationalism and its contributions to modernity. Admiring the sheer force of character required as Peter the Great and Catherine the Great "dragged the reluctant, heavy, quailing Russian society" forward into a new era, she continues:

> The ability of Peter and Catherine to do so was, of course, dependent on the nature of the relationship between the autocrat and the subjects in Russia, which was the legacy of the Muscovite kingdom, and in which the subjects had neither a will of their own nor the ability to carry such will through if they had it.[1]

This opening salvo in an otherwise insightful analysis encapsulates the negative historical preconceptions that too often shackle thinking about Russian history in general and of its eighteenth century in particular. The misconceptions about the Muscovite past with its unthinking and powerless subjects have been treated in the previous chapters. As for the eighteenth century, Greenfeld's presentation of the century with its two nodal points, the two Greats, separated by a void, allows us critical entrée to the history and historiography of this colorful period.

In this chapter and the following, we move into the eighteenth century and engage critically the issues she raises. The chapters divide thematically rather than chronologically. In this chapter we explore the manifestations of autocratic power tempered by reciprocity and responsiveness in the reigns of Russia's eighteenth-century monarchs, while in the following chapter we focus on the nature of Russian identities, question the easy assumptions that have been made

---

[1]Liah Greenfeld, *Nationalism: Five Roads to Modernity* (Cambridge, MA: Harvard University Press, 1992), p. 189.

about nations and nationalism in the eighteenth century, and emphasize imperial strategies and Russians' experience of collectivity and differentiation.

Assessment of Russia's history in the eighteenth century requires setting aside
centuries of sedimented stereotype and prejudice that have hardened into a solid
edifice, a story that begins with glorious enlightenment and martial glory but
then sinks into a morass of frivolity, favoritism, and corruption. As the story
goes, the century opened with the advent of Peter the Great, who boldly, though
admittedly with some roughness, shook the dusty, backwards-looking Muscovites out of their stupor and brought them into the vibrant world of Europe's
early Enlightenment. Due to unfortunate circumstances, he was followed on the
throne by a sequence of young boys and women who were not up to the task of
completing what he had initiated. For a taste of this flavor of historical prejudice,
a summary paragraph from Michael Florinsky's popular survey of Russian
history, published in 1954, will suffice:

> To the grotesque and fantastic procession of monarchs who mounted the throne
> in the interval between the reign of Peter I and that of Catherine II must be
> added the even more numerous and bewildering array of their favorites, the
> actual masters of the country. The exotic courts of these rulers, and the bizarre
> and sinister *cortège* of ignorant, licentious women, half-witted German princes,
> and mere children on whose shoulders in turn descended the imperial purple
> present a morbidly fascinating picture suggestive of the imaginative and unreal
> world created by some medieval craftsman and preserved in ancient Italian em-
> broideries and in stain glass windows.[2]

Entertaining though it is to follow Florinsky in a prurient romp through the sex
lives and twisted psychologies of Russia's empresses, more recent scholarship has
revivified the study of the eighteenth century by asking new questions on new
topics, and also by reposing questions of sex and gender in productive new ways,
exploring their cultural and political meanings and uses in an age of female rule.

In this chapter we reshape the standard narrative, keeping the core issues of
imperial formation and rule as our focus. We trace the consolidation of power
in the new capital city, St. Petersburg, and we track the changing forms of reciprocity that connected subjects and rulers. We find important shifts in the representation and experience of political relationships between ruler and subjects
and among and between subjects both in the historical core of European Russia
and in the ever-expanding peripheries of the *Rossiiskaia imperiia*, the Russian
empire.

---

[2]Michael Florinsky, *Russia: A History and Interpretation* (New York: Macmillan, 1954), p. 432. For
more sensible treatments of gender and rule in eighteenth-century Russia, see, among others, Benda
Meehan-Waters, "Catherine the Great and the Problem of Female Rule," *Russian Review* 34 (1975):
293–307; Isabel de Madariaga, *Catherine the Great: A Short History*, 2nd ed. (New Haven: Yale University Press, 2002), pp. 203–18; Simon Dixon, *Catherine the Great* (Profiles in Power) (New York:
Routledge, 2001).

SUCCESSION, CONSULTATION,
AND THE POLITICS OF AFFIRMATION

Peter Alekseevich came to the throne in a messy sequence of half steps and interim solutions. Born in 1672, Peter was the son of Tsar Aleksei Mikhailovich and his second wife, Natalia Naryshkina. Tsar Aleksei's first wife, Maria Miloslavskaia, bore many children, including sons (and daughters) who survived her, so Peter was low in the line of succession when his father died in 1676. Peter's oldest surviving half-brother Fedor Alekseevich succeeded his father to the throne. During his short reign, Fedor and his advisers initiated a number of important reforms that anticipated Peter's own changes. For instance, for centuries relations of precedence among the boyar nobility had been determined by a complicated system of genealogical and service-based calculations known as *mestnichestvo*, which had dictated who would receive key appointments in the military and administration. In 1682, shortly before his death, Fedor presided over a session of his boyar council that agreed to sweep away this antiquated system and replace it with a more flexible system of appointments and promotion. Peter would extend this more merit-based concept with his introduction of the Table of Ranks in 1722.

The frail Fedor died childless after only six years on the throne, leaving the succession question up in the air. By custom, the eldest surviving brother should have been the natural choice, but at sixteen years old, poor Ivan Alekseevich suffered from severe mental and physical limitations, while his twelve-year-old half-brother, Peter, was bright, strong, and energetic, if a trifle unruly. A conclave of church leaders and leading boyars, including but not limited to members of the Naryshkin clan, the family of Peter and his mother, decided to bypass Ivan and elevate Peter to the throne.

On the face of it, this preference for competence over seniority, though logical to a modern sensibility, might seem a radical overturning of age-old traditions. If the sequence of monarchs was determined by birth order, and therefore by divine will, then meddling in it should have been unthinkable. Recently, however, Paul Bushkovitch has convincingly argued that the succession had long involved an element of flexibility. As we have seen, since the Time of Troubles, when tsars rose and fell in rapid succession, rulers had incorporated rituals for declaring their claims and obtaining affirmation of their rightful rule. The public supplication to Michael Romanov and his mother in 1613, and Michael's accession to the throne shortly thereafter, enshrined this practice of enacting the *vox populi* in Muscovite tradition.

In the calmer decades that followed, the public had less opportunity to voice its opinions, but the approval of an inner circle was always necessary, and some form of public acclamation was expected. When the ritual of public approval was bypassed, as in the perfectly straightforward accession of the young Aleksei Mikhailovich following the death of his father, Michael, in 1645, disgruntled gossip might spread.[3] Looking forward to the eighteenth century, with its own tumultuous history of coronations and coups, Bushkovitch points out that those monarchs who failed to enlist the support of powerful elements at court faced poor prognoses as rulers and dramatically shortened life expectancies.[4] This vision of succession hammered out by consensus and confirmed by some collective voice runs counter to prevailing ideas about tsarist rule as absolute and utterly autocratic, shaped by the tsar's will alone, and impervious and unresponsive to any popular input. The idea that a public voice, and not the haphazard dictates of birth order or even the schemes of an elite inner circle alone, contributed to determining royal succession is a radical revision of that stereotyped view but fully accords with our understanding that the power of the Russian state rested on an implicit reciprocity and a need to win the acquiescence of key actors. Some kind of "election" or buy-in by some circle of people secured a ruler's claim to the throne.

At some level, this observation may simply state the obvious. No one individual can ever rule an empire completely single-handedly, no matter how much effort rulers and ruling elites put into creating that impression. Studies of the ostensibly absolutist monarchies of early modern Europe have pulled back the veil of myth created by the regimes' own propagandists and have revealed that even the most powerful of autocrats actually shared power with various elites and to some extent even with larger segments of the population.[5] As our discussion of heuristics and ideal types has acknowledged, large gulfs separate every model from far messier realities. In all historical instances, unlimited rule was more an aspiration than an actuality. Some degree of the reciprocity and inclusion that we underscore in the Russian case inevitably characterizes all regimes with any lasting power. Yet the point is still worth stressing for two reasons. First, Russia in particular, throughout its history, is often too glibly equated with absolutism and despotism. And second, because the line of royal succession, with its seeming biological clarity and reliance on the happenstance of birth order, is a surprising place to find human agency and broader input.

As it happened, the unconventional elevation of Peter did provoke unease, and a major uprising led by the *streltsy* or musketeers, armed guards who protected the Kremlin and served in regiments throughout Moscow, shook the regime, causing the royal family to remove itself and the court out of the city. The *streltsy* rose in defense of Ivan, Peter's older half-brother, who they believed had been murdered, and they mobilized in solidarity with the Old Belief and old ways. They attacked and killed members of the Naryshkin family, including Peter's

---

[3]Such rumors were detected and recorded in cases of lèse majesté, trials of people who spoke out against the tsar. See N. Ia. Novombergskii, *Slovo i delo gosudarevy*, 2 vols. (Moscow: Iazyki slavianskoi kul'tury, 2004).

[4]Paul Buskhovitch, "Succession, Election, Autocracy, and 'Absolutism' in Early Modern Russia," unpublished paper delivered at the Russian History Workshop, University of Michigan, October 25, 2012.

[5]Nicholas Henshall, *The Myth of Absolutism: Change and Continuity in Early Modern European Monarchy* (London: Longman, 1992).

maternal uncle. They targeted particular officers known for ill treatment of their men, and they burned down the chancellery where slavery contracts were stored. Their violence contained a precise and eloquent message about their demands, and ultimately the ruling elites capitulated on the key point: they crowned Ivan and Peter as co-tsars, ruling together under the guardianship of their sister (Peter's half-sister), the *tsarevna* Sophia.

Sophia's reign continued the reformist momentum of the previous decade. Among other initiatives, her regency oversaw the founding of the first formal school, the Slavo-Greco-Latin Academy, to meet the perceived need for skilled clerics and administrators. The founding of the academy reflected the regent's openness to the increased tempo of cultural exchange provoked by a continuing influx of foreign, mostly Ukrainian or Ruthenian, scholars and theologians, schooled in more European ways of *thinking*. In 1689, as Peter approached his seventeenth birthday and the age of majority, Sophia sharpened her bid for independent power. As regent, Sophia had followed a long tradition of female regents and guardians, but when she began to style herself "Sovereign Lady (*gosudarynia*)," the female equivalent of the male sovereign's title (*gosudar'*), she inaugurated the chain of female rulers that would predominate for the rest of the century. Sophia's efforts to secure her claim roused young Peter to action. Roaring into Moscow from the provincial estate where he had spent most of his youth, Peter abruptly terminated the regency and incarcerated his sister in a convent. A decade later, in 1698, when the *streltsy* once again rose up in the name of the former regent, Peter visited upon them such hideous punishment that, according to horrified reports of foreign witnesses, the entire city became a gallows, with the corpses of executed musketeers hanging from walls, gates, and makeshift scaffolds. Peter inaugurated his period of active rule and Westernizing reform, his enlightened agenda, with a spectacular display of cruelty.

THE PETRINE REVOLUTION AND THE IMPERIAL STATE

Russia's tsars, even in the Muscovite centuries, were not only Christian monarchs, the most pious heads of the Church, but also powerful rulers of a burgeoning bureaucratic state, conquerors, and the commanders of nobles and armies. With Peter the Great (1682–1725), the Orthodox Emperor and Orthodox Empire ceded pride of place—though without yielding altogether—to a more earthly and European ethos of conquest and imperial power. "Peter's advents gave notice that the Russian tsar owed his power to his exploits on the battlefield, not to divinely ordained traditions of succession. . . . The image of conqueror disposed of the old fictions of descent."[6]

---

[6]Richard Wortman, *Scenarios of Power: Myth and Ceremony in Russian Monarchy, Vol. I, From Peter the Great to the Death of Nicholas I* (Princeton: Princeton University Press, 1995), p. 44.

Nearly his entire reign saw Russia engaged in warfare. In the late 1690s he battled against the Ottomans and the Crimean khanate. Later he turned his attention to the north, to Sweden. The Great Northern War occupied him for two decades, from 1700 to 1721, until his ultimate victory with the Treaty of Nystad. To fuel his battlefield endeavors, he simultaneously militarized his own society. He worked relentlessly to increase revenues by taxing more and collecting more effectively. He experimented with ways to conscript soldiers and laborers into his war efforts, and exerted himself to import technologies and the experts who could bring skills to Russia for the manufacture of the weapons of war. He mandated that soldiers should be billeted in civilian households, thereby shifting the cost of maintaining his huge army onto the rest of the population.[7]

To demonstrate his European diplomatic credentials, he had one of his advisers, Peter Shafirov, compose a formal justification for Russia's long-running war against Sweden. The piece was published in large numbers and distributed in Russia and abroad (the print run amounted to 20,000 copies in various languages). The work is conventional, even dull, but as demonstrated by Pärtel Piirimäe, it signaled an important step in Peter's effort to cast his empire as European and civilized and to differentiate it from the "barbaric" Ottoman state. Russia had never before bothered to enter in the polemics of justification. The etiquette of proving one's wars as "just," essential in a Western martial tradition, had not played any role. With *A Discourse Concerning the Just Causes of the War Between Sweden and Russia*, Peter "took a novel decision to launch a campaign of public legitimation of Muscovy's attack on Sweden in 1700. The legitimations of war published during Peter's reign can be seen as essential components of his quest for the acknowledgment of Russia as a fully-fledged member of the European moral, legal, and political community."[8] Peter's successes were as much in the field of public relations as on the battlefield.

Peter embraced European technologies and foreign political structures, imposing on Russia his preference for beardlessness, Western dress, Baroque architecture, and Dutch, German, and English technical innovations. He built a new capital, St. Petersburg, in an unpropitious malarial swamp, as a "window on the West," and as a window *for* the West as well. Bringing Russian society into line with developments in the rest of Europe, he made the mysterious and misunderstood tsardom comprehensible and "legible" to Western observers, starting with its title. He rebranded the tsardom an *imperiia*, and in place of the hard-fought title of "tsar," so proudly embraced by his predecessors, he substituted the more immediately recognizable "*imperator*" in 1721. He made sure that European

---

[7] The literature on Peter is enormous. Two important works among many are Paul Bushkovitch, *Peter the Great: The Struggle for Power, 1671-1725* (Cambridge: Cambridge University Press, 2001); and Lindsey Hughes, *Russia in the Age of Peter the Great* (New Haven, CT: Yale University Press, 1998).

[8] P. P. Shafirov, *A Discourse Concerning the Just Causes of the War Between Sweden and Russia: 1700-1721* (Dobbs Ferry, NY: Oceana, 1973); Pärtel Piirimäe, "Russia, the Turks and Europe: Legitimations of War and the Formation of European Identity in the Early Modern Period," *Journal of Early Modern History* 11, no. 1 (2007): 63–86.

Engraved portrait of Peter the Great, the first Russian ruler to take the Latin title "imperator," or emperor. *Peter the First, Emperor of the Russians.* Engraving made in 1717–1718 by Jacobus Houbraken from an original oil painting by Karl (Carel) Moor, 1717.

audiences appreciated the change, even spelling the new titles out for them in Latin letters. "Peter's ideology was very much of the age of rationalism, of the celebration of reason over tradition and emotions, his contribution to the 'general welfare' of Russia legitimating his rule." The emperor was designated "father of the fatherland," and "now the relationship between sovereign and subjects was to be based not on hereditary right and personal obligation, but on the obligation to serve the state."[9]

Peter altered the terms of service to the state in more concrete ways as well. Toward the end of his reign he created the Table of Ranks, which would govern the terms of state service until the end of the Old Regime in the revolutions of 1917. The Table established a series of steps through which civil servants and military officers would climb in order to achieve higher status and more lucrative positions. Promotions could be earned through a combination of seniority and educational credentials, and although the highest nobility gained automatic entry to the highest ranks through birth, the new system also opened doors for ambitious commoners to rise into the nobility as well. The Table granted the

---

[9]Wortman, *Scenarios of Power*, I, pp. 61, 64.

status of personal nobility (that is, for themselves, but not their families) to those who reached the fourteenth rank and hereditary nobility (conferred to their children as well) to those who achieved the coveted eighth rung. The educational requirements, duplicated in Peter's preemptory demand that members of the nobility prove that they had completed the necessary level of schooling before being allowed to marry, caused an abrupt sea change. A profound generational shift in cultural orientation occurred among Russia's elites. Instead of turning inward and looking backward to Russian customs and traditions, the up-and-coming members of the upper strata looked to Europe and to imitation of foreign models.

Peter also created a new polite society for Russia. He forced his nobles to accept that Western ideas and practices were superior to old, backward Russian customs and traditions. Adopting Western ways, clothing, manners, architecture, shaving off beards, and building a Western-style capital in St. Petersburg were the first steps toward making Russia a more European country, competitive with the advanced West. Soon French would become the language of the court. "The idea of regime-sponsored Westernizing change," writes Alexander Martin, "starting at the top of society and gradually spreading downward—along with an attitude of fear and contempt toward the peasant masses—lay at the core of the regime's ideology for most of the 18th century."[10]

Peter played his part as "father to the fatherland" on a public stage by acting as a harsh patriarch commanding his subject-children. Committed to his own principle of sacrificing all to the service of the state, he hectored his own son, Aleksei Petrovich, for his laziness, lack of discipline, and disgraceful conduct. He excoriated Aleksei for his failure to maintain domestic order within his own household. In a letter dated October 11, 1715, Peter warned of the dangers posed to the entire realm if Aleksei, as heir to the throne, failed to display masculine strength and authority. He quoted a passage from Paul's epistles: "If someone does not know how to manage his own household, how can he take care of God's church?" He held him up to biblical standards and reminded him of the obligation of a righteous head of household to maintain domestic order.[11] This same son would die three years later at the hands of Peter's interrogators, as they carried out their order to torture him to discover all the details of a plot against the tsar.

Enacting a rowdier, more transgressive form of masculinity than the patriarchal one he demanded of his son, Peter performed his manhood also through extravaganzas of male excess. His conduct was calculated to disrupt traditional Orthodox mores and those of the new polite society. This was particularly on display in the activities of his much discussed "Most Foolish and All Drunken Council," a group of friends and others coerced into participating. The members

[10]Alexander M. Martin, "The Invention of 'Russianness' in the Late 18th–Early 19th Century," *Ab Imperio* 3 (2003): 127.

[11]Ernest Zitser, *The Transfigured Kingdom: Sacred Parody and Charismatic Authority at the Court of Peter the Great* (Ithaca, NY: Cornell University Press, 2004), p. 147.

enacted bawdy and irreverent revelries, displays of blasphemy, inversion, violence, and sexual power. Along with public carousing in the streets, astonishing drinking bouts, and blasphemous mocking of Orthodox rites and hierarchies, the Drunken Council elaborated an obscene vocabulary and set of rituals focused on "the royal phallus." Ernest Zitser writes that "only those members of the royal entourage who had publicly declared their wholehearted commitment to the tsar could have the dubious privilege of being referred to by the obscene word for the *membrum virile* (the virile member)." Phallic imagery and language abounded. "A picture of a giant ejaculating phallus graced the back of the handwritten booklet containing the statutes, rules, and membership list of [a foreign group formed as a spin-off of the Drunken Council,] a mock religious order."[12] Zitser describes these raucous performances as demonstrating that "the tsar and his company quite literally sought to embody the connection between religious charisma and political potency." The royal phallus served as a Baroque era coded emblem, "both a talisman and an assertion of power," signaling Peter's ability to father an heir and to lead his armies to triumph.[13]

The literature on early modern European masculinities has identified the importance of outsized consumption and projection (intake of food, alcohol, women, and projection of vomit, urine, semen, and power) as key elements in defining successful manhood.[14] Peter's performances, both on the battlefield and in the banquet hall, conform to this model. Zitser argues that even his most apparently debauched performances held religious meanings as well, and that his assaults on Orthodox propriety drew on a deep commitment to an enlightened faith. Whether or not his irreverent displays signaled outright sacrilege or coded religiosity, Peter's rule was as theatrically gendered as those of his female successors.[15] His outrageous behavior demonstrated the ruler's ability to thwart conventions that others were obliged to observe and displayed the lack of limits to the autocrat's power.

Inevitably there would be a backlash opposing this imposed Westernization, first from the traditionalists who favored Moscow over St. Petersburg, people like Peter's son Aleksei, and Aleksei's son, who reigned briefly as Peter II, from Old Believers and schismatics who saw Peter as the Antichrist and his commoner mistress and then wife, later Catherine I, as the Whore of Babylon. Eventually nostalgic intellectuals would celebrate what was unique in Russian culture and was different from Western imports, culminating in the Slavophile nationalism of the mid-nineteenth century. But for Peter the Great and his noble associates, imitation of the West was the door to success. As Greenfeld demonstrates, Peter

---

[12]Ibid., p. 163.

[13]Ibid., p. 166.

[14]Patricia Simons, *The Sex of Men in Premodern Europe: A Cultural History* (Cambridge: Cambridge University Press, 2011); Lyndal Roper, "Blood and Codpieces: Masculinity in the Early Modern German Town," in her *Oedipus and the Devil: Witchcraft, Sexuality and Religion in Early Modern Europe* (New York: Routledge, 1994), pp. 107–25.

[15]Zitser, *The Transfigured Kingdom*.

and his circle, the first generation of Westernizers, adopted European models with enthusiasm unadulterated by doubt or resentment. They were unabashed in acknowledging what they saw as the superiority of European ways and strove to inculcate European civilized politesse without any shadow of insecurity. A clear sense of "Russianness" found expression in measuring themselves against a European model and actively bringing their conduct into line. Only later did Russian nobles and intellectuals begin to confront the derogatory implications of their race to catch up with a more advanced West. At that point, "their souls would burn in the consuming flame of the sense of national inadequacy."[16] That dark turn, however, would come decades later, at the end of the century.

PETER'S SUCCESSORS: A CENTURY OF WOMEN (AND CHILDREN) ON TOP

In his Naval Statute, Peter stated that the ruler answers to no one but God. Peter certainly acted as if this were the case. In 1722 Peter decreed that the emperor could choose his own successor, turning what had been customary practice into a written law. But, given the apparently deliberate openness of the decree, the tsar could now name anyone, even a person who was not from the ruling dynasty. A long-running propaganda campaign had elevated the image of his second wife, Catherine, the ignobly and foreign-born, non-Orthodox, illiterate, ex-camp-follower, and former mistress to Peter's right-hand man, to near saintly status—an unlikely and uphill battle if ever there was one. Building on the cult of her namesake, St. Catherine of Alexandria, the wise, learned, and brave martyr who went to her death to defend her chastity and her faith, Peter's image-makers played on Catherine's wisdom in calming her fiery husband, her self-sacrifice in selling her jewels to subsidize the Russian war effort, and her suffering in childbirth as (stretched!) analogies to the chastity and wisdom of her holy counterpart.[17] The year before he died, Peter had Catherine crowned empress, and though he cooled toward her in the final years of his life and never officially designated her his successor, the dominant nobles chose her as empress on Peter's death.

Having upended the principles of dynastic succession, Peter arbitrarily set aside customary practice and set about recreating Russia. With a snap of his fingers, and at the cost of perhaps tens of thousands of laborers' lives, Peter summoned out of nothingness a sparkling new, Western-style capital on the shores of the Neva River and the Gulf of Finland. At a whim, he reset Time itself, discarding the ancient Orthodox calendar that tracked time from the moment of Creation (dated precisely at September 1, 5508 BCE) and adopting the Julian Calendar

---

[16]Greenfeld, *Nationalism*, esp. pp. 227–28.
[17]Gary Marker, *Imperial Saint: The Cult of St. Catherine and the Dawn of Female Rule in Russia* (DeKalb: Northern Illinois University Press, 2007), pp. 145–225.

on January 1, 1700.[18] By decree he ordered elite women out of their traditional seclusion and into the swirl of cosmopolitan sociability. Examples like these have caused many historians to consider Russia to be despotic, with arbitrary rulers who disregard their own laws, and Peter most despotic of all.

Yet powerful as the tsar was, his power was not unlimited, and this was all the more true for Peter's successors. We have seen how Muscovite rulers governed in close consultation with their boyars and church hierarchs. This practice continued in the eighteenth century, and in some ways intensified, tipping the balance of power in favor of the nobility over the monarch, who in some cases was a mere figurehead or placeholder. Peter himself occasionally lashed out against the corrupt self-enrichment schemes of his inner circle, the graft carried out on an unimaginable scale at the expense of state coffers, but for the most part he had to shrug and put up with it. Massive looting of state funds operated as an up-to-date version of the "gift, pillage, and largess economy" that won the support of early Kievan military retinues or of the "feeding" grants, patronage, and guaranteed supply of unfree labor that kept Muscovite elites loyal to their pious sovereign.

Historian John LeDonne goes so far as to assert that there was no "state" in any formal, institutional sense in Russia in the eighteenth century. Rather, he sees Russia as the playground of a "ruling class," as does Perry Anderson, who refers to "one great ugly bargain" between the elites and the tsar to give the monarch uncontested power and the nobles the enserfed peasantry. In a devil's pact, a "special deal" in the language we have been employing, the nobles traded away any institutionalized limits on the monarch's will for the grand economic boon and social status and power associated with exercising rights of ownership over other human beings and tying them to the land.

More recently, Ekaterina Pravilova has fundamentally reevaluated the nature of the special pact between the nobility and the imperial regime. While acknowledging the intimate bond between nobles and rulers, she proposes that we invert the dynamic of the relationship. Rather than ceding all their political clout, the nobility successfully held the regime in a moral vise: since the regime, and in particular Catherine II, won her nobles' loyalty by guaranteeing them rights in property with the Charter of the Nobility in 1785 (discussed below and in chapter 5), she and her successors took to heart their obligation to protect those rights in full, whatever the costs. Protections were granted by gift, not acknowledged as preexisting rights. The imperial regime linked its authority to guaranteeing, and not reneging on its commitments to key supporters. Property rights included not only land, but also water, forests, minerals, and, until the emancipation of the serfs in 1861, people.

Staunch protection of noble rights, Pravilova demonstrates, locked the regime into a position where it had to protect the sacrosanct claims of ownership of some people by others, and ultimately, in the nineteenth and twentieth centuries, of

---

[18]Ernest A. Zitser, "The Petrine Revolution in Time: Plural Temporality and Practical Anachronism in the *Vita* of Prince B. I. Kurakin," unpublished paper. With thanks for permission to read and cite.

Catherine the Great issued this Charter to the Nobility in 1785. The Charter granted the nobles a wide array of rights and protections and helped to consolidate the nobility as a special group with its own generous "special deal." The charter was printed, but the imperial title is handwritten in gold. Engravings of the coats of arms of all the Russian provinces frame the text, with Catherine's initial at the top and the imperial double-headed eagle at the bottom. The text proclaims Catherine's status as ruler of all the many constituent parts of the empire. The list extends beyond this grandly illuminated first page and fills the entire second page as well.

private property claims over those of any broadly conceived public. In a refreshing and ingenious inversion of commonplace assumptions, Pravilova shows that Russia suffered from an *excessive* commitment to (elite) private property, not, as one would expect, from the reverse.[19]

We find her gloss on the "devil's pact" a welcome one, and one that if anything strengthens the idea that the warm relationship between sovereigns and nobles was mutually supportive at the expense of the rest of the population. We would only add that the protective, intimate ties between rulers and subjects did not stop short at the lower ranks of the nobility. They reached to other social strata as well, at least in the emotive rhetoric of the age, and special deals of every variety abounded.

Scholars influenced by the discipline of anthropology have uncovered the family interests and nests of patronage and clientage that underlay and motivated factions at court and determined their actions. David Ransel, in particular, highlights

---

[19]Ekaterina Pravilova, *A Public Empire: Property and the Quest for a Common Good in Imperial Russia* (Princeton, NJ: Princeton University Press, 2014).

the patronage agendas at stake in the various foreign policy and institutional programs advanced by Count Nikita Panin, one of the great statesmen of the second half of the century.[20] This important interpretive work peels back layers of research that misguidedly attempted to impose modern politics and programs back on the eighteenth century. At the same time, it runs the risk of stripping all real "politics" out of the struggles at court.

One place where this risk has been realized is in discussions of the so-called Constitutional Crisis of 1730, a fascinating episode long held up as a moment when Russia *could have* adopted a democratic mode of governance but instead lapsed back into its familiar comfort zone of tyranny. In brief, on January 19, 1730, Peter II, the young grandson of Peter the Great, died on the very eve of his wedding to the daughter of one of his chief noble advisers. Without a clear successor, a small inner circle of the cream of the elite, the Supreme Privy Council, took the decision to invite Anna Ivanovna, widowed daughter of Ivan V (hence, niece of Peter the Great), to return from her home in Courland and to ascend the throne. In a radical move, they added "Conditions" to their invitation: she would not marry, wage war or conclude peace, impose new taxes, spend state revenues, or deprive members of the nobility "of their life, honor, and property without trial." In effect, the Conditions would have created a limited monarchy under the authority of the Supreme Privy Council. Anna signed the Conditions before setting out for Moscow.

In the meantime, rumors leaked out to the large numbers of nobles who had gathered in Moscow for the intended wedding of the young emperor and had stayed on for his funeral. United in opposition to the Council's power grab, groups of noblemen formulated counterproposals or addenda that floated an array of reformist schemes. Over 400 noblemen signed their names to the various plans. Most of the noble proposals demanded (or humbly requested) alleviation of the harsh conditions of service imposed by Peter the Great. They also asked for revocation of his deeply unpopular law on unigeniture, which required nobles to leave their property intact to a single heir rather than dividing it up among their sons (and sometimes daughters) as tradition and parental concern dictated. The Supreme Privy Council attempted to work up its own compromise proposals in response to noble dissatisfaction, but kept its plans veiled in secrecy, hence succeeding only in alienating the mass of the nobility still more.

By the time Anna appeared before a general assembly of the nobility on the morning of February 25, the noble opposition was ready to submit a petition (the Cherkasskii Petition) begging her to arbitrate between them and the Council. When the assembly reconvened in the afternoon, Prince Ivan Trubetskoi submitted yet another petition, backed by the cries of the Guards, imploring her "graciously to resume such Autocratic power as Your glorious and praiseworthy

---

[20]John P. LeDonne, *Absolutism and the Ruling Class: The Formation of the Russian Political Order, 1700–1825* (Oxford: Oxford University Press, 1991); Perry Anderson, *Lineages of the Absolutist State* (Verso, 2013), pp. 328–60; David Ransel, *The Politics of Catherinian Russia: The Panin Party* (New Haven, CT: Yale University Press, 1975).

ancestors possessed and abrogate the article sent to Your Imperial Majesty by the Supreme Privy Council and signed by You."[21] The new empress called for the copy of the Conditions that she had signed and dramatically ripped them up.

Generally, in the scholarship on this moment of tragically missed opportunity, the rank-and-file nobility come in for unbridled criticism and mockery, both for their failure to understand the advantages of a limited monarchy and for the pettiness of the demands that they pursued in its place. On both counts, though, the lesser nobles deserve some vindication. They raised no objections to the principle of limitations or to the requirement that the sovereign gain approval for major decisions. Their grievance, to the extent they had one, concerned the narrow definition of those empowered to approve or reject the sovereign's decisions. By institutionalizing the obligation to consult with the Council and only the Council, the Conditions excluded the broader ranks of the nobility from having a voice. They would have created an oligarchy of the highest nobles in place of the familiar practices of autocracy. The remainder of the century would confirm the petitioners' strategic thinking: the broader nobility, particularly the young officers of the Guards Regiments, would become the arbiters of power and the fulcrum of change for the next three decades. None of the actors involved in this business entertained an idea of broadly inclusive democracy; indeed, even in the constitutional monarchies of Europe at the time, the "rabble" had no formal role in political decision-making. Still, the rank-and-file nobles spoke up to protect the principle of wider, rather than narrower, consultation.

As for the presumptive pettiness of their specific demands, there has been a consistent tendency to write these off as "matters neither of dispute nor of great political importance."[22] The modern tendency to diminish these matters of service, property, and inheritance as not truly political issues misses the fact that in the eighteenth century, family politics were not distinct from high politics. And here too, the lesser nobles achieved their aims. As Empress Anna assumed the throne unhindered by any formal conditions, she nonetheless bowed to the will of her supporters and granted each of their demands, reducing the years of mandatory service, alleviating the harsh conditions of service, and, most welcome, abrogating the law of unigeniture.

This overview of the events of 1730 suggests a more fruitful approach to the politics of the age than contrasting the glories of an abstract ideal of Constitutional Monarchy with the imagined horrors of unbridled despotism. What the "Constitutional Crisis" reveals is a more nuanced, reciprocal relationship between tsar and nobles. Politics at the highest level involved an inclusive negotiation that allowed space for the empress's supporters to voice their concerns and encouraged the ruler to act on them. This finding in turn allows us, first, to situate Russian

[21]Marc Raeff, *Plans for Political Reform in Imperial Russia, 1730–1905* (Englewood Cliffs, NJ: Prentice-Hall, 1966), p. 51.
[22]Brenda Meehan-Waters, *Autocracy and Aristocracy: The Russian Service Elite of 1730* (New Brunswick, NJ: Rutgers University Press, 1980), pp. 139–40.

imperial rule in the rapidly changing cultural context of the eighteenth century; second, to question the notion that Russia deviated greatly from what went on in the rest of Europe at the time; and, third, to take seriously, rather than caricaturing as pettiness and "female foolishness," the court politics of the era.

The fact that a series of women held the throne was partly an accident of genetics: the Romanovs produced few sons in the generations between Peter I and Paul I. The arbitrary predominance of daughters in the royal line received an extra boost through the unfortunate tendency of the rulers' few male offspring to die young, whether during interrogation in the torture chamber, like Peter the Great's wretched son, Aleksei; from smallpox, like Aleksei's son Peter II (r. 1727–1730); or at the hands of their rivals, like the briefly reigning Ivan VI (r. 1740–1741), Peter the Great's great-grandnephew (who ruled as an infant for six months before spending the rest of his short, unhappy life in solitary confinement, driven mad by his lifelong isolation, and finally dying in 1764 at the hands of an assassin). Following the Y-chromosome tradition, Peter III (r. 1762) was ousted and killed during a coup perpetrated by his wife. Their son, Paul I (r. 1796–1801), would be the last to die at the hands of a close family member, assassinated with the tacit assent of his beloved son, who was immediately crowned Alexander I.

And so, it was a parade of women who sat on the Russian throne for most of the eighteenth century after Peter I's death in 1725. His wife Catherine I (r. 1725–1727) followed him. After the brief interlude of Peter II, Anna Ivanovna (r. 1730–1740) took the throne. When she bequeathed the crown to her great-nephew, the infant Ivan VI, under the guardianship of his Germanic parents, a palace coup and the ascent of Peter the Great's daughter Elizabeth put an end to the messy situation (1741). Elizabeth (r. 1741–1761) brought a welcome stability to the throne and was followed by her grandnephew Peter III. His wife overthrew him after six months and reigned gloriously for thirty-four years as Catherine II, the Great (1762–1796).

What did the reign of women entail? First of all, it is important to remember that the empresses oversaw growth according to all the standard indicators of state success. They conducted successful military campaigns and expanded the empire. The economy boomed in the eighteenth century as merchants engaged with the world market in unprecedented ways, and industry, mining, and agricultural production all intensified. Economic growth was hindered by the decidedly non-capitalist impulses of the nobility, who preferred to sink their wealth into displays of conspicuous consumption instead of investment. This tendency is satirized in Iakov B. Kniazhnin's *Misfortune from a Coach*, a play from the end of the century, that turns on the premise that a pretentious noble couple plans to sell off a serf as a military recruit in order to pay for a fancy French-style coach, lace caps, and red high-heeled shoes. "Imagine," the buffoon of a master writes to his steward on his country estate, "the disgrace it would be not only for me but for all of you if your master did not ride in this beautiful coach; and if your mistress did not buy those lovely headdresses that are also imported directly from Paris.

An honorable man should hang himself for such shame."[23] The fact that they are selling off a human being, in this case a fine young man about to be married to his true love, raises no scruples in the masters. As the play underscores, industry and agriculture continued to be fueled by unfree labor, and in gestures of great generosity to their privileged friends and clients, the empresses expanded both the territorial spread and the number of people tied in bondage. Nonetheless, the empresses oversaw economic and industrial expansion and fostered growth with some up-to-date policies, such as removing internal tariffs and tolls.

More interesting and more specific to the eighteenth century as a whole and to the female rulers in particular was a tendency to use affective means to cultivate stability. Sentimental novels and plays imported from France inspired a vogue for cultivating and displaying the most delicate sensibilities and refined pangs of the heart. Vasilii Trediakovskii, a product of the Slavo-Greco-Latin Academy, translated Paul Tallemant's *Le voyage de l'Isle d'amour* (1663) into Russian hexameter in 1766. Translations and imports of foreign philosophical treatises and sentimental novels and plays popularized the idea of literary salons that might encourage a public sphere of discussion and creativity. These stylish salons, the early modern equivalent of today's book groups, became the place to see and be seen. Salons, often run by women, allowed young men on the make to flaunt their command of the new, cosmopolitan ways of thinking and being. The great Soviet literary scholar and semiotician Iurii Lotman writes that in France, "the salon (a literary milieu) had given rise to the novel, whereas in Russia the novel was expected to give rise to a particular cultural milieu. There, reality created the text; here, the text was supposed to create reality."[24] In other words, life imitated art: literary culture modeled a new world, and the new court culture molded its lived reality, in fashion, form, and sentiment, to that bookish prototype.

In keeping with the sentimentalist culture of the age, which celebrated tender feelings, empathy, intrinsic moral sensibility, and passionate love, the empresses Elizabeth and Catherine II redirected the art of politics into strategies of winning favor among the elite by manipulating the dual languages of reason and emotion. Princess Elizabeth, for instance, lined up support for her ouster of the infant ruler Ivan VI and his unpopular German parents in deliberate and premeditated fashion. A contemporary observer reported that she "began with gaining over some soldiers of the guards of the regiment of Preobrazhenskii." At midnight on the day of the coup, with the ground already prepared, some three hundred members of the regiment, plus subalterns and private men, "all, to a man, consented to sacrifice themselves for her." Her loving and devoted supporters came out of the conspiracy well: "The first care of the Empress, after her getting possession of the imperial power, was to reward those who had served her in this

---

[23]Iakov B. Kniazhin, "Misfortune from a Coach," in Harold B. Segel, *The Literature of Eighteenth-Century Russia: A History and Anthology* (New York: Dutton, 1967), vol. 2, pp. 374–93; quote on pp. 381–82.
[24]Cited in Martin, "The Invention of 'Russianness'," p. 121.

revolution. She began with her favorite, Razumovskii, who was declared chamberlain some months after her coronation. She raised him to the post of grandmaster of the hunt, made him a count, and gave him the blue ribbon. . . . The whole company of grenadiers of the regiment of Preobrazhenskii were ennobled and promoted. The private men of them had the rank of lieutenants, and the corporals that of majors. . . . It was called the company of body-guards. Her Majesty declared herself the captain of it."[25] Expanding and sweetening traditional practices, Elizabeth secured her guards' loyalty and love through deliberate appeals and kept that loyalty with showers of rewards.

Ruling as a female presented some challenges, but these powerful women skillfully turned their sex to best advantage. Elizabeth set a precedent of demonstrating her ability to lead like a man when she donned the uniform of her favorite guards regiment. A famous 1743 portrait by Georg Christoph Grooth depicts her in uniform wearing a three-cornered hat, and riding astride like a man, not in sidesaddle. Her power is evident in her confident posture and her easy command of both her spirited horse mount and her African page. The equestrian pose and male dress, not incidentally, also allow her to show a shapely leg.

Portrait of Empress Elizabeth Petrovna on Horseback, Accompanied by a Negro Servant. This is a copy of an original by Georg Christoph Grooth, painted in 1743. It is in the collection of the State Hermitage Museum, St. Petersburg.

---

[25]Christof Herman von Manstein, *Memoirs of Russia: Historical, Political, Military from the Year 1727 to 1744 . . .* (London 1770), pp. 279–81.

Catherine II followed Elizabeth's example, with an equestrian portrait in the uniform of her own beloved guards from the regiments responsible for carrying out her own successful coup. In presenting themselves in male attire the empresses did not attempt to hide the fact of their sex. Their cross-dressing underscored their femininity, allowing them to exert masculine authority while displaying their female allure. Beginning with the reign of Elizabeth, court social events occasionally dictated that guests arrive in mandatory cross-dress attire, putting the play of gendered expectations on full display.

Overblown sentiment paired with witty repartee as the currency of the day was seen not only in the melodrama and humor of the stage, but also in private diaries and protestations of political loyalty. Catherine proved herself a master of both registers, sentiment and wit. She exchanged pointed barbs with public intellectuals such as Nikolai Novikov, an important representative of the nascent "public sphere" in which open discussion and publication was beginning to take place. And in her interactions with her advisers, supporters, and potential opponents, she demonstrated her talent in the theater of the heart.

Her first spectacular entrance onto this stage occurred in preparation for her coup, when affection for her stirred the guards' regiments, composed of the young men of the rank-and-file nobility, to a frenzy of love and loyalty. In her own description of the coup, written in a letter to a former lover, she wrote, "The ins and outs of the secret were in the hands of the three brothers Orlov, the eldest of whom . . . used to follow me everywhere and committed innumerable follies. His passion for me was openly acknowledged and that is why he undertook what he did." While the plot to remove her husband was under way, "We went to join the Ismailovskii regiment. . . . The soldiers rushed to kiss my hands, my feet, the hem of my dress, calling me their savior." She deliberately contrasts her own loving heart to that of her dead husband, whose autopsy proved beyond a doubt that he deserved his fate. Working to extinguish rumors that he was murdered (which he was), she described how a combination of fear and excessive drinking sent him to his grave. To find the cause of death she ordered an autopsy, and gloating over the findings, she reported: "He had an inordinately small heart, quite withered."[26]

The politics of power help explain Catherine's fabled sequence of official lovers, who held official title and position and were publicly proclaimed rather than hidden from view. When they chose to do so, these calculating rulers acted coquettish, strategically showering their attentions on the courtiers who surrounded them. In a practical calculus, flirtation preempted opposition: how unseemly would it be for a man to speak out against a woman who dallied with him. On a more pragmatic level, an empress's amorous or amiable advances, when publicly witnessed, raised the status of courtiers or diplomats, publicizing their closeness to power.

The memoir of the noblewoman Anna Labzina describes the tangible benefits that radiated from the empress's attention. One day, while walking in the royal gardens

---

[26]*The Memoirs of Catherine the Great*, ed. Dominique Maroger; trans. from the French by Moura Budberg (New York: Collier Books, 1961), pp. 271–74.

with her highly placed patron, Prince Grigorii Potemkin, Labzina happened to meet the empress. Potemkin "motioned for me to approach her and she took my hand. She was told who I was. From that day on I saw her frequently, all of which fed my pride and vanity, especially when I saw that everyone wished to serve me and looked into my eyes to see what I needed. I received the most noble and respectful treatment. All my needs were met then: the prince sent me everything I wanted." Such was the golden glow of connections on high that a "tax farmer whom my husband had recommended to the prince" spontaneously financed and built a house for the couple, anticipating her every desire, filling the place with her beloved "song birds and flowers." "None of this cost us a penny," she marvels, while chalking this generosity up to "friendship."[27] The reciprocal benefits from closeness and loyalty to the ruler enhanced both the nobility's status and the empress's secure hold on the throne.

In commemoration and celebration of the overthrow of the small-hearted Peter III, a painter named I. K. Kaestner produced a series of watercolors depicting the coup. Amid the crowds of people in the scene, Catherine herself is almost invisible, yielding the most visible place to her faithful guards, who decided the struggles for the throne. Here the painter acknowledges a fundamental political truth that has been overlooked in hindsight: Catherine's protestations of love to her guards were not superficial feminine indulgences but a matter of life and death. Her survival, both political and physical, depended on their loyalty. Autocracy was not for the socially inept or the isolated.

In the dismissive vein so commonly adopted in discussing Russia's eighteenth-century rulers, the whole period has been characterized as "the era of palace coups," or "autocracy tempered by assassination." It is worth noting which rulers were assassinated and which died peacefully in their beds. Those who acceded to the throne with some degree of active support—not through actual "election," of course, but with powerful backing—and those who managed to win over, to seduce, beguile, and entrance key elements in the court, the general nobility, and especially the military, lived to ripe old ages. Those who interacted in a high-handed fashion with their courtiers and troops did more than display bad manners. They egregiously violated the essence of politics: reciprocity, affective bonds, and the building of support. Rulers who had the apparent good fortune to be born to the succession, that is, the male heirs who took the throne as a matter of course, did not go through the process of building constituencies or winning support, and, not entirely coincidentally, their lives and reigns were cut short. Catherine was deeply aware of her need to build consensus. She famously recorded her riposte to the French philosophe Denis Diderot, when she tired of his caviling about the slow pace of reform in Russia:

> Mr. Diderot, I have heard with the greatest pleasure everything which your brilliant spirit has inspired in you; but with all your great principles, which I understand very well, one would make beautiful books but poor work. You forget in all

---

[27]Gary Marker and Rachel May, eds. and trans., *Days of a Russian Noblewoman: The Memories of Anna Labzina, 1758–1821* (DeKalb: Northern Illinois University Press, 2001), pp. 71–72.

I. K. Kaestner, watercolor, *Catherine II on the Balcony of the Winter Palace, Greeted by the Guards and People on the Day of the Palace Revolution on June 28, 1762.* The young Catherine is barely visible in this depiction of the coup that deposed her husband and placed her on the throne. She is seen as a shadowy shape in the window, mostly blocked by the gentleman (presumably one of the Orlov brothers), who has just climbed up and entered the room in front of her. The painting represents the coup as a popular event carried out by "the people," and downplays Catherine's own role in it.

> your plans for reform the difference of our two positions: you work only with paper, which suffers everything; it is all unified, supple, and poses obstacles to neither your imagination nor your quill; while I, poor empress that I am, I work with human skin, which is quite differently irritable and susceptible.

Elsewhere, she wrote, "Power without the nation's confidence is nothing for he who seeks to be loved and to have glory."[28] Here Catherine casually uses the word *nation*, not to mean all the people (including the tens of thousands of peasant serfs she gifted to her loyal nobles), but in reference to those closest to her, those who

---

[28]For these translations and work tracking down sources on these widely known but elusively sourced aphorisms, we thank Shoshana Keller and her undergraduate research student, who generously shared the results of their detective work. Louis Philippe de Ségur, *Memoires ou souvenirs et anecdotes*, Vol. 3 (Paris: Alexis Eymery, Libraire-Éditeur, 1826), pp. 42–43; https://books.google.com/books?id=A9lfA AAAcAAJ&lpg=PP15&ots=pAPQJWS6fB&dq=de%20segur%20memoires%20souvenirs%20 anecdotes%20tome%20iii&pg=PA42#v=onepage&q=de%20segur%20memoires%20souvenirs%20 anecdotes%20tome%20iii&f=false. Keller finds the second passage attributed to a miscellaneous note by Catherine, and, in a longer version, to a nineteenth-century biography of the empress by Charles de Larivière, who cites Book 7 of the *Collections of the Russian Imperial Historical Society*.

despised her husband, helped her to the throne, and would years later depose and murder her unfortunate son. The eighteenth century was certainly an era of autocracy, but it was tempered by elite consensus as well as by assassination and coups.

Geoffrey Hosking writes that the eighteenth-century Russian state was

> a rickety framework in a howling gale, subject to all the chance crosswinds of court intrigue and kinship feuding. It was a mere skeleton whose flesh and sinews consisted of the clannish interests of the great families who provided its continuity and its motive power. As for local government, it was notional only, feeble to the point of being non-existent: for lack of suitable personnel to staff its offices, it lapsed back into the hands of the arbitrary and venal military governors from whom Peter had tried to rescue it.[29]

At one level, Hosking is absolutely right: when we view Russia's history from the vantage point of the canals and ornate palaces of St. Petersburg, from the desks and boudoirs of the empresses and their elite circles, we are dazzled and deceived by their sparkling surfaces. In Boeck's clever aphorism, we fall victim to "decreedulity," the mistake of credulously believing that all the papers issued as formal decrees actually became reality. The empire was a far flimsier apparatus, with far less reach than its paper trail would lead us to believe. It was an amorphous, shape-shifting overlay across its vast subject terrains and populations. Yet, it was not so much an "elusive empire," as a recent book title would have it, not so much a goal just out of reach, as it was a polity built deliberately on jury-rigged particularism, on special arrangements, differentiated rules, demands, and concessions, geared to hold a kaleidoscopic miscellany together, loosely, under the tsarist double-headed eagle.[30]

The eighteenth-century rulers, like those before and after, faced the challenge of holding together their great and diverse empire, not just winning the support of a few key individuals in court circles. Catherine faced particularly formidable obstacles in her quest for legitimacy on the throne. Born a Prussian Protestant, she converted to Russian Orthodoxy upon her marriage to the heir to the throne. Appreciating the need to appear genuine in commitment to her adopted home, she immersed herself in Russian religion and language, mastering both with aplomb. Still, as a foreigner, a convert, and a woman, she already had a steep road to climb. When one adds the fact that she was already rumored to have lovers and to have given birth to an illegitimate son before her accession to the throne, and then, to complicate matters further, came to power through a coup d'état followed by the murder of her husband, the legitimately reigning monarch, the odds of mounting a successful public relations campaign were clearly enormous.

A woman of tremendous energy and intellectual ability, she succeeded beyond all expectation. Besmirching the reputation of her late-unlamented husband, he of the small, withered heart, was just a first step. Catherine carefully manipulated

---

[29]Geoffrey Hosking, *Russia, People and Empire, 1552–1917* (Cambridge, MA: Harvard University Press, 1997), p. 96.

[30]Matthew P. Romaniello, *The Elusive Empire: Kazan and the Creation of Russia, 1562–1671* (Madison: University of Wisconsin Press, 2012).

and publicized her image as wise lawmaker; Minerva, the Roman goddess of wisdom and patron of the arts, and Semiramis, the Assyrian warrior-queen, rolled into one; worthy heir of Peter the Great (witness *The Bronze Horseman*, the monumental statue she erected in St. Petersburg bearing the dedication "To Peter the First from Catherine the Second"). She cultivated her image as a cosmopolitan intellectual, involved in witty exchanges with the continent's leading minds. She made certain that her wholehearted conversion to Russian Orthodoxy was on view to a broad public. As she aged, she added to the mix an emphasis on the maternal love and care she extended to her people.

She surrounded herself with talented advisers and drew on the brightest minds of Europe. She instituted an extensive program of reform and publicized her wisdom as lawgiver, as enlightener, and as mother to the motherland. She called the various categories of people to participate in a great Legislative Commission, intended to draft new laws for the land on the basis of her own *Nakaz* ("The Grand Instruction to the Commissioners Appointed to Frame a New Code of Laws for the Russian Empire"). The commission drew representatives of various regions and social estates together to discuss models for reform. They collected reports that poured in from people and groups throughout the land, people eager to communicate ideas and to air complaints using the traditional formula of petition and supplication. Although the Commission itself collapsed before producing any formal legislation, several of its drafts bore fruit in the various Charters issued later in Catherine's reign. With the collection of ideas from "all the land" and the meetings of the Commission itself, Catherine adhered to earlier models of responsive and inclusive governance. The decisive authority of the empress was never subject to doubt, but her commitment to listening and to bringing her people into the conversation demonstrated familiarity with Russian traditions of consultation and reciprocity.

To a remarkable degree this stratagem seems to have enjoyed success as a powerful social glue. A language of love became the standard form of political encomia, elaborate and over-blown tributes, directed first to Empress Elizabeth and then to Catherine. Literary scholar Olga Greco notes that the poet Gavrila Derzhavin built on the poetry of the ancients to argue that Catherine ruled over an empire not just rivaling but superior to that of the Romans. The ancients built their empire on law and fear, while Catherine won the love of her subjects through kindness, wisdom, and virtue:

> But not through war and blood:
> But, let love, dressed in compassion
> And wisdom be your might.
> Like Zeus, hold a thunderbolt and make it shine across the skies;
> But, styling yourself more after Phoebus,
> Shine in the world, like the god of light. . . .[31]

---

[31]Olga Greco, "From Triumphal Gates to Triumphant Rotting: Refractions of Rome in the Russian Political Imagination," PhD diss., University of Michigan, 2015.

Catherine the Great Composes the Nakaz, 1768. In this portrait, Catherine shows herself as lawgiver and as hardworking heir to Peter the Great, completing the work of reform that he began. Peter's bust looks on approvingly as she composes her manifesto for legal and social reform of Russia. The open pocket watch on her writing desk signals the hours of work she devotes to the task. Although she wears only a simple coronet or tiara, her gold and diamond-encrusted orb of royal office sits by her side on a red velvet and gold-tasseled pillow, and ermine tails ornament her fur-trimmed white satin gown.

Labzina's memoir reveals the same vocabulary of love and friendship at work as a binding agent throughout society. In her interactions with members of the nobility, with tradesmen to whom she owes money, with hardened prisoners in Siberia, and with the enserfed peasants on her mother's estate, tears, protestations of love, and eternal friendship define her relationships and mask the harsh inequalities on which these "friendships" were built. When her mother received a party of menacing Tatars hospitably and appealed to their kindness, they responded "with tears in their eyes," swearing themselves not enemies but protectors of their "kind neighbor and friend." When obliged to leave her childhood home and her enserfed nanny, Labzina recalls her "poor, sad nanny, who was more dead than alive as she parted with me, her face was terribly pale. She could no longer cry, and I saw that she was staggering and barely able to stand. Her eyes were dark and wild, and I had a deep dread that something most dire would happen." At the prospect of her departure from her husband's posting in Siberia, the local convicts "soaked my hands with their tears, and I cried with them and felt for them sincerely. They were very close to my heart."

The prominent historian of Imperial Russia Marc Raeff asserted that "sentimentalism proved incapable of taking hold and evolv[ing] into a genuine intellectual force; . . . it remained a superficial literary fashion." Raeff explains that in
the Western European societies where sentimentalism struck more resonant
chords, it served as a weapon to fortify the bourgeoisie (as a repository of authentic feeling) against the frivolous and superficial aristocracy. In Russia, by contrast, "the purveyors of sentimentalism were themselves members of the nobility,
the creators and consumers of modern and potentially revolutionary values were
at the same time the social and political elites which depended on and benefited
from state service and serfdom."[32] Labzina's emotional memory of her dear serf
nanny and her tear-drenched parting offers a valuable corrective to this view.
Sentimentality not only caught on but provided righteous moral cover for the
practice of holding human beings in bondage.

In a world held together by such passionate sentiment, refined thinkers like
Labzina could imagine that love and friendship, rather than coercion and exploitation, held her comfortable world together.[33] Perhaps indeed the personal model
of loving friendship softened the experience of serfdom for those who lived on
the estates of owners so deeply affected by their own sensibilities. Or perhaps
Misfortune from a Coach (discussed above), Kniazhnin's lampoon of masters
heartlessly pursuing Frenchified refinement at the cost of their human posses-
sions, more accurately represents the experience of serfs, caught in the crosshairs
of their masters' expensive cultural aspirations and the harsh realities of legal
serfdom.

Other logics were at work on Russian estates that sharply undercut the loving
friendship model. From the seventeenth century, great numbers of Russian peasants were bound to landlords, losing former freedoms to move from their lands.
The conditions of serfdom sharpened during the eighteenth century, and what
had begun in the previous century as a system for keeping track of taxpayers and
securing laboring hands for landholders' estates devolved into a more brutally
restrictive system for policing and exploiting the peasantry. The conditions of the
peasantry varied widely across the empire, where regional arrangements were
largely preserved, in accord with the general practice of maintaining difference.
The Baltic regions, for instance, brought their own manner of serfdom into the
empire when Peter incorporated them, while Siberia remained at least nominally
free of serfdom (in practice, something very much like slavery was common
there). Even within Russia, conditions varied by region and even estate to estate.
Peasants were bound by very different terms in the fertile black-soil regions of the

---

[32]Mark Raeff, "Review of Hans Rogger, *National Consciousness in Eighteenth Century Russia, Jahrbücher für Geschichte Osteuropas* 8 (1960), p. 447.
[33]Marker and May, *Days of a Russian Noblewoman*, pp. 14, 39, 93. Mary W. Cavender finds the same
kind of sentimental cover for holding people in bondage among the nobility of Tver Province: *Nests
of the Gentry: Family, Estate, and Local Loyalties in Provincial Russia* (Newark, DE: University of
Delaware Press, 2007).

south and colder regions of the north, and the degree to which the landlord interfered in their lives depended on all sorts of factors, including regional custom, climate, and soil quality, as well as the landlords' personality and whether or not they lived on or near a particular estate. Some peasants were obligated to work directly on the landlords' lands; others could pay off their dues in kind. Still others were allowed to satisfy their debts in cash, which gave them opportunities to leave their estates and earn money in other ways. The forms and experience of serfdom, like so much else in the empire, was construed differently in different regions, as was appropriate to an imperial formation.

As a general rule, across these important differences, over the course of the eighteenth century peasants became increasingly dependent on the will of their landlords. Landlords increased their rights over their serfs, until by the reign of Catherine the Great they were being sold at auction like slaves. Orthodox Christian lords "owned" Orthodox Christian peasants and could buy and sell them, flog them, or send them into exile or the army. Serfs were required to work for their masters and suffer all manner of punishments if they did not obey. There were limits to the power of the lords, however: they were not permitted (in principle) to torture or kill peasants.

Coercion and outright brutality, exercised by the masters and backed by state violence, certainly played a part, but coercion alone could not suffice to maintain control with such lopsided demographics and remote landscapes. Historian Steven Hoch explores the inside workings of serfdom to figure out how a small handful of landowners succeeded in binding a huge population of peasants to their estates and forcing them to labor without compensation. His findings are extremely revealing. On the one hand, he finds that serfdom did in fact offer important compensations to the serfs. While from the point of view of the landlord, serfdom bound the peasants to the land, from the peasants' perspective what was attractive was that it bound the land to the peasants. A guarantee to land was a non-trivial boon for an agrarian population. On the other hand, Hoch exposes a chilling, self-enforcing dynamic that locked the peasantry into colluding in their own enserfment. Through their agents and bailiffs on site, masters enlisted the cooperation of peasant patriarchs, the male heads of households who called the shots within large family units.

By shoring up the authority of the patriarchs, the masters and bailiffs coopted them as willing participants, creating a replicating structure of hierarchical domination from top to bottom of society. Patriarchs enjoyed the right to domineer in their households and make critical decisions, such as which family members would be sold off as military recruits (the plot device seen in *Misfortune from a Coach*, and also famously critiqued in Alexander Radishchev's radical *Journey from St. Petersburg to Moscow*, published in 1790). Within the serf household itself, hierarchies of tyranny and abuse layered one over another, with the unfortunate junior daughter-in-law as the bottom of the heap, subject to the whims and abuse of her father-in-law, her mother-in-law, and her husband. With this miserable "separate deal," where nearly everyone enjoyed a small dominion, it proved difficult to find common ground for opposing the system.[34]

In spite of this insidious system of collusion and self-policing, landlords were sharply aware of the potential threat posed by their massing serfs. Although they might tell themselves warm stories of loving peasant nannies, they took steps to limit the danger of a dagger in the night. Literary scholar Thomas Newlin notes an unease hidden within noble descriptions of bucolic scenes on their estates. In a watercolor painting by the eighteenth-century nobleman and memoirist Andrei Bolotov, a serpent is hidden cleverly under a lovely pink rose, a metaphor, Newlin suggests, for the ever-present unseen menace on the serf-holding estate. Also studying the work of Bolotov, Priscilla Roosevelt remarks on the subtle differences between English and Russian landscape design in the late eighteenth century. Bolotov himself worked as a landscape designer for Catherine the Great and is credited with importing the "romantic" or "natural" English garden to replace French-style formal gardens with their stiff lines and geometric layouts. Key to the English garden was an open view that stretched to the horizon, without barriers. Bolotov and other Russian gardeners recreated that effect, but, fearing the unpredictable wrath of the peasants, dug ditches along the distant perimeters of their properties and hid protective fences down below the line of sight, barring unauthorized entry. These seem apt metaphors for the relations of masters and serfs in the age of Enlightenment.[35] In the boundless spaces of the Russian Empire, the ruling nobility was nominally obligated to protect the lowliest subjects of the realm. They attempted to convince themselves that their dominance was based on a natural order of superiors and inferiors connected by bonds of affection. At the same time they were aware (and wary) that such sentiments proved a slim reed, easily broken by conditions of the real world.

BRIEF BIBLIOGRAPHY

Anderson, Perry. *Lineages of the Absolutist State*. London: Verso, 2013.

Anisimov, E. V. *The Reforms of Peter the Great: Progress Through Coercion in Russia*. Translated by John T. Alexander. Armonk, NY: M. E. Sharpe, 1993.

Bushkovitch, Paul. *Peter the Great: The Struggle for Power, 1671–1725*. Cambridge and New York: Cambridge University Press, 2001.

Hughes, Lindsey. *Russia in the Age of Peter the Great*. New Haven, CT: Yale University Press, 1998.

---

[34]Steven L. Hoch, "The Serf Economy, The Peasant Family, and the Social Order," in *Imperial Russia: New Histories for the Empire*, ed. Jane Burbank and David Ransel (Bloomington: Indiana University Press, 1998), pp. 199–209. See also Hoch, *Serfdom and Social Control in Russia: Petrovskoe, a Village in Tambov* (Chicago: University of Chicago Press, 1986).

[35]Thomas Newlin, "Rural Ruses: Illusion and Anxiety on the Russian Estate," *Slavic Review* 57, no. 2 (1998): 295–319; Priscilla Roosevelt, "Tatiana's Garden: Noble Sensibilities and Estate Park Design in the Romantic Era," *Slavic Review* 49 (1990): 335–49.

Henshall, Nicholas. *The Myth of Absolutism: Change and Continuity in Early Modern European Monarchy.* London and New York: Longman, 1992.

Kamenskii, Aleksandr. *The Russian Empire in the Eighteenth Century: Searching for a Place in the World.* Trans. and ed. by David Griffiths. Armonk, NY: M. E. Sharpe, 1997.

LeDonne, John P. *Absolutism and the Ruling Class: The Formation of the Russian Political Order, 1700–1825.* New York: Oxford University Press, 1991.

Madariaga, Isabel de. *Russia in the Age of Catherine the Great.* New Haven, CT: Yale University Press, 1981.

Marker, Gary. *Imperial Saint: The Cult of St. Catherine and the Dawn of Female Rule in Russia.* DeKalb: Northern Illinois University Press, 2007.

Wortman, Richard. *Scenarios of Power: Myth and Ceremony in Russian Monarchy, Vol. I, From Peter the Great to the Death of Nicholas I.* Princeton, NJ: Princeton University Press, 1995.

FIVE

RUSSIANS' IDENTITIES IN THE EIGHTEENTH CENTURY
A Multitude of Possibilities

Empresses and their inner circles, members of the cultured elite, may have imagined that they lived in a community of virtue and love, but this premise had limited efficacy and reach as a form of group or collective identity. The eighteenth century in Europe was the moment in history when the word *nation* began to pick up the cluster of meanings that would make it one of the most powerful political concepts of modern times. At the same time, eighteenth- and nineteenth-century Europe might also be considered the apogee of empire. For their proponents both "nation" and "empire" were positive concepts, and many imagined that the two were neither contradictory nor irreconcilable. Yet both in discourse and practice, empire and nation tended to mix like oil and water: they appeared to blend together in a common emulsion but in fact kept their own identity and over time slipped apart.

It is important to recognize, however, that the polarities of nation and empire did not exhaust the possibilities for collective identification. Far from it. Life within the Russian Empire offered other foci for identification or affiliation. Law, custom, and experience organized people, willingly or unwillingly, consciously or unconsciously, into collectives premised on social status, place of residence, cultural competencies, and political reliability, in addition to the familiar categories of gender, religion, and language. In this chapter we consider these various dimensions that shaped identities in the eighteenth century. We begin with the important interplay of national and imperial conceptions, and then move on to other dimensions of human collective imagination.

WHAT DOES *RUSSIAN* MEAN? THINKING ABOUT NATIONS IN THE EIGHTEENTH CENTURY

Some historians, as we have seen, read national consciousness back into the Russian seventeenth century, to the Time of Troubles or the Old Believer Schism, and others see it arising at the time of Peter the Great. Michael Cherniavsky, for example, argued that a dual consciousness emerged with the Church schism of the late

seventeenth century and solidified with the reforms of Peter I: that of the Europe-
anizing gentry, which identified themselves with "Russia" and considered what they
were doing as "by definition, Russian"; and that of the Old Believers and peasants in
general who "began to insist on beards, traditional clothes, and old rituals—
creating, in reaction, their own Russian identity."[1] In this view, "national consciousness emerged as a popular reaction to the self-identity of the absolutist state, with
the threat that those things which challenged it—the absolutist consciousness of
tsar, empire, and Orthodoxy—could be excluded from Russian self-identity."[2] In a
useful corrective, James Cracraft points out that much of the reaction to the Niko-
nian and Petrine reforms, rather than constituting xenophobia or national consciousness, was in large part "an anguished opposition to a pattern of behavior
which did great violence to a world view that was still essentially religious."[3]

Undoubtedly, ideas about what constituted Russia and Russians existed, and
identities competed between and within social groups in a confused, shifting,
unsystematized discursive space in which religious and ethnocultural distinctions overlapped and reinforced one another. Russian was closely identified with
being Orthodox Christian but also with living in the tsar's realm, being a subject
of the sovereign. As the state under Peter the Great moved away from the more
traditional ethnoreligious sense of community toward a non-ethnic, cosmopolitan, European sense of political civilization, to the extent that they paid attention
or cared about such broad affiliations, people were pulled between these two understandings of the "Russian" community.

The disputes among scholars about Russian national identification and nationalism in the eighteenth century have not added much clarity to a most important discussion. The debate often founders on imprecision when defining
nation and nationalism. Cracraft, for example, argues that an imperial
nationalism—pride in empire, sovereign, and state—developed under Peter I and
preempted any other form of nationalism. His examples argue for a strong sense
of "national pride," meaning pride in the achievements of the state and the
empire, imperial dignity, and glory. The people are almost completely left out.
Cracraft concludes that "absolutism and imperialism were inherent in Russian
nationalism virtually from the beginning."[4]

Identification with Russia, at least among nobles and the educated population,
appears to have been largely contained in a sense of state patriotism, that is, identification with the state and its ruler rather than with a broader political community conceived separately from the state, namely the nation. This is evident in
Peter's own writings. In the 1709 order to his troops Peter speaks of *rossiiskoe*

---

[1]Michael Cherniavsky, "Russia," in *National Consciousness, History, and Political Culture in Early-
Modern Europe,* ed. Orest Ranum (Baltimore and London: The Johns Hopkins University Press,
1975), p. 141.
[2]Ibid., p. 140.
[3]James Cracraft, "Empire Versus Nation: Russian Political Theory Under Peter I," in *Major Problems
in the History of Imperial Russia,* ed. James Cracraft (Lexington, MA, 1994), p. 225.
[4]Cracraft, "Empire Versus Nation," p. 540.

(meaning inclusion of all peoples living in Russia) in reference to the army, mentions the *otechestvo* (fatherland), the *gosudarstvo* (state), and makes one reference to the all-Russian people (*za narod vserossiiskii*).[5] As Cynthia Hyla Whittaker demonstrates, the forty-five amateur historians of eighteenth-century Russia were principally concerned with replacing religious with new secular justifications for autocracy, based either on dynastic continuity, dynamism of the ruler, his/her concern for the welfare of the people, or the superiority of autocracy over alternative forms of government.[6] Their point of positive connection with a broader community therefore was with the state and the monarch rather than with the people as a community unto itself.

The archbishop Feofan Prokopovich, often cited as Peter's theorist of absolutism, proposed that all governments originated from an agreement of the people, a notion quite popular in Europe at the time. But once a sovereign government based on heredity had been formed, the people were required to obey that government and make no effort to overthrow it or even to judge it. In theory and practice, Peter and his spokesmen were engaged in a political effort to reinforce the state against competing elites and reform old customs and practices, but not to eliminate the privileges of the nobles and establish a despotism of a single ruler. The old families remained powerful and influential before, during, and after Peter's reign.[7]

Toward the end of the eighteenth century, Russian writers joined in the general European practice of identifying national distinctions, or what would be called "national character," something in which European Enlightenment figures from Voltaire and Montesquieu to Johann Gottfried von Herder and Johann Blumenbach engaged. This sensitivity to "national" difference was already evidenced earlier in the century by "Russian" nobles' resistance to and resentment of "foreigners" advancing too high in state service. When this principle was breached during the reign of Anna, Russian nobles protested the visibility of the German barons surrounding the empress. Here patriotism was a way not only of protecting privilege and discouraging competition for power but also of encouraging the construction of solidarities within one group against another.

In conscious reaction against the Germanophilia of Anna or Peter III, the coronations of Elizabeth and Catherine II were conceived as acts of restoration, bringing back the glories of Peter the Great. In the view of these monarchs, Peter now represented the authentic Russia, and Elizabeth made the most of being the daughter of Peter and Catherine I. The German princess who became Catherine II may have been a usurper with no legitimate right to rule, yet her seizure of power was depicted as an act of deliverance from a tyrant with foreign airs. Besides being portrayed as Minerva, the embodiment of enlightenment, she presented

---

[5]Ibid., p. 529.
[6]Hans Rogger, *National Consciousness in Eighteenth-Century Russia* (Cambridge, MA: Harvard University Press, 1960); Cynthia Hyla Whittaker, "The Idea of Autocracy Among Eighteenth-Century Russian Historians," in *Imperial Russia: New Histories for the Empire*, ed. Jane Burbank and David Ransel (Bloomington and Indianapolis: Indiana University Press, 1998), pp. 32–59.
[7]Meehan-Waters, *Autocracy and Aristocracy*.

herself as one who loved Russia and respected its Orthodox religion. Enveloped in a cosmopolitan culture that preferred speaking French to Russian, the noble elite was not above sentimental attachments to elements of Russian ethnic culture. Catherine the Great introduced a "Russian dress" with native features for women and favored plays based on historical Russian themes, even writing some herself. "Imperial patriotism with a Great Russian coloration was a theme of late-eighteenth-century history and literature."[8]

A number of specialists, most notably Hans Rogger, have argued for the origins of national consciousness in eighteenth-century Russia. Late in the eighteenth century, and accelerating in the early nineteenth, writers and the literate elite became interested in the virtues and particularities of the common folk. Partly the fallout from the French Enlightenment and the rising artistic movements of Sentimentalism and, later, Romanticism, the peasantry now appeared to be a repository of simple, unaffected life, the fount of the national culture that contrasted with the artifice of the elite and the inauthenticity and foreignness of French-influenced noble culture.

Literary and more ethnographic works produced in the second half of the century suggest that Russian nobles following intellectual developments in the West turned their attention to sifting out the particular characteristics of the Russian folk. Drawing on the same cultural stereotypes already in circulation in the seventeenth century, the newly emerging specialists in Russian ethnography came to imagine the Russian national character as "easygoing, tolerant, warm-hearted, communal, spiritual, sincere, and loyal; the shortcomings attributed to them by Russian writers—superstitiousness, drunkenness, corruption, laziness, disregard for rules—were deemed logical, even endearing corollaries to these favorable qualities."[9] Russia was great but mysterious, difficult to know, often irrational but also passionate, full of feeling.

The discovery of such depth of feeling in the crude peasantry could come as a shock to the educated elite, so pleased with themselves and their refinement of emotion. In the play *Misfortune from a Coach*, mentioned in the previous chapter, the author lampoons the dandified francophilic master and mistress for their failure to understand that their peasant-property could hold deeply felt sentiments. On the verge of selling off one of their peasants, they relent when they realize that their marketable resource speaks French, and therefore must be capable of true sentiment: "Ah,! Mon coeur! He knows French, and he's in chains! That simply will not do," exclaims the mistress. The master, apparently not remembering that he himself is Russian, responds: "Parbleu! I never would have believed that Russian people could love so tenderly.... Am I not in France? That

---

[8]Wortman, *Scenarios of Power*, Vol. 1, p. 136. On fashion as a site where Russians worked out their sense of national identity, see Christine Ruane, *The Emperor's New Clothes: A History of the Russian Fashion Industry, 1700–1917* (New Haven, CT: Yale University Press, 2009).

[9]Alexander M. Martin, "The Invention of 'Russianness' in the Late Eighteenth–Early Nineteenth Century, *Ab Imperio* (2003), no. 3: 119–34, quote on 126.

Ivan Argunov, *Portrait of an Unknown Woman*, 1784. Argunov, himself a serf-artist, painted this beautiful if sentimentalized portrait of an unknown woman in Russian peasant dress in 1784.

he feels love comes as no great surprise to me—he does speak French." When he discovered that the girl, who speaks only Russian, also understands love, he declares himself "still more amazed."[10] New trends in painting displayed the same discovery of the humanity of the simple folk and the sensitive souls of the true Russian peasants. Ivan Argunov, himself a serf on the estate of Count Sheremetev, contributed to this movement with his painting of a radiant woman in peasant dress, completed in 1784.

The discovery (or invention) of a pure, simple Russian *narod* (a or the people) posed uncomfortable challenges for the cosmopolitan elites, the nobility and educated circles in St. Petersburg and Moscow. There is little evidence that they identified with the "folk" or considered themselves part of that collectivity. In fact, they went to great lengths to differentiate themselves from the common people. To mark their elevated status, elites were required by law and fashion to dress, talk, and act according to the worldly norms of polite society, that is, according to European norms. Clean-shaven chins and plunging necklines, witty banter in French, and familiarity with the latest European fashions and philosophical currents were not only fashionable but were requirements for participating in refined society and walking the corridors of power. Yet toward the end of the century, writers recorded a growing unease with the cultural chasm that separated nobles from their good, honest Russian peasants.

---

[10]Ibid, pp. 390, 393.

As long as Petrine regulations obliged nobles to serve the state, they could justify their status through service. But once mandatory service was abolished during the brief reign of Peter III and this "emancipation" from service was confirmed by Catherine II, Russian nobles found themselves in a quandary. Freed from service, they could justify their nobility only through their cultural pretensions, but since refined culture meant European culture, their claim to nobility cut them adrift from their Russianness. No longer upholding the state through their service, alienated from the simple routines and Orthodox piety attributed to peasants, those members of the elite who spent any time thinking about it had a hard time carving out a meaningful role for themselves in society.[11]

The Russian nobility set themselves to the task of defining true Russianness with particular urgency, because they found themselves at a loss to understand their own Russianness. If the folk embodied Russia, then what was their role? Literary texts demonstrate a growing preoccupation with the good old Russian morality of the past, imagined nostalgically in opposition to the corrupt and frivolous values of the court and capital. In the plays of Denis Fonvizin or in Prince Mikhail Shcherbatov's *On the Corruption of Morals in Russia* (1797), it was the old-time provincial nobles like Starodum (Old-fashioned Thinker) who embodied these ancient virtues, and the silly social climbers who are satirized.

Yet in our opinion, none of this—the state patriotism of the elites; the sharper awareness of differences between peoples; the new interest in the simple folk, the *narod*—rises to what would become in the nineteenth century nationalism, which we define as "the sentiment or doctrine that expresses primary or ultimate loyalty to and affection for a particular nation and dedication to its promotion and advancement." While certainly a national consciousness, an awareness of what was distinctly Russian, was growing in eighteenth-century Russia, identities still centered on locality; social position in the existing hierarchy; the ruler, the dynasty, and the state; religion; and a sense of belonging to a particular ethnic community. The discourse of the nation, which emerged most forcefully with the French Revolution of 1789 and would legitimate the people's power, was only embryonically visible in the late eighteenth century.

A MULTIPLICITY OF NATIONS:
THE PEOPLES AND DIVISIONS OF EMPIRE

The great Russian Empire, however, consisted of a widely varied national palette. At the same time that they grappled with reconciling their Europeanized veneer with a yearning for national authenticity, Russian thinkers also had to confront

---

[11]Marc Raeff, *The Origins of the Russian Intelligentsia: The Eighteenth-Century Intelligentsia* (New York: Harcourt, Brace & World, 1966) argues that the freedom from service left noblemen with little to do and led them in the next century to embrace reform and even revolution. As he puts it, "The members of the intelligentsia combined the moral and intellectual tenets of the eighteenth-century servicemen with the fervor and emotional commitment to action of the Decembrists" (pp. 170–71).

the puzzle of a greater Imperial Russia that included many non-Russian subjects. By the eighteenth century, Russia was an empire in the multiple senses of a great state whose ruler exercised full, absolute sovereign power over diverse territory and subjects. How did Russians think and feel about the non-Russian native peoples among them? Beginning with the reign of Peter the Great, Yuri Slezkine tells us, curiosity about the animal, mineral, and human diversity of empire gripped the educated elite. Through the eighteenth century, travelers, explorers, and ethnographers fanned out to categorize and study the natural phenomena of Eurasia. Among those phenomena were people, and following the fashion in Germany at the time, people were to be categorized as peoples or nations. "Before describing a nation," Slezkine writes, "the scholar had to decide where one nation ended and the other began: in other words, he had to find the ethnic equivalent of Linnaeus's pistils and stamens by constructing a complex but necessarily complete hierarchy of communal traits. The first such trait was the name, invariably mentioned as the first and most obvious badge of existential autonomy."[12] Next came territory (*obitanie*), where the people lived, and geography defined the people as well. Other markers of difference were food, sexual practices, smell, way of life, hygienic practices, and relationship to the land. Through the course of the eighteenth century a group's purported customs became more central to the definition of the people.

While the Russian state continued to classify peoples by their religion, scholars and bureaucrats described them in terms of their practices and customs, which over time evolved into imputed national characteristics. In Russian the word *natsiia*, borrowed from the French *nation*, was only occasionally used; instead the Russian *narod*, which corresponded to the German *Volk*, was employed. There were many different peoples in the world, eighteenth-century ethnographers noticed, but natural law dictated that though they had different languages and customs they were essentially the same. Some had the true faith, others did not; some were more enlightened than others, who were more barbaric—filthy, smelly eaters of raw meat. Confusion and contradiction plagued efforts to understand precisely how these various peoples fit into a sense of Russia and Russianness.

Willard Sunderland stresses how a sense of territoriality developed during the Petrine period. In Peter's time, censuses of peoples, exploration of the empire, and a serious effort to create maps of Russia were undertaken. Sunderland writes, "In the same way that territorial knowledge became a vehicle for the expression of Russian state patriotism, it also became a basis for identifying (or at least trying to identify) the Russian nation."[13] Further, to claim equivalence to the great

---

[12]Yuri Slezkine, "Naturalists Versus Nations: Eighteenth Century Russian Scholars Confront Ethnic Diversity," in *Russia's Orient: Imperial Borderlands and Peoples, 1700–1917*, ed. Daniel R. Brower and Edward J. Lazzerini (Bloomington, IN: Indiana University Press, 1997), pp. 27–57; quote on p. 30. Carl Linnaeus (1707–1778) was a Swedish botanist and zoologist who worked out the modern system of categorizing plants and animals.
[13]Willard Sunderland, "Imperial Space: Territorial Thought ad Practice in the Eighteenth Century," in *Russian Empire: Space, People, Power, 1700–1930*, ed. Jane Burbank, Mark von Hagen, and Anatolyi Remnev (Bloomington, IN: Indiana University Press, 2007), p. 42.

European overseas empires, Russians grew concerned with differentiating a "Russian" metropolitan center from "colonial" peripheries. Although the word *colonies* (*kolonii*) first entered a Russian dictionary in the late eighteenth century and even then was rarely used in connection with Russia's peripheries, parallels with the imperial stature, wealth, and power of "New Spain," "New England," and "New Portugal" were self-consciously invoked. Where empires with overseas holdings had no difficulty differentiating the two, the sprawling Eurasian land-mass made that task more challenging. In order to sharpen the requisite distinction between metropole and colonies, Vasilii Tatishchev and other scholars shifted the notional border between Europe and Asia from the Don River to the Ural Mountains, confirming the division between a core "European Russia" and peripheral others, seen more as colonies.[14]

Russia took on the aspects of a colonizing empire familiar to major European states, but distinctions between colonizer and colonized were forever in jeopardy of blurring. To begin with, available terminology lacked clarity.[15] How could one distinguish linguistically between a Russian-Russian, that is, a Slavic, Orthodox, Russian-speaker, and a Russian non-Russian, that is, an ethnically, religiously, linguistically and/or territorially foreign member of the empire? Linguistically, Russians were able to employ the slightly different words *rossiiskii* and *russkii* to differentiate all-imperial Russianness and more limited ethno-linguistic Russian-ness, but the distinction was not consistently observed in the eighteenth century.

The fuzziness in terminology reflected a lack of clear division in thinking about these various categories. Sunderland writes:

> despite the fact that the Russian state came to be typed as a European-style empire consisting of a national core ("Russia proper") and a colonial periphery, members of the Russian establishment—like good imperialists—tended to identify all of the empire as Russian space. They developed this identification not just because the space was ruled by Russians, but also because they saw its vast extent as the natural outgrowth of historically Russian territory and the Russians themselves as the only people who seemed to live all over it. . . . Eighteenth-century territorial investigators, in effect, dissolved the nation into the empire and the empire into the nation, with the result that—territorially speaking—one could not really have one with the other.[16]

The problem of defining precisely what constituted Russia and Russianness grew even stickier as researchers probed into the nation's past. The German

---

[14]Mark Bassin, "Russia Between Europe and Asia: The Ideological Construction of Geographical Space," *Slavic Review* 50 (1991): 1–17; Valerie Kivelson, "Cartographic Emergence of Europe," in *Oxford Handbook of Early Modern History*, ed. Hamish Scott (Oxford: Oxford University Press, 2015), pp. 37–69, esp. pp. 59–60. Tatishchev's division also conveniently included more of Russia in Europe, which was seen as an ideological gain.

[15]The key text that discusses the various meanings of colonies, colonization, and colonialism is Jürgen Osterhammel, *Colonialism: A Theoretical Overview*, trans. Shelley L. Frisch (Princeton, NJ: Markus Wiener, 1997).

[16]Sunderland, "Imperial Space," pp. 54–55.

scholars invited to Russia to staff the newly founded Academy of Sciences and Moscow University in the eighteenth century were supposed to discover a glorious past and identity for Russia, but they found just the opposite. "The scholars brought in to describe the Russian Empire and to bring glory to its name, state, tongue, land, and people had ended up discovering that, in terms of origins and according to the best primary sources, none of these categories had anything to do with each other. The Russian land had not been 'Russian' for very long; the Russian state and the Russian name had come from Sweden; the Russian apostle Andrew had never been to Russia; and the Russian language had been—quite recently—brought in by tribes chased out of the Danube."[17] The Russian Empire was the only "national" state that the Russian people had—in the sense of a congruity of people, territory, language, religion, state, and name—but when scholars delved into its past and noted the multiplicity of peoples in the empire, "Russia's challenge seemed unusually formidable. Much of its 'sacred' heartland seemed to consist of borderlands."[18]

An influential line of historical scholarship argues that Russia followed a particular logic of empire-building, at least up to the middle of the nineteenth century. After acquiring territory, usually by conquest, often by expanding settlement, the agents of the tsar usually coopted local elites into the service of the empire.[19] But in many peripheries, like the Volga, Siberia, South Caucasia, and Central Asia, integration stopped with the elites and did not include the peasant or nomadic populations that retained their tribal, ethnic, and religious identities. Some elites, like the Tatar and Ukrainian nobles, dissolved (at least partially) into the Russian *dvoriantsvo*, but others, like the German barons of the Baltic or the Swedish aristocrats of Finland, retained privileges and separate identities.

Another school of thought suggests that from the time of Peter the Great, Russian rulers attempted to rationalize the state by eliminating the welter of particular administrative units and jurisdictions and by homogenizing structures of rule. A number of important scholars assert that once areas were conquered and subordinated to imperial rule, the Russians integrated them into the overall administrative system. Peter the Great was a self-conscious advocate of uniform practices and centralizing institutions, and he advanced a number of important reforms in this direction. He could, however, be flexible when it served his interests. He settled on a very different administrative solution in Ukraine than in the Baltic regions, where he tolerated the continued authority of noble corporations. The historian N. N. Petrukhintsev identifies an intriguing feedback loop whereby Peter's policy in the Baltic exposed Russian nobles to a model of European

---

[17]Slezkine, "Naturalists Versus Nations," p. 48.
[18]Ibid., p. 50.
[19]Marc Raeff, "In the Imperial Manner," in *Catherine the Great: A Profile,* ed. Marc Raeff (New York: Hill & Wang, 1972), pp. 197–246; S. Frederick Starr, "Tsarist Government: The Imperial Dimension," in *Soviet Nationality Policies and Practices,* ed. Jeremy Azrael (New York: Praeger, 1978), pp. 3–38.

corporate rights within their own imperial boundaries, inspiring political thinkers, including Peter, to think about the nobility in new ways. In this instance, a solution negotiated on the imperial frontier at the time of conquest led to changes in political thought at the imperial center.[20]

On the question of homogenizing administration, John LeDonne advances the interesting argument that until the late eighteenth century, Russian elites were committed to "building a unitary state in the form of an expanding core," defined by the limits of the agricultural zone, "beyond which [the Russian peasant] would not go because that world was alien to him." With the administrative-territorial reform of the 1780s, the ruling elite decided to extend that self-consciously homogenizing process: "the time had come to impose a uniform set of local agencies across the entire eastern theater, those in Krasnioarsk [*sic*] identical, at least in principle, with those in (central Russian regions) Kaluga, Orel or Voronezh."[21] This vision of Russia as "one and indivisible" would be immediately sabotaged by the emerging realities of the nineteenth century, with sharply differentiated governance of core and borderlands, but the goal and vision of homogeneity, LeDonne contends, remained influential in shaping policy. We are not fully convinced that such a vision guided imperial policy in any consistent way. Although the impulse toward homogeneous administration did color efforts at reform throughout the century, so too did efforts to create, preserve, and enshrine difference by region, social standing, and type. In our view the state's efforts at a kind of bureaucratic rationality, which accelerated in the first quarter of the nineteenth century under Alexander I, coincided, as we will show, with differentiation both horizontally across space, distinguishing the privileges of some peoples and the disadvantages of others, and vertically between those deemed distinct and superior at the top of society and the great mass of the people below.

Through the course of the eighteenth century, successive regimes undertook to reform the administrative structures of the empire. Peter experimented with dividing the entire realm into large governorships (*gubernii*), which proved unwieldy. The weakness of local governance became painfully obvious decades later at the time of the Pugachev Rebellion, a huge, violent, and remarkably successful uprising of Cossacks, industrial serfs, Bashkirs, Tatars, and Old Believers, which

---

[20]Paul Bushkovitch advances the case for Peter's flexibility by comparing Ukraine and the Baltic in Serhii Plokhy, ed., *Poltava 1709: The Battle and the Myth,* Harvard Papers in Ukrainian Studies (Cambridge, MA: Harvard University Press; Ukrainian Research Institute, 2012); T. G. Tairova-Iakovleva in the same volume sticks to a centralization narrative. On the feedback loop, see N. N. Petrukhintsev, "Konsolidatsiia dvorianskogo sosloviia i problemy formirovaniia oformliaiushchei ego terminologii," in *Praviashchie elity i dvorianstvo Rossii vo vremia i posle petrovskikh reform,* ed. N. N. Petrukhintsev and L. Erren (Moscow: Rosspen, 2013), pp. 256–283; esp. pp. 265–66. We extend our thanks to Ernest Zitser for his valuable guidance on this topic.

[21]Marc Raeff, *Imperial Russia 1682–1825: The Coming of Age of Modern Russia* (New York: Knopf, 1971), p. 44; Cracraft, "Empire Versus Nation," pp. 228, 230; John LeDonne, "Building an Infrastructure of Empire in Russia's Eastern Theater, 1650s–1840s," *Cahiers du Monde russe* 47, no. 2 (2006): 607–8.

shook the country from 1773 to 1775. The revolt began at the frontier as disaffected non-Russians rallied to the charismatic Cossack Emelian Pugachev, attracting ethnic Russians as it moved up the Volga. Rebel ranks reflected the ethnic and religious diversity of the empire, with Old Believers and Muslims joining the movement. Pretending to be the Tsar Peter III, Pugachev issued his *ukazy* (imperial decrees) both in Russian and Tatar.

After suppressing the rebellion and executing its leaders, Catherine undertook major reforms of local administration with the twin goals of making a more uniform system with more effective penetration of the countryside. The whole of Russia was demarcated into *provintsii* (provinces), and *uezdy* (districts), and, in an important turn from Petrine models, significant authority was delegated to local elites. The 1775 Provincial Reform called for the establishment of local courts for nobles, townspeople, and peasants, respectively, where their peers could judge them. It also required the creation of local welfare boards staffed by elected representatives of each social group. The reforms aimed "to create institutional structures of equivalent form (though not equal status) for all three principal social estates."[22] The formula "equivalent in form and unequal in status" captured an important element of the long-standing presumption that different groups naturally stood in different relationship to power and rule.

The Charter to the Nobility and Charter to the Towns of 1785 followed up on the move toward delegation of some degree of fiscal and administrative authority to local populations and established collective local assemblies with elected leaders. Nobles, in particular, were granted extensive rights, including security in person and property, the right to trial by their peers, and the right to travel abroad. For the first time, a small subset of Russian subjects enjoyed rights formally set in writing. Yet, significantly, these charters were conceived of separately for nobles and townspeople (with one for peasants anticipated but never forthcoming), and they confirmed the principle of stratification within each social group or *soslovie* (plural, *sosloviia*).

Soslovie status conferred on each member particular obligations but also certain protections. Like all the other divisions that crosshatched Russian society, it shaped the lives of all Russian subjects. As Alison Smith illustrates in a detailed study, *soslovie* was prescribed by law, but it was not simply imposed from on high. Since there was always some degree of mobility, both geographic and social, the practicalities of implementation were worked out on the ground by at least three sites of power and interest: central state administration; local administrative bodies; and the individuals or families concerned. This resulted in a three-way tug-of-war. The "societies," that is, the collective units that embodied *sosloviia* on the local level, participated energetically in hammering out the details and particularities of who could join and who could not, the terms and prices of registration or departure, and the legality of various positions. The extent to which the

---

[22]R. P. Bartlett, "Catherine II's Draft Charter to the State Peasantry," *Canadian-American Slavic Studies* 23, no. 1 (1989): 42.

local estate societies could decide which members to release and which to accept, what Smith calls "the freedom to choose and the right to refuse," was subject to constant negotiation between estate corporate bodies and the central authorities. *Sosloviia* were imagined to exist not only to ease the state's difficulties in collecting taxes, organizing the draft, and making its subjects visible, but also, as Catherine the Great pronounced, "for the common good and their own well-being." She insisted that clearly ascribed *soslovie* status was beneficial to her subjects themselves, because without it, they would struggle to understand who they were. She evidently had a point. Russians of all *soslovie*-estates were deeply invested in working out their own estate positions to their best advantage.[23] Following the Petrine tradition of the Table of Ranks, Catherine's legislation built on the notion that even within the encompassing social divisions, nobles, townspeople, and peasants came in many flavors, and her laws stratified rights and privileges according to fine-grained divisions. This was a society that took inequality seriously.

In many instances scholars on both sides of the debate about differentiation versus homogenization are right. It depends on whether one emphasizes the efforts at bureaucratic conformity or the myriad exceptions and special cases. "Nationalizing," homogenizing policies, integrating disparate peoples into a common "Russian" community (particularly among the nobles), coexisted with policies of discrimination and distinction. Brian Boeck documents the early-eighteenth-century transformation of the Don Cossack Host from autonomous circles of self-governing free men to loyal protectors of the imperial regime by following the modification of their "separate deal" with the state. They gradually lost their traditional right to select their own leader (*ataman*) and accepted the tsar's direct sovereignty, but they retained their distinctive organizational structures, their distinctive markers of clothing and titulature, and many of their special privileges and exemptions. They remained free from the burdensome taxes and regulations that weighed on Russian peasants, and these exemptions and distinctions won their loyal service in patrolling the empires boundaries. Well into the eighteenth century, the distinction between the freedom of the "privileged periphery" and the demeaned servility of the Russian peasants of the "underprivileged core" was maintained. Where peasant conscripts could be (and were) thrown into battle in the tens of thousands, regardless of consequences, thoughtlessly used up as involuntary labor and cannon fodder, Cossacks retained their value as protectors of the realm.

The Don could not be administratively equated with Russian districts, Boeck says. It could be incorporated, perhaps, but not integrated. Even after the Bulavin rebellion, a huge Cossack uprising of 1708–1709, was crushed by a deadly state campaign of destruction, decimating the population and leaving tens of thousands dead or dispersed, the Cossacks retained distinctive standing in the Russian Empire. "Peter I enshrined the principle of separate deals in Russian law in

---

[23]Alison K. Smith, *For the Common Good and Their Own Well-Being: Social Estates in Imperial Russia* (Oxford: Oxford University Press, 2014), pp. 14–71, 72.

his General Regulation of 1720 which ordered officials of the new administrative Colleges that he created to administer each people (*narod*) according to its distinct privileges. Henceforth, Cossacks would be classified as a privileged people within the empire."[24]

Further undermining the drive toward uniformity, regional and other distinctions continued to proliferate. Autonomous entities were brutally dismantled, at great cost of life, and yet, simultaneously, the empire undermined its own efforts toward administrative uniformity by reconstituting various manners of institutional distinctiveness and particular sets of restrictions and privileges. After subduing the Bashkir khanate in a bloody campaign, Russia gave the Bashkirs special rights as a military host in the Volga-Urals region in 1798, as they had done for the Don Cossacks slightly earlier (1786). Like the medieval princes who fought bitterly to claim the overarching mantle of "grand prince" and then blithely redivided their territories among their sons, so too the rationalizing monarchs of the eighteenth century unselfconsciously smashed and reconstituted subunits.

The incorporation of the Crimea and the territories of "New Russia" (modern-day eastern and southern Ukraine) offer a counternarrative to the story of single-minded drive toward homogeneity and territorial-administrative uniformity. In 1783 Catherine's troops won control of the beautiful Crimean Peninsula from the Khanate of Crimea, a protectorate of the Ottoman Empire. The conquest inspired a torrent of poems, odes, and ceremonies of imperial rule on the part of Catherine II's enthusiastic courtiers and publicists. The recurrent theme of Crimea as a "garden," luxuriantly planted with every kind of plant and flower, extolled the beauty of variety collected in one place. The peninsula was celebrated not as an extension of a single, undifferentiated Russia but as a showcase for the myriad species and types that made up the empire.[25] This exaltation of variety extended beyond laudatory verses. In their incorporation of the Muslim Tatars of Crimea, Russian authorities allowed for significant flexibility in the structures they established. They retained old Muslim institutions and created overlapping and replicating administrative units. All sorts of local exceptions and exemptions remained possible within a variegated imperial system.[26] Resident Tatar nobles and merchants shuffled for position in the new hierarchy, some gaining property rights that challenged or even exceeded those of Russian settlers, some losing out to more powerful claims. Policies of winning local support by welcoming Tatar elites into the new imperial ruling class were complicated by mixed perceptions of Tatar (dis)loyalty in a complex geopolitical region.

In the new territories opened up by conquest and diplomacy, Catherine the Great and her successors experimented with various policies to address the

---

[24]Boeck, *Imperial Boundaries*, pp. 54, 126–27, 117, 123, 182–83, 201.

[25]Andreas Schönle, "Garden of the Empire: Catherine's Appropriation of the Crimea," *Slavic Review* 60, no. 1 (2001): 1–23.

[26]Kelly O'Neill, *Southern Empire: The Logic and Limits of Russian Rule in Crimea* (in manuscript). With thanks for permission to cite this work.

problem of sparse population. The empress sent Russians to settle in the relatively empty lands of New Russia. She looked to other populations for potential recruits as well, and particularly to groups that she and her contemporaries viewed as model settlers: hard-working Germans, industrious Old Believers who had fled Russian persecution, Greeks, and Armenians, with the idea that they would prove good merchants and traders. They enjoyed economic and legal benefits by dint of their collective status. The essential premise of these invitations derived from stereotypes about "national character," and encouraged the continuation of differential policies.

Jews were also invited in, though with sharp restrictions on their movement. Much has been written about the discriminatory policies against Jews, who were confined to the southern and western provinces of the empire, the so-called Pale of Settlement (*Cherta osedlosti*), established by Catherine II in 1791, and were subject to a long list of requirements and limitations. Studies that take a step back and analyze policies toward Jews in the broader context of imperial strategies put these discriminatory regulations in a different light. They remind us that the regime parceled out particular conditions to all of its constituent peoples, not only to the Jews. While the specific terms varied from group to group, the general phenomenon of special deals and differential rights was a trademark of empire. Jews were limited in their movement, but they were confirmed in their right to administer themselves through the judicial institution of the *kahal*, the communal organization.[27] Other groups, like the Georgians, were allowed to keep their customary laws for a time, while less-favored populations, such as the Kalmyks, were progressively deprived of land and rights until most of them despaired of their future within a Russian orbit and undertook a grueling, ultimately deadly, trek to their ancient homeland in the Far East.[28]

Religion offered another site for the state's ambivalent competing impulses toward assimilation and integration on one hand and preservation or even manufacture of difference on the other. Certain religious groups received particularly harsh treatment, notably the Old Believers and Uniates or Eastern Rite Catholics (Ruthenian Orthodox who had joined the Catholic Church after the Union of Brest in 1569, while preserving their Slavonic liturgy and Eastern practices, such as maintaining a married clergy). These most proximate of religious "others" had broken with the Orthodox Church and therefore earned the Church's sharpest opprobrium. They were considered not just misguided and ignorant, as could be said of animist pagans and Muslim "infidels," but rather apostates, willful heretics, who therefore had to be dragged back into the fold, willingly or unwillingly. Those located along the strategic western borders of the empire, such as the

---

[27]Eugene Avrutin, *Jews and the Imperial State: Identification Politics in Tsarist Russia* (Ithaca, NY: Cornell University Press, 2010); Richard Pipes, "Catherine II and the Jews: Origins of the Pale of Settlement," *Soviet Jewish Affairs* 5, no. 2 (1975): 3–20.
[28]Michael Khodarkovsky, *Where Two Worlds Met: The Russian State and the Kalmyk Nomads, 1600–1771* (Ithaca, NY: Cornell University Press, 1992).

Eastern Rite Catholics, were particularly suspect because of their acceptance of papal religious authority and the possibility that they might maintain secret allegiance to their former Polish-Lithuanian overlords. Facing heightened Russian suspicion, these groups were harshly persecuted and forced to convert en masse.[29]

Elsewhere in the empire, other religious groups were subject to less concerted pressure to conform, or to none at all. Aside from sporadic and highly localized moves toward conversion, the state and the official Church maintained their longtime reluctance to muddy the waters through intrusive and potentially disruptive conversion campaigns. Following patterns set in the Muscovite era, Catherine the Great expressed a fervent hope that all her subjects would eventually see the light and be brought to the Orthodox faith, but insisted that conversion should be fully voluntary. Fearful of provoking unrest, she prohibited all Christianizing work among Muslims. As a result of her German Lutheran upbringing and of the currents of thought of the Enlightenment age, religious campaigns of the time stressed the need for sincere belief rather than superficial and coerced conversion. This idea of internal belief introduced a new twist to the history of Orthodox proselytism, which had traditionally deemed ritual baptism fully sufficient.[30]

In the spirit of the Enlightenment, "educated Russians in Catherine's time admired the diversity of the 'Great Map of Mankind'—indeed they took a great deal of pride in the fact that many of the peoples in the Great Map lived within the Russian empire," but they nonetheless presumed an inevitable progression of all "backwards subjects of their empire" in the direction of the superior Russians.[31] In keeping with this evolutionary vision, religious policy rested on a notional hierarchy of religions and customs that placed settled, agrarian Orthodox Russians at the top (although sometimes even they were thought to benefit from the example of hardworking Germans or sectarians) and animist pastoral nomads at the bottom.

Under Catherine II, the state was prepared to try to use whatever religion they encountered as a foundation for popular loyalty to the autocracy and a means of disciplining and regulating the heterogeneous population of their vast realm. With religion, rather than language or nationality, as the principal identification of peoples in the empire, the law required every subject to be a member of a

---

[29]Barbara Skinner, *The Western Front of the Eastern Church: Uniate and Orthodox Conflict in Eighteenth-century Poland, Ukraine, Belarus, and Russia* (DeKalb: Northern Illinois University Press, 2009); Georg Michels, "Rescuing the Orthodox: The Church Policies of Archbishop Afanasii of Kholmogory, 1682–1702," in *Of Religion and Empire: Missions, Conversion, and Tolerance in Tsarist Russia*, ed. Robert P. Geraci and Michael Khodarkovsky (Ithaca, NY: Cornell University Press, 2001), pp. 19–37.

[30]Michael Khodarkovsky, "'Not By Word Alone': Missionary Policies and Religious Conversion in Early Modern Russia," *Comparative Studies of Society and History* 38, no. 2 (1996): 287–89; Paul W. Werth, *At the Margins of Orthodoxy: Mission, Governance, and Confessional Politics in Russia's Volga-Kama Region, 1827–1905* (Ithaca, NY: Cornell University Press, 2002).

[31]Willard Sunderland, *Taming the Wild Field: Colonization and Empire on the Russian Steppe* (Ithaca, NY: Cornell University Press, 2004), p. 61.

confessional community and to obey the clerical authorities of that community. The faiths of Muslims, Jews, Buddhists, as well as the particular non-Orthodox Christians—Protestants, Catholics, and Armenian Apostolics—were eventually officially recognized and integrated into the system of local governance.

With its own recognizable institutions, mosques, shrines, and scriptural traditions, Islam seemed to have more in common with Christianity than various forms of animism, and so Catherine allowed Muslims special dispensations and special supervision. The religious and social life of Muslims was regulated by the state. After the conquest of Crimea, imams of the region were enrolled as salaried officials, and the first "spiritual assembly of Muslim law" was set up to license and regulate Muslim clerics, who had to report in Russian as well as Tatar and prove loyalty to the state. A somewhat more formal assembly was established in Ufa in 1788 with similar functions and goals. It was meant to coopt Muslim leaders, to supervise religious practice, and to smooth a path toward expansion into Muslim areas of Central Asia, while at the same time fostering religious toleration. "To domesticate Islam in the empire," writes Robert Crews, tsarist officials "opted to introduce a churchlike organization among a population that had previously known no such institutions."[32] Eventually the Orenburg Muhammad Ecclesiastical Assembly, with its *mufti* (jurists, scholars of Islamic law) appointed by the emperor, became the principal authority over the Muslims of the Volga and Urals regions. Muslim clerics among the Volga Tatars used their role as *ulema* (authoritative religious scholars) to carry out their own civilizing mission within the empire, promoting an empire-friendly version of Islam on the Kazakh steppe.[33] A novel institutional hierarchy, created in the image of a Christian ecclesiastical order, was imposed, creating new expressions of Islamic organization.[34]

Historians have usually depicted tsarist Russia's treatment of its Islamic peoples as a story of repression, Russification, and constant conflict between Christian rulers and their tens of millions of Muslim subordinates. That indelible image continues to color the analysis of Imperial Russian and Soviet rule of the Central Asian peoples, and conflicts like the Caucasian wars right up to the conflicts with Chechnya have served to confirm the idea of an eternal clash of Orthodox and Islamic civilizations. The multidimensionality of Russian encounters with Islam tells a far more complex story. Over time some Muslims adapted to the tsarist religious regime "as a potential instrument of God's will." In many instances, Muslims of the empire accepted (though not without contestation) the clerics sanctioned by the state, and turned to official religious institutions to regulate their own members and settle disputes among them. Tensions within Muslim communities could be expressed as charges of heterodoxy, and the Russian-supervised religious establishment would set itself to the unlikely task of

---

[32]Robert D. Crews, *For Prophet and Tsar: Islam and Empire in Russia and Central Asia* (Cambridge, MA: Harvard University Press, 2006), p. 33.
[33]Our thanks to Willard Sunderland for this insight.
[34]Ibid., p. 60; Elena I. Campbell, "The Autocracy and the Muslim Clergy in the Russian Empire (1850s–1917)," *Russian Studies in History* 44, no. 2 (Fall 2005): 8–29; esp. 8–9.

sorting through the right and wrongs of Islamic teaching. As Central Asian specialist Alexander Morrison notes, however, even if such charges were "a good way of discrediting an enemy in the eyes of the tsarist authorities, . . . it is naive to believe that this is anything but opportunism."[35]

Of course, Muslim subjects interacted with the state not only as Muslims, but also as subjects of a secular regime with secular concerns. At times, they might view the state as a source of protection and rely on secular authorities to resolve their differences. Court records show that the state and its clerical allies penetrated into the community and even the home to regulate the most intimate of relations. Marriage and divorce, the proper disciplining of children, as well as squabbles over property, theft, and inheritance all came to the attention of official clerics and the courts.[36]

Perhaps the most common mode of interaction for most newly colonized people was no interaction at all. Local histories written by Muslims in the steppe and Volga regions do not report reliance on the state and its appointed *ulema* to resolve religious or secular issues, and neither do they dwell on state oppression. Rather, they depict a world "in which the tsarist state is remote and irrelevant and where sacred geography and authority are very much the local creations of Muslims themselves."[37]

From respectful acceptance to opportunistic manipulation to indifference and lack of contact, none of these aspects of Russian-Muslim relations squares with a violent clash of civilizations view. Integrated into the tsarist system as they were, Muslims seldom resorted to open conflict with the regime. Though neither the loyalty of Russian Muslims nor the altruism of tsarist policy should be exaggerated, the Catherinian system seemed to work, but not for everyone nor all the time.

In their approaches toward incorporating these varied peoples, Russian authorities employed a combination of our four types of imperial rule. With the Cossacks they moved along the spectrum from indirect rule delegated to the elected *ataman* (also seen in the preservation of the Jewish *kahal*) to elimination (the destruction of the Don Cossack Host, the killing or dispersing of nine tenths of the population, also used to devastating effect against the Kalmyks and Bashkirs) to rule through difference (seen in all these cases, where special institutions—the new Bashkir host, the Muslim Spiritual Assembly, the reconstituted Cossack host with an appointed *ataman,* later replaced by more direct rule). The fourth strategy of imperial incorporation, assimilation, also came into

---

[35]Alexander Morrison, "Review of Robert Crews, *For Prophet and Tsar,*" *The Slavonic and East European Review* 86, no. 3 (July 2008): 553–57; quote on 555.

[36]Crews, *For Prophet and Tsar,* p. 20. For another view on Islam and the Russian Empire, see Elena Campbell, *The Muslim Question in Imperial Russia* (Bloomington: Indiana University Press, 2014).

[37]Morrison, "Review of Robert Crews, *For Prophet and Tsar,*" p. 555. Morrison draws on the work of Allen J. Frank.

play with occasional forced conversions (Old Believers, Uniates) and with efforts at establishing more uniform administrative units and governing practices, but always these efforts worked at cross purposes with the tendency to leave well enough alone or even to create new semi-autonomous or anomalous formations: new hosts, new religious boards, new settlements of distinctive immigrant groups encouraged, precisely because of imputed national characteristics, to operate according to their own laws and customs. What might look to some as inconsistencies might be better appreciated as examples of flexible and pragmatic approaches that contributed to the empire's longevity.

Religion remained the principal marker of difference between Russians and non-Russians, and religious identity was believed to reveal essential qualities that helped to predict behavior. Orthodox Christians were expected to be more loyal than the duplicitous Muslims. Not infrequently, "enlightened" state officials argued that conversion to Orthodox Christianity would strengthen the empire as well as bring civilization to the benighted populations of the borderlands.[38] Though efforts at such religious "Russification" were haphazard, they reinforced the perceptual connection between Russianness and Orthodoxy. But as it continued to grow, the Russian Empire was increasingly marked by differences of all kinds and by hierarchies of superiority and inferiority—confession, ethnicity, *chin* (rank), *soslovie* (estate), class, and region. Empire both maintained and produced diversity and for much of its history did not seem particularly troubled by it. That would begin to change in the nineteenth century with the steady dominance of the new discourse of the nation and the creation of nation-states.

Empires like those of Britain and France that stretched across the seas consolidated their sense of difference between the ruling Europeans and the native peoples through notions of superior and inferior cultures and civilizations. Eventually ideas of race solidified those distinctions, making passage from those ruled to those ruling exceptionally difficult. In the Russian Empire race was a minor issue, certainly until the late nineteenth century.[39] What distinguished rulers or more privileged people in the empire from those ruled were clothes, customs, the ability to speak French. Those and other distinctions were codified into law and became the system of legal estates that gave certain rights and duties to some and other obligations and disadvantages to others. Nobles could own serfs, as could Orthodox clergy prior to 1762; townsmen could not. Nobles and clergy paid no taxes; townspeople and peasants did. In the empire of the tsars inequalities were based on birth, sanctioned by the ruler, and enshrined in law. In the words of Alexander Etkind, "The Russian Empire defined its others by estate and religion; western empires defined them by geography and race."[40] We would add that the

---

[38]Michael Khodarkovsky, "'Not by Word Alone'," pp. 267–93.
[39]Marina Mogilner, *Homo Imperii: A History of Physical Anthropology in Russia* (Lincoln, NE, and London: University of Nebraska Press, 2011); and her article "Russian Physical Anthropology in Search for 'Imperial Race': Liberalism and Modern Scientific Imagination in the Imperial Situation," *Ab Imperio* 8, no. 1 (2007): 191–223.
[40]Etkind, *Internal Colonization*, p. 252.

Russian Empire defined not only its others in these ways, but also its own, sorting them into categories by rank and religion, occupation, region, gender, age, and marital status.

IMPERIAL EXPANSION IN THE EIGHTEENTH CENTURY

In this era of "cameralism," a purported science of government and economic development, European states conceived of themselves as the embodiments of human achievement. Their function, as they saw it, was to regulate society and maximize social order, economic production, and population growth. Russia, in keeping with its neighbors to the west, aspired to become a "well-ordered police state."[41] Peter I was determined to subordinate all to the interests of the state and to force each of his subjects to follow the course of selfless service set by him personally, the "first servant of the state." Catherine II's invitations to German settlers whom she thought to be frugal and industrious followed a similar impulse of maximizing economic output, putting land to productive use, and building population. "Populationism" was another motivating creed of the day, a conviction that population growth would correlate with economic and political success.

In the great diplomatic games of the era, saber rattling and warfare also played a part in establishing imperial status. It is no coincidence that the two rulers to gain the sobriquet of greatness were those most successful in adding territory to the empire's already vast holdings, although their outsized personalities and restless pursuit of radical reform surely also contributed to their status. The expansive growth already set in motion in the Muscovite era continued throughout the eighteenth century, but the opportunities for easy expansion in sparsely populated regions like Siberia had been more or less exhausted. The Caucasus, with its complex interregional politics and diplomatic risks, beckoned throughout the century, and Russia involved itself increasingly in the region. Moving toward the west in order to grow, Russia would have to bump up against major powers with well-armed militaries: Crimea, the Ottoman Empire, Sweden, Poland. Peter I inaugurated the new era of warfare just before the beginning of the new century, with clashes with the Turks at Azov in 1695 and 1696.[42] These campaigns set the stage for the coming wars: Peter learned here that peasant conscripts were cheap, abundant, and easily replaced. He wasted no time on supplying them with food, clothing, or weapons, and simply sent wave after wave of men to fight his wars. Setbacks and distractions led Peter to abandon Azov and to turn his attention to the north, where he engaged in a struggle for survival and ultimately won a

---

[41]Marc Raeff, *The Well-Ordered Police State: Social and Institutional Change Through Law in the Germanies and Russia, 1600–1800* (New Haven, CT: Yale University Press, 1983).

[42]Brian J. Boeck, "When Peter I Was Forced to Settle for Less: Coerced Labor and Resistance in a Failed Russian Colony (1695–1711)," *Journal of Modern History*, 53: 3 (2008), pp. 485–514.

decisive victory against Sweden, after the long and devastating Great Northern War. He toyed with eastern campaigns toward Persia and India as well.

Catherine the Great also engaged in successful wars on multiple fronts, expanding the empire even more than Peter the Great had. When her First Turkish War ended in victory in 1771, she demanded not only the territories won from the Turks, but also a piece of Poland, a more or less hapless bystander. This was a time when European diplomatic theory maintained that the optimal way to foster peace and prosperity was to maintain a "balance of powers." According to this understanding of international relations, the goal of diplomacy was to guarantee that no single power or bloc grew so large that it could overwhelm the others. Russia's gains against the Ottomans alarmed her European neighbors, Austria and Prussia, who also demanded slices of Poland in return for accepting the postwar settlement. This first bite at the edges of the Kingdom of Poland and the Grand Duchy of Lithuania eventually came to be called the First Partition of Poland. More were yet to come. William Fuller observes that this partition did not actually contribute to the balance of powers to which it nominally adhered. "Giving shares of Poland to the two German monarchies was the necessary price that had to be paid if Russia wanted to retain its southern conquests. The balance of power was not thereby restored; rather, Petersburg bribed Prussia and Austria into overlooking the fact that Russia had just overturned it."[43]

Catherine displayed herself as an "enlightened monarch" and reveled in her associations with French elite culture. At the moment that the French Revolution broke out in July 1789, she was preoccupied with wars against both Sweden and Turkey as well as the revelation that her current young lover, Aleksandr Mamonov, was betraying her and wanted to marry his beloved. She reluctantly consented, dismissed him from court, and took up with the twenty-two-year-old Platon Zubov, her last amour. Her former favorite, Grigorii Potemkin, was far away in the south fighting against the Turks, and his efforts to have the empress rid herself of Zubov failed. Far from Russia, however, the world was changing. When the empress turned her attention to what was happening in revolutionary France, she was appalled. But war on two fronts prevented her from coming to the aid of her fellow monarch, the besieged Louis XVI. Catherine's second war with Turkey ended with a qualified Russian victory in August 1791, a few days before her faithful Potemkin died.

The monarchs of Europe were determined to restore the French monarchy, and Catherine indicated her sympathy with these efforts. Her sympathy did not stop her from taking advantage of the moment, however. While Prussia and Austria were preoccupied with war with France, the empress turned her attention back to Poland. In May 1791 Polish nobles carried out their own revolution,

---

[43]Fuller also notes that Poland had played a part in this high-stakes game as well: "if Russia were at war with Turkey, the Poles were apt to avail themselves of that opportunity to wriggle away from St. Petersburg's unwelcome embrace." William C. Fuller, Jr., *Strategy and Power in Russia, 1600–1914* (New York: Free Press, 1992), p. 146.

abolishing the *liberum veto* (by which laws could be passed only by the unanimous vote of the entire aristocratic assembly) and establishing a stronger monarchy. Deeply concerned by this mobilization so close to home, Catherine had her army invade Poland and crush the revolution. The ensuing partition agreement carved up Poland again, granting the larger portion to Russia (3 million new subjects, including, for the first time in Russia's history, a large population of Jews) with a smaller portion reserved for Prussia. Her justifications ranged from recovery of ancient Russian lands to stamping out the revolutionary virus close to home and containing its spread to neighboring lands. Catherine was horrified by the treatment of the French king, the assassination of the Swedish king Gustav III, and the destruction of the old order in France. Isabel de Madariaga writes, "It was not Catherine who became 'reactionary' in the 1790s, but France which became revolutionary."[44] When Louis XVI was executed in January 1793, Catherine exclaimed: "C'est une véritable anarchie. Ils sont capable de pendre leur roi à la lanterne, c'est affreux."[45] ["This is true anarchy. They are capable of hanging their king from a lamppost, it's horrible."] She broke off all relations with France. She and other European monarchs were determined to suppress the revolution and restore order to the continent.

In May 1794 the Poles launched a rebellion against Russian rule. They were led by General Tadeusz Kościuszko, who had already achieved fame as a hero of the American Revolution. The Russians under General Suvorov took Warsaw after bloody battles marked by savage killing. "They are all dogs," one Russian soldier proclaimed as he used his hatchet to split the skulls of the enemy. "They have fought against us, let them perish."[46] The suppression of the insurrection led to the third and final partition of Poland, and the newly seized territories were divided into *guberniia*, the governorships standard in Russia. Poland as an independent polity vanished from the map of Europe, and even its name was eliminated from the titles of the victorious monarchs. A secret article in the Russo-Prussian agreement stated: "In view of the necessity to abolish everything which could revive the memory of the existence of the Kingdom of Poland, now that the annulment of this body politic has been effected . . . the high contracting parties are agreed and undertake never to include in their titles . . . the name or designation of the Kingdom of Poland, which shall remain suppressed as from the present and forever."[47] There would be no independent Polish state for another 123 years. The empress topped off her acquisitions by annexing the Duchy of Courland (today: western Latvia) once the local Diet was convinced to invite Catherine to become their overlord. On Catherine's aims toward Poland and the French Revolution, de Madariaga writes that "there is no doubt that until the fall

---

[44]Ibid., p. 435.
[45]Isabel de Madariaga, *Russia in the Age of Catherine the Great* (New Haven and London: Yale University Press, 1981), p. 421.
[46]Cited in ibid., p. 447.
[47]Norman Davies, *God's Playground: A History of Poland* (Oxford: Clarendon Press, 2005), p. 408.

Map 5.1. Partitions of Poland.

of the French monarchy Catherine could live with the French Revolution, whereas she could not for one minute accept the Polish 3 May constitution, which challenged both the Russian power position in Poland, and the absolute monarchy she incarnated. Catherine sensed the revolutionary undercurrent in Poland—and there is no point in pretending it was not there—and she crushed the revolution where she could most easily reach it."[48]

Although Poland and France preoccupied the empress, she continued to dream of imperial advances in other parts of the world as well. Her vaguely formulated and ill-fated "Greek Project" to take Istanbul and reestablish the Byzantine Empire, or more accurately an Orthodox Empire, under the rule of her grandson Constantine has sometimes been identified as a major influence in fostering Russian nationalism in its foreign policy.[49] In our view, this was an inherently *imperial* adventure, or an imperial reverie, that has been coopted by

---

[48]Madariaga, *Russia in the Age of Catherine the Great*, p. 451.
[49]Martin, "The Invention of 'Russianness'," p. 131.

historians to prove the solidity of a nationalist vision at the time of Catherine II. It was imperial in its grandeur, in its evocation of earlier imperial greatness, and in its ambitions to imperial conquest and incorporation. But more fundamentally, it grew out of the internal logic of Russia's imperial experience, in which tsars and emperors achieved their sovereignty by taking varied peoples of many faiths, languages, and customs under their wing and protecting them in all their differences. According to the terms of the Treaty of Kuchuk-Kainardji of 1774, negotiated at yet another all-European congress after another Russian victory against the Turks, Catherine claimed the right to protect the Christian population of the Ottoman Empire, and specifically those of the Ottoman protectorates of Moldavia and Wallachia, where Russians had had an occasional military presence and where majority Christian populations fueled imperial hopes.

Originally meant as concrete protections of all Christian residents, not just Orthodox Christians, from possible Turkish oppression, this obligation to protect became a useful pretext for Russian intervention in the Balkans for almost a century and a half. It is useful to remember the imperial landscape in which this right of protection was invoked: Russian tsars had understood it to be their business to protect and supervise their Muslim subjects already for over two hundred years, and they stated explicitly that they could not fail to do so, or other Muslim powers would see it their business to intervene. Protecting religious groups and minorities within imperial borders and beyond them was what empires did to establish their own legitimacy and shore up their position, and Catherine's Greek dreams make perfect sense in this light. Russian diplomats "assumed that the function of protection of the Ottoman Christian population belonged to the sultan, while the role of the tsar was to protest before other powers the Porte's failure to exercise its assumed functions. This formula of the relations between the tsar, the sultan and the latter's Christian subjects was in accordance with the attempts of the Russian rulers in the late eighteenth and early nineteenth century to represent the cause of Orthodoxy in the Ottoman Empire as a universal Christian concern."[50]

Catherine the Great died on November 5 (16), 1796, of a stroke. She had planned to name her grandson Alexander her successor, disinheriting Paul, her despised son. Paul and his courtiers took over the Winter Palace even as the old empress lay on a mattress on the floor slowly and in agony expiring. Although

---

[50]Victor Taki, "Limits of Protection: Russia and the Orthodox Coreligionists in the Ottoman Empire," *The Carl Beck Papers in Russian and East European History* (2015). Catherine's navy also battled to liberate Greece from Turkish control and her local commanders planned to establish for them an archduchy or, remarkably, if they preferred, a "republic." This is another telling instance of the diversity considered normal under imperial rule. See Irina Smilianskaia, Mikhail Velizev, and Elena Smilianskaia, *Rossiia v Sredizemnomor'e: arkhipelagskaia ekspeditsiia Ekateriny Velikoi* (Moscow: Indrik, 2011), pp. 38–54, 483–98; and Elena Smilianskaia, "Catherine's Liberation of the Greeks: High-Minded Discourse and Everyday Realities" in *Word and Image in Russian History: Essays in Honor of Gary Marker*, edited by Maria di Salvo, Daniel H. Kaiser, and Valerie A. Kivelson (Brighton, MA: Academic Studies Press, 2015), 7–89

Paul would exert himself to the utmost to undo everything that his mother had done, the subjects he inherited continued to demand some role or at least some recognition, however minimal, in shaping the realm, and the empire he inherited continued to operate along lines of collectivity and distinction.

BRIEF BIBLIOGRAPHY

Avrutin, Eugene M. *Jews and the Imperial State: Identification Politics in Tsarist Russia.* Ithaca, NY: Cornell University Press, 2010.

Geraci, Robert P., and Michael Khodarkovsky, eds. *Of Religion and Empire: Missions, Conversion, and Tolerance in Tsarist Russia.* Ithaca, NY: Cornell University Press, 2001.

Madariaga, Isabel de. *Russia in the Age of Catherine the Great.* New Haven, CT: Yale University Press, 1981.

Martin, Alexander M. "The Invention of 'Russianness' in the Late Eighteenth–Early Nineteenth Century." *Ab Imperio* (2003), no. 3: 119–34.

Mogil'ner, Marina. *Homo Imperii: A History of Physical Anthropology in Russia.* Lincoln: University of Nebraska Press, 2011.

Rogger, Hans. *National Consciousness in Eighteenth-Century Russia.* Cambridge, MA: Harvard University Press, 1960.

Slezkine, Yuri. "Naturalists Versus Nations: Eighteenth Century Russian Scholars Confront Ethnic Diversity." In *Russia's Orient: Imperial Borderlands and Peoples, 1700–1917,* edited by Daniel R. Brower and Edward J. Lazzerini, 27–57. Bloomington: Indiana University Press, 1997.

Smith, Alison Karen. *For the Common Good and Their Own Well-Being: Social Estates in Imperial Russia.* Oxford: Oxford University Press, 2014.

Sunderland, Willard. *Taming the Wild Field: Colonization and Empire on the Russian Steppe.* Ithaca, NY: Cornell University Press, 2004.

Werth, Paul W. *At the Margins of Orthodoxy: Mission, Governance, and Confessional Politics in Russia's Volga-Kama Region, 1827–1905.* Ithaca, NY: Cornell University Press, 2002.

Whittaker, Cynthia Hyla. *Russian Monarchy: Eighteenth-Century Rulers and Writers in Political Dialogue.* DeKalb: Northern Illinois University Press, 2003.

SIX

IMPERIAL RUSSIA IN THE MOMENT OF THE NATION, 1801–1855

Paul I (1796–1801) was in most ways a throwback to his father, the unfortunate Peter III (1762). His erratic behavior, particularly in foreign policy, quickly alienated influential nobles and the elite guards units that had already carried out several coups d'état in the eighteenth century. The reign of his mother, Catherine II, had been marked by the empress's solicitous relations with the nobility and their loyalty to her. Immediately after Catherine's death, Paul upset those who had doted on the late empress when he bizarrely arranged her funeral by disinterring the corpse of Peter III and burying it next to her. He was off to a rocky start. She had ruled by engendering affection, he by fear. Paul managed to keep the contagion of European revolution away from Russia by strict censorship and an ever more elaborate system of police spies. He levied a tax on noble estates in 1797, which historically had been tax-exempt. The same year he undermined the rights conferred by the Charter of the Nobility when he decreed that nobles convicted of a crime could be flogged. Two years later he discontinued the provincial assemblies of nobles that his mother had established, and he refused to hear loyal addresses from the aristocrats. Establishing a new "tradition," one observed inconsistently and without explicit formulation in the past, Paul decreed that in future the principle of primogeniture—the eldest son would succeed the father as emperor—was the law of the land. Paul's decree did not exclude succession in the female line, but permitted it only in the complete absence of male heirs. Here too was a slap at the mother he despised, who had seized the throne without reference to her son, the likely heir, and who planned to elevate her grandson, Alexander, as her successor rather than Paul.

In foreign policy the emperor was as capricious as in domestic affairs. Like his father, Paul loved all things Prussian, wounding the pride of patriotic Russians at court and in the military. On ascending to the throne, he astounded Europe by denouncing his mother's militant anti-French policy and proclaiming his intention to mediate a general pacification of Europe. The next year, upset that Napoleon had captured the island of Malta after Paul himself had been elected Grand Master by the Knights of Malta, he rejoined the anti-French powers—Austria, Britain, Naples,

Portugal, and the Ottoman Empire (the Second Coalition)—and declared war on Napoleon. Then the following year he abandoned his allies, withdrew from European affairs, and began planning an extravagant campaign to use the Don Cossacks in a march through Central Asia to attack India. In his last year Paul gravitated once again toward France. For Britain and Austria he had become "Bonaparte's fool."[1] Enough nobles were alienated by what they considered the tyranny of the arbitrary emperor that on March 11, 1801, they slipped into Paul's fortress-like palace in St. Petersburg and strangled him. Paul had violated the tacit rules of aristocratic politics that had characterized the previous century, and he paid for his oversight with his life. His twenty-three-year-old son, Alexander, was proclaimed tsar. Among most nobles and the educated public a sense of relief spread, hope that a new day was about to dawn.

A KIND OF CONSTITUTION

Alexander's government, like his empire, was cosmopolitan. Among his foreign ministers, for example, were a patriotic Pole (Prince Adam Czartoryski), a Baltic German (Count Karl Nesselrode), and a Greek (Count Ioann Capodistrias). In choosing his officers and officials, competence, breeding, and affection were far more important to the emperor than ethnicity. Loyalty to the dynasty and to the state was an absolute requirement for a high position. The tsar's close friend Czartoryski had earlier fought for Poland against Russia and would later emerge as the epitome of Polish patriotism. Yet in the early nineteenth century he was able to serve the tsar and develop a scheme in 1803 to unite a broad "Slavic race" that would include both Poles and Russians. Even as he conceived of a peaceful world in which each nation, with its own language and customs, feelings and point of view, would have a bounded territory of its own, Czartoryski saw Russians and Poles as two nations "descended from the same stem." What in later nationalisms would develop as two separate and often antagonistic nations, for a time, in the imagination of the prince, could coexist as a single ethno-political community that could thrive under a single monarch.[2]

The new ruler himself and his circle of close friends, the so-called Unofficial Committee, raised hopes and expectations for better days to come not only by avoiding the pitfalls of Paul's brief reign but also through lofty verbiage about reform and constitution. However, despite their seeming idealism, their degree of commitment to meaningful reform of Russia's autocratic system remains controversial, continuing to fuel debate in the historical literature after two centuries of discussion. The disagreements derive from the ambiguity of the words that were

[1]Hugh Ragsdale, "Was Paul Bonaparte's Fool? The Evidence of the Danish and Swedish Archives," *Canadian-American Slavic Studies* 7, no. 1 (Spring 1973): 52–67.
[2]Paul Brykczynski, "Prince Adam Czartoryski as a Liminal Figure in the Development of Modern Nationalism in Eastern Europe at the Turn of the Eighteenth and Nineteenth Centuries," *Nationalities Papers* 38, no. 5 (September 2010): 647–69.

circulating (what did "constitution" actually mean to the people who tossed it around?), from the distance between the visionary language of reform and the far less impressive practical results, and, probably, from Alexander's own ambivalence and mutable thinking. One school of thought, strongly advanced by Marc Raeff, maintains that neither Alexander nor his inner circle, nor even his ambitious and abrasive minister, Mikhail Speranskii, desired to limit the monarch in any substantive way. Raeff argues that the Alexandrine reformers had their own ideas of what a "constitution" might mean in Russia, one that Alexander accepted: preservation of the autocracy but with more orderly and rational administration and avoidance of arbitrariness or anything that smacked of tyranny or despotism. Whatever reforms might be brought to Russia would come from an enlightened ruler working through an efficient bureaucracy. State power, not that of the landed gentry, would be paramount. In this interpretation, Russian "constitutionalism" was hardly limited government; rather it was unlimited rule but based on a rule of law and bureaucratic consistency. This hybrid formula would prove extremely difficult to achieve, since its two premises were fundamentally at odds. Autocratic arbitrariness infected bureaucratic consistency, and regulation eventually would threaten to cramp the monarch's will. Over time, the power of the bureaucracy, the tsar's ministers, and appointed provincial governments increased at the expense of the landed nobility's assemblies and the aristocratic Senate.[3] No estate or social class would be allowed to check the monarch's supreme authority.

Yet Alexander and his friends were fascinated with the democratizing impulses of the era, and other scholars take their preoccupation with reform seriously. The idea of constitution, whatever its precise meaning, floated about, unmoored, raising hopes and expectations.[4] Throughout his reign Alexander encouraged his friends in the Unofficial Committee and kept turning to his capable minister Speranskii to develop plans for constitution and reform. He commissioned reform plans to be drawn up, including a plan for a thorough overhaul of the system of governance and a codification of the law. These grand plans produced paltry results, but they set in motion and put some kind of hesitant official imprimatur on the pursuit of reformist goals. Under Alexander's watch, six universities were established, as well as a relatively extensive system of lycées, gymnasia, and local schools, all of which contributed to training the literate bureaucrats and administrators that Russia needed. These educational institutions also augmented the cultured world of "polite society" and produced the cadres of writers responsible for Russia's nineteenth-century literary boom.

Alexander's regime took the first small steps toward emancipating the serfs, mandating the liberation of the Baltic peasants, but on deeply disadvantageous terms and without any land. The destitution that resulted from this landless

[3]Marc Raeff, *Michael Speransky, Statesman of Imperial Russia, 1772–1839* (The Hague: M. Nijhoff, 1957), p. 44.
[4]David Christian, "The Political Ideals of Michael Speransky," *Slavonic and East European Review* 54, no. 2 (April 1976): 199.

liberation drove home the lesson that any subsequent move toward emancipation should guarantee the freed peasants an adequate allotment of land. This realization raised the bar for emancipation, intensifying landlords' resistance, but also taught would-be reformers where to place their energies. Emancipation efforts moved forward but with steps that were small to the point of negligibility: the Free Agriculturalist Law of 1803 gave serfs the right to purchase their freedom, along with a bit of land, according to agreements worked out privately with the landlords. The likelihood of such polarized parties reaching mutually satisfying terms was small, and fewer than 50,000 male serfs were able to take advantage of the law, but in this sensitive area, as in many others, David Saunders argues, Alexander "had created an atmosphere in which principles could be canvassed and he had allowed discussions to take place whose effects could not be easily calculated."[5] By summoning into being a previously nonexistent category of "freed peasant," this reform set wheels in motion.

On the other hand, Alexander, with the help of the ruthless General Count Aleksei Arakcheev, created another new category of peasant-soldier, the highly regulated recruits of the "military colonies," or "military settlements," first established in 1816. Designed with the goal of building a reliable, trained reserve, the colonies combined agricultural with military labor and were run with military discipline that extended to every aspect of life. Families settled in the colonies were subject to the same harsh discipline, and sons of colonists inherited their fathers' obligatory service. The colonies provoked deep hostility and erupted in rebellion frequently. The military colonies and their hybrid serf-soldiers, like the "free agriculturalists," were part of a proliferation of new categories of people and forms of rule, produced by fiat, in the course of Alexander's reign.

Liberalizing expectations heightened after the ruler confirmed the constitutional structures and rights of Finland, incorporated into the empire in the course of the Napoleonic wars, and of Poland, reincorporated after being liberated from Russian rule and briefly reestablished as the Duchy of Warsaw by Napoleon. As an ally of Napoleon in 1808, before they parted ways, Alexander sent his troops into Finland, which had for six hundred years been a part of the kingdom of Sweden. As he put it in his "Gracious Manifesto," "In accordance with the will of the Almighty, who has blessed Our arms, we have united the province of Finland to the Russian Empire for all time."[6] Fearing that the Swedish-speaking nobles of Finland harbored loyalties to Sweden, the emperor allowed the people of his new Grand Duchy to retain all the rights and privileges, including an advisory legislature, the Diet, that they had enjoyed under Swedish rule. The Orthodox Emperor of Russia not only took on the title of Grand Duke of Finland but also became the head of its Lutheran church.

---

[5]David Saunders, *Russia in the Age of Reaction and Reform, 1801–1881* (New York: Longman, 1992), p. 25.
[6]D. G. Kirby, ed. and intro., *Finland and Russia 1808–1920: From Autonomy to Independence, A Selection of Documents* (London and Basingstoke: Macmillan, 1975), p. 12.

In a secret instruction to his governor-general in Finland, Alexander wrote, "In determining conditions in Finland, my intention has been to give the people of that country a political existence, so that they would not consider themselves conquered by Russia, but joined to it by their own self-evident interests."[7] At a Diet that he convened in 1809, he confirmed the Finnish "fundamental laws" and "constitution." As Saunders writes, "What he meant by these promises has been intensively debated. The fact that the Finnish Diet did not meet again until 1863 seems to show that Alexander did not intend to give more ground than he had to. Nevertheless, Finland occupied a place in the constitutional structure of the Russian Empire which was unique at the time of the union and was subsequently paralleled only by the position of Poland after 1815. The Finnish Grand Duchy had its own laws and own customs dues. Finns were not enserfed, not recruited into the Russian army, and had dual citizenship (of the Duchy and the Empire)."[8] The peculiar status of Finland within the Russian Empire—a Grand Duchy with reserved rights for the local gentry—was at one and the same time anomalous and a manifestation of the diversity routinely tolerated, even produced, by empire.

Alexander followed the template he had adopted in Finland when he established a Kingdom of Poland in 1815 out of the lands regained from Napoleon. Twenty years after his grandmother had erased Poland from the map, and against the judgment of his policy advisers who urged him to absorb Poland fully into Russia as part of an administratively uniform polity, Alexander conferred on Poland a remarkable constitution, guaranteeing parliamentary representation based on a relatively broad electoral base, rights of freedom of religion, press, and habeas corpus. Under the direction of his friend Czartoryski, education at all levels, including at the university of Wilno, was conducted entirely in Polish, and a cohort of great national writers found their voices.

True, he took for himself the crown of this new kingdom, but he cast this as a "personal union," a fortuitous coincidence of Polish king and Russian tsar in a single person, rather than the political incorporation of Poland into Russia. Perhaps swept up in the spirit of his own magnanimity, he gave an uplifting speech on freedom and constitutions in Warsaw. The speech reverberated throughout the realm. One of the major figures of the Decembrist Rebellion that would follow Alexander's unexpected death in 1825 would report that he was inspired by "the first speech of the late Emperor at the Diet of Warsaw, from which it was inferred that His Majesty intended to lead Russia, in due course, to a similar state."[9]

In sum, Alexander's was a complex reign, with an ambivalent agenda and ambiguous record. What is clear, however, is that he and his policymakers continued the deeply ingrained imperial tendency of ruling through difference, creating new entities and categories (Grand Duchy of Finland, Kingdom of Poland, free

---

[7]Ibid., p. 25.
[8]Saunders, *Russia in the Age of Reaction and Reform*, p. 61.
[9]Quote from Prince Sergei Petrovich Trubetskoi, cited in Marc Raeff, *The Decembrist Movement*, 2nd ed. (Englewood Cliffs, NJ: Prentice-Hall, 1966), p. 46.

agriculturalists, emancipated Baltic peasants, military colonists), enshrining differences in regional dispensations and in the law of the land. The same men who most forcefully advocated the idea of rationalizing imperial rule saw no contradiction in resting their reform efforts on structures of differential rights.

Mikhail Speranskii expressed this point explicitly when he built inequitable standing into his vision for systemic legal overhaul. "The law defining personal freedom cannot be the same for everyone." "No one ought to be deprived of it, but not everyone can have it in equal degree."[10] In this extraordinary statement, Speranskii reveals the world of difference that divides twenty-first-century ideas of freedom from those of nineteenth-century Russia. Freedom was of profound concern, but the obvious fact of its unequal distribution among different social estates was beyond question.

CLASH OF EMPIRES

Active as Alexander was in internal reform, particularly in the early years, the central, defining focus of his reign was his engagement in the Napoleonic Wars. After the fall of the Bourbon monarchy in 1789, the French Revolution descended into a "Reign of Terror" followed by an oligarchy of representatives of the propertied classes, and then a dictatorship by the extraordinary General Bonaparte. In 1804 Bonaparte proclaimed himself Napoleon I, emperor of the French. The revolutionary republic had become an empire, whose ruler set out to dominate Europe, taking on the other great states of the continent—Prussia, Austria, and eventually Russia—as well as its formidable foe on the seas, Great Britain. To the reigning monarchs of Europe, Napoleon's imperial ambitions posed an intolerable threat. His early campaigns to take Malta and Egypt failed but sharpened antagonisms between France and Britain. To punish Britain and enhance French economic dominance, in 1806 Napoleon established the Continental Blockade, preventing his allies and his defeated rivals from trading with the British.

In 1805 Russia joined Britain, Sweden, and Austria in the Third Coalition against France. But in a series of colossal battles—Austerlitz, Jena, and Auerstädt—Napoleon overwhelmed his enemies and forced Russia to accept the humiliating Peace of Tilsit in 1807, the price of which was a de facto alliance with France and opposition to Britain. Alexander's mother admonished him for accepting the treaty with France. The emperor replied that he was playing for time, "to breathe freely and to increase in the course of this most precious time the resources of strength of Russia."[11]

And he used the time well. Although he was technically supposed to be an ally of Napoleon, and he benefited from that connection in the brief war with Sweden that resulted in the annexation of Finland, Alexander proved to be

---

[10]Saunders, *Russia in the Age of Reaction and Reform*, p. 66.
[11]Quoted in William C. Fuller, Jr., *Strategy and Power in Russia, 1600–1914* (New York: Free Press, 1992), p. 183.

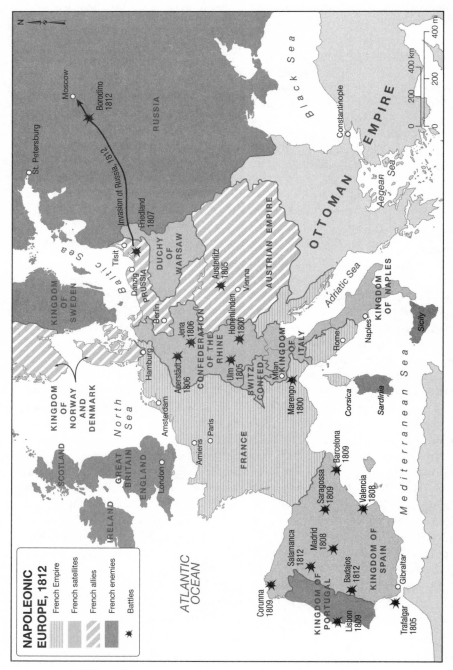

Map 6.1. Napoleonic Europe.

quite independent of his French partner. He held back his troops when Napoleon fought the Austrians, and he thwarted the French plan to keep all English goods out of Europe and thus compel the British to come to terms with France. Alexander broke the Continental Blockade in 1810 and permitted English products into Russia on neutral ships. Napoleon was furious, and both emperors steadily built up their forces for the coming clash. On June 24, 1812, Napoleon's army of nearly half a million men crossed the Neman River, then the border of the Russian Empire.

The tsar was determined not to give in to Napoleon this time. He held supreme authority over his armed forces, but his leading generals hated one another and pulled the emperor in different directions. Minister of War Mikhail Barclay de Tolly (of Scottish heritage) proposed retreat before Napoleon's larger and more battle-hardened army to draw it deeper into Russia, while his rival, Prince Petr Bagration, scion of the Georgian royal family, saw such a strategy as cowardly. While de Tolly was derided as a "German," Bagration was lauded for his forceful "Russian" patriotism. The emperor was unimpressed by the one man whom his nobles favored as commander, the one-eyed veteran Mikhail Kutuzov, an ethnic Russian, but gave in to their pressure and appointed him. Alexander deplored the strategy of retreat, which was known as *skifskaia strategiia* (Scythian Strategy), a derisive term that cast retreat as an Asian tactic inappropriate for a European power. Russians finally stood up to the invaders at Borodino, and though they lost the battle they battered the French, who were then far weaker when they marched into a deserted Moscow on September 3, 1812. Mysteriously, fires broke out all over the city, destroying almost half its buildings. To this day it is not certain if the Russians or the French set the fires, but it is most likely that Russians torched buildings in order to force the French to abandon the old capital. For thirty-three days Napoleon sat in the Kremlin waiting for the Russian surrender that never came. He ordered his army to pull back, and as the once *Grande Armée* moved back westward, the Russian army and partisan bands repeatedly attacked its flanks and picked off stragglers. When the French reached the Russian border, only one out of ten of those who had invaded Russia had survived.

Russia won this catastrophic war with France thanks to its strategy of retreat, the generalship of Kutuzov, the determination of the emperor not to give in, and the logistical difficulties faced by the French in their attempt to defeat a resistant Russia. Napoleon was unable to equip and feed his gargantuan army, while the Russians managed not only to supply their army but to cripple the French by killing almost all their horses. "The horse was a crucial—perhaps the single most decisive—factor in Russia's defeat of Napoleon," writes Dominic Lieven. "The enormous superiority of the Russian light cavalry played a key role in denying food or rest to Napoleon's army in the retreat from Moscow and thereby destroying it."[12] Winter weather, it appears, had little to do with the victory of the

---

[12]Dominic Lieven, *Russia Against Napoleon: The True Story of the Campaigns of* War and Peace (London: Penguin Books, 2009), p. 7.

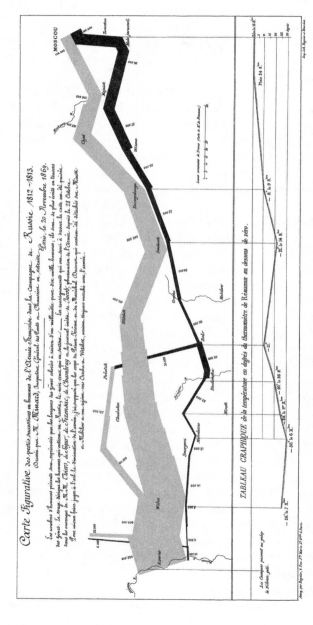

Charles Joseph Minard's 1869 map of Napoleon's invasion and disastrous retreat from Russia in 1812: *Carte figurative des pertes successives en hommes de l'Armée Française dans la campagne de Russie 1812–1813* [Figurative Map of the successive losses in men of the French Army in the Russian campaign 1812–1813]. The map is considered a masterpiece of efficient visual representation of information. Despite its deceptively simple layout, it conveys information on distances, temperature, latitude and longitude, direction of movement, and dates, as well as the number of men in Napoleon's army, with precipitous drops marked at specific points. The English translation of the explanatory text says "The numbers of men present are represented by the widths of the colored zones in a rate of one millimeter for ten thousand men; these are also written beside the zones. Red designates men moving into Russia, black those on retreat."

Russians. There was enough support and fighting spirit in the Russian ranks to hold out against the French and inflict sufficient damage on them.

In hindsight, Russian patriotic writers and historians described the country's resistance to the European army led by Napoleon as a great triumph of the people, a fervent defense of the fatherland inspired by an aroused nationalism. The war came to be known in Russian as the *Otechestvennaia voina*, the Fatherland War. The motivations of people at the time, however, were less clear-cut. In the context of our considerations of the rise of nationalism, the struggle against the French offers an interesting opportunity to assess the extent to which the Russian people were mobilized by a sense of national solidarity.

The view from the top, from the imperial palace, was largely uninflected by popular nationalism. Although the tsar and his friends had been happy to specu-late about the peaceful coexistence of various Slavic nations under an imperial mantle, this did not translate into any acknowledgment of popular sovereignty. The state, in Alexander's view, was embodied in his person. At the moment of the French invasion, Alexander I issued a rescript that concluded, "I will not lay down arms while the last enemy soldier remains in my empire."[13] No mention was made of the Russian people, and the empire was presented as a possession of the emperor. Even as the French moved toward Moscow, Alexander's advisers had to convince the reluctant emperor to go to Moscow and take on the role of national leader. His manifestos, written by the conservative poet Admiral Alexander Shishkov, "appealed to the people's patriotic and religious feelings."[14] The tsar was depicted by writers of the time as the "Angel of God," "Our Father," loved by his subject people to whom he feels great love.[15] At the same time that Shishkov was marketing this image of tsar as beloved and loving, Russian au-thorities resisted portraying the great victory as a popular triumph and instead projected it as a divinely ordained triumph of autocracy supported by a devoted people. "The people's involvement in the imperial scenario," writes Richard Wortman, "threatened the tsar's image as a superordinate force, whose title came from outside or from above, from divine mandate, or the emanations of reason."[16]

For the rulers of Russia as well as their most faithful followers, there was no distinction made between nation and state, between the loyal people and dedica-tion to the empire. What had already emerged in Europe, particularly in eighteenth-century France, the idea that the nation was distinct from the monarch and his state and possessed its own claims to sovereign power, was not only something not embraced by Russian authorities or thinkers in the reign of Alexander I but was seen as a sinister threat to autocracy.

Even so, at the height of the war, Russian officialdom gave its blessing to a particular form of folksy patriotism and shared credit for the victory over

---

[13]Wortman, *Scenarios of Power,* Vol. 1, p. 217.
[14]Ibid., p. 218.
[15]Ibid., p. 221.
[16]Ibid., p. 222.

I. I. Terebenev, *The Russian Hercules Drives Off the French*, c. 1813. The text notes that the Russian Hercules "crushed the French in the woods and beat them like a real man [*kak muzhik*]." The puny French soldiers hide and flee while the giant Russian peasant casually strides through them, waving them about in his enormous hands.

Napoleon with a manufactured figure of the "simple Russian *muzhik* (peasant man)." Popular broadsides, called *lubki* (singular, *lubok*), by Russian artists Ivan Terebenev, Ivan Alekseevich Ivanov, Aleksei Gavrilovich Venetsianov, and others, depicted friendly, honest Russian *muzhiki* dispatching their effete French foes with ease, and with no rancor. Other, more somber Terebenev prints showed the courage and unstoppable commitment of the Russians. In "A Russian Scaevola," the artist recasts in Russian terms the legend of Gaius Mucius Scaevola, a brave Roman soldier who awed the Etruscans when he thrust his own arm into a fire to demonstrate Roman courage and commitment. In the Russian version, another humble *muzhik* unflinchingly chops off his own arm. Stephen M. Norris explains that Terebenev and other *lubok* artists drew inspiration "from a legend circulating throughout the years 1812–1813 about a Russian peasant who had been captured and branded with the letter N (for Napoleon) on his arm. Rather than accept this outrage, the peasant took an axe and chopped off his arm."[17] The scrawny French soldiers reel back in horror. The accompanying text explains that the peasant would prefer to cut off his arm "in order not to serve Napoleon, the enemy of the Fatherland," and continues with praise of the "glory of the Russian

---

[17]Stephen M. Norris, *A War of Images: Russian Popular Prints, Wartime Culture, and National Identity, 1812–1945* (DeKalb: Northern Illinois University Press, 2006), p. 22.

Руской Сцевола.

Ivan Terebenev, *A Russian Scaevola*, 1813. In his 1813 print, the Terebenev recasts in Russian terms the legend of Gaius Mucius Scaevola, who cut off his arm to prove his Roman courage to the Etruscans.

[*Rossian*] in 1812 during the French invasion of Russia."[18] Norris notes that the choice of the *lubok* genre—the simple broadsheet, mass produced for popular markets, worked in simple folk style rather than in the stiff, academic style in which Terebenev and his fellow printmakers were trained—demonstrates an active decision to celebrate the art forms of "the people." At the same time, it reflects a deliberate bid to influence the hearts and minds of a broad "national" public.

In these popular art forms, endorsed though not directly commissioned by the regime and supported by a consumer market, the common man personifies all that is the best in Russia. As the explanatory texts make clear, these good, strong, simple, men and women embody Russia and Russianness and the "fatherland." The ruler and his supporters could accept this small admission of the people's contribution, because it could be reconciled with a state-patriotic vision in which the devoted people fought loyally for the emperor and his cause. "The nation and the tsar are conflated, not yet set apart. Russian patriotism depicted in the war *lubok* . . . had a 'divine' emperor whom viewers could contrast with the 'insidious' Napoleon. More importantly, the patriotism espoused in the images of 1812 stressed not only the deeds of individual Russians, but also the

---

[18]Ibid., pp. 20–35.

overarching influence and guidance of their tsar."[19] Alexander himself would eventually acknowledge this conceptual fusion of the nation with his person when he expressed appreciation for the "powerful valor of the people entrusted to Us by God," which so critically contributed to the victory.[20]

The anxieties that surrounded permissible representation of Russia's victory underscore the importance to the key players of the time of working out a solution to the relation of tsar and nation. A similar amalgam of state patriotism with elements of ethnic and national sentiments would be reproduced 130 years later in what the Soviets called the Second Great Patriotic War, that is, World War II.

The embryonic national identity and state patriotism were largely limited to the upper classes: the imperial court and the nobility; some townspeople; and intellectuals. Such sentiments most likely did not extend widely or deeply into the common people. The patriotic *muzhik* of the *lubki* may have stirred the imaginations of urban buyers, but there appears to have been no general enthusiasm among the peasants for the war with the French. Peasants were prepared to defend their villages whether against foreign invaders or against marauding Russian soldiers. On the very eve of the French invasion, the minister of war, Barclay de Tolly, had written the emperor of the need to arouse national feelings among the masses:

> We must try to raise the morale and spirit of Russia's own population and arouse its commitment to a war on whose outcome Russia's very salvation and existence will depend. I make bold to add here that for the last twenty years we have been doing all we can to suppress everything that is truly national but a great nation which changes its customs and values overnight will quickly go into decline unless the government stops this process and takes measures for the nation's resurrection. And can anything aid this process better than love for one's sovereign and one's country, a feeling of pride at the thought that one is Russian in heart and soul? These feelings can only be brought forth if the government takes the lead in this matter.[21]

Barclay de Tolly spoke of the people defending the "Holy Faith and the frontiers of the Fatherland."[22] The emperor himself told a Finnish officer that in order to unite Russians against the French it was essential to have Napoleon be seen as the aggressor and to fight the war on Russian soil.[23] Whatever worked to mobilize and inspire ordinary people to fight was deployed. At Borodino, Kutuzov and clergy paraded before the troops with the Icon of the Smolensk Mother of God.

Still, in Petersburg society there was fear that Russian peasants might rise up in support of Napoleon, who after all had abolished serfdom in the Duchy of

---

[19]Norris, *War of Images*, p. 27. On the conflation of loyalty to Orthodoxy and tsar as defining Russianness in popular texts and *lubki*, see also Jeffrey Brooks, *When Russia Learned to Read: Literacy and Popular Literature, 1861–1917* (Princeton, NJ: Princeton University Press, 1985), p. 214.
[20]Lieven, *Russia Against Napoleon*, p. 221.
[21]Quoted in Lieven, *Russia Against Napoleon*.
[22]Lieven, *Russia Against Napoleon*, p. 216.
[23]Ibid., pp. 124, 216.

Warsaw. The Russian army was made up of conscripted peasants who generally were forced to leave their homes and families and serve for twenty-five years. There were no peasant volunteers. Peasant soldiers were often treated brutally and with sneering condescension from their noble officers. The same social distinctions and divisions that separated the upper and lower classes in Russian society were reproduced in the ranks of the army. And yet the soldiers fought and died by the tens of thousands, their motivations varying from loyalty to their fellow soldiers with whom they had long served, to compliance bred by their training and socialization, to an elemental sense of self-preservation. There may have been no surge of peasant patriotism in 1812 but neither was there a rising of the serfs against their masters.[24]

IMPERIAL CONSERVATISM

Russia emerged from the Napoleonic wars even more imperial than it had been in the eighteenth century. Rather than a mobilized nation, it was *ancien régime* Russia that won the war, a multinational empire led by an autocrat and a landed gentry with the bulk of its people serfs or state peasants (that is, peasants bound to serve the state rather than private landlords). The tsar stood apart and above his people; they remained diverse not only ethnically, religiously, and in social status, but also in terms of the institutions through which they were ruled. In the newly designated Grand Duchy of Finland, the Orthodox Russian emperor, autocrat in his Russian lands, served as a constitutional monarch and observed the public law of the Grand Duchy. In the Kingdom of Poland (1815–1832), he ruled as *Tsar Polskii*, the constitutional king of Poland. At the same time, according to the Fundamental Laws codified in 1832, "the Emperor of Russia is an autocratic [*samoderzhavnyi*] and unlimited [*neogranichennyi*] monarch," while he proclaimed his realm a *Rechtsstaat*, responsibly governed by laws, and distinct from the despotisms of the East.[25]

Victorious Russia, the conservative bulwark against the principles of the French Revolution, was self-consciously the antithesis of nationalism. Alexander I expressed this personally in his post-war scheme for a Holy Alliance in which various European states would consider themselves members "of a single Christian nation" ruled over by the "Autocrat of the Christian People," Jesus Christ.[26] Russia's foreign policy during the years of the French threat had been not only defensive but "imperial," taking opportunities to expand into Moldavia and Wallachia and annexing Finland. Alexander never gave up his grandmother's dream

---

[24]For critiques of the myth of popular Russian nationalism in 1812, see Fuller, *Strategy and Power in Russia*, pp. 207–18; and Lieven, *Russia Against Napoleon*, p. 11.
[25]Marc Szeftel, "The Form of Government of the Russian Empire Prior to the Constitutional Reforms of 1905–06," in *Essays in Russian and Soviet History in Honor of Geroid Tanquary Robinson*, ed. John Shelton Curtiss (New York: Columbia University Press, 1962), pp. 105–19.
[26]Szeftel, "The Form of Government of the Russian Empire Prior to the Constitutional Reforms of 1905–06," p. 230.

of taking Constantinople and establishing "either the empire of the Slavs or that of the Greeks."[27] And though thwarted from having all of Poland by the other European Great Powers meeting at the Congress of Vienna in 1815, Alexander emerged from the Napoleonic wars as the ruler of the most powerful country on the continent.

After 1812, Russia held a different place in the world. As William C. Fuller Jr. put it, "Russia came to be regarded as the premier land power on the Continent, and the Russian autocracy and its army of 800,000 troops, as the arbiter of European order, the bulwark of legitimacy, conservatism, and stability."[28] As the victor over the upstart imperialism of the illegitimate Napoleon, who himself represented in some ways the universal principles of the French Revolution (e.g., in the *Code Napoléon*), Alexander by 1813 had moved away from his early liberalism toward defense of legitimate monarchies and religious conservatism. Hardly a coherent movement or even body of thought, conservatism in the first quarter of the century was more an inclination to reject the materialism and rationalism of the French Revolution, a preference for order, fidelity to traditional and tried practices, and gradual organic growth rather than precipitate reform. As the patriotic historian Nikolai Karamzin put it, the French Revolution "clarified our ideas. . . . Not freedom which is often calamitous, but order, justice, and safety . . . are the pillars of a happy society." He became the most dedicated defender of autocracy, which he saw as the institution that had repeatedly saved Russia from disintegration. In his secret memorandum to Alexander I, *Memoir on Ancient and Modern Russia* (1811), Karamzin argued that autocracy and a powerful state were responsible for Russia's greatness.[29] "In Russia," he wrote, "the sovereign is the living law . . . , our government is fatherly, patriarchal, the father of a family judges and punishes without a protocol. The monarch too must in conditions of a different nature follow only his own conscience and nothing else."[30] The tsar's absolute power was not to be disputed, but, Karamzin hoped, the emperor would always consider Russia's traditions and ancient customs and maintain close contact with its nobility whose privileges and prerogatives he would respect.

THE DECEMBRISTS

The emperor continued to talk about constitutionalism well into his later years, although after granting constitutions to both Poland and Finland he rejected such schemes for Russia proper. Instead, fearing sedition and revolt at home, he relied increasingly on the police to monitor what his officials were doing. The last

---

[27]Letter of Alexander I to Admiral Pavel Chichagov, cited in Lieven, *Russia Against Napoleon*, p. 182.
[28]Fuller, *Strategy and Power in Russia*, p. 177.
[29]Richard Pipes, *Karamzin's Memoir on Ancient and Modern Russia: A Translation and Analysis* (Cambridge MA: Harvard University Press, 1959; Ann Arbor: University of Michigan Press, 2005).
[30]Ibid., p. 197; Andrzej Walicki, *The Slavophile Controversy: History of a Conservative Utopia in Nineteenth-Century Russian Thought*, trans. Hilda Andrews-Rusiecka (Oxford: Oxford University Press, 1975), p. 40.

decade of Alexander's reign was known as the *Arakcheevshchina*, after his brutal but loyal lieutenant, General Arakcheev, who was said to have proudly announced, "I am the friend of the tsar and complaints about me can be made only to God."[31] Frustrated by Alexander's growing conservatism and mysticism, disappointed by unfulfilled promises of constitutional reform, and inspired by their experiences in Europe during the Napoleonic Wars, groups of young officers and nobles organized secret political societies to discuss reform and even a coup d'état. Their youthful dreams reflected the imperial world that shaped their experience as well as the radical innovations they hoped to introduce.

Pavel Pestel, leader of the most radical of the factions, began his treatise with the assertion that "Russia (*Rossiia*) is a state, one and indivisible," but then promptly enumerated all the different peoples, social estates, and functional units that comprised it. He contrasts the right to nationhood, which is enjoyed by great nations, like the Russians, with the right of convenience, which great states, like Russia, must invoke for their own security.

> ... Finland, Estonia, Livland, Courland, White Russia [Little Russia], New Russia [*Novorossiia*], Bessarabia, Crimea, Georgia, and other tribes living within the state have never enjoyed and never can enjoy their independence; they have always belonged either to Russia . . . or in general to some strong state. And in the future, too, because of their weakness, they will never be able to constitute separate states; for this reason they are subject to the right of convenience and must forever relinquish their rights to be separate nations.[32]

Poland, on the other hand, which had been independent, should be granted separate statehood "through the magnanimity of the glorious Russian people," but under conditions that guarantee Russia's safety and security.[33] Pestel's intellectual nationalism and his commitment to popular government was contained within a non-autocratic but nonetheless imperial vision of a great multinational state ruled by the Russian nation.

These young men expressed impassioned commitment to serving and improving their country and their society. They were animated by what they had seen abroad after war, by what they had read or studied in university, or simply by awareness of the lack of freedom in Russia. "The desire to be useful to humanity always filled me," Petr Borisov, a co-founder of one of the underground societies, the Society of United Slavs, testified. He explained, "Nobody imparted in me free thoughts and liberal ideas. The reading, since childhood, of Greek and Roman history . . . implanted in me a love for freedom and popular sovereignty." Such aspirations had no outlet in the oppressive circumstances of the time, where any unauthorized discussion of reform was viewed as dangerous and even members of the elite had no licit opportunity to voice their concerns. Censorship silenced efforts to work constructively within the autocratic system, so even members of

---

[31] http://www.labex.ru/page/g14_istr_lek_16.html
[32] Raeff, *The Decembrist Movement*, p. 135.
[33] Ibid.

ne privileged elite like these young officers were driven into conspiracy, against their own immediate interests. Borisov noted that he was so moved by "the cruelty displayed by commanding officers toward their subordinates . . . that I left ranks and swore to myself to abolish this kind of punishment, should it cost me my life."[34] Although the more radical among them spoke of justifiable regicide and of emancipating the serfs, the conspirators of the Northern and Southern Societies aspired to change the form of government, not to arouse the masses in revolution.

Their chance came with the sudden, unexpected death of Alexander I. When on December 14, 1825, the imperial troops gathered on Senate Square in St. Petersburg to swear allegiance to the new emperor, Nicholas I, the rebel officers called instead for his brother Konstantin to rule and for a constitution: "*Konstantin i Konstitutsiia!*" Pale with fear, Nicholas sat stiffly on his horse, as his loyal troops faced the rebels. He then ordered his soldiers to fire; several men were killed; and hundreds were arrested. The prisoners were interrogated harshly, a few "whose guilt exceeded that of all the others" were executed and others were sent in perpetual exile to Siberia. The memoirs of some of the survivors express a sense of genuine surprise that the tsar's officials, men whom these privileged young nobles had known since childhood, were prepared to mete out such merciless punishment. A. M. Muravev conveyed this sense of hurt in his memoir about the ordeal. After months of confinement in "a dirty, humid, dark, and narrow cell," he was taken for questioning to General Sukhin,

> an old veteran whom I had known as a child. He received me seated at his desk, pretending not to recognize me, and asked for my name. I answered that I was called Murav'ev and that I was an officer of the Cavalier Guards. To this he thought it polite to say: "I am quite sorry for the memory of your esteemed father who has a criminal in you." I shook on hearing this, but a sentiment of pity seized me at the view of this poor old man who was so dulled by servility that he could remain completely indifferent to the sight of someone's sufferings, of someone who did not share his views.[35]

The Decembrists learned at great cost that the space for "someone who did not share his views" was closing rapidly. Opportunities for expressions of ideas and criticisms were being driven underground, into the dark corners of revolutionary conspiracy and the subterfuge of "Aesopian" (masked, coded, allegorical) language.

Muravev and his comrades had come of age in a changing world. Born at the tail end of an era of palace coups orchestrated by the glittering inner circle of courtiers and guards regiments, they preserved a sense that the monarch was obligated, by pragmatic survival instincts as well as by graciousness and personal relationships, to listen to the elites and at least pretend to take them seriously. But

---

[34]Ibid., p. 55.
[35]Ibid., pp. 164–65.

at the same time, they grew up surrounded by "free thoughts and liberal ideas" about "the drawing together of all classes and . . . the civil reorganization of Russia." They read in newspapers and "various books on politics, such as Machiavelli, Montesquieu, and the *Contrat Social* of J. J. Rousseau." They learned about "the increase of happiness in the United States of America" due to "the superiority of the republican form of government."[36] Their conceptions of political life had strayed into a muddled intermediate zone somewhere between the intimacy and entitlement of a privileged ruling class and the national entitlements of a sovereign people.

The Decembrist revolt was easily crushed, but it left a complicated legacy. Nightmares of revolution haunted the new emperor and encouraged him to rein in the dreams of reform unleashed by his brother's rash talk of constitutions and by contact with Western ideas of freedom and popular sovereignty. On the other hand, although the rebellion itself was handily put down, the movement created its own martyrs and a durable mythology of selfless sacrifice in defense of the people against an oppressive and tyrannical state. In a curious twist, the Siberian exiles were allowed to correspond with their friends and families back in Petersburg, thereby cultivating the legend of their own noble martyrdom. The cult received a public relations boost from the equally noble and self-sacrificing choice of a number of beautiful "Decembrist wives" to follow their husbands into the wilderness. Modeling themselves on the tragic, inspiring figures of the Decembrists and their wives, the next generation of educated men and women explored avenues for serving the "the general good" within a closed society that offered few legal opportunities to serve the people. Siberia, as a space of noble suffering and exile, far distant from state oppression and from court frivolity, became a focus for dreams of true Russianness.

OFFICIAL NATIONALITY

The reign of Nicholas I (1825–1855) was a deeply contradictory one. It began with the failed coup of guards' officers, hoping to topple the autocracy and establish a constitutional regime, and ended with Russia fighting a modern, nineteenth-century war in Crimea with the antique social and political system crying out for drastic reform. The reign witnessed the emergence of the Russian intelligentsia, a serious discussion of reforms of the peasant bondage system, and an energetic push for state-directed economic and industrial development. The first railroad in Russia was laid, and a sturdy structure of police surveillance was established. Political repression coexisted with economic growth and intellectual ferment, but autocratic power was in no way compromised.

Central to the political contradictions was the character of the emperor himself. Nicholas was an imposing man, over six feet in height, described by one

---

[36] A medley of quotations from the testimony of Decembrists, from Raeff, *The Decembrist Movement*, pp. 45, 51, 54, 55.

Vasilii Golike, portrait of Emperor Nicholas I, 1843.

historian as "the most handsome man in Europe" and by a contemporary foreign observer as "the most perfect specimen of a human being, physically speaking, in all of Europe."[37] Once he sat firmly on the throne, he was stern, unyielding, and majestic when he commanded, but his courage, it was said, concealed a nervousness and excitement bordering on panic. Deeply religious, he was absolutely convinced that God was on Russia's side. He believed that the state was meant to serve God and not God the state. His greatest love was the army, and he lavished attention and rewards on it, taking special care to tend to even the minutest details concerning the military. He was a martinet at heart, and the dress uniform became the fashion of the day. What he sought was order, obedience, and a sense of duty, as one finds in a well-run army.

As the educated public grew, and writers found an audience of readers, the regime produced its own synthetic ideological formulation to counter oppositional tendencies that it saw taking shape in the widening public sphere. Elaborated by the conservative minister of education, Sergei Uvarov, the state's program known as "Official Nationality" emphasized the close ties between the tsar and the people, a bond said to originate deep in the distant past. Russians, it was claimed, had chosen their foreign rulers, the Varangians, and worshiped their successors. Russia was distinct in the love of the people for the autocrat and their devotion to the church. "Official Nationality," was summed up in the official slogan "Orthodoxy, Autocracy, Nationality [*narodnost'*]." The historic link of autocracy, Orthodoxy, and the people was present at Russia's creation, claimed the journalist Fedor Bulgarin:

> Faith and autocracy created the Russian state and the one common fatherland for the Russian Slavs. . . . This immense colossus, Russia, almost a separate continent, which contains within itself all the climates and all the tribes of mankind, can be held in balance only by faith and autocracy. That is why in Russia

---

[37]Nicholas Riasanovsky, *Nicholas I and Official Nationality, 1825–1855* (Berkeley and Los Angeles: University of California Press, 1959), pp. 2, 19.

there could never and cannot exist any other nationality, except the nationality founded on Orthodoxy and on autocracy.[38]

At the heart of Official Nationality stood the image of Russia as "a single family in which the ruler is the father and the subjects the children. The father retains complete authority over the children while he allows them to have full freedom. Between the father and the children there can be no suspicion, no treason; their fate, their happiness and their peace they share in common."[39] Nicholas played up the familial aspect in what Wortman calls "scenarios of power," formalized tableaux in which he cast himself as the "first father" and his family as first family of the land. This sentimentalized and naturalized representation of power enjoyed some success in touching his intended audience: when he presented his young son and heir to the people, witnesses reported not a dry eye in the crowd, so moved were they by the loving father and son.

The staged "loving family" of the monarchy affected Russian society in even deeper ways than the official planners might have hoped. Not only did it win the affectionate loyalty of susceptible subjects, but it also provided a model for patriarchal landholders, who internalized the role of benevolent fathers to their wives, daughters, sisters, and, of course, serfs. The familial model saturated understandings of power and gave Westernized Russian landholders a way to imagine their prerogatives as moral, intimate, and distinctly Russian. Patriarchy inflected with familial affection may have softened some interactions between serfs and the peasants they viewed as their children, but, as John Randolph observes, it also licensed the "romantic" liaisons of masters and serfs, painting an attractive veneer on profoundly unequal relations.[40] Memories of the Pugachev rebellion half a century earlier and real-life interactions on provincial estates perturbed the iconic figure of the simple, pure, arcadian peasant, but the powerful strains of early-nineteenth-century nationalism bolstered the image in the face of experience.

"Nationality," the most obscure and contested of the official trinity, was intimately linked with ideas of obedience, submission, and loyalty. This was not something akin to modern nation but a wishful idea about what the Russian people were like. As an authentically Christian people, Russians were said to be marked by renunciation and sacrifice, a deep affection for their sovereign, and dedicated resistance to revolution. At the same time Nicholas attempted to quash discussions of popular sovereignty, he russified the monarchy more intensively. At the ball that followed his coronation, nobles danced in national costumes surrounded by Muscovite decor. Russian was to be used at court; Russian language and history became required subjects at university; churches were built in a

---

[38]Cited in Riasanovsky, *Nicholas I and Official Nationality*, p. 77.
[39]Mikhail Pogodin, cited in ibid., pp. 118–19.
[40]John Randolph, *The House in the Garden: The Bakunin Family and the Romance of Russian Idealism* (Ithaca, NY: Cornell University Press, 2007); see also George Mosse, *Nationalism and Sexuality: Middle-Class Morality and Sexual Norms in Modern Europe* (Madison: University of Wisconsin Press, 1985), passim.

ısso-Byzantine style. A national anthem, "God Save the Tsar," was composed, under the emperor's supervision, and Russian authors and musicians sought what they believed were authentic Russian themes.

Although not the first "Russian" opera, Mikhail Glinka's *A Life for the Tsar* (1836) was widely lauded as genuinely Russian. "When I heard [*A Life*] for the first time, in its entirety and on the stage," wrote a critic of the time, "I was so astonished by the depth and breadth of its conception—which sought to elevate Russian folk tunes into a jewel of Nature—that all music which had been written prior to this on Russian texts seemed like childish babble."[41] Set during the Time of Troubles, the opera told the tale of a patriotic peasant, Ivan Susanin, who leads a band of Poles astray rather than reveal the hiding place of the future tsar. In the official scenario, reflected in the opera, the people adored the tsar but did not sanction or legitimize his right to rule. Nicholas dispensed with the pretense of attending to the voices of "the people" with the comfortable (though erroneous) assumption that he knew and understood his people and that they were delighted to entrust him with the burden of rule. The right to rule was conferred by God, conquest, and hereditary right. Any notion that sovereignty resided in the collective "folk" was peremptorily rejected.

"Official Nationality" was an attempt to make an ideological end run around the Western discourse of the nation and to re-suture nation to state, to the monarch and the state religion at the moment when in Western Europe the political community known as nation was becoming separable from the state, at least conceptually, and was fast gaining an independent potency as the source of legitimacy.[42] Generalizing from the Russian case, Benedict Anderson, a leading theorist of nations and national identity, defines "official nationalisms" as a category of nationalisms that appear after the first stirrings of popular linguistic and cultural nationalisms, "*responses* by power-groups—primarily, but not exclusively, dynastic and aristocratic—threatened with exclusion from, or marginalization in, popular imagined communities." Official nationalism "concealed a discrepancy between nation and dynastic realm" and was connected to the efforts of aristocracies and monarchies to maintain their empires.[43] The ideology of Official Nationality was part of the empire's adjustment to the claims of the discourse of the nation and the perceived subversive power of the European nation-form. With considerable trepidation and in its own particular way, the empire faced the challenges of a modernity defined by its Western competitors.

By the second quarter of the nineteenth century, the notion of "nation" was up for grabs. Monarchs, nobilities, and various other social groups, like the emerging middle class (the "bourgeoisie"), competed with emboldened intellectuals to

---

[41]Cited in Marina Frolova-Walker, *Russian Music and Nationalism from Glinka to Stalin* (New Haven, CT, and London: Yale University Press, 2007), p. 75.

[42]Benedict Anderson, *Imagined Communities: Reflections on the Origin and Spread of Nationalism* (London: Verso, 1983, 2006), pp. 86–87, 110.

[43]Ibid., pp. 109–10.

claim that they were the nation. Certainly the official tsarist view of what was national was deeply conservative in the sense of preserving a given state form that was being questioned by rival conceptions in the West. Looking back to an idealized past of harmony between people and ruler, Nicholas's notion of Holy Rus was contrasted to godless, revolutionary Europe. At the same time the monarchy resisted those domestic nationalists, like the Slavophile Konstantin Aksakov, who identified with the simple people (*narod*) by wearing a beard and Russian national dress. "In Nicholas' Western frame of mind, beards signified not Russians but Jews and radicals. The official view identified the nation with the ruling Western elite," and not with the mass of the people.[44]

Nicholas spent much time traveling about his empire, showing himself to the public, reassuring them (and himself) of the special powers that he held. During the cholera epidemic of 1830, he appeared in Moscow as if taking charge of the efforts to fight the disease. His faithful adjutant Aleksandr Benkendorff remarked, "it seemed to all that the disease itself would capitulate to his omnipotence." Reprising his frozen defiance of the Decembrist rebels, Nicholas faced down a riotous mob driven to frenzy by the cholera. "He threw off his coat, ordered the rioters to fall to their knees and cross themselves. He then scolded them. . . . 'Remember what you did, remember that you aren't French, you aren't Poles, but Russians'."[45]

THE INTELLIGENTSIA

In many ways the emergence of the group of critical, socially engaged thinkers known as the "intelligentsia" in the 1830s implied a social dialogue about what constituted "the nation." Made up of members from various classes, the intelligentsia lived apart from polite society (*obshchestvo*) on the one hand and from the people (*narod*) on the other. It was isolated from and alien to official Russia, questioning fundamentals about the political order and religion, yet deeply desirous of becoming close to the people and serving it. As Alan Pollard suggests, "Herein lay the intelligentsia's dilemma. The elements which created consciousness tended to be products of the West, so that the very qualities which endowed the intelligentsia with understanding, and thus with its very essence, also alienated it from national life, to represent *which* was its vital function. Therefore, the intelligentsia's central problem was to establish a liaison with the people."[46]

Where the Decembrists had been content to scheme and act on behalf of the common soldiers and peasants, their successors increasingly strove not only to serve these victimized masses but also to connect with them in some way. Young Russian intellectuals moved between the 1830s and the 1860s from contemplating

---

[44]Wortman, *Scenarios of Power, I*, p. 402.
[45]Ibid., p. 301.
[46]Alan P. Pollard, "The Russian Intelligentsia: The Mind of Russia," *California Slavic Studies* 3 (1964): 15.

the world to attempting to transform it through action. The opening event in the intelligentsia dialogue was the 1836 *Philosophical Letter* by Petr Chaadaev that Aleksandr Herzen reported had an effect like "a pistol shot in the dark night." Radically anti-nationalist, the *Letter* proclaimed that Russia was unique in that it had no history or traditions; it was a *tabula rasa* on which new ideas and forms could be written. This extreme position was diametrically opposed to Official Nationality that celebrated Russia's healthy wholeness in contrast to the rottenness of the West. After he was condemned as insane and placed under house arrest, Chaadaev published an *Apology of a Madman*, in which he argued that Russia's backwardness presented a unique opportunity for his country "to resolve the greater part of the social problems, to perfect the greater part of the ideas which have arisen in older societies."[47]

The ensuing discussion divided the intelligentsia into Westernizers, those who subscribed to a rationalist, Enlightenment agenda for Russia—reform in a generally modernist European direction—and Slavophiles, who advocated a more conservative, nostalgic reconstruction of what was thought to have made up the Russian tradition. While some Westernizing liberals appeared to be indifferent or even hostile to issues of national identity, those identified as Slavophiles were preoccupied with finding the Russian nation, characterizing it, and building on its many virtues. They followed the European Romantics and looked to the *narod* [the people], which was largely identified with the peasantry, for *narodnost'*, the essential character of the Russian or Slav. For Aleksei Khomiakov national character was contained in religion or a certain form of religiosity.[48] Slavs were the most highly spiritual, the most artistic and talented of the peoples of the earth. Peace-loving and fraternal, spontaneous, loving, and valuing freedom, they realized their fullness in an organic unity of all in love and freedom which he called *sobornost'* (roughly, spiritual collectivity or community within Orthodoxy). Russians were the greatest of the Slavs and possessed an abundance of vital, organic energy, humility, and brotherly love. In the pre-Petrine past they had lived freely and harmoniously, but Peter the Great introduced alien Western notions of rationalism, legalism, and formalism to Russia and destroyed the organic harmony of the nation. Rigid rules and impersonal procedures, in this romantic view, crushed the human element and the quality of mercy that had made Muscovy a community of love and faith.

For Konstantin Aksakov and other Slavophiles, not only was Orthodox Christianity the essential heart of Slavic nature, but the peasant commune (communal village organization) was envisioned as "a union of the people who have renounced their egoism, their individuality, and who express their common accord." Critical of the newly triumphant capitalism of the West, they feared the

---

[47]P. Chaadaev, *Philosophical Letters and Apology of a Madman*, trans. and introduced by Mary-Barbara Zeldin (Knoxville: University of Tennessee Press, 1969), p. 174.

[48]See Austin Jersild's unpublished paper, "Khomiakov and Empire: Faith and Custom in the Borderlands," presented at the AAASS annual convention, Boca Raton, Florida, September 26, 1998.

depersonalization of human relations, the dominance of things over men, that came with private property. In Andrzjei Walicki's telling analysis, Slavophilism was a "conservative utopianism" that defended community against the fragmenting effects of society.[49]

Though Slavophilism was in its origins "a cultivation of the native and primarily Slavic elements in the social life and culture of ancient Russia," this conservative nationalism later blended into a larger concern with the whole of Slavdom (Pan-Slavism), rather than a focused development of Russian national character. Slavophile Russians advocated freedom for Slavic peoples ruled by the Ottoman Empire. In its Pan-Slavic incarnation, calls for Slavic fraternity adopted an ugly, aggressive stance vis-à-vis Russia's Slavic neighbors, particularly the Catholic Poles, who were cast as rightfully subject to the manifestly superior Russians.[50]

Both the state authorities and the Westernizer intellectuals rejected the Slavophile vision. For the autocracy, the repudiation of the Petrine reforms was an unacceptable challenge and the valorization of the people threatened to undermine the premises of autocracy, while for the Westernizers the Slavophile reading of the Russian past was a narcissistic fiction. Paul Bushkovitch observes that none of these lines of thought, not even the Slavophile philosophy, endorsed a fully ethnic vision of a sovereign Russian people apart from a state.[51] Their contribution to Russian political and social thought was of a different kind and built toward different solutions. The Westernizers themselves were divided between liberals who favored capitalist development and parliamentary democracy and the radicals who proposed a particularly Russian form of socialism that would avoid capitalism and build a unique future on the collectivist sentiments of the peasantry. From Alexander Herzen's "Russian socialism" and the celebration of the peasant commune to the revolutionary populism of the 1870s, ideas of Russian exceptionalism, of overcoming the burdens of Western capitalism and moving straight on to a new communitarianism, dominated the left wing of the Russian intelligentsia.

Historians of the time entered the debate over the nature of the Russian nation and the effects of Peter the Great's intervention, usually in opposition to the Slavophile interpretation. In a series of lectures in 1843–1844, Timofei Granovskii attacked the Slavophile idealization of the people. But more long-lasting was the work of the so-called statist school of Russian historians—Konstantin Kavelin, Boris Chicherin, and Sergei Solovev—who by proposing that the Russian state was the principal agent of progress in Russia's history assured that state-centered narratives would dominate the subsequent historical discussion. The "nation," while always present as a palimpsest, was overlaid by other more pressing social and political themes.

---

[49]Walicki, *The Slavophile Controversy.*

[50]Andrzej Walicki, *A History of Russian Thought from the Enlightenment to Marxism*, trans. Hilda Andrews-Rusiecka (Stanford, CA: Stanford University Press, 1979), p. 92.

[51]Paul Bushkovitch, "What Is Russia? Russian National Identity and the State, 1500–1917," in *Culture, Nation, and Identity: The Ukrainian-Russian Encounter, 1600-1945*, edited by Andreas Kappeler, et al. (Toronto: Canadian Institute of Ukrainian Studies Press, 2003), pp. 144–161.

Even the conservative nationalist Mikhail Katkov (1818–1887), an influential journalist and political commentator, conceived of Russian identity as basically state-centered. Russian society was not ethnically homogeneous, and that condition had to be changed. Russification would provide the state with an appropriately unified ethnic nation below. Though his newspaper, *Moskovskie Vedomosti* [Moscow News], was very popular, his nationalist views had only limited appeal. The idea of a Pan-Slavic unity, perhaps headed by "the tsar of all the Slavs" and not just of Russia (an idea expressed by the poet Fedor Tiuchev among others), was continually undermined by the resistance of other Slavic peoples, most importantly the Poles, who not only did not share Orthodoxy with the Russians but whose whole self-identity was bound up in resistance to Russian domination. Closer to home, both Pan-Slavism and the more modest concept of the Russian people including both "Little Russians" (Ukrainians) and "White Russians" (Belorussians) as well as "Great Russians" was dealt a severe blow by an emerging separate national identity among Ukrainians. After the government suppressed in 1847 the short-lived Ukrainian Brotherhood of Cyril and Methodius, a radical Pan-Slavic group that advocated emancipation of the serfs and a federation of the Slavic peoples, it officially condemned Pan-Slavism as a dangerous and subversive doctrine.[52]

All this interest in "the people" led some leading figures among the educated classes to take the next obvious step: to go out and study "the people." While sentimentalized images of peasant purity had circulated in the previous century, those arcadian idylls were recognizably more imaginary than based on reality. In the 1830s, the Imperial Russian Geographic Society was founded and a flotilla of ethnographers set out to catalogue the costumes and customs of the many people of the empire. These gentleman-scholars took with them a host of preconceived notions about the folk cultures they would encounter, but nonetheless, they were able to gather a good deal of information. Initially intent on spanning the empire, their efforts quickly came to focus on the Russian peasantry over any other inhabitants of the realm. Their experience as they traveled across the roads of Russia were given a particular gloss and an exaggerated sense of coherence by the very fact that they had to stick to the routes built and maintained by the state and staffed by official coachmen. The ethnographers relied on their coachmen to explain what they saw and to pass the hours by singing laments. These coachmen, and the roads they traveled, shaped the impression of Russia brought back by learned investigators.[53]

---

[52]P. A. Zionchkovskii, *Kirilo-Mefodievskoe obshchestvo (1846–1847)* (Moscow: Izdatel'stvo Moskovskogo universiteta, 1959); Faith Hillis, *Children of Rus': Right-Bank Ukraine and the Invention of a Russian Nation* (Ithaca, NY: Cornell University Press, 2013).

[53]John W. Randolph, "The Singing Coachman or, The Road and Russia's Ethnographic Invention in Early Modern Times," *Journal of Early Modern History* 11, nos. 1–2 (2007): 33–62; Nathaniel Knight, "Science, Empire, and Nationality: Ethnography in the Russian Geographical Society, 1845–1855," in *Imperial Russia: New Histories for the Empire*, ed. Jane Burbank and David L. Ransel, pp. 108–42; Cathy A. Frierson, *Peasant Icons: Representations of Rural People in Late Nineteenth-Century Russia* (New York: Oxford University Press, 1993).

Growing preoccupation with the Russian peasantry and with all the rich local varieties of their ethnographic customs might have encouraged a sense of regional loyalty—a commitment to the particular peasant customs in Province A or B—or an enthusiasm for "the provinces" as opposed to a broader national vision. Anne Lounsbery finds quite the contrary at work within Russian literary texts. Within Russia proper "the provinces" did not win intellectuals' loyalties. The term did not actually refer to the country life of the peasantry, but rather to the stultifying world of provincial towns. Lounsbery finds in literary works the provinces shade into a homogeneous and indistinguishable nowhere, characterized by being "not the capitals," "a mass of grimly uniform places in opposition to which the capitals took their meaning." "So Saratov or Pskov? Take your pick: it usually matters little. What matters is the province-vs.-capital opposition and the fact that in Russian literature, the provinces as the embodiment of cultural lack are so often not merely drab or backward or philistine; . . . [r]ather, the provinces can be a version of hell itself, a place where banality threatens to intensify to the point of evil." To explain why this should be so, Lounsbery returns to the question of Russia's sense of backwardness relative to the West: in Europe, authors might mock provincials' striving to emulate the cultural heights of Paris, but the status of Paris as true metropolis would never be subject to doubt. "In Russia provincialism is deeply worrisome because the provinciality of the provinces can be seen to reflect the provinciality and perhaps even the "inauthenticity" of the nation as a whole."[54] The Russian capitals themselves, it was feared, were just as provincial as the actual provinces when held up to the daunting measuring stick of European metropolitan centers.

To this point we have discussed the ideas advanced by political authorities and by literate elites of various stripes. It proves far more difficult to discern popular ideas about "nationality" or identity. Since figures from the lower orders rarely recorded their perspectives, historians have to find creative ways to tap into their beliefs. Jeffrey Brooks attempts to do so by considering what ordinary Russians were likely to read and takes their reading choices as indicators of their views. He acknowledges that "We know little about the popular conception of what it meant to be Russian," and finds that "the concept of a nation of peoples with shared loyalties was not well developed."[55] He finds some clues in the recurrent themes of *lubki,* the popular broadsheets we have seen above, which consistently featured "the Orthodox Church, and, to a lesser extent, the tsar" as "the foremost emblems of Russianness throughout the nineteenth century."[56] It is difficult, however, to disaggregate the "popular" content of the *lubki* from the messages we have already seen being purveyed from on high. In any case, this Orthodox conception of Russianness would have appealed to only a limited subset of the empire's

[54]Anne Lounsbery, "'No! This Is Not the Provinces!' Provincialism, Russianness, and Authenticity in Gogol's Day," *Russian Review* 64, no. 2 (2005): 259–80; quotes on 265, 266.
[55]Brooks, *When Russia Learned to Read,* p. 215.
[56]Ibid., p. 214.

population. Figuring out the extent to which a broader sense of imperial (*Rossiiskii*) awareness or identity had developed at this time poses an even more difficult question, and leads us again to the complex position of Russia's non-Russian subjects within the empire.

EXPANSION, CONQUEST, AND REBELLION

Russia's intensive engagement with Napoleon was perhaps the most dramatic of its foreign entanglements in the first half of the nineteenth century, but the empire grew apace in other directions as well and continually confronted the downstream consequences of its expansion. Siberia has sometimes been referred to as Russia's first colony, and eventually it would become a region of intense Slavic settlement. Nicholas I sent the prominent statesman Mikhail Speranskii to survey his lands in Siberia and propose reforms to bring some order and good governance to the vast territory. The reform laws of 1822 set up a more transparent administration, curtailed the arbitrary rule of governors (to an extent), and granted the Siberian peoples, now classified as state peasants, self-governing institutions organized around clans and chosen elders. The statutes allowed indigenous Siberians to practice their religions, use their own languages in official business, and settle disputes according to their customs. Although the laws worked better on paper than in reality, and ultimate authority remained with Russian governors and bureaucrats, Speranskii's reform established rules and practices that safeguarded to a degree the native peoples' way of life until the end of the empire.[57]

At the same time, the native peoples found themselves enmeshed in the ethnographic trap of language and labeling. The slippery term *inorodtsy* meant literally, people of other blood or clan, and from the point of view of the Russians, it denoted particularly alien, and primitive peoples. The term took on strict legal definition in a related 1822 Ustav (statute) "on the administration of the *inorodtsy*." "The Ustav placed in the category of *inorodtsy* various 'Eastern' peoples, mostly nomadic or semi-nomadic Siberian natives, whose way of life was based on herding, hunting or fishing. Subsequent nineteenth-century expansion to the south and east brought new ethnic groups into the empire, and a decision had to be made in each case whether or not a given ethnic group should be assigned to the category of *inorodtsy*."[58] The term took on disproportionate significance as its ethnographic meanings shifted and hardened into legal consequences, and its mobility inevitably raised questions about the mutability or immutability of such categories. As John Slocum writes:

---

[57]Raeff, *Michael Speransky*, pp. 252–79; and his *Siberia and the Reforms of 1822* (Seattle: University of Washington Press, 1956).
[58]John W. Slocum, "Who, and When Were the Inorodtsy? The Evolution of the Category of 'Aliens' in Imperial Russia," *Russian Review* 57 (1998): 173–90; quote on 174.

In 1835, Russia's Jews were designated inorodtsy, despite the fact that Jews were a sedentary people and inhabited a European, rather than Asian milieu. The classification of Jews as inorodtsy points to a fundamental ambiguity in the underlying logic of this category: was it more an indicator of a given people's purported level of civilized development, or a legal marker of racial difference? If the former was the case, a group categorized as inorodtsy could in principle eventually qualify for "promotion" out of this status, given Enlightenment-era notions of social evolution.[59]

If the latter were the case, and differences were biological, physiological, then presumably characteristics of *inorodtsy* would be understood as immutable. Russians are generally said to have been indifferent to the category of race, but Slocum challenges that easy assumption, reminding us that these were questions very much open to debate in the early nineteenth century, and even more as time progressed.

It is difficult to gain access to the experience of Siberia's native peoples in this era or to assess their impressions of the empire, although some good work makes inroads in this direction.[60] More accessible are members of the Russian administrative and intellectual elite who served the empire in its distant reaches. One of the peculiarities of the Siberian case, later to be replicated in Central Asia as well, was that many of the key figures who staffed its ministries, served as governors, or oversaw its reforms were sent to the region as exiles. Mark Soderstrom examines the copious writings of some of these figures, some exiled, others simply blocked in their career aspirations and subject to the derogatory attitudes toward these ultimate provincials held by their more cosmopolitan counterparts in the capitals. He finds well-educated men, typical of the "enlightened bureaucrats" of the age, who were deeply committed to improving the realm, while also unambiguously attached to the monarchy, the principle of absolutism, and the person of Nicholas I, the tsar who has one of the darkest reputations for autocratic, repressive rule of all Russian rulers. In their writings they demonstrated almost religious commitment to this unlikely figure as the path to enlightenment and benefactor of all his subjects.

Where scholarship has long understood the regime's attention to crafting its own image, Soderstrom's research sheds light on the difficult problem of *reception*. Like Anna Labzina half a century earlier, these Siberian officials show in their writings that they had fully internalized the idea of autocracy as the best and only path for Russia. Particularly Peter Slovtsov, exiled, like so many of his contemporaries, and barred from service in the capitals, is a fascinating case. He expressed an ongoing commitment to the imperial regime and also was convinced that his knowledge of Siberia would allow him and his protégé, Ivan Kalashnikov, to make important contributions to furthering the imperial mission.

---

[59]Ibid., p.174.
[60]See also Yuri Slezkine, *Arctic Mirrors: Russia and the Small Peoples of the North* (Ithaca, NY: Cornell University Press, 1994).

They combined a fierce commitment to empire with a strong sense of attachment to Siberia itself.[61] Their political loyalism found a counterpart in a literary Siberia that also found voice in this period.[62]

Their regionalism highlights yet another mode of affiliation that complicates the empire-nation binary. Lounsbery observes that this kind of regionalism surfaces almost exclusively in literary works situated in "borderland spaces—non- and semi-Russian places like Siberia, Ukraine, the Caucasus, Crimea, the Asian steppe, and even the Baltics," where the particularities of the region add to the impact of the work. Pushkin's "Prisoner of the Caucasus," discussed below, or Gogol's Ukrainian tales exemplify this pattern. "In the Russian cultural imaginary the empire's various borderlands and frontiers are most often *opposed* to 'Russia,' so that the presence of all these less-than-Russian spaces within the territorially unified empire perhaps even intensified the tendency to collapse the heterogeneous regions of European Russia into the idea of 'the provinces'."[63]

The nineteenth century opened with successful advances in the South Caucasus, with the incorporation of Georgia and Persian Armenia. In later decades, securely positioned in the lowland valleys of Georgia, Armenia, and what would become Azerbaijan, Russia turned its acquisitive gaze to the highlands, to the far more challenging North Caucasus, where it became mired in fierce war against the "mountain people," a struggle with echoes even today in Chechnya and Dagestan. On the western front, the promising overtures of Alexander to his Polish subjects in 1816 soured in subsequent decades, leading to the Polish November Insurrection of 1830, and this "betrayal" in turn colored imperial policies toward the heterogeneous populations of the Ukrainian, Ruthenian, and Baltic lands.

Russia had long-standing contacts with the Georgian and Armenian populations of the South Caucasus, and was generally viewed as a protective force shielding the region's Christians from Persian and Ottoman oppression. When Russia incorporated Georgia in 1801 and the former khanate of Erevan in 1828, its dominion seems to have been welcomed by its new subjects, at least by the Christians. Some Muslims chose to exit and migrated to the Ottoman and Persian Empires; others chose loyalty and stayed under the sway of the Orthodox emperor. Official documents made much of the fact that Russia had been invited into these regions. Since Russian officials always kept an eye on their Western counterparts and compared themselves to those other empires, their reception in the Caucasus allowed them to tout themselves as liberators and to pat themselves

[61]Mark Soderstrom, "Sibiriaki na sluzhbe imperii: Sluzhba i samoznanie (sluchai P. A. Slovtsova i I. T. Kalashnikova," in *Sibirskii tekst v national'nom suzhetnom prostranstve*, ed. K. V. Anisimov (Krasnoiarsk: Siberian Federal University, 2010), pp. 27–45.

[62]Mark Bassin, "Inventing Siberia: Visions of the Russian East in the Early Nineteenth Century," *American Historical Review* 96, no. 3 (1991): 763–94; and his *Imperial Visions: Nationalist Imagination and Geographical Expansion in the Russian Far East, 1840–1865* (Cambridge: Cambridge University Press, 1999).

[63]Lounsbery, "No! This Is Not the Provinces!" 265.

on the back as a kinder, gentler empire. Favorable policies allowed Armenians to maintain a large degree of autonomous self-rule within local communities and empowered the Catholicos, the head of the Armenian church, to supervise religious and spiritual matters and to impose censorship on Armenian works published anywhere in the empire, to establish and run religious schools, and to call on state forces to enforce his decisions.

At the same time, Russian rhetoric circulated deprecating and even vicious stereotypes of their new subjects. Armenians in many ways benefited from their inclusion in the empire and even from the cultural stereotypes about them that Russians believed to be true. In particular, the entrenched image of Armenians as able merchants and traders worked in their favor, leading first Catherine II and then her grandson to privilege them with tax exemptions and permission to travel freely both within the empire and abroad. In the anomalous treatment of Armenia and Armenians, we see once again the persistence of patterns of differential rights. As Ann Stoler observes about empires as a general phenomenon: "imperial formations are macropolities whose technologies of rule thrive on the production of exceptions and their uneven and changing proliferation."[64]

Armenians had long been scattered about the world, forming settlements from India to Italy. After centuries of dispersion, they lacked a coherent sense of themselves as a people or nation distinct from an ethnoreligious community. The newly established *Armianskaia oblast'* (Armenian Region) attracted nearly 100,000 Armenians from Persia and Turkey, which increased interaction and exchange among members of this reassembled diaspora. Occurring as it did in the early nineteenth century, this condensation coincided with the explosion in thinking and writing about national identity. Ideas about nationality funneled into Russian Armenia through the work of Armenians educated in Venice, one of the leading centers of Armenian intellectual life. Armenian national thinkers, however, were not in a position to militate for national sovereignty or independence, nor, given their appreciation for their new "liberation" from Muslim rulers and their favorable position within the Russian empire, did they particularly want to do so. Instead, as we have seen in other cases, they paired their commitment to Armenian identity with solid loyalty to the empire. In his study of Armenian history, Ronald Suny labels them the "Armenian patriotic intelligentsia."[65] Their patriotism in this case was for the state that protected them, and the culture that offered, from their perspective, attractive benefits of membership, that is, Western-style education, opportunities for advancement, and roads to enrichment.

The Armenians and Georgians had religious reasons to welcome Russian dominion. More surprising perhaps were those Muslim populations that also made common cause with the Russians as they continued to penetrate into the steppe,

---

[64]Ann Laura Stoler, "On Degrees of Imperial Sovereignty," *Public Culture* 18, no. 1 (2006): 128.
[65]Ronald Grigor Suny, *Looking Toward Ararat: Armenia in Modern History* (Bloomington: Indiana University Press, 1993).

Crimea, the Caucasus, and Central Asia in the late eighteenth and early nineteenth centuries.

Following patterns set by Catherine the Great, the Russian state relied on the structures and institutions of the imamate that the regime itself had established and supported as an instrument of imperial rule. In the early nineteenth century, however, and particularly in the wake of the Polish uprising of 1830, the Russian authorities grew wary of non-Orthodox clergies, and inserted themselves in disputes between ordinary Muslims and the clergy. Parallel to the particular forms of attachment to empire that we have seen among Armenians, some Russian Muslims articulated an imperial form of loyalty that allowed them to maintain a clear sense of their communal religious identity while at the same time claiming proud membership in the broader community of imperial subjects.[66]

For the most part, imperial power worked through, not against, the religious institutions of its varied population. Conversion still remained largely off the table. Robert Crews writes: "For millions of tsarist subjects, the state did more than tolerate other confessions; it presented itself as a defender of certain forms of Islam, Judaism, Buddhism, Protestantism, and other faiths."[67] Only later did the series of Russian-Ottoman wars, particularly the Crimean War (1853–1856) and the War of 1877–1878, and the growth of nationalism among Poles and other subject peoples, give rise to Russian anxieties about the loyalty of the empire's Muslims. Conservative Russian nationalists, like Mikhail Katkov and the novelist Fyodor Dostoevsky, questioned the policy of tolerance. As Russian Pan-Slav writers fantasized about the unity of all Slavic peoples, observers feared that parallel ideologies, Pan-Turkism or Pan-Islamism, might seduce Muslims within Russia to support the Ottomans. While the policy of tolerance continued until the end of the empire, powerful voices proclaimed that the diversity of faiths weakened the empire and that Russia should follow the lead of European nation-states and work toward greater homogenization of its population. Yet even in the revolution of 1905 and the period of constitutional monarchy from 1905 to 1917, Muslims continued to work within the system to the extent that they were able, electing representatives to the state dumas and petitioning for civil rights and equal treatment.

Significantly, Russia cast itself as defender of only *certain forms* of religion. One that fell decidedly outside of the zone of protection was the form of Sufism that played a critical role in mobilizing the armed resistance of the peoples of the North Caucasus—Chechens, Circassians, Avars, Kumyks, Kabardinians, and Adyghes—to Russian incursions. The great range of the Caucasian Mountains, the highest mountains in Europe, is known as the "Mountain of Tongues"

---

[66]On the oldest Muslim community in the Russian Empire, the Volga Tatars, see Michael Kemper, "Imperial Russia as Dar al-Islam? Nineteenth-Century Debates on Ijtihad and Taqlid Among the Volga Tatars," *Islamic Law and Society: A Global Perspective*, guest ed. Sabrina Joseph, special issue of *Encounters: An International Journal for the Study of Culture and Society* 6 (Fall 2015): 95–124.
[67]Crews, *For Prophet and Tsar*, p. 2.

Map 6.2. Russian expansion in the Caucasus.

because of its huge diversity of languages and peoples. Most North Caucasians are Muslims but many are Christian or practice local religious rites. Ruled by khans and chieftains, imams and sheiks, the Caucasians were nominally under the rule of the Ottomans from the early sixteenth century. At about the same time, Ivan the Terrible expanded his realm southward to Astrakhan on the Caspian Sea and settled Cossacks on the Terek River just north of the Caucasian Mountains. From the 1780s, when Russians began creeping into the region, a series of Sufi leaders declared holy war against the invaders. In the late eighteenth century, Russians built the "Georgian Military Highway" through the mountains to link Russia with the Georgian kingdoms to which they pledged support. In the 1820s, taking advantage of a period of weakness of the two powers that had traditionally held sway in the region, Persia and Turkey, Russia began edging into the region more forcibly, sparking what would prove to be a long (endless), murderous war.

Initially the Russians attempted to implement their usual technique of coopting local elites, but the region proved frustratingly fractious and fractured. Identifying a set of elites with any real authority was difficult, and the absence of a single, unified political entity made the usual approach impracticable. In campaigns against the elusive tribesmen of the mountains, the Russian Empire set aside its general preference for ruling through difference and instead adopted a horrific path toward eradication. The "special deal" prescribed for the North Caucasians was an immeasurably grim one. In 1829, following an important victory over Persian forces that opened the path for Russian advance, Nicholas I bluntly urged General Paskiewicz to "set his sights on a glorious and most vital enterprise of direct utility [to Russia]—the permanent pacification of the mountain peoples or the annihilation of those who do not submit."[68] Since submission was not forthcoming, annihilation became Russian policy. Passing through the mountainous region in 1829, the great poet Alexander Pushkin reported in short, abrupt sentences the results of this bloodthirsty policy: "The Circassians hate us. We have driven them from their pastures; whole *auls* [villages, settlements, encampments] belonging to them have been sacked; entire clans destroyed."[69]

Russia's bitter and bloody war with the native peoples was marked by the "policies of terror" employed by General Aleksei Ermolov, the tsar's all-powerful viceroy in the Caucasus (1816–1827). The largest and most tragic ethnic cleansing of non-Russians in the tsarist empire followed the defeat of the North Caucasian peoples in the prolonged wars in the mountains that stretched from the middle of the reign of Alexander I through the entire rule of Nicholas I into the early years of Alexander II (roughly 1817 to 1864). One might even note that violent conflicts between Chechens and other mountain peoples and the Russian state have continued until the present.[70]

The mountaineers rose repeatedly to resist the Russian conquest, eventually rallying around powerful charismatic Islamic leaders. Preaching and enforcing strict *sharia* law, banning vices such as drinking, smoking, dancing, and unregulated relations between men and women, the imams successfully organized the local tribes to fight the invaders for decades. The most effective leader was Shamil, who during the Crimean War even threatened the Russians' Caucasian capital, Tiflis. The rebels of the Caucasus were effectively allies of the Ottoman enemies of the tsarist state. The Europeans planned to invade the Caucasus and join up with the anti-Russian resistance, but the end of the Crimean War

---

[68]Quoted in Gary Hamburg, "War of Worlds: Commentary on the Two Texts in Their Historical Context," in *Russian-Muslim Confrontation in the Caucasus: Alternative Visions of the Conflict between Imam Shamil and the Russians, 1830–1859*, ed. Gary Hamburg and Thomas Sanders, Soas/Routledge Studies on the Middle East (Abingdon, Oxon, and New York: Routledge, 2004), p. 157.
[69]Quoted in ibid.
[70]Vladimir O. Bobrovnikov, *Musul'mane Severnogo Kavkaza: obychai, pravo, nasilie. Ocherki po istorii i etnografii prava Nagornogo Dagestana* (Moscow: Vostochnaia literatura RAN, 2002).

allowed the Russians to subdue the Caucasians.

In the early 1860s the Russian authorities decided to reduce the vulnerability of their Caucasian frontier by ridding the region of certain peoples. They first removed Adyghe and Cherkess (Circassian) tribes and settled Cossacks on their lands. These policies encouraged the mass emigration of hundreds of thousands of North Caucasians southward to the Ottoman Empire. Alexander Knysh writes,

Shamil, c. 1860.

> The refugees were motivated by a variety of factors, such as the dislocation and resentment produced by the Russian resettlement schemes and oppressive rule, hopes for a happy life under friendly Muslim rule in Anatolia (inspired in part by Ottoman propaganda), and the religious rulings issued by Muslim religious authorities, which proclaimed living under infidel rule to be a grave sin for any Muslim who had other options. Once the emigrants found themselves on board ships headed for Ottoman Turkey, they were readily preyed upon by Ottoman slave-traders and greedy crews who charged their passengers by the head and therefore packed as many of them as possible into each ship.[71]

Upwards of half a million Caucasians fled, half of whom would perish on the journey. Other hundreds of thousands were moved by the Russian government to places where they could be supervised more closely by Cossacks. Sporadic revolts continued, most notably during the Russian-Turkish War of 1877–1878, but essentially the Caucasus became part of the Russian Empire though never fully pacified or effectively integrated into the imperial administration.

The battle lines during this conflict were less clear-cut than a "holy war" or "clash of civilizations" explanation would suggest. A century of varied interactions between Russians and the people of the mountains had produced an assortment of people of mixed allegiances, affiliations, and loyalties that profoundly complicated any easy claims about imperial powers and colonized subjects. Hadji Murat, an Avar warrior who became the protagonist of Tolstoy's 1904 novella, moved back and forth

---

[71]Alexander Knysh, "'al-Kabk' ('The Caucasus'): The Period 1800 to the Present Day," in *The Encyclopedia of Islam, 2d edition (Supplement)*, fasc. 7–8 (2003), pp. 486–501.

between the forces of the resistance and the Russians, driven by personal experiences and jarred by assaults on his dignity and his family rather than by any rigid cultural attachments. In another short novel, "The Cossacks," Tolstoy depicts a world of Cossacks deployed to the North Caucasian offensive line, where their lives have far more in common with their tribal adversaries than with their cultured Russian officers, and where lines between Cossack and Adyghe, between Christian and Muslim, between the languages and practices of invaders and resisters have become blurred.

Groups of Christian sectarians, considered "apostates" by the Orthodox authorities in St. Petersburg, similarly shook up comfortable categories when relocated in the mountainous frontier. Dukhobors, Molokans, and Subbotniks, sectarian groups that were condemned as heretics, settled in large numbers both in the North and South Caucasus beginning in the 1830s. Driven from their Russian homes by persecution, they came as exiles or fled seeking freedom to practice their religion, but their new homes in the mountainous frontier transformed them in a variety of ways. From the point of view of St. Petersburg, the former heretics became model colonists and exemplars of Russianness. For the settlers, living in new ecological surroundings and confronting the harsh realities of scratching out a living in unfamiliar terrain, relations with their indigenous neighbors became matters of life and death. Historian Nicholas Breyfogle charts the ways in which these sectarians interacted with their neighbors, learned from them, competed and fought with them, and adapted to entirely new environmental demands. The categorical divisions that had defined them and led to their exile proved ephemeral in the plains and high mountain air.[72]

In a work of historical reconstruction, Michael Khodarkovsky traces the life of a historical figure who lived on precisely this hazy divide and had to make "bitter choices": a certain Semyon Atarshchikov. Raised as a Russian Cossack but born to Chechen parents, Atarshchikov followed a back-and-forth trajectory remarkably similar to Hadji Murat's, playing a dangerous, ultimately lethal, game of shifting allegiances between his Russian fellows and his Muslim roots.[73] Another boundary crosser, Shamil, the great leader of the anti-Russian resistance, was captured and spent the end of his life as an important personage in St. Petersburg, receiving visits from the curious elite. The public feted the defeated Shamil, treating him nostalgically as a noble warrior. He married an Armenian captive, who converted to Islam and stayed with him in a loving relationship for life. It is remarkable to discover that even on the most sharply contested frontiers of empire, crisscrossing loyalties and antagonisms compromised divisions between invaders and local populations. Empire was both about differentiating peoples one from another and a cosmopolitan mixing that produced hybrid combinations of colonizer and colonized.

Not only the people caught in the turbulent winds of imperial conquest expressed ambivalence about the process of mixing. Ambivalence and indecision

---

[72]Nicholas B. Breyfogle, *Heretics and Colonizers: Forging Russia's Empire in the South Caucasus* (Ithaca, NY: Cornell University Press, 2005).
[73]Michael Khodarkovsky, *Bitter Choices: Loyalty and Betrayal in the Russian Conquest of the North Caucasus* (Ithaca, NY: Cornell University Press, 2011).

continued to mark official state positions toward incorporation of its multitude of subject peoples as well. Many historians have remarked on the drive on the part of the Nicolaevan regime to institute uniform policies and to integrate all their holdings and people into a single, clear, Russian whole. Yet, as we have argued, recourse to differentiation continued apace, alongside and perhaps beneath half-hearted homogenizing campaigns.

The Jews of the Pale of Settlement offer a case in point. Eugene Avrutin argues that beginning in the 1830s, the Russian regime confronted the difficulties presented by the large Jewish population that they had absorbed from Poland-Lithuania in the late eighteenth century. Jews presented particular problems of "legibility." Instead of the formally regulated baptismal practices that made Christian births easy to record and Christian names easy to track, Jews kept no official records of births (deaths were a different matter). Moreover, during their lives they went by all sorts of different names and nicknames, making it hard for the authorities to keep straight who was who. The state therefore launched a two-pronged effort to register the Jews of the Pale and to "civilize" them, to bring them into line with Russian ideas of propriety and cleanliness. They should register births, adopt and record stable first and last names, and abandon their traditional dress in favor of up-to-date urban couture.

But here the Russian plan ran into a stumbling block: what to do if Jewish subjects took them up on their offer and chose to adopt Russian names? If Moishe the Fishmonger became Ivan Ivanovich Ivanov, if he set aside his dark overcoat and cut his sidelocks, how would one know he was a Jew? This possibility unnerved the authorities, who had mixed feelings about truly "russifying" the Jews, and they continually tinkered with policies in order to guarantee some distinctions. Jews had to take last names, but they had to be identifiably Jewish last names. New forms of sartorial distinction came into play, and modern sumptuary laws regulated precisely who could wear what. The Jews themselves had mixed responses to the web of requirements that enmeshed them. Some tried to evade the strictures of registration and documentation, while others saw the benefits of playing along and even actively sought ways to register themselves in the system.[74]

Russia confronted its "Jewish Problem" as a consequence of one of its most significant imperial relationships, the fraught interactions with Poland, whose large Jewish population suddenly fell under Russian jurisdiction following the partitions. As we have seen, ambitious empires campaigned across Poland during the Napoleonic wars and batted the region back and forth between them. After the defeat of Napoleon and the reassertion of Russian rule, Alexander I's granting of constitutional rule and (nominal) separate monarchical status allowed for a heady, though brief, honeymoon, which soon turned sour as Russian rule manifested its far less attractive reality. In 1830 a group of young Polish military cadets, inspired by nationalist rhetoric and constitutionalist aspirations, sparked

---

[74]Eugene M. Avrutin, *Jews and the Imperial State: Identification Politics in Tsarist Russia* (Ithaca, NY: Cornell University Press, 2010).

a rebellion against increasingly oppressive Russian rule. Their constitutional protections ignored, their authors stifled by Russian censors, their great university closed, the Poles mobilized a broad-based rebellion, but were handily crushed by the Russian army. Nicholas rescinded all vestiges of Polish independence and declared Poland fully incorporated in Russia.

The meaning of this rebellion would seem self-evident: a nationalist uprising in an era of fervent nationalism and commitment to popular sovereignty. Yet loyalties could be as complex and multivalent among Polish nationalists as among the warriors of the Caucasus. The rebels cast their movement not as a fundamental clash between Poles and Russians, but as a struggle to reinstate constitutional prerogatives. They drew inspiration from the Decembrists, whose commitment to freedom they shared. Their slogan, "For your freedom and ours," reflected a misplaced confidence that the Russian people would rise up alongside them. Prince Adam Czartoryski, a leader of the insurrection, wrote in the midst of the uprising, "No nation has the right to impose its opinion upon another, especially [upon] the powerful Russian nation, but [the Russian nation] should know that we, the Poles, wish them happiness, value their brotherhood, and want a union of the Slavs to come into being."

Czartoryski, whom we encountered earlier in this chapter, embodied the impossibility of fitting the people of empire into neat boxes as oppressors or oppressed, colonizers or colonists, or even Poles or Russians. Born into a Polish noble family, Prince Adam took part as a very young man in the anti-Russian insurrection of 1795. Soon thereafter, following the defeat of the insurrection and on the heels of the Third Partition of Poland, he moved to St. Petersburg and, through the prerogative of rank and culture, found a warm welcome in circles of equally aristocratic and educated young men at court. He became in short order a close friend of none other than the young Alexander I and then a member of the Unofficial Committee. Sent back to Poland to reform the educational system, the prince found the reformist aspirations for an autonomous Kingdom of Poland increasingly submerged under Nicholas's repressive rule.

In 1830, somewhat inadvertently he emerged as leader of the opposition, but only slowly relinquished his hope that Poles and Russians, a great, unified Slavic "nation," together could challenge the erosions of freedom. Czartoryski, like others of his contemporaries whom one would expect to adopt a firmly anti-Russian position, instead clung as long as he possibly could to a dual identity as ardent Polish patriot and loyal subject of empire.[75] Exiles who served the empire loyally from distant postings in Siberia, translators wrenched from their natal villages in the Caucasus, Baltic Germans and Greek diplomats in the service of the state, all were able to combine identities and perform loyal service to the empire. Yet these same people, frustrated by imperial intolerance, unable to find congenial modes to realize their "national" aspirations, might then turn to rebellion. Categories that seem transparent and self-evident today and divisions that

[75]Brykczynski, "Prince Adam Czartoryski as a Liminal Figure," pp. 647–69.

we try to impose retrospectively on historical actors are confounded by shifting loyalties of people in complex changing circumstances.

IMAGINING THE RUSSIAN "NATION": BETWEEN WEST AND EAST

Russian writers and thinkers were intrigued by the new languages of politics that flowed from Europe, and already in the eighteenth century and early in the nineteenth they shared the European search for the medieval origins of nations. People were fascinated by the discovery of the ancient poems of Ossian, ostensibly the work of a third-century Celtic bard. Their popularity spread through Europe, even though from the beginning there were suspicions that they were clever forgeries by their discoverer, the Scottish writer James Macpherson (as they indeed were). Ossian was translated into Russian in 1788 and again in 1792. Even more important was the publication in 1800 of the *Slovo o polku Igoreve* (The Tale of Igor's Campaign), a grand medieval saga of heroic battles and tragic losses in defense of the Rus land. The *Tale* was vivid enough to compete with any of the many folk epics in vogue at the time and seemed to capture something of an authentic and vibrant Russian past. The manuscript was found in a provincial monastery as part of a concerted campaign to unearth and place in circulation literary monuments of the Russian past. It was published by Count Aleksei Musin-Pushkin, who then claimed that the sole manuscript copy had lamentably burned along with his entire library and indeed most of the city of Moscow in 1812, leaving only a flawed copy for posterity. Doubt and speculation have attached to this too-good-to-be-true national treasure over the centuries, and like Ossian, the authenticity of this purported twelfth-century epic is suspect. Nonetheless it satisfied a hunger for antiquity and authenticity in a search for a true and distinctive Russian past.[76]

As with other peoples and states of Europe in the post-revolutionary period, intellectuals, particularly historians, were in a sense thinking nations into existence or at least elaborating and propagating the contours, characteristics, symbols and signs that would make the nation familiar to a broader public. From Karamzin's multivolume *Istoriia gosudarstva rossiiskogo* (History of the Russian State) (1816–1826) through the great synthetic works of Sergei Solovev and Vasilii Kliuchevskii, historians treated Russia as a persistent, recognizable polity, something like a nation-state, from the very earliest days of Rus. In many ways their idea of Russia conformed to Western European models though they acknowledged and even emphasized its uniquely multiethnic composition. Karamzin's contribution was particularly significant, for his work was extremely popular among educated readers, and it provided a colorful, patriotic narrative of Russia's past up to the Time of Troubles. The poet Alexander Pushkin proclaimed,

---

[76]Edward L. Keenan, *Joseph Dobrovsky and the Origins of the Igor Tale* (Cambridge, MA: Huri and Dores, 2003).

"Karamzin, it seemed, discovered ancient Rus', as Columbus discovered America."[77] This search for the past of Russia as a nation coincided with the development of an ideology of imperialism and the emergence of Russian schools of ethnography and geography, and was refracted through poetry, novels and short stories, music, and the visual arts.[78]

Convinced of their cultural, not to mention material, superiority over the southern and eastern peoples of their empire, Russian intellectuals and statesmen evolved a modernist program of developing, civilizing, categorizing, and rationalizing through regulations, laws, statistical surveys and censuses the non-Russian peoples of the borderlands. Whatever sense of inferiority Russians might have felt toward Europeans, particularly the Germans and the English, they more than made up for in their condescension toward their own colonized peoples. Occasionally, however, the immensity of the civilizing mission overwhelmed even the most enthusiastic advocates of expansion. Mikhail Orlov, for example, wearily (and prophetically) remarked, "It is just as hard to subjugate the Chechens and other peoples of this region as to level the Caucasian range. This is something to achieve not with bayonets but with time and enlightenment, in such short supply in our country."[79]

The conceptual work of imagining Russia as both national and imperial intensified in the second third of the nineteenth century, as Russian soldiers moved over the mountains into the Georgian principalities, the Muslim khanates, and Armenia. The Russian colonial encounter with the Caucasus coincided with an intense phase of the intelligentsia's discussion of Russia's place between Europe and Asia. In the first decades of the nineteenth century, scholars laid the foundations of Russian orientalism, and through their perception of the Asian "other," Russians conceptualized ideas of themselves. Russian "civilization," usually taken to be inferior to the West, was at least superior to the "savagery" of the Caucasian mountaineers or Central Asian nomads. A compensatory pride marked the complex and contradictory attitudes toward and images of the Caucasian Orient, where Russian authors imagine emotional intensity and primitive poetry mixing with macho violence.

Russian writers created their own "literary Caucasus" that contributed to Russian discourses of empire and national identity that in turn shaped perceptions and self-understandings of the Russian nineteenth-century elite. Admiration for the natural spontaneity of "Noble Savages" paired with a sense that their freedom was excessive, integrally tied to violence and lawlessness. A case in point, Pushkin's evocative poem, "The Prisoner of the Caucasus" (1822), was at one and the same

---

[77]Cited in Olga Maiorova, *From the Shadow of Empire: Defining the Russian Nation Through Cultural Mythology, 1855–1870* (Madison: University of Wisconsin Press, 2010), p. 4.

[78]See, for example, Susan Layton, *Russian Literature and Empire: Conquest of the Caucasus from Pushkin to Tolstoy* (Cambridge: Cambridge University Press, 1994); and Austin Jersild, *Orientalism and Empire: North Caucasus Mountain Peoples and the Georgian Frontier, 1845–1917* (Montreal: McGill–Queen's University Press, 2002).

[79]Quoted in Layton, *Russian Literature and Empire*, p. 108.

time romance, travelogue, ethnography, geography, and even war correspondence. It tells of a Russian soldier taken prisoner by Circassian tribesmen. Both captive and captivated by the life-affirming culture of the mountain folk, the Russian regains his vital fire, nearly extinguished by his jaded, disenchanted cosmopolitan existence. He falls in love with a dark-eyed Circassian girl, who reciprocates his passionate feelings. After she helps him escape, she proves her ardent love by casting herself in the river rather than live life without him.

The poem provided the template and the tropes for many subsequent treatments of the Caucasus. It glories in the sublime landscape: "What scenes of splendor! Mountain peaks, thrones of eternal snows, seemed to the eye like a motionless blank of clouds, and in their midst Mount Elbrus, huge and majestic, twin-headed colossus glistening with crown of ice, gleamed white in the azure sky." It dwells on the "outlandish people of those parts that the European found most fascinating. . . . He liked the simplicity of their lives, their hospitality, their love of fighting, the speed and deftness of their movements, their lightness of foot, their strength of hand." And it situates the "European" Russian in a curious position as the "good prisoner," noble victim, a captive conqueror, beguiled by his fierce captors, but also, ultimately outmanning them, winning both the girl and the battle.

Anthropologist Bruce Grant provides an illuminating reading of Pushkin's epic, which, he says, inaugurated an important trope of self-justification in Russian literature of imperial conquest. The "good captive" brings to the barbaric mountain people the "gift" of civilization, and the best among the tribes-people, sensitive souls like the Circassian heroine, appreciate that gift. The conquered people should be thankful for the Russian's generous civilizing mission, and their resistance shows ingratitude.[80] Pushkin's epilogue supports Grant's interpretation. The closing lines of the poem celebrated the military conquest of the Caucasus and introduced a dissonant note into his meditation on the purity, generosity, and liberty of the mountaineers.

> I shall celebrate our hero Kotliarevskii,
> scourge of the Caucasus:
> wherever his thunderous presence loomed,
> his coming, like the black death,
> brought havoc and destruction to the mountain tribes. . . .[81]

Pushkin's close friend, the romantic poet Petr Viazemskii, was appalled at Pushkin's praise for the Russian generals, Kotliarevskii and Ermolov, who had

---

[80]Bruce Grant, *The Captive and the Gift: Cultural Histories of Sovereignty in Russia and the Caucasus* (Ithaca, NY: Cornell University Press, 2009).

[81]Alexander Pushkin, "A Prisoner in the Caucasus," in *Eugene Onegin and Four Tales from Russia's Southern Frontier: A Prisoner in the Caucasus; The Fountain of Bahchisaray; Gypsies; Poltava* (Ware, Hertforshire: Wordsworth Editions, 2005), p. 137. The notion of the "good prisoner" comes from Bruce Grant, "The Good Russian Prisoner: Naturalizing Violence in the Caucasus," *Cultural Anthropology* 20, no. 1 (2005): 42–43. Shamil "gifted" his son, Jamal al-din, to the Russians as a sign of good faith. Personally raised by the tsar, Jamal became an officer in the Polish guards.

brutally subdued the Caucasians. "If we had educated the tribes, then there would have been something to sing. Poetry is not the ally of executioners; they may be necessary in politics, and then it is for the judgment of history to decide whether it was justified or not; but the hymns of a poet should never be eulogies of butchery."[82]

The young Mikhail Lermontov expressed some of this ambivalence and censure in his poem "Izmail-Bey" (1832): "And the tribes living in those gorges are savage/Their god is freedom, their law is war."[83] For some the "civilizing mission" of Russia in the south and east was paramount; for others, like military volunteers, adventure and a "license to kill" was what they sought. In "Izmail-Bey" and Elizaveta Gan's oriental tales the mountaineers also become the sexual aggressor, "real men" both terrifying and seductive, a threat to the wounded masculine pride of the more restrained Russian. The East invited Russian fantasies about alternate gender orders. For the radical literary critic Vissarion Belinskii, "a woman is created by nature for love," but the Caucasians go too far, making them exclusively objects of passion. Russian writers treated Georgia as a dangerous woman, capable of murder, who had to be dominated for her own good. This deeply entrenched trope about "vengeful Georgian girls" who lay with Russian men appears even in the epilogue of Pushkin's "Prisoner of the Caucasus," intruded as a kind of free association about the eroticism and danger that companioned imperialism. Literature expressed currents of terror, violence, and desire that accompanied imperial advance. It articulated Russian fear of the physical prowess of the Caucasians that extended from the battlefield to the bedroom.

As we have already emphasized, the cohesion of the empire was maintained by more than simple coercion. Although the scorched *auls* in the North Caucasus and the brutal suppression of rebellion in Poland and Lithuania testify to the empire's willingness to use unrestrained violence, in most imperial encounters, people on the margins could benefit in some ways from the connection to the imperial center. In both the empire of the tsars and the empire of the soviets, one occasionally glimpses what Alexander Etkind has called a "reversed imperial gradient," that is, those in the peripheries might live better than those in the metropole.[84] Culture too provided a connective tissue throughout the Russian realm. Political order may have come with the uniformed Russian officers, but so too did Russian literature, painting, and later photography. "In the long run, Russian literature proved to be an extremely successful instrument of cultural hegemony," Etkind tells us. "With its classics, heretics, and critics, it conquered more Russians, non-Russians, and Russian enemies than any other imperial

---

[82]T. J. Binyon, *Pushkin, A Biography* (London: HarperCollins, 2002), p. 148. See also Layton, *Russian Literature and Empire*, p. 53.

[83]Quoted and discussed in Harsha Ram, "Prisoners of the Caucasus: Literary Myths and Media Representations of the Chechen Conflict," *Berkeley Program in Soviet and Post-Soviet Working Papers* (Berkeley, CA, 1999), p. 4.

[84]Alexander Etkind, *Internal Colonization: Russia's Imperial Experience* (Cambridge, UK, and Malden, MA: Polity Press, 2011), pp. 143–44.

endeavor."[85] And yet there was "an uneasy dialectics. The more productive a literary text was in the machinery of hegemony, the more destructive it became to the hierarchy of domination."[86] The circulation of ideas, texts, and historical myth and memory proved to be a dangerous by-product of imperial domination. Just as Russia's rebellious Decembrists provided unintended inspiration to Poland's rebels, Russian literary classics with their humanist values and moral conflicts planted seeds of opposition to the repressive empire in which they had been created.

While expanding in territory and upholding the traditional principles of autocracy and orthodoxy, the Russian monarchy imagined Russia as a modern Western state. But the "West" had changed since Peter's time. No longer embracing the ideal of absolutism, progressive Europe (the one that attracted Russia's intellectuals) increasingly celebrated the principles of nationality and popular sovereignty, industrialism and free labor, constitutionalism and representative government. The task for the ideologists of empire in mid-century was to reconceive Russia as "modern" and rethink its relationship to its own imagined "West." Setting out the terms of what would become an interminable debate, the conservative Moscow university professor, Stepan Shevyrev, wrote in 1841, "The West and Russia, Russia and the West—here is the result that follows from the entire past; here is the last word of history; here are the two facts for the future."[87]

While observers looking back from the future might believe that the great empires of the nineteenth century were doomed to be replaced by nation-states, which in many cases would eventually happen, the imperialists themselves were confident that their empires were viable, indeed admirable, forms of governance that would long reign over and civilize their subjects. They were prepared neither to give in to nationalism nor to accept that empires were archaic. But in the global competition with nations, imperial elites in all the great landed empires—Russia, the Ottoman, and Austro-Hungary—came to realize that they could no longer do business as usual. They needed to face the challenge from their European rivals and America and modernize—whatever that meant and however precarious the road ahead appeared.

BRIEF BIBLIOGRAPHY

Bassin, Mark. *Imperial Visions: Nationalist Imagination and Geographical Expansion in the Russian Far East, 1840–1865.* Cambridge and New York: Cambridge University Press, 1999.

Grant, Bruce. *The Captive and the Gift: Cultural Histories of Sovereignty in Russia and the Caucasus.* Ithaca, NY: Cornell University Press, 2009.

---

[85] Ibid., p. 169.

[86] Ibid., p. 253.

[87] S. Shevyrev, "Vzglad russkogo na sovremennoe obrazovanie Evropy," *Moskvitianin*, no. 1, p. 219; cited in Nicholas Riasanovsky, *Nicholas I and Official Nationality in Russia, 1825–1855* (Berkeley and Los Angeles: University of California Press, 1967), p. 134.

Hillis, Faith. *Children of Rus': Right-Bank Ukraine and the Invention of a Russian Nation.* Ithaca, NY: Cornell University Press, 2013.

Lieven, D. C. B. *Russia Against Napoleon: The True Story of the Campaigns of* War and Peace. New York: Penguin, 2009.

Maiorova, O. E. *From the Shadow of Empire: Defining the Russian Nation Through Cultural Mythology, 1855–1870.* Madison: University of Wisconsin Press, 2010.

Norris, Stephen M. *A War of Images: Russian Popular Prints, Wartime Culture, and National Identity, 1812–1945.* DeKalb: Northern Illinois University Press, 2006.

Raeff, Marc. *The Decembrist Movement.* 2nd ed. Englewood Cliffs, NJ: Prentice-Hall, 1966.

Randolph, John. *The House in the Garden: The Bakunin Family and the Romance of Russian Idealism.* Ithaca, NY: Cornell University Press, 2007.

Riasanovsky, Nicholas V. *Nicholas I and Official Nationality in Russia, 1825–1855.* Berkeley: University of California Press, 1959.

Slocum, John W. "Who, and When Were the Inorodtsy? The Evolution of the Category of 'Aliens' in Imperial Russia." *Russian Review* 57, no. 2 (1998): 173–90.

Suny, Ronald Grigor. *Looking Toward Ararat: Armenia in Modern History.* Bloomington: Indiana University Press, 1993.

SEVEN

WAR, REFORMS, REVOLT, AND REACTION

Russia's engagement with the concept of nation is punctuated by its victories and defeats in wars, nowhere more clearly than through the nineteenth century. The victory over Napoleon in 1812 was claimed by the monarchy, and the role of ordinary people only grudgingly acknowledged. In Russian literary imagination the Caucasian wars distinguished civilized Russians from savage others, though in actual experience the lines were blurred and porous. Confident of its role in the world after Waterloo and the occupation of Paris, Russian authorities boldly intervened in national revolts abroad, encouraged the Greeks, suppressed the Hungarians, and confidently asserted their prerogatives to protect their fellow Orthodox Christians in the Ottoman Empire. When the French emperor Napoleon III forced the sultan to recognize French and Catholic protection of the holy sites in Palestine, Nicholas I countered by sending his troops toward the principalities of Moldavia and Wallachia, then part of the Ottoman lands, to assert his right to protect their Orthodox Christians. Pride and power led to the Crimean War, an unnecessary war so bloody and costly that the folly of war was confirmed in the death of almost 800,000 men, just over half on the Russian side. While blame for the war can be spread to a number of state leaders, "the outbreak of this war," writes David Goldfrank, "was especially the result of the power, policies, and personality of an autocrat who exhibited plenty of 'ill will' as well as pride and poor judgment."[1] Nicholas may have been most responsible, but Orlando Figes notes, "This was a war—the first war in history—to be brought about by the pressure of the press and by public opinion."[2]

---

[1] David M. Goldfrank, *The Origins of the Crimean War* (London and New York: Longman, 1994), p. 271.
[2] Orlando Figes, *The Crimean War, A History* (New York: Henry Holt, 2010), p. 147.

A FOOLISH WAR

Three imperial powers—Britain, France, and the Ottoman Empire—and one ambitious nation-state, Sardinia, allied to take on the Russians after Nicholas's
forces initially defeated the Ottoman fleet at Sinop on the Anatolian coast at the
end of November 1853. Russia dominated the Black Sea from its port of Sevastopol
in Crimea, and the Allies decided to lay siege to the fortress. The war that gave us
Lev Tolstoy's *Sevastopol Stories*, the Charge of the Light Brigade, Raglan sleeves,
the cardigan, and Florence Nightingale—known as both the Crimean War and the
Eastern War—might more accurately be named the Balkan-Crimean-Caucasian-
Baltic-White Sea War, as it was fought from Eastern Europe to Caucasia and
north to the White Sea with a few skirmishes in the Pacific. New technologies,
like explosive naval shells, along with incompetent commanders and medical
failures, led to colossal human losses. The Crimean War was the first major international conflict that people were able to follow almost in real time, thanks to the
advent of war correspondents, the telegraph, steamships, photography, and the

Map 7.1. Crimean War, 1853–1856.

burgeoning availability of newspapers. The death of the emperor on February 18 (March 2) 1855 and the fall in September of Sevastopol after a long siege convinced the new tsar, Alexander II (1855–1881) to sue for peace. The European Powers met in Paris and agreed to guarantee the integrity of the Ottoman Empire. Russia was humiliated and forced to retreat from the Danubian provinces and the fortress of Kars in eastern Anatolia. The Romanov rulers turned inward to assess what had happened and what they had to do about it. Defeat inspired reform.

For the next generations of Russians, rather than the humiliating defeat, the heroism of simple Russian soldiers and the brave, futile defense of Sevastopol became points of national pride. Tsar and nobles could not take credit. This war was seen, most notably by the young Tolstoy, as evidence of something particularly Russian. "Men will not put up with terrible conditions like these," he wrote from the scene of battle, "for the sake of a cross or an honour, or because they have been threatened: there must be a higher motivation. This motivation is something that surfaces only rarely in the Russian, but lies deeply embedded in his soul—a love for his native land." The soldiers with which he served were "joyfully prepared to die, not for the town but for their native land. Long will Russia bear the imposing traces of this epic of Sevastopol, the hero of which was the Russian people."[3]

THE GREAT REFORMS: NATIONS, SUBJECTS, AND CITIZENS

During the thirty-four-year reign of Alexander II, many of the basic premises that had structured Russian imperial rule were challenged by rapidly changing circumstances. The most profound changes were precipitated by the emancipation of the serfs, which at a stroke transformed the meanings of belonging to the empire. Emancipation and the accompanying reforms in other aspects of governance (landholding, law and justice, military conscription, education, health, local governance, economy) opened radically new ways for the imperial subjects to imagine themselves and their collective affiliations with the realm. New categories swirled in political discourse, and new possibilities for reinventing imperial rule through separate deals clashed with the truly radical new concepts of horizontal equality of citizens and uniform guarantees of rights.

The Great Reforms of the mid-nineteenth century at first glance pose a conundrum: why would a non-liberal, self-consciously autocratic regime, wary of diminishing its unfettered authority and openly suspicious of even the most patriotic nationalism, initiate a potentially destabilizing overhaul of society on such a scale? Although numerous factors played into these decisions, the most straightforward answer is that the humiliating loss of the Crimean War (1853–1856) taught the

---

[3]Lev Tolstoy, *The Sebastopol Sketches*, trans. D. M. McDuff (London, 1986), pp. 56–57.

regime that modern wars could not be won on the backs of unfree conscripts, and neither could a creaky economy based on serf labor compete in a world of industrial capitalism. The Crimean War, which bridged the reigns of Nicholas I and his son, Alexander II, brought Russia into conflict with the combined forces of England, France, and the Ottoman Empire, and while all sides suffered huge numbers of casualties, at the end of the day Russia was forced to acknowledge a thorough and mortifying defeat.

Even prior to this loss, the famously rigid and conservative Nicholas I had been considering major reforms, largely with the intention of ameliorating the position of the peasants, streamlining the conscription system, and maximizing the efficiency and effectiveness of the military without bankrupting the state. He had established a commission to investigate the possibility of emancipating the serfs, but considered this a long-term rather than immediate or practicable goal. He implemented only small, piecemeal steps. "At the *present* time," he pronounced to the Council of State in 1842, "any thought of such an undertaking would be neither more nor less than a criminal infringement on domestic tranquility and the welfare of the state. The Pugachev rebellion showed what the turbulence of the mob can produce."[4] Recognition of the imperative to put an end to serfdom, nonetheless, clearly predated the Crimean catastrophe and was impelled by other developments as well.

It proves difficult to quantify the contributions of various factors—economic, military, social, cultural—but all played a part. Aside from the incontrovertible fact of Russia's resounding military defeat, the other pieces of the equation seem to have loomed large in the minds of contemporaries. Participants pointed to economic necessities: the need to modernize the economy to compete on the world market, and create both a pool of free industrial labor and a more motivated and productive agricultural workforce by allowing peasants to farm their own land. Most recent historical studies conclude that Russia's economy was growing at mid-century; agriculture even under conditions of low-yield farming was enormously profitable on the international grain market, and the system had accommodated to the irrationalities of bonded labor and had developed ways to work around the peasants' limited movement. Yet the *perception* that serfdom posed an economic liability pushed political leaders to venture along the risky path of reform. Similarly, regardless of the actual threat posed, which seems to have been minimal, reports on rising numbers of peasant revolts alarmed landholders and policymakers, and memories of the Pugachev rebellion of 1773–1775 were never far from their minds. Where the shade of Pugachev bolstered Nicholas's decision to postpone the disruption that would inevitably accompany reordering the entire society, two decades later, fear of rebellion propelled the move toward emancipation. When Alexander II pointedly remarked to an assembly of the marshals of the Moscow gentry, "It is better to begin abolishing serfdom from

---

[4]Quoted in Daniel Field, "The Year of Jubilee," in *Russia's Great Reforms, 1855–1881*, ed. Ben Eklof, John Bushnell, and Larissa Zakharova (Bloomington: Indiana University Press, 1994), p. 42.

above than to wait for it to begin to abolish itself from below," this was precisely the specter that haunted them all.[5]

Along with perceived need for military and economic reform and social redress, cultural currents swept in the era of reform. Forward-thinking European empires were putting an end to slavery in their territories, and the moral weight of abolitionism was tipping the scales of social thought. Russia (along with the United States, whose own internal dispute about this issue was heated and bloody) was an outlier in this regard, and its reputation as a nation of brutal landlords and debased serfs undermined its aspirations to be taken as an exemplar of Christian monarchy. So powerful was this sweeping revulsion to the idea of human bondage, that it can be counted as an active force, a participant in advancing the cause of emancipation in Russia. Even the staunch conservative historian M. P. Pogodin, ideological supporter of Nicholas I and contributor to the policies of Official Nationality, stated that "the old system has outlived its time."[6] The force of this tidal wave was such that by the mid-nineteenth century even the nobility, who saw serfdom as "neither more nor less than a reliable device for providing them with income," could not defend serfdom on moral grounds. "Even for them, serfdom had no vitality or moral validity of its own."[7]

Despondent over the course of the war, Nicholas succumbed to pneumonia, and it fell to his son, Alexander II, to bring fundamental reforms into being. Alexander's tentative first foray reflected the kind of particularized, piecemeal approach that we have remarked on throughout as a characteristic of imperial rule: he dispatched the reactionary General V. I. Nazimov to collect ideas and opinions from the gentry in the northwest part of the country, near the Baltic regions with their already free peasantry. More comfortable with the idea of stripping the cheap labor supply from Polish noble landholders than from Russian ones, the regime chose this region as a starting place.

In January 1857, Alexander moved a step closer to general emancipation when he established a Secret Committee on the "Peasant Question" and staffed it with a stodgy collection of supporters of the status quo. Word of the Committee's existence leaked out, thanks in part to the lightened censorship regime that Alexander had already initiated, and soon the monarch found it advisable to broadcast publicly the fact that reforms were in the works. The Nazimov Rescript, published toward the end of that same year, set out an unambitious plan, but opened discussion and ignited fears and hopes. Further, the Committee, now renamed the Main Committee since it was no longer secret, called on assemblies of provincial gentry to gather together and submit their ideas about the Peasant Question. This invitation to the gentry to participate in the great, formative

---

[5]David Saunders, *Russia in the Age of Reaction and Reform 1801–1881* (London and New York: Routledge, 2014), p. 217.

[6]Quoted in Larissa Zakharova, "Autocracy and the Reforms of 1861–1874 in Russia: Choosing Paths of Development," in *Russia's Great Reforms*, ed. Eklof, Bushnell, and Zakharova, p. 22.

[7]Daniel Field, *The End of Serfdom: Nobility and Bureaucracy in Russia, 1855–1861* (Cambridge, MA: Harvard University Press, 1976), pp. 359–60.

decisions of the realm, even if only by floating suggestions, has been hailed in the historiography as a vital turning point in imperial politics. Perhaps, but we have certainly seen similar openings in earlier centuries, whether with the Assemblies of the Land from Muscovite times or the Legislative Commissions of the eighteenth century. At any rate, by the standards of the nineteenth century, this was a major overture, an opening to elite society.

Gentry reports flowed in, mostly expressing vehement opposition to the whole idea of serf emancipation or demanding inflated payments for everything from landed property to physical freedom, but some, notably the liberal wing of the nobility of Tver Province, endorsed full emancipation with generous land allotments. The job of creating coherent legislation from this tangle of suggestions fell to the Main Committee under the leadership of Iakov Rostovtsev, a former staunch conservative turned dedicated advocate of landed emancipation. On February 19, 1861, the Tsar-Liberator issued the decree of Emancipation, which proved a very mixed bag.

"Emancipation" did not confer instantaneous, sweeping, and generous liberation, the "Golden Charter" imagined by the peasants. Rather it came as a complex, highly differentiated set of regulations, subdivided (as one might expect) by region into four areas (Russia, Eastern and Western Ukraine, and the North-West) and by zones of agrarian productivity, with different rules pertaining to each. Further typological distinctions differentiated various kinds of pre-emancipation bondage: state peasants (those without private landlords), proprietary or seigniorial serfs, and household serfs, each entitled to different terms and settlements. The notion of granting a single, uniform freedom or ensuring what the tsar himself earlier alluded to as "equal justice and equal protection for everyone, so that each can enjoy in peace the fruits of his own righteous labors," was not on anyone's practical agenda.[8] Freedom, to the extent that it was allowed, was apportioned differentially.

The terms of emancipation shaped the lives of peasants and landlords for all of the remaining decades of the Old Regime. Having seen what they considered the unhappy results of the enclosure movement in the industrialized West and, closer to home, of the landless emancipation in the Baltic, the Russian planners understood the importance of providing newly freed peasants with small plots of land. The Russian tradition of enserfment, which, as we have seen, tied peasants to the land but also land to the peasants, may have further eased the way toward a landed solution. But that commitment required expropriating property from the landlords, not an easy prospect in a system governed by and for the ruling class. A few years later the United States would follow a very different course. General Sherman's wartime promise of "40 acres and a mule" would prove chimerical, and nearly 4 million former slaves would be freed with no land at all.

---

[8]George Vernadsky et al., eds. *A Source Book for Russian History from Early Times to 1917*, 3 vols. (New Haven, CT: Yale University Press, 1972), Vol. 3, p. 589.

Seeking to balance the nobility's anxieties about losing their land and labor on the one hand and the perils of creating an incendiary mass of landless peasants on the other, the reforms worked out a compromise solution. Peasants would be granted personal freedom and an allotment of land, but both would come in stages and at significant cost. Emancipation would be delayed for two years, while local "peace mediators" investigated the conditions of each estate and set the terms of land division and payment. Until the formal payment process began, peasants remained in a state of "temporary obligation," that is, prolonged serfdom. Payments would be paid in installments over forty-nine years, but the state extended credit to the peasants, allowing them to make their redemption payments to landlords up front and leaving the state bank shouldering the peasant debt. The emancipation set up a complicated calculus for determining land allotments and payments in a way intended to maximize sustainability for both sides, while in actual fact leaving both sides disgruntled and feeling cheated. Recently, historian Stephen Hoch has suggested that the outcome, with all parties left equally unhappy, suggests a pragmatic and well-intentioned even-handedness in the process, a clear-eyed resolution of an impossible problem.[9]

Along with the commitment to securing land for the freed peasants, the emancipators ensconced a second fundamental principle in the terms of liberation. The peasants were to be freed not individually, but collectively. They would receive their land and be held responsible for redemption payments jointly with their fellow villagers in their communes. The commune took different forms in different parts of the country, but the classic model, the repartitional commune, had traditionally been governed by male heads of households, who wielded significant local power. Household plots and kitchen gardens, farming tools and livestock were held separately by multigenerational extended families, but plowland was held collectively by the whole commune and was redivided at intervals and reallocated among families according to their need and labor power. The fields were common property, but families worked their temporarily held strips separately, thereby locking the countryside into a pattern of low yield. The repartitional commune combined the meager returns of small-scale farming with disincentives to invest in improvements on properties allotted for short-term use.

Through the insidious strategy of "collective responsibility (*krugovaia poruka*)," landlords and state authorities for centuries had made peasants responsible for the behavior of their peers, thereby extending the scarce personnel and resources of state control and coopting the population into policing itself. Following these collectivist practices that were so integral to Russian imperial governance, peasants after emancipation were imagined and addressed by the state as they had been previously: in clumps. Since redemption payments were

---

[9]Steven Hoch, "The Great Reformers and the World They Did Not Know: Drafting the Emancipation Legislation in Russia, 1856–61," in *Everyday Life in Russian History: Quotidian Studies in Honor of Daniel Kaiser,* eds. Gary Marker, Joan Neuberger, Marshall Poe, and Susan Rupp (Bloomington, IN: Slavica, 2010), pp. 247–77.

assessed on communes and responsibility was shared among members, the newly liberated agriculturalists were not freed into a world of independent smallholders but of a collectivized peasantry. Agricultural patterns persisted unchanged across the 1861 divide: peasants continued to function in communal economies; and landlords continued to rely on payments from peasant agriculturalists, essentially sharecroppers, rather than investing in more intensive, large scale farming. As Field writes:

> To minimize disruption, the reformers took the economic characteristics of serfdom as their point of departure. For example, the size of the allotments set by statute derived from the size of the allotments under serfdom. The reformers retained the commune, although they supposed it to be a barrier to agricultural progress; they preferred, as the serfholders had, to rely on it as an intermediary, sparing the regime the necessity of dealing directly with twenty-two million ex-serfs.[10]

Even those peasants who chose to leave the village and find work in growing cities or factories would continue to be tied by ascription (*prikreplenie*) to their natal communes, as they had been under the old order. This was meant to prevent the development of what was seen as a dangerous class of impoverished, rootless people who might be disposed to violence. Concerned reformers also felt that the commune would protect peasant agriculturalists from the depredations of profiteers and exploiters. Both of these concerns emerged out of fundamental convictions about Russia and its difference from the West. Peasants were considered vulnerable to schemers because of their supposed guileless simplicity and selfless collective spirit, just as the massing proletariat of Europe's smoke-belching factory towns was seen as emblematic of Western soulless capitalism and anomie.[11] The former had to be defended; the latter avoided at all costs. The preservation of the commune carried another form of collectivism and constriction into the post-emancipation age.

Preservation of the commune was not the only step that the government took toward maintaining social control. Once the proprietary relationship between masters and serfs was severed, the state could no longer rely on the manorial courts and arbitrary authority of the landlords to police the countryside. The regime found itself facing the daunting task of governing its severely under-governed population. In Iaroslavl Province in 1857, 244 policemen oversaw a population of 950,000, spread across nearly 14,000 square miles.[12] A sequence of necessary reform measures ensued. In them, the familiar reliance on

[10]Daniel Field, "The Year of Jubilee," in *Russia's Great Reforms*, ed. Ben Eklof, John Bushnell, and Larissa Zakharova, p. 53.

[11]On the impact of ideological conceptions of peasant collectivism and "backwardness" in shaping visions of progress and reform, see, among others, Yanni Kotsonis, *Making Peasants Backward: Managing Populations in Russian Agricultural Cooperative, 1861–1914* (London: Palgrave Macmillan, 1999).

[12]Robert J. Abbott, "Police Reform in the Russian Province of Iaroslavl, 1856–1876," *Slavic Review* 32 (1973): 293.

categories of legal differentiation warred with an incipient, and for Russian authorities, uncomfortable, impetus toward the horizontal equalities and protected rights of *citizens* of a nation. As the Chair of the Editing Commission wrote in 1859, liberating the serfs would allow the tsar to "create a people in Russia such as had hitherto never existed in our fatherland."[13]

The first, radically equalizing measure, was the reform of the military. The Crimean War had cast a harsh light on the shortcomings of the military: it was too large, and hence cripplingly expensive, but the prospect of releasing large numbers of active-duty soldiers into reserves posed pressing danger. Torn by the draft from their former villages and families, non-serving soldiers had no place to go, and hence threatened to create the nightmare menace of unattached, destitute men equipped with arms. Moreover, the particularities of the old conscription process meant that the military was manned by carefully selected undesirables. In the face of mandatory conscription quotas, landlords, bailiffs, and peasant patriarchs had traditionally colluded to round up the weak and the troublemakers for the draft, ridding themselves of unwanted mouths to feed by foisting them off on the state. Treatment of these miserable soldiers was brutal, training minimal, munitions and supplies chronically inadequate, and military results consequently unsatisfactory.

With emancipation, the military faced new challenges. No longer reliant on serf-conscripts, Dmitrii Miliutin, the war minister, instituted radical changes. In 1874, the draft became the most egalitarian and universal institution in the realm: at the age of twenty almost every male, from noble to peasant, was eligible to be called. Yet there were many exceptions in accordance with the imperial vision that still informed even the most equalizing reforms. Tribal peoples of Central Asia were exempted until 1916 when the effort to conscript them into labor battalions in the midst of the First World War would provoke ferocious resistance. Muslims in the Caucasus were not drafted but could volunteer to serve; Finns were required to serve but only in Finland; and Jews were not permitted to become officers.[14] In place of the brutal treatment of recruits and soldiers, Miliutin instituted a more dignified process, and he developed for the first time serious programs for educating and training his troops. Under his leadership, the military became a forward-looking supporter of education, even opening higher education and medical schools to women.[15]

---

[13]M. D. Dolbilov, "The Emancipation Reform of 1861 in Russia and the Nationalism of the Imperial Bureaucracy," in *The Construction and Deconstruction of National Histories in Slavic Eurasia*, ed. T. Tayashi (Sapporo: Hokkaido University Press, 2003), p. 209.

[14]Robert F. Baumann, "Universal Service Reform and Russia's Imperial Dilemma," *War and Society* 4, no. 2 (1986): 131–49; and his "Subject Nationalities in the Military Service of Imperial Russia," *Slavic Review* 46, nos. 3/4 (Autumn–Winter 1987): 489–502; and David Schimmelpenninck and Bruce Menning, eds., *Reforming the Tsar's Army: Military Innovation in Imperial Russia From Peter the Great to the Revolution* (Washington, DC: Woodrow Wilson Center; Cambridge: Cambridge University Press, 2004).

[15]Christine Johanson, *Women's Struggle for Higher Education in Russia, 1855–1900* (Kingston, Ontario: McGill–Queen's University Press, 1987).

PARTICIPATORY POLITICS
AND CATEGORIES OF DIFFERENCE

Facing a population of former serfs, the government took steps to concoct new modes and nodes of governance. Although peasants would be included in some of the new administrative bodies, they were generally treated differently and given their own special institutions. At the most local level, beyond the commune, a network of administrative units called *volosti* (singular, *volost'*) was established for the peasants. Run by men elected by and from the peasantry, the *volosti* directly undercut any impression that the peasants were being integrated into an equal citizenship. At the broader provincial level, responsibility for provincial administration and infrastructure was turned over to newly created bodies that included all classes of residents. These bodies were called "*zemstva* (singular, *zemstvo*)," derived from the word for "land"—*zemlia*—the same root familiar from the *Zemskii sobor*, the Assembly of the Land. As its root implied, the *zemstvo* concept was meant to draw the "people" into the work of administration.

As the glance back to the Muscovite assemblies and other historical examples (Muscovite "elected" elders, the Cossack *krug*, Catherine the Great's Legislative Commission, and the provincial assemblies and assemblies of the nobility instituted in 1785) suggests, the attempt to involve a public in administration or governance was not unknown in the Russian experience. Even the peasants had experienced their own flavors of electoral politics and policymaking within the communal *skhod*, or village council prior to emancipation.[16] Nonetheless, the scale, scope, and practical authority delegated to the *zemstva* were unprecedented. The government entrusted the new institutions with responsibility for local policing, for building and maintaining infrastructure, for the health, welfare, and economic prosperity of the population, and for primary education, a not insignificant remit. They were authorized to impose taxes locally to fund their undertakings.

Given Russia's reputation as a pure autocracy with a crushed and silenced population, glimpsing these forms of participation and seeing them strung together in something of a sequence serves as a reminder that Russia's imperial rulers recognized the importance of allowing at least some of the people some room to express their ideas. As we will see, when these spaces constricted and avenues for expression closed down, important elements of the population were pushed to renounce the system, to stop playing by the rules, to turn to subversion, terror, and revolution.[17]

Zemstva were created at two levels: the district (larger and more socially inclusive than the peasant-only *volosti*); and then higher-level provincial *zemstva*,

---

[16]S. Frederick Starr, *Decentralization and Self-Government in Russia, 1830–1870* (Princeton, NJ: Princeton University Press, 1972).

[17]We find useful the model provided in Albert O. Hirschmann, *Exit, Voice, and Loyalty: Responses to Decline in Firms, Organizations, and States* (Cambridge, MA: Harvard University Press, 1970).

elected by the delegates to the district level assemblies. Calls for additional assemblies at the *volost'* and at the national level were roundly rejected at the top. *Volost'*-level *zemstva* would have conceded unprecedented authority to the peasants without the disciplinary oversight of their "betters." Likewise, a national level *zemstvo* was off the table. Too similar to a parliament, it was seen as crimping the authority of the tsar.

In the tug-of-war between homogenization and differentiation of the empire's population, the *zemstva* were located dead center. While introducing institutions of self-governance, the reformers stumbled over their inability or unwillingness to think beyond categories of difference. District-level representatives were elected separately by three distinct (though potentially overlapping) categories of people: landowners, urban property holders, and peasants (elected from the *volosti*). Female property holders were accommodated through another form of indirect vote, cast by male relatives. Peasants who accumulated enough wealth to purchase land in the countryside or in towns might qualify as voting members of the top two "curia," but in general peasants remained an indigestible category, one that required its own separate representative box. Differential and hierarchical imperial distinctions remained largely intact, and any notion of equal citizenry was decisively blocked.

The same typological distinctions spilled over into the court reforms. A fundamental overhaul of the justice system in 1864 introduced trial by jury and the defense of the accused by professional lawyers. Courtrooms were opened to the public. Judges were granted life tenure, meaning immunity from removal on arbitrary or political grounds. At the district level, courts with jurisdiction over misdemeanors were staffed by Justices of the Peace elected by the district *zemstva* from among educated landholding residents. Courts were open to all. Yet, *volost'* courts remained a set-apart legal venue where peasants could pursue their legal disputes outside the general judicial system. The reformers argued for this on protective grounds. A leading reformer, Prince Vladimir Cherkasskii, reportedly said: "Only such an order [*soslovie-* or social estate–based peasant administration] will be able to resist the nobility's efforts to keep all of the peasant population in patrimonial administrative or at least economical dependency."[18] Jane Burbank shows how avidly the peasants used these courts and how keenly they developed a sense of the promise and pitfalls of the law.[19]

The peasants were not the only anomalous group singled out for special treatment. The entire *zemstvo* project was limited to territories and populations in the core European Russian lands. Neither the three Baltic provinces nor the nine western provinces constituted from the former holdings of Poland-Lithuania received *zemstva*. They were excluded on the grounds of insufficient Russianness. The State Council vetoed the option of creating *zemstva* in the Baltic province in

---

[18]Quoted in Dolbilov, "The Emancipation Reform of 1861," p. 228.
[19]Jane Burbank, *Russian Peasants Go to Court: Legal Culture in the Countryside, 1905–1917* (Bloomington: Indiana University Press, 2004).

1887, "for, in its opinion, no matter how skillfully self-government would be organized, it would be entirely in the hands of the German nobility," the preponderant landowning group in the region.[20] German nobles were suspect on the basis of their collective identity alone. Similar reluctance to create institutions that might be dominated by Polish nobles complicated the creation of *zemstva* in the western borderlands. The Don Cossacks experienced a brief period of *zemstvo* administration between 1876 and 1882, but it fell apart precisely on the issue of categorization: the Cossacks resisted what they perceived as the *zemstvo*'s threat to their unique standing as a privileged military caste.[21] The *zemstvo* system was not extended to Siberia, which was governed by a separate administrative structure. In the Caucasus, only recently and incompletely "pacified," the idea was a non-starter, and in Central Asia, where the empire was making significant advances at just the same time as the reforms were instituted, the state asserted its rule in a more conventionally colonial manner. The government extended the system to several more provinces in the early twentieth century, but in each case, the argument for extending the system wrestled with the tendency toward differentiation. The familiar push and pull between integrated uniformity and rule through distinction thus was fully in evidence. Many intellectuals and some reformist government officials were intrigued by new concepts of community based on citizenship and equality before the law.[22] Others were passionate about ethnic, linguistic, and cultural "Russianness," however they understood it, and wanted to preserve the privileged status of one people over others.

WHO ARE WE? MORE QUESTIONS
OF NATIONAL IDENTITY

In light of the changing relationship between the emperor and his subjects, or the state and its citizens, the questions about who or what constituted "the nation" that had troubled early-nineteenth-century thinkers took on even more edge. Figuring out a coherent basis for collective identity in the imperial context proved deeply divisive. Cultural historian Olga Maiorova contends that with Russia's devastating defeat in the Crimean War, Russian intellectuals and political leaders began to see the nation as something urgently needed, something to be created or recreated or restored, on which human beings could act and improve. The search for the "authentic Russia" yielded varied results. For the nostalgically inclined Slavophiles, it was what had existed before Peter the Great. For Tolstoy, writing a

---

[20]Quoted in Kermit E. McKenzie, "The Zemstvo and the Administration," in *The Zemstvo in Russia: An Experiment in Local Self-government,* ed. Terence Emmons and Wayne S. Vucinich (Cambridge: Cambridge University Press, 1982) p. 34.

[21]Aleksei Volvenko, "The Zemstvo Reform, the Cossacks, and Administrative Policy on the Don, 1864–1882," in *Russian Empire,* ed. Jane Burbank, Mark von Hagen, and A. V. Remnev (Bloomington: Indiana University Press, 2007), pp. 348–65.

[22]On citizenship, see Eric Lohr, "The Ideal Citizen and Real Subject in Late Imperial Russia,"*Kritika: Explorations in Russian and Eurasian History,* n.s., 7, no. 2 (2006): 73–194.

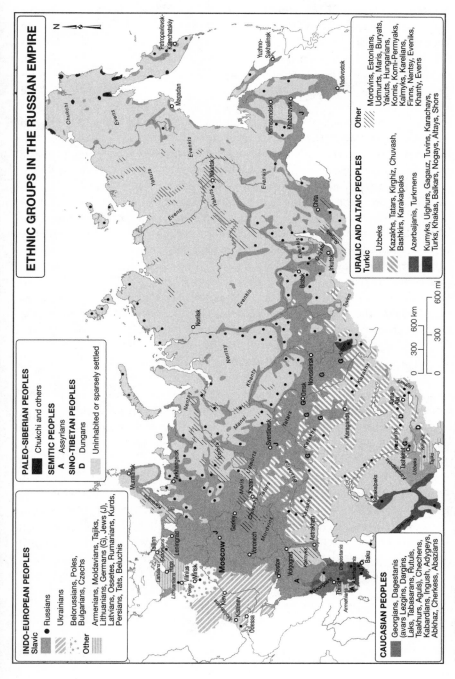

ETHNIC GROUPS IN THE RUSSIAN EMPIRE

INDO-EUROPEAN PEOPLES

Slavic

• Russians

Ukrainians

Belorussians, Poles,
Bulgarians, Czechs

Other

Armenians, Moldavians, Tajiks,
Lithuanians, Germans (G), Jews (J),
Latvians, Ossetes, Rumanians, Kurds,
Persians, Tats, Beluchis

PALEO-SIBERIAN PEOPLES

Chukchi and others

SEMITIC PEOPLES

A Assyrians

SINO-TIBETAN PEOPLES

D Dungans

Uninhabited or sparsely settled

URALIC AND ALTAIC PEOPLES

Turkic

Uzbeks

Kazakhs, Tatars, Kirghiz, Chuvash,
Bashkirs, Karakalpaks

Azerbaijanis, Turkmens

Kumyks, Uighurs, Gagauz, Tuvins, Karachays,
Turks, Khakas, Balkars, Nogays, Altays, Shors

Other

Mordvins, Estonians,
Udmurts, Maris, Buryats,
Yakuts, Hungarians,
Komis, Komi-Permyaks,
Kalmyks, Karelians,
Finns, Nentsy, Eveniks,
Khanty, Evens

CAUCASIAN PEOPLES

Georgians, Dagestanis
(avars Lezgins, Dargins,
Laks, Tabasarans, Rutuls,
Tsakhurs, Aguls), Chechens,
Kabardians, Ingush, Adygeys,
Abkhaz, Cherkess, Abazians

Map 7.2. Ethnic groups in the Russian Empire.

195

bit later, it was represented by the Cossacks, people close to nature, brave, a bit reckless, spiritual, and unpretentious. (His celebration of Cossacks as the quintessential Russians is somewhat ironic, in light of the fact that Cossacks defined themselves in earlier centuries as free men, in explicit contradistinction to servile and enserfed Russians.) For the Westernizer Alexander Herzen, true Russianness lay in the peasant commune with its village council and periodic repartition of land. Herzen saw in this collectivist commune a kind of simple socialism that could be the salvation not only of Russia but of Europe as well.

Advocates of a specifically Russian nationalism encouraged a boom in ethnographic examination of the particularities and charms of the Russian peasants, the *narod*. Supporters of a more broadly inclusive Orthodox or Slavic nationalism embraced the Ukrainians, Belorussians, Lithuanians (proprietarily called Little, White, and Red or Black Russians), and sometimes also others farther afield: Orthodox Slavs in Ottoman-held Bulgaria, Moldavia, and Wallachia. Ethnography provided fodder for these kinship claims, since Slavic languages, folklore, and material culture shared a great deal across nominal boundaries. In a grand gesture meant to solidify these supposedly ineluctable linkages among the Slavic people, enthusiasts organized a great Slavic Congress in 1867, to which they invited representatives from their "brother nations."

The conservative historian Mikhail Pogodin marveled at the pilgrimage of ardent Slavs to the event: "Moscow has become the pantheon of the Slavic world. The Slavs are coming here to venerate [the ancient city]." Adopting a similar tone, the Slavophile Ivan Aksakov asserted that Moscow had become "the focus of moral [and political] energy for all Slavdom." Mikhail Katkov, conservative nationalist journalist and editor, put the case for Russia's political preeminence among the Slavic brethren in blunt terms: "The history of Moscow is a harsh history. . . . But were it not for that harsh past, where would the Slavic world be now and what would have come of the Slavic cause?"[23] In her analysis of the Congress, Maiorova wryly notes that Russian writers may have missed some of the pushback of their worshipful "little brothers" against their political ambitions: "The Russians' thirst for political domination became so obvious at the congress that the Czech delegation felt the need to assert its right to an independent future and demand that the Russians repent their brutal suppression of the Polish uprising."[24] The national aspirations of the smaller Slavic peoples confronted and challenged the imperial nationalism of the self-styled "Great Russians," who identified their national greatness with their empire and its civilizing mission.

In spite of the opening of local governance and the relaxations on censorship that accompanied the Great Reforms, the imperial regime did, as Maiorova suggests, block avenues to mass participation in political life. As its squeamishness about establishing a national-level *zemstvo* demonstrated, the regime feared the

---

[23]Quoted in Olga Maiorova, *From the Shadow of Empire: Defining the Russian Nation Through Cultural Mythology, 1855–1870* (Madison: University of Wisconsin Press, 2010), pp. 170–71.
[24]Ibid., pp. 170–71.

prospect of mass mobilization in any politicized form. Congresses of a handful of professors and dreamers might be tolerated, and assemblies of loyal subjects in officially scripted ceremonies might even be desirable, but once talk turned to the notion of an energized abstraction, "the people," mobilized in pursuit of a political goal, the emperor balked. The conservative patriots who orchestrated the Slavic Congress saw themselves as ardent loyalists and imagined the pious Russian/ Slavic people as worshipfully devoted to the tsar. Yet, to their bewilderment and disappointment, the emperor responded to their efforts with almost as much sus- picion as if they were waving a flag of revolution. Only in manifestations of patri- otic support for the empire's military adventures, where the state relied on popular fervor to win its wars, or in collective rites of worship, would mass mobilization be allowed. Maiorova underscores the ominous effects of this narrowing of channels for popular involvement and expression: aggression, militarism, and righteous violence became the only forms of national activism condoned by the state. Mili- tarism and Orthodoxy together "became a symbolic substitute for mass engage- ment." Reform-era nationalism, she argues, forged and reinforced "a profound linkage between advocacy of war and the empowerment of the Russian people."[25]

Russia's international image, as well as its ability to participate in the imperial practices of the other Great Powers, had been damaged by the defeat in Crimea. The emperor, Alexander II, was determined to reassert Russian interests in Europe and the Ottoman Empire and found an opportunity when the Ottomans brutally suppressed their Christian subjects in the Balkans in the so-called Bul- garian Horrors of 1875. Slavic supra-nationalists known as Panslavists used the increasingly influential newspapers and journals in Russia to stir up public opin- ion in favor of Russian intervention in the Balkans. Although the Ottoman sultan Abdülhamid II (1876–1909) promulgated a constitution to placate European pressure, Alexander was not satisfied. On April 24, 1877, the emperor declared, "The Porte has remained immovable in its categorical refusal of every effectual guarantee for the security of its Christian subjects. . . . Turkey, by its refusal, places us under the necessity of having recourse to arms."[26] The war was short and decisive. Hundreds of thousands of Ottoman soldiers, all of them Muslim (since only Muslims were eligible as soldiers), were killed. Russians quickly ad- vanced within striking distance of Istanbul in the west and Erzurum in the east.

Flush with victory, the Russians imposed the harsh Treaty of San Stefano on the Ottomans and forced them to give up most of their Balkan territories. Serbia, Montenegro, and Romania became independent states; Bulgaria was granted au- tonomy under a Christian prince; and Bosnia-Herzegovina became an Austrian protectorate. Russia gained territory in Caucasia: the towns of Batumi, Kars, and

---

[25]Ibid., pp. 182, 190.
[26]"Manifesto of the Emperor of Russia Announcing War with Turkey," St. Petersburg, April 24, 1877; in *The Map of Europe by Treaty, Showing the Various Political and Territorial Changes Which Have Taken Place Since the General Peace of 1814, IV, 1875–1891*, ed. and comp. Sir Edward Hertslet (London: Her Majesty's Stationery Office, 1891), pp. 2588–89.

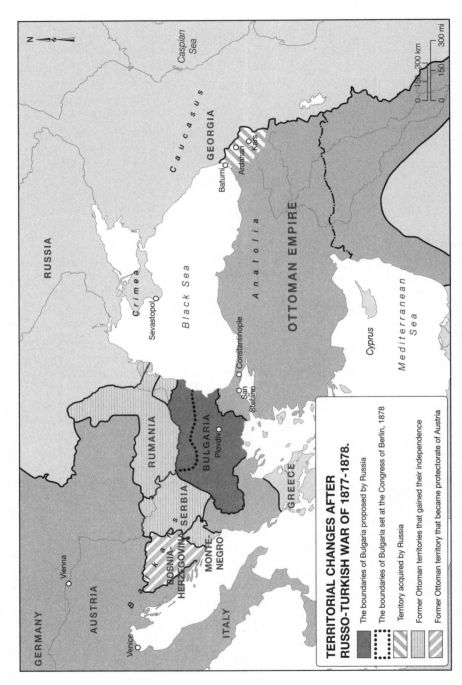

TERRITORIAL CHANGES AFTER RUSSO-TURKISH WAR OF 1877-1878.

- The boundaries of Bulgaria proposed by Russia
- The boundaries of Bulgaria set at the Congress of Berlin, 1878
- Territory acquired by Russia
- Former Ottoman territories that gained their independence
- Former Ottoman territory that became protectorate of Austria

Map 7.3. Territorial changes after the Russo-Turkish War of 1877–1878.

Ardahan, and the surrounding villages. Article XVI of the treaty compelled the Sublime Porte to carry out "the improvements and reforms demanded by local requirements in the provinces inhabited by the Armenians, and to guarantee their security from the Kurds and Circassians."[27] The Russians would continue to occupy the regions until the reforms went into effect.

Russian imperialism justified itself as a mission to protect and liberate fellow Slavs and Christians, as well as "less enlightened" peoples of other religions, but its European rivals saw the tsarist empire as implacably expansionist and a danger to the balance of power on the continent. Although they won the war, the Russians lost the peace. The Treaty of San Stefano was too advantageous to the Russians to be acceptable to the other European powers. The Ottomans found a firm supporter in Great Britain, at least for a few more years, and on June 4, 1878, secretly signed the infamous Cyprus Convention by which the British received the island of Cyprus in exchange for a pledge to fight against Russia should the tsar attempt to keep his conquests in eastern Anatolia.[28] Internationally isolated, Alexander II agreed to send his representatives to a congress in Berlin, convened by the "honest broker," German chancellor Otto von Bismarck, to work out a definitive treaty between Russia and the Ottoman Empire, which reduced Russia's territorial and political gains. Article LXI of the Treaty of Berlin called for reform within the Ottoman Empire but without any mention of a timetable or Russian military presence to ensure compliance. The Armenians living in eastern Anatolia were not to be protected by Russia but by all European powers, which meant they were left largely to the mercies of the Ottoman authorities.

The Congress of Berlin was the last major meeting of the "Concert of Europe," for the Great Powers soon divided into antagonistic alliances. Eventually Russia would ally with Great Britain and France in the Triple Entente, while the "Central Powers," Germany and Austro-Hungary, grew closer to the Ottomans. This was the ultimate configuration that led the powers into the "Great War" of 1914–1918, the first of the two world wars.

RUSSIFICATION, DIVERSITY, AND EMPIRE

By the last quarter of the nineteenth century a robust Russian nationalism—a fervent love for ethnic Russia and its imperial ambitions—inspired both conservative intellectuals and many state officials. But that imperial nationalism (or national imperialism) took different and often conflicting forms. Most perniciously it was expressed in xenophobia and anti-Semitism; more benignly (at

---

[27]Cited in Manoug J. Somakian, *Empires in Conflict: Armenia and the Great Powers 1895–1920* (London and New York: I. B. Tauris, 1995), p. 7. See also Brad Dennis, "The Debate on the Early 'Armenian Question' 1877–1896: Strengths, Weaknesses, Lacunae and Ways Forward," *Middle East Critique* 20, no. 3 (Fall 2011): 271–89.

[28]For an overview of British policy toward the Ottoman Empire and the Armenians, see Arman J. Kirakossian, *British Diplomacy and the Armenian Question from the 1830s to 1914* (Princeton, NJ: Gomidas Institute, 2003).

least in the minds of the powerful and privileged) it assumed the role of benefactor, bearing the gifts of learning and progress to the less fortunate and less developed. The most conventional image of late tsarism's nationality policy is that it was dedicated to Russification. But this image, in which every action from administrative systematization to repression of national movements is homogenized into a seemingly consistent program, is sorely deficient. In Russia, Russification had at least three distinct meanings. For Catherine the Great and Nicholas I, Russification was a state policy of unifying and making uniform the administrative practices of the empire. Second, there was a spontaneous process of self-adaptation of people to the norms of life and language in the Russian Empire, an unplanned Russification that was quite noticeable among the peoples of the Volga region and the western Slavic peoples and continued to be particularly powerful in the middle decades of the nineteenth century when the empire was inclusive and relatively tolerant (except toward Poles and Ukrainians). Learning the ropes—linguistically, pragmatically—appealed to non-Russians as an available path to European enlightenment and progress, or simply as a way to advance and survive in an imperial environment. The third form of Russification was the effort to "make Russian" in a cultural sense. Cultural Russification was a latecomer to the arsenal of tsarist state-building and was a reaction to the nationalisms of non-Russians that the governments of Alexander III and Nicholas II exaggerated beyond their actual strength.[29] The government considered all Slavs potential or actual Russians, and to lend force to that article of faith, officials restricted Polish higher education and the use of Ukrainian.[30] The Polish university in Wilno [Vilno] was closed after the rebellion of 1830–1831, only to be reopened later in Kiev as a Russian university. Alexander III's advisers Dmitrii Tolstoi and Konstantin Pobedonostev equated Russianness and Orthodoxy and were particularly hostile to Catholics and Jews. Even Orthodox students were to be educated in Russian, whether or not they considered themselves Ukrainian, Belorussian, Georgian, or Bessarabian.

Inconsistency and contradiction were hallmarks of tsarism's policies toward non-Russians. Rather than make everyone in the empire "Russian," Russian colonizers adopted the notion of "civility" (*grazhdanstvennost'*) as a way of expressing both the civilizing mission of the empire and a sense of the civic virtues that would

[29]On the varieties of Russification, see Edward C. Thaden, ed., *Russification in the Baltic Provinces and Finland, 1855–1914* (Princeton, NJ: Princeton University Press, 1981), pp. 7–9, passim.
[30]Theodore R. Weeks, *Nation and State in Late Imperial Russia: Nationalism and Russification on the Western Frontier, 1863–1914* (DeKalb: Northern Illinois University Press, 1996), pp. 70–79; Darius Staliunas, "Between Russification and Divide and Rule: Russian Nationality Policy in the Western Borderlands in mid-19th Century," *Jahrbücher für Geschichte Osteuropas*, n.s., 55, no. 3 (2007): 357–73. Dolbilov argues that "Russification" policies varied dramatically, depending not so much on the actual circumstances in situ but on the particular traits considered essentially "Russian," and hence deserving protection. Thus he returns the problem full circle to the cultural conundrum of defining true Russianness (Mikhail Dolbilov, "Russification and the Bureaucratic Mind in the Russian Empire's Northwestern Region in the 1860s," *Kritika* 5, no. 2 [2004]: 245–71).

bring "the other" into a multinational Russian world.[31] Yet at the
same time, as an imperial polity
engaged in both discriminating as
well as nationalizing policies in the
nineteenth century, the Russian
state maintained vital distinctions
between Russians and non-Russians, Orthodox and non-Orthodox peoples, as well as between
social estates. Whole peoples, designated *inorodtsy* (people of other
ethnic origins) and *inovertsy*
(people of other faiths), continued
to be subject to special laws, among
them Jews, peoples of the North
Caucasus, Kalmyks, nomads,
Samoeds and other peoples of
Siberia. Many educated, upwardly
mobile, Russian-speaking non-
Russian subjects, even as they ac-
culturated to imperial society,
found their access to the civil service and upper ranks of society
blocked to a degree. This frustrated
mobility contributed to the growth
of nationalism among peripheral
elites.[32] Both larger and smaller nationalities argued that their ethnicity or religion ought to give them
privileged access to state positions
and that other peoples should be
barred. Tsarism remained ambivalent about nationality until the end.

Hayk or Haig, said by the medieval chronicler Movses Khorenatsi to be a descendant
of Noah, is the legendary founder of Armenia, the eponymous hero of the Armenians.
The myth claims that the mighty Hayk slew
the giant Bel, with an arrow from his powerful bow, thus freeing his people whom he
then led to the lands around Mount Ararat
(*Masis* in Armenian). The image of Hayk
became a vivid assertion in the nineteenth
century and onward of the independent
spirit of the Armenians, who were repeatedly conquered by others but maintained
their ethnoreligious essence.

Yet, the regime's ambivalence of-
fered educated non-Russians some openings. Empire in a variety of ways—by enforcing differences and distinctions, educating non-Russians, and repressing
outward expressions of nationalism—was the crucible of national consciousness.

[31]On *grazhdanstvennost'*, see the essays by Dov Yaroshevski and Austin Lee Jersild in Daniel R.
Brower and Edward J. Lazzerini, eds., *Russia's Orient: Imperial Borderlands and Peoples, 1700–1917*
(Bloomington: Indiana University Press, 1997), pp. 58–79, 101–114; Paul Werth, *At the Margins of
Orthodoxy: Mission, Governance, and Confessional Politics in Russia's Volga-Kama Region, 1827–1905*
(Ithaca, NY: Cornell University Press, 2001).
[32]Anderson, *Imagined Communities*, p. 57.

As a state that valued the conservative values associated with faith in God, the tsarist government was concerned that people have access to religious instruction in their own faith. Therefore, it permitted the establishment of Catholic, Protestant, Armenian, Muslim, and Jewish schools and occasionally allowed non-Orthodox education in languages other than Russian. Non-Christian confessional schools were also allowed to have instruction in other languages, while non-Christian state schools had to use Russian. An Orthodox educational reformer, Nikolai Ilminskii, argued persuasively that the heathen had to hear the Gospel in their own language, and in 1870 the so-called Ilminskii system establishing a network of missionary schools in local languages began to effect "some kind of profound spiritual transformation" in the lives of non-Russian converts and among their Orthodox instructors themselves, who were encouraged to rethink their ideas about the interiority of faith.[33] A regime often accused of Russification in fact promoted the languages of the "small peoples."

Language was the battlefield where empire met national aspirations. The Georgian nationalist poet, Ilia Chavchavadze (1837–1907), proposed a triad for his nation—fatherland, language, faith—and insisted that the duty of women was to bear children and teach them the mother tongue.[34] In the 1880s, young Armenians resisted the tsarist government's closure of their school, depriving them of education in their own language. The shift from religious to linguistic and ethnic identification of peoples as a politically salient category was the unintended consequence of state religious policy. The first Russian census in 1897 differentiated the population on the basis of both language and religion. As elementary school enrollment in Russia increased fivefold from 1856 to 1885 and another fourfold by 1914, the issue of language of instruction became a major concern of the government. Non-Russianness was associated more and more with language, and the government intervened more frequently in favor of Russian education.[35] In 1887, for example, elementary schools in the Baltic region were allowed to teach in Russian, Estonian, or Latvian for the first two years, but were required to teach exclusively in Russian in the last year, except for religion and church singing. Twenty years later, about 1910, "'nationality' had become a politically salient category within imperial Russia. . . . Language-based nationality achieved the status of the primary criterion for distinguishing Russians from non-Russians (and one group of non-Russians from another) by overturning an earlier official definition

---

[33]Werth, *At the Margins of Orthodoxy*, p. 230. Werth corrects the common notion that the Ilminskii system was in any way a formalized system or official policy. See also Isabelle Kreindler, "A Neglected Source of Lenin's Nationality Policy," *Slavic Review* 36, no. 1 (March 1977): 86–100.

[34]Mariam Chkhartishvili, "Georgian Nationalism and the Idea of Georgian Nation," *Codrul Cosmonilui* 19, no. 2 (2013): 189–206.

[35]As John Slocum suggests, "a state policy aimed at language rationalization, when pursued simultaneously with the implementation of a system of public education, induces a politics of nationality when the state encounters entrenched societal actors (in this case, non-Orthodox religious hierarchies) with a vested interest in upholding alternative worldviews." (John Slocum, "The Boundaries of National Identity: Religion, Language, and Nationality Policies in Late Imperial Russia," PhD diss., University of Chicago, 1993, p. 10.)

of the situation, according to which religion was the primary criterion for determining Russianness and non-Russianness."[36] From a politics of difference based primarily, but not entirely, on religion Russia passed to a politics in which nationality counted as never before.

"PACIFYING" THE PERIPHERIES

Russia's reputation as an imperial overlord differs greatly depending on point of view. In general, Russian administrators and military leaders liked to cast themselves as benevolent colonizers, as the gentler, more generous alternative to their Western counterparts. In a poem called "The Two Unions," written in 1870 by one of Russia's leading poets, Fedor Tiutchev, Bismarck's Germany was "a union bonded by iron and blood," "But we will attempt to bond ours with love—And we shall see which is the more lasting."[37] The conventional narrative of many non-Russian peoples and their chroniclers, by contrast, depicts a particular nationality standing up to and opposing the Russifying policies of the imperial state. The story can be told in a lachrymose vein, as a tragic story of oppression, or as a heroic epic of resistance and defense of rightful autonomy. In either flavor, these tales of opposition rest on a certitude about the fixity and sanctity of a primeval national essence. Yet intellectuals and activists were still uncertain about what constituted a nation and what its relationship to the empire should be.

The tsarist government itself actually promoted sub-imperial national cultures at certain times in order to foster greater allegiance to the empire. In 1863, for example, Alexander II granted the Finnish language equal status with Swedish, the official language, in the Grand Duchy of Finland. Such concessions were made to the Finns in order to keep them loyal to Russia and distant from Sweden. Two years later Governor-General Rokassovskii reported to the tsar that there were separatist aspirations in Finland, and he feared that new concessions would not "satisfy the radical party, but merely lead to new desiderata impossible to fulfill."[38] Nevertheless, Alexander III, the tsar most identified with campaigns to Russify his subjects, reinforced the Finnish language decree in 1886.

In the middle of the nineteenth century, Armenian merchants in the Caucasus, who benefited from the *Pax Russica* that the tsar's troops and officials had established beyond the mountains, readily adopted Russian forms for their last names. Georgian nobles, who a generation earlier had rebelled against the imposition of Russian authority and the abolition of the Georgian monarchy and their own ancient privileges, became loyal servitors of the Russian state. During the Viceroyalty of Prince Mikhail Vorontsov (1844–1853) the cosmopolitan city of Tbilisi (Tiflis) enjoyed official promotion of European arts, an opera house, European fashion, and the Georgian and Armenian elite adapted easily to the

[36]Ibid., pp. 4–5.
[37]Quoted in and translated by Maiorova, *From the Shadow of Empire*, p. 174.
[38]Kirby, *Finland and Russia*, p. 55.

advantages offered by imperial authority. The threats suffered in earlier centuries from Ottoman and Persian invaders receded, and the road was opened to young men to travel north to study in Russia. Europe came to the Caucasus through Russia. Imperialism fostered embryonic national intelligentsias, who for decades accommodated themselves to the realities of Russian rule.

The affinity between the national and the imperial did not last forever, however. By the 1870s a number of non-Russian intellectuals emphasized their difference with Russians and saw the empire as a restraint, if not repressor, of their national aspirations. In Georgia some of the very nobles who had fought loyally for the empire now became prominent critics of the regime. Count Dmitri Qipiani's winding odyssey illustrates the evolution of Georgian attitudes. From a rebel against tsarism in the 1830s, this patriotic Georgian became a faithful servant of the Russian state during the emancipation of the serfs, only to turn against the Russian policy of limiting Georgian language learning in the 1870s. Qipiani broke decisively with the regime in 1885–1886 when he denounced the policies of the

Tiflis (Tbilisi) was the cosmopolitan capital of the South Caucasus (Transcaucasia to the Russians). The royal city of the eastern Georgian kingdom, Kartli, it was the administrative capital of the region after the tsarist conquest. Blending elements of East and West, the city served as the political center of the Transcaucasian Soviet Federated Socialist Republic (ZSFSR) from 1922–1936, the capital of the Georgian Soviet Socialist Republic (1921–1991), and the capital of the independent Republic of Georgia since 1991.

Viceroy and demanded that the Russian Exarch of the Georgian Church, who had called Georgian "the language for dogs," leave the country. Instead the government exiled Qipiani to Stavropol where he was murdered by unknown assailants.

What changed between the early 1860s and the 1870s for non-Russians and Russians alike was the intensification of the contest over identities, over the nature of Russianness, and the imperial government's growing fear of non-Russian national sentiments. Often taken as a significant turning point is the January 1863 insurrection of the Poles. Once again accumulated grievances and humiliations, frustrated hopes that the new emperor would restore Poland's former autonomy, and the plans to draft Polish men into the tsarist army exploded into an uprising. Quickly a provisional Polish government was formed, divided between more radical Reds, who were prepared to turn the land over to the peasants, and more moderate Whites, who opposed extensive land reform. The fighting was bloody, and the Russian repression cruel. The rebels hoped for support from Russian revolutionaries and the Great Powers of Europe—Britain, France, Prussia, and/or Austria-Hungary—but no one came to their aid. Even the most progressive Russians viewed the rebellion as an act of treachery and rank ingratitude to their Russian overlords. The same cultural figures who had been grappling with the task of defining and finding (or, more accurately, creating) the Russian nation viewed the Polish uprising with a combination of envy (at their national unity and commitment) and horror. Russian writers drew important lessons about national mobilization, and in reacting against the Polish movement expressed a newly activated solidarity. In a perverse twist, the poet Tiutchev described the Poles as vampires rising from the dead in 1863 to feast on innocent Russian blood. They had been trounced once and for all in 1830, he suggested, and should have had the decency to stay dead.

> A horrid dream has been burdening us,
> A horrid, monstrous dream:
> Drenched in blood, we grapple with dead men
> Arisen in order to be buried again.[39]

Mikhail Dolbilov explains that a remarkable shift in attitudes toward the Poles had taken place since the earlier rebellion of 1830. At that time, the Russians had celebrated their military triumph and the thorough defeat of their foe. After 1863 Russians painted a very different picture, evident in Tiutchev's vampiric metaphor. In defeating these latest rebels, Russians claimed to be throwing off "a Polish yoke" that had long burdened them. They were liberating ancient Russian lands, defending themselves from Polish "poison" or "contagion." In the context of emancipation, they congratulated themselves for freeing the Polish peasants from the oppression of the *szlachta* (nobility). "Such a discursive transformation was completely unthinkable without the 1861 reform. Indeed, the peasant emancipation loosened the Imperial power's tongue, and the tongue was

---

[39]Quoted, translated, and analyzed by Maiorova, *From the Shadow of Empire*, pp. 130–43.

an extremely powerful weapon for promoting the idea of Russianness in the highly contested area of the Western provinces."[40] Inherent in the reform-era formulation was the idea of peasants as innocents, victims of noble exploitation, and embodiments of national authenticity. In Russian vindications of their crushing of the rebellion, the rottenness, superficiality, artificiality, and falsity of the Polish nobility was axiomatically accepted, and the plight of the downtrodden peasants therefore was seen as all the more tragic, especially when those peasants were Orthodox Ruthenians.

Ultimately thousands of Poles were exiled to Siberia, hundreds were hanged. Torn between the usual policy of class-based affinity with local elites against their peasants and the particular revolutionary potential of the Polish nobility, the authorities in this case violated the principle of aristocratic solidarity and mutual support. In one of the empire's ongoing special deals, the peasants, largely Orthodox and Ukrainian-speaking, were categorized as "Russians," and were given expedited emancipation with generous land allotments and rights at the expense of the defeated Polish nobles.

Poland's awkward position in the empire illustrates the persistence of Russia's tendency to rule through distinction, whether in bestowing privileges or constricting them. Poland had been stripped of its status as a kingdom in 1832 when Nicholas I declared the "eternal incorporation" of Poland into Russia and appointed a military viceroy to rule the Poles. With these two measures, the imperial regime attempted to pursue a contradictory double-barreled approach, aiming to eradicate any residual autonomy while at the same time holding the rebellious region at arm's length, underscoring its difference. In the aftermath of 1863, additional repressive measures silenced the lively sphere of political and scholarly discussion that had blossomed in university classrooms and in print. In 1869 Polish was eliminated from secondary schools in Russian Poland, where Polish political agitation had so clearly revealed its dangerous side. A decades-old effort to homogenize the Polish with the Russian economy, long delayed by financial considerations, finally bore fruit, and the Polish currency, the *zloty*, gave way to the ruble. Ekaterina Pravilova notes that the Finance Ministry's drive to develop a "single state-wide currency system" represented an atypical impetus toward homogenization in "Russia's otherwise diverse platform of imperial policies." Even with an explicit goal of unifying the empire's currency, because of the vagaries of international finance, it took over thirty years to achieve that homogenization in Poland. Further, Pravilova remarks, in the spring of 1860, just before the Finance Ministry triumphantly integrated the Polish currency into a broadly revised empire-wide monetary system, a fiscal crisis impelled Russia to grant Finland its own separate currency. She writes: "The introduction of the new Finnish currency is a vivid reminder of the fact that while the Ministry of Finance may have aspired to and even vigorously pursued 'universal principles,' it also never

[40]Dolbilov, "The Emancipation Reform of 1861," p. 231.

developed an entirely consistent conceptualization of regional fiscal policy."[41] Ap-plying this insight to the empire as a whole, it becomes apparent that it could never aspire to "an entirely consistent conceptualization" of anything at all.

Even though the 1863 revolt was centered primarily in the former Congress Kingdom of Poland, and not in the right-bank (western) Ukrainian regions, the tsarist government and important Russian public intellectuals turned against the Little Russian and Ukrainian movements. In July 1863 Minister of Internal Affairs Petr Valuev issued his infamous circular that claimed that the Ukrainian language was a mere dialect of Russian that had been corrupted by Polish in-roads. "There was not, is not, and cannot be any special Little Russian language," he proclaimed, echoing the even more extreme statement of the influential Russian journalist Mikhail Katkov that "Ukraine has never had its own history, its own government, and the Ukrainian people are purely Russian people."[42] (One might respond to these bits of nineteenth-century arrogance with an adage sometimes attributed to the Yiddish linguist Max Weinreich: "A language is a dialect with an army and navy.") After Valuev's circular, publishing in the Ukrainian language nearly ceased within the Russian Empire. Hostility toward potential separatists extended even to the circle of self-designated "Little Russianists," a faction that in fact supported amalgamation of the Ukrainian speakers with the other Russians within the imperial setting. There was an ugly side to the Little Russian ideal: it rested its case for the unity of Ukrainians and Russians posi-tively on their common identity and negatively on their common cause against Poles and Jews.

Looking westward, the tsarist government sensed threats from potentially separatist movements in Finland, Poland, and Ukraine. Two conflicting policies were attempted after 1863 to bring the western provinces under imperial control. Valuev and Katkov both favored working with the "best people," elites of what-ever nationality or religion (even Jews!), in estate-based institutions like the pro-posed *zemstva*, which were still in the planning phase, and city councils. Their belief was that class lines were to be exploited in order to diminish nationality loyalties. They could point to the many Polish nobles who had stayed loyal to the empire, as well as Jewish merchants who worked closely with the government and benefited through that connection, profiting richly from the expansion of the sugar beet industry in the south. But another group of officials favored working only with "Russians," by which they meant East Slavs of the Orthodox faith, re-warding them with estates confiscated from rebel Poles. To men of Valuev's ilk, this move would have undercut the economic prosperity of the region by disem-powering successful industrialists and merchants, while encouraging potentially

---

[41]Ekaterina Pravilova, "From the Zloty to the Ruble: The Kingdom of Poland in the Monetary Poli-tics of the Russian Empire," translated by Willard Sunderland, in *Russian Empire*, ed. Burbank, von Hagen, and Remnev, p. 316.

[42]Faith Hillis, *Children of Rus': Right-Bank Ukraine and the Invention of a Russian Nation* (Ithaca, NY: Cornell University Press, 2013), p. 66.

dangerous political activism among the "Little Russians." Ultimately the minister decided to forego implementing the *zemstva* in the western provinces, postponing that incendiary question for several generations until it created a new crisis for the regime in the years just before World War I.

Neither encouraging local culture nor repressing it helped the government to eliminate either the consolidating popular nationalism among Poles or the growing move toward Ukrainian consciousness. In 1876 Alexander II issued the futile Ems Decree prohibiting almost all publication in Ukrainian. The decree, which in part read, "All theatrical performances and lectures in the Little Russian dialect, as well as printing of text to musical notes, are forbidden," only stirred greater animosity toward tsarism. In Galicia, across the border in Austria, Ukrainian activists continued their work promoting Ukrainian identity against the *moskale* (Muscovites) as well as against Poles and Jews. As Jews became prominent in the capitalist development of Kiev and in the profitable sugar beet industry, anti-Semitic attitudes melded with social resentment and fear of being displaced by "foreigners." Strains of both Polish and Ukrainian nationalism, as well as pro-imperial Little Russianism, targeted the Jews as alien exploiters. In the 1840s–1860s, Ukrainian intellectuals and "activists presented Little Russian peasants as the guardians of authentic Rus traditions and celebrated their struggle against Poles and Jews who allegedly had endeavored to destroy their culture."[43] After the assassination of Alexander II on March 1, 1881, anti-Jewish pogroms broke out in Kiev, Kishinev, and other cities, particularly in the southwest. Workers combined their anti-Semitic and anti-capitalist sentiments in a ferocious popular bloodletting.

In those regions where the majority of the population was Muslim, Russian policy was sometimes flexible, sometimes inept, but rarely driven by commitment to procedural or principled uniformity. From the time of Catherine II's conquest of the region in 1783, Russian policy in Crimea, for instance, responded with some suppleness to local practices, both by necessity and by design. Russian preconceptions about wealth and property were confounded in the peninsular world by the different definitions and material realities that placed a higher premium on water than on peasant labor, rendering moot the engrained Russian sense that it was labor that infused land with value. The standard imperial policy of incorporating indigenous nobilities was complicated in Crimea by the incompatibility of Tatar and Russian notions (vague in and of themselves) of what constituted nobility.[44] Missionizing work was prohibited, the geopolitical situation of the region making it far too risky to irk either the local Muslims or their Ottoman

---

[43]Hillis, *Children of Rus'*, p. 13.

[44]Kelly O'Neill, "Rethinking Elite Integration: The Crimean Murzas and the Evolution of Russian Nobility," *Cahiers du monde russe* 51, no. 2 (2010): 397–417; and her "Constructing Imperial Identity in the Borderland: Architecture, Islam, and the Renovation of the Crimean Landscape," *Ab Imperio* 2 (2006): 163–92.

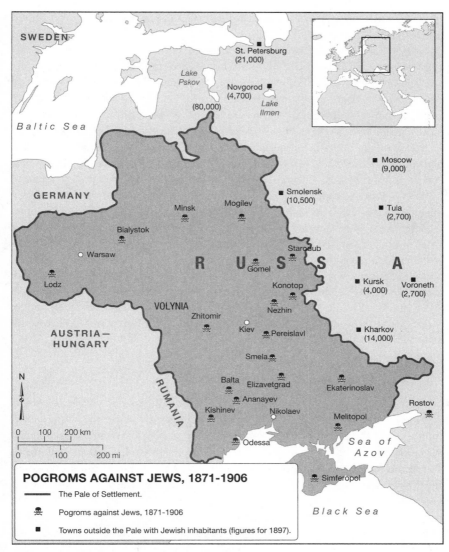

Map 7.4.   Pogroms against Jews, 1871–1906.

co-religionists across the Black Sea. Interestingly at odds with this prohibition on conversion, Russian ideologues placed great weight on Christianizing the beautiful Crimean land, particularly during and after the Crimean War. Looking to medieval chronicle descriptions of Grand Prince Vladimir's conversion in Kherson (Chersones) in Crimea, Russian leaders attempted to deepen their claim to the region by recasting it as a holy land and the cradle of Russian Christianity, but like their forbearers in Muscovite Siberia, their campaign involved constructing churches and consecrating shrines, a pointillist hallowing of sacred spaces rather than a blanket Christianization.[45]

During and after the Crimean War, the tsarist regime grew suspicious of the Tatars and began to introduce harshly oppressive policies, justifying them on political not religious grounds. In spite of the Crimean Tatars' proven record of loyal service in the empire's endless wars, the St. Petersburg authorities came to fear that they were betraying the empire, and no amount of protestation allayed those suspicions. Crimeans documented their military service in the Napoleonic wars and in the intervening decades, and the official Muslim legal official, the *mufti*, ordered his flock to "be faithful to the tsar and homeland." In Crimea itself, witnesses almost without exception affirmed the Tatars' complete reliability, but back in the capital, Alexander II stated that "free[ing] the territory from this unwanted population" would be a "beneficial action." Here was a case where the affective disposition of Russian authorities toward a subject people created a sense of threat that the targeted people were unable to dispel. Emotional attitudes of the rulers, based in anticipated future threats, drove otherwise loyal subjects into opposition or emigration. The turn against the Tatars was so sharp that in 1860–1861 an estimated 200,000 of a total Tatar population of 300,000 emigrated to Turkey. The Russian General Totleben reported that: "The Tatars continued to emigrate in crowds, with tears they said farewell to their homeland, taking earth with them from the graves of their fathers."[46]

CONQUERING CENTRAL ASIA

Intellectuals and government officials believed in the special character of the Russian people, something different from and inherently better than the chaotic amoralism of the West. This sense of superiority provided Russian policymakers with motivation and justification for imperial expansion to the east and colonization of the "empty spaces" of Siberia and Central Asia. The voluminous writings of a conservative nationalist like Mikhail Pogodin, for example, a historian who worshiped Karamzin and held the first chair in Russian history at Moscow University, contained all these themes: Russian exceptionalism, Pan-Slavism, and a civilizing mission in the east.[47] As Russian forces moved into Central Asia, they engaged in imperial conquest of independent, autonomous polities and extended colonial rule through military might. Whereas in the west, Russia met resistance

---

[45]Mara Kozelsky, *Christianizing Crimea: Shaping Sacred Space in the Russian Empire and Beyond* (DeKalb: Northern Illinois University Press, 2009).

[46]Brian Glyn Williams, "Hijra and Forced Migration from Nineteenth-Century Russia to the Ottoman Empire: A Critical Analysis of the Great Crimean Tatar Emigration of 1860–1861," *Cahiers du monde russe* 41, no. 1 (2000): 79–108; quotes on pp. 92, 99.

[47]Pogodin's writings are scattered but can be sampled in N. Barsukov, *Zhizn' i trudy M. P. Pogodina*, 22 vols. (St. Petersburg, 1888–1910); M. P. Pogodin, *Bor'ba ne na zhivot, a na smert', s novymi istoricheskimi eresiami* (Moscow, 1874); idem., *Sobranie statei, pisem i rechei po povodu slavianskogo voprosa* (Moscow, 1978). Riasanovsky, *Nicholas I and Official Nationality*, passim., discusses Pogodin at length.

to its expansion—the Crimean War, the Treaty of Berlin (1878)—and rebellion (the Polish insurrections of 1831 and 1863), the east offered opportunities. With the defeat of Imam Shamil in the North Caucasus, battle-hardened troops were available to be deployed further east. Imperial expansion was motivated by a mélange of motives. Russia's principal concern in Central Asia was neither economic nor religious, probably more strategic at first. Whatever frontier they established had to be defended, and peripheral instability led to pushing the frontier further east and south. Ambitious men in uniform saw opportunity, and instabilities in the Muslim polities only encouraged adventures.[48] Caught up in a drama of international competition and espionage over Afghanistan and Central Asia between Russia and Great Britain known as the "Great Game," Russia marched into Bukhara, Samarkand, and across Turkestan. The energetic General Mikhail Cherniaev seized Tashkent in 1865, creating facts on the ground. Russia's cautious foreign minister, Prince Alexander Gorchakov, opposed annexing the Khanate of Khokand, but abolishing the khanate's autonomy eventually gained powerful supporters in the government. The emirate of Bukhara had its own ambitions in the region, and the British in India were also imagined by some as a threat to Russian hegemony in Central Asia.

The new masters incorporated their new territories through force and ruled them as colonies, some under direct military rule, others indirectly through local leaders. After Konstantin von Kaufman defeated Bukhara and Khiva, they were made dependencies of the Russian tsar but allowed to keep their autonomy. This policy of "indirect rule," familiar to many empires, reinforced the power and privileges of the traditional indigenous elites and preserved customary forms of social and political practice. Efficient as a way of pacifying a foreign people without building a new infrastructure, indirect rule had long-run costs. It consolidated archaic power relations, entrenched hierarchies, and stymied change in a world that was changing. Even in those areas where Russians ruled directly, the military remained in charge, with all of its rigidity and authoritarianism. Civilians became more influential in Central Asia after 1886, yet the administration, manned by petty and ill-educated officials, was marked by callous and arbitrary treatment of the local peoples and pervasive corruption. A cultural and class chasm separated Russian administrators and settlers from the Muslim peoples. Educated Muslims either entered the Islamic clergy or accepted the benefits of European knowledge, mediated through Russian. The Muslim reformers, known as Jadidists (followers of the "new method"), attempted to bring Western learning to Central Asia but found themselves caught between suspicious Russians on one side and hostile Muslim clerics on the other.[49]

---

[48]Alexander Morrison, "Introduction: Killing the Cotton Canard and Getting Rid of the Great Game: Rewriting the Russian Conquest of Central Asia, 1814–1895," *Central Asian Survey* 33, no. 2 (April 2014): 131–42.

[49]Adeeb Khalid, *The Politics of Muslim Reform: Jadidism in Central Asia* (Berkeley–Los Angeles: University of California Press, 1999).

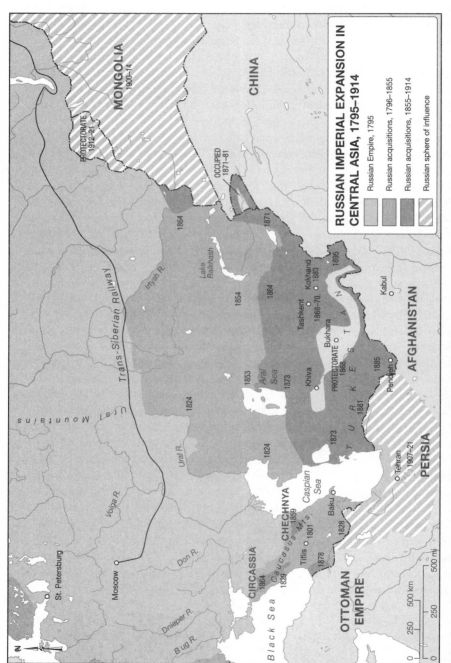

RUSSIAN IMPERIAL EXPANSION IN CENTRAL ASIA, 1795–1914

- Russian Empire, 1795
- Russian acquisitions, 1796–1855
- Russian acquisitions, 1855–1914
- Russian sphere of influence

MONGOLIA 1900–14

PROTECTORATE 1912–21

CHINA

OCCUPIED 1871–81

1864

1871

1895

Kabul

1864

Kokhand 1883

Tashkent 1865

1868–70

Bukhara

AFGHANISTAN

Lake Balkhash

1854

Irtysh R.

Trans-Siberian Railway

Ural Mountains

1853

Aral Sea

1873

Khiva

PROTECTORATE 1868

1885

Pendjeh

1824

Ural R.

1824

Caspian Sea

1873

1881

T U R K E S T A N

1907–21

Tehran

PERSIA

Volga R.

Baku

1828

St. Petersburg

Moscow

Don R.

CIRCASSIA

1864

Caucasus Mts.

CHECHNYA

1829

Tiflis 1801 1859

1878

Black Sea

Dnieper R.

Bug R.

OTTOMAN EMPIRE

0   250   500 km

0   250   500 mi

N

Map 7.5. Russian imperial expansion in Central Asia, 1795–1914.

The images we have of the Russian conquest of Central Asia derive in part from the powerful work of the great military painter Vasilii Vereshchagin (1842–1904). Born into an affluent provincial gentry family, the young Vereshchagin was largely raised by a serf nursemaid, Anna, whom he loved more than his own parents. He developed a concern for the common people, like many other Russian *intelligenty*, and eventually gave up the military career that his parents had planned for him and took up painting. Influenced by the realist philosophy of the radical journalist and activist Nikolai Chernyshevskii, he enthusiastically adopted the creed that art should reflect reality and work to educate and liberate humanity. Trained in St. Petersburg and Paris, Vereshchagin made several trips to the Caucasus where he sketched the local peoples in their exotic garb, in keeping with the current interest in things "Oriental." But his most famous works came from his assignment to the mission of General Kaufman in Central Asia. He believed in the Russian "civilizing mission" in Turkestan, but he was curious to learn the "real nature of war, of which I had read and heard, and to which I was so near in the Caucasus."[50] In 1867 he fought in defense of the Russian fortress at Samarkand and learned firsthand of the brutality of hand-to-hand combat. His paintings from this period made him famous and even brought him to the attention of the tsar. Exhibiting the paintings in London, he wrote in the catalogue: "The barbarism of the Central Asian population is so apparent, its economic and social situation is so low, that the sooner European civilization, from one side or another, penetrates that region the better."[51] In the Orientalist tradition then popular throughout Europe, they depicted the indigenous Muslims as exotics who smoked opium, celebrated victory by beheading Russian corpses, and traded small children for sex.

Despite their exoticism, Vereshchagin's pictures did not glorify the conquest of Central Asia. His series of Turkestan paintings, which combined beauty and barbarism in scenes that illuminated the horrors of war, was bought by the industrialist and art collector Pavel Tretiakov for his Moscow gallery. In 1877–1878 he traveled with the Russian army in the Balkans, once again showing the raw, ugly side of warfare, refusing to glorify Russian arms. Most horrifying of his depictions of war scenes is his *Apotheosis of War* (1874), an unforgettable scene showing a huge pile of skulls, pecked at by crows, in a barren, sunbaked desert.

The tsar, his heir, the grand prince, and the Minister of War Dmitrii Miliutin were all appalled at the paintings and considered Vereshchagin to be unpatriotic, a revolutionary subversive, a nihilist. In response, the painter decided to give up the subject of war. He turned first to religious paintings and then to a series on the momentous events of 1812. But, again, he swam against the patriotic current, refusing to depict Alexander I as the architect of victory. Ironically, the artist who had testified to war's horrors and had escaped death many times was killed on

[50]Vahan D. Barooshian, *V. V. Vereshchagin, Artist at War* (Gainesville: University Press of Florida, 1993), p. 22.
[51]Ibid., p. 34.

Sale of a Child Slave, painted by Vasilii Vereshchagin, 1872.

Apotheosis of War, painted by Vasilii Vereshchagin, 1871.

board the battleship *Petropavlovsk,* sunk by the Japanese during the Russo-Japanese War of 1904–1905.

Like Caucasia, Central Asia can be viewed as a Russian colony.[52] In both areas Slavic settlers migrated into the region, particularly into the fertile valleys of Central Asia, where they competed with the local peoples for the best land and access to the scarce resource of water. Russian officials envisioned both the South Caucasus and Central Asia as a potential source for the all-important crop of cotton that could then supply the textile mills of central Russia with the "white gold" it required. One governor of Caucasia described the cotton growers in 1833 as "our Negroes," but it was only in the 1860s and afterwards, when American cotton exports were curtailed because of the Civil War and the Russian state more securely held Central Asia, that the domestic Russian imperial cotton production took off. By the 1880s, Turkestan supplied a quarter of the cotton for Russian industry, and by 1909 more than half.[53] The growing of cotton was initiated by "thousands of economic actors—smallholding peasants, merchants, and entrepreneurs—in Turkestan itself," who were assisted by tax breaks and subsidies from the state.[54] The practice of transforming the nomadic and settled Muslim peoples of Central Asia into producers of a cash crop was only an idea in tsarist times but continued into the Soviet period with all the attendant social changes and ecological disasters that the ambitious, confident, and shortsighted imperialists failed to anticipate.[55]

COUNTER-REFORMS
AND POLITICAL POLARIZATION

Limited though the Great Reforms were, they opened up political life and a public sphere in ways that had no precedent in Russia. Alterations in censorship laws allowed for animated conversation, and more liberal legislation for universities opened lecture halls to an influx of aspiring non-nobles, non-Russians, women (in segregated courses), and scholarship students. New university charters guaranteed significant autonomy within the walls of the institutions and extended protections to students and faculty from police intrusion and harassment. Selection of department chairs and deans fell to the professoriate, a radical democratizing of higher education. The newly opened law courts drew mobs of spectators, and sensational trials received voluminous commentary, not always complimentary, in the burgeoning newspapers and "thick journals," popular compendia of scholarship, commentary, and literary works. In spite of the negative press it

---

[52]See the discussion in Willard Sunderland, "The Ministry of Asiatic Russia: The Colonial Office That Never Was but Might Have Been," *Slavic Review* 69, no. 1 (2010): 120–50.
[53]Sven Beckert, *Empire of Cotton: A Global History* (New York: Knopf, 2014), p. 347.
[54]Beatrice Penati, "The Cotton Boom and the Land Tax in Russian Turkestan (1880s–1915)," *Kritika: Explorations in Russian and Eurasian History* 14, no. 4 (2013): 774.
[55]Ibid., pp. 741–74.

received, "the jury was simply the most democratic institution in tsarist Russia." Jurors, though all male, came from all classes of society, and "yesterday's serfs could decide the fates of their former masters."[56]

In the midst of all this ferment, the momentum for reform proved short-lived. Already within a decade, the regime attempted to turn back the clock, to slam doors shut or at least push them mostly closed. The trajectory of the courts illustrates this trend: after a series of trials that culminated in unfortunate outcomes in the eyes of the state, many of the protections of public trial were rescinded. The state wanted to take no chances.

Scandalous acquittals of confessed murderers contributed to the retrenchment on the part of the government and disillusionment on the part of educated society. The newly hatched defense attorneys took seriously the task of representing their clients, and through them, exposing the ills of society. In 1878 for instance, the brilliant lawyer Vladimir Spasovich won the exoneration of his client, a certain S. L. Kronenberg, from charges of brutally beating his daughter. Although the man was clearly guilty (the girl's bloodstained clothes and the birch rod were advanced as evidence, and an eyewitness testified that "Now the child sits alone and does not speak to anyone"), the theatrical Spasovich pleaded that the father was simply a product of the brutal society. He argued that Kronenberg should not be penalized for following the violent patriarchal mores of the world he inhabited. The argument convinced the jury, but many, including Fedor Dostoevsky, were shocked by what they saw as crass manipulation of the court. The great writer was one of many intellectuals of the age who viewed the courts as sites of corruption and bureaucratic indifference to the suffering of real people, and he immortalized his critique of the courts in his fiction. The coldness, pettiness, and apathy of judges and juries drew his ire in *The Brothers Karamazov*, where the trial of Dmitrii Karamazov goes terribly awry, due to what Dostoevsky calls an "organic error," that is, what he saw as the fundamental rottenness of formal, legalistic, merciless (in)justice.[57]

The opportunity for lawyers like Spasovich to hone their oratory before rapt courtrooms, to paint dark pictures of the people's miserable lives, made the authorities wary. The courts earned even sharper opprobrium when they allowed revolutionaries and political terrorists public grandstands for propagating their radical creeds. For instance, in 1878 an educated and highly principled young revolutionary, Vera Zasulich, walked calmly into the office of General Fedor Trepov, the governor of St. Petersburg, and shot him in retribution for subjecting a university student to a humiliating beating in violation of his rights. Her lawyer, the same Spasovich, convinced the jury to acquit her by explaining that it was her

---

[56]Louise McReynolds, *Murder Most Russian: True Crime and Punishment in Late Imperial Russia* (Ithaca, NY: Cornell University Press, 2012), p. 8.

[57]Yanina Arnold, "Writing Justice: Fiction and Literary Lawyers in Late Imperial Russia, 1864–1900," PhD diss., Ann Arbor, MI, 2014. Harriet Murav discusses the Kronenberg case as a site for thinking about what constitutes Russianness: *Russia's Legal Fictions* (Ann Arbor: University of Michigan Press, 1998), pp. 125–56.

victim who should be held guilty, whereas she was acting out of pure altruism, sacrificing herself for the good of the people. It is no surprise, then, to learn that in the aftermath of Zasulich's acquittal, political trials were closed to the public, jury trials were drastically scaled back, and judges lost their life tenure, making them more pliable to the demands of the state.

Zasulich won the hearts of the jury by her selfless commitment to service and sacrifice for the good of the much-discussed "people," a commitment that resonated powerfully in educated society. To some extent, the rise of radicalism and terror in Russia testifies to the success of the government's efforts over the previous century or two. Since Peter the Great, Russia's rulers had encouraged their nobles to serve the state, and increasingly service required education. With increasing social mobility, through the Table of Ranks, which allowed non-nobles to rise in state service, and through the opening of schools and universities, ever-increasing portions of the population partook of European-style education.

Already with the Decembrists, the potential dangers of this kind of schooling were manifest. In an era of increasing focus on the *narod*, the traditional emphasis on service took a sharp turn, for those of a radical bent, away from service to the soulless state with its disappointing policies of watery reform, and toward service to the long-suffering, brutally exploited, people. Politically charged notions of citizenship, rights, dignity, and equality and currents of Romantic nationalism intertwined with the intelligentsia's commitment to service and sacrifice. Added to the mix, even for staunchly secular materialists, was Christian reverence for saintly martyrdom. "There are times, there are entire ages, when there is nothing more beautiful, more desirable, than a crown of thorns," Zasulich wrote. "That crown of thorns attracted me to those who perished, inspiring my passionate love for them too. . . . I would seek them out and try to make myself useful to their struggle."[58] This explosive combination had radical implications. In other words, the regime had been right to fear the rise of nationalism. The reciprocity that had always tied Russian elites to their monarchs was compromised. A more meaningful bond for young men and women of conscience was that with the *narod*, to whom many of them owed their comfort, wealth, and privilege. Women, deeply inculcated with lessons about virtue and self-sacrifice, took a prominent role in the radical movement, which also gave them meaningful work and venues for self-expression and serious thinking in a society where they were constricted by both general censorship and gendered silencing. A number of them wrote memoirs, leaving moving accounts of their suffering in pursuit of a virtuous ideal, liberating an oppressed population. One of the means they chose for this campaign was carefully orchestrated assassination.

The radical student movement took many twists and turns on its way to revolution. Mid-nineteenth-century radicals adhered to a variety of political and

---

[58]Vera Zasulich, in *Five Sisters: Women Against the Tsar. Memoirs of Five Young Anarchist Women of the 1870's*, ed. and trans. Barbara Alpern Engel (Boston: Allen and Unwin, 1975), p. 69.

philosophical positions. In 1874 a large group of students and radicals headed out to the countryside with the "To the People" movement, hoping to teach the peasants to revolt, or, alternatively, to learn from them. Some of these people found employment as what was called the "third element," that is, educated professionals—doctors, physicians assistants, teachers, agronomists, statisticians— in the employ of the provincial *zemstva*; others devoted themselves to full-time agitational work. The peasants by and large did not take well to these godless revolutionaries, and the crusaders were treated to a hard welcome. In large numbers they were beaten up, turned in, arrested, and tried. "Going to the People" failed, but subsequent movements developed along a variety of paths, some working toward education, radicalization, and mobilization of the growing class of urban workers, others following a more clandestine agenda of destabilizing the state and society by a campaign of assassination and terror.

In earlier centuries and through to the middle of the nineteenth century, the Russian Empire was fairly cosmopolitan in its recruitment into elites and into government service. But in the last third of the century, in reaction to the 1863 Polish Insurrection, the tsarist authorities became increasingly suspicious of non-Russian nationalisms—of Armenians, Finns, Ukrainians, and others—and favored ethnic Russians for positions in the state and military. The most influential non-Russian official in that period was the assimilated Armenian count Mikhail Loris-Melikov, who served Alexander II in his last years as minister of interior. Pursuing a policy of simultaneous reform and repression, Loris-Melikov hunted down and persecuted revolutionaries while proposing that the emperor allow a consultative assembly to assist him in formulating new laws. The nearest approximation to a national-level representative body that had any chance of gaining approval, this purely consultative assembly would have had no binding force but would have granted one of the central aspirations of reform-minded Russians. This plan offered a fleeting hope of reforging a connection between regime and society and sanctioning a form reciprocity and interchange that was so important to maintaining imperial rule. It never came into being. On March 1, 1881, the very day that the tsar planned to sign the proposal, the so-called Dictatorship of the Heart ended abruptly, when radical populists, a group called The People's Will (*Narodovoltsy*), succeeded in assassinating the tsar. A carefully placed cache of explosives blew up the tsar's carriage. Unhurt himself, Alexander II, liberator of the serfs, climbed out of the carriage to check on his driver. A second blast extinguished his life.

The terrorists had hoped that by killing the tsar, exposing his fallibility and weakness with his bloody corpse, they would dispel the people's naïve faith in the autocrat as a godlike figure with unquestioned right to rule over them. Instead, educated society abandoned any sympathy it had felt for the appealing young radicals, and the common people too seem to have been appalled. In a memoir documenting his transformation from pious peasant to radicalized worker, S. I. Kanatchikov recalled his father's hostile (if poorly informed) response to the assassination. Jews and "nahilists [*sic*]," landowners and students,

Mykola Pimonenko, *Victim of Fanaticism* (1899). Rather than sympathizing with the Jewish victims of pogroms, this painting by a Russian-Ukrainian artist reverses the moral lens and chooses to illustrate Jewish intolerance, persecution by Jewish neighbors of a Jewish woman who converted to Orthodoxy to marry her beloved.

"killed the Tsar-Liberator because he'd given freedom to the peasants. They are all 'Freemazons,'" he added, "they believe in neither God nor Tsar."[59]

Alexander II's son and successor, Alexander III (1881–1894), abandoned the planned reforms and heeded his Russian nationalist advisers who insisted Loris-Melikov be replaced by a "true Russian." The institutions of the empire reflected discrimination against non-Russians, even those in the elite. The *zemstva*, as we have seen, were not extended to the peripheries of the empire (Poland, the Baltic lands, Caucasia, Muslim lands) where the upper classes were made up largely of non-Russians. Both Russian and Polish anti-Semitism (and Alexander III was himself infamous for saying "In the depth of my soul, I am always happy when they beat the Jews, but still we must not allow it") kept Jews trapped in the so-called Pale of Settlement, legislated restrictions on their activities, and prevented them from participating in local government.[60] When mobs roamed through

---

[59]Semen Kanatchikov, *A Radical Worker in Tsarist Russia: The Autobiography of Semen Ivanovich Kanatchikov*, trans. and ed. Reginald Zelnik (Stanford, CA: Stanford University Press, 1986), p. 4.
[60]Richard S. Wortman, *Scenarios of Power: Myth and Ceremony in Russian Monarchy, Volume II, From Alexander II to the Abdication of Nicholas II* (Princeton, NJ: Princeton University Press, 2000), p. 238.

towns beating or killing Jews, the authorities either took no action or were slow to prevent the killings.

EMPIRE AND THE REVOLUTIONARY MOVEMENT

The new ruler, a great bear of a man, Alexander III, set out to quash any and all traces of radicalism. Nonetheless, underground revolutionary political mobilization continued beneath the leaden pressure of state repression, as did reluctantly sanctioned social activity. When a devastating famine struck in 1891, the regime found itself incapable of addressing the situation and was forced to turn to the *zemstva* and other voluntary aid organizations for help. Conscientious nobles, both women and men, liberal and conservative, threw themselves into the relief effort, reanimating the tradition of elite service to the people. Energized by the magnitude of need, the nobles militated for a body that could coordinate relief efforts at a national level, but this request roused the suspicion of the autocrat, who saw it as a sideways bid to forming a nationwide *zemstvo*. In their exchange with the tsar, the enlightened nobility experienced a taste of meaningful participatory politics and then felt the sting of autocratic reaction.

While conservatives generally supported the autocracy and the social hierarchies as they existed, liberals hoped for reform rather than revolution. But their dilemma was that reform, as so often in the past, could come only from the top, from the tsar, and by the end of the nineteenth century the last two tsars abandoned reform in favor of maintaining the autocratic system as much as possible. Meanwhile, radical political movements continued to gain steam in underground organizations. The German philosopher and economist Karl Marx's (1818–1883) important work, *Das Kapital*, slipped past the censors in 1872 and drew readers in its Russian translation. Paralleling the socialists' propagandizing work among the peasants, Marxist groups agitated among the rapidly growing population of urban industrial workers, luring them into literacy circles and study groups and spreading a doctrine of class liberation and revolution to throw off their oppressors. Despite the enormous gulf that divided these two currents of political activity, the conservative and the revolutionary, both stemmed from a deep commitment to serving the people, a sense of entitlement or even obligation to participate in the political life of the country, and ever-mounting frustration with the refusal of the autocratic regime to include them in any way in governance and decisionmaking. Where the mainstream elites saw their commitment directed toward the betterment of the *narod*, the folk, understood as the nation, radicals increasingly defined "the people" in class terms. New collective identities rearranged the already murky social terrain. Heading into the twentieth century, Russian political thinkers and activists reimagined collective identities, solidarities, and affiliations, continuing to mobilize and regulate through categories of difference. Increasingly people spoke of a new social distinction, class, one based on economic position, worker versus capitalist, peasant versus landlord. Class jostled with earlier groupings of estate, ethnicity, language, and religion. Propagated widely by those activists inspired by Marx's revolutionary message, class identification became one of the most salient senses of self for millions of ordinary people.

By the 1890s a major alternative to nationalist solidarity was becoming more widespread: the varieties of international socialism that emphasized class allegiance and the creation of an inclusive movement of all ethnic groups and religions. In many of the peripheries of the Russian Empire—the southwest, Poland, the Baltic region, and the Caucasus—worker movements blossomed. Those socialists advocating a broad-based peasant socialism emanating from the villages—the Populists (*narodniki*)—and those who favored the urban workers—the Marxists or Social Democrats—competed with nationalists for the allegiance of the lower classes. It should not be assumed that national rather than social identity always triumphed, nor was the score sheet always tilted in the other direction. The powerful modernizing message of Marxism convinced tens of thousands of Georgian workers and peasants to align themselves with the Social Democrats rather than the Georgian nationalists. In Finland, workers also gravitated toward the Social Democrats rather than the most fervent nationalists. Movements that were primarily nationalist found support among a few major nationalities—Poles and Armenians in particular—but even with these peoples nationalism and socialism were interwoven. Often the most successful oppositional movements among non-Russians in the empire combined a social resistance to the regime and the rejection of capitalism with the emotions and language of a national, anti-imperial struggle. The popular Polish Socialist Party (PPS), for example, mixed its socialism with a heavy dose of Polish patriotism, while the more orthodox and internationalist Marxist party, the Social Democracy of the Kingdom of Poland and Lithuania (SDKPiL), remained a minor splinter party.

Russia's educational system had contradictory effects on non-Russians. The state set up elite *gymnazii* (classical high schools) in which instruction was in Russian. Although the purpose was to create Russified literate professionals, the combination of a conservative, Russifying education and the actual discrimination and condescension toward non-Russians often produced alienated intellectuals who gravitated to the liberal or revolutionary opposition. The young Georgian Iosip Jughashvili, son of a cobbler and a seamstress, attended the Georgian Orthodox Seminary in Tiflis (Tbilisi) at a time when a chauvinistic Russian administration was hostile to all things Georgian and attempted to turn the young seminarians into priests faithful to church and tsar. Instead, a significant number of the students left the seminary, not as clerics, but as rebels against the tsarist order. Jughashvili never completed the course, joined the Marxist Russian Social Democratic Workers' Party (RSDRP), and later adopted the nom-de-guerre "Stalin." Upwardly mobile, he soon identified himself as an *intelligent*, a member of the cosmopolitan all-Russian intelligentsia, rather than as a Georgian proletarian.

In the early twentieth century, both social-political movements and nationalist movements gained strength. The anxieties produced by capitalist and industrial modernization, the insecurities faced by former peasants as they migrated into unforgiving cities, and the new associations that they made with fellow workers made class even more than ethnicity or religion the most palpable and meaningful identity for tens of thousands of newly proletarianized peasants. Yet both in Russia and on the peripheries of the empire, those abused in society often expressed their social distress in difficult times as if it had been caused by their perceived ethnic and religious enemies. In the revolutionary year of 1905, Azeri Turks and Armenians clashed in the eastern Caucasus; Orthodox Russians in Tbilisi turned on Georgian socialist workers; and in Ukraine, where anti-Semitism ran rampant, the triumph of October 17, when the tsar granted his subjects basic civil rights, turned from liberal and socialist celebrations into vicious pogroms. In the next twelve days, violence, stimulated by right-wing and anti-Semitic organizations with the compliance and assistance of tsarist authorities, exploded into almost seven hundred riots in which over three thousand Jews were killed, over fifteen thousand wounded, and thousands of buildings burned to the ground. Nationalists and monarchists saw Jews as subversive revolutionaries, foreigners exploiting and undermining "true Russians." "Here is your freedom," they shouted, "here is your constitution, here is your revolution."[61] Tsar Nicolas II wrote to his mother: "In the first days after the manifesto, the bad elements boldly raised their heads, but then a strong reaction set in and the whole mass of loyal people took heart. The result, as is natural and usual with us, was that the people (*narod*) became enraged by the insolence and audacity of the revolutionaries and socialists; and because nine-tenths of them are Yids, the people's whole wrath has turned against them. That is how the pogroms happened."[62] Social Democrats condemned the anti-Jewish violence, appalled that many workers participated in the pogroms.[63] "Anti-Semitism is the socialism of fools," they proclaimed, but the equation of Jews with the Left, on one hand, and with capitalism, on the other, proved amazingly durable. This contradictory, but emotionally volatile branding of Jews as agents of capital and communism would resonate through the first half of the twentieth century in the fascist movements that proved extraordinarily powerful in the period between the world wars.

While images of decline and failure often have marked the portrait of late imperial Russia, they belie a roiling, dynamic society undergoing rapid, profound transformations. From the early 1890s until the revolution in 1917 Russia experienced periods of accelerated industrialization, punctuated by economic breakdowns. As in any capitalist society booms were followed by busts, only to revive after painful bouts of unemployment and scarcity experienced by the most vulnerable. The traditional, stable expectations of village life were shaken by the unpredictability and insecurity of an emerging capitalist market economy. For

[61]Victoria Khiterer, "The October 1905 Pogroms and the Russian Authorities," *Nationalities Papers* 43, no. 5 (2015): 1–2.

[62]Cited in ibid., p. 10; and in Antony Polonsky, *The Jews in Poland and Russia, II: 1881 to 1914* (Oxford: The Littman Library of Jewish Civilization, 2010), p. 56.

[63]Charters Wynn, *Workers, Strikes, and Pogroms: The Donbass - Dnepr Bend in Late Imperial Russia, 1870–1905* (Princeton: Princeton University Press, 1992).

many, "all that's solid melted into air," as Marx wrote in *The Communist Mani-festo,* and movement from the countryside into teeming, unfamiliar cities opened the new migrants to new influences. Labor markets in capitalist economies were built on generalized insecurity: there was no guarantee that a person could find a job or that once found that he or she could keep it.[64] Workers found some solace and support from their families, from kinship networks, and with people from their own villages or of the same nationality. They formed *zemliachestva* (home-land groups), worked in collectives of their compatriots or fellow workers (*arteli*), and were exposed to the messages propagated by the older, skilled workers or socialist agitators.

These dynamic changes brought people of the same class together on the fac-tory floor, in workers' barracks, or grimy lower-class ghettos. The effects of invol-untary proximity sometimes strengthened ethnic allegiances, at other times exaggerated social differences within a nationality. Some Jews, Armenians, or Ukrainians were more rapidly upwardly mobile; they learned to read and entered the free professions as doctors, lawyers, agronomists, and so forth; others stayed close to their original occupations as tailors, shoemakers, or petty traders. Coming to town as a villager from a particular region or an ethnic non-Russian from an imperial borderland, workers of the first generation took on new identi-ties consistent with their new lives. Older hierarchical categories based on social estate (*soslovie*) or religion steadily gave way to new loci of identity based on class, occupation, and ethnicity (*narodnost'*). Many married partners of a different nationality—Jews found Russian or Ukrainian wives and vice versa—but few married below their social class.[65] Political activists appealed to them to join their movement. The Jewish Bund worked among Yiddish-speaking Jewish workers; the *Dashnaktsutiun* recruited exclusively among Armenians; but in the multieth-nic imperial setting of the early twentieth century, movements that appealed to a multinational class solidarity, like the Marxist Social Democrats, proved to be more effective in attracting followers than the more nationalist parties.[66]

The major revolutionary movements, Populism (*narodnichestvo*) and Marxist Social Democracy, reflected the imperial setting in which they emerged. Much anti-tsarist protest expressed itself through peasant and worker movements, or liberalism among the middle classes and professionals, rather than as nationalist movements aimed toward ethnic nation-building. Class and nationality over-lapped and reinforced one another more often than undermining and weakening the other. This socioethnic amalgam was expressed forcefully in the language of a class-based movement, like Social Democracy or the Socialist Revolutionary Party, which proclaimed as its goal a universalistic, egalitarian, non-discriminatory

---

[64]Vivek Chibber, *Postcolonial Theory and the Specter of Capital* (London and New York: Verso, 2013), p. 118.

[65]Riga, *The Bolsheviks and the Russian Empire*, pp. 269–70.

[66]"New class identities were gradually organizing around ethnicity. To the extent that socioeco-nomic position was experienced, it was through these more immediate ethnic associations, com-munities, and residential neighborhoods." [Ibid., p. 27]

Table 7.1 Political Parties in Russia, Late Tsarist and Early Soviet Period.

Right

Russian Rightists and Nationalists	made up a group of small political parties—the Union of the Russian People, Russian Assembly, Union of the Archangel Michael—often referred to as the "Black Hundreds." They were vocally anti-Semitic and called for "Russia for the Russians." They supported absolute monarchy, were close to the imperial court, and opposed any significant liberalizing reform. Their social base included a mix of wealthy landlords and disgruntled lower classes in the cities. Their influence dissipated temporarily during the revolution but revived in the White movement during the Civil War (1918–1921).
Octobrists (The Union of October 17)	was a conservative reformist party led by Alexander Guchkov that desired gradual reforms of the autocracy toward a constitutional monarchy. Supported by nobles, bureaucrats, and businessmen, the Octobrists abhorred revolution or radical changes and supported the reforms of Petr Stolypin until 1910. Influential in the Third and Fourth State Dumas, they became largely irrelevant once World War I broke out.

Center

Kadets (Constitutional Democrats)	were the leading liberal party, appealing primarily to the urban middle class and intellectuals and favoring a constitutional monarchy. Led by the historian Pavl Miliukov, the Kadets were particularly important during the First and Second State Dumas, after which the government changed the voting laws to disenfranchise the lower classes and the Left. During the revolution of 1917 the Kadets were a leading party in the Provisional Government working toward a democratic state, but they moved steadily to the right as the socialists gained in influence.

Left

Socialist Revolutionaries (SRs)		the heirs of the Populist Movement of the 1860s and 1870s, the SRs were the principal party that appealed to the peasantry and believed in a democratic socialist revolution by the peasants. Like the Populists, they used individual terrorism as a revolutionary tactic and favored socialism based on the peasant communes.
	Right SRs	during the revolutionary years 1917–1918, this wing of the SR party allied with moderate Social Democrats, the Mensheviks, and supported a bourgeois democratic revolution rather than an immediate transition to a socialist revolution. They won the elections in late 1917 to the Constituent Assembly and fought against the Bolsheviks (Communists) during the Civil War.

Table 7.1. *(continued)*

Left		

	Left SRs	were the more radical pro-peasant socialists who broke with their moderate comrades and sided with the Bolsheviks in favor of Soviet Power and a rapid transition to a socialist revolution. Left SRs were in a coalition government with the Bolsheviks from November 1917 until March 1918, when they opposed the Treaty of Brest-Litovsk and launched a rebellion against the Soviet government.
Social Democrats (SDs) or the Russian Social Demo- cratic Workers' Party (RSDRP)		were the major Marxist political party in Russia. They favored a bourgeois democratic revolution in Russia before 1917 but split into two factions, later independent parties, over questions of organization and the speed of the transition to a socialist revolution.
	Mensheviks	were the moderate wing of the Social Democratic Party, led primarily by Iulii Martov, and favored a bourgeois democratic revolution throughout 1917 and the Civil War. In general, they were more inclusive and democratic in their politics than the more militant Bolshevik wing of the party. During the Civil War they were a nonviolent opposition to the Communists and were forced eventually to dissolve their party organizations. Many of the leaders emigrated abroad. The Mensheviks were particularly popular in Georgia, where they governed an independent republic from 1918 until expelled by the Communists in 1921.
	Bolsheviks (Communists)	were the radical wing of the Social Democratic Party, led by Vladimir Lenin, and shifted in 1917 to advocate a rapid transition to a Soviet Power and socialist revolution. Lenin favored a tightly organized political party that would convey the message of Marxism to the workers, developing their revolutionary consciousness. They came to power in October Revolution, changed their name to Communists in 1918, established a one-party dictatorship, and ruled Russia and the Soviet Union until 1991.
Anarchists		were particularly influential among peasants and sailors and favored a stateless socialism. Not as popular as the SRs or the SDs, anarchists found support among peasants in Ukraine during the Civil War and the sailors of the Kronstadt, who rebelled against the Communists in March 1921.

political order that would respect the cultural differences and rights of the empire's constituent peoples. Russian socialism in the early twentieth century accepted the multinationality of the country of its birth and proposed a future society without class discrimination but at the same time a society with respect for distinct and different cultures.[67] Or, as historical sociologist Liliana Riga puts it, "their socialist universalism contained a certain tension: it was radical in its class attack on Tsarist autocracy but conservative in its desire to preserve the empire."[68]

BRIEF BIBLIOGRAPHY

Burbank, Jane. *Russian Peasants Go to Court: Legal Culture in the Countryside, 1905–1917.* Bloomington: Indiana University Press, 2004.

Emmons, Terence, and Wayne S. Vucinich, eds. *The Zemstvo in Russia: An Experiment in Local Self-government.* Cambridge: Cambridge University Press, 1982.

Engel, Barbara Alpen, ed. and trans. *Five Sisters: Women Against the Tsar. The Memoirs of Five Young Anarchist Women of the 1870's.* Boston: Allen and Unwin, 1975.

Field, Daniel. *The End of Serfdom: Nobility and Bureaucracy in Russia, 1855–1861.* Cambridge, MA: Harvard University Press, 1976.

Figes, Orlando. *The Crimean War, A History.* New York: Henry Holt, 2010.

Hillis, Faith. *Children of Rus': Right-Bank Ukraine and the Invention of a Russian Nation.* Ithaca, NY: Cornell University Press, 2013.

Khalid, Adeeb. *The Politics of Muslim Reform: Jadidism in Central Asia.* Berkeley: University of California Press, 1998.

Kotsonis, Yanni. *Making Peasants Backward: Managing Populations in Russian Agricultural Cooperative, 1861–1914.* London: Palgrave Macmillan, 1999.

Maiorova, Olga. *From the Shadow of Empire: Defining the Russian Nation Through Cultural Mythology, 1855–1870.* Madison: University of Wisconsin Press, 2010.

Riga, Liliana. *The Bolsheviks and the Russian Empire.* Cambridge: Cambridge University Press, 2012.

Starr, S. Frederick. *Decentralization and Self-Government in Russia, 1830–1870.* Princeton, NJ: Princeton University Press, 1972.

Thaden, Edward C., ed. *Russification in the Baltic Provinces and Finland, 1855–1914.* Princeton, NJ: Princeton University Press, 1981.

Weeks, Theodore R. *Nation and State in Late Imperial Russia: Nationalism and Russification on the Western Frontier, 1863–1914.* DeKalb: Northern Illinois University Press, 1996.

Werth, Paul W. *At the Margins of Orthodoxy: Mission, Governance, and Confessional Politics in Russia's Volga-Kama Region, 1827–1905.* Ithaca, NY: Cornell University Press, 2002.

Wortman, Richard. *Scenarios of Power: Myth and Ceremony in Russian Monarchy, Volume II, From Alexander II to the Abdication of Nicholas II.* Princeton, NJ: Princeton University Press, 2000.

Kritika: Explorations in Russian and Eurasian History, n.s., 7, no. 2 (2006): 73–194.

---

[67]Liliana Riga, *The Bolsheviks and the Russian Empire* (Cambridge: Cambridge University Press, 2012); Ronald Grigor Suny, *The Baku Commune, 1917–1918: Class and Nationality in the Russian Revolution* (Princeton, NJ: Princeton University Press, 1972), passim.

[68]Riga, *The Bolsheviks and the Russian Empire,* p. 263.

EIGHT

IMPERIAL ANXIETIES: 1905–1914

No polity exists forever, and many historians and social scientists have been most interested in why empires decline and collapse. Several have concluded that crisis and collapse of empires is written into their very nature. Alexander J. Motyl believes that "imperial decay appears to be inevitable. . . . Empires, in a word, are inherently contradictory political relationships; they self-destruct, and they do so in a very particular, by no means accidental and distinctly political, manner." Collapse stems "from the policies that the imperial elites adopt in order to halt state decline." Whether it was war, in the case of the Habsburgs, the Romanovs, and the Ottomans, that crushed the central state, or the revolution from above, as in the case of Mikhail Gorbachev's Soviet Union, the implosion of the center allowed the subordinate peripheries to "search for independent solutions to their problems."[1] Yet unless one sees an inevitable tendency in empires to enter losing wars, something that can happen to any state, or one believes that events like the selection of Gorbachev as party leader or the adoption of his particular form of reform was unavoidable rather than contingent, then there is no inevitability in the collapse of empires based on policy choices. Empires like those of the Romanovs or the Ottomans proved to be quite viable for several centuries, and the Communist regime proved cohesive enough to withstand the powerful threats and foreign invasions it faced in the civil war and World War II.[2]

Here we suggest that empires dealt effectively over long periods with many internal problems and external threats, but in modern times three principal challenges proved to be particularly difficult to defeat. The increasingly powerful discourse of the nation presented two of those challenges. First, it required that

---

[1] Alexander J. Motyl, "From Imperial Decay to Imperial Collapse: The Fall of the Soviet Empire in Comparative Perspective," in *Nationalism and Empire: The Habsburg Empire and the Soviet Union,* ed. Richard L. Rudolph and David F. Good (New York: St. Martin's Press, 1992), pp. 36–37, 40.
[2] On the surprising longevity of revolutionary regimes, see Steven Levitsky and Lucan Way, "The Durability of Revolutionary Regimes," *Journal of Democracy* 24, no. 3 (July 2013): 5–17.

states represent a more homogeneous and coherent population, which designated itself the "nation," and that its rulers come from that nation, requirements fundamentally at odds with imperial structures. Second, it demanded more egalitarian, representational, and democratic forms of rule that severely undermined imperial justifications. It called for forms of participation that far surpassed the rituals of mercy and inclusion that had bound subjects to sovereigns in the past. Finally, there was what one might call "the imperial dilemma," an unexpected consequence of empires' efforts to address the ideological and political challenges posed by these national ideas. When empires attempted to devise alternative legitimizing formulas, like the *mission civilisatrice* (civilizing mission) of the French to elevate the natives of Africa and Asia or "the White Man's Burden" of Christian missionaries and imperialists bringing Christianity to those they considered heathens, such propositions produced their own subversive effects. Empires claimed to be effective civilizers and modernizers, bringing progress to backward peoples, but when they indeed educated them to the empire's standards, produced effective entrepreneurs, competent civil servants, and free-thinking intellectuals and gave them the tools that enabled self-rule, the colonizers' own logic made the continuance of the imperial relationship of subordination of the peoples of the periphery superfluous. In the eyes of the colonized, that relation came to be seen as hypocritical and a hindrance to further development. In the Russian case, as in some others, it was not so much the failures of the tsarist and Soviet empires that led to collapse but the success of their imperial mission.

THE FATE OF EMPIRES
IN THE TWENTIETH CENTURY

While empires were among the most long-lived polities in premodern history, they operated within a legitimating paradigm completely different from that of the nation—one based on rights of conquest, divinely ordained rulers, and/or mandates bestowed through dynastic continuity. The designated superiors believed they had the right to rule over the inferior, and for long periods those designated as inferior to some extent accepted that inequality as a defining condition of life. Of course, resistance movements and rebellions threatened imperial rule throughout its history: we have touched on fierce revolts of the peoples of the Volga in the sixteenth century, the Bashkirs and Cossacks in the seventeenth and eighteenth century, and the Poles in the eighteenth and nineteenth, and the histories of other premodern empires chronicle equally sharp resistance. Something changed radically in the late eighteenth and through the nineteenth century, however, when the inherited hierarchies that had been acceptable by those ruled no longer were tolerable.

Yet, what looks from the present to have been the inevitable replacement of empires by nations and more democratic forms of governance was not a view accepted by imperial authorities through the nineteenth and most of the twentieth centuries. None of the great European empire states of the late nineteenth and early twentieth centuries—Russia, the Ottoman Empire, Austro-Hungary, or Germany—passively accepted inexorable decline. The great contiguous state-empires of Eastern Europe and the Middle East—the Russian, Persian, and Ottoman Empires—resisted democratization, fearful that concessions to the people would undermine the right to rule of the dominant imperial elite and the hierarchical and inequitable relationship between metropole and periphery in the empire. They borrowed what they could from the West, the model of what passed for modernity, and attempted to adjust to the new constellation of national states, to reform their imperial structures, reshape their ideological underpinnings, and define their own alternative "modernity." Western technology, industrialization, and capitalist relations were introduced into societies with limited social mobility for the majority of the population, privileges based primarily on birth rather than achievement, and autocratic government without institutional avenues of communication from the tsar's subjects upward to people in power.

Imperial modernizers envisioned the empire as a progressive civilizing force leading benighted peoples into a prosperous and secure future. Even Karl Marx and Friedrich Engels, fervent anti-nationalists and anti-imperialists in their own self-conception, accepted the view that the British in India and the Americans, in their dealing with Mexicans, were engaged in progressive projects of introducing bourgeois civilization.[3] The great landed empires dealt with their internal problems of governance in radically different ways. The Russians tried at different times repression, concession, and Russification; while the Ottomans tried constitutional reform, greater centralization, and the multiculturalist approach known as Ottomanism before turning to the most desperate and disastrous policy, that of physical elimination of designated peoples.[4] Austro-Hungarian imperial policy dealt more tolerantly with its constituent peoples, making concessions to the various non-German peoples. These imperial survival strategies, ultimately aborted by the catastrophe of World War I, were attempts at a kind of imperial refurbishing aimed at creating a political community that was multinational or multireligious—a civil "imperial nation"—rather than a single ethnic nation, while at the same time building a more modern state better able to confront the challenges of representation, popular mobilization, and the bureaucratic efficiencies of Western nation-states.

Contiguous empires, like the Habsburg, Ottoman, tsarist Russian, and Soviet, did not have hard borders within the empire, and therefore migration created

---

[3]On Marx and Engels, see Neil A. Martin, "Marxism, Nationalism and Russia," *Journal of the History of Ideas* 29, no. 2 (1968): 239–42; Anthony Brewer, *Marxist Theories of Imperialism: A Critical Survey* (London: Routledge, 2002); and Kevin Anderson, *Marx at the Margins: On Nationalism, Ethnicity and Non-Western Societies* (Chicago: University of Chicago Press, 2010).

[4]Karen Barkey, *Empire of Difference: The Ottomans in Comparative Perspective* (Cambridge: Cambridge University Press, 2008), p. 21, fn. 39. See also Ronald Grigor Suny, *"They Can Live in the Desert But Nowhere Else": A History of the Armenian Genocide* (Princeton, NJ: Princeton University Press, 2015).

mixed populations, highly integrated economies, and shared historical experiences and cultural features—all of which made extrication of the core or any of the peripheries from the empire extremely difficult without complete state collapse. Understandably, in three of the four cases at hand—the Habsburg, Ottoman, and tsarist—defeat in war preceded the end of the empire. And while secession of peripheries weakened these empires, in two of the four cases—the Ottoman and the Soviet—it was the secession of the core from the empire—Mustafa Kemal's nationalist Turkey in Anatolia and Boris Yeltsin's Russia—that dealt the final blow to the old imperial state.

Imperial regimes regularly practiced population politics, fixing some people in place and moving others from place to place. "Tsarist officials," write Lewis H. Siegelbaum and Leslie Moch, "sought to slow definitive departures of peasants from the village by reinforcing communal authority at the same time as they made seasonal migration possible and paternalistically guided resettlement. The Pale of Settlement served to keep Jews away from the Russian interior—until World War I sent hundreds of thousands of them streaming eastward. Similar restrictions kept Chinese settlers confined to border regions in the Far East. Distinguished administrators and lowly soldiers alike found themselves assigned far from home; and thousands of revolutionaries and ordinary criminals went into exile in the Far North, to Siberia and beyond."[5] Slavic peasants moved eastward in large numbers with the often vain hope of farming the Siberian or Central Asian steppe. Demarcating and differentiating subordinated peoples facilitated the empire state's capacities to send people where it wished. Whether it was the Ottoman policy of forced deportations (*surgun*) or Britain's settlement of Englishmen in Ireland or the Jackson administration's driving the Cherokee and other tribes onto the "Trail of Tears," differentiation was the first step in placing some populations at the disposal of a state's imperial and colonizing practices.

When the contiguous landed empires of Eastern Europe and the Middle East were defeated in the Great War of 1914–1918, the victors, led by President Woodrow Wilson, enforced the principle of national self-determination as the new basis of legitimacy. The leader of the radical party that had seized power in Russia in October 1917, Vladimir Lenin, had preceded Wilson as an advocate of national self-determination and fought with some of his closest comrades who as internationalist Marxists wanted no concessions to nationalism. Marxist anti-colonialism, which became part of the Soviet Union's foreign policy and aimed to promote anti-imperialist, national liberationist, and socialist movements, would compete for the hearts and minds of colonized peoples against the liberal anti-colonialism of the United States, which was geared to ending the European colonial empires and opening up the world to free trade, capitalism, and democracy.[6]

---

[5]Lewis H. Siegelbaum and Leslie Moch, *Broad Is My Native Land: Repertoires and Regimes in Migration in Russia's Twentieth Century* (Ithaca, NY: Cornell University Press, 2014), p. 3.
[6]Erez Manela, *The Wilsonian Moment: Self-Determination and the International Origins of Anti-Colonial Nationalism* (Oxford: Oxford University Press, 2007).

Migrant farmstead in the settlement of Nadezhdinsk with a group of peasants. Golodnaia Steppe (Hungry Steppe), Kazakhstan, by pioneering color photographer Sergei Mikhailovich Prokudin-Gorskii, from the album *Views in Central Asia, Russian Empire*, taken in 1911.

Many of the new nation-states that emerged after the collapse of the landed empires had utopian ambitions to empower a single ethnicity—usually the titular nation (Poles in an enlarged Poland, Hungarians in what was left of the Hungarian lands, Turks in Anatolia)—within their borders. Thus nation-making created in its wake ethnic minorities, often plagued by discrimination, forced assimilation, or even the threat of physical annihilation. Just as modern empires attempted to nationalize and modernize to deal with the institutional and discursive shifts that took place with the rise of the nation-state, so emerging nations harbored imperial ambitions. Like the defenders of empires, nationalists thought of themselves as bearers of their own form of progress and civilization. Forced, involuntary assimilation has long been part of nation-making and, given the inequity of power between the dominant assimilating "nation" and what were constituted as "minorities," may be considered profoundly imperial. Despite being brought within the nation, the assimilated often live in a world of continued distinction and inferiority. The homogenization projects of nationalizers, as Ernest Gellner pointed out, make up the "basic deception and self-deception practiced by nationalism," which involves the "general imposition of a high culture on society, where previously low cultures had taken up the lives of the majority, and in some cases of the totality, of the population."[7]

---

[7]Ernest Gellner, *Nations and Nationalism* (Ithaca, NY: Cornell University Press, 1983), p. 57.

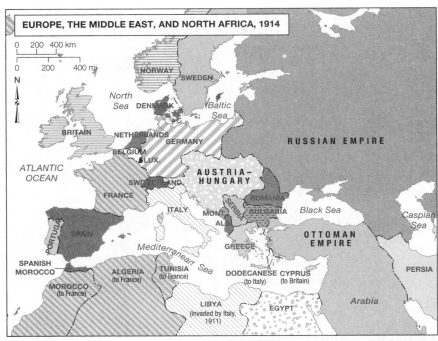

EUROPE, THE MIDDLE EAST, AND NORTH AFRICA, 1914

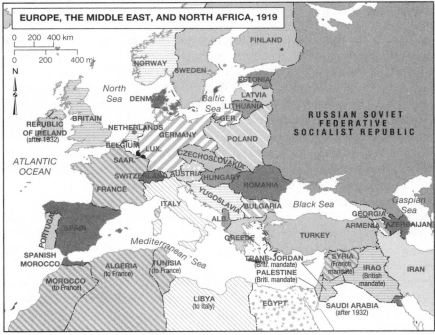

EUROPE, THE MIDDLE EAST, AND NORTH AFRICA, 1919

Map 8.1. Europe, North Africa, and the Middle East in 1914 and 1919.

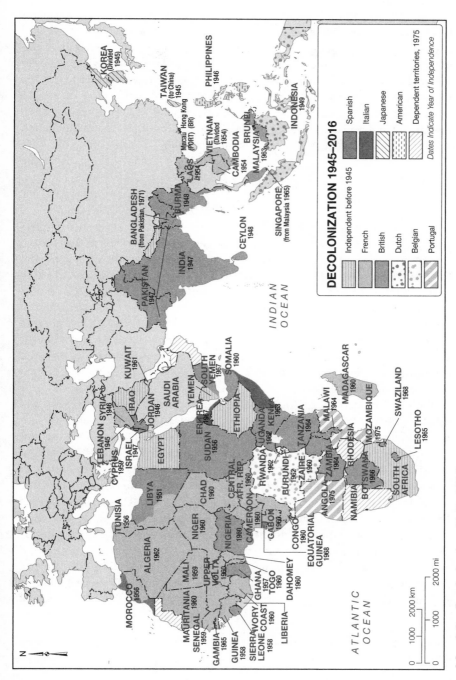

Map 8.2. Decolonization, 1945–2016.

233

Nationalism, then, can easily take on a colonizing form, just as empires are
capable of "nationalizing" their populations, particularly peoples of the peripheries. Assimilation by decree and force could be adopted as a technique of imperial
rule, even though in some ways it runs counter to the preeminent trait of empires, that is, diversity and distinction. In nationalizing projects, when minority
populations were forced to shed their languages and cultures in order to join the
national "we," inclusive impulses were undercut by the imperial or at least imperious enforcement of assimilative requirements. The result in such cases is often
resentment and resistance, and distinctions persist between the dominant nation
and the peripheral, subordinated, assimilated peoples.

THE MODERNIZING EMPIRE
AND ITS DISCONTENTS

In the popular imagination, as well as in the work of many historians, empires
are thought of as backward, traditional, and doomed to disappear in the modern
age. In contrast, we have been arguing that as political formations empires—and
the Russian Empire along with others—were constantly reacting to and adapting
to the monumental changes that took place within and around them. At no time
was this so evident as it was in what is customarily referred to as "modern times,"
the period following the French Revolution, through the nineteenth century into
the twentieth. For all its conservatism, tsarism accomplished much of what the
French Revolution did to *ancien régime* France, ridding it of provincial and local
privileges, abolishing internal duties and tariffs, and standardizing weights and
measures over a broader space.

But the "modernizing" and homogenizing practices of eighteenth- and
nineteenth-century Russian emperors and bureaucrats coexisted with and contradicted programs and policies that moved in another direction, creating new
or reinforcing old differences, distinctions, privileges, disadvantages based on
social class, region, ethnicity, or religion. There was no program, as in France, to
educate and affiliate millions of people around an idea of the nation, turning
linguistically diverse "peasants into Frenchmen."[8] Here the parallels between
England's success in integrating Scotland and Wales and failing in Ireland, or
France's success in nationalizing the "hexagon" (continental France) and failing
in Algeria, are suggestive in the Russian case.[9] Russian nationalists in the final
decades of tsarist rule were dedicated to promoting either a *velikaia derzhava*, a
great imperial state (which we call imperial nationalism), or a single ethnically
Russian nation (ethnonationalism). Other political actors, usually the liberal and

---

[8]Eugen Weber, *Peasants into Frenchmen: The Modernization of Rural France, 1870–1914* (Stanford,
CA: Stanford University Press, 1976).

[9]Ian Lustick, *State-Building Failure in British Ireland and French Algeria* (Berkeley: Institute of International Studies, University of California at Berkeley, 1985). England's success story is looking
less shiny given the powerful resurgence of independence movements in both Scotland and Wales.

revolutionary oppositions, advocated a multicultural political community (civic nationalism) in which all the peoples of the empire were included.

Over and over again Russian officials deferred to a regime of differentiation of rights, advantages, and privileges, or liabilities for the empire's subjects, even as intellectuals and reformers enchanted by Western discourses of universal and equal rights attempted to move the regime in another direction. "[T]he Russian imperial rights regime," writes historian Jane Burbank, "founded on the state's assignment of rights and duties to differentiated collectivities, created conditions for including even lowly subjects in basic practices of governance. Imperial law and imperial administrators recognized status, confessional, and ethnic difference as normal to social and political life. The practice of rule based on difference readily generated appeals for its opposite—general and universal law—among elites, but even after the mid-19th century in an era of self-conscious reform and desired standardization . . . officials defaulted in practice to the habit of manipulable, unequal rights."[10]

Long-engrained imperial practices repeatedly overwhelmed efforts to make Russia more like Western nation-states with their purported horizontal equivalence of homogenous citizens. Rights did not rise up from a sovereign people, though they might be recognized as traditions inherited from the past by particular peoples. "Rights could not be had except through the state," writes Burbank, "and through official identification as a member of one or another kind of collectivity. The recognition of "natural" social collectivity went hand-in-hand with the imperial practice of assigning rights to groups. The state kept for itself the authority to assign, reassign, and take away rights, duties, and privileges from the groups that comprised the empire's population."[11] Rights of even the highest-born were not natural but ascribed, and the nobles understood that their "rights" came from the state and could be withdrawn.

Ruling through difference may have been the general impulse of Russian imperial governance, but at certain times efforts at greater uniformity were attempted. After the annexation of the Georgian kingdoms and principalities in the early nineteenth century, and the recognition and acceptance of the traditional law code and customary laws, the state bureaucrats attempted to harmonize Georgian serfdom and landholding with Russian practices.[12] Intellectuals and officials in Moscow and St. Petersburg periodically flirted with ambitions to make Russia more uniform, more easily legible to state authorities. In the mid-nineteenth century the statist thinker Nikolai Ustrialov saw Russian strength enhanced by

---

[10]Jane Burbank, "An Imperial Rights Regime: Law and Citizenship in the Russian Empire," *Kritika* 7, no. 3 (Summer 2006): 400.

[11]Ibid., p. 403. Also see Ekaterina Pravilova, *A Public Empire: Property and the Quest for the Common Good in Imperial Russia* (Princeton, NJ: Princeton University Press, 2014).

[12]Ronald Grigor Suny, "Russian Rule and Caucasian Society in the First Half of the Nineteenth Century: The Georgian Nobility and the Armenian Bourgeoisie," *Nationalities Papers* 7, no. 1 (Spring 1979): 53–78; and his "'The Peasants Have Always Fed Us': The Georgian Nobility and the Peasant Emancipation, 1856–1871," *Russian Review* 38, no. 1 (January 1979): 27–51.

the "gradual merging of unlike elements into one whole, one unbounded state, where every one submits to the one Russian law, where the Russian language reigns supreme, and the Orthodox Church is triumphant."[13] Although differentiation remained basic to Russian imperial governance, the Fundamental Laws, a kind of limited constitution promulgated by Nicholas II after the 1905 revolution, spoke of Russia as "unified and indivisible" and Russian as the "general language of state." Still, the statute allowed for "special laws" on the usage of other languages in state and public institutions. Even when in 1906 peasants were given the same right as nobles to enter state service, the so-called *inorodtsy*, those "native aliens," thought to be primitive, were not granted these rights.[14]

IMPERIAL OVERREACH: TSARIST MODERNIZATION AND EXPANSION

The late nineteenth century was a time of intense imperialist competition. Along with the "Scramble for Africa" and the rapid acquisition of new European colonies in the subcontinent and in Asia, the great empires extended their physical hold over the far reaches of their states by importing the latest advances of Western science and technology. In the Russian and Ottoman empires as in the Western European empires, space and time were first conquered by the telegraph, built at great effort over vast distances. Railroads and steamships followed. Russian authorities were convinced that railroads could work as a tool of imperial consolidation and control and were fascinated by the possibilities of more rapid movement around their immense realm. A young engineer who later rose to become Russia's first minister of communications exclaimed, railroads had been "invented for Russia more than for any other country in Europe."[15] Railroads were an important means of securing imperial authority over peripheries and even to extend influence across borders. Warsaw in Russian Poland was closer to the Rhine than to Moscow, and the poor roads connecting the two cities made the distance even greater until railroads were built.[16] Nicholas I used the railroad to send his troops to crush revolution in Hungary in 1849, and his son followed suit to put down the Polish insurrection in 1863. When Finance Minister Sergei

---

[13]N. G. Ustrialov, *Istoricheskoe obozrenie tsarstvovaniia gosudaria Nikolaia I* (St. Petersburg: Tipografiia Ekspeditsii zagotovleniia gosudarstvennykh bumag, 1847), p. 167; cited in Willard Sunderland, *Taming the Wild Field: Colonization and Empire on the Russian Steppe* (Ithaca, NY: Cornell University Press, 2004), pp. 126–27.

[14]Burbank, "An Imperial Rights Regime," pp. 419, 422–23.

[15]Pavl Melnikov, cited in Frithjof Benjamin Schenk, "Mastering Imperial Space? The Ambivalent Impact of Railway-Building in Tsarist Russia," in *Comparing Empires: Encounters and Transfers in the Long Nineteenth Century,* ed. Jörn Leonhard and Ulrike von Hirschhausen (Göttingen: Vandenhoeck & Ruprecht, 2011), p. 61.

[16]Frithjof Benjamin Schenk, "Travel, Railroads, and Identity Formation in the Russian Empire," in *Shatterzone of Empires: Coexistence and Violence in the German, Habsburg, Russian, and Ottoman Borderlands,* ed. Omer Bartov and Eric D. Weitz (Bloomington and Indianapolis: Indiana University Press, 2013), p. 140.

Witte laid out the Trans-Siberian railroad to the Pacific Ocean, he promoted a line through Manchuria, the Chinese Eastern Railroad, which encouraged fantasies of eastern expansion for the Nicholas II.[17] Russia competed with Great Britain, France, and Austria-Hungary for influence in the troubled Ottoman Empire. The Germans worked with the Ottomans to link Berlin to Baghdad in a trans-imperial project, and the Russians did what they could to prevent the Ottomans from building railroads near the Caucasian border.

Russia's railroads were a state project built for state purposes. By 1900 the empire had the second-largest rail network in the world, but its colossal size meant that the density of rail connections lagged far behind smaller states like Germany, Switzerland, or the Netherlands. Russia's technological progress did not translate into Western-style political reform. As the dissident Westernizer Aleksandr Herzen ominously warned in an open letter to Alexander II, Russia would use the most progressive elements of the West to reinforce tsarist despotism, creating "something on the order of Chingis-Khan with telegraphs, steamboats, railroads."[18] Movement and mixing of peoples had contradictory effects. On the one hand, migration to distant parts of Russia knitted the empire more tightly together, with Russians settling in Siberia, the Kazakh steppe, and the Far East. On the other hand, the expectations that railroads would integrate and consolidate the empire were contradicted by travelers who as they moved through the landscape did not experience "images of territorial integrity but, on the contrary, strengthened the awareness of the multiethnic and multi-religious character of the huge country."[19] They no longer heard Russian, except among their fellow passengers, and noticed in particular the presence of Jews, the eternal internal "other," in the western borderlands.[20] Five million settlers moved by rail from the western provinces of Russia to settle in Siberia and the Far East, to the dismay of the indigenous populations and earlier local settlers who feared that Siberia would become an exploited colony of European Russia.[21]

The scale of peasant resettlement was so vast that it transformed both the human and natural terrain. Writing on this massive migration, Willard Sunderland identifies peasant colonization of Siberia as "a matter of imperialism."[22] Technological integration of the empire not only exposed the fundamental political and

---

[17]Ibid., p. 65. See also Frank W. Wcislo, *Tales of Imperial Russia: The Life and Times of Sergei Witte, 1849–1915* (Oxford: Oxford University Press, 2011).

[18]Cited in Marsha Seifert, "'Chingis-Khan with the Telegraph': Communications in the Russian and Ottoman Empires," in *Comparing Empires*, ed. Jörn Leonhard and Ulrike von Hirschhausen, p. 78.

[19]Schenk, "Travel, Railroads, and Identity Formation," pp. 142–43.

[20]Ibid., pp. 142–45.

[21]Schenk, "Mastering Imperial Space?," pp. 67–68; see also Donald W. Treadgold, *The Great Siberian Migration: Government and Peasant in Resettlement from Emancipation to the First World War* (Princeton, NJ: Princeton University Press, 1957); and Barbara A. Anderson, *Internal Migration During Modernization in Late Nineteenth-Century Russia* (Princeton, NJ: Princeton University Press, 1980).

[22]Sunderland, *Taming the Wild Field*, p. 3.

social contradictions of a modernizing society with a state resistant to political liberalization but created new problems. The same rail lines that facilitated tsarist troop movements to Poland in 1863 were a conduit for Polish nationalist literature and "agents of the Polish cause" moving in the other direction.[23] Railroads needed railroad workers, and as one of the largest groups of organized and strategically placed labor groups railroad workers had a profound effect on the stability of tsarist rule. In the 1880s, railroad workers were prominent participants in anti-Semitic pogroms.[24] In October 1905 the participation of railroad workers in the general strike was key to forcing the emperor to grant the liberalizing reforms promised in the October Manifesto. As Lenin demonstrated in 1917 and during the Russian civil war, revolutionaries could use the telegraph and the railroads just as effectively as the former state authorities.

The modernization of Russia—its administrative reforms and industrialization—was intimately connected with its position in the world and its imperial nature. The Empire lived in a world of rival imperial powers and struggled from the 1860s to restore its status as a Great Power. The last third of the nineteenth century was a period in which the imperialist appetites of European powers could be satisfied only at the expense of weaker nations and in conflict with the interests of rival powers. The "empty" spaces of Africa became the target of the infamous "Scramble for Africa" when Britain, France, and Germany placed their flags wherever on the continent they were able. At the turn of the twentieth century, the areas of contention that remained were the Balkans, other parts of the Ottoman Empire in the Middle East, and the Far East at the expense of China and Korea. In 1897 Russia seized the Chinese city of Port Arthur. When the Boxer Rebellion against European concessions broke out in China in 1900, Russia exploited the opportunity to occupy Manchuria, ostensibly to protect the Chinese Eastern Railroad that they were building. Britain and Japan tried but failed to force them to withdraw and concluded an alliance to prevent further Russian advances.

The tensions in the Far East escalated in the next few years. Japan and other powers had their own interest in Manchuria, and the United States favored China being opened to the commercial activities of all countries. World opinion, fueled by news of the anti-Semitic pogrom in Kishinev in April 1903 and the stories of bleak prison camps described in George Kennan's *Siberia and the Exile System*, turned against Russia, which was depicted as a cruel, aggressive, expansionist state. A bellicose mood festered in St. Petersburg, and the powerful minister of the interior, Viacheslav von Plehve, declared, "Russia has been made by bayonets not diplomacy . . . , and we must decide the questions at issue with China and Japan with bayonets and not with diplomatic pens."[25] Russian diplomats spoke of

---

[23]Schenk, "Travel, Railroads, and Identity Formation," pp. 141–42.

[24]I. Michael Aronson, "Geographical and Socioeconomic Factors in the 1881 Anti-Jewish Pogroms in Russia," *Russian Review* 39, no. 1 (January 1980): 31.

[25]Barbara Jelavich, *A Century of Russian Foreign Policy, 1814–1914* (Philadelphia: J. B. Lippincott, 1964), p. 243.

"Sitting by the Sea, Waiting for the Right Weather," a Russian political poster at the time of the Russo-Japanese War (1904–1905).

a "short victorious little war" and could not imagine defeat at the hands of Asian states. As with each of their previous military engagements, Russians saber-rattled and thumped their chests at home in print and image, convincing themselves of the rightness of their cause and the certainty of their victory. Some familiar images recurred. A striking cartoon recycled the same jolly, imperturbable Cossack who had been dealing with minor irritants like Napoleonic invaders for the past century. This time his tiny, laughable foes were Japan and China, shown as child-sized puppets, manipulated by the only slightly more substantial figures of John Bull and Uncle Sam. This war was nothing to worry about.

War imagery took on a novel twist with this war, however, with the hideously racialized representation of the foe as not simply negligible or comical but as bestial, subhuman.[26] The Japanese were represented as monstrous creatures: "'animals, Mongols,' 'slant-eyed,' and 'yellow-faced dwarves.'"[27] Most often, they were called "monkeys," and depicted as such.

Here, though acting against the righteous disapproval of other major powers, Russia drew on a common stock of imperial tropes, demonstrating Russia's full

---

[26]Stephen M. Norris, *A War of Images: Russian Popular Prints, Wartime Culture, and National Identity, 1812–1945* (DeKalb: Northern Illinois University Press, 2006), pp. 107–34.
[27]Ibid., 107.

Cartoon on the cover of *Budil'nik* (Alarm Clock) magazine portrays the commander-in-chief of the Japanese navy, Admiral Tōgō, as "Chief 'Monkey' of the Japanese Navy."

participation in a world caught up in imperial competition. The visual reinforced and drew energy from a newly racialized discourse that was creeping into Russian understandings of the world. Race, as we have seen, was not entirely absent earlier, but had not hardened into a naturalized understanding of differences in human quality, capability, or virtue based on physiological distinctions or skin color. This was one of the first clear signs that race had joined the other categories of difference that organized the world in the educated Russian imagination. Still not rising to forefront in terms of domestic categorization, race fed enthusiasm for the war.

Without warning, on the night of January 26–27, 1904, the Japanese launched a surprise attack on Port Arthur, seriously damaging the Russian fleet and blockading the harbor. The Japanese army invaded the Kingdom of Korea (and some years later annexed it) and Manchuria. A year later, in May 1905, the Russian Baltic Fleet, which had sailed for seven months halfway around the world, was destroyed in the Tsushima Straits by the Japanese. Ignominiously defeated, the tsar's government had no choice but to accept the mediation of U.S. president Theodore Roosevelt, sign the Treaty of Portsmouth, and give up its gains in the Far East. The war isolated and humiliated Russia. Even more ominously, it fueled massive discontent at home that exploded in revolutionary violence.

THE FIRST REVOLUTION, 1905

The last emperor of Russia, Nicholas II, came to the throne in 1894, succeeding his powerful father, Alexander III. Nicholas was young, handsome, not very tall, unsure of himself, and widely seen as weak and indecisive. He ruled over a vast empire divided among hundreds of nationalities, hierarchically structured by *sosloviia* (social estate) and increasingly polarized along class lines. Society was pulling apart between a privileged upper class—nobles, landlords, capitalists, industrialists, and many professionals and intellectuals—on one side, and workers and peasants, the vast majority of the population, on the other. While society and the economy were becoming more capitalist and industrialist, more mobile, and socially differentiated, the state was in many ways an archaic structure dominated by nobles, bureaucrats, and the imperial family, most of whom were determined to prevent the enfranchisement and empowerment of the lower and middle classes, the peasants, the workers, and even the bourgeoisie. New ideas, infiltrating from the West—nationalism, as we have already seen, but also liberalism, constitutionalism, and socialism, particularly in its Marxist variant—were providing social actors with new languages and new aspirations that made it increasingly difficult to maintain the autocratic, hierarchical, anti-egalitarian social and political order.

Throughout society, as the paltry protections traditionally afforded by membership in the empire's various collectivities of estate, commune, or denomination crumbled, demands for new kinds of rights grew. The modes of inclusion and reciprocity that had sufficed to bolster tsarist authority in earlier centuries no longer were enough to still the aspirations of the empire's people. Neither the paternalistic rhetoric and occasional displays of mercy that had qualified as reciprocity in the seventeenth century, nor the protestations of affection and demonstrations of generosity that served to tie elites to the crown in the eighteenth century, came close to satisfying new demands for real rights and responsive and responsible governance. As people became increasingly adept at using the courts to defend their interests, legal consciousness deepened among all levels of the population, from peasants to educated society. Professional and corporate groups agitated for rights and protections that would create conditions where they could work and profit, and they spoke out in favor of a lawful and law-abiding government. Liberal thinkers considered the possibilities for creating a form of citizenship for Russia. Yet the autocratic regime, the law as it existed, and the feeble notion of citizenship tolerated by the state offered few hopeful avenues for reform. Eric Lohr concludes, "Late imperial Russia's particularity lay perhaps in the absence of faith among contemporaries that existing law, institutions, and traditions could provide the basis for an evolutionary move from powerless subject to rights-endowed citizen. Lacking a usable past, for better and for worse, many Russian liberals turned to categorical imperatives and universal, moral sources to define the ideal citizen."[28] In the case of liberals, these universals took the form of advocacy of effective laws and a set of "natural rights" belonging to all human beings. Radicals turned to more militant philosophies: anarchism, nihilism, and socialism. The tensions between society and the state, and the contradictions between an emerging capitalist industrial society in the towns and the autocratic authority, as articulated and propagated by the radical and liberal intelligentsia, exploded in a series of revolutionary upheavals.

---

[28]Eric Lohr, "The Ideal Citizen and Real Subject in Late Imperial Russia," *Kritika: Explorations in Russian and Eurasian History*, n.s., 7, no. 2 (Spring 2006): 173–94; quote on 194.

Small brooch most likely made soon after Tsar Nicholas and Tsaritsa Alexandra's wedding, November 26, 1894; now in the collection of the Estate of Marjorie Merriweather Post at Hillwood in Washington, D.C.

Execution, painting by S. V. Ivanov, 1905. Tsarist soldiers fire on a workers' demonstration during the 1905 revolution.

The year 1905, in its historic sense, actually began nine days after the New Year. Thousands of workers, led by the radical priest Father Gapon, marched in solemn procession, holding icons and singing "God Save the Tsar," to the tsar's Winter Palace in Saint Petersburg. Their pleas were met with a volley of rifle shot that left at least 130 dead and 299 seriously wounded.[29] The January snow ran red in Russia's capital city, and the events reverberated throughout Russia and the world as "Bloody Sunday." "The indiscriminate shooting of unarmed people seeking to petition their sovereign for 'justice and protection'," writes a historian of 1905, "had severed the psychological ties between the ruler and many of the ruled, ties that were intangible but indispensable for the maintenance of order. Masses of Russians no longer felt bound to obey the commands of a sovereign whose power had previously been accepted as hallowed by God and tradition."[30]

As the year unfolded, strikes and demonstrations, mutinies and armed clashes of workers and police, battles between peasants and soldiers on horseback, nearly brought the three-century-old monarchy down. Later the sporadic turbulence would be known as the "revolution of 1905," and those out on the streets, as well as those in the palaces, certainly felt that they were in the midst of a revolution. "1905 unsealed the lips of all," wrote Leon Trotsky. "The country that had been silent for a thousand years began to speak for the first time."[31] In October 1905, a broad coalition of workers, middle-class people, and intellectuals carried out a mammoth mass strike and forced the tsar to make significant reforms that seriously compromised the autocratic powers of the emperor and gave Russia, for the first time in its history, a kind of semi-constitutional regime. The October Manifesto, wrung from a reluctant emperor, granted important political concessions, including freedom to organize, speak, and assemble. It also authorized the establishment of a representative duma, that is, a nationwide elected representative assembly with legislative power. At last, the reformers' long-held dream of crowning the system of provincial *zemstva* with a national-level representative body was to be realized.

The rare convergence of interests that had mobilized so many segments of society to join their voices in demanding reform lasted only a few months. The huge cross-class national alliance fractured in December, when workers in Moscow and other cities moved to more radical positions, defending their local councils (the soviets) and breaking ranks with the middle classes, who were by and large content with the tsar's concessions, however unwillingly given. The revolutionary energy dissipated, and political activism turned to organizing for elections to the dumas.

The fundamental contradictions of Russian society and governance were not resolved, however. The new industrialized economy, with its growing number of

---

[29]Abraham Ascher, *The Revolution of 1905: Russia in Disarray* (Stanford, CA: Stanford University Press, 1988), pp. 91–92.
[30]Ibid., pp. 206–7.
[31]Trotsky, *Stalin*, pp. 65–66.

Map 8.3. Demonstrations, strikes, disturbances, 1905–1907.

factory workers, managers, and industrial entrepreneurs, fit awkwardly in a system still constrained by autocracy. The revolutionary clashes would continue, particularly in the empire's peripheries, like Poland, the Baltic region, and the Caucasus, for the next two years.

In its last twelve years the Russian government was a kind of "constitutional autocracy," that is, a regime in which the monarch refused to renounce his autocratic powers but which in fact operated with a parliament and some regulations that restricted his arbitrary and absolute rule. The inherent contradictions in this oxymoronic formulation played out over those twelve years in a hostile dance between the emperor and the elected body he had so unwillingly authorized.

Tsar Dadon Meets the Shemakha *Tsarevna* (illustration to *The Tale of the Little Golden Cockerel* by Alexander Pushkin) by Ivan Bilibin, 1906.

Saddled with a legislative assembly that he deemed antithetical to his imperial authority, the emperor blocked Duma initiatives, meddled with the electoral law, and, when unable to limit its activities, prorogued or disbanded its sessions. Similarly, his ambivalence toward his own manifesto led to draconian measures to undercut the freedoms granted by the new "constitution." So dire were the regime's attacks under one powerful prime minister, Petr Stolypin, that people spoke of the nooses deployed to strangle revolutionary movements as "Stolypin neckties."

In spite of the regime's hostility to the reforms it had been forced to concede, in the years between 1905 and the start of the First World War, Russians took advantage of the slivers of freedom allowed them. Culturally, this dynamic period gained the label the Silver Age. Great artists, novelists, poets, composers, dramatists, dancers, and choreographers won international praise for their avant-garde work: the writers Andrei Belyi, Alexander Blok, and Anna Akhmatova; the choreographer Sergei Diaghilev; set and costume designer Leon Bakst; composers Sergei Prokofiev and Alexander Skriabin; dancers Vaslav Nijinsky and Anna Pavlova. . . . The list goes on.

Philosophers delved into mysticism, spiritualism, and the aesthetics of decadence. The social avant-garde explored alternative sexualities in explicit and implicit expressions. A vibrant silent film industry was just starting, and an even more vibrant consumer market made everything imaginable available to buyers, from cheap newspapers to family photographs to ready-made clothing. Collectors could even purchase a full set of ornamental porcelain figurines of the peoples of the empire in full costume: what better than to display them all in one's kick-knack cabinet?[32] More than any earlier time in Russia's history a civil society appeared, and people were able to associate publicly with one another more freely than they had before 1905.

Political life, both authorized and revolutionary, also took on new dynamism, in spite of official displeasure. Elections to the First State Duma were held in 1906, with a surprisingly broad and inclusive suffrage. Almost all men over the age of twenty-five were entitled to vote. True to the empire's tradition of rule through difference, however, qualifications for suffrage varied by region and social standing. The first European country to allow women to vote was the Grand Duchy of Finland, semi-autonomous within the Russian Empire. Voting throughout the empire was conducted separately by social class, and not all votes weighed equally. *Soslovnost'* (the estate system) continued after 1905 to be the imperial way of ruling. "Estates" (*sosloviia*) were legal categories into which each person in the empire was initially fixed by virtue of their birth. The tsar's subjects were born into particular estates: noble, peasant, clergy, or townsperson. Through their lives they might be able to move up (or down) to another estate, but mobility was restricted, unlike the more fluid class system of the capitalist West. Each effort to eliminate *soslovnost'* failed, and so did efforts to foster an all-estate, imperial replacement.

In this momentous first election campaign and in the subsequent ones of 1907, 1908, and 1912, political parties competed for the allegiance of potential voters by appealing to both class and ethnic grievances. Growing in influence among factory workers and radical intellectuals, the formerly underground Marxist party, the Russian Social Democratic Workers' Party (RSDRP), was largely blind to ethnicity and drew activist Jews, Georgians, Latvians, Ukrainians, as well as Russians, into its ranks. In most of Russia, except for the Caucasus, the Social Democrats, whose more radical wing (the Bolsheviks) were led by Vladimir Lenin, boycotted the elections to the first Duma, leaving the field to the liberal Constitutional Democrats (Kadets), pro-peasant activists, and nationalists. In Georgia the moderate Social Democrats (Mensheviks) swept the elections, but in Kiev the liberals who emerged victorious were met by accusations that they favored "Jews and professors."[33] Ukrainian intellectuals and activists, like the Ukrainian historian Mykhailo Hrushevskyi, were upset with the liberals, who though they favored gradual reform and greater democracy, seemed indifferent to

[32]Willard Sunderland, "Shop Signs, Monuments, Souvenirs: Views of the Empire in Everyday Life," in *Picturing Russia: Explorations in Visual Culture*, ed. Valerie Kivelson and Joan Neuberger (New Haven, CT: Yale University Press, 2008), pp. 104–8.
[33]Faith Hillis, *Children of Rus': Right-Bank Ukraine and the Invention of a Russian Nation* (Ithaca, NY, and London: Cornell University Press), p. 190.

Figurines of "Russians" and "Peoples of Central Asia," from the series *Peoples of Russia, Produced by the Imperial Porcelain Factory in St. Petersburg, 1909–1913.*

their national aspirations for recognition. While Ukrainian nationalists called for autonomy, the principal liberal party in Russia, the Kadets, called for equal rights for all peoples and a unitary Russian state. (See Table 7.1 for list of parties.)

The first empire-wide elections yielded a quite varied set of deputies, including Jews and Muslims, as well as liberal and labor representatives. On the far Left were the Social Democrats and peasant deputies; in the center were the Kadets and affiliated liberals; on the Right were conservative monarchists and Russian ethnonationalists. When the Duma put forth proposals too radical for the

This carefully posed photo taken in a professional photography studio in Baku reminds us that a bourgeois, consumerist society was developing not only in Russia's capital cities but in major provincial centers as well. What looks like a typical middle-class family in Baku in late 1895 contains many secrets. The stern father is actually a German engineer, Wilhelm Richard Sorge, who married a Russian, Nina Semionovna Kobieleva. In the back row is an older woman in a kerchief, perhaps Nina Seminonovna's mother or a servant. The 8-month old baby in this cosmopolitan family, Richard Sorge, grew up to be a famous Soviet spy. Converted to Communism in Germany, he infiltrated the Nazi Party and was posted to the German Embassy in Tokyo during World War II. There he reported back to Moscow, informing Stalin about the coming German invasion. Stalin did not heed Sorge's warning. Discovered by the Japanese and Germans in 1941, Sorge was hanged in 1944. Novels and films have been written about his extraordinary exploits.

emperor, he disbanded it after only a few months. A second set of elections sent even more radical representatives to the assembly. Fed up, the emperor and the prime minister, Stolypin, dissolved the Second Duma and engineered the so-called Third of June (1907) coup d'état, a thorough, unilateral reworking of the electoral law that underrepresented workers and peasants and overrepresented nobles and people of property. Though discontent and resistance continued throughout the country for a few more years, the regime managed successfully to put in place a Duma more compliant with the emperor's wishes.

WHEN NATIONALISM GOES PUBLIC: REIMAGINING EMPIRE

The revolutionary years 1905–1907 witnessed an explosion of intellectual interest in nationalism. As a growing educated public engaged with politics, ideas of the nation offered an appealing way to reimagine the empire. Nationalist newspapers of all varieties appeared in greater number; nationalist committees were formed; political "parties" expressing national agendas were established. Very often, ethnic Russians living in ethnically non-Russian areas, like the western provinces, Ukraine, or South Caucasia, were ferociously nationalist. They were represented in the (Russian) Nationalist Party, which flourished in the western provinces, and chauvinist publicists like Vasilii Velichko, with his anti-Armenian diatribes, became influential in the Caucasus.[34] Among non-Russians, similar hostilities ignited nationalist sentiments. Many Georgians and Caucasian Muslims saw Armenians as a privileged bourgeoisie that threatened their traditional ways of life. What Jews represented to many Poles and Ukrainians in the western provinces—an alien, rapacious harbinger of capitalism—so the Armenians were to Georgians. When the revolutionary wave receded and government authority came down on political activists, popular interest in nationalist solutions to social and political problems declined. Still, the issue of "nations" within the empire had been repeatedly raised, and determined intellectuals and activists kept the question of national rights alive.

Perceptive thinkers and politicians realized that the empire faced the possibility of collapse and disintegration. Hostile foreign powers like Germany, Austria, and the Ottoman Empire, and domestic opponents like the liberals, populists, and Marxists presented palpable threats to the empire and autocracy. Influential writers and officials agonized over the problem of civil integration—how to create a sense of solidarity within the population. In his forced retirement the former prime minister, Count Sergei Witte, a thoughtful analyst of autocracy, noted the

---

[34]Robert Edelman, *Gentry Politics on the Eve of the Russian Revolution: The Nationalist Party* (New Brunswick, NJ: Rutgers University Press, 1980); Ronald Grigor Suny, *The Making of the Georgian Nation* (Bloomington, IN, and Stanford, CA: Indiana University Press in association with the Hoover Institution Press, 1988; second edition: Bloomington: Indiana University Press, 1994), p. 142.

principal difficulties faced by traditional empires as they entered the twentieth
century. In his memoirs Witte agonized over how difficult it was "to preserve
autocracy" when the monarch commits "not only inappropriate but fatally
flawed" acts and the popular masses have become more politically conscious
nurtured by the "liberation movement."[35] To these failures of the center and the
mobilization of the masses, Witte added the threat presented by growing nationalism among the empire's subject peoples:

> The borderlands . . . began to avenge very real discrimination that had gone on
> for years, as well as measures which were entirely justified but unreconciled
> with the national feelings (*natsional'noe chuvstvo*) of conquered ethnic groups
> (*inorodtsy*). . . . The big mistake of our decades-long policy is that we still today
> do not understand that there hasn't been a Russia from the time of Peter the
> Great and Catherine the Great. There has been a Russian Empire. When over
> 35 per cent of the population are ethnics, and Russians are divided among Great
> Russians, Little Russians, and White Russians, it is impossible, in the 19th and
> 20th centuries, to conduct a policy that ignores . . . the national particularities
> (*natsional'nye svoistva*) of other nationalities who have entered the Russian
> Empire, their religion(s), their languages, and so on. The motto of such an
> empire cannot be "I will make them all true Russians"—this is not an ideal that
> will inspire all subjects of the Russian Emperor, unify the population, create
> one political spirit.[36]

Among the more interesting ideas of how to save the empire was the program
promoted by the Ministry of War and military reformers of building a *civic nation*—
one that would include all the peoples of the empire, make them equal under the
law, and end any discriminations based on ethnicity or religion. This ministry had
advanced remarkably progressive agendas since the Great Reforms, when Minister
of War Dmitrii Miliutin argued the pressing need for creating a reformed army of
free men, and accepted female physicians into the ranks of military doctors. Now,
shattered by Russia's defeat in the war with Japan (1904–1905), some military thinkers saw the revolution that followed as an opportunity. The reformers began with
the general conviction that "the Russian empire was ethnically diverse, socially
stratified, and devoid of a strong sense of community." Moreover, "they were fully
aware that the autocratic political system was antinational."[37] For the military reformers the failures in the Russo-Japanese War demonstrated that Russia had not
achieved the kind of nationhood that the West and Japan had achieved. While conservatives, particularly in the Ministry of Internal Affairs, feared nationalism and
the mass mobilization it implied, military reformers wanted to create active citizens
with a sense of a united political community who were ready to fight for their

[35]Francis C. Wcislo, "Witte, Memory, and the 1905 Revolution: A Reinterpretation of the Witte
Memoirs," *Revolutionary Russia* 8, no. 2 (December 1995): 175.
[36]Ibid., p. 176.
[37]Joshua Sanborn, "Family, Fraternity, and Nation-building in Russia, 1905–1925," in *A State of Nations: Empire and Nation-Making in the Age of Lenin and Stalin,* ed. Ronald Grigor Suny and Terry
Martin (New York: Oxford University Press, 2001), p. 94.

country. Their conservative opponents focused their fears on the mobilized population in 1905, which they saw as an enormous danger that had nearly toppled the monarchy. They too valued the shared sense of patriotic duty that the nation implied but feared the more liberal and democratic consequences of nationhood. General A. N. Kuropatkin, minister of war and commander of Russian troops in the war, fretted, "belief in God, devotion to the tsar, [and] love of the fatherland," factors that previously had made the "uneducated peasantry . . . fearless and obedient" had dissipated. "These principles have latterly been much shaken among the people."[38]

Among the competing visions for the empire that emerged during and after the revolutionary years 1905–1907, the most extreme was that of the "true Russian" nationalists, particularly powerful and influential in southwestern Russia. They proposed that the empire favor all Orthodox East Slavs, support them in their historic struggle against Catholic Poles and the Jews, and change electoral laws so that they promoted people of Russian nationality over others. They were prepared to move from the estate principle favoring nobles and people of great property to a national principle favoring a particular ethnicity, namely East Slavs, that is, in their view "true Russians."

A third vision was to maintain the empire in all its contradictions on the basis of the estate principle. This meant continuing to promote the interests primarily of the landed gentry while taking into account the increasingly forcefully expressed interests of others, namely middle-class entrepreneurs, workers, and peasants. The estate principle had been the basis of imperial rule for centuries and after 1905 was supported vigorously by Witte, the tsar's first minister during the crisis of 1905. But in the age of growing nationalism those who wanted to move beyond the estate principle found a powerful champion in Petr Stolypin, the most skillful and influential imperial politician in the period after 1905. Stolypin shared the views of Russian nationalists and proposed to establish *zemstva* in the western borderlands, at long last. He wanted their delegates to be elected on the basis of nationality in a system calculated to favor Orthodox Russians and disadvantage the Polish gentry. In what became known as the "Western *Zemstvo* Crisis" of 1910, the lower house of the State Duma passed Stolypin's bill, but when the bill came to the State Council it met opposition from those nobles who understood (correctly) that this new principle seriously undermined the distinctions based on *soslovie*, which for many were fundamental principles of the imperial system. The bill was defeated. Stolypin then, with the tsar's agreement, went ahead and implemented the bill while the Duma was not in session. This high-handed maneuver lost the government the support of Stolypin's center-right backers, the Octobrist Party, in the Duma, and left him weak and vulnerable in the last year before he was assassinated. In his reckless gamble Stolypin won the battle to promote nationality, but the supporters of social differentiation, *soslovnost'*, won the war.

---

[38]Cited in Josh Sanborn, "The Mobilization of 1914 and the Question of the Russian Nation: A Reexamination," *Slavic Review*, LIX, 2 (Summer 2000), p. 284.

A fourth vision was that of non-Russian nationalists who claimed that their people constituted a nation, which by virtue of its culture and history deserved national rights, perhaps a degree of autonomy, and a designated territory of its own. As a major Ukrainian spokesman, Hrushevskyi spoke of Russia as "an empire of nations" (*imperiia narodov*) that in the future needed to grant national-territorial autonomy to the various subject peoples. In the nationalist narratives, nationalism is the natural and inevitable outcome of human history, the eventual expression of a repressed national essence long denied by imperial powers. Yet even in the last years of the Russian Empire most of the non-Russian peoples under tsarist rule had neither formed cohesive mass national movements nor even managed to convince large numbers of their potential supporters of the advantages of a national path rather than continuing to live within the empire.

Nationalism usually arose first among intellectuals as an idea that a certain group of people shared common features—language, culture, history, folk songs, perhaps even biological origins. Those ideas filtered down to wider circles of people through newspapers, schooling, and political movements. Only with great effort by activists and educators did the idea of a nation take hold on the masses of ordinary people. For most ethnicities in tsarist Russia, that third, mass stage of national awareness appeared only with the First World War, the revolution, the civil war of 1918–1921, and the early years of the Soviet state.[39]

Both conservative Russians and non-Russian activists remained uneasy about the place of ethnicity, culture, and national political expression in the empire. The government was concerned enough to hold a series of conferences on nationality matters just before the world war, one on Pan-Turkism and another on the education of *inorodtsy*, those peoples designated as particularly backward culturally. The organizers of the latter conference hoped to attract *inorodtsy* into the general educational system of the Russian-language state schools, to develop the use of Russian "as the state language," though forcible Russification was to be avoided. This was clearly an abandonment of the Ilminskii approach, discussed in the previous chapter, for now instruction, except in the first and possibly the second year of primary school, was to be in Russian. The goal no longer was the development of backward peoples within their own culture along with the Orthodox religion but assimilation of non-Russians to the greatest extent possible. The conference opposed "artificial awakening of self-consciousness among separate *narodnosti* [peoples], which, according to their cultural development and numerical size, cannot create an independent culture."[40] As the conference report concluded, "The ideal school from the point of view of state unity would be a unified school for all the *narodnosti* of the Empire, with the state language of instruction,

---

[39]The stages of the development of nationalism are developed thoroughly in Miroslav Hroch, *Social Preconditions for National Revival in Europe: A Comparative Analysis of the Social Composition of Patriotic Groups Among the Smaller European Nations* (Cambridge: Cambridge University Press, 1985).

[40]Slocum, "The Boundaries of National Identity," p. 214.

not striving for the repression of individual nationalities [*natsional'nosti*], but cultivating in them, as in native Russians, love of Russia and consciousness of her unity, wholeness [*tselost'*], and indivisibility."[41] This resounding call to integration gained little traction in official circles. The state was prepared to use its resources to gain converts to Orthodoxy and the Russian language but also seemed to realize that "the majority of the empire's population was not and never would be truly Russian."[42] In the view of Russian state officials, religious boundaries were real and were to be enforced, while nationalism and separatism were to be repressed. The formulation most acceptable to the administration, as expressed in the conference goals quoted above, posited a sense of unity and belonging to an imperial "whole" that would bind together a kaleidoscope of religious and ethnic groups. While retaining their distinctiveness, all would be loyal subjects of the empire, uncontaminated by separatist or nationalist ambitions.

Nationalists had to compete with liberals, who were closely identified with intellectuals and the middle class, populist peasant socialists, and pro-worker Marxists for the allegiance of the common folk. Ultimately it was appeal to class solidarities, not nationalist ones, that mobilized Russia to revolution. Over time, thanks to the persistence of the Social Democrats, workers increasingly identified with the imagined community of the working class. Peasants most often saw themselves as members of a particular village or a region and identified with their religious affiliation rather than primarily with a national community. There was no significant "bourgeois nationalism" in tsarist Russia, either among ethnic Russians or among the non-Russian middle classes. Those in Russia who actually qualified as "bourgeois," entrepreneurs and manufacturers in the main, stayed out of oppositional politics and remained closely tied to the state, which provided both capital and opportunities for investment.

Because in Russia the urban middle class was so small and politically insignificant, any hope of "bourgeois revolution" by a purported middle class, like that in England in the 1640s or France in the 1790s, rested with the working class and its Marxist leaders. Their struggle up to 1917 aimed at bringing about democracy and the expansion of the possibilities of capitalist development, not an immediate transition to socialism, which in their view lay far in the future of peasant Russia. The weakness of liberalism was matched by the limited reach of nationalism among Russians. The discourse of the nation was potentially powerful, but it would take decades more, and further efforts of poets, politicians, and educators, to inculcate that view of history and belonging to ordinary people. Much of the hard intellectual and political work to make nations, ironically, would be carried out in the ostensibly anti-nationalist, self-proclaimed internationalist Soviet system.[43] Empire remained a going concern, despite the fractures between state and

---

[41]Ibid., p. 216.
[42]Ibid., p. 256.
[43]This is essentially the argument of Ronald Grigor Suny, *The Revenge of the Past: Nationalism, Revolution, and the Collapse of the Soviet Union* (Stanford: Stanford University Press, 1993).

society. In fact, to some it might have seemed that the imperial regime had successfully adapted to the pressures of modern times. With its fully functioning, legislative Duma, its vibrant cultural production, and its thriving consumer market, it appeared to be a modern and modernizing empire. At the turn of the twentieth century and into World War I, neither its rulers nor many observers in the West imagined that the Russian Empire was entering its last decades.

BRIEF BIBLIOGRAPHY

Ascher, Abraham. *The Revolution of 1905: Russia in Disarray.* Stanford, CA: Stanford University Press, 1988.

Kivelson, Valerie A., and Joan Neuberger, eds. *Picturing Russia: Explorations in Visual Culture.* New Haven, CT: Yale University Press, 2008.

Pravilova, Ekaterina. *A Public Empire: Property and the Quest for the Common Good in Imperial Russia.* Princeton, NJ: Princeton University Press, 2014.

Schenk, Frithjof Benjamin. "Travel, Railroads, and Identity Formation in the Russian Empire." In *Shatterzone of Empires: Coexistence and Violence in the German, Habsburg, Russian, and Ottoman Borderlands,* edited by Omer Bartov and Eric D. Weitz. Bloomington: Indiana University Press, 2013.

Siegelbaum, Lewis H., and Leslie Moch. *Broad Is My Native Land: Repertoires and Regimes of Migration in Russia's Twentieth Century.* Ithaca, NY: Cornell University Press, 2014.

Sunderland, Willard. *Taming the Wild Field: Colonization and Empire on the Russian Steppe.* Ithaca, NY: Cornell University Press, 2006.

Treadgold, Donald W. *The Great Siberian Migration: Government and Peasant in Resettlement from Emancipation to the First World War.* Princeton, NJ: Princeton University Press, 1957.

Wcislo, Francis W. *Tales of Imperial Russia: The Life and Times of Sergei Witte, 1849–1915.* Oxford: Oxford University Press, 2011.

NINE

CLASH AND COLLAPSE OF EMPIRES: 1914–1921

Historians have debated the origins and causes of World War I since its unexpected outbreak in the summer of 1914. The assassination of the Archduke Franz Ferdinand, the heir to the Austro-Hungarian throne, and his wife was the spark that ignited the accumulating tinder of inter-state political and economic rivalries. Vienna immediately accused Serbia of complicity in the assassination and issued an ultimatum to Belgrade. Germany backed Austria, giving their ally the infamous "blank check" to avenge the killing. Russia and France mobilized to contain Germany, and Britain joined their Entente allies to oppose the Central Powers. After months of hesitation, the Young Turk regime in the Ottoman Empire, urged on by the Germans, attacked the Russians and expanded the war to the Middle East. While more moderate socialists across Europe joined the war effort and defended the efforts of their own governments, most Russian Social Democrats, particularly Lenin and the Bolsheviks, saw the war as an imperialist struggle for markets, colonies, and strategic advantage and refused to back the tsar. Only after years of massive killing and a seemingly irresolvable stalemate between the Entente and the Central Powers did the European Left and masses of ordinary people begin to abandon their earlier enthusiasm for the war and wearily long for its end.

THE GREAT WAR

The threat of war finally forced the tsarist regime to rethink its entrenched suspicion of even the most patriotic nationalism and to try to find ways to put it to use. Both in anticipation of the coming war, and when the mobilization in 1914 began, Russian military authorities appealed to Russian patriotism and a sense of nation, something they hoped to find but also to create. Their greatest fear was division, disunity, and the fracturing of the country. Their hope was unity, and for conservatives this was centered until quite late on the tsar. A deputy to the Fourth Duma from the conservative Octobrist party, Mikhail Rodzianko, proclaimed proudly, to great applause, in January 1915: "The Russian tsar, with his sensitive heart, divined the feelings of the people, and he has heard here the response of a united, harmonious Russian family. . . . And presently, after a half of a year of unprecedented bloodshed, Russia stands . . . indivisible, firm in will, and strong in spirit."[1] This was wishful thinking on his part, but war did indeed unleash some apparently heartfelt expressions of solidarity from large segments of the population, and the military did what it could to foster it.

Metaphors and language about family were deployed to inculcate a kind of national feeling among Russians, to build affective bonds between people, particularly soldiers. "The nation was like a family," writes Joshua Sanborn, "as was the army, as indeed was the primary battle group to which the soldier belonged."[2] Loyalty to family was understood to be far more important than to the imagined community we might call the "nation." To rally people to fight for their country, the recruiters and propagandists had to convince peasant soldiers that defense of the country was the same as defense of their family. The very image of the family deployed by the military changed during World War I: it metamorphosed from an image of a patriarchal family that emphasized the commander as father to a more fraternal one of the soldiers as a band of brothers, comrades-in-arms. Commanders and soldiers were to be linked in mutual trust and love, a political metaphor reminiscent of eighteenth-century rhetoric, but played now in a masculine, martial key, stripped of the tearful sentiment of its earlier incarnation.

When the war broke out, there was a burst of patriotic fervor, attacks on German shops (even on Singer sewing machines since the name sounded German, though it was an American company); the city of St. Petersburg, its name taken from Dutch but sounding German, was renamed Petrograd, attaching a Slavic root for "city" onto Peter. Soldiers swore an oath to be loyal to tsar and motherland; if they broke that oath they were deemed "unworthy to your fellow brothers and sons of Russia." "Russia was the mother, and all officers and soldiers were 'fellow brothers'."[3] These images of family and motherland became part of a broad discourse, which non-Russians adopted and used themselves in appeals to the government. When Kyrgyz representatives who did not want to be drafted petitioned the Duma, they made their appeal in the language of common familial ties: "We Kirgiz consider ourselves the equal sons of a unified Russia and sincerely hope that the victorious war will serve as a stimulus for the introduction of a rule of law for our motherland, for the passage of reforms necessary for the good of the fatherland, and for the establishment of fraternity between the tribally variegated sons of the fatherland."[4]

Scholars have come down differently on this question of Russian "nationness" in the first decades of the twentieth century. In his study of patriotism during

---

[1] Cited in Sanborn, "Family, Fraternity, and Nation-building in Russia," p. 96.
[2] Ibid., p. 97.
[3] Ibid., p. 101.
[4] Cited in ibid., p. 102.

ШВЕЙНЫЯ МАШИНЫ
КОМПАНІИ ЗИНГЕРЪ

КОМПАНІЯ
ЗИНГЕРЪ

The Singer Sewing Machine Company, an American enterprise, responded to growing Russian nationalism with this advertisement featuring a seamstress decked out in traditional Muscovite garb. This did not save it from being attacked as a "German" company at the start of the war.

World War I, Hubertus F. Jahn writes, "Patriotic imagery reveals that Russians had a pretty clear idea against whom they were fighting in the war, but not for whom and for what. If a nation is a community imagined by its members as Benedict Anderson convincingly argues, then Russia was not a nation during World War I."[5] Sanborn, on the other hand, concludes that imperial Russia and eventually the Soviet Union did form national attachments, or at least that military leaders and others had a clearly national project in mind as they carried out reforms from above.[6] S. A. Smith acknowledges that "the war strengthened rather than weakened national identity," but one should not "underestimate the extent

[5]Hubertus F. Jahn, *Patriotic Culture in Russia During World War I* (Ithaca, NY: Cornell University Press, 1996), pp. 171–73.
[6]Sanborn, "The Mobilization of 1914 and the Question of the Russian Nation: A Re-examination," *Slavic Review* 59, no. 2 (Summer 2000): 267–89; and his *Drafting the Russian Nation: Military Conscription, Total War, and Mass Politics, 1905–1925* (DeKalb, IL: Northern Illinois University Press, 2011), pp. 201–08. See also Scott Seregny, "Zemstvos, Peasants, and Citizenship: The Russian Adult Education Movement and World War I," ibid., pp. 290–315.

to which nation, empire, and class pulled in different directions from 1916. . . . By the summer of 1917, politics had become polarized between an imperial language of nation, used mainly by the privileged and educated strata, an anti-imperial language, used mainly by the elites of the non-Russian nationalities, and a language of class, used mainly by the subaltern classes."[7] Once state authority broke down and civil war broke out in 1918, the equation shifted again, ultimately with national identity proving to be much more robust, for non-Russians particularly, than class identity.[8] Geoffrey Hosking has most consistently contended that only in Soviet times, most dramatically in the resistance to the Nazi invasion, was the state and party able to link "civilian and military, empire and local community" together in ways that the tsars had failed to accomplish. "The Second World War did more than any other event to crystallize Russian nationhood."[9]

With the creation of a new public sphere through Duma elections and attention to national politics, the idiom and rhetoric of nation had become more widespread from 1905 and was omnipresent during World War I. Yet the actual cohesion of a national community in Russia remained weak. At the same time that military bands stirred patriotic feelings, people all over the country resisted the draft. Women protested the mobilization of their men and throughout the war desertion remained a serious problem. Patriotic sentiments supporting the imperial state grew ever weaker as the war effort worsened for Russia. Kazakhs resisted the end to their traditional exemption from the draft when they were called up to serve in labor battalions in a last-ditch war effort in 1916. Tens of thousands of Kazakhs, and other Muslim peoples, already upset with Russian farmers encroaching on the lands of the nomads, joined the revolt; hundreds of thousands were displaced from their homes or fled to China. With popular insurrection in their rear, Russian troops had to be diverted to put down massive opposition to the war, conscription, and Russian settlers.[10] As the death toll mounted on various fronts and defeat followed defeat, the war became more unpopular. The tsarist regime was seen as foreign, corrupt, debauched, manipulated through the person of the German-born empress, by the enemies of the state. The conduct of the war was so incompetent that liberal politicians accused the regime of treachery.

---

[7]S. A. Smith, "Citizenship and the Russian Nation During World War I: A Comment," ibid., pp. 317–29.

[8]Ibid., p. 329. For the nationalizing effects of the war on the empire, without an explicit argument that a Russian nation is being formed, see also Eric Lohr, *Nationalizing the Russian Empire: The Campaign Against Enemy Aliens During World War I* (Cambridge, MA: Harvard University Press, 2003).

[9]Geoffrey Hosking, *Russia and the Russians, A History* (Cambridge, MA: Harvard University Press, 2001), p. 505.

[10]Martha Brill Olcutt, *The Kazakhs*, 2nd ed. (Stanford, CA: Hoover Institution Press, 1995), p. 124. The best account of the revolt is Marco Buttino, *La Rivoluzione Capovolta* (Naples, 2003), updated and translated by N. Okhotina into Russian: *Revoliutsiia naoborot: Srednaia Aziia mezhdu padeniem tsarskoi imperii i obrazovaniem SSSR* (Moscow: Zvenia, 2007).

The idea of fraternity was powerful, but rather than a fraternity of citizen-soldiers the ordinary soldier in his actual day-to-day service experienced a regime of hierarchy and patriarchy. Sanborn argues the nation was "a tangible force. When the seven years of total war came to an end, this national identity was new and shaky, but it was stronger than any other nonlocal appeal."[11] Yet once the tsar was overthrown, the chasm separating the rank-and-file and the officers would be starkly exposed. The officers would side with the new liberal government, while soldiers gravitated to the soviets, councils elected by workers, soldiers, and peasants. Reality overcame rhetoric; fraternity was associated not with the "vital forces of the nation," as moderate socialists would hope, but with the *demokratiia*, a term that signified not the political form of "democracy," but rather, solidarity of the lower classes—peasants, workers, and soldiers. Whatever buds of nationhood the military had cultivated withered in the social polarization and rise of class, regional, village, and ethnic identities that overwhelmed the cross-class connections of a civic Russian nation.

Even if one does not buy into the Leninist concept of World War I as an "imperialist war" fought primarily by Great Powers eager to secure territory and colonies to stave off the inevitable collapse of capitalism, it appears evident that it was a war of empires fearful that their rivals might best them in what they conceived as a Darwinian struggle for survival. Within each of the warring empires, subject peoples found opportunities to act independently, to make choices about loyalties and identities, either accepting the polities in which they had lived or following nationalist intellectuals and activists into uncharted waters. On the Eastern and Caucasian fronts, four empires and a cluster of smaller nation-states began the war, which concluded with the emergence of more than a dozen new nation-states, some for the first time in history, a few not to survive the final postwar settlement. Competitive nationalist movements undermined the efforts of liberals, conservatives, and socialists to hold the old empires together. Social and class conflicts in the fragmenting Russian Empire, as well as in belligerent states, seemed to confirm Lenin's prediction that as empires fell apart, the imperialist war would metastasize into civil wars.

At the imperial level the war might be imagined as sibling rivalries, or a brutal contest of cousins, but a change of focus from the monarchies and ministries of foreign affairs and war to the movements of ordinary people reveals that more subterranean processes were at work that would ultimately undermine the existing state structures. Beyond the walls of diplomatic salons were the mobile worlds of food supply, labor migration, and the intricate interconnections of what had already become a globalized capitalist economy. All that was solid was melting into air once again. Some analysts believed that integrated markets would render war impossible, but others, like Lenin and Rosa Luxemburg, were convinced that the current stage of capitalism would make conflict all but inevitable.

---

[11]Sanborn, "Family, Fraternity, and Nation-building in Russia," p. 106.

At a macrohistorical level, World War I was the moment when inter-imperial rivalries led to the collapse of continental empires in Europe. World War II would have a similar effect on overseas empires. For much of the nineteenth and twentieth centuries, imperial regimes, both landed and overseas empires, failed to domesticate nationalism even though they resorted to the most brutal forms of "pacification"—deportations, ethnic cleansing, and genocide. Yet during the ferocious bloodletting of the world war, instead of consistently repressing nationalist impulses, empires often contributed to them intentionally. Not about to give in and give up to nationalism, empires were determined to use such sentiments instrumentally to further their own imperial projects. In the heat of battle from 1914 to 1918, warring empires manipulated, even encouraged, the aspirations of ethnicities.[12]

The Great War was an open opportunity for states to shift their borders at the expense of their foes. The long-disputed and unresolved Eastern Question—what was to be done with the Ottoman "Sick Man of Europe"—was a trigger that unbalanced the balance of power in Europe, and ambitious politicians and warriors anxious to fight looked toward their neighbors hungrily. Central Europeans considered Russia, as well as the Ottoman Empire, to be so sickly that healthier and more vigorous powers could take advantage. Not only imperial governments but also famished nationalists prepared for what they hoped would be a banquet of spoils. The self-styled nation-state of Romania tried to entice Romanian-speaking subjects in Bessarabia, which was part of the Russian Empire, to its side. The prewar years, and even more so the war years, were moments when maps could be reimagined. Borders were both sacred and manipulable. New homelands were being conceived for "nations" that were still cohering around national myths, common languages, and articulated histories.

Empires were rethinking how they might prosper in a fluid and unpredictable world. No longer committed to upholding a balance of powers, competing states battled for higher stakes. Empires fought to maintain their power and expand their territories; aspiring nations struggled for independence and recognition. The question on the agenda was survival in a fiercely winner-take-all, zero-sum-game competition. Peoples who were in the way had to be removed—Jews, Ajars (Georgian Muslims), and Armenians—and running roughshod over them was justified by new science that confidently asserted that some races were superior to others. Existing nation-states and stateless nations had their own ambitions—to expand their territory, regain ancient lands, or even the capital, Constantinople or Vilnius, of a long-deceased imperial state. The immediate danger presented by war produced an upsurge in patriotism, even in Russia where class loyalties had strongly challenged ethnic loyalties. On the Left, socialist internationalism collapsed throughout Europe in 1914 before patriotic concerns,

---

[12]Much of this section is taken from "Introduction: Bringing Empire Back," in *The Empire and Nationalism at War,* ed. Eric Lohr et al., Russia's Great War and Revolution 2 (Bloomington, IN: Slavica, 2014), pp. 1–7, and reflects the findings of the authors collected in that volume.

with notable exceptions—the martyred Jean Jaurès in France, the Bolsheviks and internationalist Social Democrats in Russia, and the Bulgarian "Narrows"—who would have to wait until war weariness would resurrect transnational class affinities. Religion as well, Christianity and Islam, failed to transcend national boundaries, and coreligionists inspired by God and Country killed each other with a sense of just cause.

Notoriously empires did not limit their borders to the national composition of desired territories. They were promiscuous in expanding for whatever reason seemed appropriate. Sometimes strategic concerns were paramount; at other times consolidation of the "nation" might be deployed as justification for diplomatic or military aggression. Russian rulers, who thought of Ukrainians as "Little Russians" and therefore an integral part of the Russian people, were anxious (in the words of General Aleksei Brusilov) to "take back" Galicia, the part of the old Polish state held by the Austrian Empire, "which despite its being a constituent part of Austria-Hungary is a Russian land, populated, after all, by Russian people."[13] Here an empire justified its expansion in the name of the national principle, recovery of ostensibly long-lost territory. Through convenient, self-serving definitions of membership in the Russian "nation," the empire cast expropriation of territory as happy reunification, righting the wrongs of history and bringing brothers back into the embrace of their rightful kin. The Ottomans did the same in their campaigns into Caucasia, discovering the Turkic connection with the local "Tatars" (today's Azerbaijanis) and encouraging Caucasian Muslims to declare an independent Azerbaijan.

When convenient, however, the imperialist claims could be made on religious or state security grounds in addition or instead. Just as the Russian Empire hoped to win Galician Ukrainians "back" from Austria and into the Russian camp, so Wilhelmine Germany and its Austrian allies, playing the same game, urged Ukrainians to align with them and to detach the western borderlands of the Romanov Empire from the tsar's domain. On November 5, 1916, the two emperors promised that a self-governing Poland would be created after the war out of lands in the Russian Empire. The Central Powers recruited prisoners of war as potential nationalist opponents of imperial Russian rule, while the Russian General Staff permitted the organization of Slavic prisoners of war from Austria-Hungary into armed units. The number of prisoners of war on the Eastern Front was staggering: 3,343,900 Russians in the hands of their enemies and almost 2,000,000 Central Powers soldiers held by the Russians.[14] In a clear case of unintended consequences, the formation of a Czechoslovak Legion from captured Austrian Slavs under one Russian government led to events a few years later that helped to initiate the Russian Civil War against another. Future leaders of

---

[13]Mark von Hagen, *War in a European Borderland: Occupations and Occupation Plans in Galicia* (Seattle: University of Washington Press, 2007), p. 19.
[14]Joshua A. Sanborn, *Imperial Apocalypse: The Great War and the Destruction of the Russian Empire* (Oxford: Oxford University Press, 2014), p. 130.

RUSSIAN PRISONERS IN PRZEMYSL

Russian prisoners of war after their defeat at the Battle of Tannenberg, August 1914. Over 10,000 German soldiers were killed, nearly 80,000 Russian; and over 90,000 Russian soldiers were taken prisoner. The humiliated Russian commander, General Alexander Samsonov, committed suicide.

Eastern European states, among them Josef Pilsudski and Josef Broz Tito, served time in Russian military camps.

Nationalists also worked with empires opportunistically, attempting to exploit the rivalry between Germany and Russia. Poles dreamed of war between the powers that had partitioned their country over a century before. Georgian nationalists sought German assistance in their drive for independence, and even some moderate socialists flirted with a German orientation. Once established, the "nation-states" that proliferated late in the war and at its conclusion turned out not to be ethnically homogeneous as anticipated in the slogan of national self-determination, but more often than not multinational states or even little empires disguised as nation-states. Certainly in postwar Poland, with its inclusion of vast lands in which Ukrainians, Belorussians, Germans, and Jews lived, "making" a Polish nation meant assimilation of some, e.g., the Slavic peoples, and the exclusion of others, e.g., Jews and Germans.[15]

In Galicia, once in the orbit of Rus, later part of Poland, then Austrian, and in the future brought by the Soviets into Ukraine, the tale of national identity was particularly tangled. The Habsburgs had encouraged Ukrainian nationalism in

---

[15]Rogers Brubaker, *Nationalism Reframed: Nationhood and the National Question in the New Europe* (Cambridge: Cambridge University Press, 1996), pp. 84–103.

the prewar years to distance their Ukrainians from Russia, but when the war broke out the Austrians arrested tens of thousands of Ukrainians, suspecting them to be Russophilic. Crowded into concentration camps, thousands perished.[16] In 1914 the Russian army moved in, occupied Lvov (Lemberg, Lviv), and rounded up thousands of people who were thought to be enemies of Russia. In the first year of fighting the Russian military expelled half a million Jews from lands it had occupied and stood by while Cossacks and Poles looted the stores and homes of Jews. Tens of thousands of Germans living in Russian Poland suffered the same fate, and as a result they were compelled to identify more intensely as Germans than as the Russian subjects they had been. When the Germans drove the Russians back in 1915, Germans and Austrians adopted policies designed to foster Ukrainian identity in order to distance the local peasants from the Russians. The tsar's government responded by softening its opposition to Ukrainianness.[17]

Nationality became an instrument wielded by competing empires to win the hearts and minds of the peoples who lived in their borderlands. The war may have been an imperial conflict, a struggle for survival by bloated, ambitious imperial states, but as they bled their poorest subjects, imprisoned or deported others, they reinvigorated the search for national or state patriotic identifications of people caught in the middle. Such permissive violence and enforced discrimination only sharpened the lines between religions and ethnic groups, particularly in the shatter zone of Russia's western borderlands. The lands contested by rival empires had been battlefields on which differences of all kind and presumptions of entitlement were fought over long before they became the "Bloodlands" that some have argued were the result of particular dictatorial regimes.[18]

Before and during the First World War, Russian political analysts debated the future contours of their multinational state. Liberal intellectuals, most notably the leader of the Kadet Party, Pavel Miliukov, generally supported the war aims of the Russian Empire. Miliukov advocated expansion of the empire to include all of Poland and the eastern provinces of Ottoman Anatolia in order to form coherent national autonomies of Poles and Armenians under the scepter of the tsar. But he not only linked empire to nation in his design but also favored Russian

---

[16]Sanborn, *Imperial Apocalypse*, p. 41.

[17]Peter Gatrell, *A Whole Empire Walking: Refugees in Russia During World War I* (Bloomington and Indianapolis: Indiana University Press, 1999); and Eric Lohr, *Nationalizing the Russian Empire: The Campaign Against Enemy Aliens During World War I* (Cambridge, MA: Harvard University Press, 2003).

[18]For the latter argument, see Timothy Snyder, *Bloodlands: Europe Between Hitler and Stalin* (New York: Basic Books, 2010). For alternative viewpoints, see the essays in Omer Bartov and Eric Weitz, eds., *Shatterzone of Empires: Coexistence and Violence in the German, Habsburg, Russian, and Ottoman Borderlands* (Bloomington: Indiana University Press, 2013). *Bloodlands* makes a relatively straightforward argument attributing the massive violence and killing of the 1930s and 1940s in Eastern Europe to the persons and personalities of Hitler and Stalin, while *Shatterzone of Empires* takes a more contextual and even environmental approach to the contest of empires and nationalist movements and states, broadening the chronological sweep to nearly two centuries and the geographical frame to include the important case of the Ottoman Empire.

Map 9.1. The Eastern Front and losses from the Treaty of Brest-Litovsk.

conquest of Constantinople and the Straits as essential for the empire's future. Other liberal visions for maintaining Russia as an empire came from Russians' familiarity with British historical writing on the British Empire. Former Social Democrat turned liberal Peter Struve was enamored of the British model, as he understood it from his reading of the Cambridge University historian John Robert Seeley. In his influential book, *The Expansion of England* (1883), Seeley had written that the empire was England writ large, a collection of dominions and colonies.

British writers proposed a vision of "liberal imperialism." To resolve the fundamental contradiction of a "free people" ruling despotically over their imperial subjects, the imperial power must establish good government to improve the welfare of the colonial peoples.[19] Maxim Kovalevskii, Russia's leading sociologist and a principal leader of the Progressivist Bloc, also saw the British Empire (or at least a well-scrubbed idealized version of that empire) as a model for Russia.[20] The war, revolution, and anti-colonial movements in the colonies would soon expose the dilemma of empire when the well-intentioned reforms of the imperial powers only fed the appetites of the colonized to increase their autonomy or fight for independence altogether.

The Russian Left, as well as non-Russian nationalists, went further than the imperial visions of leading Kadets and Progressivists and advocated that Russia develop a nationality policy that recognized the full cultural development of the peoples within the empire while simultaneously promoting a universal imperial citizenship for all subjects of the empire. The Left Zionist Abram Kastelianskii favored nations as the political form of the future, condemning empires to history's dustbin. In the Duma, deputies from the borderlands debated the failures of Russian colonialism. The Georgian Social Democrat Nikolai Chkheidze castigated the government for what it characterized as its "liberationist" militarism and asked rhetorically, "what liberation did you gentlemen bring to Galicia, when you were the victors? . . . And what did the liberation of Armenia bring? How many Turkish Armenians remain among the living?" The Muslim deputy Mamed Iusif Jafarov accused the regime of breaking the social contract with the peoples of Central Asia when it called up Muslims to work in labor battalions and then brutally suppressed their insurrection. He and the Russian deputy from Saratov, Alexander Kerensky, made a formal report on the 1916 revolt in Central Asia, and Kerensky worried that Russian policies were discrediting the imperial mission of the state in the colonialized regions. Russia now appeared in the eyes of "the natives" to have lost its patina of civilization because of its "planned and systematic terror unacceptable not only in a cultured European state but also in any sort of eastern despotism." It would be difficult for Russians "to speak now about Turkish atrocities in Armenia, very difficult to talk about German atrocities in Belgium, given that what happened in the mountains of Semirechie (during the 1916 Kazakh revolt in Central Asia) has never been seen before."[21]

Appalled by the ferocity as well as the stupidity of the war, Lenin, the leader of the most radical Social Democrats, the Bolsheviks, tried desperately to understand it from his Marxist perspective. For him the war was imperialist—annexationist, predatory, and plundering, a war for the redivision of the world,

---

[19]Karuna Mantena, *Alibis of Empire: Henry Maine and the Ends of Liberal Imperialism* (Princeton, NJ: Princeton University Press, 2010); and Adam Tooze, *The Deluge: The Great War and the Remaking of Global Order* (London: Allen Lane, 2014), pp. 15–16, 386.
[20]Alexander M. Semyonov, "Russian Liberalism in Imperial Context," in *Liberal Imperialism*, ed. Matthew Fitzpatrick (London: Palgrave Macmillan, 2012), pp. 67–89.
[21]Cited in Sanborn, *Imperial Apocalypse*, pp. 185–87.

the partition and reparation of colonies, spheres of influence, and of finance capital. Taking power in October 1917, his party, he confidently asserted, would change all of that—if Europe obliged by carrying out the international socialist revolution that Russia had attempted to ignite.

Tsarist Russia's collapse did not occur because of nationalisms from the peripheries, but because of the progressive weakening and disunity of the center. Much of the legitimacy of the autocracy and its imperial enterprise had withered away by 1917. Elites withdrew support from the monarchy, and more broadly the regime was alienated from the intelligentsia and workers, strategically located in the largest cities. Policies of industrialization and the limited reforms after 1905 had created new constituencies in tsarist society that demanded representation in the political order that the tsar refused to grant. In its last years the dynasty appeared increasingly to be incompetent and even treacherous. As Russians suffered defeats and colossal losses in World War I, the fragile aura of legitimacy was stripped from the emperor and his wife, who were widely regarded as distant from, even foreign to, Russia. Elite patriotism, frustrated non-Russian nationalisms, worker discontent, the anxieties of ordinary soldiers, and peasant weariness at intolerable sacrifices for a cause with which they did not identify combined lethally to undermine the monarchy. When tsarism failed the test of war, its last sources of popular affection and legitimacy fell away, and in the crucial test of the February Days of 1917 Nicholas II was unable to find the military support to suppress the popular resistance to its rule in a single city.

NATIONALITY AND CLASS
ACROSS THE REVOLUTIONARY DIVIDE

The fall of the three-hundred-year-old Romanov monarchy occurred in a few days in the capital, Petrograd. First, women workers, followed by their male comrades, came out into the streets in the dark, cold days of late February to protest food and fuel shortages. Their numbers grew day by day even as soldiers and police turned their weapons on the crowds. Soon soldiers joined the protestors, and the tsar, who was at the front, was unable to return to the capital. High officials and officers convinced him that saving his throne was impossible, and in early March Nicholas II abdicated. A republic was soon declared. The February Revolution of 1917 would prove only the first in a year of revolutions.

Two competing authorities emerged immediately in Petrograd: a Provisional Government made up of liberal and conservative Duma deputies; and councils (soviets) of workers' and soldiers' deputies elected by ordinary people in the city. While the Provisional Government was recognized by foreign powers and was supported by the middle and upper classes, as well as military officers, the Petrograd Soviet had the backing of soldiers, workers, and the lower classes. Formal power lay with the Provisional Government; real power was in the hands of the Soviet. By May the government invited leading members of the Soviet to join the cabinet since governing alone had become impossible. But the government was torn between those who wanted to preserve as much of the old order as possible

"Down With the Monarchy, Hail the Republic," a demonstration during the February Revolution, 1917.

and those more liberal forces who pushed for reforms. Landlords wanted to keep their estates, while peasants seized the land and chased the nobles from their mansions. Industrialists found it impossible to continue to raise wages to meet inflating prices, and workers suspected plots by the owners to subvert the revolution. Soldiers no longer wanted to fight a losing war, while officers obeyed the government's call to launch a disastrous offensive in June.

The country was pulling apart. The lower classes—peasants, workers, and ordinary soldiers and sailors (who were identified as the *demokratiia*)—became increasingly hostile to the middle and upper classes (referred to either as *burzhui* [bourgeois] or *tsenzovoe obshchestvo* [propertied society]). Class conglomerates were the basic loci of social identification at the center of the revolution.

Before the fall of tsarism, nationalist movements, both among those who touted ethnic "Russianness" and those who identified with other national groups within the empire, were still largely centered in the ethnic intelligentsias, among students and the lower middle classes of the towns, with at best a fleeting following among broader strata. Among Belorussians, Lithuanians, and Azerbaijanis, the paramount identification was with people nearby with whom one shared social and religious communality, rather than a sense of ethnic nationality. For these peoples neither nationalism nor socialism was able to mobilize large numbers into the political struggles that would decide their future. For several other nationalities, among them the Latvians and Georgians, class-based socialist movements were far more potent than political nationalism. For still other nationalities, like the Ukrainians and the Estonians, nationality competed with a sense of class for primary loyalty of the workers and peasants, with neither winning a dominant position. Among Armenians a socialist-nationalist party, the *Dashnaktsutyun*, dominated. Faced by the threat of annihilation at the hands of Ottoman Turks, Armenians rallied around an inclusive, all-class nationalism.[22]

For the Muslim populations of Caucasia and Central Asia, religion served as the most potent collective affiliation and mobilizing issue. Referred to as *temnye* (dark) by the urban Christians and often considered to be an unenlightened, benighted people by members of educated society, migrant Muslim villagers found themselves in towns dominated by Russians and other Christians. In South Caucasia the sense of inferiority and of victimization at the hands of the Christian overlords and bourgeoisie kept local Muslims, referred to as "Tatars," apart from the non-Muslim population. The town of Baku, which until 1902 produced as much oil as the whole of the United States, was complexly segregated, with Russians and Armenians in the central part of the town and Muslims clustered in distinct districts. Poor Muslim workers developed resentments against skilled workers and employers, most of whom were Christians. Armenians and Russians were either blind to the concerns of Muslims or condescending in their behavior. By virtue of property holdings and a legal quota on Muslim representation, the Baku city duma remained in the hands of wealthy Armenians and Russians. Even though incorporation into the Russian Empire provided a new outlet for educated Muslims, some of whom turned from their religious upbringing to a more secular outlook, social resentments festered, particularly in times of political uncertainty. Ethnoreligious differences defined the battle lines in bloody clashes between Caucasian Muslims and local Armenians both in 1905 and 1918. When observers spoke about politics or class interests the language was about consciousness and rationality, values coded as masculine; when they spoke about ethnic impulses, it was about something more elemental, irrational, feminine. In the fall of 1917, for example, a reporter on unrest in Baku told his listeners: "The population of Baku and the industrial districts [where the inhabitants were mostly Muslim] feels extremely nervous about the supply problems. An intelligent attitude is noticeable among only a few. The dark forces are not sleeping and are using the situation being created to carry on hooligan agitation. . . . Crowds of uninformed Muslims appear with reproaches that no one cares about them. Behind them appears a crowd of similarly uninformed Russian women, claiming that it is mostly Muslims about whom [the authorities] care."[23] The word in Russian for politically "uninformed" was usually *nesoznatel'nyi*, literally "unconscious."

The February Revolution of 1917 ended the empire and inaugurated formally a multinational republic of equal nationalities. Empire and imperialism, with all

---

[22]For a comparative account of nationalism and socialism during the Russian Revolution, see Suny, *The Revenge of the Past*, particularly pp. 20–83.

[23]*Baku*, no. 204, September 13, 1917; cited in Ronald Grigor Suny, *The Baku Commune, 1917–1918: Class and Nationality in the Russian Revolution* (Princeton, NJ: Princeton University Press, 1972), p. 115.

their oppressive, coercive, and anti-egalitarian practices, were anathema to the revolutionaries and their supporters. Yet when decisions had to be made as to what rights to give to the constituent peoples of Russia, those in power found it difficult to make concessions to national aspirations. Confronted immediately by existential questions of war and peace, land reform, and the future shape of the new state, the liberal and moderate socialists who came to power were extraordinarily confident that juridical solutions could ameliorate deep social and ethnic conflicts. Women were given the vote, and restrictions on Jews and other peoples were abolished. The evils that had led to class and nationality hostilities were laid at the doorstep of tsarism, and it was argued that proper legislation in a Western, liberal direction would solve all such problems. Just a few weeks after the tsar's abdication, newspapers announced that the government intended to abolish all legal restrictions based on religion, nationality, and "class" (here referring primarily to *soslovie*—estate—and *chin*—rank). When Prime Minister Lvov signed the law on March 20, it was greeted by an editorial in the conservative *Novoe vremia* (New Time) that expressed both the fear that "the developing centrifugal forces and separatist aspirations of the nationalities that compose Russia" presented a "real danger of the gradual decomposition of the state into its component parts" and the hope that "[n]ow all obstacles to mutual understanding among the peoples of Russia have withered away in the light of liberty dawning over the country." Such optimism that "liberty will unite" demonstrated faith in legal solutions but also prepared the ground for bitter disappointment when problems associated with nationality proved to be far more intractable than imagined.

Toward the end of March, when the government worked out its provisions for local self-government, the principle of nationality was taken into consideration in two ways, the first, acknowledging particular groups' collective claims to some degree of recognition; the second, limiting rights on the basis of perceived ethnic characteristics. In forming the provinces of Estland and Lifland, "the natural boundaries" between them were to be delimited according to ethnicity. But in extending the *zemstva* to Siberia and Arkhangel'sk province, the government exempted those areas occupied by the nomadic Samoeds, various other *inorodtsy*, and Cossacks, for whom special regulations and institutions would be implemented. Special laws were issued for Turkestan (where local authorities would decide if *zemstva* were appropriate for various districts and peoples), the Kalmyk steppe, and the lands of the Kyrgyz Inner Horde. Plans for extending *zemstva* to South Caucasia and the Cossack regions of southern Russia were still being formulated when the Provisional Government was overthrown seven months later. The habit of working out particular solutions for various kinds of people, the practice of elaborating multiple separate deals, bridged the revolutionary divide and continued to color the policy of the Provisional Government, in spite of its commitment to overturning the pernicious practices of its imperial predecessor.

Nationality was clearly a consideration in the formulation of policy, but the Provisional Government and the principal parties were much more concerned about the unity of the state in a time of acute danger. The leading liberal party, the

Kadets, opposed national territorial political autonomy, a federal structure for the new Russia, and any form of separatism. They saw themselves as the champions of equal rights of *people*, rather than *peoples*, within a unitary Russian state. Representation would be geographic, rather than based on nationality. Proclaiming themselves for "Russia, One and Indivisible," the Kadets saw manifestations of nationalism as signs of pro-German disloyalty. Pavel Miliukov told his fellow Kadets in May that "the Party of the People's Freedom will endeavor to find a solution that, while giving an opportunity to the various regions of Russia to create their local autonomy on the principle of local legislation, will not at the same time destroy the unity of the Russian State. The preservation of the unity of the Russian State is the limiting factor conditioning the decisions of the Party. The division of the country into sovereign, independent units is considered by the Party as absolutely inadmissible." For non-Russians the liberals were almost as imperial-minded (though without the restrictions on national rights) as the monarchical regime that they had deposed. By the fall of 1917, not surprisingly, leading Kadets had become political allies of the Cossacks, the traditional defenders of Russian statehood.

While the various parties in the Provisional Government debated the fine points of their positions on nations and federalism, their actual power was severely limited. Two competing political authorities faced each other for most of 1917: the Provisional Government and the Petrograd Soviet. The Petrograd Soviet, which was the leading organ of the so-called *demokratiia* (the lower classes), was seldom in agreement with the government, which was identified in the minds of most workers and soldiers with the propertied classes. In the midst of the increasingly devastating war and with the entire future of Russia still desperately uncertain, with frequent strikes and militant actions by disgruntled soldiers and hungry workers and peasants, with factional strife dividing parties on the left and on the right, the "national question" was not a major concern for most activists. Yet, the question was inextricable from the various groups' visions for the Russia that they hoped would emerge from the chaos. Among the parties of the Left represented in the Soviet, the neo-populist Socialist Revolutionaries (the SRs) devoted most of their energy to three issues, summed up in their slogan— later adopted by the Bolsheviks—"Peace, Land, and Bread!" In 1917 the SR party continued to favor federalism but now opposed separation. At the third party congress, in May 1917, the SR rapporteur on state organization, M. V. Vishniak, envisioned Russia as Switzerland writ large, a federal state with a collegial executive, but, nevertheless, a single state.

In contrast to the SRs, the Marxist Social Democrats, who promoted the claims of the workers, were committed to national self-determination, and Lenin took that slogan farthest—to envisioning a right of voluntary separation from the empire in his programmatic plan for the state. National parties, particularly the Jewish Bund and the Armenian *Dashnaktsutyun*, advocated allowing ethnicities certain extraterritorial national-cultural autonomy and rights, such as granting each nationality representation in parliament as an ethnic voting bloc, no matter

Vladimir Lenin, leader of the Bolshevik (later Communist) Party, addressing a crowd of soldiers in Moscow's Red Square.

where its members lived. In contrast, the Bolsheviks favored regional autonomy without demarcation into ethno-territorial units. In the revolutionary year the Bolshevik position foresaw giving nationalities a stark choice: either full independence and separation from the rest of Russia or becoming part of a future unitary socialist state with all cultural and civil rights guaranteed for working people. Lenin believed that if Russians offered this choice between full national independence on one hand and continuing membership in the Russian state on the other, this tolerance would actually make non-Russians less likely to opt for independence. Lenin asked the Seventh Conference of the Bolsheviks in April 1917 rhetorically, "Why should we Great Russians, who have been oppressing more nations than any other people, deny the right to secession for Poland, Ukraine, or Finland?" He declared that the Bolshevik attitude toward the separatist movement should be "indifferent, neutral. . . . We are for Finland receiving complete freedom because then there will be greater trust in Russian democracy, and the Finns will not separate."[24] With considerable acuity, Lenin understood the dangers of trying to throw Russian weight around. He warned his comrades not to repeat the mistakes of the old regime's "Great Russian chauvinism" and to renounce its heritage of injustice toward the non-Russians of the empire.

---

[24]*Sedmaia (Aprel'skaia) Vserossiiskaia konferentsiia RSDRP (bol'shevikov), Protokoly* (Moscow: Gosizdatpolit, 1958), pp. 216–19.

Lenin was both aware of the power of nationalism (even as he hoped to harness it to the proletarian revolution) and ready to concede the need to ally with "bourgeois nationalists." Many of his comrades, like Nikolai Bukharin and Giorgii Piatakov, staked out a more radical position and opposed any concessions to nationalism. Like the famous and influential Polish Jewish Marxist Rosa Luxemburg, they consistently favored subordinating nationalism strictly to promotion of class considerations. "In a class society," she wrote, "'the nation' as a homogeneous sociopolitical entity does not exist. Rather, there exist within each nation, classes with antagonistic interests and 'rights.'"[25] For Lenin, nationalism reflected only the interests of the bourgeoisie; the proletariat's true interests were supranational; and the end of colonialism would diminish the power of nationalist sentiments. Nationalism and separatism were neither natural nor inevitable, but were contingent on the sense of oppression that nationalities experienced from imperialism.

In the terms of the theories of nationalism discussed above, Lenin was a "constructivist" before his time. In contrast to his party comrades on the Left, Lenin refused to oppose the independence of Finland, Poland, and Ukraine. Though he hoped that such separations could be avoided and reserved the option to oppose specific moves toward independence on principle, he was unequivocal in his public commitment to "the full right of separation from Russia of all nations and nationalities, oppressed by tsarism, joined by force or held by force within the borders of the state, i.e., annexed." At the same time, he argued that the goal of the proletarian party was the creation of the largest state possible and the rapprochement (*sblizhenie*) and eventual merging (*sliianie*) of nations. Such a goal was to be reached, he optimistically predicted, not through force, but voluntarily, by the will of the workers.[26] The question remained open, however: what would Lenin and the Bolsheviks actually do if non-Russians chose to leave Russia?

The first year of the Russian Revolution was a period in which social issues articulated in a language of class overwhelmed specifically ethnic concerns. Baku oil workers drew together in a coordinated movement to pressure the industrialists to raise their wages, and when persuasion failed, they launched a victorious industry-wide strike. Though ethnic tensions appeared in the newly elected municipal duma in Tiflis, as Georgians replaced the formerly hegemonic Armenian middle class, they were contained within a political framework that promised democratic solutions to these perennial problems. Traumatized by the mass killings and deportations in Turkey, the Armenians maintained their separate national agenda, hoping that constitutional reforms would grant them a degree of autonomy and self-rule within a democratic Russia. Most of the peoples of the now-defunct Russian Empire expressed interest in remaining within the new,

[25]Rosa Luxemburg, "The Right of Nations to Self-Determination," in *The National Question—Selected Writings by Rosa Luxemburg*, ed. and intro. Horace B. Davis (New York and London: Monthly Review Press, 1976), p. 135.
[26]From the brochure *Zadachi proletariata v nashei revoliutsii (Proekt platformy proletarskoi partii)*, written in April 1917, first published in September. V. I. Lenin, *Polnoe sobranie sochineniia* [henceforth, *PSS*] (Moscow: Izdatel'stvo politicheskoi literatury, 1958–1965), Vol. 31, pp. 167–68.

democratic Russia, but at the same time they wanted guarantees of their ethnic as well as individual rights. They were not as determined in 1917 to secede from the new democratic state as they would become during the years of civil war (1918–1921). Their faith lay in a constitutional solution within a renewed multinational state, which overrode the risky choice of going it alone in time of war.

In one of its first acts the Provisional Government restored the constitution of the Grand Duchy of Finland and recognized its full "internal independence." The Finnish Social Democrats, the dominant party in the Finnish Diet, went further and pushed for a law that ascribed sovereignty to the Finnish parliament. But neither the Provisional Government nor the Petrograd Soviet, committed as they were to formal and complete independence for Poland, was willing to grant the same to Finland or Ukraine. Since Germany was in control of most of Poland by early 1917, political support for Polish independence in no way threatened the war effort. But the concession to Poland only increased the appetites of the Finns and the Ukrainians, and the inherent conflict between the principle of national self-determination and the commitment of the leading political actors to the unity of the Russian state emerged into open political struggle within the first weeks of the revolution.

In Kiev a locally elected assembly, the Rada, issued its First Universal, declaring autonomy for Ukraine and itself the supreme political authority. Late in June, delegates from the Provisional Government conferred in Kiev with representatives of the Rada, and after heated discussions the Petrograd delegation reluctantly decided to recognize the Rada's competence to work out reforms in Ukraine and run the region until the convocation of the Constituent Assembly, the promised electoral body tasked with working out a new form of government for Russia. Back in the Russian capital, however, liberal party leaders balked at the concessions made in favor of autonomy for Ukraine. The attempt at compromise with the Ukrainians led to a crisis within the Provisional Government, and several members of the Kadet party resigned in protest against political concessions to the Ukrainians.

In Finland the attitude of the Petrograd authorities stimulated even more support for independence, and through May and June the Finnish Social Democrats pushed for a law (the *valtalaki*), passed in mid-July, that ascribed almost full sovereignty to the Finnish parliament, leaving only foreign and military policy to Petrograd. The Russian socialists, however, hoped to delay the final disposition of Finland until the Constituent Assembly. The First All-Russian Congress of Soviets adopted a broad resolution on the national question, proclaiming its support of decentralization of the state and broad political autonomy for regions that differ ethnically and socioeconomically from one another. It called on the government to issue a declaration recognizing the right of self-determination of all peoples, including separation, but left the final disposition of the various regions to be realized through a covenant with the national Constituent Assembly. Until the very last days of its existence the Provisional Government refused to concede full independence to Finland and proved willing to use armed force to enforce its policy.

The war exacerbated the economic collapse within the country and radical-ized the soldiers, most of whom no longer wanted to fight in a futile conflict. The Bolsheviks, as the most radical party in the country, reaped the whirlwind. To please the Western Allies and contribute to the war effort against the Central Powers, the minister of war, Alexander Kerensky, launched a disastrous offensive against the enemy in June, but as news of Russian defeats reached the capital, workers, sailors, and soldiers demonstrated against the war and the government, even calling on the Soviet to take power in its own name and to end the debilitat-ing and unstable compromise of dual rule. The moderate socialists refused, and at one point the impatient crowd seized one of these moderate socialists, Victor Chernov, the minister of agriculture. Chernov had to be rescued by Leon Trotsky, a recent addition to Lenin's Bolshevik Party, having switched his allegiance from the less centralized Menshevik Party. In the confusion of the "July Days" (July 3–5 [16–18][27]), militant elements—workers, soldiers, and radical activists—supporting the Bolsheviks pushed to seize power from the Provisional Govern-ment. Lenin believed that taking power by force was premature at this point and opposed the radical move. When order was restored by troops loyal to the gov-ernment and soviet, Lenin was forced to go into hiding in Finland. The liberal prime minister, Prince Lvov, resigned, and the moderate socialist Kerensky formed a new coalition government.

Through the summer of 1917, workers and soldiers increasingly gravitated to the Bolshevik program for a rapid end to the war, "workers' control" of industry, and "All Power to the Soviets!" The peasants carried out their own land reform by seizing land without sanction from the government. Liberal and conservative forces became more wary of the lower classes and called for an authoritarian gov-ernment to restore order. Briefly, the hopes of the Kadets, army officers, and much of the middle and upper classes fell on the ponderous General Lavr Kornilov—whom his commander General Brusilov claimed "had the heart of a lion but the brain of a sheep"—when he called for discipline, restoration of the death penalty in the rear, and curtailing the powers of the soviets and revolutionary commit-tees. When he marched on Petrograd, believing (inaccurately) he had the support of Kerensky, Kornilov met resistance from armed workers and soldiers and was arrested. But in the aftermath of this counterrevolutionary "mutiny," the lower classes moved swiftly toward the Bolsheviks, electing them the majority party in both the Petrograd and Moscow soviets by early September. The warnings of the Bolsheviks that Kerensky and company wanted to reverse the gains made by the workers and soldiers appeared to be confirmed by the *Kornilovshchina*.

Preparations began for the convening of the Second Congress of Soviets, at which, it was believed, a majority of Bolsheviks and their allies, most importantly

---

[27]Here and subsequently, bracketed numbers represent the dates according to the Gregorian calen-drical system adopted by the Bolsheviks in 1918. Previously, Russians had used the Julian calendar, which in the twentieth century was thirteen days behind, represented here by the unbracketed numbers.

the Left Socialist Revolutionaries, would proclaim "Soviet power" and eliminate Kerensky's government. Still an outlaw hiding in Finland, Lenin urged his followers to take power immediately and not wait for the Congress. He feared that Kerensky would move first against the Bolsheviks. "History will not forgive us," he told his comrades, "if we do not take power now." In the second half of October, the Military-Revolutionary Committee of the Petrograd Soviet, led by Trotsky, began establishing its authority over the garrisons of the city. On the morning of October 24 (November 6), Kerensky made his move to suppress the Bolsheviks and prevent the insurrection that everyone knew was coming. But in the crucial hours the prime minister found his support weak or nonexistent. Even the Cossacks deserted him, and only the Women's Battalion of Death stood between the Soviet forces and the government in the Winter Palace. Though workers did not actively participate in the insurrection, the Bolsheviks found the military muscle to take power. By dawn on October 25 (November 7), the city was in the hands of the Military-Revolutionary Committee, and Lenin went before the Second Congress of Soviets and declared that power had passed to the soviets. For the Bolsheviks and their allies, the October Revolution was the logical and necessary extension of what had begun in February. For liberals, conservatives, and moderate socialists, it was the perversion of what they had hoped for eight months earlier.

SOVIET POWER

In Petrograd and Moscow, where the main action of the revolution took place, nationalism did not serve as a mobilizing ideology, except perhaps in the misdirected patriotic commitment to pursuing a losing war that doomed the Provincial Government to collapse. Other forms of solidarity, particularly of class, and other priorities, namely peace, land, and bread, animated the revolutionary movement. In the complex push and pull between national and imperial identities that we have traced throughout this book, *neither* proved the victor or inspired the workers, soldiers, peasants, or socialist revolutionaries. Although the nation-form had seemed poised to sweep aside empires and emerge as the triumphant political model of the twentieth century, Russia followed a different course. Imbued with many of the democratic principles of national discourse, the *demokratiia* understood sovereignty to rest in the working people. They aspired to dignity and equality—for working people—and participatory and responsive government. They sought economic rights and, more concretely, control of the land and factories. But for the most part they did not respond to the strains of nationalism. Other kinds of affiliation and political thinking made for a forking rather than one-way road from old regime empire to modern state.

The October insurrection eliminated the middle and upper classes from political participation. Soviet power meant that only working people would be eligible to elect people to the new representative councils. This radically new order instituted a new, inverted, class-based mode of distinction and exclusion. When the moderate socialists, the Mensheviks and Right Socialist Revolutionaries, protested the Bolshevik seizure of power and walked out of the Congress, they essentially left only those furthest to the Left, the Bolsheviks and Left Socialist Revolutionaries, able to form a new government. The Socialist Revolutionaries saw themselves as the party that best represented the peasants, the vast majority of the country, but through 1917 the party split between a left wing that drew close to the Bolsheviks and a right wing that allied with the Mensheviks. Lenin hoped to have the Bolsheviks form a one-party government, even though the workers, soldiers, and party activists who supported the October Revolution in fact preferred a multi-party government of all the socialist parties. Within a month, however, the Bolshevik leader was forced to concede significant seats to the Left Socialist Revolutionaries, and until March 1918 Soviet Russia had a Left socialist coalition government.

The Bolsheviks and Left SRs came to power in 1917 largely because their program to form a lower-class government, end the war, and give the land to the peasants won significant support by late summer and fall, as society pulled apart and confidence in the Provisional Government evaporated. The Soviet government immediately acted on its major promises. It withdrew Russia from the war and decreed that the peasants should take over and redistribute the land. Yet the new Soviet government remained weak and insecure outside of Petrograd, Moscow, and a few other large cities. In November 1917 elections were held to a Constituent Assembly, a kind of founding congress for the new republic. Many hopes were riding on this elected body, which was intended to work out the new form of government for the country through a legitimate representative process. The Bolsheviks failed to win a majority, winning only 24 percent of the votes cast, while the Right Socialist Revolutionaries, who successfully carried the elections in the countryside, emerged with the largest plurality with 40 percent. But Lenin did not intend to surrender his hard-won position, and after allowing a single day's meeting (January 5 [18], 1918), the Soviet government dispersed the Constituent Assembly, Russia's most freely elected parliamentary body until the early 1990s.

By this act, even more than the seizure of power in October, the Leninists who in 1918 would begin to call themselves Communists, declared war on all those forces that had supported the first revolution of 1917 but not, like the Bolsheviks and Left SRs, the second. Almost immediately after October, Socialist Revolutionaries attempted an armed attack on the Bolshevik government. Cossacks in southern Russia rallied around Kornilov and other generals to launch what would become a full-fledged civil war. In South Caucasia, Ukraine, Belorussia, Central Asia, Finland, and the Baltic region, unlike in Russia proper, nationalism contributed to violent resistance to the new Bolshevik government. Non-Russian nationalist (and often socialist) parties seceded from Russia and formed independent states supported either by the Germans, Turks, or the Western Allies. Enemies that ranged from reactionary monarchists to liberals, moderate socialists, and peasant anarchists opposed Lenin's government. The Germans occupied Ukraine, Belorussia, and the Baltic region; the Ottoman Turks moved into South

Caucasia; and Britain, France, Japan, and the United States sent armies to Russia to bring her back into the war or overthrow the Bolsheviks.

The battle lines in the Civil War pitted "Reds," the Bolsheviks and their allies, against the "Whites," everyone from monarchists to liberals, and various peasant armies, the "Greens," which shifted from side to side. To their advantage the Reds occupied the heartland of Russia, which had been reduced to roughly the core lands of early modern Muscovy, along with both capitals, Moscow and Petrograd. The Whites, to their disadvantage, were divided and spread out from the Baltic region in the northwest, Ukraine, Crimea, and the Don River region in the south, and Siberia to the east. The nationalist and separatist movements were also located in the peripheries of the old empire: South Caucasia, Ukraine, Poland, Finland, the Baltic region, and Central Asia. The Reds had the shorter supply lines and the prestige of holding the capitals, while the Whites were unable to link their various armies on distant fronts together in a concentrated advance on the capitals.

Building a centralized party organization, a 5 million man Red Army headed by Trotsky, and relying on broad support in the central regions of Russia, the Communists won the Civil War by early 1921. Against all odds, they managed to defeat their opponents and establish the Soviet state, a task akin to building a ship in a stormy sea. Even though workers soon found themselves unemployed as the industrial economy nearly shut down and many grew disaffected with the Communists, most of them still supported Soviet power. Soldiers "voted with their feet" and deserted the fronts, yet most who remained continued to back the Communists. Peasants were pleased by the Bolshevik land decree that gave them the land outright without compensation to the former owners, and they carried out a radically egalitarian repartition of the land. But when during the Civil War the Communists forced peasants to give up their grain to feed the Red Army and the cities, peasants turned against the Soviets. Nonetheless, when caught between the Reds, who had given them the land, and the anti-Bolshevik Whites, who would take it back, peasants generally chose the Communists as the lesser of the two evils.

If Russian workers, peasants, and soldiers were for the most part positively disposed toward the new socialist government—or at least willing to acquiesce in its rule—the same cannot be said of the non-Russian populations of the former empire. The Bolsheviks were not numerous in many non-Russian areas, with the exception of industrial centers like Baku, and their sudden seizure of power and radical message did not resonate in smaller towns and villages. When the Soviet government withdrew unilaterally from the war, even before their withdrawal was formalized in the Treaty of Brest-Litovsk in March 1918, Russian troops from the Caucasian and Western fronts left for home. In the borderlands what had been social struggles along class lines rapidly turned into inter-ethnic conflicts. In Caucasia the danger of a Turkish invasion threatened some nationalities (the Armenians and Georgians) and was seen as an opportunity by others (the Azerbaijanis). When Russian troops at the end of 1917 abandoned the Caucasus,

Armenian volunteer military units, which had fought on the Caucasian Front since late 1914, found that they possessed one of the most powerful military forces in the region. For Armenians the principal source of danger came from their ethnic and religious enemies, the Ottoman Turks and the Azerbaijanis, and the very acuteness of that danger completed what two decades of nationalist propaganda had been working to accomplish—the effective mobilization of the Caucasian Armenian population to vote for and fight for the national future as defined by their leading party, the Dashnaktsutyun. Like almost all the other nationalist movements within the Russian Empire, the Dashnaks called for autonomy within the Russian state through 1917 rather than complete independence from it.

But with the October Revolution non-Russians reassessed their future connections to the center. Russia began to fragment into independent states. With the outbreak of civil war in mid-1918 semi-independent governments sprang up in the borderlands. The Georgian Mensheviks acted swiftly to disarm the Russian garrison in Tiflis and establish local soviet power. Refusing to recognize the Bolshevik government in Petrograd, the South Caucasian socialist parties (with the exception of the local Bolsheviks) gradually separated the region from the rest of Russia. A brief experiment in Transcaucasian autonomy (February to April 1918) was followed by an even briefer one in an independent federative republic of Transcaucasia (April to May), and finally the establishment of three

Map 9.2. Transcaucasia, 1918–1921.

separate republics (May 1918 to 1920–1921). This brief phase of independent statehood lasted only until the Red Army was able to occupy Azerbaijan (April 1920), Armenia (December 1920), and Georgia (February 1921).

The revolution and civil war engulfed the millions of Russians and non-Russians in a common maelstrom of imperial collapse and social revolution. The Communists were not everywhere the enemy of non-Russian actors but were seen by many as the preferred alternative to a national independence promoted by a small nationalist elite in the name of a peasant majority. The difficult choice for both Russians and non-Russians was whether to support the central Soviet government and the revolution as now defined by the Leninists or to accept a precarious existence in alliance with undependable allies from abroad with their own agendas. The Russian Whites did not present an attractive alternative to non-Russians. While the Reds backed the "right of national self-determination," the monarchists and their compatriots proclaimed a unitary Russian state. Non-Russians calculated the relative advantages to be gained from the options available, which in turn were influenced by realistic estimations of who might support their interests. In hard-fought regions like the Baltic, Finland, Poland, and South Caucasia, anti-Communist nationalists found allies in foreign interventionists—the Germans in the northwest and Ukraine, the Ottomans and British in Caucasia. Civil war overlapped with ethnic war, which overlapped with international conflict between competing empires. In this complex context, threatened with violent overthrow, the Communists fought to maintain the largest state they could, using whatever means they felt were needed: terror, propaganda, persuasion, and promises. Their state would be built by mobilizing millions and ultimately winning the war against great odds.

Like the liberals and moderate socialists, the Communists wanted to preserve the great Russian state, but for both ideological and pragmatic reasons, Lenin and Joseph Stalin, the People's Commissar of Nationalities in the new Soviet government, decreed national self-determination including separation from Russia and full cultural and political rights for the non-Russian peoples of the Soviet state. Lenin's hope that permitting separatism would actually discourage it proved false. In the euphoria of revolution and the confidence that came with surviving civil war, Lenin and the Bolsheviks gave in to their most utopian hopes: that the world would soon be made anew by international revolution. National borders would be swept away, and a new organization of human society would gradually replace capitalism and bourgeois parliamentarianism. Already in the appeal "To All Muslim Toilers of Russia and the East," issued just one month after the Bolsheviks came to power in November 1917, the powerful rhetoric of self-determination, liberation, independence, and anti-imperialism established a unity of the struggle against colonial and national oppression.

> Now, when war and desolation are demolishing the pillars of the old order, when the entire world is blazing with indignation against the imperialist brigands, when the least spark of discontent bursts out in a mighty flame of revolution, . . . now it is impossible to keep silent. Lose no time in throwing off

the yoke of the ancient oppressors of your land! Let them no longer violate your
hearths! You must yourselves be masters in your own land! You yourselves must
arrange your life as you yourselves see fit! You have the right to do this, for your
fate is in your own hands!
Comrades! Brothers!
Advance firmly and resolutely towards a just and democratic peace!
We inscribe the liberation of the oppressed peoples of the world on our
banners!
Muslims of Russia!
Muslims of the East!
We look to you for sympathy and support in the work of regenerating the
world.[28]

To win the war and bring the non-Russian territories back into the new state,
the Communists did not hesitate to use violence and terror, even against peasants and workers who resisted their rule. As fighting escalated throughout
the land, much of the democratic promise of the revolution of 1917 was lost.
Terrible atrocities occurred on both sides. Red Terror was matched by White
Terror. The Communists killed clerics and nobles, the bourgeois and other
class enemies as they defined them. The Whites targeted the Jews in particular,
whom they considered equivalent to Communists, and in sheer numbers
slaughtered more civilians than did the Reds. The fledgling Soviet state fought
for three years, 1918–1921, against monarchists, moderate socialists and liberals,
peasant rebels, and foreign interventionists. To win over non-Russians the
Communists stepped back from their most radical aspirations and made significant policy concessions. Not only did the new regime proclaim the right to
national self-determination, including separation from Soviet Russia, but it
agreed that rather than a unitary state the new republic would become a federal
state with units based on nationality.

SOVIET NATIONALITY POLICIES

Soviet Russia was conceived by the Bolsheviks not as an ordinary national state,
and certainly not as an empire, but as the first stone in a future international socialist edifice. The reach of the Russian Revolution was to be limitless. With a
confidence born of recent victories and faith in a Marxist eschatology, the Communists used all the means available to realize their dream of international revolution. For Communists of the Civil War period, internationalism was less the
servant of the Soviet states than the Soviet states were the servants of internationalism. Lenin saw Russia as the springboard from which the international revolution could be launched, after which workers of other countries would aid
backward, peasant Russia to build a socialist society. But the imperatives of holding power and operating in an international system of states soon forced the

[28]https://www.marxists.org/history/ussr/government/foreign-relations/1917/December/3.htm.

Communists after the revolutionary euphoria faded to act more like a normal state: to establish diplomatic relations with other powers and to subordinate the international revolution to Soviet state interests.

The Bolsheviks' pre-revolutionary thinking on the national question, which opposed autonomous ethnonational units and federalism, did not survive their taking power. With little real ability to enforce its will in the peripheries, the Soviet government made a strategic shift in response to the growing number of autonomies and accepted by January 1918 the principle of federalism. Adding a third possibility to Lenin's earlier binary policy, wherein ethno-national units either could opt out altogether and establish national independence or opt into the Soviet state and renounce their (obsolete) separatism, the revised party position now allowed ethno-territorial subdivision with significant autonomy within the broader state. Though dressed in entirely new, socialist garb, this pragmatic solution had a good deal in common with tsarist efforts to create unity through difference. The new Soviet state would be both federative, at least in name and theory, and based on ethnic political units. Nationalities would have their own territorial homelands within the Russian Soviet Federative Socialist Republic. Even diasporic communities, those living outside a designated national territory, were to be given cultural and educational institutions, and in many cases their own political bodies. Whereas the imperial regime had claimed extraterritorial authority over Orthodox Christians and fellow Slavs abroad as justification for meddling in the affairs of its neighbors, the Soviets granted extraterritorial rights to these diasporic peoples within Soviet borders. Indeed for more than a decade following the Civil War, nationalities like the Jews and Armenians, and Ukrainians in Russia, enjoyed extraterritorial privileges that they had been seeking since late imperial times. They were authorized to operate their own schools and soviets in republics of other nationalities. Soviet practice combined ideological desiderata, such as the struggle against Russian chauvinism, with practical considerations of state unity. The aim was to erode separatist nationalism while developing class loyalties. But the concessions to the national principle led not to the disappearance of ethnic cultural affiliations as Lenin expected but to the consolidation of nationality. Rather than a melting pot, the Soviet Union became the incubator of new nations.

The Soviet state, however, was being put together in the midst of civil war and foreign military intervention. Decisions about alliances and the use of force were made pragmatically, even opportunistically, despite the stated goal of recognizing national rights and independence. As they launched a military campaign in Ukraine, where Red, White, Green (peasant), anarchist, and foreign forces were contending for power, the Bolsheviks backed those most sympathetic to their revolution. They announced that they recognized the Central Executive Committee of Soviets of Ukraine as "the supreme authority in Ukraine" and accepted "a federal union with Russia and complete unity in matters of internal and external policy." By the end of January 1918 the Third Congress of Soviets resolved: "The Soviet Russian Republic is established on the basis of a free union of free nations, as a federation of Soviet national republics."[29] Both federalism and national-territorial autonomy were written into the first Soviet constitution, adopted in July 1918. As Richard Pipes has noted, "Soviet Russia . . . became the first modern state to place the national principle at the base of its federal structure."[30]

Ukraine secured its independence from Russia for a short time by subordinating the new republic to the Central Powers—Germany and Austria—at Brest-Litovsk in early 1918. Bolsheviks were driven out of Ukraine, and German and Austrian soldiers guaranteed the country's limited sovereignty. For many Ukrainian nationalists, the Treaty of Brest-Litovsk, the first treaty of the end of war settlement, has been regarded as a positive step in the history of Ukrainian state-building. For Russians, Brest-Litovsk was another "Tilsit Peace," like the humiliating concessions made to Napoleon by Alexander I. Huge territories in the western parts of the Russian Empire, including Ukraine, Belorussia, and the Baltic lands, passed under the hegemony of the Germans, who supported local anti-Bolshevik nationalists. For Russian nationalists (and for Vladimir Putin today), Brest-Litovsk was an act of treason by the fledgling Bolshevik regime. The Treaty is still seen by many Russians as proof that European imperialism has always been anxious to weaken Russia by stripping it of its borderlands.

Now that the Ukrainian nationalists had a country of their own, albeit one dependent on the bayonets of foreign soldiers, they had to make more complete Ukrainians—to promote the Ukrainian language and integrate the Russian-speaking cities into the new Ukrainian state. Under the Ukrainian parliament, the Rada, as well as under the Hetmanate and the Austrian-sponsored "Red Prince," Wilhelm von Habsburg, moderate programs of Ukrainization were carried out, laying a foundation for later Soviet indigenization policies. Not to be outdone, the Bolsheviks (at least Lenin) also preached acceptance of nationalities making their own decisions about their future. A month after taking power, Lenin spoke boldly about the Soviet policy toward the most important non-Russian nationality, the Ukrainians.

> We now observe the national movement in Ukraine, and we say: we uncondi-
> tionally stand for the full and unlimited freedom of the Ukrainian people. We
> must break with the old, bloody, filthy past, when the Russia of capitalist op-
> pressors played the role of executioner of other peoples. . . . We say to the Ukrai-
> nians: as Ukrainians, you can run your own lives as you wish. But we extend a
> fraternal hand to the Ukrainian workers and say to them: together with you we
> will fight against your and our bourgeoisie. Only a socialist alliance of laborers
> of all countries eliminates any ground for national persecution and fighting.[31]

Toward the end of 1919, while reflecting on the factors that had led to Bolshevik victory in 1917, Lenin turned once again to Ukraine to underscore the importance

---

[29]Richard Pipes, *The Formation of the Soviet Union: Communism and Nationalism, 1917–1923* (Cambridge, MA: Harvard University Press, 1954), p. 111.
[30]Ibid., p. 11.
[31]V. I. Lenin, *PSS*, Vol. 35, p. 116.

of tolerance in nationality policy. Reviewing the Constituent Assembly election results, in which Ukrainian SRs and socialists outpolled the Russian SRs among Ukrainian voters, he noted: "The division between the Russian and Ukrainian Socialist Revolutionaries as early as 1917 could not have been accidental." Without holding that national sentiments are fixed or permanent, he suggested once again that internationalists must be tolerant of the changing national consciousness of non-Russians, which, he was confident, was part of the petty-bourgeois vacillation that had been characteristic of the peasantry throughout the Civil War.

> The question whether the Ukraine will be a separate state is far less important [than the fundamental interests of the proletarian dictatorship, the unity of the Red Army, or the leading role of the proletariat in relation to the peasantry]. We must not be in the least surprised, or frightened, even by the prospect of the Ukrainian workers and peasants trying out different systems, and in the course of, say, several years, testing by practice union with the RSFSR [Russian Soviet Federative Socialist Republic], or seceding from the latter and forming an independent Ukrainian SSR, or various forms of their close alliance....
>
> The vacillation of non-proletarian working people on *such* a question is quite natural, even inevitable, but not in the least frightful for the proletariat. It is the duty of the proletarian who is really capable of being an internationalist ... to leave it to the non-proletarian masses *themselves* to *get rid* of this vacillation as a result of their own experience.[32]

Lenin's position contrasted starkly with the policies adopted over the centuries by his tsarist predecessors, who, as we have seen, experimented with a variety of manifestations of autonomy and differentiation but never tolerated actual secession.

In the ferocity of the civil war, many Communists, particularly those in the peripheries or of non-Russian origin, opposed Lenin's rhetoric about national self-determination, fearing the dissolution of the unitary state. As early as December 1917, Stalin argued that the freedom of self-determination should be given only to the laboring classes, not to the bourgeoisie. At the Eighth Party Congress in March 1919, Nikolai Bukharin, at the time a militantly leftist member of the Bolshevik inner circle, supported Stalin's position and tried to divide the national from the colonial question. Only in those nations where the proletariat had not defined its interests as separate from the bourgeoisie should the slogan of "self-determination of nations" be employed. Lenin answered Bukharin sharply. All nations, he reasserted, have the right to self-determination, and Bolshevik support for this principle would aid the self-determination of the laboring classes. The stage of a given nation as it moved from "medieval forms to bourgeois democracy and on to proletarian democracy" should be considered, he stated, but it was difficult to differentiate the interests of the proletariat and the bourgeoisie, which had been clearly defined only in Russia proper.[33]

---

[32]V. I. Lenin, *PSS*, Vol. 40, p. 20; V. I. Lenin, *Collected Works* (Moscow, 1960–1970); Vol. 30, p. 271.
[33]*Vosmoi s"ezd RKP (b). Mart 1919 goda. Protokoly* (Moscow: Gosudarstvennoe izdatel'stvo politicheskoi literatury, 1959), pp. 46–48, 52–56.

Map 9.3. The Russian Civil War, 1917–1922.

The final resolution of the Congress was a messy compromise between Lenin's tolerance of nationalism and the more militant opposition to it. The Bolsheviks reached no consensus on nationality policy, and the conflict between those who, like Lenin, considered the national agenda of non-Russians and those who, like Stalin, subordinated the national to the "proletarian," continued until the former's death and the latter's consolidation of power within the party. On the ground, Communists themselves decided who was the carrier of the nation's will, and after the initial recognition of independence for Finland, Poland, the Baltic republics, and (for a time) Georgia, few other gestures were made toward "separatists."

The final disposition of Russia's border territories was decided by expedience, opportunity, and physical force. Bessarabians, for example, at first identified primarily with the Russian Empire in which they had lived for over a century. In the year of revolution, 1917–1918, when socialists dominated local politics, national activists sought autonomy within a federal democratic state. But with the Bolshevik victory in Petrograd and the collapse of the Russian economy, nationalists made a desperate choice to unite with the Romanian state with which most Bessarabians (Moldovans) shared a common language. Lithuanians were torn between a Russian and a German orientation. Their principal enemy, the Poles, dominated Vilnius and other cities and had ambitions to include the traditional Lithuanian capital in their resurrected state. After losing Vilnius to Poland in 1920, Lithuanian nationalism focused on recovering the treasured city, even though its population was heavily Polish and Jewish. The Soviets returned Vilnius to Lithuania in 1939 but at a high price—occupation.

In the vast landscape of Central Asia Russian settlers carried out a colonial counterrevolution against the native Muslims. The struggle for food and social order pitted Muslims who favored greater autonomy against Soviet forces that promoted subordination to the center. Tashkent Communists fiercely fought against various Muslim forces, in one case in alliance with Armenian nationalists. Alliances formed and were broken between "bandits" and Reds, until ultimately Bolshevik Moscow considered the Turkestan Muslims too unreliable to be granted significant local authority.

The Civil War, like all of Russia's wars, was fought by men and women whose complicated, mixed lineages and geographical and social mobility defined them as products of empire. Through the life of one individual, Baron Roman Feodorovich von Ungern-Sternberg, historian Willard Sunderland tracks the personal, ethnic, religious, national, ideological, and international whirlwind of the twilight of the Russian empire. Ungern was raised at the intersection of two great land-based empires (the Austro-Hungarian and Russian), and his later ambitions placed him at the boundary between two others (the Russian and the Chinese). His upbringing, education, military service, and his own political-ideological campaigns took him back and forth across Russia's imperial terrain, encompassing most of Eurasia. His life encapsulates the movement and the mixing of populations that such imperial currents generated. A Baltic German baron turned Cossack, schooled in Estonia and St. Petersburg, serving his emperor in Siberia, Mongolia, and along the western borders of Russia in the First World War, Ungern was a product and a champion of empire. Once the Bolsheviks toppled the Provisional Government, Ungern, posted at the time in the Trans-Baikal region (eastern Siberia), joined the counterrevolution, engaged in brutal warfare, and formulated a grandiose plan to reconstitute the Russian and Chinese Empires from his base in Outer Mongolia, where he had established himself as warlord and ruler. Briefly empowered through his tremendous audacity, in the Far East he not only enjoyed free rein for his murderous impulses, but he also developed a semi-mystical political philosophy that licensed his anti-Semitic and anti-socialist violence. His brief imperial escapade came to an end when the Bolsheviks captured him in 1921 and shot him. A signature product of empire, Ungern served one empire and died at the hands of another while dreaming of building a third.[34]

---

[34]Willard Sunderland, *The Baron's Cloak: A History of the Russian Empire in War and Revolution* (Ithaca, NY: Cornell University Press, 2014). Any number of other individuals could illustrate the

As the strategic situation improved for the Bolsheviks and their allies by the summer of 1920, the "national-colonial question" was put squarely on the agenda. The British were leaving the Russian periphery, and the Communists had gained their first foothold south of the Caucasus with the relatively easy Sovietization of Azerbaijan in April. The balance of forces in Central Asia and in Transcaucasia clearly favored the Soviets, even though Georgia and Armenia remained independent for almost another year. The Soviets established direct links with the Turkish secular nationalists under Kemal Atatürk in Anatolia, effectively squeezing the South Caucasian republics between them. On April 26, Kemal sent an official communication to Moscow expressing his appreciation of Moscow's fight against imperialism and his readiness to take upon himself "military operations against the imperialist Armenian government" and to encourage Azerbaijan "to enter the Bolshevik state union."[35] In May, Soviet troops and the Persian revolutionary Kuchuk Khan established the Soviet republic of Gilan on the southern coast of the Caspian Sea, and though the situation in Persia remained extraordinarily fluid, the government at Tehran appeared prepared to distance itself from the British and open negotiations with the Soviets. With the anti-Bolshevik "White" General Anton Denikin defeated, the reactionary Admiral Kolchak, who had fought the Reds in Siberia, dead, and the Red Army marching against Józef Piłsudski's Poland, the latter half of 1920 turned out to be a high point of revolutionary enthusiasm and direct Bolshevik promotion of the revolution in the East.

The Congress of the Peoples of the East, held in 1920 in Baku, the newly liberated capital of Soviet Azerbaijan, has rightly been described as a display of revolutionary millenarianism, impractical and poorly planned from the beginning. Excessively rhetorical, it reflected the enthusiasms and style of its chief organizer, Lenin's lieutenant, Grigorii Zinoviev, and has been vividly memorialized in Warren Beatty's film, Reds, largely for its fatal effects on the American Communist John Reed. More than two thousand delegates, primarily from Caucasia and overwhelmingly Muslim, attended.[36] Zinoviev opened the congress with a rousing speech that ended with a call for "a true people's holy war" against both imperialism and capitalism.[37] An alliance of convenience was to be forged between Communists and anti-imperial nationalists to carry the revolution into the Middle East and Asia.

Lauded as the first congress of the peoples of the East, the Baku Congress turned out to be the last as well. The export of revolution proved far more difficult than had been imagined. Lenin publicly praised the Congress, but privately he

---

ways that Russia's imperial makeup constituted the people of empire. See the short biographies in Stephen M. Norris and Willard Sunderland, eds., Russia's People of Empire: Life Stories from Eurasia, 1500 to the Present (Bloomington: Indiana University Press, 2012).

[35]Richard G. Hovannisian, "Armenia and the Caucasus in the Genesis of the Soviet-Turkish Entente," International Journal of Middle East Studies 4 (1973): p. 147.

[36]Pervyi s"ezd narodov Vostoka (Petrograd: Kommunisticheskii internatsional, 1920); Congress of the Peoples of the East: Baku, September 1920: Stenographic Report, transl. and annotated by Brian Pearce (London: New Park, 1977).

[37]Congress of the Peoples of the East, pp. 23–27.

Two Muslim men prepare a banner for the Congress of the Peoples of the East. As part of their international revolutionary effort, the Communists appealed to leftist activists to come to Baku in September 1920 to help organize an anti-imperialist struggle in the colonized world. The appeal was directed to "the enslaved masses of Persia, Armenia, and Turkey." The Congress has rightly been described as a display of revolutionary millenarianism, impractical and poorly planned from the beginning. Excessively rhetorical, it reflected the enthusiasms and style of its chief organizer, Grigorii Zinoviev, and has been vividly memorialized in Warren Beatty's film, *Reds*, largely for its fatal effects on the American Communist John Reed, who died soon afterwards. More than two thousand delegates, primarily from Caucasia and overwhelmingly Muslim, attended.

was dismayed by Zinoviev's unbounded enthusiasm for the nationalists. "Don't paint nationalism red," he admonished.[38] Within a few months the Armenian republic, facing an invasion by the Kemalist Turks, capitulated to the Communist forces stationed on its border as the lesser evil. In February 1921, the Red Army drove the Mensheviks out of Georgia. Both of these South Caucasian "revolutions" were far more artificial and external than had been the collapse of independent Azerbaijan in April 1920, where Communists enjoyed considerable support from Baku workers. In Armenia and Georgia, where there was no significant wellspring of support for Communism, the party remained an isolated political force until time, inertia, and coercion brought grudging acquiescence from the population.

---

[38] *M. N. Roy's Memoirs* (Bombay: Allied Publishers, 1964), p. 395.

The first phase of the Comintern's involvement with the peoples of the East was over by late 1921. The revolutionary wave had receded, and as the Soviet government began to see itself as one state among many, albeit with a different historical role, the link between the national question within the USSR and the anti-imperialist struggle abroad became more tenuous. Both in its domestic nationality policies and in its anti-imperialist foreign policy, the experience of the Soviet leadership demonstrated a series of concessions and adjustments of theory to reality, of desire to necessity, and of ideology to pragmatism. Bolsheviks were a minority party representing a social class—industrial workers—that had nearly disappeared in the Civil War. With the collapse of industry, workers starving in the cities left for their ancestral villages. Others joined the Red Army, where they at least could expect military rations. With no political or cultural hegemony over the vast peasant masses and with exceptional vulnerability in the non-Russian regions, the Communist parties moderated their own leap into socialism. The years of the New Economic Policy (1921–1928) were a period of strategic compromise with the peasantry in both Russia and the national republics, a time of retreat and patience awaiting the delayed international revolution. It was also a time of greater accommodation to the non-Russian peoples of the periphery. National cultures were promoted; native languages were taught; and local officials were elevated into positions of power, displacing Russians over time.[39]

Until his last active days Lenin continued to advocate caution and sensitivity toward non-Russians, whereas many of his comrades, most notably Stalin and his close Georgian associate, Sergo Orjonikidze, were less willing to accommodate even moderate nationalists. In his last struggle, Lenin fought with Stalin over the form that the new Union of Soviet Socialist Republics would take. While he won the initial battle for a looser federation, Lenin ultimately lost the war to Stalin's push for greater centralization.[40] Perhaps most ominously, in the light of a resistant reality in which the anticipated inevitable movement toward communism appeared stalled, the gap widened between the actual practices of Bolsheviks and the inflated rhetoric that disguised them. The language of national liberation and anti-imperialism remained a potent discursive cloak under which an empire of subordinated nations was gradually built.

BRIEF BIBLIOGRAPHY

Gatrell, Peter. *A Whole Empire Walking: Refugees in Russia During World War I.* Bloomington: Indiana University Press, 1999.

Hirsch, Francine. *Empire of Nations: Ethnographic Knowledge and the Making of the Soviet Union.* Ithaca, NY: Cornell University Press, 2005.

---

[39]For thorough discussions of Soviet nationality policies in the 1920s, see Terry Martin, *Affirmative Action Empire*, and Francine Hirsch, *Empire of Nations: Ethnographic Knowledge and the Making of the Soviet Union* (Ithaca: Cornell University Press, 2005).

[40]See Moshe Lewin, *Lenin's Last Struggle* (New York: Random House, 1968; Ann Arbor: University of Michigan Press, 2005).

Hosking, Geoffrey A. *Russia and the Russians, A History.* Cambridge, MA: Harvard University Press, 2001.

Jahn, Hubertus. *Patriotic Culture in Russia During World War I.* Ithaca, NY: Cornell University Press, 1996.

Lewin, Moshe. *Lenin's Last Struggle.* Ann Arbor: University of Michigan Press, 2005.

Lohr, Eric. *Nationalizing the Russian Empire: The Campaign Against Enemy Aliens During World War I.* Cambridge, MA: Harvard University Press, 2003.

Lohr, Eric, et al., eds. *The Empire and Nationalism at War.* Bloomington, IN: Slavica, 2014.

Martin, Terry D. *The Affirmative Action Empire: Nations and Nationalism in the Soviet Union, 1923–1939.* Ithaca, NY: Cornell University Press, 2001.

Norris, Stephen M., and Willard Sunderland, eds. *Russia's People of Empire: Life Stories from Eurasia, 1500 to the Present.* Bloomington: Indiana University Press, 2012.

Pipes, Richard. *The Formation of the Soviet Union: Communism and Nationalism, 1917–1923.* Cambridge, MA: Harvard University Press, 1954.

Sanborn, Joshua A. *Imperial Apocalypse: The Great War and the Destruction of the Russian Empire.* Oxford: Oxford University Press, 2014.

Sunderland, Willard. *The Baron's Cloak: A History of the Russian Empire in War and Revolution.* Ithaca, NY: Cornell University Press, 2014.

von Hagen, Mark. *War in a European Borderland: Occupations and Occupation Plans in Galicia and Ukraine, 1914–1918.* Seattle: University of Washington Press, 2007.

TEN

MAKING NATIONS, SOVIET-STYLE: 1921–1953

In the early decades of the twentieth century, empires still shone brightly in much of the Western world, since Britain, France, the Netherlands, Portugal, and Germany still proudly boasted of their imperial stature. The concept of "empire" itself fell into disrepute in the course of decolonization, tarnished by the belated realization, already voiced clearly by Lenin and others, that imperial power trampled on the rights of conquered peoples. Once European empires shed their formal colonial holdings, the word became available as a term of opprobrium, and began to be applied to the Soviet Union, destroyer and prison of nations. Ronald Reagan emblazoned the label in popular memory with his memorable condemnation of the Soviet Union as the "Evil Empire" in 1983.

This vision of the USSR as imperial oppressor and destroyer of nations had great staying power. In the nationalist discourses of movements for self-determination in the late Soviet Union and afterwards, the long experience with Soviet rule was often depicted as the destruction of the many non-Russian peoples held in its grip. Repression and forced Russification, imposed modernization and the suppression of national traditions, the destruction of the traditional village, even an assault on nature are combined into a powerful series of images that show Soviet power as the enemy of the nation. Lost in this powerful nationalist rhetoric is any sense of the degree to which the long and difficult years of Communist Party rule actually continued the "making of nations" of the pre-revolutionary period. Under Soviet rule, "nationalities" were ensconced as the official constituent parts of the socialist union. Not without its own contradictions and paradoxes, the Soviet experience resulted in nationalities stronger, more coherent and conscious than when they entered the federation at its inception.

Premised on an ideology based on class and advertising itself as the first workers' state, the Soviet Union was also the first state in history to be formed of territorial units defined as ethnic political entities, a pseudo-federal union that eliminated political sovereignty for its nationalities while guaranteeing them territorial identity, educational and cultural institutions in their own language, and the promotion of native cadres into positions of power. The policy of "nativization" (*korenizatsiia*), encouraged by Lenin and supported by Stalin, established alphabets for peoples who had no writing, opened schools for those who had none under tsarism, and set up hundreds of national soviets (governing councils) for peoples living outside their national region.

Steadily, members of local nationalities were appointed as leaders, replacing ethnically Russian officials, and the 1920s witnessed the growth of "national communisms," variant roads to the future, in many republics. In Armenia the Communists spoke of the resurrection of Armenia from the ashes of what later would be called genocide, and while they drove out or arrested the anti-Bolshevik nationalists, they began the rebuilding of an Armenian state to which refugees from other parts of the Soviet Union and the world could migrate. The cosmopolitan capitals of Georgia and Azerbaijan now became the seats of power of native Communists who laid the foundational infrastructure of national states, complete with national operas, national academies of science, national film studios, and education in the national language. Histories were rewritten to tell the stories of the formation of modern Soviet nations. In Kazakhstan, where native Kazakhs clashed with Russian settlers, the Soviet government launched a land reform in favor of the Kazakhs and expelled thousands of Slavs and Cossacks in 1921–1922. "The center quickly lost control of the land reform. . . . Entire Russian villages were in twenty-four hours . . . driven out into the frost," and the government ended the reforms. The Russian population of Kazakhstan fell by almost 20 percent and lost 50 percent of their land.[1] These policies, brutal as they were, were intended to ease ethnic tensions and consolidate the native population in the territory designated as their national homeland.

While nation-states might aspire to gathering in all those who identify as members of the nation, increasing the ethnic homogeneity of the state, empires adopt more ambivalent policies. Dedicated to the principle of collective difference and frequently bent on identifying particular peoples with particular territories, empires are also characterized by the mixing of populations, of peoples moving around and settling in a vast cosmopolitan space. In the Soviet Union, migration strengthened the titular nationalities, that is the recognized group that gave its name to each republic, consolidating the identification of ethnicity with territory. But in the larger cities, particularly Moscow and Leningrad, and in desirable areas like the Baltic republics (after their annexation in 1944), people of all nationalities flocked to find jobs and higher standards of living. When the USSR collectivized agriculture in the 1930s, it tied peasants to their place of origin and work, eliciting unwelcome mutterings about a second enserfment. But at the same time, the rapid and forced industrialization of the country drew people from every nationality to the building sites and new towns raised from the empty steppe.[2] Like earlier

[1]Terry Martin, "The Origins of Soviet Ethnic Cleansing," *Journal of Modern History* 70, no. 4 (December 1998): 827.
[2]Stephen Kotkin, *Magnetic Mountain: Stalinism as Civilization* (Berkeley and Los Angeles: University of California Press, 1995), pp. 84–85; John Scott, *Behind the Urals: An American Worker in Russia's City of Steel* (1942; Bloomington: Indiana University Press, 1989), p. 215.

imperial incarnations, the Soviet Union allowed, even promoted, the mixing of peoples, while contemporaneous nation-states were more often than not about the homogenizing, gathering in, or even *unmixing* of peoples.[3]

In the pre-revolutionary centuries South Caucasia had been a region of high mobility, with tribes and peoples moving constantly from one area to another. After the Russo-Persian and Russo-Turkish wars, Muslims left for the empires to the south and Armenians migrated north into Erevan province and to the major cities, Tiflis and Baku. The population of towns was mixed, with Armenians being the most urbanized of the three peoples, but in the Soviet period high rates of ur-banization led to solid majorities of Azerbaijanis in Baku and Georgians in Tiflis. Yet even as ethnic consolidation rose, anomalous enclaves of ethnic minorities re-mained: in Mountainous Karabakh (Nagorno-Karabakh), an autonomous region in Azerbaijan, over three-quarters of the population were Armenian; in Abkhazia, an autonomous republic in Georgia, the Abkhaz minority was threatened by the growing Georgian plurality. Dozens of Azerbaijani villages remained in Georgia and Armenia; Armenian and Georgian villages could be found in Azerbaijan; and Armenian villagers and urban dwellers lived in Georgia. In the 1920s the central Soviet government was committed to defending the cultural particularities of all peoples, but the territorialization of ethnicity and the increased power of the titu-lar nationality left minorities with few guarantees when the dominant nation in the three republics worked assiduously to "nationalize" their populations.

The man in charge of the "nationality question" in the first years after the revolu-tion was the People's Commissar of Nationalities, Joseph Stalin. Himself an ethnic Georgian and recognized as the Communist Party's authority on the non-Russian nationalities, Stalin shared Lenin's views on fostering national cultures and ethnic elites. Rather than forced Russification or elimination of ethnic difference, there would be nationality without nationalism, that is, without aspirations to political autonomy. The various ethnic cultures would be national in form, socialist in con-tent, phrases that together explained the link between promoting ethnic cultures and cadres while educating and leading people toward a socialist future. Up to the early 1930s wherever a significant number of non-Russians lived, national schools were established. Ukrainians in Russia, Jews or Armenians in Ukraine, were taught in their own languages. Even national soviets were set up in ethnic villages. Ethnic-ity was promoted for everyone with the deliberate exception of Russians, who to the Marxists had been chauvinistic imperialists and now needed to be reined in.

The marriage of Marxism, which emphasizes the importance of social class, with nationality, which links all members of the same ethnicity in a shared com-munity, was an uneasy one. In the last years of his mentor's life (1922–1924), Stalin resisted Lenin's ideas for a looser Soviet federation. Suspicious of the na-tionalistic tendencies of non-Russians, Stalin preferred a more centralized union and considered Lenin too soft in his approach to non-Russians. The party went

---

[3]This argument is made convincingly by Rogers Brubaker, *Nationalism Reframed: Nationhood and the National Question in the New Europe* (Cambridge: Cambridge University Press, 1996).

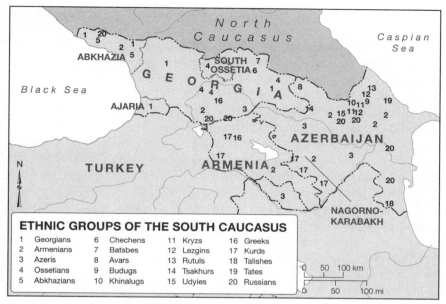

Map 10.1. Ethnic groups of the South Caucasus.

along with Lenin's plans for a Union of Soviet Socialist Republics, but once Lenin was incapacitated with a series of strokes that led to his death in January 1924, Stalin was able gradually to carry out his own program of centralized control over the republics. He fought against "national Communists," those party leaders who too energetically promoted their own nationality against the center.

The Tatar Communist Mirsaid Sultan-Galiev, who had worked closely with Stalin in the Commissariat of Nationalities, grappled with the problem of a nationalized Muslim communism to his detriment. Since the Muslim regions of the Russian Empire had very few industrial towns and few workers who could be considered proletarians, Sultan-Galiev proposed that all Muslim peoples by virtue of their colonial oppression were proletarian peoples. He called for the Russian revolution to be exported to the East and led by Muslim Communists. For such radical notions, he was accused of collaborating with anti-Communist Muslim forces, repeatedly arrested, and eventually executed in 1940.[4]

Through the 1920s the various national Communist parties in the republics were Bolshevized, subordinated to Moscow, and its more national-minded cadres

---

[4]On Sultan-Galiev, see Alexandre Bennigsen and Chantal Quelquejay, *Les mouvements nationaux chez les musulmans de Russie: Le «sultangaliévisme» au Tatarstan* (Paris et La Haye, Mouton & Co, 1960); their *Sultan Galiev, le père de la révolution tiers-mondiste: "Les inconnus de l'histoire"* (Paris: Fayard, 1986); Alexandre Bennigsen and S. Enders Wimbush, *Muslim National Communism in the Soviet Union* (Chicago: University of Chicago Press, 1979); and Maxime Rodinson, *Marxism and the Muslim World*, trans. Jean Matthews (London: Zed Press, 1979).

removed. In many of the non-Russian republics native Communists were few, and new members were recruited from ethnic parties or other socialist parties. In Ukraine former members of the *Spilka* (Ukrainian Social Democratic Union) and Ukrainian Socialist Revolutionists joined the Communist Party of Ukraine. In Azerbaijan partisans of the left-leaning Azerbaijani *Himmet* party made up a large part of the local Communist organization, and one of its leaders, Nariman Narimanov, became the leading Azerbaijani politician in the country. When his preferences for a Muslim revolution rather than the class-based socialist revolution became too evident, this "national Communist" was "promoted" to serve in Moscow. In neighboring Georgia, national Communism dominated the republic's Communist party in the early 1920s until Stalin and his local ally, Sergo Orjonikidze, purged its ranks.

Promotion of Yiddish culture and laws against anti-Semitism attracted many Jews to the Communist cause, both within the USSR and abroad. A special section of the Communist Party, the *Evektsiia*, was established to work on Jewish issues.[5] Zionism and Judaism, however, were attacked. In line with Stalin's view that nations had to have distinct territories, in 1931 the Soviets formed a Jewish Autonomous Region in inhospitable Birobidzhan, far from the centers of Europe and near the Chinese border. The "Jewish homeland" was conceived to resolve several other ongoing issues for the Soviets: to populate a strategically important yet remote and underpopulated border region, to refashion a population of traders and middlemen into peasants, a category more acceptable to Communist ideology, and to tidy up the problem of the Jews as a "people" without the requisite "homeland." Although some Jews did respond to the appeal of a place where not only schools but also public institutions would use Yiddish as the language of choice, the numbers remained small. Even when it encouraged literacy in native languages, cultures, and the development of native Communists, the regime was uneasy about the potential threat of nationalism. In Birobidzhan, established with the explicit promise of allowing for Yiddish schools and public life, the head of the local government, Josef Liberberg, was arrested in 1938 for trying to "establish the JAR (Jewish Autonomous Region) into the center of Jewish culture in the Soviet Union," which would have seemed to have been precisely the point. The wife of the local party head was accused of trying to poison Lazar Kaganovich, a close associate of Stalin, with "homemade gefilte fish" during his visit to the region in 1936. She was sentenced to labor camp, along with her husband.[6]

The process of nativization, which made republics more ethnic and homogeneous, was challenged by the Soviet program of economic development and

[5]Zvi Gitelman, *Jewish Nationality and Soviet Politics: The Jewish Sections of the CPSU, 1917–1930* (Princeton, NJ: Princeton University Press, 1972); Jeffrey Veidlinger, *The Moscow State Yiddish Theater: Jewish Culture on the Soviet Stage*, new ed. (Bloomington: Indiana University Press, 2006).
[6]Robert Weinberg, *Stalin's Forgotten Zion: Birobidzhan and the Making of a Jewish Homeland: An Illustrated History, 1928–1996* (Berkeley: University of California Press, 1998), pp. 67–68.

social modernization, which promoted mobility and the mixing of populations. For many Communists the first priority was economy, the building of an industrial society with a large, vigorous proletariat. In the economic sphere the emphasis was on efficiencies that very often disregarded ethnocultural factors. While creating national territorial units with broad cultural privileges, the new government's overwhelming concern was that the new multinational federal state be a single integrated economy. On this point there was to be no compromise. Economic policy was statewide, and each federal unit was bound to others and to the center by economic ties and dependencies. An intense debate raged in the Communist Party in the 1920s over the priority of economy over national culture, with the more-economically oriented, like Avel Enukidze, promoting administrative division of the country according to an economic rationale (*raionirovanie*), and officials in the People's Commissariat of Nationality Affairs (*Narkomnats*) and representatives of various non-Russian peoples favoring boundaries that corresponded to ethnicity.[7]

While much attention was paid to regional and cultural particularities, at least in the 1920s, over time economic regionalization became an extra-ethnic practice, and party members were regularly encouraged, even in the 1920s, to consider specialization, education, and training over ethnic qualifications in cadre policy. Stalin's lieutenant in Georgia, Orjonikidze, told his comrades that expertise was more important than nationality as a criterion for selecting economic officials: "It is necessary to work for the economic renaissance of our country, and for this it is not enough to be a Georgian, one must also know one's business."[8] The very repetition of this call indicates, of course, that ethnic favoritism as underlined by the *korenizatsiia* (indigenization) policy was seen to be working against economic efficiency.

THE STALIN YEARS, 1928–1953

Stalin's "revolution from above" and his radical transformation of Soviet state and society was at one and the same time a revolution and a counterrevolution, both a heroic and tragic period for the Soviet people. Peasants were forced into collective farms; industries were rapidly, haphazardly built; the market system was abolished in favor of a state-driven economy; and all these colossal social changes were made under the strict supervision of the police. The standard of living declined; the amount that people had to eat or spend diminished; housing and consumer goods deteriorated. While Stalin declared that "life was becoming more joyous, comrades," in fact daily existence was desperately difficult for most people. Millions of people would die in the frantic rush to collectivize agriculture

---

[7]An excellent discussion of economic and ethnic *raionirovanie* is in Martin, *Affirmative Action Empire*, pp. 33–55; see also Hirsch, "Toward an Empire of Nations," pp. 205–13.
[8]Ronald Grigor Suny, *The Making of the Georgian Nation* (Bloomington: Indiana University Press, 1988, 1994), p. 230.

and create a modern, urban, industrial society and in the bloody Great Terror of the late 1930s. Early egalitarian reforms were reversed by Stalin, and strict hierarchies divided the more privileged skilled laborers and professionals from ordinary workers and peasants. The radical experiments in art, film, and literature that had lifted revolutionary Russia into the ranks of the avant-garde were replaced by a more conventional realist style and propagandistic, prosaic content, wrapped up in the official school called "Socialist Realism." Whereas in the 1920s women had enjoyed new freedoms—divorce was made easier, abortions were legalized, and "illegitimate" children received rights—in the 1930s divorce and abortion were made difficult and same-sex relations punishable, all in an effort to shore up the Soviet family and promote a natalist policy encouraging parents to have as many children as they could. Observers characterized the Stalinist turn away from the revolutionary impulses of 1917 and the 1920s toward a more conservative and conventional society as the "Great Retreat" or a Soviet Thermidor, akin to the turn to the Right in the French Revolution.[9]

Once Stalin had consolidated his autocratic powers by the early 1930s, nationality policy took yet another sharp turn. For more than a decade Russian "Great Power Chauvinism" had been considered a greater danger to Soviet internationalism than the nationalism of small nations, even as real power to make binding decisions steadily accrued to the central authorities. Beginning roughly in 1932, Soviet nationality policy began a gradual shift away from this Russophobic program toward a growing identification of the Russian nation with the Soviet project. *Korenizatsiia* was scaled back; many national Communist leaders who had promoted their own peoples were purged, jailed, or executed; Russian heroes and history were celebrated as the models for a new state patriotism.[10]

Russians became the state-bearing nation in the full sense as the country approached and then went through World War II. As defense of the "motherland" (*rodina*) became paramount in the mind of Stalin, the USSR became a nationalizing empire intent on founding its identity and security on a new "imagined community," the Soviet people. But this new people, made up of dozens of nations and nationalities, were now to be largely identified with the practices and values stemming from the imperial Russian past. Ethnic interests were even more radically subordinated to considerations of economic efficiency and productivity. What was good for the Five-Year Plan—high targets for industrialization, impossible goals

[9]Nicholas Timasheff, *The Great Retreat: The Growth and Decline of Communism in Russia* (New York: E. P. Dutton & Co., 1946; Leon Trotsky, *The Revolution Betrayed: What Is the Soviet Union and Where Is It Going?* (Garden City, NY: Doubleday, Doran and Co., 1937).

[10]On the uses of history and heroes in building Stalin's vision of the USSR, see Ronald Grigor Suny and Terry Martin, eds., *A State of Nations: Empire and Nation-Making in the Age of Lenin and Stalin* (New York: Oxford University Press, 2001); David Brandenberger, *National Bolshevism: Stalinist Mass Culture and the Formation of Modern Russian National Identity, 1931–1956* (Cambridge, MA: Harvard University Press, 2002); and Serhy Yekelchyk, *Stalin's Empire of Memory: Russian-Ukrainian Relations in the Soviet Historical Imagination* (Toronto: University of Toronto Press, 2004).

for grain requisition—were brutally enforced, while the former promotion of national cultural development was curtailed.

Smaller nationalities lost their special schools and soviets, and assimilation into larger nationalities accelerated. The policy of forced assimilation of smaller peoples continued until the end of the Soviet Union. In Azerbaijan, for example, the Persian-speaking Talysh were eventually formally melded into the Turkic-speaking Azerbaijani nation. In 1959 they were eliminated as a census category, as though they had physically ceased to exist. The campaigns to collectivize Soviet agriculture in the early 1930s, resisted by hundreds of thousands of peasants, were in the non-Russian areas a devastating blow to traditional patriarchal village leadership, and they coincided with attacks on the Church and the Mosque. In Azerbaijan and Central Asia women were compelled to give up the veil.[11] In Armenia, the head of the national church was murdered. The industrialization of South Caucasia and Central Asia resulted in social and geographical mobility that further broke up traditional patterns of authority and cultural practices. Education was nationalized but also secularized, and the old elites were eliminated in favor of the Communists and their allies. Stalin systematically arrested and either exiled or executed almost all the leaders of the non-Russian republics, even those who had supervised earlier purges in accord with central party commands. In 1938 Levon Mirzoyan, an Armenian who had served as secretary of the Azerbaijani party and first secretary of the Communist Party in Kazakhstan, complained in a letter to Stalin about the exiling of Soviet Koreans to Kazakhstan and the activities of the secret police. He was arrested and a year later shot. Among the few top leaders of national republics who survived were the ruthless Lavrenti Beria in Georgia and his satrap, Mir Jafar Bagirov, in Azerbaijan.

A Soviet Marxist discourse replaced the prohibited nationalist discourses, and the lines were blurred between Soviet and Russian culture. By the end of the 1930s, Russian-language study was compulsory in all schools. Though native languages were also taught, they were often seen as insufficient for successful careers in politics or science. Despite the modifications in the nativization policies of the 1920s and the promotion of Russian language and culture under Stalin, the demographic and cultural developments set in motion by *korenizatsiia* continued and by the 1960s had largely achieved their goals in the non-Russian regions and republics. Most republics had become national in character, not only demographically, but politically and culturally as well. What had been in effect "affirmative

---

[11]There is an extensive literature on the unveiling campaigns in Muslim republics. See Gregory J. Massell, *The Surrogate Proletariat: Moslem Women and Revolutionary Strategies in Soviet Central Asia, 1919–1929* (Princeton, NJ: Princeton University Press, 1974); Douglas Northrop, *Veiled Empire: Gender and Power in Stalinist Central Asia* (Ithaca, NY: Cornell University Press, 2004); Marianne Kamp, *The New Woman in Uzbekistan: Islam, Modernity, and Unveiling Under Communism* (Seattle: University of Washington Press, 2008); and Adrienne Lynn Edgar, "Emancipation of the Unveiled: Turkmen Women Under Soviet Rule, 1924–29," *Russian Review* 62, no. 1 (January 2003): 132–49.

"Drawing, Music, and Singing Lessons. Without a Doubt They Raise the Culture of the Pupils." A Soviet poster extolling the virtues of the arts in education.

action" programs promoted cadres from the titular nationalities, often to the detriment of the more urbanized and educated Russian (and in Azerbaijan and Georgia, Armenian) population.[12] Territorial nations had been formed, but without their own full political expression. What Tom Nairn calls a "Reservation culture" had been established: ethnolinguistic culture without political nationalism was the only permissible, "healthy" nationhood.[13] The form of the state was that of a multinational federation, but real sovereignty shifted from the republics to Moscow and all the republics, including the Russian Soviet Federal Socialist Republic (RSFSR), were strictly subordinated to the central party apparatus. The usurpation of sovereignty—that is, all important decision-making—by the center, along with the differentiation and subordination of nationalities (Russians

---

[12]In Georgia, for example, the Communist Party was 76.1% Georgian in membership in 1970, though in that year Georgians made up only 66.8% of the republic's population. Armenians made up 9.7% of the population but only 8.0% of party membership, while Russians were 8.5% of the population and 5.5% of the party. [*Kommunisticheskaia partiia Gruzii v tsifrakh (1921–1970 gg.) Sbornik statisticheskikh materialov* (Tbilisi, 1971), p. 265; J. A. Newth, "The 1970 Soviet Census," *Soviet Studies* 24, no. 2 (October 1972): 215.] At the same time, ethnic Georgians accounted for 82.6% of the students in higher education in the republic, while Russians made up only 6.8% and Armenians 3.6%. [Richard B. Dobson, "Georgia and the Georgians," in *Handbook of Major Soviet Nationalities,* ed. Zev Katz (New York: Free Press, 1975), p. 177.]

[13]Tom Nairn, "Beyond Big Brother," *The New Statesman & Society* 3, no. 105 (June 15, 1990): 31.

included) and social classes (most importantly, the peasantry) to the Communist Party elite, constituted the very essence of the Soviet rule.

This pseudo-federation was in many ways a new form of empire. Its very success arrogating all power to Moscow transformed the state from an imperial patchwork into a unitary, centralized "pseudo-federal union" that paid lip service to the autonomy of its constituent parts but subjected them all to dictatorial enforcement of Kremlin mandates. Stalin's Soviet Union succeeded where earlier governmental forms had failed at creating a centralized state with power flowing out from the center and pervading far reaches, diminishing only a little with distance. The party's pervasive, dictatorial rule in some ways obviated the kind of regional differentiation and practices of indirect rule with considerable autonomy that defined earlier forms of empire. Rhetorically, the Soviets proclaimed equality and democracy, voicing a commitment to a kind of horizontal homogeneity antithetical to traditional definitions of empire. In practice, however, the state continued to rely on imperial distinctions among its peoples, classes, and territories. The various nationalities of the USSR were given greater or lesser status according to a Marxist evolutionary calculus that some peoples were more developed, more proletarian or closer to achieving socialism, than others.

The whole population carried on their persons legal institutionalized distinctions that led to discrimination, sometimes to their advantage, sometimes to their peril. After 1932, the internal passports that they were required to keep with them recorded their class and ethnicity, labels freighted with meaning for their lives. Coded by class and nationality, some groups were collectively deemed loyal and reliable, while others were declared prone to treason and sabotage. Imperial modes of conceptualizing the population remained operative with often deadly effect. Yet at the same time the Soviet Union presented itself as the major opponent of imperialism and colonialism. Under Stalin the anti-imperialist Soviet Union had assumed characteristics of a self-denying empire.

BEATING PEASANTS INTO SUBMISSION

Millions throughout the Soviet Union died during Stalin's campaign to collectivize agriculture, and the largest number of deaths—estimated to be over 4 million—occurred in Ukraine in the *Holodomor* (Death Famine) of 1932–1933. The original denial that famine had devastated Ukraine and other parts of the USSR occurred during the events themselves and continued until the end of the Soviet period. The stark and completely false claim that no famine ever took place was propagated by journalists at the time, most notoriously William Duranty of the *New York Times*, who simply did not report what was evident. Others like Malcolm Muggeridge of the *Manchester Guardian* and Gareth Jones honestly chronicled that people were starving. Duranty won a Pulitzer Prize, and Jones was banned from the USSR. Ever since historians have been divided over whether the *Holodomor* was the result of ill-conceived policies of grain requisitioning and blatant disregard of the effects on ordinary peasants, or a deliberately engineered state program to destroy Ukrainians as a nationality.

Few today dispute that mass mortality took place. But one side claims that the killings were intentionally aimed at destroying Ukrainians or at least Ukrainian nationalism embedded as it was in the Ukrainian peasantry. Therefore this was genocide. The other side claims that the Soviet dictator was primarily concerned that the grain requisition targets be fulfilled because the state needed those quotas for its industrialization and foreign-exchange goals. With the opening of the Soviet archives after 1991, historians determined that Stalin was convinced (or convinced himself) that Ukrainian peasants, along with Ukrainian party officials, were resisting the absurd, unreasonable quotas imposed on Ukraine. He considered their recalcitrance to be nationalist resistance to Soviet power and ordered that the last grain reserves be requisitioned even though he knew that millions would die. Rather than an act of nature, the famine was an act of humans, artificially, deliberately created. The regime callously watched as people starved to death, and only in 1933 when the crisis threatened the loyalty of Soviet soldiers, many of them Ukrainians, did the government send grain into Ukraine and end its destructive policies.[14]

If, as we have argued, nations emphasize the homogeneity and equality of their citizens, the fraternal bonds that hold the nation together and make it different from others, and empires, in contrast, base their power on the institutionalized differences among peoples and the hierarchical distance between those who have the right to rule from those subordinates who are to be ruled, how does the destruction of the Soviet peasantry and the *Holodomor* fit into our concept of imperial rule? Unlike nations in which the collective "we" defines those who are to be included in the benefits of government, empires systematically and legally define—even produce—differences that privilege some and disadvantage others. Difference gravitates toward inequity and is used to legitimize the superiority of some and the inferiority of others. If a great state demarcates some peoples as different and therefore exploitable in some way from those who make up the superior group (or the core of the nation, its genuine members), then that discriminating imperial relation facilitates policies that can destroy those others who stand in the way of the power and prosperity of those favored. Just as the late Ottoman Empire under the Young Turks designated specific ethnoreligious groups, Armenians and Assyrians, to be deported and massacred, and the British in India sentenced vast numbers of their colonial subjects to starvation by forcibly shifting cultivators from subsistence agriculture to the production of cotton for export, so Stalin's Soviet empire marked off millions of people for annihilation.[15]

---

[14]Terry Martin, *The Affirmative Action Empire: Nations and Nationalism in the Soviet Union, 1923–1939* (Ithaca, NY: Cornell University Press, 2001).

[15]Mike Davis, *Late Victorian Holocausts: El Niño Famines and the Making of the Third World* (London: Verso, 2001); Sven Beckert, *Empire of Cotton: A Global History* (New York: Random House, 2014).

Stalinists singled out Soviet peasants, particularly Ukrainians, as the source of grain to be extracted at any price, even the death of its own agricultural producers. Their very identities were marked; they were made visible as a distinct group and eliminated, labeled as alien by their imperial overlords.[16] Their foreignness was defined both by ethnicity and class (Ukrainians were overwhelmingly peasants) and attacked because of their politics (Ukrainian peasants refused to accept collectivization). Social separation, ethnic and class differences, constituted the principal marks of distinction that made peasants the victims of state policies.[17] Class distinctions among peasants were unstable within villages, reflecting age and life cycle more than fixed social standing, but the Soviets turned the label *kulak* (wealthy peasant, literally "fist") into a marker of fixed, and dangerously retrograde, identity. Those identified as kulaks were rounded up and deported in vast numbers.[18] Stalin was willing to punish them, render them unable to resist further, teach them a harsh lesson through starvation.

As those historians who question the famine as genocide have shown, that punishment extended far beyond Ukraine to the Volga and other regions of Russia itself. A fierce campaign to procure grain and transform traditional ways of life in Kazakhstan, eliminating the elites and forcibly settling the nomads, killed more persons per capita than in Ukraine.[19] Stalin did not intend to eliminate totally either Ukrainians or the peasantry or render them unable to reproduce themselves. Rather, peasants, former nomads, Kazakhs, and Ukrainians were to be made obedient Soviets and to lose what the Communists labeled their nationalism. The famine resulted from the seizure of grain and the choice to starve peasants in order to feed cities and soldiers and to export grain for hard currency.[20] Rather than genocide, the *Holodomor* and other famines throughout the USSR, as well as the decimation of the Kazakhs, were extraordinarily lethal examples of state repression to achieve goals set by a distant elite operating in a high-handed, imperial style.

EMPIRE-STATE AND STATE OF NATIONS

By the mid-1930s, Joseph Stalin had established himself not only as the heir of Lenin and the supreme leader of the Soviet Union but as an autocrat more powerful than any tsar. His quarter century of undisputed rule, the period conventionally

[16]Kate Brown, *A Biography of No Place: From Ethnic Borderland to Soviet Heartland* (Cambridge, MA: Harvard University Press, 2004).

[17]Ronald Grigor Suny, *The Revenge of the Past: Nationalism, Revolution, and the Collapse of the Soviet Union* (Stanford, CA: Stanford University Press, 1993).

[18]Moshe Lewin, *The Making of the Soviet System: Essays in the Social History of Interwar Russia* (New York: Pantheon Books, 1985).

[19]Niccolò Pianciola, "Famine in the Steppe: The Collectivization of Agriculture and the Kazakh Herdsmen, 1928–1934," *Cahiers du monde russe* 45, nos. 1–2 (January–June 2004): 137–92; Isabelle Ohayon, *La sédentarisation des Kazakhs dans l'URSS de Staline. Collectivisation et changement social (1928–1945)* (Paris: Maisonneuve & Larose–Institut Français d'Études sur l'Asie Centrale, 2006).

[20]See Terry Martin's response to a review of his book, *The Affirmative Action Empire*, in *Reviews in History* [http://www.history.ac.uk/reviews/review/278].

labeled Stalinism, was a time of upheaval, one social and demographic crisis after another. Collectivization of peasant farms, the deadly political purges in which over 700,000 people were executed, the Second World War during which the USSR lost 27,000,000 citizens, and the forced movement of non-Russians from border-lands meant that millions of people were on the move—deported from their homes, fleeing advancing armies, or "volunteered" or coerced to settle wherever the state needed them for industrial, agricultural, or security reasons.

Borderlands and their mixed populations were seen as potentially rife with treason and consequently were subject to particularly energetic policies of mas-sive resettlement. After Finns and Karelians fled westward to Finland after the Winter War of 1939–1940, "Russians" (which could have included Ukrainians or other peoples) were brought in to settle the new borderlands. After the war and the expulsion of Germans from the newly annexed Baltic republics, tens of thou-sands of "Russians" migrated to the region, reducing the percentage of Karelians, Latvians, and Estonians in their homelands. When parts of interwar Poland became part of Soviet Belorussia and Ukraine, locals considered suspect were exiled to Siberia or Kazakhstan. In the late 1940s and early 1950s the Stalinist regime deported Armenians from Armenia, Georgia, and Azerbaijan; Azerbai-janis from Armenia; and other minorities like the Meskhetian Turks living in Georgia on the border with Turkey. Sometimes they were "returned" to their titular republic in which they had never lived or, in more brutal cases, sent on trumped-up charges eastward to the Urals, Central Asia, or Siberia.[21]

Under Stalin the state tried within its means to restrict migration as well as to direct it to where workers and peasants were needed. "Some practices of Impe-rial Russian migration regimes reappeared in Soviet times," Siegelbaum and Moch note:

> . . . the state continued to organize resettlement and assign soldiers, prisoners, and administrators far from home; newcomers to the cities required permission both to leave the countryside and to take up urban residence; passports once again governed internal migration. Yet, in the Soviet era, and particularly under Stalin, state attempts to control the movement of people assumed un-precedented proportions. For example, the way the Soviet government handled the threat that enemy occupation posed to civilians during the Great Patriotic War was fundamentally more ambitious than what its tsarist predecessor had done during the First World War. The goal of the Stalinist state became the ra-tional distribution of population in accordance with the location of natural re-sources and in contrast to its vision of bourgeois societies in which people moved about willy-nilly. An elaborate hierarchy of "regime" and nonregime cities with corresponding registration procedures substituted for the price structures of a capitalist housing market to bar some categories of people and

[21]N. N. Ablazhev, "Repatriatsiia i deportatsiia Armian vo vtoroi polovine 1940-kh godov," *Vestnik NGU* 10, no. 1 (2011): 116–21; Arpenik Aleksanian, *Sibirskii dnevnik, 1949–1954* (Erevan: Gitutyun, 2007). Thanks to Harutyun Marutyan for this memoir of his mother's exile under Stalin. For the full story of migration in the USSR, see Siegelbaum and Mott, *Broad Is My Native Land*.

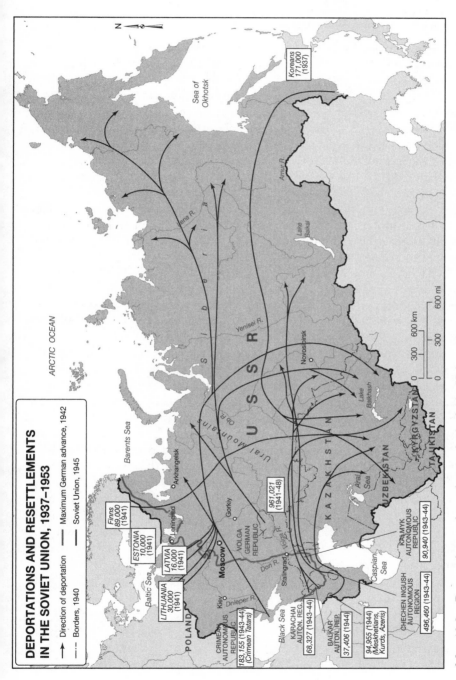

DEPORTATIONS AND RESETTLEMENTS IN THE SOVIET UNION, 1937–1953

→ Direction of deportation
── Maximum German advance, 1942
---- Borders, 1940
── Soviet Union, 1945

ARCTIC OCEAN

Barents Sea

Sea of Okhotsk

Koreans
171,000
(1937)

Amur R.

Lena R.

Lake Baikal

Yenisei R.

Novosibirsk

Ob R.

U S S R

Siberia

Ural Mountains

Arkhangelsk

Finns
89,000
(1941)

ESTONIA
10,000
(1941)

LATVIA
16,000
(1941)

LITHUANIA
30,000
(1941)

POLAND

Baltic Sea

Leningrad

Moscow

Gorkiy

Kiev

Dnieper R.

961,021
(1941-48)

VOLGA
GERMAN
REPUBLIC

Volga R.

Don R.

Stalingrad

Black Sea

CRIMEAN
AUTONOMOUS
REPUBLIC

183,155 (1943-44)
(Crimean Tatars)

KARACHAI
AUTON. REG.

68,327 (1943-44)

BALKAR
AUTON. REP.

37,406 (1944)

CHECHEN INGUSH
AUTONOMOUS
REGION

496,460 (1943-44)

94,955 (1944)
(Meskhetians,
Kurds, Azeris)

Caspian
Sea

Aral
Sea

KALMYK
AUTONOMOUS
REPUBLIC

90,940 (1943-44)

KAZAKHSTAN

UZBEKISTAN

KYRGYZSTAN

TAJIKISTAN

Lake
Balkhash

0   300   600 km
0   300   600 mi

N

Map 10.2. Deportations and resettlements in the Soviet Union, 1941–1953.

303

permit others. Only at the end of the Stalin era did compulsory resettlement and deportation give way to moral suasion and material incentives, which predominated in subsequent decades."[22]

To Siegelbaum and Moch's reminder of the compulsory nature of much of this movement, we would add that the Stalinist state also moved people around at will to serve less economically rational purposes than those listed here, notably the mass deportations of peasants. Whereas in the 1920s, the Soviets had favored nationalities like diaspora Poles, Koreans, and other peoples living along Soviet borders, showing them off as positive examples of the benefits of the Soviet system to their compatriots on the other side of the border, in the 1930s, with fear of approaching war in the air, a Soviet paranoia gripped the leadership. Diaspora peoples within the USSR were now thought to be potential traitors. Between 1935 and 1938, diaspora nationalities—either living outside of their designated republics or those without a Soviet space assigned to them—were ruthlessly rounded up and exiled to Central Asia and Siberia, many of them perishing on the journey, others summarily executed.[23] Koreans had settled in the Soviet Far East to escape the Japanese occupation of their country, but during the collectivization campaigns ethnic clashes occurred between local Russians and Koreans. In 1937 the entire Soviet Korean population, more than 170,000 people, was deported to Kazakhstan and Uzbekistan, their collective farms taken over by demobilized Soviet soldiers. They were the first nationality to be deported in its entirety. Resettled in Central Asia, those who survived were given—in a perverse parody of Leninist nationality policy—Korean collective farms, Korean-language schools, a publishing house, and their own newspaper.[24] Most of the top Korean Communists were executed. From a state open to foreign immigration in the NEP period, the USSR became in the Stalin years a closed fortress state vigilantly guarding its borders and turning on its own citizens suspected of foreign loyalties.

As in any empire, sovereignty belonged only to the center: the Communist elite, the metropole of the Soviet empire. The periphery, both Russian and non-Russian, was ruled in the name of a Soviet version of the *mission civilisatrice* (civilizing mission) that British, French, and Portuguese empires claimed to pursue in their overseas colonies, an arrogant mission to elevate backward peoples into a higher civilization. More ambitiously, however, the Bolsheviks sought to create a new kind of human being, *Sovetskii chelovek*, the Soviet Man and Woman, as well as a shared culture in which the peoples of the USSR would draw closer together (*sbilizhenie*) and perhaps ultimately assimilate (*sliianie*) into an integrated *Sovetskii narod* (Soviet People) free of nationalism and of national characteristics.

If one looks at the whole history of Soviet nationality policies, major contradictions and tensions between their imperial aspects and their nationalizing

[22]Siegelbaum and Moch, *Broad Is My Native Land*, p. 3.
[23]Martin, "The Origins of Soviet Ethnic Cleansing," pp. 813–61.
[24]Ibid., pp. 850–52.

This Soviet poster made by N. Tereshchenko in 1955 promotes the idea of the healthy Soviet Man. Robust and athletic, muscular and optimistic, the Soviet person, male and female, was to be an example to others, a dedicated builder of socialism, confident about the future. The text quotes the great poet Vladimir Mayakovsky: "There isn't more beautiful clothing in the world than the bronze of muscles and freshness of skin."

projects appear to run through the whole seventy years of Soviet power. Even as the Soviet project proclaimed that the peoples of the USSR would gradually grow together and eventually meld into a new, modern Soviet people, the promotion of folklore and folk culture emphasized what was different, unique, and authentic about a particular people. A similar ambivalence characterized official attitudes toward nationalities already under the Old Regime, which both extolled the diversity of the empire while it also aspired to the creation of a supra-national imperial cohesion. In tsarist times, no one took the time to sort these strands or made the effort to establish a single strategy for the entire realm. Under the Soviets these contradictory subcurrents hardened into explicit policy. Nationalities were defined and designed as distinct from one another. Literature, painting, and music were to be based on motifs and melodies judged to be "national," which usually meant that they were related to past traditions or folk art.

Soviet nationality policy emphasized that the distinctive cultures of separate *narody* and *natsional'nosti* rooted peoples in their national republics, hardening identities through passports and policies. The reification of national distinctions may have slowed down the formation of a common sense of Soviet identity. And yet, decades would pass; another vicious world war would be fought; and over time bonds of sentiment, fostered by shared historical traumas, bureaucratic red tape, public rituals of celebration and grieving, youth summer camps, and working the harvest, tied the diverse peoples together. These shared experiences to a significant degree succeeded in forging a single Soviet affective community, a community connected as much if not more by feelings and emotions than calculated interests.[25]

The encouragement of ethnonational cultures of the non-Russian peoples (*korenizatsiia*), complete with their own assigned territories and the trappings of statehood, coexisted with the acculturating, integrative program of modernizing a "backward" peasant country. The Communists were confident that the socialist solvent would homogenize the dozens of different social and ethnic groups. Up until the disintegration of the Soviet Union, *korenizatsiia* remained part of Soviet nationality policy, even as the word itself dropped out of common usage. Soviet culture was supposed to be multinational. Russian, non-Russian, and cosmopolitan Soviet components could be found in the art, literary, and musical productions that Soviet people consumed. But even as Soviet cultural development promoted the multiplicity and variety of Soviet cultures, at the same time it limited the specific ethnic idioms in which the nationalities could express themselves. Certain traditions were considered retrograde.

Marxists saw religion as superstition, a drug that blurred perception of reality. Karl Marx had written, "Religious suffering is, at one and the same time, the expression of real suffering and a protest against real suffering. Religion is the sigh of the oppressed creature, the heart of a heartless world, and the soul of soulless conditions. It is the *opium* of the people."[26] While religions were never fully banned, and private religious practice went on, the state occasionally carried out vicious campaigns against clerics, systematically discouraged or even persecuted religious practices, prohibited proselytizing religious faith, and turned churches into warehouses or cinemas. Marriage rituals that ran over several days and other festivals and holidays were criticized, and the veiling of Muslim women was repeatedly attacked.

Intellectuals and officials took on the role of ethnic police, defining and enforcing what was acceptable and unacceptable for the nationalities. When Armenian villagers sang Azerbaijani songs that they had heard on Radio Baku (as Ron Suny witnessed on a visit to Soviet Armenia in the 1970s), they angered local intellectuals who were dismayed by the Armenian *zhoghovoord* (people) not singing the songs they were supposed to sing, not acting as Armenian folk were supposed to act. Here the more cosmopolitan Soviet sharing of cultures came up against the ethnonational preferences of those locals who guarded the boundaries of what was "authentically" national. Still, in the official ideology, the folk elements identified with the past were supposed to be overcome eventually as the society moved toward socialism. For the time being, it seemed, as one writer on Soviet folk art

---

[25]James von Geldern, *Bolshevik Festivals, 1917–1920* (Berkeley and Los Angeles: University of California Press, 1993); Karen Petrone, *Life Has Become More Joyous, Comrades: Celebrations in the Time of Stalin* (Bloomington: Indiana University Press, 2000).

[26]Karl Marx, "A Contribution to the Critique of Hegel's Philosophy of Right," first published in *Deutsch-Französische Jahrbücher* (Paris), February 7 and 10, 1844. https://www.marxists.org/archive/marx/works/1843/critique-hpr/intro.htm.

put it, "It was absolutely possible to be a 'good' communist and still feel pride about one's national identity, as long as it did not exceed a certain accepted level."[27]

The making of a shared Soviet sense of belonging was not a linear process. National integration and connections rose and fell. Apart from the enthusiasts of the Communist party, the first decade of Soviet power was more a period of restoration and reconstruction than the effective achievement of a transnational Soviet national identity. In the 1930s Stalin embarked on an integrative project with the goal of creating a single Soviet identity and fostering exclusive loyalty to the Soviet Union. In an abrupt policy reversal, he ended the extreme variant of bolstering linguistic and cultural distinctiveness and supporting schools and presses for non-Russian nationalities that had marked the Leninist and NEP (New Economic Policy, 1921–1928) years. Instead he inaugurated an attack on manifestations of what he called local and bourgeois nationalism. In his anti-nationalist campaign, he purged the first generation of national Communists, concentrating state power in Moscow, and imposing a form of specifically *Russian* Soviet patriotism on the country as a whole—Soviet in form, Russian in content. The upheavals of collectivization, the devastating famines, and the Great Purges divided the population into multitudes of losers and a few victors, with contrasting and conflicting loyalties.

The tensions between the imperial aspects of the USSR and the ostensible goal to form a multinational state of equal nations were never overcome. The Soviet Union was at one and the same time an empire-state and a state of nations, a unitary state in federal guise. Both the Stalinist and post-Stalinist Soviet state manifested qualities of empire while maintaining features akin to a multinational nation-state with its promotion of nationality among the non-Russian peoples. Its internationalist ideology and its self-proclaimed historical project of building world socialism further complicate the task of applying any straightforward label. Its commitment to international socialism and to the workers of the world, though growing increasingly tepid as time went by, was antithetical to both the asymmetries and inequities of empire and the narrow exclusions of the nation-state.

No simple teleological path led from empire to nation-state, and these two poles did not contain the universe of possibilities and permutations vying for dominance in the Soviet experience. Perhaps these strains were what Soviet Marxists would have called "dialectical," the coming together of contradictory elements—a rhetoric of democracy, equality, internationalism, and a common Soviet community in tension with everyday practices of discrimination, disenfranchisement, and emphasis on ethnic communities—in a fusion into something new, but never fully resolved. Yet they contributed to the deep structural problems and discursive confusions that marked the Soviet experience. Russia's long history as an empire weighed heavily on the Soviet endeavor to create a non-imperial

---

[27]Philip Herzog, "'National in Form and Socialist in Content' or Rather 'Socialist in Form and National in Content'? The 'Amateur Art System' and the Cultivation of 'Folk Art' in Soviet Estonia," *Narodna Umjetnost* [*Croatian Journal of Ethnology and Folklore Research*] 47, no. 1 (2010): 122.

alternative. The Soviet Union's national subdivisions remained officially distinct and disempowered, endowed with different legal rights and standing, and imperial forms of rule remained palpable in spite of new language and commitments.

We should stop to ask at this point whether these particular forms of differentiation along national lines were inherited from the imperial era, whether they sprang from habits of mind and practice that could not be shaken, or whether they were invented afresh through a Marxist logic. The answer would have to be some of each. Lenin's sensitivity to nationality issues derived from his own experience of empire, from his distaste for the way his fellow Great Russians set themselves above the rest, as much as from his Marxist commitments. And Lenin set important precedents for Soviet development.

Nationality was not the only or even the primary axis along which the Soviets imagined collective distinctions and hierarchies. As under the tsars, other forms of collectivity jostled with nationality for primacy, but now class proved salient. The regime emphasized class as a primary identification, and Western scholars interviewing Soviet emigrants after World War II confirmed the salience of social along with ethnic identities.[28] Alex Inkeles, Raymond A. Bauer, and Clyde Kluckhohn, then at Harvard University, found that

> The basic social and political values of our respondents, their attitudes toward the Soviet regime, and their life experiences were on the whole strikingly little determined by their nationality as compared with their social origins or their class position in the Soviet system. On most questions a Ukrainian or Georgian lawyer's or doctor's responses are more like a Russian lawyer's or doctor's than like a Ukrainian or Georgian peasant's. And the same goes for the Russian member of the intelligentsia as against the Russian peasant. . . . Thus, we may conclude that basically a man's nationality is not a good predictor of his general social and political attitudes in the Soviet system, but rather that these attitudes are better predicted by knowledge of his occupation or social class.[29]

Still, Ukrainians reported that they did less well than Russians occupationally, and more frequently than Russians they said that nationality was important when it came to marriage and family life. More anti-Russian than anti-Soviet, older Ukrainians were more knowledgeable about Ukrainian culture and folklore than were the younger, who were "least likely to charge the regime with mistreatment of the Ukrainian people."[30] Ukrainians who had left the USSR were more than twice as likely as Russians to recommend dropping an atom bomb on Moscow.[31]

[28]The Harvard Project on the Soviet Social System provides an excellent and easily accessible window into popular and intelligentsia attitudes about the effects of Stalinist nationality policies. [http://hcl.harvard.edu/collections/hpsss/index.html].
[29]Raymond A. Bauer, Alex Inkeles and Clyde Kluckhohn, *How the Soviet System Works: Cultural, Psychological and Social Themes* (Cambridge, MA: Harvard University Press, 1956; New York: Vintage Books, 1961), pp. 238–39.
[30]Alex Inkeles and Raymond A. Bauer, *The Soviet Citizen: Daily Life in a Totalitarian Society* (Cambridge, MA: Harvard University Press, 1961), pp. 239–40, 347, 353.
[31]Ibid., p. 353.

The researchers on the Harvard Project noted that refugees "from the less well-developed areas point to the positive achievements in the direction of racial equality, increased educational opportunities, and technological and industrial advance." They credited the Soviet regime "for improved medical facilities, the increased literacy rate, the growth of the theater and cinema, and other developments."[32] Muslims, however, more than any other non-Russians, felt "deprived of their cultural heritage," and the "relative isolation from the center of many Moslem [sic] groups and the wide gulf between their culture and that of the European Russian probably facilitate the relative endurance of a Moslem subsociety in the villages which is both an actual and a potential source of passive resistance to Soviet and Russian penetration."[33] All in all, nevertheless, the researchers concluded that the USSR was a relatively stable society and that the nationality issue was not one that threatened that stability.

> Time is mainly on the side of the regime as far as the nationality issue goes, particularly because of the trend among the youth noted above. Population transfers and purges of the national, political, and cultural leaderships, while increasing the resentments of articulate elements in the national populations, have even further reduced the possibility of their raising an effective opposition against the regime. Most of the various minority borderlands are increasingly dependent on Moscow because of more and more economic specialization. Local situations in some cases (e.g., Armenian fears of the Turks and jealousy of a strong Georgia) also reinforce ties to the center. Most of all, the drift through time is enhanced by urbanization, industrialization, and increasing Union-wide literacy in Russian. Project data show rather dramatically the extent to which, even a decade ago, attitudes had become homogenized along social class rather than nationality lines. However, the very process of minimizing national differences in the USSR produces resentments, especially in the trouble spots of the moment.[34]

As tenacious as affiliation with one's ethnic nation was in many cases, social position successfully competed as a source of identity. Later, in the post-Stalin years, long after the government had proclaimed that class struggle had ended in the Soviet Union, class was removed from the internal passport. Nationality remained as a key source of distinction and definition, coexisting and at time contending with Soviet patriotism and an acceptance of Soviet values.

BUILDING NATIONAL BOLSHEVISM

Correcting Marx and Engels who asserted that the proletariat had no fatherland, Stalin asserted in 1931 that now the proletariat did indeed have a fatherland, the Soviet Union. The Stalinist 1930s were the years of the formation of what David Brandenberger has called (following the dissident Communist Martemian

---

[32]Bauer, Inkeles, and Kluckhohn, *How the Soviet System Works*, p. 243.
[33]Ibid., p. 236.
[34]Ibid., p. 243.

Riutin) "National Bolshevism," the introduction of a "new pragmatism" in Soviet ideology that "eventually settled upon a russocentric form of etatism as the most effective way to promote state-building and popular loyalty to the regime."[35] Nativist, even nationalist, this new direction was not aimed "to promote Russian ethnic interest . . . so much as . . . to foster a maximally accessible, populist sense of *Soviet* social identity through the instrumental use of russocentric appeals."[36] The intention of Stalin and the Stalinists was to promote patriotic loyalty to the party and state, but unwittingly they generated "a mass sense of Russian national identity within Soviet society" that "proved durable enough to survive the fall of the USSR itself."[37]

While Lenin had actively discouraged "Great Russian Chauvinism," Stalin sought to reverse the degrading of Russian national identity. New Soviet histories written on Stalin's orders were replete with heroes whom one could emulate and events that generated pride and militant enmity to the country's enemies. The appeal to Russian nationalism was not without its challenges, however. Cultivating affective identification with an entity called "Russia" still required careful work of the same kind necessary to build identification with abstract collectives such as "the proletariat" or "workers and peasants." In her study of popular opinion in the 1930s, Sarah Davies notes the fragility of a sense of Russian nationness among ordinary workers and peasants and its articulation primarily at the margins of contact with others such as Jews and Armenians.[38] While Russians expressed ethnic pride and a sense of unique Russian characteristics in their proverbs and songs, or their visceral hostility toward the Jews and others, the broader identification with abstract nation remained amorphous. Yet the ascription of nationality, its fixedness in the internal passport after 1932, reified what earlier had been a more fluid identification.[39]

Historian Terry Martin argues that "Friendship of the Peoples" replaced the Affirmative Action Empire of the 1920s and early 1930s (1923–1933) to become the accepted form of imagined community of the Soviet state.[40] The slogan "Friendship of the Peoples" (*Druzhba narodov*) was introduced into the Soviet vocabulary in December 1935, partially supplementing the term "brotherhood" (*bratstvo*), which had enjoyed currency in the more radically egalitarian early years of Soviet rule. While the two terms, friendship and brotherhood, were variously used for different purposes, it should be emphasized that the transition from one to the other implied an important emotional shift in official rhetoric.

---

[35]David Brandenberger, *National Bolshevism: Stalinist Mass Culture and the Formation of Modern Russian National Identity, 1931–1956* (Cambridge, MA: Harvard University Press, 2002), p. 2
[36]Ibid., p. 4.
[37]Ibid., p. 9.
[38]Sarah Davies, *Popular Opinion in Stalin's Russia: Terror, Propaganda, and Dissent, 1934–1941* (Cambridge: Cambridge University Press, 1997), pp. 88–89.
[39]David Shearer, "Elements Near and Alien: Passportization, Policing, and Identity in the Stalinist State, 1932–1953," *Journal of Modern History* 76, no. 4 (December 2004): 835–81.
[40]Martin, *Affirmative Action Empire*, pp. 432, 436–42.

While brotherhood suggests greater intimacy, it also involves hierarchy between older and younger brothers, and Soviet citizens were aware which nationality would soon become the "elder brother."[41] The trope of friendship had the advantage of an emphasis on equality among the Soviet peoples. Friends after all are equivalent to one another; their relationship is about trust, devotion, dependability, affection, and reciprocity. Moreover, one chooses ones friends. Rather than determined by blood and fate, friendship is an active act of conscious, emotional agents. Equality and hierarchy were brought together (dialectically!) in Stalin's toast to mark the anniversary of the October Revolution in 1938: "Old Russia has been transformed into today's USSR where all peoples are identical. . . . Among the equal nations, states, and countries of the USSR, the most Soviet and the most revolutionary is the Russian nation."[42]

FROM HOT WAR TO COLD WAR: EXTERNAL EMPIRE AS DEFENSIVE EXPANSION

Many historians have argued that during the Second World War, Sovietism, or the elevation of an overarching Soviet patriotism, was pushed aside in the name of Russian nationalism. But this formulation misses the peculiar amalgamation of nationalism and Soviet patriotism that marked those years. Speaking on the anniversary of the Bolshevik Revolution in 1941, Stalin told the "nation" that "you must draw inspiration from the valiant example of our great ancestors," and then went on to name them: Aleksandr Nevskii, Dmitrii Donskoi, Kuzma Minin, Dmitrii Pozharskii, Aleksandr Suvorov, Mikhail Kutuzov—all Russians to be sure, but defenders of the fatherland. Here was a Georgian with his accented Russian calling these military leaders "our ancestors." They were not merely ancestors of ethnic Russians but of the Soviet people as a whole. In much wartime rhetoric images from the Russian past blended with those of the Soviet past and present. In the famous Soviet poster by a collective of graphic artists known as the Kukryniksy, the ghosts of the medieval Russian warrior Aleksandr Nevskii, the eighteenth-century Russian general Aleksandr Suvorov, and the simple Red Army commander Vasilii Chapaev call on the Red Army men to advance.[43] A supranational but Russified patriotism was grafted onto Leninist internationalism, replacing the class element with a new primacy placed on Russia's past. To some extent, this renewed emphasis on Russia and Russian history played on the persistent loyalties of ethnicity and nation that had been suppressed before the war. Soldiers, men and women, went into battle and to their death shouting "For

---

[41]For a comprehensive discussion of themes of friendship in the Soviet Union, see Thomas Hooker, "'A Comrade in Need is a Friend Indeed': Friendship and Communism in Soviet Russia, 1921–1980," Phd dissertation in history, Harvard University, 2016.

[42]Brandenberger, *National Bolshevism*, p. 284, n. 43.

[43]"We are fighting heartily and bayoneting daringly, grandchildren of Suvorov, children of Chapaev" (Kukryniksy, 1941; depicted in Brandenberger, *National Bolshevism*, p. 117).

"We are fighting heartily. And bayoneting daringly—grandchildren of Suvorov, children of Chapaev." A wartime poster (1941) by the famous caricaturists, the Kukryniksy (M. Kurpriianov, P. Krylov, and N. Sokolov), which depicts the medieval Russian warrior prince Aleksandr Nevskii, the tsarist General Aleksandr Suvorov, and the Red Army commander Vasilii Chapaev, thus linking Russian nationalism with Soviet patriotism.

the Motherland, for Stalin." As party leader Aleksandr Shcherbakov suggested to journalist-novelist Ilya Ehrenburg, "Borodino is closer than the Paris Commune," that is, a battle from imperial Russia's war against Napoleon evoked more emotional response than an epic moment in the history of class struggle.[44] Despite two decades of exposure to communist ideology, the history of the Russian motherland touched emotional depths, particularly among mobilized peasants, that the march of the working class could not reach. There is a significant irony here. As discussed in earlier chapters, Russia had never developed the kind of relatively uncomplicated national identity that so many other European groups constructed during the nineteenth century, so this turn "back" to a putatively natural identification with and love of a Russian mother- or fatherland reflected as much a novelty as a recovery of or return to some earlier, purer state.

Invaded by Nazi Germany on June 22, 1941, the Soviet people fought for almost four years against Germans, Austrians, Finns, Hungarians, Romanians, and other peoples allied with Hitler. Millions of people were displaced, died in the fighting, or were murdered by the invaders. Much of the mass killing of the Holocaust against the Jews took place on lands at some point Russian or Soviet

---

[44]Ilya Ehrenburg, *Liudi, gody, zhizn'*, p. 322; Brandenberger, *National Bolshevism*, p. 150.

territory. Twenty-seven million Soviet citizens lost their lives, and millions of others were wounded or crippled. The Nazis allowed, indeed encouraged, local anti-Semites and anti-Communists to take vengeance on those they despised and hated. The Germans systematically starved to death millions of Soviet prisoners of war. The brutality of the Nazi war in Eastern Europe was far greater than on the Western Front. But the losses were in part the fault of Stalin's miscalculations and his own ruthlessness. The Generalissimus, as he would be referred to later, refused to accept the warnings of his agents of an imminent German attack in 1941. He seemed to trust that Hitler would keep to the infamous agreement he had made with the USSR in August 1939, the Nazi-Soviet Pact. Stalin rejected sound advice from his generals, which led to huge territorial and human losses. Convinced that whole nationalities were guilty of collaboration with the enemy or treason, he exiled hundreds of thousands of Volga Germans, Chechens, Ingush, Kalmyks, and others to Siberia and Central Asia. Uncounted tens of thousands died in the forced deportations.

In the Soviet experience the "Great Fatherland War," as World War II was called, was both interruption and acceleration, unbearable sacrifice and transcendent triumph. Nazi Germany was an ideological, imperialist state that in the vision of its leader required the conquest of Eastern Europe and Russia to realize its dream of a German-led empire. Adolf Hitler was simultaneously anti-Communist and anti-capitalist, anti-Slavic and anti-Semitic, and sought to eliminate "inferior" races and establish German dominance over the enslaved survivors. In the prewar period the Soviet Union officially condemned anti-Semitism, and in the view of the Nazis, Communists and Jews were blood brothers. In Poland, Ukraine, Lithuania, and elsewhere the Nazis found sympathizers who made the same fatal equation of Bolsheviks and Jews, and in their anti-Communist fury they murdered Soviet officials, party members, and Jews. A brutal racist empire expanding from Central Europe met and was ultimately defeated by another brutal empire, but one that preached not the superiority of some races over others but egalitarian, internationalist socialism.

Timothy Snyder calculates that the massive killing in East Central Europe (his "Bloodlands"), most viciously in Ukraine, ran to 14,000,000 victims in the years when Hitler and Stalin were in power. He makes the powerful point that these horrors were the result of two rival colonial projects—Nazi and Soviet—aimed at subduing the contact zone between Germany and Russia.[45] As revealing as comparing and conflating these campaigns may be, historians must at the same time note the profound differences between imperial ambitions. The Nazi Empire was exterminationist and aimed to depopulate the region of Jews and Slavs and re-populate them with Germans, a truly colonial project, while the Soviet was developmentalist and aimed to create a modern industrial society that would promote national cultures within its self-defined "socialist" framework, a project that

---

[45]Timothy Snyder, "Integration and Disintegration: Europe, Ukraine, and the World," *Slavic Review* 74, no. 4 (Winter 2015): 695–707.

more closely resembles an imperial civilizing mission. The practices of the Nazis only too well matched their exterminationist and expansionist ideology, while the practices of the Soviets failed to live up to their Enlightenment ideology of equality and socialist democracy.

If early Bolshevik efforts to reintegrate and subordinate breakaway pieces of the former Russian Empire into their newly hatched Soviet Union smacked of imperialism, then the wholesale incorporation of East Central Europe in the aftermath of the Second World War was incontrovertibly so. The West reluctantly acknowledged that the Soviet Army "liberated" the countries of East Central Europe from the Nazis. At the Yalta Conference in February 1945, U.S. president Franklin Delano Roosevelt, British prime minister Winston Churchill, and Stalin agreed that the USSR could expect to have friendly governments in the states along its western borders and material reparations from defeated enemies to assist the recovery in the war-devastated Soviet Union. The USSR emerged as a major military power on the European continent but also as a hollowed-out landscape of ruined cities and villages. Stalin was determined that no power hostile to the Soviets would again rise and dominate the countries closest to the USSR. Although the incorporation of each Eastern European country unfolded differently, with varying degrees of internal support for such an alignment, the postwar map is an unambiguously imperial one, with formerly independent polities subordinated through military conquest and control maintained through differentiated, more or less indirect rule, terror, and force. In the late Stalin years Moscow determined the political and foreign policy choices of its East Central European satellites.

This form of indirect rule of the periphery had been foreshadowed in the very first Soviet "satellite," Mongolia, which for seventy years from 1921 on was ostensibly an independent state but in fact under the dominion of the USSR. Expanding its rule to lands once subject to tsarist dominion, such as Poland, or subject to tsarist ambitions, such as Bessarabia (Moldova), or historically beyond the reach of the tsarist state, such as East Germany or Czechoslovakia, the Soviet sphere of influence subsumed the countries of Eastern and East Central Europe in an imperial manner for forty years.

These new forms of empire—controlling both foreign and domestic policy with or without formal absorption of the states—broadens the palette of imperial models. Here imperialism should be distinguished from hegemony, that is, what other great powers, like the United States, practiced. Hegemony over other states was a looser but powerful influence that eschewed much interference in the domestic arena but demanded loyalty to the hegemonic state in foreign policy. Latin American states learned the lesson that they had to consider the interests of their powerful northern neighbor in their allegiances, programs, and choice of allies. Similarly, the Soviets practiced hegemony over Finland in what was known as Finlandization. Finland remained independent, democratic, and capitalist but coordinated its international actions under the stern gaze of the Kremlin. The twentieth century also witnessed the creation of dependencies cloaked in

putatively non-imperial guises: protectorates, territories, and puppet governments proliferated, reaching their logical conclusion in the proxy wars of the
Cold War era, fought between militaries aligned with one side or the other.

World War II transformed the history of imperialism. The two superpowers
that survived the war—the United States and the USSR—were both committed to
decolonization of the European overseas empires and anti-imperialism, except in
their own spheres of influence. Europe was divided into an American-dominated
West and a Soviet-dominated East. The Warsaw Pact, established by the Soviets
and including its satellites in East Central Europe, eventually faced a far more
powerful NATO bloc and more affluent European Union. The elimination of European overseas maritime empires—the last one fell in 1975 with the retreat of
Portugal from Africa—left new kinds of empires confronting one another globally. The Soviet external empire was a contiguous territorial subordination of half
a dozen states—East Germany, Poland, Czechoslovakia, Hungary, Romania, Bulgaria, and Mongolia—that over time evolved unevenly into a looser system of
states that looked more and more like Soviet hegemony rather than direct colonial control of both foreign and domestic policy. East Central European states
increasingly developed their own "roads to socialism" under Moscow's watchful
eye. If they strayed too far, the Soviets intervened militarily, as in East Germany

Map 10.3. Europe during the Cold War, 1945–1991.

in 1953, Hungary in 1956, and Czechoslovakia in 1968. The American military and economic dominance in much of the rest of the world was far looser, less coercive, and generally voluntarily accepted by its allies, but still a powerful influence with which all other states had to contend and negotiate.

During those decades, Soviet authorities would experiment with a range of policies in their satellites. Stalin initially toyed with the idea of Soviet hegemony over the countries along the western borders but without full Communization, but after 1947 and the outbreak of Cold War, Stalin pitilessly installed Communist Party dictatorships in East Germany, Poland, Czechoslovakia, Hungary, Romania, and Bulgaria. Yugoslavia and Albania were also ruled by Communists but were able to maintain independence from the command of the Soviet Union since their parties had come to power largely without Soviet assistance. Estonia, Latvia, and Lithuania were directly absorbed into the USSR and became Soviet Socialist Republics. Purges of "national Communists" were carried out, and in the last years before Stalin's death in 1953 police regimes closely supervised by the Soviets closed off the Soviet Bloc from the West. In the 1950s and 1960s the Soviets permitted significant cultural independence without full political autonomy (Nikita Khrushchev's "goulash communism" in Hungary) along the lines of that permitted to the Soviet nationalities; at other times and in other places they enacted harsh policies of surveillance and repression.

Germans in East Berlin resisting the Soviet repression of the workers' uprising, June 1953.

Regardless of the variation in control from Moscow, it would be hard to mistake the imperial quality of Soviet domination of its holdings. But this mid-twentieth-century imperialism perforce took on different coloring and spoke a different language from its nineteenth-century predecessors. Simple conquest no longer justified possession, and the ideological imperative to honor national self-determination complicated matters. Ideological conformity with Soviet communism and the military presence in or near their territories kept the satellites in line. The countries of East Central Europe nominally joined in concert with the Soviets by their own volition rather than by force (the circumstance of each varied), and subsequently were not folded into a greater Soviet Union. They maintained their status as independent states, while the USSR monitored them closely from Moscow.

COLD WAR AT HOME: THE INTERNAL EMPIRE

The sacrifices endured by the Soviet peoples in the Second Great Patriotic War fostered hopes that victory would bring about a relaxation of the harshest aspects of Stalinism. Perhaps the collective farms would be disbanded and land returned to the peasants. Perhaps censorship would be eased, and writers and artists would be able to pursue their own inspiration. Perhaps there would be an opening to the West and a flow of goods and ideas from abroad would ease the burdens of recovery and rebuilding. Such hopes were quickly dashed. An aging, infirm Stalin grew ever more suspicious of Western powers, returning POWs, and even those of his own people who had mobilized and won the war. The West closed itself off from the USSR and the "Communist menace," and the Kremlin now saw its recent allies in Europe and America as a pernicious threat. The censors went back to work with new vigor in a cultural campaign known as *Zhdanovshchina* after the Leningrad party chief Andrei Zhdanov. Major artists—the poet Anna Akhmatova, satirist Mikhail Zoshchenko, composers Dmitrii Shostakovich, Sergei Prokoviev, and Aram Khachaturian, among others—were severely criticized as a warning to their fellow writers and musicians.

Diaries, letters, and official reports testify that the war had heightened national feelings, both Russian and non-Russian, and ethnic pride was accompanied often by ethnic hostility toward others. There was a new expression of and a greater permissiveness toward anti-Semitism during and after the war that metastasized into the Anti-Cosmopolitan Campaign targeting prominent Jewish intellectuals and the crackdown on the supposed "Doctors' Plot," a trumped-up case against primarily Jewish doctors that led to arrests and executions.[46] Until the Second World War Jews had both suffered and benefited significantly from Soviet power. In the early decades of Soviet rule, the majority of Jews had lived in the small towns (shtetls) in the Pale of Settlement along Russia's western borders

---

[46]Amir Weiner, *Making Sense of War: The Second World War and the Fate of the Bolshevik Revolution* (Princeton, NJ: Princeton University Press, 2001), pp. 114–22, passim.

to which they had been confined in the imperial era, but by 1939 almost 90 percent of Soviet Jews lived in cities, most of them in the largest eleven cities. While their religion was frowned upon and Zionism persecuted, Jews made up a large and influential segment of the "Soviet bourgeoisie," highly represented in the party leadership and the secret police, in the intelligentsia, among artists, in higher education, the diplomatic corps, and the spy service. They were among the most loyal Communists until well into the 1950s.

In a fascinating and provocative study, Yuri Slezkine argues that Soviet Jews "represented modernity and internationalism" to their compatriots, and because Jews were so prominent in Bolshevism, many gentiles identified Bolshevism with the Jews.[47] Soviet people, like many if not most people in the world, conceived of ethnicity as something fixed, given, and indicative of one's morality, character, and abilities. Such views were contrary to the Marxism of Marx with its historicist and constructivist emphasis, but in the 1930s Soviet nationality policies moved steadily toward an essentialization, even biologization, of nationality. Even after they left the shtetl, Judaism, and Yiddish behind and assimilated into their beloved Russian culture, Jews remained labeled as Jews with their identity inscribed in their passports. The Nazi invasion only reinforced their Jewish identification, and war experiences and the creation of the State of Israel in 1947 further ethnicized Soviet Jews in the eyes of their Russian compatriots.

The usual explanation of the anti-cosmopolitan campaign of the late 1940s starts with Stalin and his innate anti-Semitism, but such an explanation does not explain the upward mobility of Jews in the heyday of Stalinism before the war. Slezkine argues that Jewish success clashed with the rise of educated Russians in an environment in which the importance of ethnicity (not class any longer, as in the first fifteen years of Soviet power) made it no longer acceptable that Jews dominate the very realms into which Russians and others aspired to move. Anti-Semitism only increased with the emphasis on ethnicity and the re-ethnicization of Soviet Jews after the Holocaust and the founding of Israel. "The two trends—the ethnicization of the Soviet state and the nationalization of ethnic Jews—kept reinforcing each other until Stalin and the new Agitprop [Department of Agitation and Propaganda] officials made two terrifying discoveries. First, the Jews as a Soviet nationality were now an ethnic diaspora potentially loyal to a hostile foreign state. . . . Second, according to the new Soviet definition of national belonging and political loyalty, the Russian Soviet intelligentsia, created and nurtured by Comrade Stalin, was not really Russian—and thus not fully Soviet. Russians of Jewish descent were masked Jews, and masked Jews were traitors twice over."[48]

Stalin essentially reflected the interests of the upwardly mobile new Russian educated class, the backbone of the regime. He made a "Big Deal" with a new Soviet establishment: In place of the appeals of the past to the socialist cause, the

---

[47]Yuri Slezkine, *The Jewish Century* (Princeton, NJ: Princeton University Press, 2004), pp. 217, 237.
[48]Ibid., p. 297.

regime offered consumer benefits—wristwatches, bicycles, fringed lampshades, vacations—to the technical and professional intelligentsia and managerial class. This new social compact reset the thermostat, replacing the heroic sacrifice demanded of the first generation of Bolsheviks and of the population at large during the war with a more sustainable commitment to Stalinism and stability, secured through material comfort and rewards. To motivate the administrative, managerial, and technical cadres, the planned economy slowly shifted gears, allowing limited production of consumer goods previously held in contempt as frivolous and petty-bourgeois. A range of lowbrow literature validated this new celebration of comfort and domesticity and established models of how the emerging managerial class should live. The "Big Deal" entailed not merely paying off loyal servitors with fringed lampshades and wristwatches, but also the decimation of the older elite to allow a new one to emerge.[49] And though Jews recovered somewhat after Stalin's death, Slezkine's epitaphs are telling: "The Russian and Jewish Revolutions died the way they were born—together." "Communism lost out to both liberalism and nationalism and then died of exhaustion."[50]

Like World War I, so the second great global war stimulated nationalism and stirred anti-imperial impulses. In specific cases, as in western Ukraine or the Baltic region, the nationalism of non-Russians newly incorporated into the Soviet Union after the war was directed against the Soviets. Anti-Communist guerrilla movements operated in the border regions well into the 1950s, covertly aided by the American Central Intelligence Agency.[51] Tens of thousands of Soviet officials and soldiers, and equal numbers of anti-Soviet insurgents, were killed before the Soviets crushed the resistance of the "Forest Brothers" in the Baltic region and the Bandera movement in western Ukraine. Hundreds of thousands of Ukrainians were deported from the newly annexed regions. But in many other parts of the USSR, a lasting effect of the war was the political and affective integration of Soviet and national identifications. For many people, the Soviet Union became the "fatherland" (*otechestvo*) and even the "motherland" (*rodina*). On the heels of shared suffering and sacrifice, this affective connection with the Soviet Union took on an internal reality. Victory solidified and sanctified the Soviet regime and Stalin; history seemed to be truly on their side.

When the fruits of that victory were challenged by the nuclear-armed capitalist West, which condemned Soviet expansion into East Central Europe, insecurity and fear, pride and faith heightened the feelings of many toward the *patrie en danger* (the fatherland in danger). As if to emphasize its distance from its earlier

[49]Vera Dunham, *In Stalin's Time: Middleclass Values in Soviet Fiction* (Durham, NC: Duke University Press, 1990).
[50]Slezkine, *The Jewish Century*, pp. 330–31, 359.
[51]Geraint Hughes, *My Enemies' Enemy: Proxy Warfare in International Politics* (Eastbourne: Sussex Academic Press, 2012), p. 43. See also Peter Grose, *Operation Rollback: America's Secret War Behind the Iron Curtain* (Boston: Houghton Mifflin, 2000); and Jeffrey Burds, "The Early Cold War in West Ukraine, 1944–1948," *The Carl Beck Papers*, no. 1505 (Pittsburgh: Center for Russian and East European Studies, University of Pittsburgh, 2001).

Monument to the Victory at Stalingrad, in the city of Volgograd. The heroic portrayal of a Soviet soldier, with a gigantic Mother Russia holding a sword aloft, were monumental examples of how the victory over fascism became the Soviet central myth after 1945, in many ways displacing the importance of the October Revolution of 1917. A political myth is not necessarily false but is deployed for political purposes, to justify the structures of power in society and the state.

internationalism, the Stalinist leadership of the late 1940s turned xenophobia into a mark of loyalty to the socialist fatherland. Nativist pride in Russia's past was combined with deep hostility toward the West. The postwar synthesis involved severely restricting non-Russian nationalisms, which the regime considered potentially anti-Soviet. Stalin apparently told filmmaker Sergei Eisenstein: "We must overcome the revival of nationalism that we are experiencing with all the [non-Russian] peoples."[52] The Russian imperial historical narrative was advanced as the foundation of Soviet patriotism, and the struggle and victory in the Second Great Fatherland War was deployed to solidify the pan-national identification with the Soviet Union. In the following decades and even into the post-Soviet period, the victory in the war was a far more powerful source of loyalty and deep affection for the Soviet Union than the revolution or civil war.[53]

---

[52]Brandenberger, *National Bolshevism*, p. 187. Brandenberger added the words [non-Russian].
[53]Nina Tumarkin, *The Living and the Dead: The Rise and Fall of the Cult of World War II in Russia* (New York: Basic Books, 1995); Amir Weiner, *Making Sense of War: The Second World War and the Fate of the Bolshevik Revolution* (Princeton, NJ: Princeton University Press, 2002).

Through the years of Stalin's rule, Soviet historians and party officials fought bitterly over the "correct" formulation of Soviet patriotism and impermissible nationalism. Tsarist Russia as "gendarme of Europe" and "prisonhouse of peoples" was cast, at least in Zhdanov's rendition (1936), as "the lesser evil" for non-Russians. Pride in the Russian past became sacrosanct. Party ideologues occasionally opened doors a crack to accommodate the local cultures of various nationalities, but the openings were ambivalent and inconsistent, and the doors would be slammed shut with grim consequences for the people involved. Some courageous figures like the historian Anna Pankratova, operating in conditions of what Reginald Zelnik called "constrained dissent," tried to document the achievements of non-Russians and to advocate for expanding "national rights." Pankratova's own life charts the challenges of broaching nationality questions in Stalin's time. A powerful figure in the historical profession, Pankratova herself suffered periods of exile. When she was banished to Kazakhstan, she developed her interest in Kazakh history and culture, and endured the arrest of her husband.[54]

During the war, film studios in the national republics put out their own equivalents to Eisenstein's great anti-German epic, *Aleksandr Nevskii*, which celebrated a medieval prince's battles against the Teutonic Knights. Non-Russian republics produced analogous epic films dedicated to national heroes who defended their native lands against the incursion of foreigners: Armenia's *David Bek*, Georgia's *Giorgi Saakadze*, and Ukraine's *Bohdan Khmelnytsky*. Ultimately, though, the task of reconciling national histories with the Russian imperial story proved insurmountable. As Serhy Yekelchyk concludes in his study of Ukrainian historiography, "The casualties of this cohabitation were many: historians accomplished little, ideologues could not completely control the writing and teaching of history, and teachers apparently struggled to instill in students both pride in their nation's past and an appreciation of Russian imperial credentials."[55] But "once the exigencies of 1941–1943 had faded, party ideology reverted to an extreme version of the post-1937 line on the Russian people's ethnic primacy within Soviet society . . . [which] emerged from the wartime experience in a much more russocentric and etatist form than it had been before the outset of the conflict."[56]

As Stalin proclaimed in his famous toast in May 1945, the Russian people were "the most outstanding nation of all the nations in the Soviet Union," "the Soviet Union's leading force among all the peoples of our country . . ." and possessed "a clear mind, hardy character, and patience."[57] Lenin's deathbed warning to beware of Russian chauvinists—even if they were of another nationality—had been cast aside. The Soviet national anthem adopted in 1944 to replace the *Internationale* neatly summarized the Stalinist national patriotic synthesis: "Unbreakable union

---

[54]Reginald E. Zelnik, *Perils of Pankratova: Some Stories from the Annals of Soviet Historiography* (Seattle: University of Washington Press, 2005).

[55]Serhy Yekelchyk, *Stalin's Empire of Memory: Russian-Ukrainian Relations in the Soviet Historical Imagination* (Toronto: University of Toronto Press, 2004), p. 107.

[56]Ibid., pp. 130, 131.

[57]Cited in ibid., pp. 130–31.

of free republics, forged together through the centuries by Great Rus! Hail the united, mighty Soviet Union created by the will of the peoples. Hail our free Fatherland, Friendship of the Peoples is our reliable stronghold! The Soviet banner, the people's banner, let it wave from victory to victory!"[58]

In this postwar celebration of Russian primacy, the diverse histories of non-Russians were brutally subordinated to the Russian narrative. In 1948 the Armenian Communist Party condemned scholars for "idealizing the historical past of the Armenia." Three years later it castigated the nineteenth-century novel *Kaitser* (Sparks) by the nationalist writer Raffi that it had approved for republication just four years earlier. Stalin's Russia/USSR—the two words were used interchangeably in the late 1940s–early 1950s—might be labeled an empire of nations with the Russians as the privileged imperial nation. In its system of official nationalities and divisions of republics and regions, it maintained and cultivated the ethno-territorial distinctions that had constituted its imperial predecessor. The preeminence of Russia as the first among nations and of Moscow as the metropolitan hub clearly maintained the inequitable distribution of power characteristic of empire.

Unlike the tsarist empire, however, the Soviet Union worked assiduously and consistently under Stalin to create an integrative Soviet affective community, and it enjoyed some success in creating such a supranational community. With this campaign, the Soviets displayed a distinctly nationalizing impulse: to efface differences and to create a homogenous whole. Pre-revolutionary Russia had only haphazardly and sporadically attempted Russification. Equipped with far more effective means of propagating their message, the Soviet regime spread its chosen ideas through mandatory education, mass conscription, the pervasive voice of state-controlled radio and television, and ubiquitous visual reminders that the Party offered a glorious road to the future, and that one should wash one's hands. Even as they developed the notion of a Soviet people, the Communists, like the tsars, maintained and even reinforced differences between nationalities and between the elite with its special perquisites and the general population.

Although class distinctions lessened over time, especially after Stalin's death, they continued to mark people in both obvious and disguised ways. Some people had access to special stores; others could hang their coats in designated cloakrooms; still others were allowed to travel abroad or live in restricted cities. Equality existed in law but not in everyday life. And money, the great equalizer and separator in capitalist societies, played less of a role than who you were and whom you knew. The distinctions of national populations and the unequal division of power between the center and peripheries, between the party elite and the people, continued to bring imperial flavor to the mix. Uneasily the Soviet people coexisted with the nationalities within a distinctly modern and reconfigured incarnation of empire.

---

[58]Translated from Russian by Ronald Suny.

ПОД ВОДИТЕЛЬСТВОМ ВЕЛИКОГО СТАЛИНА—ВПЕРЕД К КОММУНИЗМУ!

A Soviet propaganda poster displays the happy union of nationalities, the Friendship of Peoples. Against a backdrop of a map of the Soviet Union, representatives of different nationalities, costumed in their national garb, smile up at Joseph Stalin. Throngs of their fellow Soviets recede in the background. The poster was published by the Iskusstvo Publishing House, 1950 (?). The caption reads: "Under the Leadership of Great Stalin - Forward to Communism."

SOVIET DISCURSIVE POWER

Stalin's Soviet Union was a highly centralized state with a dictator more powerful than the pre-revolutionary autocrats. No tsar, with the possible exception of Peter the Great, had had as much command over his subjects, but not even he had the means that Stalin had to reach deep into the population and far beyond the borders of his country. No opposition survived for long; Communists at home and abroad were dedicated to Stalin's vision; and the victory in the war made him an invulnerable, deified figure to the faithful. In a country marked by material privation, the regime disciplined and mobilized the population through fear and propaganda.

During the early Cold War years (1945–1953) Western scholars conceived of the Soviet system as totalitarian, that is, similar in structure and ambition to the defeated Nazi regime. In the totalitarian model, citizens were seen as politically passive, manipulated atoms largely incapable of effective resistance against the all-powerful state. The social contract between state and society was based on the mass loyalty by ordinary people in exchange for security and the minimum delivery of goods and services necessary for survival. Deviation was quickly punished. The totalitarian model captured something of Stalin's intent to control society as much as possible, but it misled Western analysts into predicting that the USSR could not evolve from mass terror to a regime based more on persuasion and propaganda, as it did after Stalin's death. Totalitarianism led to expectations that the Soviet Union, like Nazi Germany, was war-bound and perpetually expansionist, when in fact it was relatively satiated by its territorial acquisitions once it secured its sphere of influence in East Central Europe. Learning a misconstrued lesson from history, Western leaders and their publics came to accept that negotiation with the Kremlin was equivalent to appeasement, a policy that had fed Hitler's appetites and led to world war.

Soviet society and politics were far more complicated than the totalitarian lens allowed observers to see. Indeed they were messy and disorganized. From the top to the bottom of society little Stalins ran republics, regions, factories, and farms. As absolute and arbitrary as their sway might be far from Moscow, local party and state leaders were constantly threatened from above by the displeasure of the higher bosses, particularly Stalin. From below they were challenged by possible disturbances of dissatisfied constituents, and from all sides by rival factions and personalities. The powerful and popular chief Communist in the Soviet Riviera Black Sea republic of Abkhazia, Nestor Lakoba, for example, was secure in his seat as long as his friendship with Stalin was intact. But when the ambitious Georgian Communist Lavrenti Beria turned against him, his fate was sealed. Invited to Tbilisi to dine with Beria and his wife, Lakoba became sick and died, probably poisoned. His clients in Abkhazia soon fell, replaced by those of Beria.[59]

Below the party elite, those that Stalin referred to as "little screws" (*vintiki*) managed in a variety of ways to muddle through, to make things work, to acquire what they needed. Citizens could try to alleviate their hardships or satisfy desires by petitioning those in power. Historian Oleg Khlevniuk gives this picture of how citizens turned to Beria once he was recognized as the lord of his native republic.

> Residents of Georgia appealed to Beria to resolve all sorts of issues. Peasants asked to be resettled because of the threat of mountain avalanches. Collective farm workers complained about hunger resulting from crop failures or asked that schools be opened in their villages. An engineer raised the issue of railroad construction. A Georgian playwright asked for help in staging his plays in a Moscow theater. Anonymous and signed statements reported malfeasance among Georgian officials. These and many other statements show how Beria was perceived by wide layers of Georgian society to be the republic's protector, appeals to whom had great chances of success because of particular relationships. This perception of "political intimacy" (in one of the letters Beria is referred to as "a beloved person of the Georgian people") is enhanced by the fact that many of the letters

---

[59]Timothy K. Blauvelt, "Abkhazia: Patronage and Power in the Stalin Era," *Nationalities Papers* 35, no. 2 (May 2007): 203–32.

Head of the political police Lavrenti Beria with Svetlana Allilueva, Stalin's daughter, on his lap, and Stalin at work in the background, 1930s.

were written in Georgian and translated into Russian in Beria's secretariat. As a rule, citizens of Georgia appealed to "their" protector in their shared language.[60]

The practices of supplication described here replicate the forms familiar from Muscovite and Imperial times. Deploying the personalized language of love and invoking the protective obligations of their patrons like their pre-revolutionary forbearers, Soviet citizens addressed those with whom they could plausibly claim a personal connection: in the case of Beria, that is, a tie of Georgian nationality. Reciprocity, delivered through the conventional forms of patronage and clientelism, continued to play an important role in allowing the system to work, even at the height of Stalinism.

The Stalin era did not simply replicate earlier conventions, of course. New ideologies and new forms of social cohesion also came into play in this era. Ideological changes, in particular, effected not only official, public transformations but interior accommodations on the part of individuals as well. Recently, scholars have elaborated more subtle and complex views of Soviet subjectivity than

---

[60]Oleg V. Khlevniuk, "Kremlin—Tbilisi. Purges, Control and Georgian Nationalism in the First Half of the 1950s," in *Georgia After Stalin: Nationalism and Soviet Power,* ed. Timothy K. Blauvelt and Jeremy Smith (London: Routledge, 2016), pp. 14–15.

allowed for by the totalitarian model, looking closely at the ways in which Soviet people understood themselves, the world around them, and their relationship to official Soviet discourses. Whereas some scholars emphasize the centrality of Marxist ideology as determining the Soviet experience, the "subjectivists" believe "ideology may be better understood as a ferment working in individuals and producing a great deal of variation as it interacts with the subjective life of a particular person."[61] Ideology was not only top down—in some sense the official dogma was dead ideology—but "a living and adaptive force" that operated "in living persons who engage their selves and the world as ideological subjects."[62] Soviet citizens had to reconcile their enthusiasms and convictions with the evident shortfalls and repression of everyday Stalinism. In the view of historian Jochen Hellbeck, by "rationalizing unfathomable state policies," Soviet citizens became "ideological agents on a par with the leaders of party and state."[63] Hellbeck's Soviet man and Soviet woman, at least as evidenced by the handful of ideologically attuned diarists he investigates, were introspective, and their tortured efforts at self-fashioning were directed toward remaking themselves into politically conscious citizens who fused with the cause of the revolution and the building of socialism. Soviet socialist subjectivity did not prize individual autonomy or private values; these were the signs of bourgeois consciousness, liberal individualism, which needed to be eradicated.

Hellbeck's diarists lived in an environment structured by an authoritarian regime, enforcement of ideological conceptualizations, and a thick web of discursive constructions within which they were constrained to operate and think. Their search for an authentic Soviet subjectivity was sincere, he claims, but, as one critic of the Soviet subjectivity school argues, it was not carried out in a space full of alternatives. "They were sincere, but they were not free."[64] Our own view is that Soviet discursive power was pervasive but not total, not without fissures and self-contradictions that opened space for variation in subjectivities. In Stalin's USSR there were still people who had come of age before Bolshevism; there were religious believers of many stripes; millions who were untouched or only very slightly affected by the urban based, thinly stretched regime; criminals, dissenters, ornery outsiders, and principled opponents.[65]

---

[61]Jochen Hellbeck, *Revolution on My Mind: Writing a Diary Under Stalin* (Cambridge, MA, and London: Harvard University Press, 2006), p. 12.

[62]Ibid., p. 13.

[63]Ibid.

[64]Alexander Etkind, "Soviet Subjectivity: Torture for the Sake of Salvation?" *Kritika* 6, no. 1 (Winter 2005): 177.

[65]For a sense of the variation of Soviet subjectivities, see Nina Lugovskaia, *The Diary of a Soviet Schoolgirl, 1932–1937* (Moscow: Glas, 2003); the first-person narratives in Veronique Garros, Natasha Korenevskaya, and Thomas Lahusen, eds., *Intimacy and Terror: Soviet Diaries from the 1930s* (New York: New Press, 1995); and Sheila Fitzpatrick and Yuri Slezkine, eds., *In the Shadow of Revolution: Life Stories of Russian Women from 1917 to the Second World War* (Princeton, NJ: Princeton University Press, 2000).

In a study of postwar Ukrainians in Kyiv (Kiev), historian Serhy Yekelchyk demonstrates how the regime used ritual, ceremonies, elections, and the media to shape the practices and attitudes of Soviet citizens, and how the careening shifts in official discourse could ultimately undermine confidence in the regime.[66] Immediately after the liberation of Kyiv from German forces, a language of hatred and revenge was propagated, first against the Nazis, then against "internal enemies" like Ukrainian nationalists, and finally, during the anti-cosmopolitan campaign, obliquely against Jews. After Stalin's death and the surprising withdrawal of the accusations against the Jewish doctors, people began to doubt the reliability of official Soviet statements, an erosion that would accelerate a few years later with Khrushchev's "Secret Speech" attacking Stalin. The seemingly solid block of official ideology left spaces for even the most ardent socialist subjects to make choices from among competing and contradictory positions.

BRIEF BIBLIOGRAPHY

Brandenberger, David. *National Bolshevism: Stalinist Mass Culture and the Formation of Modern Russian National Identity, 1931–1956.* Cambridge, MA: Harvard University Press, 2002.

Brown, Kate. *A Biography of No Place: From Ethnic Borderland to Soviet Heartland.* Cambridge, MA: Harvard University Press, 2004.

Davies, Sarah. *Popular Opinion in Stalin's Russia: Terror, Propaganda, and Dissent, 1934–1941.* Cambridge: Cambridge University Press, 1997.

Dunham, Vera. *In Stalin's Time: Middleclass Values in Soviet Fiction.* Durham, NC: Duke University Press, 1990.

Hellbeck, Jochen. *Revolution on My Mind: Writing a Diary Under Stalin.* Cambridge, MA: Harvard University Press, 2006.

Inkeles, Alex, and Raymond Augustine Bauer. *The Soviet Citizen: Daily Life in a Totalitarian Society.* Cambridge, MA: Harvard University Press, 1959.

Kotkin, Stephen. *Magnetic Mountain: Stalinism as Civilization.* Berkeley and Los Angeles: University of California Press, 1995.

Lewin, Moshe. *The Making of the Soviet System: Essays in the Social History of Interwar Russia.* New York: Pantheon Books, 1985.

Martin, *The Affirmative Action Empire: Nations and Nationalism in the Soviet Union, 1923–1939.* Ithaca, NY: Cornell University Press, 2001.

Northrop, *Veiled Empire: Gender and Power in Stalinist Central Asia.* Ithaca, NY: Cornell University Press, 2004.

Petrone, Karen. *Life Has Become More Joyous, Comrades: Celebrations in the Time of Stalin.* Bloomington: Indiana University Press, 2000.

---

[66]Serhy Yekelchyk, *Stalin's Citizens: Everyday Politics in the Wake of Total War* (New York: Oxford University Press, 2014). Isaiah Gruber makes a similar case for the costs of rapid shifts and reversals in official discourse in his study of the Time of Troubles at the beginning of the seventeenth century: *Orthodox Russia in Crisis: Church and Nation in the Time of Troubles* (DeKalb: Northern Illinois University Press, 2012).

Slezkine, Yuri. *The Jewish Century*. Princeton, NJ: Princeton University Press, 2004.

Timasheff, Nicholas S. *The Great Retreat: The Growth and Decline of Communism in Russia*. E. P. Dutton & Co., 1946.

Trotsky, Leon. *The Revolution Betrayed: What Is the Soviet Union and Where Is It Going?* Garden City, NY: Doubleday, Doran and Co., 1937.

Tumarkin, Nina. *The Living and the Dead: The Rise and Fall of the Cult of World War II in Russia*. New York: Basic Books, 1994.

von Geldern, *Bolshevik Festivals, 1917–1920*. Berkeley: University of California Press, 1993.

Weinberg, Robert. *Stalin's Forgotten Zion: Birobidzhan and the Making of a Jewish Homeland: An Illustrated History, 1928–1996*. Berkeley: University of California Press, 1998.

Weiner, Amir. *Making Sense of War: The Second World War and the Fate of the Bolshevik Revolution*. Princeton, NJ: Princeton University Press, 2002.

Yekelchyk, Serhy. *Stalin's Citizens: Everyday Politics in the Wake of Total War*. Oxford: Oxford University Press, 2014.

———. *Stalin's Empire of Memory: Russian-Ukrainian Relations in the Soviet Historical Imagination*. Toronto: University of Toronto Press, 2004.

ELEVEN

IMPERIAL IMPASSES
Reform, Reaction, Revolution

Stalin's death in 1953 was greeted with heartfelt weeping. Surprising though it is
to most Western readers, his casket on display in Moscow drew vast numbers of
mourners and the streets thronged with people beside themselves with grief.
Police futilely tried to control the mourners. Hundreds were trampled to death in
a stampede. There must have been plenty of people who felt no need to grieve for
Stalin, but they kept their views to themselves.[1]

A scuffle for power followed, with a short-lived triumvirate giving way in
short order to the emergence of Nikita Khrushchev as First Secretary of the Communist Party (1953–1964). Khrushchev oversaw sharp reorientations in policy,
particularly after he denounced the destructive violence and sheer cruelty of his
predecessor in a "Secret Speech" at the 20th Party Congress in February 1956. In
his speech, which was not destined to remain secret for long, he lambasted Stalin
for cultivating a "cult of personality," and he exposed the horrors of the purges,
the forced confessions, the faked evidence, and the destructive distrust that
caused him to see enemies everywhere. Speaking for four hours, Khrushchev
drew attention to Stalin's failure to include the Soviet people in his governance,
to win them over rather than beat them into submission:

> Stalin acted not through persuasion, explanation, and patient cooperation with
> people, but by imposing his concepts and demanding absolute submission to
> his opinion. Whoever opposed this concept or tried to prove his viewpoint, and
> the correctness of his position was doomed to removal from the leading collec-
> tive and to subsequent moral and physical annihilation. This was especially true
> during the period following the 17th party congress [1934], when many

---

[1] Yevgeny Yevtushenko, *A Precocious Autobiography* (New York: E. P. Dutton, 1963). A nice account
of the range of responses to Stalin's death is found in Solomon Volkov, *Conversations with Joseph
Brodsky: A Poet's Journey Through the Twentieth Century*, trans. Marian Schwartz (New York: Free
Press, 1998), p. 30.

prominent party leaders and rank-and-file party workers, honest and dedicated
to the cause of communism, fell victim to Stalin's despotism.[2]

With this passage, Khrushchev gestured to one of the central themes of our analysis: the ongoing recognition (with notable periods of exception) of the importance of reciprocity in successful governance of the Russian Empire. The passage
sets a low bar for responsive government. It does not criticize the lack of representative government or even of opening channels of communication from below. It
merely advocates explaining nicely, instead of imposing by force, whatever the
Party has decided. And yet, along with condemning the cult of personality, exposing atrocities, and appealing for a return to "revolutionary Socialist legality,"
the speech emphasizes the importance of a more benevolent relationship of rulers
and ruled. Along with "the decisive role of the Marxist party in the revolutionary
fight for the transformation of society," he acknowledged "the people as the creator of history and as the creator of all material and spiritual good of humanity."
Although its central import derived from its attack on Stalin and Stalinism, the
speech implicitly raises the questions we have been addressing all along, about
how to think about "the people" of a state or nation and how state and society
should interact.

     With the end of the police regime of Stalin, the loosening of central control
under Khrushchev led as well to some easing of the extraordinary restrictions
on ethnic expression, but the path had many turns and switchbacks. A tug of
war began between Moscow and the party leaders in the republics. National
political elites in each republic began to test the limits of what Moscow would
tolerate. In Azerbaijan and Latvia the Communist leaders strengthened the
teaching of the national language of the republic in 1956, only to lose their positions soon after. In 1958 Khrushchev pushed back against non-Russian language enthusiasts with an educational reform that gave parents the right to
choose in which language their children could study, thus effectively ending
the requirement to learn the national language of the republics.[3] In Ukraine
under party secretary Petro Shelest (1963–1972), expressions of Ukrainian national consciousness were tolerated for a while, but when the Kremlin feared
that nationalism was spreading too far too fast, a tough enforcer of central
party policy, Volodymyr Shcherbytsky (1972–1989), was installed in Kiev. In
Ukraine, as in Belorussia, the teaching and promotion of the Russian language
was intensified.

     The struggle against what party officials occasionally referred to as *mestnichestvo*
(localism) remained a persistent problem for the center. In South Caucasia and
Central Asia long-lasting local party elites created a corrupt system of patronage,
favoritism toward the titular nationality, and a widespread practice of bribe-taking

[2]http://digitalarchive.wilsoncenter.org/document/115995.pdf?v=3c22b71b65bcbbe9fdfadead9419c995.
[3]Jeremy Smith, *Red Nations: The Nationalities Experience in and After the USSR* (Cambridge:
Cambridge University Press, 2013), pp. 208–15.

and payoffs.[4] With the rise of complex networks of patrons and clients, "family circles," and the notorious illegal, private "second economy," party leaders who enjoyed Khrushchev's favor became enmeshed in the corruption and favoritism that characterized normal Caucasian and Central Asian political and economic practices. Here too by the early 1970s Moscow grew suspicious of the consolidated local elites that placated the local populations with moderate concessions to national feelings and a high degree of economic permissiveness. In a tense dynamic typical of imperial rule, regional satraps loosened the bonds that the center used to restrain them, and eventually Moscow either reined them in or, in most cases, removed them.

By the end of the 1960s the regime of Leonid Brezhnev (1964–1982), which in general backed the entrenched party cadres, could no longer tolerate the continued frustration of its economic plans, especially in the republics of the southern tier of the USSR. In order to break through the complex networks of friends, clients, and relatives that local party bosses had erected, the central party leaders turned to new personnel outside the dominant party apparatuses. In July 1969, Heidar Aliev, a career KGB officer, was selected as first secretary of the Azerbaijani Communist Party. Three years later, in September 1972, his colleague in the Georgian security forces, Eduard Shevardnadze, was named leader of the Georgian party. That same year Russians were brought into Armenia to serve as second secretary of the Central Committee and head of the KGB, and in November 1974, Karen Demirchian, a young Armenian engineer educated outside of Armenia, became party chief in Armenia. The mandate given these men was the same: to end economic and political corruption, to stimulate economic growth, to end ethnic favoritism, to contain the more overt expressions of local nationalism, and to promote a new governing elite able to carry out the policies of the Communist Party.

Because of the traditional Caucasian and Central Asian reliance on close ties with family and friends, acquaintances and clans, the underground economy and corrupt political practices in the south proved to be invulnerable to reform.[5] Favors done or received were the operative currency of both social and political relations, and the networks built up through favors and personal ties made it possible to circumvent the official state economy and legal forms of political behavior. These practices, often seen as characteristic of these peripheral southerners, were not exclusive to that region but could be found endemically present through much of the Soviet Union.[6] Since the political and police structures had also been penetrated by such personal networks, protection from punishment was a

[4]John H. Miller, "Cadres Policy in Nationality Areas—Recruitment of CPSU First and Second Secretaries in Non-Russian Republics of the USSR," *Soviet Studies* 39, no. 1 (January 1977): 35.
[5]Gerald Mars and Yochanan Altman, "The Cultural Bases of Soviet Georgia's Second Economy," *Soviet Studies,* 25, no. 4 (October 1983): 549.
[6]Erik R. Scott, "Edible Ethnicity: How Georgian Cuisine Conquered the Soviet Table," *Kritika: Explorations in Russian and Eurasian History* 13, no. 4 (Fall 2012): 831–58; and *Familiar Strangers: The Georgian Diaspora and the Evolution of Soviet Empire* (New York: Oxford University Press, 2016).

frequent favor, and noncompliance with the law held fewer risks than breaking family codes or ties between former schoolmates, army buddies, or other close associates. Even after the state came down hard on the "black" or "gray" so-called second economy, and the risks involved in circumventing the law increased, the networks persisted. No form of private business, no profit-making enterprises, were permitted by law. Kinship or friendship ties served as an effective form of national or simply social resistance against the ways of doing business imposed by the Soviet polity. Once Stalinist terror was reduced—and in the absence of effective democratic control from below—many regions and republics were essentially ruled by local or national "mafias" that were centered within the Communist parties and state apparatuses whose reach extended throughout society.[7]

Besides a pervasive "official nationalism" within the party and state bureaucracy and sanctioned among the intelligentsia and population, a dissident or "unorthodox nationalism" expressed by a few human rights activists and even revolutionary separatists first appeared in the 1960s, accompanied by counternationalisms of the minorities within the republics. "Official nationalism," or what was defined by Soviet authorities as "patriotism," became a permissible form of expression in the more laissez-faire atmosphere of the 1950s–1960s, but central authorities, fearing the growth of ethnic chauvinism or political separatism, periodically tried to rein in the more vocal proponents of local nationalism. The new republic leaders of 1969–1974 brought a renewed emphasis on the need for Russian-language education and the curbing of what Shevardnadze called "national narrow-mindedness and isolation." As in the late tsarist period and the early Soviet years, language and cultural rights once again became the battlefield where all-Union needs and national republic desires clashed. State and society struggled over the definition of national rights in the Brezhnev years, and an openly defiant dissident movement risked arrest and exile to express its discontents. As early as March 1956 students in Tbilisi took to the streets to protest the removal of a monument to Stalin and were met by gunfire from the army. The demonstrations had begun as a protest by Georgian patriots, who felt humiliated at the demotion of Stalin in Khrushchev's "secret speech" denouncing the crimes of the late dictator. But once the regime used the army against the demonstrators and dozens were killed, Georgians turned sharply against the Soviet system. Repression gave birth to a growing dissident nationalism.[8] Almost a decade later, on April 24, 1965, thousands of Armenians marched in an unofficial demonstration to mark the fiftieth anniversary of the Armenian Genocide. Then First Secretary Iakov Zarobian rejected the use of force, tried to calm the crowds, and ultimately made concessions to Armenian national sentiments. A monument to the victims

---

[7]The corrupt practices in the post-Stalin period were foreshadowed earlier. For a thorough study of how corruption permeated the Soviet system, see James Heinzen, *The Art of the Bribe Under Stalin: Corruption Under Stalin, 1943–1953* (New Haven: Yale University Press, 2016).

[8]For archivally based articles on the events and aftermath of 1956 in Georgia, see Blauvelt and Smith, eds., *Georgia After Stalin*.

of the massacres and deportations of 1915 was built on Tsitsernakaberd, a hill in Erevan, and each year on April 24, a spontaneous procession of people filed up to the eternal flame to lay flowers. But Zarobian, who had achieved considerable popularity in Armenia for his conciliatory attitude toward Armenian national sentiments, was removed from power within a year after the demonstration.

Discussions were held in the mid-1970s about eliminating the federal structure of the Soviet state and declaring Russian the state language of the Union, but neither proposal went very far. The republics were able, within limits, to stand up to the center and win modest concessions to national sentiments. In April 1978, in a more successful challenge to central authority, or at least one without the negative consequences suffered by Zarobian, hundreds of students and others in Tbilisi took to the streets to protest a government plan to change the clause in the Georgian constitution that proclaimed Georgian to be the state language of the republic. Shevardnadze addressed the crowd, estimated at five thousand, before the building of the Council of Ministers, and informed them that he had recommended retention of Georgian as the state language.[9] Not only was Georgian retained but Moscow prudently abandoned similar proposed changes in the constitutions of Armenia and Azerbaijan. No party leaders suffered from this open expression of anti-Russian sentiment, an early manifestation of the re-emergence of civil society in the Soviet Union and a harbinger of *perestroika* (rebuilding) from below.

What could not be tolerated, however, was "unorthodox nationalism," which included both a small number of revolutionary separatists, like the Armenian National Unity Party, and more moderate intellectuals who formed human rights organizations, like the Helsinki Watch Committees that attempted to awaken international public opinion to the denial of national and other human rights within the Soviet Union.[10] Dissidents in Georgia, for example, at first became interested in the seemingly anodyne pursuit of preservation of Georgia's historic and religious monuments, but some of the more daring soon took up the plight of the Meskhetians, the Muslim Georgians who had been forcibly moved in 1944 from their homes along the border with Turkey to Central Asia and wanted to return. Russian nationalism found some expression in similar pursuits, organizing around protection of religious and historic monuments and agitating to found nature preserves. Ukrainian dissenters protested the suppression of Ukrainian

---

[9]The new article in the constitution was to have read: "The Georgian Republic ensures the use of the Georgian language in state and public agencies and in cultural and other institutions and . . . , on the basis of equality, ensures the free use in all these agencies and institutions of Russian, as well as other languages used by the population." *Zaria vostoka*, April 15, 1978; in *CDSP*, 30, no. 17 (May 24, 1978): 12.

[10]A full treatment of the Helsinki Watch Committees in Transcaucasia can be found in Yaroslav Bilinsky and Tonu Parming, *Helsinki Watch Committees in the Soviet Union: Implications for the Soviet Nationality Question* (Final Report to the National Council for Soviet and East European Research, 1980). See also Ludmila Alexeyeva, *Soviet Dissent: Contemporary Movements for National, Religious, and Human Rights* (Middletown, CT: Wesleyan University Press, 1985).

language and literature, a policy they sometimes provocatively pointed out were violations of Leninist nationality policies. After the Israeli victory over Arab states in the Six-Day War of 1967, Jewish activists protested against restrictions on Jewish traditions and petitioned to emigrate from the Soviet Union. Jews who lost their jobs and prospects upon filing to emigrate to Israel and then had their petitions refused or long delayed came to be called "Refuseniks." Their cause was vigorously supported in the United States and Europe and embarrassed and annoyed the Soviet leaders. When the nationalists proved difficult to tame, they were shut down by the head of the political police, Iurii Andropov. By the early 1980s the dissidents had either disappeared underground or been exiled abroad.

Officially loyalty to one's nationality was supposed to give way to feelings of Soviet patriotism, but because the close association of Sovietism with Russia continued right up to the end of the Soviet Union, hundreds of millions of Soviet citizens faced the dilemma of reconciling their ethno-national affiliations and affections with their supranational loyalties. Some, like most Estonians, forcibly integrated into the USSR after the war, simply rejected the Soviet Union and along with it Russia, and lived as much as possible within their own ethnic community. Others, like the hundreds of thousands of Armenians who either lived in or emigrated to Russia and other republics, assimilated into Russo-Soviet culture, and though their nationality was emblazoned on their passports, they were effectively "Russian" in language, culture, and attitude. After a generation or two they intermarried, and their passport identity might disappear. Between those two poles were others who tacked back and forth between identities or created hybrid identities, becoming situationally Soviet in some circumstances, ethnic in others. Nationality was so powerful a marker in late Soviet society that in many circumstances it was used instrumentally, e.g., for political or social advancement within a national republic or to emigrate from the Soviet Union (Jews, Germans, Armenians, Koreans, and others).

POLICY AND EXPERIENCE:
FRIENDSHIP OF THE PEOPLES

On the ground, the policies written in Moscow could take on different hues and registered on people's experiences in contradictory ways. Life in the Soviet Union was defined by rigid bureaucratic norms and by their subversion, by sclerotic residues of Marxist-Leninist ideology, by effusive displays of nationality, by standardized currency, time, geographic orientation, and consumer products, and by material shortages. Many factors contributed to the development of an increasingly unified Soviet culture, still diverse ethnically but peopled by a homogeneous Soviet population. Soviets across the USSR's eleven time zones marked official time on clocks set to Moscow time, and caught planes and trains at hours oddly out of joint with the passage of the sun but coordinated to the Kremlin's timepiece. Those same Soviets could ask for different kinds of chocolates in colorful wrappers by their universal names, *Belochka* (Little Squirrel) or *Mishka kolosopaty* (Little Pigeon-toed Bear), wherever they traveled, whether in Leningrad or Vladivostok. Comfortingly familiar menu items (Chicken Kiev; Chicken *Tabaka*; *Stolichnyi* salad) would greet them if they ever had occasion to dine in a restaurant. Georgian food became a universal Soviet menu item.[11] Less benign commonalities also united Soviets' experiences: lines, with all their accepted etiquette and protocol, deficits (shortages of goods and food products), unpaid "voluntary" workdays (called Lenin Saturdays), exhortations to improve themselves in a variety of ways, enormous billboards featuring propaganda written in the regime's favored red and black lettering. Soviet children went off to camp in ritual summer migrations, and older ones worked on annual potato harvests. Camp memories created a shared set of nostalgic memories, sometimes tinged with bitterness. Across the expanse of the Soviet Union, people celebrated the big holidays—Day of the Revolution, International Workers' Day, International Women's Day—and observed the small, bizarre ones—Day of the Soviet Border Guard, Day of the Soviet Tank Driver—by wearing and exchanging cheap metal badges (*znachki*). Workers from factories across the country were entitled to receive special boxes of hard-to-come-by goods and to relax at workers' spas and vacation resorts.

Even as such quotidian commonalities strengthened a horizontally shared sense of what it meant to be Soviet, other impulses pushed in different directions. For example, the constant reminders of ethno-national diversity that were so central to the Friendship of Peoples rhetoric conflicted with building any overriding Soviet identity. As Adrienne Edgar points out, no checkbox allowed one to declare "Soviet" as one's official nationality, so even those who felt themselves to be "Soviet" were forced to identify instead with some other subcategory. Edgar notes the painful situations created for children of mixed marriages in a world where each individual, at the age of sixteen, was obliged to select one and only one nationality to inscribe in his or her passport, and "Soviet" was not a nationality option. Even in Central Asia, where national categories were late introductions, often created by the Soviet functionaries in charge of divvying up regions and populations, the act of ascription took on potent meaning in people's lives. Edgar finds that the children of mixed marriages often internalized ideas about the greater or lesser value of their parents' groups of origin, and their intermediate status could be painful in a world that demanded sharp divisions.[12] Soviet nationality policies thus spawned a variety of unanticipated and unwanted downstream effects. They undercut the development of an uncomplicated affective commitment to Soviet nationhood, accelerated the mobilization of national movements agitating for rights or autonomy, stripped people of mixed origin of

---

[11]Scott, "Edible Ethnicity: How Georgian Cuisine Conquered the Soviet Table."

[12]Adrienne Edgar, "Children of Mixed Marriage in Soviet Central Asia: Dilemmas of Identity and Belonging"; with thanks for her permission to cite this unpublished work. See also the caution against accepting Soviet nationality categories as fixed, unitary, and essential in Dmitry Gorenburg, "Rethinking Interethnic Marriage in the Soviet Union," *Post-Soviet Affairs* 22, no. 2 (2006): 145–65.

secure identity, and undermined the status of certain groups to the benefit of others. Identification with nationality had become a permanent feature of the Soviet experience that thwarted assimilatory efforts by the central state.

If the ascription and inscription of nationality might reinforce stereotypes, positive and negative, and lock individuals into particular roles and views, the celebration of diversity could also inculcate a sense of imperial belonging or even imperial dominion in its participants. Public parks such as the VDNKh (*Vystavka Dostizhenii Narodnogo Khoziaistva* or Exhibition of the Achievements of the National Economy) in Moscow placed the friendly peoples of the USSR on display in an iconic fountain and in individual structures dedicated to the resources and products of each republic. Filmmakers from Kyrgyzstan to Ukraine made films in their national idiom, creating "scenes of national belonging that did not contradict a highly centralized and Russian-dominated political and cultural system." Soviet Ukrainian filmmakers in the 1960s, for example, reimagined "a core Soviet concept—multinationality (*mnogonatsional'nost'*)—shifting its emphasis from incorporation, assimilation, and modernization to difference, authenticity and tradition."[13] At the same time most Russian and non-Russian filmmakers were trained at GIK, the State Cinema Institute in Moscow, in styles that were generically Soviet. Newlyweds across the Soviet Union took their wedding pictures at their local monuments to World War II; in Kazakhstan bride and groom took another set of photos at an Islamic tomb, amalgamating several invented traditions. Pride was evident among members of smaller nationalities that they were part of a great state and could travel and vacation on the Baltic, in Crimea, or climb mountains in the Caucasus or Altai. Continuing a prerevolutionary tradition, Soviet manufacturers produced ceramic collectables and sets of dolls representing heterogeneous population types. Following Willard Sunderland's analysis of the tsarist prototypes, the act of collecting the full set might have instilled a proprietary and participatory sense of empire in the purchasers, allowing them to display the full array in the massive standard-issue glass-fronted display cabinets that occupied space in so many small Soviet apartments.

On the other hand, the shared experience of viewing, collecting, displaying, and performing the friendship of peoples revealed both the true differentiation and segmentation that constitutes empire and brings us back toward the homogenization of nation. In the bizarre closing ceremony of the Moscow Olympics of 1980, boycotted by the United States and other Western nations in protest of the Soviet invasion of Afghanistan, participants dressed in the myriad costumes of the diverse Soviet peoples marched onto the field and together sang the famous Soviet Russian wartime song, *Katiusha*. For Soviet film buffs the finale could very well have been the final scene in the 1930s film *Circus*, in which people of various nationalities, having triumphantly vanquished an evil Nazi, sing the soaring

[13]Joshua First, *Ukrainian Cinema: Belonging and Identity During the Soviet Thaw* (London and New York: I. B. Tauris, 2015), p. 1.

The Fountain of Friendship of the Peoples at the Soviet Exhibition of the Achievements of the People's Economy (VDNKh) built in Moscow, 1951–1954.

Soviet song, *Broad Is My Native Land*. Also known as *Song of the Motherland* and sung by the popular movie star Liubov' Orlova, the song was an enormous popular hit and "became the unofficial anthem of the Soviet Union."[14] The Soviet peoples were a single family, the song proclaimed, that protected its motherland as it would its bride or mother.

Given all these conflicting pushes and pulls, it proves hard to fit the Soviet experience into a single box. It defies the easy taxonomies of political science and was a hybrid formation in constant flux. People lived their lives under circumstances that preserved and extended an imperial attitude, fostered oppositional nationalism, created a unity of nations under a Soviet rubric, or rendered popular identities and affiliations meaningless under the crushing mantle of an authoritarian center. All these possibilities were inherent in the contradictory policies and practices of the Soviet Union.

A STRANGE EMPIRE

When reflecting on the peculiarity of their own nation within the Soviet empire, many ethnic Russians saw the whole Soviet Union as their patrimony. Symptomatic of the conceptual fusion of Russia with the entire USSR, the Russian Republic, unlike all the other republics, lacked republic-level institutions of its own; all-Union institutions served in that capacity. As Yitzhak Brudny puts it, "[T]he

---

[14]Petrone, *Life Has Become More Joyous, Comrades*, pp. 54–55.

A Young Pioneers unit in Yalta, Crimea, USSR, 1950s. The Young Pioneers was a youth organization established by the Communist Party in Russia in 1922. From the collection of the State Central Museum of Contemporary History of Russia, Moscow.

Russian population in general, and Russian nationalists, in particular, viewed the USSR as essentially a Russian nation-state rather than an empire. The problem with the USSR, they insisted, was that it was not Russian enough."[15] This sense that the whole country was theirs, though parts of it seemed foreign, reminds one of Nikolai Karamzin's observation almost two hundred years earlier in his "Letter from Riga." Here was a highly educated and sophisticated nobleman traveling in the Baltic region of the empire, recounting in his *Sentimental'noe puteshestvie* (Sentimental Journey), "I had not yet travelled outside of Russia, yet I was already a long time in foreign lands."[16] At the same time that they clearly had privileges that other nationalities lacked, Russians complained that they were in an inferior and exploited position vis-à-vis the non-Russian nationalities. South Caucasians, for example, enjoyed greater freedom in some domains (and better food) than did Moscow. Georgia was distinguished by the highest number of doctors and automobiles per capita of any republic. Armenia opened the only museum in the USSR dedicated to modern and abstract art, works that were forbidden elsewhere in the USSR. Russians loved traveling, even emigrating, to the Baltic republics,

---

[15]Yitzhak M. Brudny, *Reinventing Russia: Russian Nationalism and the Soviet State, 1953–1991* (Cambridge, MA: Harvard University Press, 2000), p. 7.
[16]N. M. Karamzin, "Pis'ma russkogo puteshestvennika (Pis'mo iz Rigi, 31 maia)," in his *Izbrannye sochineniia v dvukh tomakh*, Vol. 1 (Moscow and Leningrad: Khudozhestvennaia literatura, 1964), p. 88. Our thanks to Willard Sunderland for this quotation.

which had a higher standard of living and possessed a kind of European (at least Scandinavian) style. The Soviet Union was a strange empire in which the peoples of the periphery, in the minds of many, lived better and had greater advantages than the people of the metropole.

Supporters of a Russian nation-making nationalism resurfaced in the last decades of the Soviet Union and advocated an exclusively ethnic Russian nation (*russkaia natsiia*). This Russian ethnic nationalism would eventually contest the civic nationalism of the Yeltsin years (1991–1999) that proposed an inclusive, ethnically undifferentiated Russia, using the term "*rossiiskaia*," which refers to all the people and peoples living in Russia, in place of the narrower, culturally and ethnically specific, "*russkaia*" (ethnic Russian).[17] Once the heavy hand of Stalin was removed by his death in 1953, Russian nationalism gradually won the support of influential intellectuals. Initially in the early and mid-1950s, led by the journal *Novyi Mir* (New World), essayists and village prose writers depicted the devastation of the Russian countryside with its implicit critique of the Stalinist legacy and its nostalgic appreciation of threatened peasant traditions and values. The central character in Aleksandr Solzhenitsyn's "Matryona's House," for instance, a simple, big-hearted, long-suffering peasant woman, depicted as both victim and heroine, is presented as an evocative symbol of Russia. Groups began to organize to protect the environment and preserve the nation's architectural heritage, particularly churches and other monuments of Orthodox Christianity. This tentative opening of a public sphere in the Soviet Union was closely linked to Nikita Khrushchev's de-Stalinization campaigns and was only tangentially nationalist. But the Khrushchev and Brezhnev regimes tolerated these mild critiques by poets and short story writers, even as more explicitly political writers were forced into the *samizdat* (illegal self-publishing) underground. As Marxist ideology lost its mobilizational force, the regime of Leonid Brezhnev allowed Russian nationalists, who advocated spiritual renewal as a remedy to the nation's ills, to express their views within the permissible realm of expression. The party tolerated their control of the Russian writers' union and their publication in prominent thick journals. Russian nationalists ranged from liberal to reactionary. The more conservative elements were dedicated to a more statist vision and opposed the liberalization of Soviet politics. Even with a degree of state support, however, the nationalists' politics of culture failed to move beyond an intelligentsia discussion, and when civil society reemerged in the Gorbachev years, nationalists were unable to succeed in the arena of mass politics. The alliance of conservative and radical nationalists was defeated in the 1990 elections to the newly created RSFSR Congress of People's Deputies. Nationalism continued to hold more weight outside the dominant Russian core than within it.

By the last decades of Soviet power, nationalities in the republics experienced an unprecedented degree of local autonomy. Moscow was confident that it had solved the nationality problem with its combination of enforced order and

---

[17]Brudny, *Reinventing Russia*, pp. 7–8.

national permissiveness. Interethnic tensions continued, despite a broad sense shared by many that they were all Soviets. Some nationalities were extremely resistant to Sovietization. Lithuanians remained dedicated to the Catholic Church, and a visitor to Vilnius could observe people kneeling and praying in the street before the shrine of a saint. A young Estonian basketball player was willing to play with a foreigner but not to speak to him in Russian even though he plainly understood the language.[18] Military recruits of various ethnicities, particularly from the Central Asian or Caucasian republics endured rough hazing from older soldiers, often Russians or other Slavs, a practice known as *dedovshchina* (the rule of the grandfathers). Yet the Soviet Union did not experience mass ethnic clashes; there were no pogroms as there had been in tsarist Russia; and no ethnic wars were fought until the very last years of Soviet power when the state lost its grip on society. In part this can be explained by the presence of police and the army, but to a large extent the Soviet experience gave both protection and cultural rights to nationalities. It effectively, if briefly and tenuously, integrated them into an affective community of Soviet socialist affiliation and superpower pride. That gossamer web of community would dissolve after the disintegration of the USSR, but the older generation remembered with nostalgia and regret how "we all lived together."

THE SOVIET UNION IN THE WORLD

Over many centuries, with a few brief exceptions, Russian, and later Soviet, foreign policy, was principally guided by its leaders' belief that their country was relatively weak, insecure, and therefore vulnerable vis-à-vis its international and near-to-home competitors. Among the most fundamental sources of weakness were (and still are): Russia's size and place on the globe combined with a lack of clearly defined borders, a low density of population, and a relatively underdeveloped social and communications infrastructure. The neighborhood in which it exists was and is dangerous for Russian security, territorial integrity, and well-being. Russia's own sense of weakness and insecurity was (and is still) related to the actual dangers and perceived threats felt to come from peripheries within the country (e.g., Chechnya today), from the Near Abroad (e.g., the spread of Islam, dangers presented by the expansion of NATO, the defections of Georgia and Ukraine to the West), and the Great Powers. The long legacy, the structure and ideology of empire, the costs and constraints of an imperial system, were (and remain) related to a lack of dynamism, resistance to reform, and therefore the perennial problem of relative economic backwardness.

Diplomats and political commentators have treated Russia and the Soviet Union alternately as states that like other states act in their national interest or as ideologically driven states that operate from a particular identity, e.g., "the Third

---

[18]These were the experiences of Ron Suny traveling in the Baltic countries in 1966 during his research year on the U.S.-USSR cultural exchange program.

Rome" or the Vanguard of the Proletariat. "National interest" has often been invoked as an objective, unavoidable, permanent "fact of life" that must be a feature of a country's foreign policy if disaster is to be avoided. Certainly the most well-known and succinct statement of this view was by the nineteenth-century British prime minister Lord Palmerston: "England has neither permanent friends nor permanent enemies; she has permanent interests."[19] In this view, the USSR is a rational actor suspicious of other states, which anticipates danger and seeks to increase its power whenever possible. It does not matter who is in charge of Russia. Whether it is Nicholas I, Joseph Stalin, or Vladimir Putin, Russia will be Russia, that is, a state acting as a great power, seeking to become a hegemon, at least in its own region, if not globally. In this "realist" perspective, Russia, like all other great states, is a power maximizer, concerned about relative power, not absolute power.[20]

In contrast to the view that the national interest is objective and permanent, constructivist international relations theorists have argued that in actuality ideas of national interest are subjective understandings of the way the world works, particular views of what the "interests" of the country are, and a cognitive and emotional calculation of what must be done to preserve, protect, or advance the "interests" of the country.[21] Unlike the various forms of realism, constructivism "assumes that the selves, or identities, of states . . . likely depend on historical, cultural, political, and social context."[22] A prominent constructivist, Alexander Wendt, points out, "Identities are the basis of interests. Actors do not have a 'portfolio' of interests that they carry around independent of social context; instead, they define their interests in the process of defining situations."[23] For constructivists, power is both material and discursive; that is, it is also about the generation of meanings that are shared intersubjectively, that is, between different actors. Ideas constitute interests; indeed, "in some sense interests *are* ideas."[24] Action gains legitimacy, even motivating force, only in the context of specific discourses. Constructivists hold that conflict and cooperation are intimately tied to perceptions of threats embedded in historical experiences. The experience of their history and how they understand it is what determines how Russian and Soviet leaders determined who they were and what their interests were. Regime

---

[19]The actual quotation by Henry John Temple, 3rd Viscount Palmerston (1784–1865), was: "We have no eternal allies and we have no perpetual enemies. Our interests are eternal and perpetual, and those interests it is our duty to follow." [Remarks defending his foreign policy in the House of Commons, March 1, 1848; *Hansard's Parliamentary Debates*, 3rd Series, Vol. 97, col. 122].

[20]John J. Mearsheimer, *The Tragedy of Great Power Politics* (New York: Norton, 2001), p. 37.

[21]For an appreciative statement of the constructivist approach, see Ted Hopf, "The Promise of Constructivism in International Relations Theory," *International Security* 23, no. 1 (Summer 1998): 171–200. The classic text is Alexander Wendt, *Social Theory of International Politics* (Cambridge: Cambridge University Press, 1999).

[22]Hopf, "The Promise of Constructivism," p. 176.

[23]Alexander Wendt, "Anarchy Is What States Make of It: The Social Construction of Power Politics," *International Organization* 46, no. 2 (Spring 1992): 398.

[24]Wendt, *Social Theory of International Politics*, p. 114.

types matter. They constrain some leadership choices and promote others. Different kinds of states have different self-conceptions and ambitions, even though certain factors, such as geopolitical position and the anarchic international environment, stay relatively constant. Empires act differently from nation-states, dictatorships from democracies, a relatively cautious Stalinist state from an aggressive, militaristic Hitlerian state, given the constellation of people and groups who can influence policy and express their interests.

While Russia's leaders have often thought in realist terms, or what is known as *Realpolitik*—the play of raw physical power between states—their perceptions of their "national interest" were and are related to their own self-conceptions (identities), ideas of history, and narratives about the past and future. Ideology (in the broad sense of a discourse of politics), rather than simple *Realpolitik* (itself an ideology), has played an important motivating, sometimes distorting, role in determining policy. As a multinational state with an imperial history, Russia found (and still finds) itself both internally and in its own region with a fragile, fragmented "national" identity that has had consequences for its generation of "national interests."

The successors of Stalin faced a world in which the Soviet state was considerably weaker and poorer than the democratic capitalist states hostile to it. The Western powers were united in an anti-Communist alliance and felt threatened by the Soviet Union's ambitions to supersede capitalism and liberal democracy. Both sides in the global standoff actively and aggressively built up nuclear arsenals that were capable of ending life on the planet. The United States was the pioneer in developing atomic weapons and had used them twice in 1945 to end its war with imperial Japan. Given its greater wealth and technological and scientific prowess, the United States usually initiated the major developments of new weapons systems, but once the Soviets possessed their own atomic and hydrogen bombs and the long-range missile system capable of delivering them, the balance of power appeared to be more even. In 1957 the USSR shocked and impressed the world when it launched the first satellite, *Sputnik*, and in 1961 the first man, Iurii Gagarin, into space. Yet these spectacular achievements and Soviet propaganda failed to conceal the actual economic and military imbalance that favored the West. Soviet foreign policy operated from a position of relative weakness and, therefore, in contrast to Khrushchev's bombastic rhetoric—"We will bury you!"— and occasional reckless adventurism (initiating crises over divided Berlin and placing missiles in Cuba), was for the most part relatively cautious and looked for opportunities to improve relations with the West.

Already in the first years after Stalin's death, the Soviets cut back their naval buildup (concentrating instead on rocketry), returned a military base to Finland, agreed to an armistice in the Korean conflict, and a treaty to end the occupation of Austria. Hardliners in the Kremlin opposed Khrushchev's advocacy of "peaceful coexistence," as did Mao Zedong and the Communists in China. Soviet policy tacked between threatening moves like the building of the Berlin Wall in 1961 and introducing nuclear missiles in Cuba in 1962 and negotiations on arms reductions (the nuclear test ban treaty of 1963). President John F. Kennedy forced the Soviets to withdraw the missiles in Cuba, which brought the world to (and back from) the brink of nuclear war. Khrushchev was seriously weakened within the Soviet elite, and he was removed as Soviet leader in October 1964. This "second October Revolution" brought his more conservative and staid comrade, Leonid Brezhnev, to power.

In his eighteen years at the top of the Soviet power hierarchy (October 1964– November 1982), Brezhnev was compelled to deal with three major foreign crises: Czechoslovakia (1968), Vietnam (1965–1975), and Afghanistan (1979–1989). When the Czechoslovak Communists turned toward radical reform under the liberalizing Alexander Dubček, the Soviets feared that one of their satellites might defect to the West and undermine their domination of their borderlands, as the Hungarians twelve years earlier had threatened to do. The "Prague Spring" introduced free discussion, the end of censorship, and tolerance of dissenting views. In August 1968 Soviet troops moved into Prague, eventually deposed Dubček, and installed a rigid party boss subservient to Moscow. The so-called Brezhnev Doctrine claimed the right to intervene in any of its neighboring Communist countries to safeguard Soviet security.

At the same time, however, anxious to improve contacts with the United States and Western Europe, the Soviets embarked on a policy of *razriadka*, easing of tensions, which in the West was known as "détente." The administrations of both Richard Nixon (1969–1974) and Gerald Ford (1974–1977), then engaged in a long war in Vietnam and desperately searching for an exit strategy, were receptive to the idea of unfreezing the Cold War. Nixon and Brezhnev signed an important arms control agreement, SALT I (Strategic Arms Limitation Treaty), in 1972, and three years later the Soviets agreed to the Helsinki Accords, which guaranteed postwar European borders, established mechanisms to protect human rights, and established the Conference on Security and Co-operation in Europe (CSCE). Détente came crashing to a halt with the intervention of the Soviets in Afghanistan.

The tension within the Soviet leadership between their ideological (Marxist-Leninist) framing and realist (also ideological!) understanding of international affairs was very evident in their tortured decision to intervene in Afghanistan in 1979. The USSR had had largely untroubled relations with Afghanistan from its earliest days when it backed the reformist efforts of Amanullah Khan and supported successive royalist regimes. Perfectly comfortable in their dealings with Afghan royals, the Soviets were, somewhat surprisingly, disturbed by the coming to power of the leftist People's Democratic Party of Afghanistan in April 1978. They resisted repeated calls by the party's leader, Nur Mohammad Taraki, for Soviet military aid. The Soviets were fearful both of the costs of intervention and of allowing the Afghan government to fall to its enemies. The United States through the Central Intelligence Agency (CIA) was secretly arming Islamic rebels to overthrow the leftist government and to provoke the Soviets to invade. President Jimmy Carter's national security adviser, Zbigniew Brzezinski, informed the president that the Soviets could be drawn in, giving them their own Vietnam.[25] Only after the more radical Hafizullah Amin had Taraki murdered and appeared to be moving away from the Soviets did the Kremlin send in troops, kill Amin, and replace him with the moderate Babrak Karmal. The aging Soviet leadership felt compelled for both strategic and ideological reasons to back the Afghans and to prevent the revolution from spinning out of control. Their aims were embedded in their perceptions of the world, their identities as "socialists," and their fears of the American "other."[26] Their involvement proved to be disastrous. Islamic rebels backed by the United States, Pakistan, and China ultimately forced the Soviets to withdraw from Afghanistan ten years later. The last Communist leader, Muhanmad Najibullah, fell from power in 1992, and four years later when the Taliban took the capital, Kabul, they castrated him, dragged him behind a truck, and hanged him in public.

STAGNATION

By the early 1980s the Brezhnevian system was grinding to a halt. The long years of Brezhnev's reign, which soon would be dubbed the "period of stagnation (*zastoi*)," had been characterized—on the political level—by a deep conservatism, an unwillingness to reform, a remarkable stability in the leadership, and a vigorous and confident military and foreign policy. The deep conservatism of the "administrative-command system" was the fundamental legacy of Stalinism. In the words of Seweryn Bialer, "The United States might *have* a military industrial complex, but the Soviet Union *is* a military industrial complex."[27] Party leaders in the 1950s through the 1970s had shared a consensus to defend and work through this very stable, highly centralized political apparatus, which directed and attempted to mobilize the whole of society. Soviet civilian and military leaders shared basic values; they saw the world in similar ways, even when they defended particular institutional interests against rivals. The post-Stalin years were marked by remarkable consistency, though temperaments differed, and circumstances changed. As George Breslauer put it, "whereas Khrushchev's strategy fostered and built upon an elite atmosphere of urgency, fear, and yearning for revitalization, Brezhnev's strategy fostered and built upon elite yearning for stabilization and steady, measured progress, based on growing confidence that problems could be managed, and tensions contained, without a *vozhd* [supreme leader] to show them the way."[28]

---

[25]David. N. Gibbs, "Afghanistan: The Soviet Invasion in Retrospect," *International Politics* 37 (June 2000): 233–46.

[26]Archival documents on the Soviet intervention into Afghanistan are available from the Cold War International History Project, online at http://wwics.si.edu/index.cfm.

[27]Seweryn Bialer, *The Soviet Paradox: External Expansion, Internal Decline* (London: I. B. Tauris, 1986).

[28]George Breslauer, *Khrushchev and Brezhnev as Leaders: Building Authority in Soviet Politics* (London, Boston, and Sydney: Allen & Unwin, 1982), p. 12.

But at a deeper social and economic level, enormous changes in Soviet society were undermining the political system and the economic machine that had pushed the population into less and less satisfying labors. Soviet leaders were convinced that neither the older form of rule through terror characteristic of Stalinism nor a move toward some kind of market socialism, such as the Yugoslav Communists were attempting, nor real political democracy was in their interest. Some reform was permissible, but only within the contours of the system as it had existed since the 1930s. The system might be improved, tinkered with, but not fundamentally changed. A Soviet joke summed up the differences between the last three leaders of the USSR. Stalin, Khrushchev, and Brezhnev were sitting in a train that suddenly stopped. Nothing seemed able to make it move again. "Shoot the driver," shouted Stalin. Still the train did not move. "Tell the driver's partner that Communism is just round the corner," shouted Khrushchev. Still the train stood still. Brezhnev then suggested: "Let's pull down the blinds and pretend the train is moving."

While this consensus kept the political establishment in place and resistant to challenges from forces outside the ruling elite, far-reaching changes in Soviet society and in the outside world were rendering the programs of the Soviet leadership increasingly irrelevant. The Soviet Union became a primarily urban society in the early 1960s. Whereas fifty years earlier, only 26,300,000 people lived in

These nesting dolls (*matroshki*) of the Soviet and post-Soviet leaders repurpose an invented Russian tradition from the nineteenth century of supposedly folk craftwork as a lucrative source of tourist dollars. From smallest to largest, the dolls represent Tsar Nicholas II, Lenin, Stalin, Khrushchev, Brezhnev, Gorbachev, Yeltsin, and Putin. A smaller doll, another Putin, has been added to the lineup from another set. Photo: Moscow. 2000.

towns, by 1974 six times as many (153,100,000) were town or city dwellers. Whereas fifty years earlier only two cities had more than 1 million inhabitants, by 1974 there were thirteen such cities. Moreover, Soviet cities were desirable places to live. Millions flocked from the countryside to enjoy the higher standard of living in the cities, desperately seeking *propiska*, the official permission required to live in the largest cities. Housing difficulties persisted, though improvements were marked—40 percent of Soviet families shared their apartments or bathrooms with others in the early Brezhnev years. By 1975 over 70 percent of worker and employee families lived in unshared apartments. The average living space increased from 10.1 square meters per urban dweller in 1964 to 11.8 in 1973. In the post-Stalin years living standards steadily rose. Consumerism became normal in Soviet society as it had long been in the West. In 1965, only 24 percent of people had a television; by 1974, 71 percent had a television. In 1965 only 11 percent had a refrigerator; that figure rose by 1974 to 56 percent. Those owning washing machines increased by three times in the same period.[29]

The Soviet Union was a relatively egalitarian society. If one compares the ratio of average earnings of the top 10 percent of the population to the bottom 10 percent, one would have found that in the United States in 1968 the average income of the top 10 percent was 6.7 times as great as the bottom 10 percent, and these differences would only grow larger in the coming half century. In Eastern Europe that ratio was 3 times. In the USSR it was 4.4 times in 1956, 3.7 in 1964, and 3.2 in 1970. The greatest percent increase in income between 1965 and 1973 was for farmers and farm workers. If one considered not only wages as sources of income and well-being but the ownership of capital, inequality of wealth was far greater in the United States where owing capital was far more important. A study at the University of Michigan in 1983 found that 10 percent of American families (7,500,000 households) owned 84 percent of the nation's assets; 1 percent (840,000 households) owned 50 percent of the country's wealth; while 90 percent of Americans had little or no net worth.

Yet discontent grew through the Brezhnev years. Beginning at the top of society, disaffection and dissatisfaction with the Soviet system spread slowly but steadily, especially in the late Brezhnev years when economic progress slowed down. Part of the bargain struck by the Communist Party in the Stalin and post-Stalin years was that the Soviet regime would eventually "deliver the goods" and life would become easier. This raised expectations that ultimately could never be fulfilled fast enough, at least not for the entire population. Significant differences remained between those who enjoyed exceptional privileges (special stores, hotels, access to goods and information) and those who did not. Money was far less important than whom you knew and what position you occupied. The rise of desire for better, finer things and the scarcity of consumer goods led to the widespread development of black and grey markets, of beating the system by

---

[29]The social, economic, and demographic changes in the USSR are discussed at length in Basile Kerblay, *Modern Soviet Society* (New York: Pantheon, 1983).

working around it, by cheating, bribing, holding back goods and distributing them to friends and relatives. Few could make it without cheating. A Soviet curse exclaimed, "May you be forced to live on your salary." People joked about the "Six Wonders of Soviet Life":

there is no unemployment, but no one is working;
nobody is working, but everyone has money;
everyone has money, but there is nothing to buy;
there is nothing to buy, but the refrigerators are full;
the refrigerators are full, but everyone is complaining;
everyone is complaining, but the votes are all unanimous.

The greatest victory of the Soviet working class was that they enjoyed complete job security. Once one had a job it was almost impossible to be fired from it. Low wages and job security led to low labor productivity. People joked, "They pretend to pay us, and we pretend to work."

While it was difficult to find rewarding work or work commensurate with one's abilities, people wanted to improve themselves, move out of the working class and the peasantry. For most Soviet citizens work was not something that they valued. There were many signs of deep job dissatisfaction. Thirty percent of Soviet workers changed jobs every year. Increasingly, the private sphere of life, one's friends and family, were most important. In the Brezhnev years it became more difficult for people to move out of their class. The society seemed frozen. Parents tried to pass privileges on to their children. Crime increased, along with child abuse, divorce, alcoholism, the spread of fundamentalist religion, and mortality rates. Health and diet declined. The Soviet Union led the world in alcohol consumption per capita. Forty-three percent of the food budget went to alcohol.

Basically, an educated, mobile, expectant society had been created in the Soviet Union by Stalinism and the post-Stalinist bureaucratic economic system. The imperial civilizing mission of the Bolsheviks had borne fruit. But the possibility of realizing one's ambitions, or of full expression of one's opinions and interests, was precluded by the undemocratic political order and the petrified ideology of Marxism-Leninism. Moshe Lewin wrote in the late 1980s, "One thing is clear: Soviet society needs a state that can match its complexity. And in ways sometimes overt, sometimes covert, contemporary urban society has become a powerful 'system maker,' pressuring both political institutions and the economic model to adapt. Through numerous channels, some visible, some slow, insidious, and imperceptible, Soviet urban society is affecting individuals, groups, institutions, and the state. Civil society is talking, gossiping, demanding, sulking, expressing its interests in many ways and thereby creating moods, ideologies, and public opinion."[30]

---

[30]Moshe Lewin, *The Gorbachev Phenomenon: A Historical Interpretation* (Berkeley, Los Angeles: University of California Press, 1988), p. 146. An enlightening study of the forms this disaffection could take is Alexei Yurchak, *Everything Was Forever, Until It Was No More: The Last Soviet Generation* (Princeton, NJ: Princeton University Press, 2006).

In the years of Soviet power, a civil society had emerged in the USSR with no place to go. A deep, dull, persistent conflict developed between the stagnant state structure and the society created by the system. At the same time, Western capitalist societies appeared to be developing in more attractive ways than Soviet society. Even when the Soviet economy was growing at a faster rate than the American, the wealth gap between the two superpowers was so great that the Soviets found it difficult to catch up. The international context put great pressure on the Soviet system to reform in order to compete effectively with the more developed West (and Japan) in technology, economic growth, and military capability. Moreover, the non-Russian peoples, who made up about half the Soviet population and had long lived under the tutelage of the Communist elite, had through the decades of the USSR become compact, conscious, coherent nations with their own cultural and political agendas.

On November 10, 1982, Brezhnev died. Within a few days Iurii Andropov, the former head of the KGB, became leader of the party. An authentic and typical product of the Soviet system, he knew that his country faced serious problems. He soon emerged as a moderate reformer who promoted other reformers to positions of influence and power. One of those Andropov promoted was a young party leader in his home province of Stavropol, Mikhail Gorbachev. In his brief reign Andropov struggled against corruption and tried to improve labor discipline. But his long bout with a fatal kidney disease and the tragic shooting-down of a Korean airliner in September 1983 prevented him from realizing his plans for better relations with the United States. Andropov died on February 9, 1984, of kidney failure at the age of sixty-nine, after only fifteen months in office. He was succeeded for an even shorter time by a Brezhnev loyalist, Konstantin Chernenko (February 1984–March 1985), the last Soviet leader from the older generation that had come up through the ranks of Stalinism. His brief reign proved to be but a short interregnum between Andropov's moderate reforms and the more radical transformations under Gorbachev.

Nineteen eighty-four was a metaphor for danger in the future, the title of George Orwell's classic warning about a war-rife totalitarian world. In the USSR that year was marked by a high degree of stability and continuity, a kind of calm before the storm. Essentially the same ruling elite that had been formed in the long years of Brezhnev's rule remained in power. Relations between the superpowers continued to be tense, and serious negotiations on arms control were suspended for over a year. The USSR and most of its allies refused to participate in the Los Angeles Olympics and held their own Friendship Games in Moscow, a graphic symbol of the deep division between the Soviet Bloc and the Atlantic alliance. In the United States attention was on the re-election campaign of President Ronald Reagan, and in the Soviet Union focus was on structural economic problems, the maintenance of military defense, the continuing war in Afghanistan, and an ambitious educational reform. Western attention was already focused on Gorbachev, who in late December 1984 traveled to Great Britain. After their meeting, conservative Prime Minister Margaret Thatcher declared, "I like

Mr. Gorbachev. We can do business together." Chernenko died on March 10, 1985, and within twenty-four hours the Politburo recommended Gorbachev, then fifty-four, to the Central Committee for election as general secretary.

GORBACHEV AND THE TEST OF PERESTROIKA

When the young reformer Mikhail Gorbachev came to power as general secretary of the Communist Party in March 1985, few predicted that within less than a decade the USSR would cease to exist as a political system and a single sovereign state. However, in the first year following his accession to the top post in the party, Gorbachev gradually laid out radical plans to liberalize, eventually democratize, the one-party state; encourage economic rationalization, eventually granting greater reliance on the market; decentralize the imperial structure of the Soviet Union, eventually permitting limited sovereignty to the republics; and end the Cold War, eventually surrendering what had evolved into Soviet hegemony over the states of East Central Europe.

At first he hoped to use the powerful instrument of the Communist Party and the support of the Soviet intelligentsia to promote his reforms, but the party had for the most part become rigidly conservative and resisted change. At the same time, significant voices from the intelligentsia boldly criticized the pace and limits of Gorbachev's program and called for even more radical and rapid changes. Trying at one and the same time to act as Pope and Martin Luther, Gorbachev was caught between conservative Communists who stalled any reforms and the rush by his critics from the Left to move quickly toward a capitalist market economy and Western-style liberal political system. His own loyalties were to a more democratic socialism, but his reforms, it turned out, were largely destructive rather than constructive. Gorbachev proved to be far more effective in tearing down than building up. As with Marx and Lenin's plans to build a communist society, there were no blueprints for what the future political structure and social supports would be. Just as in the past, much of Soviet practice and planning, rather than working from some clear design, were improvised adjustments to momentary imperatives. If Lenin built an authoritarian Soviet Union when the ship of state was at sea, Gorbachev's *perestroika* (rebuilding) was like fashioning and furnishing a democratic ship while the seas were roiling and smashing the vessel to pieces.

At first there was great optimism in the USSR that a new generation with new ideas had come to power. Gorbachev recalled his conversation with the man he would appoint foreign minister, the Georgian party chief Eduard Shevardnadze: "We said that we could not go on living the way we had been living. . . . We compared everything, and then he said that everything was rotten through and through."[31] A convinced socialist, Gorbachev believed that above all, socialism meant democracy, greater freedom, and power exercised for the people and by

---

[31]Mikhail Gorbachev, *Memoirs* (New York: Doubleday, 1996).

the people. "Our task," he said, "is to combine the socialist approach with private interest through modernizing property relations. Then we will have a mixed economy: state ownership, joint-stock ownership, etc. All in all, there will be co-operative ownership, ownership by the people and, in some form and to some extent, private ownership as well."[32]

Having taken power more quickly than any of his predecessors, Gorbachev was in a position to reshape not only the top levels of the Soviet bureaucracy but the Soviet system as well—if he could maintain a broad coalition of supporters including both the more entrenched conservatives and the younger reformers. Impressive as a man who combined toughness with personal charm and graciousness, he introduced a new style of leadership, more open and practical, willing to adopt ideology to circumstances. In foreign policy he introduced "new thinking," the need to retreat in order to rebuild, to make significant concessions in the hope of receiving similar adjustments from the West. Threatened by Ronald Reagan's "star wars" program, Gorbachev and Shevardnadze hammered away at the need for containing the nuclear arms race and restricting development of new weapons in space. But even as the Soviet government encouraged "openness" in domestic discussion and better management of the state machine, a massive nuclear accident at Chernobyl brutally exposed old habits of state secrecy and deeply rooted inefficiencies and disorganization.

The nationality issues continued to divide the country and threaten a peaceful evolution to a new political system. The story of Gorbachev's failure to reform the Soviet internal imperial structure can be said to begin with the nationalist resistance movements in Armenia, Georgia, and the Baltic republics. Estonia, Latvia, and Lithuania had been forcibly annexed to the Soviet Union by Stalin, and most people in the Baltic republics never reconciled themselves to Soviet imperial rule. With Gorbachev's new policies, people in those republics formed independent popular front groups, protested the Nazi-Soviet Pact of 1939 that had allowed Stalin to invade the republics, and rapidly escalated their demands from greater autonomy to complete independence. The most telling "test for perestroika" that Gorbachev failed was in the conflict between Armenians and Azerbaijanis over the mountainous region of Karabakh, which in Soviet times was constituted as an Autonomous Region (*oblast'*) within Azerbaijan but with a significant Armenian population. Karabakh was emblematic of the ethnonational problems facing Gorbachev and one that turned particularly intractable and violent. Armenians demanded integration of the region into the neighboring republic of Armenia, while Azerbaijanis opposed the dismemberment of their republic. About the same time Abkhaz and South Ossetians resisted Georgian dominance within

[32]*United States-Soviet Relations, 1991: Joint Hearings Before the Subcommittees on Arms Control, International Security, and Science, and on Europe and the Middle Committee on Foreign Affairs, House of Representatives, and the Joint Economic Committee, One Hundred Second Congress, first session, May 16, June 4, June 18, June 25, July 9, July 31, and October 2, 1991,* Vol. 4, p. 304.

Map 11.1. The Nagorno-Karabakh War.

their autonomies.[33] Suddenly, unpredictably, on February 13, 1988, the Karabakh Armenians began a series of demonstrations in favor of incorporation into Armenia. Five days later Gorbachev tried to placate them by offering to hold a special session of the Central Committee to discuss state policy toward the nationalities. The very next day thousands marched in Erevan in support of an Armenian Karabakh, and an unprecedented ethno-political crisis faced the Kremlin. In a historic move the local Karabakh legislative council, usually nothing more than a transmitter of party policy, voted, 110 to 17, to intercede with the Supreme Soviet of the USSR for the transfer of Karabakh to Armenia.[34]

When authorities in Moscow hesitated to act and appeared to be confused, the movement grew, until by the last week of February hundreds of thousands were marching in Erevan in continuous demonstrations. Azerbaijanis, reacting to the Armenian demands, also took to the streets. For two days, February 28–29, rioters in the Azerbaijani industrial town of Sumgait roamed the streets in search of Armenians. They stopped buses and searched them; they invaded hospitals and apartments. Before military forces could quell the riots, thirty-one were dead and hundreds beaten. Azerbaijani intellectuals and officials condemned the riots but

---

[33]On the conflicts between Azerbaijanis and Georgians, see Elizabeth Fuller, "The Azeris in Georgia and the Ingilos: Ethnic Minorities in the Limelight," *Central Asian Survey* 3, no. 2 (1984): 75–85.
[34]For a full and balanced discussion of the continuing crises over Karabakh, see Thomas De Waal, *Black Garden: Armenia and Azerbaijan Through Peace and War* (New York: New York University Press, 2003, 2013).

maintained that Karabakh was historically a part of their homeland. The Gorbachev government was faced with a political crisis for which neither the Soviet Constitution nor political precedent provided much guidance—to settle a violently contested territorial conflict between two union republics. Both nationalities set out historic claims to the region. Given their demographic majority in Karabakh, Armenians bolstered their claims with arguments based on democratic principles and even Leninist notions of self-determination. Azerbaijanis countered with defenses of territorial integrity and constitutionalism. Both sides of the conflict implicitly accepted the notion, a legacy of successive imperial regimes and reified by Soviet nationality policies, that ethno-national groups could and should claim bounded territorial spaces. Both Armenian and Azerbaijani combatants worked from the premise—by no means a natural one—that political-administrative units based on those ethno-national boundaries were meaningful enough to fight for, even to die for.

The complete breakdown of the fragile interethnic symbiosis in Azerbaijan and Armenia that had lasted for almost seventy years, compounded by the simultaneous demands for greater autonomy in the Baltic region, led Gorbachev to warn non-Russians that the future of his reform program, *perestroika*, was at stake. "We are one family," he pleaded, "we have one common home."[35] But anger and fear in both Armenia and Azerbaijan, as well as the Baltic republics, could not be overcome with pleas or postponements, and Gorbachev's hesitant and inconsistent policies toward the non-Russian nationalities eroded any sympathy and support he had initially enjoyed.

As we have seen, efforts to foster commitment to a unified, overarching homeland surfaced within Russia's highly differentiated empire from time to time from the seventeenth century on, but the attempts to foster unity never fully succeeded in overcoming the structural legacies of stratification and segmentation. Whether the aspirational "wholeness" invoked by late-nineteenth-century imperial patriots, the "burning feeling of boundless love" for the Soviet homeland propounded by *Pravda* in 1935, or Gorbachev's last-gasp entreaty to attend to "family" and "common home," each foundered, sent adrift by competing crosscurrents of alternative identities, by the patent manipulation of sentiment by a repressive center, or simply by the fragility of a unifying vision.

Unlike the national struggles in the Soviet Baltic, which had been largely constitutional and free from popular violence, the Armenian-Azerbaijani conflict over Karabakh was far more volatile, less easily manipulated by political authorities, and more subject to rapid and unpredictable escalation. At the same time, Gorbachev and his comrades were forced to face the most fundamental of Soviet dilemmas—how to democratize and modernize the largest country on the globe while maintaining the last multinational empire.

By the end of 1989 the nationalist movements had all but displaced the official power structure in the South Caucasian and Baltic republics. Mass rallies called for

---

[35]*New York Times*, November 28, 1988.

the separation of Azerbaijan from the USSR, and in January 1990 groups of extremists and unsettled migrants broke from a large rally and began massacring Armenians in Baku. After a year and a half of trying to avoid direct military intervention, Gorbachev declared a state of emergency in Azerbaijan and dispatched troops, first to Karabakh and then to Baku. By the time the army entered the city, most of the killing had ceased and the Armenians evacuated from the city. Hundreds of Azerbaijanis were killed, dozens arrested, as the Soviet army in a desperate campaign attempted to restore authority to the discredited Azerbaijani Communist Party. For the Azerbaijanis the "invasion" marked what came to be known as "Black January," a turning point in their disaffection from the Soviet Union.

Communist power rapidly eroded; nationalists dominated the newly permitted elections throughout the USSR, with the exception of Central Asia and Russia. In the Russian Republic a popular movement for greater democracy, with Boris Yeltsin, former Communist mayor of Moscow, at its head, threatened to undermine Gorbachev's support among Russians. In April 1989 Georgian protestors in Tbilisi were attacked by the army and nineteen were killed. After the Lithuanian Supreme Soviet declared the Nazi-Soviet Pact invalid (August 22, 1989) and massive demonstrations the next day, to mark the fiftieth anniversary of the Nazi-Soviet Pact, the Central Committee of the Communist Party condemned separatist tendencies in the Baltic republics. But no reprisals were taken against the Baltic leaders. A Ukrainian national movement Rukh (Movement) was founded in Kiev. The Azerbaijan People's Front called a general strike in the republic. Toward the end of 1989 the Lithuanian Communist Party declared itself independent of the all-union party. Reluctant to use force to deal with the nationality issue, Gorbachev called for a return to Lenin's nationality policy, a real federalism, not the Stalinist emasculation of the federation. He spoke of restoring the violated rights of the peoples deported by Stalin: Soviet Germans, Crimean Tatars, Meskhetian Turks, Kalmyks, Balkars, Karachai, Chechens, Ingush, Greeks, Koreans, and Kurds. But he stated that this was not the time for redrawing the administrative boundaries in the USSR.

Confronted by resistance in both the Soviet external and internal empires, Gorbachev had to deal with one of the longest-lasting effects of centuries of imperial rule: the mixing and mobility of people without regard of historically ethnic territory. For centuries Caucasia and Central Asia, for instance, had been part of the Russian and Soviet empires, and millions of migrants had moved in and settled there, some voluntarily, others not. Vast transfers of populations had transformed the demographics of Central Asia to the point that many regions had Slavic majorities and admixtures of people from all over the Soviet Union. In the nineteenth and much of the twentieth century, Caucasia, particularly in the cities, was home to mixed populations. Muslims lived in neighborhoods and villages next to Georgian and Armenian Christians. Tbilisi, the capital of Georgia at various points in time, had an Armenian plurality up to the revolution of 1917. This imperial legacy of mixing and mobility of populations throughout the empire was reversed in the late Soviet period and even more rapidly with the disintegration of the USSR. Unmixing of populations and ethnoterritorial homogenization became the dominant trend in many Soviet republics in the last decades of the Soviet period and after. For instance, following independence, the Baltic states would prove inhospitable to their large Russian populations. Stringent language requirements barred them from citizenship and drove these long-time residents, many of whom had been born in Soviet Estonia or Latvia, "back" to Russia. Yet populations remained mixed throughout the Soviet republics. Thousands of Armenians lived in Baku, the capital of Azerbaijan, and other towns in the republic, and tens of millions of Russians and Ukrainians lived scattered throughout the USSR outside the Russian SFSR. The breakup of a great state would leave these diaspora peoples left outside their ostensible homelands.

Gorbachev's program of *perestroika* (rebuilding) and *glasnost'* (openness) created a new political environment in the Soviet Union, a new playing field with new rules. The possibility now existed, if people were courageous enough to try, for an open politics: public appeals, articles in the press, public protests and street demonstrations. Among those who learned quickly to play in the new political arena were self-proclaimed democrats like Yeltsin and fervent nationalists in the non-Russian republics. At the same time that Moscow was losing its control over the non-Russian republics within the USSR, beyond the borders of the Soviet Union, within the Eastern Bloc, independence movements gained steam. In Poland the Communist leadership began "round table talks" with the outlawed Solidarity Union in April 1989 that would soon result in free, contested elections and the fall of the Communist government. One after another, the socialist governments of Eastern Europe toppled, and, with no opposition from Gorbachev, their successors withdrew from the Soviet penumbra. The end of the Communist monopolies on power in Eastern Europe and the abrupt end to the Cold War division of Europe encouraged the non-Russian peoples within the Soviet Union to accelerate their drive for full independence.

Gorbachev's magnanimous foreign policy was hailed in the West, but in the USSR it appeared as if the victories of World War II were being lost. In 1988–1989 he withdrew Soviet troops from Afghanistan, where they had been fighting since 1979 to support an unpopular Communist government. Gorbachev restored ties with China in 1989, after more than thirty years of hostility between the two countries. By 1989 Gorbachev's policies had undermined the Communist monopoly of political power, failed to revive the stagnating Soviet economy, and threatened the unity of the Soviet Union. Confronted by economic collapse and growing nationalism in the non-Russian Soviet republics, he used both force and persuasion to prevent separation of these republics from the Soviet Union. When Lithuania declared itself independent in early 1990, he used economic pressure to keep it from leaving the Union. Soon one republic after another made similar declarations. On June 12, 1990, the Russian Republic, now led by its popularly elected president, Boris Yeltsin, the brash and boorish opponent of Gorbachev, declared itself to be a sovereign, democratic state within the USSR. Gorbachev watched as the power of the Soviet center withered away.

Faced with the breakup of his country, Gorbachev offered a new union treaty granting greater autonomy to the republics in November 1990. The Union was to be a federation, with federal laws supreme, one currency, a federal budget and taxes. The republics would be responsible for setting the rules for secession from the union and accepting new members into the union. The center was to control implementation of security, war and peace, and foreign policy. There were few takers. In January 1991 Gorbachev sent tanks into Lithuania to prevent further moves toward independence, and bloody clashes took place. By this time the revolution that he had initiated from above appeared to be spinning out of control, and former supporters of Gorbachev feared that democracy would soon fall victim to social chaos and political conservatism. On March 17, 1991, the Soviet people were asked to vote on the following resolution: "Do you think it is necessary to preserve the Union of Soviet Socialist Republics as a renovated federation of equal sovereign republics in which the rights and freedoms of individuals of all nationalities will be fully guaranteed?" Almost 150 million people voted, and 76.4 percent voted for the union. Six republics refused to participate in the referendum: Latvia, Estonia, Lithuania, Armenia, Georgia, and Moldova. Both the drafting of the union treaty and the referendum indicate that the Soviet Union had fallen into two parts: the independence-minded republics (the Baltic three, Moldova, Georgia, and Armenia); and the Muslim-Slavic mass that voted for union. The vote to keep the Union in the March referendum, however, turned out to be a Pyrrhic victory.

The "nationality question" did not in and of itself bring down the Soviet Union, but it contributed to the erosion of the center's power. Radical and poorly conceived reform by Gorbachev from the top weakened the Communist Party and the power of the state.[36] Gorbachev's commitment to *glasnost'* jeopardized his regime, as an increasingly outspoken press allowed expression to dissidents and nationalists of all camps. Freedom of the press outstripped effective democratic or economic reform. Faith in the socialist project had long eroded among educated people, and the subversive power of the new criticism undermined what was left of the authority and influence of the party apparatus. The will of the party elite, the *nomenklatura*, to resist the popular discontent, now legitimized by the policy of *glasnost'*, dissipated. By 1991 even the army and police could not be trusted to carry out its usual duties.

In the non-Russian regions and republics the nationalists' demands for greater autonomy or full independence increasingly employed the images of Russian-Soviet empire and imperialism and depicted their movements as anti-colonial resistance to an oppressive imperialist yoke. Whereas to this point calling the USSR an empire had been the nearly exclusive talk of Western conservatives like President Ronald Reagan, who labeled the Soviet Union "an evil empire," envisioning it as empire had now become the common coin of nationalists and militant reformers.

---

[36]Suny, *Revenge of the Past*.

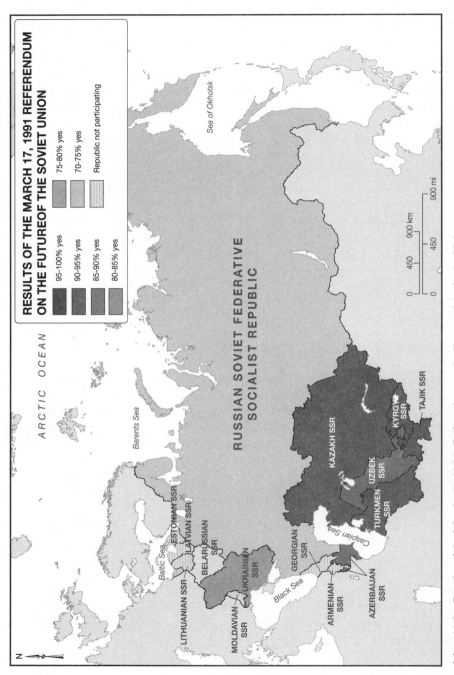

ARCTIC OCEAN

Barents Sea

Sea of Okhotsk

RESULTS OF THE MARCH 17, 1991 REFERENDUM ON THE FUTUREOF THE SOVIET UNION

95-100% yes

90-95% yes

85-90% yes

80-85% yes

75-80% yes

70-75% yes

Republic not participating

RUSSIAN SOVIET FEDERATIVE SOCIALIST REPUBLIC

KAZAKH SSR

UZBEK SSR

TURKMEN SSR

KYRGYZ SSR

TAJIK SSR

Caspian Sea

ESTONIAN SSR

LATVIAN SSR

LITHUANIAN SSR

BELARUSSIAN SSR

UKRAINIAN SSR

MOLDAVIAN SSR

GEORGIAN SSR

ARMENIAN SSR

AZERBAIJAN SSR

Baltic Sea

Black Sea

0   450   900 km

0   450   900 mi

Map 11.2. Results of the March 17, 1991, Referendum on the Future of the Soviet Union.

Gorbachev's own reluctance to use the police and military to enforce obedience to the central state (Azerbaijan and a few other cases were notable exceptions) allowed more radical reformers to influence much of society. When Soviet forces used violence against crowds, as in the Baltic republics and Georgia, repression only encouraged opposition to the regime. Conceding ground to the republics, Gorbachev negotiated a new draft of the "union treaty" that essentially turned the USSR into a confederation of fifteen republics with enhanced powers relative to a newly weakened center. But on the eve of the signing of the treaty in August 1991, conservative Communists carried out a coup against Gorbachev. In a startling display of civic mobilization, masses of people turned out in Moscow to oppose the coup. The would-be leaders summoned the military to crush the demonstration. Tanks rolled into the center of the city. A small number of martyrs to the cause died under the treads of the tanks before the soldiers, sympathetic to the movement, joined the cause. Yeltsin, President of the Russian SFSR, made his mark as a leader of the anti-coup demonstrators, seizing the moment to make his voice heard and his image seen. A now iconic photo shows him standing on a tank in front of the "White House," the building that housed the Supreme Soviet, speaking to the crowd. More republics seized the opportunity of the vacuum of power in Moscow to declare themselves sovereign and independent states. Gorbachev returned to Moscow only to find his power evaporating, the union treaty a dead letter, and Yeltsin the most powerful politician in the land.

Boris Yeltsin before the White House in Moscow defying those who carried out a coup against Gorbachev, August 19, 1991.

The rightist coup in Moscow radically changed the political balance of power in the Soviet Union and made continuation of political union nearly impossible. The United States pressured Gorbachev to set the Baltic republics free and officially recognized their independence before the Soviet leader was willing to do so. The administration of the American president George Herbert Walker Bush cautiously favored "a gradual weakening of the Soviet structure and gradual change and reform" to prevent nationalist violence as the republics moved toward independence. The American interest, a senior adviser to the president later remembered, was "stable decline" of the USSR.[37] Preserving some center that could control the nuclear arsenal was essential, but if possible that center would be far weaker than had existed before *perestroika*. Pushed by the Americans, both Gorbachev and Yeltsin agreed that in exchange for U.S. economic aid the Soviets would end their support of their allies Cuba and Afghanistan, as well as assistance to the Palestinians and other national liberation movements. In its last years the USSR essentially gave up its East Central European empire and curbed its global commitments. In its desperation to stem decline, the Soviet Union surrendered the territorial and political gains it had won at staggering cost in World War II. Historian Serhii Plokhy calls these concessions to the West a "fire sale of Soviet foreign policy assets."[38]

In the fall of 1991, just months before the USSR would no longer exist, a bitter struggle for power raged within the Russian and Soviet political elites. Once again Russia experienced "dual power": on one side Yeltsin's Russia, on the other, what was left of Gorbachev's Soviet power. When Ukraine's parliament declared independence at the end of August, the Russians were reluctant to allow their sister Slavic republic to leave the Union, and they momentarily threatened that new borders would have to be negotiated. Yeltsin and his most radical allies wanted Russia to take over the property, power, and authority of the decrepit Soviet Union. The union in their plans would become a confederation dominated by Moscow, now in the hands of the Russian republic's leaders. Ukraine, Kazakhstan, and other republics opposed Russia's grab for power. The largest republics preferred only a common economic market. Gorbachev futilely held out for a stronger center and a new union. On October 18, Russia and most of the other republics (excluding the Baltics and Ukraine) created an economic community of independent states. That same day Yeltsin ended funding of most all-Union ministries in order, as he put it, "to do away with the remains of the unitary imperial structures as quickly as possible."[39]

At the very moment when the USSR was becoming less imperial, less centralized, and moving toward a looser collection of autonomous republics, the term *imperial* in this late-twentieth-century usage had come to mean the integrative

---

[37]Plokhy's interview with Ambassador Nicholas Burns, June 15, 2012, in Serhii Plokhy, *The Last Empire: The Final Days of the Soviet Union* (New York: Basic Books, 2014), p. 64.
[38]Ibid., p. 205.
[39]Cited in ibid., p. 226.

institutions of an oppressively unitary state, quite the opposite of the heterogeneous structures and bodies that had defined differentiated rule of Russia's earlier empires. The word *empire* had taken on a new and entirely negative valence. Nearly inverting its earlier meaning, or rather singling out one aspect (absolute, unlimited power located at an imperial center) of its original layered meaning, it now signified all that was bad in despotic centralism.

The duel between Gorbachev and Yeltsin continued through the last four months of 1991. Yeltsin announced that radical economic reforms—freeing of prices, the end of subsidies, and privatization of state-owned property—would be implemented in Russia. With his unilateral transfer of power from the Soviet Union to the Russian Republic he usurped whatever clout Gorbachev still had. At the same time "shock therapy," as Russia's market reforms would be known, undermined any notion of serious coordination and cooperation with the other Soviet states who were supposed to become members of a new economic community. Gorbachev desperately tried to preserve some semblance of political unity among the Soviet states. Either some union would continue with Gorbachev as president or the fifteen republics would go their own way. He made a last stand on November 14, threatening to resign as president. He strong-armed the heads of the other republics (again Ukraine was absent) to agree to support a Union of Sovereign States in the form of a democratic confederative state with a president (presumably himself) elected by popular vote in the whole union.

Within two weeks that agreement unraveled, and on December 1, 1991, Ukrainians voted in a referendum overwhelmingly for independence. Nine months earlier, 70 percent of Ukrainian voters had supported a reformed Soviet Union. But the August coup shifted opinion dramatically, and in December over 90 percent voted for independence. A week later Yeltsin and his counterparts in Ukraine and Belarus met without Gorbachev and unconstitutionally declared the Soviet Union dissolved. They took this action once Ukraine adamantly refused to consider any form of union. Concerned that the Central Asian and other republics might object to their decision, Yeltsin and the others immediately consulted with Nursultan Nazarbaev, the president of Kazakhstan, overcame his reluctance to leave the Soviet Union, and secured the agreement of the Central Asian leaders to join the new Commonwealth of Independent States. On December 25, Gorbachev resigned as president of the country that he had hoped to save.

In the space of nine months the now-former Soviet Union had transformed from a floundering unitary state desperately trying to reconstruct itself into a more decentralized and egalitarian multinational one to a looser, more democratic federation of Soviet republics, on to a still looser Commonwealth of Independent States, and finally to fifteen fully independent sovereign republics. The empire was history—at least for the time being. Russia assumed much of the property and many of the prerogatives of the defunct USSR. It inherited enormous resources that it no longer needed to share with the non-Russian republics. The loss of the "colonies" in many ways benefited the former imperial center, many of whose citizens had resented being "exploited" by the non-Russian

Map 11.3. The breakup of the Soviet Union.

republics. Yet citizens of the newly minted Russia now nurtured a new resentment, growing from the experience of loss, contraction, and diminution. With
the collapse of the Soviet Union, even people who supported what they hoped
would be a "transition to democracy" voiced regret. They spoke of a sense of loss
that stemmed from a widely shared emotional tie to the regions that had been so
familiar to them since childhood, that had filled chapters of school textbooks,
had ornamented the various parks and chambers of "friendship of the peoples,"
and had provided the beach and mountain resorts that so many Soviet workers
enjoyed as part of their employment packages. Discussions of loss often turned
into nostalgic memories of trips to the beaches of the Baltic and the Black Sea,
and particularly Crimea. The centuries-long imperial project had succeeded in
inculcating at least in many ethnic Russians and others resident in the capital
cities a possessive sense that the empire's expanse and its many nationalities were
part of their patrimony.

Discussing the disintegration of the USSR, Serhii Plokhy writes: "Once Gorbachev introduced elements of electoral democracy into Soviet politics in 1989, the newly elected politicians in Russia were suddenly empowered to say whether they were willing to continue bearing the burdens of empire, while the politicians in the non-Russian republics faced the question of whether they wanted to remain under imperial rule. Eventually, both groups answered in the negative." In the last four months of 1991 the political elites of Ukraine and Russia could not agree on a formula to keep the union together. "It was the unwillingness of their political elites to find a modus vivendi within one state structure that drove the final nail into the coffin of the Soviet Union."[40]

The ultimate collapse of the Soviet system and the dissolution of the Union (two different but related phenomena) were primarily the result of ill-considered decisions and practices of the very summit of the Communist Party. The underlying ethnonational structure provided capacities and possibilities that empowered the leaders of the republics, undermined Gorbachev's efforts to create a unified but more democratic and decentralized state, and facilitated the transition to fifteen (or more) independent republics. Plokhy's argument that Soviet structures and the choices of politicians were key to the Soviet disintegration challenges the common views that the fall of the Soviet Union was largely the work of the United States or the popular aspirations of the Soviet people themselves. The American administration in fact wanted to preserve the USSR as the better alternative to civil war and nuclear proliferation. Most Russians, Slavs, and the peoples of the traditionally Muslim republics were not driven by the desire for independence. In each republic some pulled toward a reformed USSR, while others wanted out. The Baltic and Caucasian republics, along with Moldavia, which made up about 11 percent of the Soviet population, were the republics most fervent about sovereignty and eventually independence. As late as March 1991 about 75 percent of Soviet voters had voted to preserve the Soviet Union, just as the most precarious months of its existence began.

However one might feel about the evil of the USSR, in its last decades, it had evolved from an earlier form of empire into a distinctively different one. Just when the negatively charged imperial label caught on internally, among the national republics, and externally, on the other side of the "Iron Curtain," the waning Soviet Union had become a pseudo-federal unitary state with both imperial and national aspects and practices. The USSR was still nominally structured as a federal union premised on shared sovereignty and local autonomy, but in the Khrushchev and Brezhnev years the Kremlin struggled, not always successfully, to undercut those rights and to retain its highly centralized control. The differentiated rights regime, legal categorization of distinction, and rule through collectivity and difference that had characterized Russian rule for so many centuries were replaced by nominal parity across groups and regions and efforts to subordinate all equally to the heavy control of the center. The official language of the

---

[40]Ibid., pp. xviii, xx.

Soviet state emphasized that the various peoples of the USSR were moving closer together (*sblizhenie*) and would eventually merge (*sliianie*). Challenged for two centuries by the potent ideology of nationalism, the late Soviet empire evolved in the direction of political homogeneity but not in the direction of a homogeneous sovereign nation of and by the people. Regional distinctions continued in spite of overall trends toward homogenization: Central Asia's cotton monoculture locked the region into an ongoing economic dependency, while the Baltic republics' manufacturing situated them in an advantageous position.[41] Communist bosses with long tenure in office achieved an uncertain degree of autonomy from the center, but if they strayed too far from what Moscow desired they could be removed or punished. In spite of the fact that the periphery in many ways lived better than the center, the *perception* that the Soviet Union exploited its "colonies" fueled the national movements that would ultimately contribute along with the erosion of central power to bringing the Soviet era to an end.

The USSR suffered from what we have called "the dilemma of empire." What happens if the civilizing mission actually civilizes the people? After seventy years of Communist rule, a country that had been over three-quarters peasant had become a land in which over three-quarters lived in towns and cities. An agricultural economy had been driven into an industrial powerhouse. A formerly largely illiterate population learned to read and write and could find out about the world around them. The Soviet empire had been successful enough in its developmentalist program to convince ordinary Russians and non-Russians that they were able to go into the future on their own without the paternalism of the party. The road to modernity that Communists claimed as a key element in their rationale for one-party rule no longer ran through Marxism and Russia. The former Soviet republics embarked on an unfamiliar road at a time when the major powers of the West triumphantly proclaimed that the future belonged to liberal democracy and neoliberal capitalism. Elections, civic rights, and the market, they were confident, would succeed where state "socialism" had failed.

The nation-form and nationalism can be seen as a form of self-defense against encroaching danger, whether of anarchic disintegration, invasion by foreign forces, or oppression by imperial overlords. People of a specific nation seek their own place in the world independent of the demands of great imperial powers. By the end of the twentieth century the nationalists' teleological view of history in which empires were doomed and all peoples would have their own nation-state had become the common coin of international politics. Empires and nation-states were imagined to be mutually exclusive and inevitably antagonistic. But the history of Russia and the USSR demonstrates that in their actual discourses and practices empires and nation-states, as well as varieties of multinational states, have more often than not combined characteristics of the other forms of statehood and ways of ruling. The USSR began as an attempt to create an egalitarian

[41]Donna Bahry, *Outside Moscow: Power, Politics, and Budgetary Policy in the Soviet Republics* (New York: Columbia University Press, 1987).

multinational state but quickly devolved into an imperial state of nations. Already under the harsh authoritarianism of Stalin and continuing into the last decades of Soviet power, the differentiation of populations ethnically and socially was matched by state efforts at homogenization, the creation of a *Sovetskii narod*, and after 1953 a looser hold of the center over the peripheries. The federation forged (in both senses of the word) by Stalin maintained some distinctions (e.g., ethnicity), dissolved others (class as a legal category), and through homogenization and administrative conformity created a pseudo-federal unitary state. With the lifting of systematic terror after Stalin's death, the pseudo-federal USSR maintained both imperial and nation-making practices. Discursively the regime emphasized rapprochement and merging of the peoples of the USSR—a distinctly Soviet nation-making project, though understandably seen as a colonial idea by many non-Russians. But the embedded structures of the Soviet Union thwarted the amalgamation so desired by the Kremlin. Sovereignty remained in imperial Moscow until the very last years of Soviet rule. A bitter contest between the nations consolidated in the Soviet years and the center ultimately weakened an already compromised central authority, and the last vestiges of Russia's reach over Eurasia evaporated . . . at least for a while.

BRIEF BIBLIOGRAPHY

Alexeyeva, Liudmila. *Soviet Dissent: Contemporary Movements for National, Religious, and Human Rights.* Middletown, CT: Wesleyan University Press, 1985.

Bahry, Donna. *Outside Moscow: Power, Politics, and Budgetary Policy in the Soviet Republics.* New York: Columbia University Press, 1987.

Bialer, Seweryn. *The Soviet Paradox: External Expansion, Internal Decline.* London: I. B. Tauris, 1986.

Brudny, Yitzhak M. *Reinventing Russia: Russian Nationalism and the Soviet State, 1953–1991.* Cambridge, MA: Harvard University Press, 2000.

Breslauer, George W. *Khrushchev and Brezhnev as Leaders: Building Authority in Soviet Politics.* Boston: Allen & Unwin, 1982.

De Waal, Thomas. *Black Garden: Armenia and Azerbaijan Through Peace and War.* New York: New York University Press, 2003, 2013.

Gorbachev, Mikhail. *Memoirs.* New York: Doubleday, 1996.

Kerblay, Basile H. *Modern Soviet Society.* New York: Pantheon, 1983.

Lewin, Moshe. *The Gorbachev Phenomenon: A Historical Interpretation.* Berkeley: University of California Press, 1988.

Plokhy, Serhii. *The Last Empire: The Final Days of the Soviet Union.* New York: Basic Books, 2014.

Smith, Jeremy. *Red Nations: The Nationalities Experience in and After the USSR.* Cambridge: Cambridge University Press, 2013.

Yevtushenko, Yevgeny. *A Precocious Autobiography.* New York: E. P. Dutton, 1963.

Yurchak, Alexei. *Everything Was Forever, Until It Was No More: The Last Soviet Generation.* Princeton, NJ: Princeton University Press, 2006.

TWELVE

THE END OF EMPIRE, 1991–2016 . . . OR NOT?

In the twentieth century, Russia and later the Soviet Union experienced two chaotic, transformative instances of de-imperialization. In 1917–1918 and again in 1989–1991, what had been empires were deliberately propelled into a process of imperial disintegration and the abrupt formation of alternative forms of statehood. At these fleeting moments of possibility, when the world and the Russian state could be radically reimagined, intellectuals, activists, and politicians brought forth a flurry of ideas of how to reform the polity: perhaps a multinational state; maybe a confederation of states; or a new form of federalism under the umbrella of an internationalist doctrine—socialism or democracy. Eventually the ultimate arbitrators of the next stage of state formation were those who managed to seize power in the former imperial centers, St. Petersburg or Moscow, or successfully resisted the pull of the former empire and struck out on their own path. In 1918 the Bolsheviks moved pragmatically from a conception of a unitary, non-federal state of territorial units to the acceptance of national-territorial federalism and what eventually became the Union of Soviet Socialist Republics. In the last years of the Soviet Union, Gorbachev futilely attempted to rebuild the state while it floundered in the turbulent sea of nationalist and democratizing movements. He reduced control from the Kremlin and delegated authority to the fifteen union republics in the ill-fated Union Treaty of 1991. This arrangement would have authorized a shift to a true rather than pseudo-federalism. Despite his efforts and the expressed preference of the vast majority of the Soviet people, a conspiracy of three republic leaders—Yeltsin of Russia, Stanislav Shushkevich of Belarus, and Leonid Kravchuk of Ukraine—dissolved the USSR.

The Commonwealth that was to replace it turned out to be moribund almost from inception. However, the emergent Russian republic, which declared itself the heir of the USSR, retained the form bequeathed to it by Leninist nationality policy: at present it is a federation of eighty-five territorial units at the national level, or, in official terms, "subjects," twenty-seven of which are defined as "belonging" to a titular national group.[1]

The Soviet Union was gone but history could not be erased. Forms and practices of rule had lasting effects on the fifteen independent republics that emerged from the collapsed empire. Each of the republics embarked on a nationalizing project, to create a stable nation-state within the former Soviet republic. The Russian Federation became much less imperial internally, much more like a multinational state of equivalent citizens, but distinctions and differences, habits of imperial rule, were never totally eliminated. In the first quarter century after the Soviet flag was lowered over the Kremlin, Russians experimented with forms of democracy and federalism, struggled over what it meant to identify as Russian, and what role this giant state would play in the "Near Abroad," the other former Soviet republics. Would Russia once again act as an empire vis-à-vis its neighbors—that is, attempt to control both their domestic and foreign affairs— or would it try to become a regional hegemon—that is, satisfy itself with friendly relations, economic dominance, and a degree of coordination in foreign policy?

The 1990s in Russia might be called the "Yeltsin Era," followed in the 2000s by the "Age of Putin." If Yeltsin and his supporters had any unifying political commitment, it was to eliminate Gorbachev and the Communists from power and dismantle as rapidly as possible the remnants of the Soviet command economy and polity. With the introduction of market reforms and the collapse of state-run industry, Russia soon went into severe recession. Millions of people were instantly impoverished, while a handful of entrepreneurs, soon to be known as oligarchs, became enormously wealthy in the privatization fury that sold off Soviet assets to energetic, often unscrupulous or criminal, entrepreneurs and cronies of the government. The Supreme Soviet, the parliament that had supported Yeltsin, turned against him, and after protracted clashes over the constitution, Yeltsin found enough support in the military to overthrow the legislature in a bloody confrontation in October 1993. Tanks once again rolled into Moscow, and in an astonishing display, the president ordered them to fire at his own parliament, housed in the very same White House in front of which Yeltsin had made his heroic stand just two years earlier. The new regime solidified its control with a horrifying demonstration of just how shaky the new democratic forms and institutions were.

The new constitution that he pushed through established a powerful presidency and a relatively weak legislature, now called the Duma. Intra-elite divisions were temporarily resolved in favor of the Yeltsin camp. But the president himself steadily lost popularity, and in order to maintain his power he became dependent on the

---

[1] The literature on the disintegration of the USSR is enormous. One of the best works that focuses on the breakup of the state is Edward Walker, *Dissolution: Sovereignty and the Breakup of the Soviet Union* (Lanham, MD: Rowman and Littlefield, 2003). See also Ronald Grigor Suny, *The Revenge of the Past*; and Stephen Kotkin, *Armageddon Averted: The Soviet Collapse, 1970–2000* (New York: Oxford University Press, 2001).

The White House burning, October 1993. Russian president Boris Yeltsin ordered his troops to fire on the parliament resistant to his political reforms.

oligarchs, the security forces, friendly media, and regional governors to whom he had conceded local power. In his reelection campaign in 1996 Yeltsin came from behind to defeat the Communist Party candidate, but analysts saw this as a vote against the old order and the Communists rather than a vote for Yeltsin. Russia was a weak state with what looked on paper (after 1993) to be a powerful presidency. But the man who held that office, Boris Yeltsin, was himself sick, often drunk, distracted, and capricious. Suffering from a chronic heart condition and alcoholism, Yeltsin needed to find a competent successor who would carry on the Yeltsin program and protect him and his family from prosecution for corruption.

Far less powerful and influential on the global stage than the Soviet Union had been, Yeltsin's Russia reluctantly went along with the international agenda of the single superpower in the world, the United States. Instead of the bipolar conflict of the Cold War superpowers, the New World Order that replaced it was defined by unipolarity. But Moscow neither accepted the Western view that it had "lost the Cold War" nor that it was a defeated power that was forced to accept American global hegemony. The Kremlin was prepared, however, to accept that Russia's future required integration into the global capitalist system and at least an effort to democratize the polity. Its diminished international status meant that Russia recognized the independence of the fourteen other former Soviet republics and gave up territorial claims or ideas of changing borders. Russian leaders agreed that the end of history would not be Communism as the Marxists had hoped, but they were not convinced that history's telos was capitalist democracy as the liberals both in the West and in Russia proclaimed. The rules of the economic game were adopted, but Russia demanded that it be respected as an equal participant, even as a partner, in the international arena.

In August 1998 Russia suffered a severe economic crisis. Banks defaulted, the currency collapsed, and millions of people lost their savings. In desperation Yeltsin turned to a Gorbachev loyalist, Evgenii Primakov, appointing him prime minister. An expert in international affairs, Primakov sought to restore Russia's status in foreign affairs, challenging the "new world order" in which the United States stood as an unchallenged hegemon. On a flight to the United States he dramatically ordered his plane to turn back midway across the Atlantic when he learned that the United States and its NATO allies had begun bombing Serbia, which Russia considered an ally, without the sanction of the United Nations. Increasingly popular, Primakov stabilized the economy and made it clear that he would rein in the oligarchs and investigate corruption. This was too much for Yeltsin, who sacked him and looked for someone more pliable.[2]

In the years of Yeltsin's presidency the Russian Federation was marked by the weakness of the center and the power of regional barons in the federal republics and regions, most of whom were holdovers from the late Soviet period. Political scientist Richard Sakwa refers to this system of undemocratic asymmetrical regional autonomy as "segmented regionalism," a hodgepodge of bilateral arrangements between Moscow and the different provincial authorities.[3] Such arrangements harkened back to the practices of differentiation that had long characterized the Russian Empire, but which had subsequently been modified in Stalin's centralizing bureaucratic homogenization. Yeltsin bargained away many of the center's powers in order to hold the state together and preserve the new government in Moscow. Difference was institutionalized; some republics like Tatarstan or Yakutia were granted broad control over their considerable natural resources (in oil and diamonds, respectively). Local mafia-like officials were allowed to exploit their regions as long as they remained loyal to Yeltsin. The North Caucasian republic of Chechnya declared itself independent in November 1991, and for a time was allowed to operate as an independent state. Yeltsin himself in his campaign to undermine Gorbachev had invited the regional leaders in August 1990 to "take as much sovereignty as you can swallow." But rather than a true federalism, in which both the center and the periphery cooperate to a degree and recognize legitimate areas of mutual responsibility and limits on the power of the other, the Yeltsin state was a competitive arena in which a vicious zero-sum game over privileges and exclusions was fought. Forty-two power-sharing treaties granting unequal rights and privileges to different regions were signed between Moscow and leaders of various regions and republics. "By the end of Yeltsin's

---

[2]On the choice not taken—Primakov instead of Putin—see Jonathan Steele, "Yevgeny Primakov Obituary: Outstanding Russian Foreign Secretary Who Served Under Gorbachev and Yeltsin," *The Guardian*, June 28, 2015.

[3]Richard Sakwa, *Russian Politics and Society*, 4th ed. (London and New York: Routledge, 2008), pp. 255–285. See also Richard Sakwa, *Putin, Russia's Choice*, 2nd ed. (London and New York: Routledge, 2008).

presidency Russia was not only a multinational state," writes Sakwa, "but was also becoming a multi-state state, with numerous proto-state formations making sovereignty claims vis-à-vis Moscow."[4]

In another odd twist, just when the former empire definitively shed its colonial territories, renouncing claims on the now independent republican peripheries, it began to reinstitute imperial patterns of differential rule within Russia, returning to the particularity and distinction that had been gradually erased by late Soviet pseudo-federalism. Citizens were unequal before the law as it was in fact exercised . . . or not exercised at all. In essence they were dependent on local lords, subjects of the arbitrary authority of those in office or those nearby who had appropriated the wealth and property of the former Soviet state. The "vertical of power" disappeared, and the threat of dissolution of the federation was palpable to many of its fearful constituents. Not since the time of Appanage Russia or at moments of revolutionary disintegration like the Time of Troubles or 1917–1920 had the vast territory of Eurasia been so fragmented and loosely connected. One of those who worried about the weakness of the central state was a young KGB officer whom Yeltsin had brought to Moscow from St. Petersburg: Vladimir Putin. Yeltsin first appointed him prime minister, and on the eve of the new millennium engineered his succession as president.

VLADIMIR PUTIN
AND THE REBUILDING OF THE STATE

Russia has been ruled by grand dukes and boyars, tsars and nobles, dictators and the Communist *nomenklatura*, and at the end of the twentieth and beginning of the twenty-first centuries by strongmen, oligarchs, and their allies. Autocracy had always been tempered by factional struggles within the ruling elites and by ideas of reciprocity—the people got something, however minimal, out of the bargain. Boyars, clans, highly placed families, sons of the emperor, ambitious pretenders and claimants backed by guards regiments, powerful ministries, the Church, or sinister spiritual advisers—all played their appointed roles in the complex court politics that determined, confused, or shifted state policies. Whether called "family clans," *atamanshchina* (warlord enclaves), networks, or factions, these fluid groups competed for the ear of the supreme ruler. Family and friends, school chums, or colleagues could make up the circle of trusted loyalists on whom the boss might rely. Trust was tempered by the ever-present fear of betrayal. Stalin never forgave his once-close ally Nikolai Bukharin for meeting secretly in a cave with his rival, Lev Kamenev, and Yeltsin bore a festering grudge against Gorbachev, who had sacked him in 1987 as Moscow's mayor.

Those below the top rungs of the social ladder also believed they could expect something from those in power. In Soviet times the social contract between the

---

[4]Sakwa, *Putin, Russia's Choice*, p. 192.

state and the people meant that jobs were secure, and in exchange for loyalty and quiescence, a minimum of welfare and material goods would be provided. The state was not always able to carry through on its promises, especially in the late Brezhnev and Gorbachev years. The Soviet people had endured periods of distress and hardship before. In the 1930s workers were crowded into the burgeoning industrial center at Magnitogorsk before even the most minimal housing or provisioning was in place, and during the grim years of the Second World War starvation was widespread despite efforts to distribute food efficiently. At these earlier moments of systemic stress, however, the promises of the socialist bargain remained active, even if the system failed to deliver on those promises.[5] But with the sudden shift to economic "shock therapy" in 1992, the social safety net was shredded; pensions were either not paid or were meaninglessly tiny; housing and high-quality medicine were privatized; and jobs were no longer safe and secure. The conservative novelist Aleksandr Solzhenitsyn lamented that "Yeltsin and his entourage, the corrupt bureaucrats, the financial magnates . . . are united by one great fear: that people will take from them everything they have stolen, that their crimes will be investigated and that they will be sent to jail."[6] Yeltsin's decision to have Putin succeed him fulfilled his expectations that he and his family would be protected. In his first official act as president, Putin granted his predecessor and his family immunity from prosecution for any charges that might be brought against him.

There would not, however, be favors for everyone. Elected president by a healthy majority in 2000, Putin made it clear immediately that the status quo was unacceptable. "We are a rich country of poor people. And this is an intolerable situation," he declared.[7] The state had to be rebuilt, but the redistribution of property after the fall of state socialism, unjust and unpopular as it was, would not be reversed. There would be no second social revolution after 1991. The boom in oil and gas prices allowed Putin to increase wages and pensions. The oligarchs who had enriched themselves during the Yeltsin years were put on notice that in exchange for the preservation of their ill-gotten gains, their interference into politics would no longer be tolerated. If the oligarchs behaved themselves and were loyal to the government, Putin made clear, the state and the new bourgeoisie, the "New Russians," could coexist. Instead of the freewheeling, anarchic *laissez-faire* of the last decade, however, the economy would be more closely tied to the state and its interests.

Putin regretted the disintegration of the USSR, which he called "a major geopolitical disaster of the century."[8] Appealing to an affective community of Soviet citizens who would understand his sense of loss, he said, "Anyone who does not

---

[5]John Scott, *An American Worker in Russia's City of Steel* (Boston: Houghton Mifflin, 1942); Kotkin, *Magnetic Mountain*.

[6]Cited in Sakwa, *Putin: Russia's Choice*, p. 28.

[7]Ibid., p. 37.

[8]Annual Address to the Federal Assembly of the Russian Federation, April 25, 2005, http://archive .kremlin.ru/eng/speeches/2005/04/25/2031_type70029type82912_87086.shtml.

regret the passing of the Soviet Union has no heart. Anyone who wants it restored has no brains."[9] Rather than rejecting all Soviet symbols as Yeltsin had, Putin compromised with images and representations sacred to an older generation. Lenin monuments still stood, and his preserved remains stayed in the mausoleum on Red Square. The red flag was restored as the emblem of the military, and the old Soviet national anthem was resurrected with new words by the same author who had penned the original. The new president married the traditions of the old regime with the transformations introduced by the new one.

Although federalism is about shared sovereignty, claims by the regions and republics within the Russian Federation that they were sovereign were now declared illegitimate. Just as he centralized and concentrated power in the Kremlin by weakening the oligarchs who had profited from the shift to a capitalist economy, so Putin used his legal powers and political muscle to end the power of the regional barons. Using language redolent of textbook celebrations of the "gathering of the lands" in the fifteenth century, he proclaimed, "We must gather the state and we will do this." Putin held that the constitution demanded that laws of the regions and republics had to conform to the highest law of the Russian Federation. Favoring a stronger central state, he called for "the dictatorship of the law" to prevent any further devolution of authority from the center to the regions. In other words, he shifted course yet again, putting the brakes on Yeltsin's neo-imperial system of bilateral agreements and particular deals and turned back in the direction of implacable centralized rule. Following the example of his personal hero, Peter the Great, who had organized Russia into eight enormous regions, the man from Peter's city divided the country into seven large administrative districts headed by all-powerful plenipotentiaries appointed by the president. In 2005 he abolished the direct election of governors of the regions and made them appointed officials. Formerly, the heads of the regional governments had made up the Federation Council, the upper chamber of the central Russian parliament. Putin gradually turned that body into a much weaker chamber made up of nominees of the appointed governors. Russia was soon on its way back to pseudo-federalism not unlike what had been the pattern in the USSR. Governors became functionaries of the central state, and most of the republics and regions fell into line. Some of those whose power had been reduced complained. Ruslan Aushev of Ingushetia grumbled, "What kind of federation is it if the president can remove the popularly elected head of a region or disband the regional legislature?" Nikolai Fedorov of Chuvashia echoed the thought: "We all aimed for and tried to build a state with the rule of law. But it turns out now that society—or at least the prevailing atmosphere—is such that the will of the emperor, the will of the president, is law."[10] Even when Putin's successor, Dmitrii Medvedev, restored

---

[9]Interview with German television channels ARD and ZDF, May 5, 2005, http://archive.kremlin.ru/eng/speeches/2005/05/05/2355_type82912type82916_87597.shtml.
[10]Cited in Sakwa, *Putin, Russia's Choice*, p. 211.

gubernatorial elections in 2012, the Kremlin's influence and power was so great that almost all the governors came from the presidential party, United Russia.

Yet Putin's policies were popular. To the Russian public he appeared strong, decisive, and competent, the right man to save the country from collapse. Putin handily won the contests with both the oligarchs and the regional bosses. Russia progressively became less democratic, more authoritarian. Demonstrations were broken up; dissidents arrested; prominent journalists were murdered, and in the West and among the opposition in Russia the finger was pointed at Putin and his cronies. The president's allies grew enormously rich. Power flowed to and from the center. No one was too rich or powerful not to be brought down by Putin. When Mikhail Khodorkovskii, the richest man in Russia, defied Putin's wishes that oligarchs stay out of politics, he was arrested, his assets were taken from him, and he was sent to a Siberian prison camp for over a decade. Putin's strong-arm methods were not only acceptable to many Russians but were believed to be essential for the survival of the state. As Oleg Morozov, one of Putin's close advisers, put it in plain Russian, "Russia is a country that, in principle, cannot exist without a strong central authority. Attempts to weaken this strong central authority lead by no means to the strengthening of democracy in the state, as certain people naively hope. They lead to the intensification of centrifugal tendencies in the country and create a threat to its stability and territorial integrity." Or as stated even more bluntly by Viacheslav Volodin, first deputy leader of the Russian Federation Presidential Staff, "If there is Putin, there is Russia. If there is no Putin, there is no Russia."[11]

Most of the non-Russian regions and republics were willing to work within the new Russia and negotiate what privileges and autonomy they might be able to wheedle out of Moscow. The Volga republic of Tatarstan declared itself sovereign in the early 1990s and controlled its rich resources, including oil, but under Putin much of its autonomy was curtailed. The sovereignty movement sought political powers but in the end managed primarily to enhance the cultural assertiveness of the Tatars and turn the republic's capital, Kazan, into a lively cosmopolitan city.[12] Its constitution laid out the republic's complex relationship to the center: "The Republic of Tatarstan is a democratic constitutional State associated with the Russian Federation by the Constitution of the Russian Federation, the Constitution of the Republic of Tatarstan, and the Treaty between the Russian Federation and the Republic of Tatarstan *On Delimitation of Jurisdictional Subjects and Mutual Delegation of Powers between the State Bodies of the Russian Federation and the State Bodies of the Republic of Tatarstan,* and a subject of the Russian Federation. The sovereignty of the Republic of Tatarstan shall consist in full

---

[11]Mikhail Rostovskii, "Testimony of Retired Kremlin Official Oleg Morozov," *Moskovskii Komsomolets,* July 9, 2015; translated in Johnson's Russia List 2015=#137, July 20, 2015.
[12]Ross Oermann, "Kazan's New Spirit: Lasting Social Effects of Tatarstan's Sovereignty Movement," lecture at the Kennan Center, Woodrow Wilson International Center for Scholars, Washington, DC, July 7, 2011, reported by Blair Ruble, https://www.wilsoncenter.org/publication/kazans-new -spirit-lasting-social-effects-tatarstans-sovereignty-movement.

possession of the State authority (legislative, executive and judicial) beyond the competence of the Russian Federation and powers of the Russian Federation in the sphere of shared competence of the Russian Federation and the Republic of Tatarstan and shall be an inalienable qualitative status of the Republic of Tatarstan."[13] In simpler terms, Tatarstan is about as sovereign as the state of Texas.

When a region or republic refused to conform to the centralizing plans of the Kremlin, Moscow's imperial impulses became particularly visible. The most recalcitrant and resistant republic was Chechnya, which became the negative example for the rest of the country of the costs of separatism. The local leader of Chechnya at the time of the Soviet collapse, Jokhar Dudaev, declared the republic independent, and Chechens fought the Russians to a standstill between 1994 and 1996. The war was very unpopular within Russia proper, and in August 1996 a treaty was signed at Khasavyurt that effectively gave Chechnya de facto independence. Rebel leader Aslan Maskhadov was elected president but proved unable to prevent the lawlessness and terrorism tearing Chechen society apart. Shortly after Yeltsin appointed Putin prime minister—and his likely successor—a second Russian war with Chechnya broke out when Chechen insurgents infiltrated the neighboring republic of Dagestan. Putin feared that the separatist contagion would spread through the North Caucasus and eventually up the Volga. Bombs exploded in Moscow and other cities. Fear grew, and hostility to Chechens increased. A full-scale invasion of Chechnya was launched in September 1999. By February 2000, just before Putin's election as president, the Russian army took the Chechen capital, Grozny.

For Putin the Chechen insurgency "was a continuation of the collapse of the USSR. . . . If we don't stop it immediately, Russia as a state in its current form would no longer exist."[14] He spoke brutally of "washing the bandits in the shithouse" (*banditov v sortire zamochim*). Contrasted with the doddering Yeltsin, Putin the judo champion appeared to be the macho man of iron that Russia needed to deal with the terrorists.[15] His popularity soared. Thousands on both sides were killed in the Chechen wars, and tens of thousands crippled. Adopting a practice well-known to empires, Putin delegated authority to a tough thug, Ramzan Kadyrov, successor to his father who had been assassinated. Indirect rule meant that Kadyrov and his loyal military could govern without restraint. The Chechens installed by Moscow to run the republic mercilessly crushed any resistance or opposition. Moscow warily watched the practices of its satrap but did not interfere. At the end of February 2015, Boris Nemtsov, the liberal politician and critic of both Putin and Kadyrov, was murdered on the street just

[13]"The Constitution of the Republic of Tatarstan," www.kazanfed.ru/en/docum/konstit/2.
[14]Ibid., pp. 228–29. On Russian policy and Chechnya, see Hanna Smith, *Russian Greatpowerness: Foreign Policy, the Two Chechen Wars and International Organisations* (Helsinki: University of Helsinki, 2014).
[15]Elizabeth Wood, "Hypermasculinity as a Scenario of Power: Vladimir Putin's Iconic Rule, 1999–2008," *International Feminist Journal of Politics* (2016) [http://dx.doi.org/10.1080/14616742.2015.1125649].

Grozny, the capital of Chechnya, after years of war and devastation by Russian troops.

outside the Kremlin. Russian authorities claimed that Chechens had committed the murder without the sanction of the Russians. With his own personal army numbering tens of thousands, Putin's viceroy in Chechnya appeared to be acting independently of his sovereign. Putin's critics countered that the murder of a political opponent of the stature of Nemtsov was simply too convenient to be chalked up solely to Chechen initiative. In either case, it is noteworthy that the Putin regime was willing to spread the idea that the agent was wriggling free of the principal, publicly proclaiming the limits of its control.

Putin's Russian Federation is an authoritarian state but not an empire as we have understood the concept. The legacy of the Soviet imperial practices remain, as is clear in Chechnya, in the formal distinctions between ethnic and non-ethnic units of the federation, but overall the liberalizing reforms of Gorbachev and Yeltsin have also left an imprint. Differences between peoples exist, though the official designation of nationality was removed from passports. Russian citizens are equal under the law. With the restoration of greater order, citizens benefit from a legal structure that provides horizontal equivalence rather than division by institutionalized and hierarchical differences. Money talks more than inscribed privilege, but it is no guarantee against the government's ultimate will, as some of the oligarchs discovered. The center remains powerful, fully sovereign with delegated authority to federal units, but centralized power is not sufficient to qualify the new Russia as an empire without stretching any reasonable definition past its limits. Even though Putin's Russia has become a state marked by a soft authoritarianism, the uneasy passage into capitalism and democracy reduced the overweening power of the central state over citizens and the economy. A market

society has been firmly established, and a middle class of professionals and entrepreneurs operates within the bounds set by the state. Civil society and
inter-factional elite struggles thwart a complete transformation into autocracy.
Ilya Gerasimov and Marina Mogiliner, two of the founding editors of the journal
Ab Imperio, perhaps the most important voice in "new imperial history" of Russia
and the Soviet Union, go so far as to claim:

> For the first time since the collapse of the USSR, we are witnessing
> the triumph of the nation-centered social imagination in Russia,
> accompanied, not surprisingly, by all the attributes of the discourse
> of the wholesome national body (be it antigay propaganda, the cult
> of sports, antifeminism, xenophobia, or the rhetoric of "ancestral
> territories"). For the first time in its history, Russia is turning into
> a classical nation-state. . . .[16]

Floundering for a coherent ideology after the elimination of communism,
Russians and other post-Soviets found inspiration in a variety of ideologies and
faiths. With the fall of Communism, religion became a viable option. Russian
Orthodoxy enjoyed a renewed popularity, particularly among governmental
leaders and state functionaries, although its illicit cooperation with the Soviets
left it tarnished in the eyes of many. Alternative stripes of Christianity won ad-
herents in the wake of the collapse. Baptisms boomed in the "Old Belief," a schis-
matic offshoot of Orthodoxy that came to be associated with an authentic Russian
path. Evangelical missionaries flooded into the regions of the former Soviet
Union bringing material aid, supportive understanding, and promises of salvation. In Muslim regions, comparable bundles of religion and aid were delivered
through quickly forming *waqf* charitable trusts.[17] Radical Islam took hold in the
North Caucasus, allied for a time with the Chechen movement for independence.
In Muslim republics like Azerbaijan and Uzbekistan, however, former Communists turned nationalist leaders suppressed expressions of Islam that were critical
of the regime.

In a secular vein, an assortment of rightist intellectuals, post-Gorbachev
Communists, and state officials in the late Soviet period and through the first
post-Soviet decades championed the idea of Russia as a unique Eurasian state
bridging the cultures of two continents. They found inspiration in the works of
earlier generations of Eurasianist thinkers, particularly those of Lev Gumilev,
an errant scholar with a most distinguished pedigree. The son of two of
twentieth-century Russia's greatest poets, Nikolai Gumilev and Anna Akhmatova,
Gumilev had both a successful career as an author and ethnographer and

---

[16]Ilya Gerasimov and Marina Mogiliner, "Deconstructing Integration: Ukraine's Postcolonial Subjectivity," *Slavic Review* 74, no. 4 (Winter 2015): 722.
[17]Catherine Wanner, *Communities of the Converted: Ukrainians and Global Evangelism* (Ithaca, NY:
Cornell University Press, 2007); and Mark Steinberg and Catherine Wanner, eds., *Religion, Morality, and Community in Post-Soviet Societies* (Bloomington, IN: Indiana University Press, 2008).

repeatedly fell from grace into the prisons and camps of the Soviet regime. Gumilev drew on the teachings of a group of early-twentieth-century émigrés who had created a "Eurasianist" school of thought while struggling to make sense of the fate of their country from afar. Beginning in the 1920s, they proposed alternatives to the Bolshevik visions of state and nation. Primarily intellectuals from Russia's western borderlands who had experienced the traumas of the Russian civil war and abhorred the idea of antagonistic Ukrainian and Russian nations, the Eurasianists repudiated tsarism's colonial policies toward the non-Russian peoples. They aimed, as did the Bolsheviks, for a formula that would keep the huge, continental space of the old empire united but without the negative practices of imperialism. Their solution was to imagine the multiplicity of peoples in Russian Eurasia as a "symphonic personality," a multinational nation made up of dozens of peoples united in an indivisible space, Eurasia, and a single state. The Eurasianists veered into a mystical conception of a Eurasian geography that imbued the peoples living within it with a common culture.

Eurasianists believed that Russia was neither a nation-state nor an empire but a part of a multinational supra-nation. In the words of Eurasianist historian George Vernadsky, "There is only one Russia, 'Eurasian' Russia, or Eurasia."[18] Aligning his ideas with this intellectual tradition, Gumilev argued that as an empire, tsarist Russia was relatively benign in its relations with its subject peoples. His two ideological enemies were the Soviet regime and the Jews, the two intimately tied together in his vision. The Soviet leaders destroyed old Russia, and Jewish revolutionaries suppressed the Russian people. He also despised liberals and dissenting intellectuals, while he applauded the USSR's Cold War confrontation with the West and Stalin's "anti-cosmopolitan" campaign against Soviet Jews.

This bizarre mélange of ideas struck a deep nerve in post-Soviet intellectual and governmental circles. Gumilev's greatest fame came at the end of his life and posthumously when Russian nationalists and members of the post-Soviet ruling elite embraced his work. His idea found a hungry audience among the growing circles of Russian nationalists in both the late Soviet and post-Soviet years. Upset with what they perceived to be privileges given to non-Russian peoples and disadvantages placed on ethnic Russians by the Soviet state, the nationalists appreciated Gumilev's opposition to "hybridization" and the merging of peoples, his irreverence directed at Soviet power, and his anti-Semitism. During the Gorbachev years of radical reform, he sided with the "empire-savers," who resisted the reforms of *perestroika* and the opening to the West. Like other conservative opponents of the First Secretary, he feared the breakup of the USSR. His Eurasianist ideas caught fire within the Soviet establishment, even in the Ministry of

---

[18]Igor Torbakov, "Becoming Eurasian: The Intellectual Odyssey of Georgii Vladimirovich Vernadsky," in *Between Europe and Asia: The Origins, Theories, and Legacies of Russian Eurasianism,* ed. Marc Bassin, Sergey Glebov, and Marlene Laruelle (Pittsburgh: University of Pittsburgh Press, 2015), pp. 113–36. See also Mark Bassin, *The Gumilev Mystique: Biopolitics, Eurasianism, and the Construction of Community in Modern Russia* (Ithaca, NY: Cornell University Press, 2016).

Foreign Affairs. After his death in 1992, his popularity as a critic of democratization and Westernization carried his ideas through the chaotic Yeltsin years into the era of twenty-first-century Putinism. The reactionary Communist leader Gennadii Zhiuganov took up his banner, and Vladimir Putin deployed language— like "unity in diversity"—that was identified with the Eurasianists. In 2011 Kazakhstan's president Nursultan Nazarbaev proposed forming a Eurasian Union of former Soviet republics, and Putin became its most enthusiastic supporter.

DEMOCRATIC RECESSION IN THE POST-SOVIET STATES

The end of the Soviet Union ushered in a brief euphoria both in the former Soviet states and the West that democracy and free market, neo-liberal capitalism was on the rise. Empire and autocracy, dictatorship and state-run economies, appeared to have been thrown on the "trash heap of history." Western powers gloated that they, and the logic of the free market, had triumphed over the dark forces of communism, and that democracy would soon be in full bloom across the former Eastern Bloc. As it happened, while some post-Soviet states, like those in the Baltic region, were able to establish and consolidate democratic governments, most were not. Since roughly 2007 the world has experienced what some political scientists have called a "democratic recession." Whereas the years from 1985 through 2007 were marked by a collapse of authoritarian and communist dictatorial regimes, the years after 2007 witnessed the failure or decline of democracies. Armenia and Kyrgyzstan started off most promisingly on the path to democracy, but war and civil strife led to less democratic leaders coming to power in both republics. In Georgia and Azerbaijan nationalist anti-Communists briefly came to power with the fall of the USSR, but both republics fell into bloody civil conflicts that overthrew the nationalists and brought former Communist bosses—Eduard Shevardnadze in Georgia and Heidar Aliev in Azerbaijan—back as heads of state, but now as leaders of the nation rather than satraps of Moscow. A world-famous liberal reformer, Shevardnadze stabilized Georgia, tamed its independent militias, but ruled largely through conciliation and concessions, thus fostering, not fighting, corruption.[19] Ultimately, he lost power in the "Rose Revolution" of November 2003, when the young, dynamic, impulsive Mikheil Saakashvili led an anti-corruption campaign that overthrew the "White Fox." In Azerbaijan Aliev was far more repressive and ultimately passed the baton to his son Ilham in 2003. The German sociologist Max Weber would have called Aliev's move "Sultanism," a political form in which domination operates primarily on

[19]Eli Feiman, "Why Parties of Power? Elite Strategies and Institutional Choice in Post-Soviet Eurasia," PhD dissertation in political science, University of Michigan, 2015; Christoph H. Stefes, *Understanding Post-Soviet Transitions: Corruption, Collusion, and Clientelism* (New York: Palgrave Macmillan, 2006).

the basis of the ruler's discretion.[20] Tajikistan suffered a bloody civil war in which tens of thousands perished before the old Communist elites reestablished their authority. In Kazakhstan, Turkmenistan, and Uzbekistan the Communist first secretaries simply stayed in power, now in drag as nationalists.

Ukraine swung between presidents favored by the anti-Russian western provinces and those preferred by the more Russophilic eastern regions. Although corruption and incompetence marked government throughout the 1990s and the following decade, masses of Ukrainians took to the streets in the Orange Revolution of 2004–2005 and again in 2013–2014 to defend their fragile democracy. Belarus was the republic most reminiscent of the old Soviet Union. By the mid-1990s a former farm bureaucrat, Aliaksandr Lukashenka, was elected president to fight corruption, only to establish his own authoritarian regime. Finally, Moldova, a small state that has the dubious distinction of being the poorest country in Europe, was divided between a relatively strong Communist Party and opponents to its right and left. Plagued by the secession of the Slavic region of Transdneistria, and a nearly bankrupt economy, Moldova struggled with ethnic and political conflicts and waves of emigrants leaving the country in order to survive. Unlike most of the other former Soviet republics that opted for strong presidencies, in Moldova the parliament was supreme.

Russia descended quickly from a failed democratic transition to an authoritarian system in which one president deftly handed power to another. The people in power controlled the media and made sure that oppositional candidates were not given much air time. "No election in post-communist Russia can be considered to have been free and fair," Sakwa reminds us.[21] Just as Yeltsin had engineered his own succession, ceding his office to his personal choice Vladimir Putin, so Putin in 2008 decided that instead of changing the constitution to allow himself a third term he would have Dmitrii Medvedev, his faithful lieutenant, become president, with himself as prime minister. There would be change but no change. Again, in 2012, Putin replaced Medvedev and retook the presidency in another engineered succession. Democracy, which by definition is about competitive elections and popular choice, was supplanted and subverted by elite manipulations of the electoral process.

As post-Soviet rulers in Russia and in most other formerly Soviet republics (with the exception of the Baltic republics, Ukraine, and Moldova) reestablished their own monopoly of power, not unlike their Soviet predecessors, the media came increasingly under the influence of the state and alternative elite figures were disciplined or punished. As journalist Masha Gessen reports, "Three months after the inauguration [of Putin], two of the country's wealthiest men [Boris Berezovskii and Vladimir Gusinskii] had been stripped of their influence and effectively kicked out of the country [by threat of arrest and general fear of the

---

[20]Max Weber, *Economy and Society: An Outline of Interpretive Sociology* (Berkeley: University of California Press, 1978), p. 232.
[21]Richard Sakwa, *The Crisis of Russian Democracy: The Dual State, Factionalism and the Medvedev Succession* (Cambridge: Cambridge University Press, 2011), p. 3.

government]. Less than a year after Putin came to power, all three federal television networks were controlled by the state."[22] Post-Soviet politicians—according to Russian political scientist Vladimir Gel'man—"consciously and consistently 'poisoned' political institutions for the sake of maximizing their own power and restraining (if not eliminating) their rivals."[23] Electoral laws were passed to favor incumbents, and elections were manipulated. The people in power designed the rules of the game to their own advantage. A soft authoritarianism with manipulated elections and state dominance of the media, but without widespread terror, became the norm in Russia and most of the other former Soviet republics.

Politics was not about winning, losing, negotiating, and compromising but about winning at any cost and holding on to power without surrendering it. Lenin and Stalin would have understood well this form of politics as warfare rather than negotiation. Russia's authoritarian regime is comparatively less repressive than many other non-democratic, semi-democratic, and dictatorial regimes in the world. Media is controlled but allowed a degree of autonomy. The state is most concerned to maintain its hold over television, the medium through which most Russian citizens learn about domestic and foreign affairs. Demonstrations and protests are allowed but restricted. Elections are hardly truly competitive but they are performed. An opposition is tolerated, its members occasionally jailed; journalists investigate corruption and are occasionally bumped off.

But Putin always enjoyed high ratings as a competent and popular leader thanks to the social order and prosperity that coincided with his years in power. Putin returned civic pride to Russians and restored their self-image as living in a state to be reckoned with. When all else failed, he was prepared to play the nationalism card, draw close to the Orthodox Church, and flex his military muscle in the so-called Near Abroad, the former Soviet republics. Gel'man claims that Putin and his associates have nearly the same goals as the fictional Vito Corleone, the Godfather, and his clan—"maximizing their own power and wealth."[24] Both men use patronage and cronyism as the base of their power. Putin's own popularity and his control of the Duma doomed any efforts at opposition. The old Communist Party became politically moribund as Putin managed to revive the state and the economy, while the liberals were discredited as responsible for the chaos and costs of the "democracy" of the 1990s.

It was not Putin but Yeltsin who was the initial gravedigger of Russian democracy, digging the grave in the name of democracy. Western powers and political scientists so feared a Communist restoration that they looked away as Yeltsin overthrew parliament, pushed through his constitution, and essentially stole the election of 1996. Gel'man argues that Russia had a good chance to become

[22]Masha Gessen, *The Man Without a Face: The Unlikely Rise of Vladimir Putin* (London: Granta, 2012), p. 174.

[23]Vladimir Gel'man, *Authoritarian Russia: Analyzing Post-Soviet Regime Changes* (Pittsburgh: University of Pittsburgh Press, 2015), p. 25.

[24]Ibid., p. 75. See also Karen Dawisha, *Putin's Kleptocracy: Who Owns Russia?* (New York: Simon & Schuster, 2014).

democratic in 1991, but in the struggle of political actors for power, the weakness of institutional and political constraints allowed them to maximize their power more than their counterparts elsewhere in the world.[25] Yeltsin, unlike Gorbachev, did not hesitate to use military force against his determined (and formerly loyal) opposition in October 1993 with his siege of the parliament building.

Putin's regime has been described as "managed democracy," "sovereign democracy," "façade democracy," "electoral authoritarianism," "competitive authoritarianism"—the list goes on. Putinism is a hybrid of constitutional forms that reflect democratic aspirations, the actual practice of authoritarianism, and a mix of both state capitalism and neo-liberal reliance on markets local and global. Putin used his military and police to subdue Chechnya as well as protestors in the streets of Russian cities. He successfully coopted potential opponents in the elites or had them arrested or driven out of the country, while much of society remained passive or supportive of his actions. "Over two decades of regime changes in post-Soviet Russia," writes Gel'man, "when at certain critical junctures Russia's political actors faced the choice between moving in an authoritarian or a democratic direction, they opted for the former option almost every time."[26] In making those choices Yeltsin and Putin differed most profoundly from Gorbachev, whose hesitant moves tended toward expansion of liberalism and democracy and reluctance to use physical force. Yet Gorbachev is far less admired by ordinary Russians than either Yeltsin or Putin. He is seen as the man who destroyed the Soviet Union, weakened and impoverished Russia. Gorbachev, and democracy more generally, are equated in the popular mind with the chaos and collapse of the 1980s and 1990s.

Political scientist Adam Przeworski contends that authoritarian regimes are built on three pillars: "lies, fear, and economic prosperity."[27] The third pillar—economic prosperity—did much to bolster Putin's popularity during his first two terms, but the world economic crisis, which hit in the first year of Medvedev's presidency, shook the regime briefly. Recovery was steady, but in the parliamentary elections of 2011 the liberal and democratic opposition did surprisingly well. Protests were held, and much discontent was expressed when Putin resumed the presidency for his third term in what looked like a rather cynical handoff of power. The regime reacted by exploiting the nationalist, religious, and anti-Western sentiments of parts of the population. The punk protestors of the all-female political performance art group Pussy Riot were arrested; laws prohibiting "homosexual propaganda" were passed. Gessen argues that Putin's queer-baiting tactic, far from being peripheral to his politics, helped him "back into" a new, post-Soviet ideology, something Russian leaders had been explicitly seeking since 1991. His anti-homosexual campaign allowed him to pose as defender of vaguely defined "traditional values civilization," against the decadent

---

[25]Gel'man, *Authoritarian Russia*, p. 10.

[26]Ibid., p. 13.

[27]Adam Przeworski, *Democracy and the Market: Political and Economic Reforms in Eastern Europe and Latin America* (Cambridge: Cambridge University Press, 1991), pp. 58–59.

Vladimir Putin, president of Russia and de facto ruler of Russia from 2000 to the present (2016).

values of the West.[28] With the annexation of Crimea in 2014 and the war in eastern Ukraine, xenophobic nationalism became a constant in the media. Fear of the West, along with lies about the war in Ukraine, played a larger role in propping up the regime. Intervention in Ukraine was bolstered by anti-Western rhetoric, including again the need to protect the "traditional values civilization" from assault. Gessen reports that the chairman of the Russian Parliament's Foreign Relations Committee said in a resolution on Ukraine in December 2013, "if Ukraine moves west, that will broaden the sphere of influence of gay culture, which is the official position of the European Union."[29] Gessen's observation is an important one, moving the issue of gay-bashing from the peripheries into the center and helping to situate Putin's performance of his own "hypermasculinity"—shooting tigers, horseback riding bare-chested, retrieving amphorae from undersea archeological sites—in a meaningful political context.[30]

Those in power had no incentives to change the system in the direction of democracy, which would have led to their loss of power and property. The democratic opposition was no real threat to the Kremlin. The country muddles through, the regime hangs on, and Russia and the Russians suffer from a slow petrification of politics. As in much of Russian history, to paraphrase the Communist theorist Antonio Gramsci, the state is strong and society gelatinous.

---

[28]http://wallenberg.umich.edu/medal-recipients/2015-masha-gessen.
[29]Ibid.
[30]We take the term from Wood, "Hypermasculinity as a Scenario of Power."

Members of the punk band Pussy Riot during the trial in which they were convicted of "hooliganism motivated by religious hatred."

POST-SUPERPOWER RUSSIA AND NATO EXPANSION

International politics, in the view of realist theorists, is a ruthless game in which power determines winners and losers. For the administrations of George Herbert Walker Bush (1989–1993) and Bill Clinton (1993–2001), Russia was too weak to offer much effective resistance to American plans to enhance its position in Europe and the Middle East. In negotiations around the reunification of East and West Germany, Gorbachev agreed to withdraw Soviet troops from the countries of the Warsaw Pact with assurances that East Germany would not be militarized and—as Secretary of State James Baker promised the Soviet president on February 9, 1990, "there would be no extension of NATO's jurisdiction one inch to the east."[31] German foreign minister Hans-Dietrich Genscher told Eduard Shevardnadze, his Soviet counterpart, "One thing is certain: NATO will not expand to the east." But the United States and NATO, responding to requests from Eastern European countries, admitted Poland, Hungary, and the Czech Republic to the alliance in March 1999; the three Baltic republics Estonia, Latvia, and Lithuania, along with Bulgaria, Romania, Slovakia, and Slovenia five years later; and Albania and Croatia four years afterwards. In May 2016 NATO formally invited the tiny Slavic, Orthodox country of Montenegro (700,000 citizens), a favorite destination for Russian tourists, to join the alliance. Promises were

---

[31]Richard Sakwa, *Frontline Ukraine: Crisis in the Borderlands* (London: I. B. Tauris, 2015), pp. 44–45. See also Mark Kramer, "The Myth of a No-NATO Enlargement Pledge to Russia," *Washington Quarterly* 32, no. 2 (April 2009): 39–48.

made to other former Soviet republics, most notably Georgia and Ukraine, that they would be granted eventual membership.

NATO expansion was seen by its members as enhancing their security, but in fact it may have put them in greater danger by creating a security dilemma, a situation that occurs when states seek to increase their own security but by doing so are seen as offensive and a greater danger by other states.[32] By increasing its own side's security, NATO was seen as offensive by the Russians, who then had to react by increasing their security. While the West saw its moves eastward as benign and non-threatening, the Kremlin felt that the West thought and acted as if its interests alone were legitimate, never considering whether Russia would see the movement of a potentially hostile military alliance closer to its borders as a serious threat to its national security. Reflecting on the expansion eastward of NATO, former American ambassador George F. Kennan, himself a foreign policy realist, told a *New York Times* columnist, "I think it is a tragic mistake. There was no reason for this whatsoever. No one was threatening anyone else. . . . We have signed on to protect a whole series of countries, even though we have neither the resources nor the intention to do so in any serious way."[33]

Most Russian elites as well as ordinary Russians remained convinced that they lived in a Great Power. Even the few who no longer were convinced mourned loss of the status. But we might reasonably ask, How great was Putin's Russia? The year Putin first became president his country's economy was just a bit larger than that of the Netherlands. The European Union by 2008 was twelve times larger economically than Russia and the United States thirteen times larger. China's economy was twice as big. America's defense spending was greater than the next nine or ten countries in the world combined, and NATO's (75 percent of which comes from the United States) was more than ten times larger than Russia's.[34] Russia was outspent on defense by China, and in some accounts by Saudi Arabia. Despite his country's relative weakness, Putin repeatedly reminded the world that Russia, a nuclear-armed state, must be taken seriously, that it should not be shunned, isolated, disregarded, or humiliated. He was frustrated by the West's lack of consultation with Russia over important foreign policy issues and angered by the Americans' unilateral abrogation of the Anti-Ballistic Missile Treaty. Europe and the United States further antagonized Russia with their recognition in early 2008 of the independence of the former autonomous Yugoslav region of Kosovo. Putin set out from his first election to stabilize the country and reassert Russia's status as a great power. But even as the economy benefited from high oil and gas prices, Putin had a weak hand to play. During his first two terms as president, the Western military alliance, NATO, continued to expand eastward to

---

[32] Alexander Wendt, "Anarchy Is What States Make of It: The Social Construction of Power Politics," *International Organization* 46, no. 2 (1992): 397.

[33] *New York Times*, May 2, 1998.

[34] Nafatali Ben David, "Just Five of Twenty-Eight NATO Members Meet Defense Spending Goal, Report Says," *Wall Street Journal*, June 22, 2015, www.wsj.com/articles/nato-calls-for-rise-in-defence-spending-by-alliance-members-1434978193.

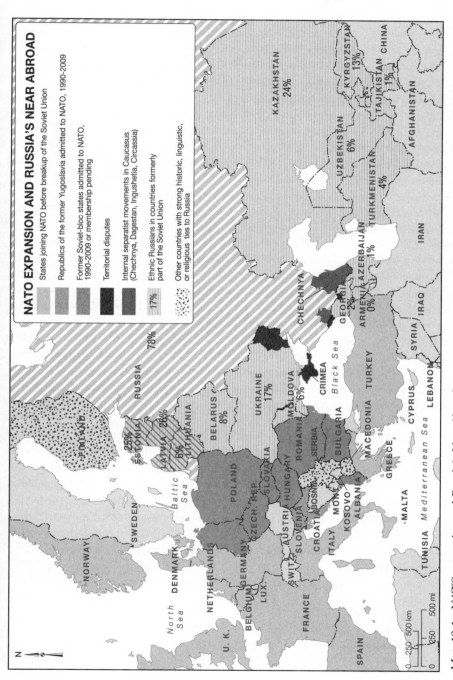

NATO EXPANSION AND RUSSIA'S NEAR ABROAD

States joining NATO before breakup of the Soviet Union

Republics of the former Yugoslavia admitted to NATO, 1990–2009

Former Soviet-bloc states admitted to NATO, 1990–2009 or membership pending

Territorial disputes

Internal separatist movements in Caucasus (Chechnya, Dagestan, Ingushetia, Circassia)

Ethnic Russians in countries formerly part of the Soviet Union

Other countries with strong historic, linguistic, or religious ties to Russia

Map 12.1. NATO expansion and Russia's Near Abroad.

include most of the former Soviet Bloc countries as well as the three former Soviet Baltic republics.

Faced by a far more powerful United States and the NATO alliance, Russia could throw its weight around only in its "Near Abroad," the regions formerly controlled by the Soviet Union. Putin's ambitions for Russia to become at least a regional hegemon, the dominant power, in its own neighborhood brought the country into confrontation with the far greater ambitions of the United States to enhance its position as a global hegemon able to oppose any regional threats to its power in Europe, the Middle East, Latin America, and East Asia. Opposed to the unipolar world that emerged after the fall of the USSR, with the United States as the single most powerful nation on the globe, Russia promoted multipolarity and the use of the United Nations instead of NATO and U.S. military force as the international arbitrator.

After 2007 Putin shifted Russia's foreign policy from supporting the status quo to actively working to change the balance of power on the globe.[35] The sense that Russia was not being given its due, that it was not adequately respected by its European and American "partners," was reflected in President Putin's February 10, 2007, speech at the Munich Conference on Security Policy. Later referred to as an introduction to a new Cold War, the speech outlined in very frank terms Putin's opposition to what he believed was the United States' attempt to create a "unipolar world" with one great superpower, "one center of authority, one center of force, one center of decision-making." He rejected the notion that force could be used if sanctioned by NATO or the European Union and proposed instead that the only legitimation for armed force against another state was through the United Nations. He bristled at the idea that Russia could be lectured on democracy or that its internal affairs should be the concern of other states and called for greater respect for Russia's counsel.[36]

As he put forth his views, Putin's policies were neither imperialist, in the sense of aiming to incorporate new territories through conquest or coercion, nor a reversion to Soviet imperialism but realist, statist, and nationalist. He even chided Lenin for his lack of concern for Russia and lack of realism: "Lenin said he didn't care about Russia. What was important for him was achieving a world socialist system. The Russian people didn't expect this. They were deceived. . . . Russia today has no intention of repeating the tsarist experience or what happened in Soviet times. . . . We should be true to ourselves, respectful of others, and good partners."[37] His international policy was the corollary of his domestic policy: a stronger state, preservation of the present internal distribution of power, economic prosperity (though with too little investment in the future), stability, and continuity.

---

[35]Sakwa, *Frontline Ukraine*, pp. 30–31.
[36]Vladimir Putin, "Speech at the 43rd Munich Conference on Security Policy," http://www.securityconference.de/konferenzen/rede.php?sprache=en&id=179.
[37]Jonathan Steele, "Putin's Legacy Is a Russia That Doesn't Have to Curry Favour with the West," *The Guardian*, September 18, 2007.

His call for multipolarity was a reversion to a Yalta-type spheres of influence view of the world, which the United States and NATO rejected. Using what limited instruments it had—energy diplomacy, trade restrictions, and the occasional military muscle flexing—Russia aspired to exercise paramount influence in the former Near Abroad, that is, become the recognized regional hegemon. But in the eyes of many of its neighbors, Russia's ambitions appeared to be imperial—to reassert the kind of control over internal as well as external policy that had characterized the Soviet Bloc.

RED LINES IN THE NEAR ABROAD: GEORGIA AND UKRAINE

In the political imaginary of Russia's elite, the Caucasian frontier is the most volatile and vulnerable borderland, and in this region, the new parameters of Russia's engagement with its former republics and with the world at large have been shaped and tested. Post-Soviet Russia's policies toward the South Caucasus, and the Near Abroad more generally, went through several distinct phases from the fall of the USSR to the present.[38] In its first year (1991–1992) the Yeltsin government pursued what might be called a "policy of neglect" toward the countries of the former Soviet Union, working largely through the hastily created Commonwealth of Independent States (CIS). The Russian policy elite was divided as the country's leaders scurried to find a stable identity and sense of interests in the new world, and its policies toward the Near Abroad were confused and contradictory. But already in the last years of the Soviet Union and the first years of the new Russian Federation, Russians were drawn into the Abkhaz, Ossetian, and Karabakh conflicts. Non-Georgians in Georgia preferred rule by Russia to remaining within the new, rabidly nationalist Georgian republic. Attempts by the Georgians under its first president, Zviad Gamsakhurdia, to end the autonomy of South Ossetia and Abkhazia and create a unitary "Georgia for the Georgians" led to ethnic and civil war, his own defeat and death, and the de facto separation of Abkhazia and South Ossetia. Russia supported the non-Georgians and eventually negotiated ceasefire agreements separating the combatants.

From January 1993 to June 1996, Russian policymakers more clearly articulated a sense that the Near Abroad was a "sphere of vital Russian interests" and saw the CIS border as Russia's security border that it had the right to defend. In late 1994 and early 1995, Yeltsin and his foreign minister, Andrei Kozyrev, publicly declared their support for the reintegration of the countries of the former Soviet Union, first economically, but then militarily and perhaps even politically. What might have been called the "Yeltsin doctrine" could be interpreted as recognition of the independence and sovereignty of the existing states (along with a paramount role for Russia in the southern tier), an explicit claim for dominance

---

[38]See Ria Laenen's dissertation, "Russia's 'Near Abroad' Policy and Its Compatriots (1991–2001): A Former Empire in Search of a New Identity," Katholieke Universiteit Leuven, 2008.

in the realm of security and, perhaps, a special role in protecting Russians and other minorities. From roughly June 1996 to the emergence of President Putin, Russia maintained that it was a "Great Power" (*Velikaia derzhava*) and promoted its *derzhavnost'* (Great Power status). But this rhetorical muscle-flexing remained largely performative until roughly 2008. More practically, Moscow gave up its program of reintegrating the supposed successor of the Soviet Union, the CIS, and promoted bilateral relations with the former Soviet states. At the same time, Russia vigorously pursued integration into the globalized capitalist economy, raised prices for its oil to world market levels, and attempted to be accepted as a major economic player.

Moscow was very concerned about the so-called colored revolutions (Serbia, 2000; Georgia, 2003; Ukraine, 2004; and Kyrgyzstan, 2005), which overthrew corrupt leaders and promised greater democracy. To the Kremlin these popular movements appeared to be manipulated by outside forces and aimed against Russia. Sadly for the countries that experienced the brief exuberance of the Rose or Tulip or Orange revolutions, the change in leaders turned out to be a mere shuffling of elites and usually reverted back to corruption and mild authoritarianism.

For most of his first and second presidential terms Putin usually acted as a "stabilizer" and a mediator both in South Caucasian conflicts and throughout the Near Abroad.[39] Through the first decade of the twenty-first century, Moscow refrained from supporting secession in eastern Ukraine, Crimea, or northern Kazakhstan, where Russian or Russian-speaking populations are relatively compact, and it abandoned any encouragement of the Russians in the Baltic republics who experience discrimination from the Latvian and Estonian governments but evince no desire to move to Russia. Rather than respond to those "imperialists" at home who called for immediate integration of Abkhazia and South Ossetia into Russia, and recognition of the independence of Nagorno-Karabakh, Putin worked to expand Russian influence gradually—extend citizenship, mediate contested elections, and maintain uneasy truces. Although Putin's government had been more interventionist in Georgia than anywhere else in the former Soviet Union, it did not hinder Georgian president Mikheil Saakashvili's reintegration of the Muslim Georgian region of Ajara into Georgia.

The ambiguous status quo in Abkhazia and South Ossetia, so satisfactory to the Russians, was increasingly intolerable for the Georgians, as Russia gradually integrated Abkhazia and South Ossetia into their own sphere of influence, granting locals Russian passports, welfare payments, and other privileges. Saakashvili made it clear that he was determined to win back those lands that Georgians consider part of their historical patrimony. Even though he had been warned

---

[39]Andrei P. Tsygankov, "If Not by Tanks, Then by Banks? The Role of Soft Power in Putin's Foreign Policy," *Europe-Asia Studies* 58, no. 7 (November 2006): 1079–99; esp. 1080. Tsygankov argues that Putin is a "stabilizer" willing to use "soft power" to achieve limited goals, rather than a "Westernizer" or an "imperialist."

Map 12.2. The Russo-Georgian War of 2008.

by Secretary of State Condoleezza Rice not to react to Russian provocations, Saakashvili may have been influenced in another direction by his powerful friends in the United States, Vice President Richard Cheney and Republican presidential candidate John McCain, and believed that the United States would come to his aid. Just as Napoleon III in 1870 had been lured by Bismarck into foolishly initiating a war with Prussia, so Saakashvili reacted to the growing violence along the Georgian-Ossetian border and launched a massive attack, escalating the conflict from sporadic shootings into a major international war.[40]

For the first time in the Georgian-Russian conflicts, one side—the Georgians—used heavy weaponry against civilians, indeed against people it considered citizens of its own country, members of the "Georgian" nation. The American-trained Georgian troops quickly overran much of the Ossetian enclave, nearly taking the capital, Tskhinval. Observers reported that tanks fired into the basements of buildings where civilians sought refuge. The goal appears to have been a rapid occupation that would result in a flight of Ossetians and convince the Russians not to counterattack. Indeed tens of thousands of Ossetians fled north into Russia, and those left behind faced the hostility of the invading Georgians. But the Russians returned with a ferocious counterattack, retaking the capital and upping the ante with bombing outside of South Ossetia. Atrocities followed, almost

---

[40]There is much controversy over which side started the war and whether the Russians had provoked the Georgians to attack. One of the best early accounts was C. J. Chivers and Ellen Barry, "Accounts Undercut Claims by Georgia on Russia War," *New York Times,* November 7, 2008.

exclusively committed against Georgians by Ossetians, whom the Russians did little to constrain. Although there was a seemingly gratuitous bombing of civilian buildings in the city of Gori and massive deliberate destruction of property, weapons, and ships in Poti and elsewhere, the Russians acted with some restraint. They did not damage the Baku-Tbilisi-Cehan pipeline, and despite some calls for the forceful removal of Saakashvili, Moscow decided not to go that far.

The outcome of the one-week war worsened relations between Russia and the West. But more important, Russia's victory was a message to the states of the Near Abroad that it would not tolerate further expansion of NATO (this message was particularly directed at Ukraine), even if the governments and people of those countries so desired. Russia was more concerned with strategic gains on the ground than elusive advantages like reputation. For the first time in the post-Soviet period, Russia had forcefully thwarted American preferences. With Europe unwilling to take as hard a line toward Russia as the hawks in the Bush administration, and with the Americans consumed by their wars in the Middle East and Afghanistan and the presidential campaign that ended with Barack Obama's victory, Russia had successfully exploited a rare moment to assert its independence in foreign policy.

Political scientist Charles King argues that the preservation of non-state entities like South Ossetia, with their autonomy protected but with its official state status up in the air, proves useful for all concerned. He points to the "utility of deadlock" in South Ossetia and also in Abkhazia, Karabakh, and Transnistria, another unrecognized entity in a "frozen conflict zone" bristling uncomfortably between Ukraine and Moldova.[41] These fragmented states are forged along the boundaries of former empires and torn between the ambitions of competing great powers, in a world where the language of national self-determination still holds clout. Their precarious status and stable indeterminacy are symptomatic of an emergent order, where irresolution may offer the best solution to intractable problems. Russia has been content to settle into a relation of hegemony rather than incorporation of the states within its Near Abroad.

With the situation in the Caucasus poised in a state of favorable ambiguity, the theater of confrontation with both the West and the Near Abroad shifted to Ukraine, where Russia would experiment with altogether different approaches and seek more resolute outcomes. The Ukrainian crisis began in a competition between Europe and Russia for paramount influence in Ukraine. The European Union proposed in 2009 an "Eastern Partnership" for six countries in the former Soviet Union to bring them closer to the West. At roughly the same time Russia initiated a customs union of former Soviet republics that eventually became the Eurasian Economic Union. The biggest prize for each side was Ukraine, with its population of nearly 50 million citizens. At the same time, Putin continued to advocate a Gorbachev-like concept of

[41]Charles King, "The Uses of Deadlock: Intractability in Eurasia," in *Grasping the Nettle: Analyzing Cases of Intractable Conflict*, ed. Chester A. Crocker, Fen Osler Hampson, and Pamela Aall (Washington, DC: U.S. Institute of Peace Press, 2005).

a "Greater Europe from Lisbon to Vladivostok" and tried to interest Europe in an arrangement whereby Ukraine would associate with both the European and the Eurasian unions. The Europeans effectively rejected including Russia in their discussions with the Ukrainians. Negotiations became a winner-take-all contest for the soul of Ukraine. Putin complained, "They just slammed the door in our face telling us to mind our own business."[42]

The Ukrainian government led by President Viktor Yanukovych maneuvered between the two sides, searching for the better deal. His political opposition believed that Ukraine could secure its future only by shedding its colonial dependence on Russia and siding decisively with Europe. At first Yanukovych flirted with the Europeans' "Association Agreement," which promised free trade with the EU but required introducing legal changes in line with the European Union and alignment with the Western bloc's security policies. Putin upped the ante by promising large loans and reductions in the cost of Russian energy sent to Ukraine. On November 21, 2013, Yanukovych decided not to decide but to postpone signing the Association Agreement. A month later he accepted Putin's economic package. His decision would ultimately prove fatal to his presidency and to Ukraine's fragile unity.

Demonstrations began in November on the Maidan, the central square in Kiev, first, as economic protests against the corruption and greed of the Yanukovych regime. Soon the crowds demanded Yanukovych's resignation and a decisive commitment to a European orientation. Powerful Ukrainian oligarchs who opposed Yanukovych and his allies from eastern Ukraine financed the protests, and the United States made clear its preference for the democratic aspirations of "Euromaidan." The government's brutal but half-hearted attempts to disperse the crowds on Maidan only served to stimulate greater opposition. The statue of Lenin was pulled down in the capital. Maidan became more militantly nationalist, and paramilitary forces filled the square. As the situation in central Kiev degenerated into violence, Yanukovych pulled back, began talks with the opposition, and prepared to step down. On February 20, 2014, snipers fired on the crowds, killing demonstrators and police. The next day Yanukovych capitulated, and the foreign ministers of France, Germany, and Poland co-signed an agreement with the Ukrainian government and opposition leaders to ease his departure in a few months. Radicalized Maidan, however, rejected the deal. As police disappeared from the streets of Kiev, Yanukovych fled to Russia, fearing for his life. A pro-Western government quickly took power and was immediately accepted by the United States and Europe. Moscow called the events of February 2014 a coup d'état. All over Ukraine some 100 statues of Lenin were torn down. The anti-nationalist, anti-imperialist opponent of Great Russian chauvinism, Lenin, had become for many Ukrainians a symbol of Russian colonialism. For many others, however, particularly in Crimea and the eastern regions of Ukraine, his removal was a signal that fascists had taken power in Ukraine.

---

[42]Sakwa, *Frontline Ukraine*, p. 78.

Almost immediately after the change in government in Kiev, Putin met secretly with his closest security advisers and plotted his countermove—the annexation of the largely Russian-populated Crimean peninsula. "Little green men"—soldiers without insignias—appeared in the streets, and the principal airport was seized. A referendum was quickly held on March 16, and it was reported that 83 percent of Crimea's eligible voters supported "reunification" with Russia. In a public address that played with potent motifs of nation, religion, and empire, Putin laid out his case for this historical injustice of Crimea's transfer to the Ukrainian Republic under Khrushchev, a travesty that had severed the good Russians of the peninsula from their rightful homeland. "In the hearts and minds of people, Crimea has always been and remains an inseparable part of Russia," he declared. "The people of Crimea clearly and convincingly expressed their will [in the referendum]—they want to be with Russia." Arguing for the rightful, natural, organic unity of the "nation," he said, "Millions of people went to bed in one country and awoke in different ones [after the USSR's collapse], overnight becoming ethnic minorities in former Union republics, while the Russian nation became one of the biggest, if not the biggest ethnic group in the world to be divided by borders." Deepening Russia's historical claim, he gestured back over a millennium, to ancient Rus: "Everything in Crimea speaks of our shared history and pride. This is the location too of ancient Khersones, where Prince Vladimir was baptized." Like many nationalist versions of history that emphasize organic continuity of the nation from the primeval ooze to the present, his account elided the intervening centuries, painting an unbroken picture of Russian Crimea.

Notably, and with a degree of implied threat of expansion in the name of religious solidarity, Putin also drew the rest of Orthodox Slavdom into his vision of a greater Russian people: "[Prince Vladimir's] spiritual feat of adopting Orthodoxy predetermined the overall basis of the culture, civilization and human values that unite the peoples of Russia, Ukraine and Belarus. The graves of Russian soldiers whose bravery brought Crimea into the Russian empire are also in Crimea."[43] His verbal embrace of Orthodox Slavic brethren beyond Russia's current borders echoes his imperial predecessors' extraterritorial ambitions, from the eighteenth century on, to "protect" people they claimed as their own. With a nod to imperial diversity he recognized that "Crimea is a unique blend of different peoples' cultures and traditions," but that made it just like the rest of Russia, a happy mix of people "retaining their own identity, traditions, languages and faith." "True," he admitted, referring to the mass deportation under Stalin, "there was a time when Crimean Tatars were treated unfairly," but that too, he explained, was part of the shared tragedy of Russia as a whole. Left out of his history lesson was Russia's military conquest of the peninsula and its subjugation of the Tatar population in the eighteenth century, the mass relocation of Muslims to the Ottoman Empire in the nineteenth century, and the uneventful sixty years of Crimea's membership in Ukraine.

---

[43]http://en.kremlin.ru/events/president/news/20603.

Drawing on a variegated set of tropes, evoking glorious imperial precedents and calling up potent affective attachments to nation and faith, the speech, and the annexation it justified, were enormously popular in Russia. Putin's ratings soared. By these actions Russia secured its control over Sevastopol, the home of its Black Sea fleet, but by violating international law and its own treaty obligations, it brought economic sanctions down upon itself and isolated Russia more than at any time since the end of the Cold War. What looked to Moscow at the time as a geopolitical imperative, and to most Russians as ethnonational rectification, was carried out in a moment of panic about an unpredictable future. Opportunism in a moment of crisis and the desire to turn defeat in Ukraine into national achievement in Crimea were part of the mix of motives that led Putin to risk a second Cold War. Putin wanted a neutral or friendly Ukraine that was not strategically aligned with NATO, but the seizure of Crimea drove Ukraine further into the arms of Europe, fostered a far more homogeneous and nationalistic, anti-Russian society in much of western and central Ukraine, and encouraged pro-Russian forces in the east to take up arms, drawing Russia into an undeclared, de facto war with its Slavic neighbor.

Russia acted as a beleaguered and humiliated nation-state, an aspiring Great Power that wanted, then demanded, more respect from other powers. To both neighbors and many in the West, Russia was an imperial state, one in which its very conception of itself as a nation harbored imperial actions and ambitions.

Map 12.3. The struggle for Ukraine.

Instead of Cold War, a hot war broke out in the Donetsk and Luhansk regions of eastern Ukraine when pro-Russian insurgents declared autonomy, then independence, and resisted Kiev's attempts to take back those territories.

The crisis over Ukraine brought the post–Cold War status quo in Europe to an end. Russia had repeatedly proposed its own answer to unipolarity by pushing for multipolarity, but its actions in Ukraine, particularly in Crimea, unified the West in opposition to Moscow's ambitions to dominate in the former Soviet sphere. Putin hoped that his proposed Eurasian Union would be an effective counterweight to the European Union, but instead his support of the anti-Kiev rebels in eastern Ukraine frightened other former Soviet countries that might have joined his Eurasian Union. Support of the insurgents in Ukraine had the effect of undermining Putin's attempt to become the regional hegemon in the former Soviet space and increased American power and European influence in Russia's western borderlands. His hardline against the West increased Russia's stature in the eyes of China and some Middle Eastern countries, but at the cost of far more valuable relations with the leading economic actors in the West. Still operating from a position of relative weakness vis-à-vis the West, Putin's Russia boldly flexed its muscles in the Syrian civil war, backing its ally in Damascus, and desperately asserting that it was a significant player on the global stage. No longer an empire but imagined by its neighbors to have imperial ambitions, Russia in the sixteenth year of Putin's reign was a crippled hegemon isolated from both major and minor powers near and far from Moscow.

BRIEF BIBLIOGRAPHY

Bassin, Mark. *The Gumilev Mystique: Biopolitics, Eurasianism, and the Construction of Community in Modern Russia.* Ithaca, NY: Cornell University Press, 2016.

Gel'man, Vladimir. *Authoritarian Russia: Analyzing Post-Soviet Regime Changes.* Pittsburgh: University of Pittsburgh Press, 2015.

Gerasimov, Ilya, and Marina Mogiliner. "Deconstructing Integration: Ukraine's Postcolonial Subjectivity," *Slavic Review* 74, no. 4 (Winter 2015): 715–722.

Gessen, Masha. *The Man Without a Face: The Unlikely Rise of Vladimir Putin.* London: Granta, 2012.

Kotkin, Stephen. *Armageddon Averted: The Soviet Collapse, 1970–2000.* Oxford: Oxford University Press, 2001.

Laenen, Ria. "Russia's 'Near Abroad' Policy and Its Compatriots (1991–2001): A Former Empire in Search of a New Identity." PhD dissertation, Katholieke Universiteit Leuven, 2008.

Putin, Vladimir. "Speech at the 43rd Munich Conference on Security Policy," http://www.securityconference.de/konferenzen/rede.php?sprache=en&id=179.

Sakwa, Richard. *The Crisis of Russian Democracy: The Dual State, Factionalism and the Medvedev Succession.* Cambridge: Cambridge University Press, 2011.

———. *Frontline Ukraine: Crisis in the Borderlands.* London: I. B. Tauris, 2015.

————. *Putin, Russia's Choice.* 2nd ed. London and New York: Routledge, 2008.

Steinberg, Mark D., and Catherine Wanner, eds. *Religion, Morality, and Community in Post-Soviet Societies.* Bloomington: Indiana University Press, 2008.

Walker, Edward W. *Dissolution: Sovereignty and the Breakup of the Soviet Union.* Lanham, MD: Rowman and Littlefield, 2003.

Wanner, Catherine. *Communities of the Converted: Ukrainians and Global Evangelism.* Ithaca, NY: Cornell University Press, 2007.

Wood, Elizabeth A. "Hypermasculinity as a Scenario of Power: Vladimir Putin's Iconic Rule, 1999–2008," *International Feminist Journal of Politics* (Summer 2016): 1–22.

CONCLUSION

The hoary images persist: Russia is once again seen as aggressive and expansionist. Only force, it is said repeatedly, can restrain its unrestrained ambitions. To many in the West Russia was, is, and always will be an empire—autocratic and undemocratic within and an imperialist danger to others abroad. By its very nature, it is said, Russia is doomed to be despotic and imperialist. Its inherent disposition is to confound the humanistic aspirations of civilized people, to dominate its neighbors, and to oppress its own people. Russia is now personified by Vladimir Putin, just as it has at times been subsumed into the images of Ivan the Terrible, Peter the Great, or Stalin. Characterizing the state leader—and selectively chosen examples of leaders at that—has long been a simple substitution for deeper analysis. German chancellor Angela Merkel fretted that Putin lives "in another world." Secretary of State John Kerry echoed her words when he mused that Putin is "creating his own reality." When Hillary Rodham Clinton was running for president the first time in 2008, she was dismayed by the fact that Putin had been a KGB agent and declared that he "does not have a soul." Putin replied sardonically that a presidential candidate "at a minimum should have a head."[1] As with any overly Manichaean imagery of good versus evil, these stereotypes of Russia are as much the product of one side's self-serving need for demons as they are overly simplified explanations of situations with complex and multiple causes. Russia has always been available for others to avoid looking inward into their own acts and intentions, to blame the "enemy" for problems whose origins lie in more complicated competitive relationships.

The two analytical strands that have run together throughout this book, the workings of empire and the forms of inclusion and reciprocity, help us address these persistent, pernicious ideas about Russia and to dig deeper into her history to derive clearer understanding. The preceding chapters have traced these themes as they apply, and have marked where they fail to apply, to the successive eras of the Russian past. In our historical excursion we have tried to show that Russia

---

[1] Sakwa, *Frontline Ukraine*, p. 33.

experimented repeatedly with various forms of governance, often with the potential vulnerabilities of fragmentation and collapse before their eyes. Before there was a state in Russia, or anything resembling an empire, there were the warrior princes of Kiev and other towns and cities, who fought and bartered with one another and foreign enemies to secure power and wealth. What has been called Kievan Rus was a constellation of power centers with no potent hub or bureaucracy until the conversion to Christianity provided greater coherence culturally, religiously, and administratively. There was some hazy sense of a people who shared language and customs but who at the same time were divided by fratricidal warfare. Raiding and trading constituted the economic base that in time supported a gorgeous literary and architectural heritage. Rus developed in the orbit of the great Byzantine Empire, and took much from that experience, but neither fell under nor emulated its imperial rule. A princely, not imperial, realm, Kievan Rus and Appanage Russia loosely held together in the knowledge that Rus princes ruled over a land and a people in some ways understood as Rus. This fragile association fell into disarray, losing what semblance of minimal statehood had occasionally been achieved. Even the memory of Kiev faded until the emergence of Muscovy and a reinvention of a mythical Kiev as the foundational state in Russian history. Continuity came with culture, and the perennial reality of difference between peoples and polities provided the field on which the future empire would play.

The Mongols brought empire with them in the thirteenth century and incorporated Russian lands into their vast network of tributary states. They established a basic imperial technique of governance, indirect rule: Russian princes were left to rule their realms as long as they were loyal and paid tribute to the khans. The princes generally collaborated with their Mongol overlords from whom they received permission to tax their own people. As the Mongol Empire weakened and fragmented, one of its most loyal subjects, Moscow, rose to primacy in Rus and steadily drove back Mongol suzerainty. By the reign of Ivan IV "the Terrible" in the sixteenth century, Muscovy was an autocracy and an empire, an increasingly powerful state that ruled through difference and distinctions, social and territorial, and conquered the Tatar Khanate of Kazan, thus for the first time annexing a distinctly non-Russian people and territory. Moscow became the sovereign power in the Russian lands, its tsar taking on the qualities of both Byzantine emperor and khan. Orthodox Christianity, universalist in its religious claims, became particularized as the faith of the Russian people and Muscovite state. Russia was the New Israel and Russians the Chosen People. Their tsars were divinely entrusted with playing a special role in the scenario of salvation.

The vagaries of birth and death led Muscovy into the chaos of the Time of Troubles and a frantic search for a legitimate ruler to lead the state. From the highest and lowest ranks people mobilized to resist foreign invaders, reconceiving Russia as more than the tsar's domain and including the people's voice as well. Hardly a national awakening in a modern sense, the election of the first Romanov tsar in 1613 was nevertheless the outcome of a popular collective mobilization, the recognition by many of the "political ethnicity" of the Russian lands, and a sense of entitlement of broad segments of society to be included in the political order.

Russia in the eighteenth and early nineteenth century most closely approached the ideal type of traditional empire. Confidently, proudly exalting in its grandeur, its territorial expansion, and its appropriation of European modernity, the empire of Peter the Great and Catherine the Great governed through institutionalized differentiation even as it harmonized bureaucratic and administrative forms and practices. Coercion by the hyperactive Peter was ameliorated to a degree under his successors through the fantasy of reciprocal love and sensitivity that the rulers and noble elites imagined held the realm together during the reigns of Anne, Elizabeth, and Catherine. What looks like precocious national consciousness or even nationalism to some historians, we regard as largely limited, on one hand, to the nobility's state patriotism and allegiance to the sovereign, and, on the other, to a more popular affiliation to the land, religion, customs, and language of Orthodox Russians. But mingled within and alongside state patriotism and ethnic affinities were the myriad other sources of loyalty to non-Orthodox religions, to Old Belief, to localities, social estates, regions like Siberia, and to one's own non-Russian people, faith, and experiences. And growing among the Westernized nobility was a puzzlement in sorting out who they were, what made them Russian, if everything that qualified them as noble—their European education, clothing, mores, and manners—set them apart from the bearded Russian *muzhiki* and their kerchiefed wives.

Empire not only describes the state form and manner of rule but also a set of institutions, practices, and discourses that worked against the easy achievement of a coherent, self-conscious, and unitary nation or more democratic forms of governance. Rather than a horizontal equivalence between citizens, the empire ruled through social discrimination, with some people possessing the right to rule over others precisely because they conceived themselves as superior. Even when millions of serfs were ostensibly emancipated, the privileges of noble landlords and obligations of peasants were reproduced, if somewhat modified, in the legal and financial complexities of the actual forms in which serfs became "free." Separate legal systems and hierarchies of advantages and disadvantages for different social estates and nationalities continued to the end of the empire. As Russia consolidated its hold on its far-flung holdings and expanded into Central Asia in the nineteenth century, practices of differentiation of groups and regions continued to pull against efforts to centralize control and erect more uniform administrative structures.

The revolutions of 1917 ended one empire and laid a foundation for another. The Soviet Union moved within the first half decade from an ideologically driven attempt to build a socialist, class-based, multinational state to a pseudo-federal state with sovereign power concentrated in the political center. The Soviet Union was a supra-state that in Lenin's time anticipated other states joining it in a global project of building socialism, "a revolutionary waiting-room that any country could join, once it had overthrown capitalism."[2] Concessions initially extended to

[2] Perry Anderson, "Incommensurate Russia," *New Left Review*, 2d ser., 94 (July–August 2015): 37–38.

entice non-Russians into the Bolshevik fold were cut back in the 1930s as Stalin not only further centralized power but promoted a synthetic Soviet identity based on Great Russian historical experiences. This Russian-infused Soviet patriotism became the touchstone of a supranational affective community that along with ethnic nationalisms would carry the Soviet people through the trials of World War II. With the victory over fascism in the Second World War, the nationalizing, Russocentric Soviet identity competed with the distinctive and different ethnonational identities of the various Soviet nationalities. No clear resolution was achieved, and in the last four decades of the USSR, center and periphery, Moscow and the non-Russians, battled over degrees of autonomy and conformity.

Eventually the fragility of the peculiar amalgam of imperial and national identities failed the test of radical reform launched by Gorbachev, who had not anticipated that socialism had lost its power to promise a better future. The late Soviet Union was a somewhat looser empire than under Stalin, and the republics achieved enough self-confidence that when Gorbachev weakened the Communist Party and the Soviet state they were prepared to go off on their own.

Yeltsin's and Putin's Russia, like the USSR, balked at being labeled empire. In the context of our examination of Russia as empire, it is worth reiterating that the valence, and even the very meaning of the term have shifted in the era of global decolonization. Empire has accrued evil, repressive, and destructive associations, completely at odds with its glorious image (if not its coercive realities) in its heyday. The term in conventional and popular usage today is highly normative and has been equated with arbitrary, despotic central or one-man rule, a characteristic common but not at all distinctive to imperial governance.

Our original definition of empire recognized four contributing elements, which we can here boil down into two general tenets. First, empire is about unlimited sovereignty, often concentrated in the hands of one individual, who rules a disadvantaged periphery to the benefit of a privileged center. Second, empire is constituted unequally and hierarchically, and maintained in difference. The various elements of this definition became more or less salient in Russia's imperial trajectory at different times, and not all apply at any given time.

When Soviet and post-Soviet regimes became more authoritarian and implemented more unitary rule, the distinctiveness of constituent parts and peoples grew less pronounced while the ruler's absolute sovereignty and the imperial role of the center were preserved and, under Stalin, enhanced. Moreover, precisely the kind of high-handed centrism that contradicts our second principle— diversity and distinction as essential characteristics of empire—fulfills the first requirement—unlimited authority of the center and disempowerment of the rest. It is the multiplicity of definitions of "empire" that make the term both useful and slippery. Our intent has been to try it out in all its maddening openness and to see where it can help us see patterns or exceptions, trends and turns, that might otherwise have gone unnoted.

For instance, we have pointed out the limiting cases where empire does not provide a satisfactory label. Kievan Rus was not an empire but a realm without a state.

It anticipated some of the terms, the collectivity and distinction of human groups and categories, that would be foundational to later imperial formations. At the other end of the chronological spectrum, both the late Soviet and Putin regimes, with their harsh central control, efforts at state integration, and diminishing of constitutive diversity, fit the pseudo-federalist form far better than the traditional imperial model, but for all their nationalizing efforts, their enforcement of the absolute sovereignty of their political center retained an imperial tinge. The habit of addressing populations distinctively in collective terms or allotting rights differentially never disappeared. In spite of deliberately integrative policies, homogenizing administrative structures, mass education, and universal emphasis on party doctrine, particular groups enjoyed the benefits or more sharply suffered the consequences of affiliation with their collective units. In the Stalin years, entire peoples, such as the Crimean Tatars, Chechens, and Volga Germans, were forcibly deported; other groups, particularly the Jews after World War II, were targeted by defamation campaigns and barred from entrance into universities or from areas of employment. And when the Soviet Union collapsed, its constituent pieces, the ethno-national republics, stood ready to break off as independent nation-states. In Yeltsin's time different deals were made with different regions and nationalities. Putin homogenized administration, ran roughshod over the delegated powers briefly enjoyed by the federal units, and promoted a shared civic Russian (*rossiiskaia*) identity. But in imperial fashion he also fought a war with Chechnya, bringing it back into the Federation with brutal force, and set up a vicious thug as his satrap in the republic.

Just as in tsarist times Russia was understood by officials and members of the educated elites as the civilizing force that claimed to bring enlightenment to the imperial peripheries, so in Soviet times Russians were presented in official discourse as the "older brother" of the other Soviet peoples, able in their own special way to raise the others to socialism. The Soviet Union had two very particular but interrelated civilizing missions, the first internally within the Soviet state and society to turn a largely agrarian, peasant country into a proletarian, industrial powerhouse, and, second, globally to lead the way beyond capitalism, nationalism, and bourgeois democracy to international socialism. The legacies of those imperial experiences live on. In post-Soviet times Russia continues to see itself as exceptional in Eurasia (and even the world) as a unique case of political development that retains something of its own to contribute to the rest of the globe. In much of their own rhetoric Russians declare themselves different from the West and superior to the East. In this way Russian exceptionalism parallels American ideas that the United States is the "indispensable nation."

Russia's imperial might and its claims to exceptionalism have long been entangled in its convoluted relation to the West. Russia is often presented to the world, and to Russians themselves, in terms set by outsiders. Even its own intellectuals have been steeped in the values and invidious comparisons that always set the West above and always find Russia lacking. Not only has Russia been at many historical junctures weaker than the West, and not only has it been economically dependent on other dominant states, but many of its intellectuals have read and written versions of Russian history framed in relation to an idealized West. "Contemporary Russia's identity," writes the Russian scholar Viatcheslav Morozov, "critically depends on its (post-)imperial self-image as a great power, where greatness is still defined by referring to the Soviet past. . . . Russia's discursive space has been fully Europeanised during several centuries of catch-up modernization, and its social structure has evolved in such a way that there are no groups within the country capable of developing an alternative articulation of Russian identity."[3] Even when Russians most self-confidently lauded themselves—as triumphant military power, as spiritually richer than a soulless West, or as ideologically superior to a decadent capitalist world—the reference was almost always to a putative (and purely imaginary) civilized West with "unquestionable normative authority."[4] Russia is spoken for by others and appears unable either to escape its subaltern, inferior position in the international system or to create its own credible alternative discourse to the West's hegemonic construction of world history that normalizes and privileges capitalism, democracy, and Western values.

In one sense Russia is imperial, and in another it is itself colonized, part of the West but kept apart from it and unable to fully identify or assimilate, Morozov argues. It is what he calls a "subaltern empire." On the other hand, as Marshall Poe points out, Russia's empire was "a remarkable success." "Around the globe, one imperial enterprise after another succumbed to European and later Western imperialism. Russia did not. . . . Where other empires, having been imperialized to one degree or another by the Europeans, joined Europe as economic partners (America) or clients (Africa and Asia), Russia achieved a good measure of economic, technical, and military success independently, or at least largely so."[5] Morozov puts a different spin on Poe's point: "Since its emergence as a sovereign polity in the fifteenth century, Russia has never been colonised by anyone but itself," even as "it created a vast and powerful empire."[6]

In this book we have tried to understand what might be meant by empire and how such a concept can explain a state's behavior and perceptions. As an ideal type, empire is a kind of state formation that differs in significant ways from other rival state formations, such as principality, nation-state, federation, nonstate entity, or multinational nation-state. Empire in its ideal form is also a way of ruling that characterizes certain states: rule through institutionalized difference between superior and inferior groups of people in which the very quality of superiority gives some the right to rule over others. Autocracy, dictatorship, the usurpation and centralization of sovereignty in the metropole, and the rule of a designated elite, ethnic or social, over inferior subjects are all practices with which empires have an affinity.

---

[3] Viatcheslav Morozov, *Russia's Postcolonial Identity: A Subaltern Empire in a Eurocentric World* (London and New York: Palgrave Macmillan, 2015), pp. 9, 11.
[4] Ibid., p.11.
[5] Marshall T. Poe, *The Russian Moment in World History* (Princeton, NJ: Princeton University Press, 2006), pp. xiii–xiv.
[6] Morozov, *Russia's Postcolonial Identity*, pp. 12–13.

Empires, thus, are antithetical to democracy, equal rights of free citizens, true popular sovereignty, and the civic or ethnic homogeneity of the population that are characteristic of (or at least are the aspirations) of nation-states. But as we have shown in this book, the real world seldom approximates tidy ideal types, no matter how useful they may be heuristically. In the history we have traced empires, especially in the period after 1789, have attempted at times to homogenize institutions and peoples in order to compete successfully with the efficiencies of nation-states, or simply to function more efficiently with a single set of administrative and linguistic practices and norms. They have, moreover, made significant concessions to winning support of at least some of their subjects through promises of reciprocity and practices of inclusion. The aura of absolute, unmitigated imperial power broadcast by the double-headed eagle or the red star can easily leave such gestures unremarked, in the shadows, or make them appear insignificant. Political participation and inclusion come in many forms, just as empires do, and electoral democracy and legislative parliaments are simply one form, admittedly an effective one, out of many.

The people of Rus, of Muscovy, of Imperial Russia, and of the Soviet Union all would have understood, had they given it any thought, the sharp and immediate limits on their ability to shape their political landscapes, to oppose their rulers, or to make demands on the state. And yet, in each of these periods, we have seen people mobilized to do all of those things. Kievan townspeople gathered and voiced support or opposition for contending princes, and their will carried the day, at least according to the chronicle account. In Muscovite times and through the 1905 Bloody Sunday march on the Winter Palace, subjects of the tsars presented their demands in the form of humble petitions, but in a marvelously passive-aggressive, and often effective way, reminded their rulers of their God-given obligation to protect their pitiful flock and to extend their mercy. Petitions often won results, though far from always, as 1905 reminds us. In times of crisis, Russian subjects took more extreme action: vanquishing the Polish and Swedish invaders and selecting a new tsar in 1613; overthrowing ungenerous emperors who did not play by the reciprocal script in 1741, 1762, and 1801; rising in mass rebellion time and time again until the culminating rebellions of 1917 and 1991; and fighting for their country in the Great Patriotic War.

One should not exaggerate the degree of popular empowerment that these non-democratic forms permitted. In many circumstances, common people were left to endure the abuses of those more powerful, or of each other, without any protection from the regime, either far from the eye of the state or with its full or tacit approval. Not infrequently, the regime itself was responsible for inflicting its own exploitation and horrific abuses. And yet, simply by noticing the subtler forms of political interaction and the sense of some small degree of entitlement by a population otherwise assumed to be supine—passive or crushed—we enrich our understanding of how non-democratic regimes function and are often able to last a long time.

Reciprocity and resistance drew elites (in the palace coups) and peasants (as petitioners) into political engagement. They involved Russians and non-Russians from the heart of the court to the most distant peripheries. And to these actions taken autonomously by Russian subjects, we can add the host of official ways in which the imperial and then the Soviet regime actively invited their subjects/ citizens to participate: in local tax-collection and policing; assemblies of the land; legislative assemblies; provincial assemblies and courts; *zemstva*; dumas; soviets; May Day marches; party congresses; elections without competing candidates; and myriad rituals demonstrating fealty to the ruler. Empires are profoundly anti-democratic, but we find strong grounds to argue that they do, and in fact must, find other ways to involve their people in their imperial project, to gain their participation in the difficult work of governing an empire, and to win their tacit acceptance if not their active loyalty.

Empires must perforce make concessions to segments of their population if they hope to survive, and thus at times act somewhat less autocratically than their reputation allows. Concessions to the populace can hardly be called either "democratic" or "national," but at times they can approximate the practices of a nation-state based on ideas of citizenship. Conversely, nation-states often act imperially both in domestic and foreign policy. Forcing a diverse population to assimilate into a dominant nationality or distinguishing some peoples as minorities to be treated differently, usually disadvantaging them, or deporting or massacring designated populations, are practices that nations have engaged in and that empires would have easily understood as part of an imperial repertoire.

For much of its history Russia and its Soviet successor were empires, at times engaged in nationalizing projects, but these were always undercut by their own ambivalence about creating a coherent national community and thwarted by the structures, discourses, legacies, and practices of empire. Within Russia itself Yeltsin and Putin have attempted to form a coherent national community. Russia today is as close as it has ever been to being a coherent multinational state, but once again ethnic and social distinctions, centralization of power in Moscow, discursive confusion about Russian identity, and the erosion of democracy and real popular sovereignty have hindered nationhood. Rhetoric and imagery move in one direction while actual practices and everyday life move in another. Tajik gardeners and Uzbek fruit sellers in Moscow are well aware that they are not equal to the metropolitans for whom they work. Once members of the same country as the Muscovites, subjects of the same Russian and Soviet empires, they are now foreign laborers, former colonials now colonized in a new post-imperial structure. Even as post-Soviet Russia has looked far less like an empire than a multinational state of citizens distinguished by ethnicity but equal under the law, it continues to flex imperial muscles both within the state, as in its relationship to Chechnya, and abroad, as in Ukraine and the Caucasus. Russia's seizure of Crimea and its current entanglement in Ukraine are simply the most obvious of these residual aftereffects of empire. The fact that Mikheil Saakashvili, the former president of Georgia, was called to serve as the governor of the Ukrainian Odessa Oblast', and Maria Gaidar, daughter of former prime minister of Russia, became his deputy, encapsulates the explosive swirl of human movement and interaction produced by empire and activated by its collapse.

Over the past decade, a great deal of scholarly work has appeared applying imperial and postcolonial theory to Soviet and post-Soviet spaces. We think of much of Russian policy in the Near Abroad as a program of hegemony rather than empire, dominion without full control of domestic and foreign policy of its subordinates. But to its neighbors and much of the world, Russia appears unable to surrender its ambitions in Eurasia. The annexation of Crimea and the ongoing crisis in Ukraine have reinforced this impression. The images and practices of autocracy and empire continue to overwhelm the possible alternatives that Russia might choose in its ongoing search for what it could be.

CREDITS

Chapter 7

p. 201: Photo courtesy of the Library of Congress; p. 204: Photo courtesy of the Library of Congress; p. 214: (top) Tretyakov Gallery, Moscow, Russia/Bridgeman Images; p. 214: (bottom) Tretyakov Gallery, Moscow, Russia/Bridgeman Images; p. 219: Kharkov Art Museum, Kharkov, Russia/Bridgeman Images

Chapter 8

p. 231: Library of Congress; p. 239: © Pictures From History/The Image Works; p. 240: Russian Academy of Sciences Library; p. 242: (top) Hillwood Estate, Museum & Gardens; p. 242: (bottom) HIP/Art Resource, NY; p. 245: akg-images; p. 247: (top) The Russian Museum of Ethnography, Saint Petersburg; p. 247: (bottom) The Russian Museum of Ethnography, Saint Petersburg; p. 248: © RIA-Novosti/The Image Works

Chapter 9

p. 257: Russian State Library; p. 262: Photo courtesy of the Library of Congress; p. 267: © ITAR-TASS/Sovfoto; p. 271: © Sovfoto; p. 287: Photo courtesy of International Institute of Social History, Amsterdam

Chapter 10

p. 298: © Sovfoto; p. 305: © Sovfoto; p. 312: HIP/Art Resource; p. 316: Associated Press; p. 320: Andriy Kravchenko/Alamy Stock Photo; p. 323: © Sovfoto; p. 325: © ITAR-TASS/Sovfoto

Chapter 11

p. 337: John Lander/Alamy Stock Photo; p. 338: HIP/Art Resource, NY; p. 345: © ITAR-TASS/Sovfoto; p. 357: Associated Press

Chapter 12

p. 366: Velenguri/EPA/Newscom; p. 373: AP Photo/Alexander Zemlianichenko; p. 380: Alexei Druzhinin/Associated Press; p. 381: Sergei Chirikov/Epa/Newscom

INDEX

A

Ab Imperio, 374
Affirmative Action Empire, 310
Afghanistan, 343
Agitprop. *See* Department of Agitation and Propaganda
agriculture, 291
Akhmatova, Anna, 374
Aksakov, Konstantin, 161–62
Aleksandr Nevskii (Eisenstein film), 321
Aleksei Mikhailovich (tsar), 60, 73, 74, 91–92; government of, 74; religion of, 60; seal of, 74
Aleksei Petrovich (tsarevich), 96–97, 103
Alexander I (emperor), 141–45; character of, 149; constitution of, 142; death of, 156; government of, 141; politics of, 154; religion of, 143, 153; Unofficial Committee of, 141; at war, 145, 147, 149
Alexander II (emperor), 172, 186–87, 197; death of, 208; on language, 203; for reform, 187; reign of, 185
Alexander III (emperor), 203; anti-Semitism of, 219–20; on radical movement, 220
Aliev, Heider, 331, 376
allies, of Soviet Russia, 285
America; dominance of, 316; economy of, 346; power of, 381
American Revolution, 80
Amin, Hafizullah, 344

Anna Ivanovna (empress), 101, 102, 118
Anderson, Benedict, 5, 160, 257
Anderson, Perry, 99
Andropov, Iurii, 334; death of, 348; reign of, 348
Anti-Ballistic Missile Treaty, 382
anti-capitalism, 208
anti-Communism, 342
Anti-Cosmopolitan Campaign, 317–18
anti-imperialist nationalists, 286
anti-Semitism, 199–200, *219*; of Alexander III, 219–20; laws against, 294; in media, 238; in Russia, 222
Apology of a Madman (Chaadaev), 162
Appanage Period, 33, 36
Arakcheev, Aleksei, 143, 155
Archpriest Avvakum, 60; death of, 61
Argunov, Ivan, *120*
aristocracy, 141; politics of, 141
Armenia, 169, 268; demands of, 350–52; founding of, 201p; massacre of, 353; Soviet Armenia, 306; at war, 277–78
Armenian Communist Party, 322
Armenian *Dashnaktsutyun*, 268, 270, 278
Armenian Genocide, 332–33
army. *See also* military; land for, 53; peasants in, 152–53; in education, *298*; as national, 305; art of Vereshchagin, 213, *214*, 215; war in, 151–52
Assembly of the Land, 59

Association Agreement, 389
Atarshchikov, Semyon, 174
autocracy; boyars in, 52–53; in empires, 2;
    legitimacy of, 266; power of, 52; practice
    of, 402; regime of, 241; religion in, 52;
    responsibilities of, 89, 107; in Russia,
    192; Witte on, 249–50
Autonomous Region, 350
autonomy; of Mongol khans, 41;
    of nationality, 339–40; as
    Transcaucasian, 278
Avrutin, Eugene, 175
Azerbaijan, 350–53
Azerbaijani Communist Party, 331, 353
Azerbaijan People's Front, 353

B

Bagirov, Mir Jafar, 297
Baku Congress, 286
Barth, Frederic, 85
Battle of Tannenberg, 262
Bauer, Raymond A., 308
Bekbulatovich, Simeon (tsar), 51
Beketev, Petr, 68
Benkendorff, Aleksandr, 161
Beria, Lavrenti, 297, 324, *325*
Berlin Wall, 342
Bessarabians, 284–85
Bialer, Seweryn, 344
Bilibin, Ivan, *245*
Birobidzhan. *See* Jewish Autonomous
    Region
Blessed Is the Host of the Heavenly Tsar,
    64, *65*
Bloody Sunday, 243
Bluntschli, Johann Kaspar, 82–83
Boeck, Brian, 71–72, 109, 127
Bogoliubskii, Andrei, 32–33; legacy of, 36
Bolotov, Andrei, 114
Bolsheviks, 224, 225, 246, 255, 261, 265,
    270, 271, 272, 274–286, 288, 304, 313,
    314, 319, 347. *See also* Social Democrats;
    Jews in Bolshevik Party, 318
Bonaparte, Napoleon, 145, 147, 149;
    invasion of, *148*; victory over, 149–50
Borisov, Petr, 155–56
bourgeois nationalism, 253
boyars, 52–53

Brandenberger, David, 309–10
Breslauer, George, 344
Brezhnev, Leonid, 331, 339; death of, 348;
    reign of, 343–44; strategy of, 344
Brezhnev Doctrine, 343, 344
Brooks, Jeffrey, 165
Brotherhood (*bratstvo*), 310, 311
The Brothers Karamazov (Dostoevsky), 216
Brudny, Yitzhak, 337–38
Budil'nik (Alarm Clock), *240*
Bukharin, Nikolai, 272, 283, 368
Bulgarin, Fedor, 158–59
Burbank, Jane; on empires, 13–15; on
    rights, 235
Bush, George Herbert Walker, 358
Bushkovitch, Paul, 55, 91, 163
Byzantine Empire, 19, 41

C

Caliphate, 5
capitalism, 222; anti-, 208; economy of,
    223; rise of, 241
Catherine I (empress), 97
Catherine II (empress) (Catherine the Great),
    99, 118–19; character of, 89, 106, 110;
    death of, 138–39; in French Revolution,
    136–37; funeral of, 140; as lawmaker, 110;
    legitimacy of, 109; lovers of, 106–7; loyalty
    to, 106–9; for nationalism, 137–38; as
    nationalist, 137–38; policies of, 126–29,
    208; portrait of, *108*, *111*; reign of, 103,
    106–10; religion of, 109–10, 130–31; at war,
    135–37
Caucasian Mountains, 171
Caucasus, 249; of Russia, 178–79
Central Asia, 210–12, 214; conquest of,
    213; cotton in, 215; expansion in, *212*;
    Slavic in, 215
Central Europe, 260
Central Executive Committee of Soviets
    of Ukraine, 281
Central Intelligence Agency (CIA), 319, 343
centralization, 288
Chaadaev, Petr, 162
challenges; of empires, 4, 229; with reform,
    193; for rulers, 105–6; of Russia, 8; for
    women, 105–6
Chapaev, Vasilii, 311

character; of Alexander I, 149; of
Catherine II, 89, 106, 110; of Lenin, 288;
of Nicholas II, 240; of Paul I, 140; of
Peter I, 89; of Russian national, 119
Charter to the Nobility, 99, *100*, 126
Charter to the Towns, 126
Chavchavadze, Ilia, 202
Chechnya, *373;* as independent, 367,
372–73; invasion of, 372–74
Cherkasskaia, Kuchenei Temriukovna, 55
Cherkasskii, Vladimir, 193
Chernenko, Konstantin, 348
Cherniaev, Mikhail, 211
Cherniavsky, Michael, 116–17
Chernov, Victor, 274
Chernyshevskii, Nikolai, 213
China, Communist Party in, 342
Chinese Eastern Railroad, 238
Chingis Khan (also Genghis Khan), 7n5, 39
Chingissid, 55–56
Chkheidze, Nikolai, 265
Chosen People mythology, 56
Christianity, 20, 54; conversion to, 22–23;
monogamy in, 22; renewing of, 374; as
social glue, 28
Christianization, 23
Christian missionaries, 228
Church, 22. *See also* Christianity;
Orthodox Church
Churchill, Winston, 314
Church of the Intercession, *24*
CIA. *See* Central Intelligence Agency
civil rights, in Russia, 222
civil society, in USSR, 348
Civil War. *See* Russian Civil War
Clinton, Hillary Rodham, 394
Cold War, 311–14, 316; divisions of, 27; era of,
315; Europe during, *315;* in USSR, 317–23
collectivization, 295–7, 301–2, 304, 307
colonization, 6; acquisition for, 236;
nationalism and, 234; in Russia, 200–201
Commonwealth, 364
communism. *See also* Communist Party;
Jews in, 222, 294; as national, 290–91;
Tashkent Communists, 285
The Communist Manifesto (Marx), 223
Communist Party, 3, 11, 276, 281; in China,
342; defeat of, 366; demise of, 353–55; for
economy, 295; expectations from, 346–47;
in Georgia, 294–95; for modernity, 362;

as national, 316; policies of, 280, 331; on
race, 295; in republics, 293–94; support
for, 279–80, 287; at war, 277
community; as national, 11, 86; of Russia, 117
concentration camps, 263
Conference on Security and Co-operation
in Europe (CSSE), 343
Congress of the Peoples of the East, 286
conservatism, 153–54
Constantine Porphyrogenitus, 19–20
Constituent Assembly, 273
constitution; of Alexander I, 142; of Soviet
Russia, 282
Constitutional Crisis of 1730, 101–2
Constitutional Democrats (Kadets),
246–47, 269–70
Constitutional Monarchy, 102
constructivism, 341
consultation, 91–93
consumerism; rise in, 346; Stalin for, 318–19
conversion; to Christianity, 22–23;
prohibition of, 208–10; in religion,
55–56, 68–69; of Siberia, 70
Cooper, Frederick, 4; on empires, 13–15
corporations, 76
Cossacks, 59; and Jews, 263; culture of, 66;
counter-revolution, 276; in Revolution,
270, 275; origins of, 71; relations with
Muscovites, 72; religion of, 69–70;
resistance from, 194, 196; revolts of,
126–28; role in Muscovy, 127–28; values
of, 71–72; zemstvo, 269
Council of Ministers, 333
Council of State, 186
counter-reforms, 215–20
courts. *See* judicial system
Cracraft, James, 117
Crews, Robert, 131, 170
Crimea, 128
Crimean War, 184, *184,* 191; loss of,
185–86; cross-dressing, 105–6
CSSE. *See* Conference on Security and
Co-operation in Europe
cultural homogeneities, 4
culture; of Cossacks, 66; of empires, 174–75;
evolution of, 33–34; in geography, 34; of
Georgia, 335; of nation, 84; of peasants,
120–21; rise in, 296; of Russia, 116–21;
of Russification, 199–203; of salons, 104;
of Siberia, 166–67; Silver Age of, 245;

superiority of, 178; of USSR, 334–36, 338–39; of Yiddish, 294
currency, in Kievan Rus, 30
Czartoryski, Adam, 141, 144, 176

D

Dashnaktsutyun, 268, 270, 278
Davies, Norman, 72
Davies, Sarah, 310
Decembrist Rebellion, 144
Decembrists, 154–55; revolt of, 157; slaughter of, 156; wives of, 157
Declaration of the Rights of Man, 86–87
decolonization, 233
de-imperialization, 364
Demirchian, Karen, 331
democracy, 49; decline of, 376–77; empires compared to, 400; introduction of, 359; socialism compared to, 349–50, 364–65
democratic recession, 376–80
demonstrations, map of, 244
Denikin, Anton, 286
Department of Agitation and Propaganda (Agitprop), 318
deportations and resettlements, in USSR, 303
Derzhavin, Gavrila, 110
Dictatorship of the Heart, 218
Diderot, Denis, 107–8
Dmitrii Ivanovich (Tsarevich), 57–58
Doctors' Plot, 317
Dolbilov, Mikhail, 205
Donskoi, Dmitrii (grand prince), 39
Dormition Cathedral, 45
Dostoevsky, Fedor, 216
Drunken Council, 97
Dubček, Alexander, 343
Duby, Georges, 28
Dudaev, Jokhar, 372
Duma, 251, 254
Duranty, William, 299

E

East Slavic Orthodox, 35
economy; of America, 346; of capitalism, 223; collapse of, 266–67, 274; Communist Party for, 295; crisis in, 367;

of industry, 243–44; of Mongols, 41; of peasants, 186; reform of, 187; under women, 103–4
education; art in, 298; of language, 252, 297; of religion, 202; in Russia, 158, 200, 221; system of, 252
Ehrenburg, Ilya, 312
Eisenstein, Sergei, 320–21
elections, 247, 249; laws of, 377
Elizabeth Petrovna (empress), 49, 103–5; portrait of, 105
emancipation; of peasants, 142–43, 187–90, 205–6; terms of, 188–90
emperors, 2–3. See also empire
empire. See also Byzantine Empire; Ottoman Empire; Roman Empire; Russian Empire; autocracy in, 2; borders of, 261; Burbank on, 13–15; challenges of, 4, 229; colonizing of, 123; concept of, 116, 290, 358–59, 396–99; Cooper on, 13–15; culture of, 174–75; decline of, 229; as defined, 4; democracy compared to, 400; division of, 121–34; expansion of, 261; fate of, 228–31, 234; framework of, 12; government of, 74; historians on, 5; history of, 2–3; lifespan of, 5; longevity of, 227–28; manifestation of, 15–16; modernity in, 15, 229, 234–36; of Mongols, 40; as multinational, 62; nationalism in, 262; nation compared to, 12–13, 75; people of, 121–34; railroads for, 237; relevance of, 5; of Rome, 2–3; of Russia, 1; state as, 77–78; survival of, 6, 260, 401; types of, 3; of USSR, 337–40; utility of, 6; visions for, 251–52; workings of, 394–95
empire-state, 301–9
Engels, Friedrich, 229
Ermolov, Aleksei, 172
Esipov, Savva, 69
ethnic groups, 84–85; in Russian Empire, 195; social position of, 309; of South Caucasus, 293
ethnic police, 306
ethnic pride, 317
ethnographic map, 81
ethnonationalism, 234
Etkind, Alexander, 14, 67–68, 133, 180–81
Eurasia, 374–76
Eurasian Union, 392
Europe; during Cold War, 315; map of, 315

European Enlightenment, 118
European Union, 5, 315, 388
Evsektsiia, 294
evolution; of culture, 33–34; of Rus, 17–43;
  of Russia, 4–8
expansion; in Central Asia, *212;* of
  empires, 261; of Moscow, 73; of
  Muscovites, 70–71; of NATO, 381–85,
  383; resistance of, 210–11; of Russia,
  66–67, 166–67, *171;* of Russian Empire,
  63, 134–39
The Expansion of England (Seeley), 264

F

False Dmitrii, 57–59
family; of Peter I, 103; war within, 32–33,
  37; during World War I, 256
famine, 299; as genocide, 301; mortality of,
  300; relief effort for, 220; in Ukraine, 300
fascism, 389
fatherland, 311
Fatherland War, 149
February Days of 1917, 266, *267*
"February Revolution of 1917," 268–69
federalism, 365, 370
Federation Council, 370
Federov, Nikolai, 370
Fedor II Alekseevich (tsar), 91; female rule,
  103–4
Ferdinand, Franz, assassination of, 255
Field, Daniel, 190
Figes, Orlando, 183
figurines, *247*
Finance Ministry, 206
Finland, 143–44
Finnish Social Democrats, 273
Florinsky, Michael, 90
Ford, Gerald, 343
foreign policy; of Gorbachev, 354; of
  Russia, 384; of USSR, 340–44
Franklin, Simon, 23, 29
fraternity, 259
Free Agriculturalist Law, 143
French Revolution, 60, 80, 87; Catherine II
  and, 136–37
Friendship of the Peoples (*Druzhba narodov*),
  310–11, *323;* experience with, 334–37;
  fountain of, *337;* policies of, 334–37

Fuller, William C., Jr., 154
Fundamental Laws, 236
fur, 19–20, 67–68

G

Gagarin, Iurii, 342
Gaidar, Maria, 401
Galicia, 208
Galician-Volynian, 34
Gamsakhurdia, Zviad, 385
Gellner, Ernest, 231
Gel'man, Vladimir, 378–79
Generalissimus. *See* Stalin, Joseph
Genghis Khan. *See* Chingis Khan
genocide; famine as, 301; by Stalin, 300
Genscher, Hans-Dietrich, 381
geography; culture in, 34; of Russian
  Empire, 122
Georgia, 169; Communist Party in, 294–95;
  conflicts with, 385–88; culture of, 335;
  language of, 204–5, 333; Muslims in, 333
Gerasimov, Ilya, 374
Germanophilia, 118
Germany, *316. See also* Nazi Germany; in
  Russian Empire, 123–24; war with, 256
Gessen, Masha, 377, 380
Giovanni di Plano Carpini, 38
Glinskaia, Elena, 55
God, 25; will of, 69
Godunov, Boris, 57, 67–68
Golden Charter, 188
Golden Horde, 35, 39; collapse of, 62
Goldfrank, David, 183
Golike, Vasilii, *158*
Gorbachev, Mikhail, 227; agreement with,
  359; death of, 376; foreign policy of, 354;
  legacy of, 379–80; police of, 357; policies
  of, 350–52; proposals by, 355; reign of,
  349; on socialism, 349–50; Thatcher on,
  348–49; vision of, 349
Gorchakov, Alexander, 211
Gorskii, A. A., 30–31
government, 192; of Alexander I, 141; of
  empire, 74; of Kievan Rus, 29; of Aleksei
  Mikhailovich, 74; as multi-party, 276;
  nationalism in, 252; of nations, 82; racism
  in, 207–8; social control by, 190–91
Gramsci, Antonio, 380

Grand Duchy of Lithuania, 34–35, 55
grand prince, 28. *See also Velikii kniaz'*;
  Vladimir of Kiev; image of, 30; as ruler,
  30–32
Granovskii, Timofei, 163
Grant, Bruce, 179
Great Fatherland War. *See* World War II
Great Patriotic War, 400
Great Power, 340. *See also velikaia
  derzhava* (Great Power); politics of, 27
Great Power Chauvinism, 296
Great Powers of Europe, 205
Great Purges, 307
Great Reforms, 185–91, 196, 215
Great Retreat, 296
Great Russian Chauvinism; Lenin on, 310;
  Stalin on, 310
Great Russians, 308
Great Schism, 26
Great Terror, 296
Great War of 1914–1918. *See* World War I
Greco, Olga, 110
Greek Orthodoxy, 54, 60
Greenfeld, Liah, 89, 97–98
Gruber, Isaiah, 57–58, 60
Guards Regiments, 102
Gumilev, Nikolai, 375

H

Habsburg, Wilhelm von, 282
Halperin, Charles, 26, 56
Hanseatic League, 34
Harvard Project, 308–9
Hellbeck, Jochen, 326
Herder, Johann Gottfried von, 80
Herzen, Aleksandr, 162–63, 237
hierarchy; in Church, 22; of Orthodox
  Church, 41; of peasants, 113–14
historians, 1; on empires, 5
history; of empires, 2–3; of Moscow, 196;
  of Rus, 7; of Russia, 1, 12–13, 15–16, 90
Hitler, Adolf, 313
Hoch, Stephen, 189
Holocaust, 312–13
Holodomor (Ukrainian Famine), 299–300
Hosking, Geoffrey, 13, 109, 258
Hrushevskyi, Mykhailo, 246–47, 252
Hypatian Codex, 25

I

Iakut people 67; importance to regime of,
  68–69; massacre of, 68; religion of, 68–69
Iaroslavl Province, 190–91
image; of grand prince, 30; of nation, 258;
  of Nicholas I, 157–58, *158*; of Putin, 371;
  of Russia, 159, 161, 386, 394, 402; of
  Russian Empire, 75, 87
imperial competition, 239–40
imperial conquest, 62, 64, 66–74; vision
  for, 61
imperial England, 15
imperial France, 15
imperialism; as conservatism, 153–54; as
  elite, 86; hostility to popular
  mobilization, 13; mission of, 199; as
  national identity, 15; in religion, 199;
  reputation of, 75; World War II on, 315
imperial modernizers, 229–30
imperial nationalism, 199–200, 234
Imperial Russia, 1, 12, 15; adapting of, 87
Imperial Russian Geographic Society, 164
Imperialism, liberal, 265
imperium. See empires
independence; of Chechnya, 367, 372–73;
  declaration of, 358; of Ukraine, 282
industry; economy of, 243–44; of jewelry,
  33; in Kiev, 32; of railroads, 238; in
  Siberia, 67–68
inheritance, 32
Inkeles, Alex, 308
inorodtsy, 166–67
intelligentsia. *See* Soviet intelligentsia
intelligenty, 213
Iron Curtain, 361
ISIS. *See* Islamic State of Iraq and Syria
Islamic State of Iraq and Syria (ISIS), 5
Israel; founding of, 318; victory of, 334
Istoriia gosudarstva rossiiskogo (History
  of the Russian State) (Karamzin), 177
Ivan III (Ivan the Great) (Grand Prince);
  coronation of, *46;* reign of, 44; religion
  of, 61; seal of, 45, *46;* victories of, 61
Ivan IV Vasilevich (Ivan the Terrible)
  (tsar), 171; abdication of, 49–51; early
  period of, 47–49; *Oprichnina* of, 49–51;
  political culture of, 51; reign of, 1–2, 47;
  religion of, 47, 51–52; sanity of, 50–51;
  suspicions of, 61; taxes for, 48; as tsar,

50; victories of, 62; violence of, 52; warnings from, 66

Ivanov, S. V., *242*

Ivan V Alekseevich (tsar), 91–93, 101

Ivan VI Antonovich (emperor), 103

J

Jadidists, 211

Jafarov, Mamed Iusif, 265

Jahn, Hubertus F., 256–57

Japan, 240

JAR. *See* Jewish Autonomous Region

Jaurès, Jean, 261

jewelry, *33*

Jewish Autonomous Region (JAR), 294

Jewish Bund, 223, 270

Jews. *See also* anti-Semitism; Yiddish; activism of, 334; in Bolshevik Party, 318; in communism, 222, 294; deportation of, 398; monarchs on, 222; nationalism on, 222; of Pale of Settlement, 175; persecution of, 263, 317–18; pogroms against, *209*; registering of, 175; restrictions on, 129; in Russian Empire, 129; vote for, 269

Jones, Gareth, 299

Journey from St. Petersburg to Moscow (Radishchev), 113–14

judicial system; manipulation of, 216; political trials in, 216–17; reforms of, 193; revolutionary movement in, 216

Jughashvili, Iosip (Stalin), 221. *See also* Stalin, Joseph.

K

Kadets. *See* Constitutional Democrats

Kadyrov, Ramzan, 372

Kaestner, I. K., 107, *108*

Kaganovich, Lazar, 294

Kaitser (Sparks) (Raffi), 322

Kalashnikov, Ivan, 167

Kamenev, Lev, 368

Kanatchikov, S. I., 218

Das Kapital (Marx), 220

Kappeler, Andreas, 13

Karamzin, Nikolai, 154, 177–78, 210, 338

Karmal, Babrak, 344

Kastelianskii, Abram, 265

Katkov, Mikhail, 164, 196, 207

Kaufman, General Konstantin von, 211, 213

Kazan, conquest of, 64

Kemal, Mustafa (Atatürk), 230

Kennan, George F., 238, 382

Kerensky, Alexander, 265, 274–75

Kerry, John, 394

KGB, 331, 348

Khlevniuk, Oleg, 324–25

Khodarkovsky, Michael, 66, 174

Khodorkovskii, Mikhail, 371

Khomiakov, Aleksei, 162

Khrushchev, Nikita, 327; for peace, 342; on reciprocity, 330; removal of, 343; rule of, 331–32; on Stalin, 339

Kiev, 32

Kievan Golden Age, 23

Kievan Rus, 397–98. *See also* Rus; currency in, 30; demise of, 38; government of, 29; Ostrowski on, 29; period of, 7; religion in, 23, 25–27, 34–35; as state, 29, 31; as stateless head, 30; structure of, 28

King, Charles, 75–76, 388

Kingdom of Poland, 35

Kingdom of Rus, 34

Kliuchevskii, Vasilii, 177

Kluckhohn, Clyde, 308

Kniazhnin, Iakov B., 103, 112, 119–20

Knysh, Alexander, 173

Kollmann, Nancy Shields, 49–50

Koreans, Soviet; exile of, 297; movement of, 304

Kornilov, Lavr, 274

Kovalevskii, Maxim, 265

Kozyrev, Andrei, 385

Kremlin, 9–10, 36, *45*, 57

Kronenberg, S. L., 216

Kukryniksy, 311

Kulikovo Field, 39

Kuchuk Khan, 286

Kuropatkin, A. N., 251

L

Labzina, Anna, 106–7, 111–12, 167

Lakoba, Nestor, 324

land; angels for, 25; for army, 53; fragmenting of, 32; for peasants, 53, 274; reform of, 291; of Rus, 17–20

language; Alexander II on, 203; education of, 252, 297; of Georgia, 204–5, 333; of Russia, 9–10, 202–3; of Ukraine, 207; of USSR, 361–62; Yiddish as, 294

laws; against anti-Semitism, 294; and inequality, 145; electoral, 245, 249; Free Agriculturalist Law, 143; Fundamental Laws (Finland), 144; Fundamental Laws (1832), 153; of elections, 377; of *Russkaia Pravda*, 30; of *soslovie*, 126–127; of succession, 98, 140; on unigeniture, 101, 102; rule of law in Muscovy, 50–51; *sharia*, 172; Siberian (1822), 166; *Sudebnik* of 1497, 44; *Sudebnik* of 1550, 47–48

LeDonne, John, 99, 125

Left Socialist Revolutionaries, 274–76

legacy; of Bogoliubskii, 36; of Gorbachev, 379–80; of Putin, 15

Lenin, Vladimir, 230, 238, *270;* character of, 288; compromise of, 276; death of, 293; on Great Russian Chauvinism, 310; on nationalism, 286–87; platform of, 272; predictions of, 259; as symbol, 389; on Ukraine, 282–83; vision of, 280; on war, 265–66

Leninists. *See* Communist Party

Lermontov, Mikhail, 180

Lewin, Moshe, 347

liberals, 241, 246–47, 249, 253, 259, 270, 275–77, 279, 280

Lieberman, Victor, 3, 29

Lieven, Dominic, 147

literature, in Russia, 180

Lithuania, 34, 285–86, 350, 353–55, 381

Lithuanians, 267, 285, 340

Litsevoi letopisnyi svod (Illustrated Chronicle Compendium), 45, 47

Lohr, Eric, 241

Loris-Melikov, Mikhail, 218–19

Lotman, Iurii, 104

Louis XVI (king), 135–36

Lounsbery, Anne, 165, 168

Lukashenka, Aliaksandr, 377

Luxemburg, Rosa, 259, 272

M

Macpherson, James, 177

Madariaga, Isabel de, 136–37

Main Committee, 187–88

Maiorova, Olga, 194

Makarii, Metropolitan, 47, 51, 64

Manifest Destiny, 64

marriage as dynastic politics, 26–27, 34–35, 44, 55

Martin, Alexander, 96

Martin, Terry, 310

Marx, Anthony, 85

Marx, Karl, 220–21, 229, 306

Marxism, 230, 253, 292. *See also* Marx, Karl; revolutionary movement; Soviet Marxism; decline of, 339; eschatology of, 280; on religion, 306

masculinity, 96–97

Maskhadov, Aslan, 372

Mazzini, Giuseppe, 80–81

media, anti-Semitism in, 238

Medvedev, Dmitrii, 370–71, 377

membrum virile (virile member), 97

Memoir on Ancient and Modern Russia (Karamzin), 154

Mensheviks, 224, 225, 276, 278, 287. *See also* Social Democrats

merchants, in Novgorod, 34

Merkel, Angela, 394

Michael of Chernigov (prince), 38

Michels, Georg, 60

migration, under Stalin, 302

Mikhail Alekseevich (tsar). *See* Romanov, Michael

Mikhailova, Yulia, 25–26

military; Muslims in, 197; reform of, 187, 191; shortcomings of, 191

Military-Revolutionary Committee, 275

Miliukov, Pavel, 263, 270

Miliutin, Dmitrii, 191, 213, 250

Miloslavskaia, Maria, 91

Minard, Charles Joseph, *148*

Minin, Kuzma, 58

Mirzoyan, Levon, 297

Misfortune from a Coach (Kniazhnin), 103, 112, 119–20

missionaries, 70, 208

mission civilisatrice (civilizing mission), 228, 304

Moch, Leslie, 230, 302, 304

modernity; Communist Party for, 362; in empires, 15, 229, 234–36; railroads as, 237; of Russia, 238

Mogiliner, Marina, 374

monarchs, 266; on Jews, 222; reciprocity for, 217

Mongolia, 317

Mongols (Mongol khans), 39, *42*, 210, 395; autonomy of, 41; collapse of, 42–43; domination by, 64; economy of, 41; empire of, *40;* Ostrowski on, 41; religion of, 38, 41; ruler of, 62

Mongol-Tatar, 7; power relations of, 42

Monomakh, Vladimir, 37

Monument to the Victory, *320*

Morozov, Oleg, 371, 399

Morrison, Alexander, 132

Moscow, 35–36. *See also* Muscovy; attacks on, 58; expansion of, 73; growth of, 62; history of, 196; nationalism in, 275; Olympics in, 336; royalty of, 39; as widowed, 58

Moskovskie Vedomosti (Moscow News), 164

mothers, 57–58

Motyl, Alexander J., 227

Muggeridge, Malcolm, 299

Murat, Hadji, 174

Muravev, A. M., 156

Muscovites. *See also* Moscow; advance of, 66–67; attacks of, 64; Cossacks for, 72; expansion of, 70–71; religion of, 64, 66

Muscovy, 7–8, 35–36, 395–96; as state, 44–45, 47

Musin-Pushkin, Aleksei, 177

Muslims, 55, 169–70, 285, 374; in Georgia, 333; incorporation of, 128; migration of, 168; in military, 197; persecution of, 306; religion of, 268; states of, 62

N

Nagorno-Karabakh, 350–53, 385–88; map of war, *351*

Nairn, Tom, 298

Najibullah, Muhanmad, 344

namestniki (vicegerents), 48

Napoleon. *See* Bonaparte, Napoleon

Napoleonic Europe, map of, *146*

Napoleonic Wars, 145

Narimanov, Nariman, 294

narod (the people, folk), 77–87, 120–22, 128, 161, 162, 196, 217, 220, 222, 252. *See also,* Sovetskii narod

narodnost' (nationhood), 158, 162, 223

Naryshkina, Natalia, 91

Naryshkin family, 92–93

nation, 76; association of, 82; concept of, 79–80, 116, 160–61, 165; cultures of, 84; discourse of, 78–87, 121; empire compared to, 12–13, 75; etymology of, 79; government of, 82; image of, 258; making of, 231; in modern science, 83; as primordial, 82; of Russia, 177–81; state compared to, 149; state for, 77

national anthem, 160, 321–22

National Bolshevism, 309–10

national-colonial, 286

national identity, 194, 196–97, 199, 397; imperialism as, 15; of USSR, 307

nationalism, 80–81, 249–51, 253–54; association of, 82; Catherine II for, 137–38; as colonizing, 234; in empires, 262; in government, 252; on Jews, 222; Lenin on, 286–87; in Moscow, 275; motivation of, 85; as official, 332; in Petrograd Soviet, 275; power of, 272; rise of, 121, 252; supporters of, 339; as un-orthodox, 332

nationalist movements, 221–22

Nationalist Party, 249

nationality; autonomy of, 339–40; concept of, 159–60, 165; importance of, 308; instrument of, 263; policy of, 306; across revolutionary divide, 266–75

nationality policies, 306; conflicts with, 284; of Soviet Russia, 280–88

nation-state, 77–78

nativization, 294–95

NATO, 315, 367; expansion of, 381–85, *383;* map of, *383*

Naval Statute, 98

Nazarbaev, Nursultan, 376

Nazi Germany; brutality of, 313; invasion by, 312

Nazimov, V. I., 187

Nazi-Soviet Pact, 313

Nemtsov, Boris, 372

Nevskii, Aleksandr, 311

New Economic Policy (NEP), 288, 307

New Israel, 57

Newlin, Thomas, 114

New Russians, 369

New World Order, 366

Nicholas I (emperor), 156, 167, 186; fashion of, 158; illness of, 187; image of, 157–58, *158;* reign of, 157–61; religion of, 158

Nicholas II (emperor), 222, *242;* abdication of, 266; character of, 240; reign of, 240–41

Nixon, Richard, 343

Norris, Stephen M., 150–51

Novgorod, *24,* 34

Novikov, Nikolai, 106

Novyi Mir (New World), 339

Nun-Ingerflom, Claudio Sergio, 59–60

O

October Revolution, 275; second of, 343

Octobrist party, 255

Official Nationality, 158–60, 187

Old Believer Movement, 60

Old Regime, 95, 188

Olympics, 348; in Moscow, 336

Oprichnina; interpretations of, 50; of Ivan IV, 49–51

Orjonikidze, Sergo, 288, 294–95

Orlov, Mikhail, 178

Orlova, Liubov', 337

Orthodox Church, 7, 20, 27, 165; contesting of, 35; hierarchy of, 41; support of, 61; unity of, 35

Orthodox Slavs, 62

Orwell, George, 348

Ossian (Celtic poet), 177

Ostrowski, Donald; on Kievan Rus, 29; on Mongol khans, 41

Ottoman Empire, 64, 183, 185, 260; religion in, 197, 199

Ottomanism, 229

P

pagans, 25–26

Pagden, Anthony, 2, 3n2

Pale of Settlement, 175

Panin, Nikita, 101

Pankratova, Anna, 321

Patriarch Iov, 57

Patriarch Nikon, 60–61

patriotism; Jahn on, 256–57; in Russia, 117–18; during war, 149–50

Paul I (emperor); character of, 140; death of, 141; policies of, 140–41

peasants, *231;* in army, 152–53; commitment to, 189; culture of, 120–21; customs of, 165; economy of, 186; emancipation of, 142–43, 187–90, 205–6; equality for, 236; hierarchy of, 113–14; land for, 53, 274; landlords of, 112–13; of Peter I, 134–35; in radical movement, 218; religion of, 113, 206; resettlement of, 237–38; submission of, 299–301; votes for, 192; at war, 277

Pecheneg, 26

people. *See also zemlia;* of empire, 121–34; of Rus, 18–20, 21–23, 25–27; of Russian Civil War, 285

People's Commissariat of Nationality Affairs, 293, 295

People's Commissar of Nationalities, 292

The People's Will, 218

persecution; of Jews, 263, 317–18; of Muslims, 306; of religion, 32, 85; in revolutionary movement, 218

Pestel, Pavel, 155

Peter (Tsarevich of the Horde), 56

Peter I Alekseevich (Peter the Great) (emperor), 89–99, 101, 103, 109, 111, 112; character of, 89; family of, 103; as father, 96; peasants of, 134–35; policies of, 124–25; reign of, 93–99; rule of, 8–9; successors of, 98–114; vision of, 90, 98–99; in war, 134–35; Zitser on, 96–97

Peter II (emperor), 97, 101, 103

Peter III (emperor), 118, 121, 126; death of, 106–7

Petrograd Soviet, 266, 270, 273; nationalism in, 275

Petrukhintsev, N. N., 124–25

Philosophical Letter (Chaadaev), 162

Piatakov, Giorgii, 272

Piłsudski, Józef, 286

Pimokenko, Mykola, *219*

Platonov, S. F., 58–59

Plehve, Viacheslav von, 238

Plokhy, Serhii, 73, 358, 360
Pogodin, Mikhail (M. P.), 187, 196, 210
Poland, 34, 144, 155, 205; exiles from, 206; incorporation of, 175–76; map of, *137*; partitions of, 135–7; prejudice in, 207–8; uprisings; of 1830, 168, 175–7; of 1863, 205–7; vampires, 205; war with, 135–37
police; corruption in, 331, 355, 357; of Gorbachev, 357
policies; of Catherine II, 126–29, 208; of Communist Party, 280, 331; contradiction of, 337; of Friendship of the Peoples, 334–37; of Gorbachev, 350–52; of nationality, 306; of Paul I, 140–41; of Peter I, 124–25; of Putin, 371, 384; on religion, 129–34, 201; of Russian Empire, 125; in Russification, 200n30; on vices, 172
Polish-Lithuanian Commonwealth, 35; politics of, 70–71
Polish Socialist Party (PPS), 221
political ethnicity, 3
political parties, 224t–225t
politics, 1; of affirmation, 91–93; of Alexander I, 154; of aristocracy, 141; goal of, 378; of Great Power, 27; of Polish-Lithuanian Commonwealth, 70–71; of USSR, 324; working class in, 275–76
Pollard, Alan, 161
polyglot, 35, 37
population; differentiation of, 363; of Russian Empire, 134; solidarity in, 249; unmixing of, 354
population politics, 230
Populism, 223, 224
postcolonial theory, 402
power; of America, 381; of autocracy, 52; distribution of, 2; of nationalism, 272; of Stalin, 301–2; struggle for, 358
Pozharskii, Dmitrii, 58
PPS. *See* Polish Socialist Party
Prague, 343
Pravilova, Ekaterina, 99–100, 206–7
president; Putin as, 368; of Ukraine, 377; Yeltsin as, 366–68
Primakov, Evgenii, 367
primogeniture, tradition of, 22
prince, claim as, 29–30
Progressivist Bloc, 265
Prokopovich, Feofan, 118

Prokudin-Gorskii, Sergei Mikhailovich, 231
property rights, 99–100
Provisional Government, 266, 269, 273
Przeworski, Adam, 379
Pugachev, Emelian, 126, 186
purges under Stalin, 294, 296–7, 302, 307, 309, 316
Pushkin, Alexander, 168, 172, 177–78
Pussy Riot, 379, *381*
Putin, Vladimir, 1, *380*, 397; anger of, 382; anti-gay policies, 374–5, 379; image of, 371; intent of, 401; legacy of, 15; policies of, 371, 384; popularity of, 379, 391; as president, 368; rebuilding by, 368–76; regime of, 379; strategies of, 390; on USSR, 369–70

Q

Qipiani, Dmitri, 204

R

race; Communist Party on, 295; in government, 207–8
radical movement. *See also* revolutionary movement; Alexander III on, 220; failures for, 218; peasants in, 218; philosophies of, 241; in Russia, 87; students in, 217–18; women in, 217
Radishchev, Alexander, 113
Raeff, Marc, 112, 142
Raffensperger, Christian, 26
Raffi (writer), 322
railroads, 236; for empires, 237; industry of, 238; as modernity, 237; for state, 237
Ransel, David, 100–101
Razin, Stenka, 59
Razin Rebellion, 59
Reagan, Ronald, 290, 348; star wars program of, 350; on USSR, 355
Realpolitik, 342
rebellion; by Pugachev, 186; women of, 258
reciprocity, 6–13, 49, 51, 89, 92, 102, 107, 110, 218, 241, 311, 325, 368, 394, 396, 400; conscience of, 217; Khrushchev on, 330; modes of, 241; for monarchs, 217

Reds (film), 286
Red Terror, 280
Reed, John, 286
reform; Alexander II for, 187; challenges
    with, 193; of economy, 187; of judicial
    system, 193; of land, 291; of military,
    187, 191
regime; as autocratic, 241; distrust of, 258;
    of Putin, 379
reign; of Sophia Alekseevich, 93; of
    Alexander II, 185; of Andropov, 348; of
    Brezhnev, 343–44; of Catherine II, 103,
    106–10; of Gorbachev, 349; of Ivan IV,
    1–2, 47; of Nicholas I, 157–61; of
    Nicholas II, 240–41; of Peter I, 93–99; of
    women, 103–4
religion. *See also* Christianity; God; Greek
    Orthodoxy; Orthodox Church; Russian
    Orthodoxy; of Alexander I, 143, 153; in
    autocracy, 52; of Catherine II, 109–10,
    130–31; classifying as, 122; conversion
    in, 55–56, 68–69; of Cossacks, 69–70;
    defender of, 170; education of, 202;
    feuds of, 60; of Iakut people, 68–69;
    imperialism in, 199; of Ivan III, 61; of
    Ivan IV, 47, 51–52; in Kievan Rus, 23,
    25–27, 34–35; in marriage, 35; Marxism
    on, 306; of Mikhailovich, 60; of Mongol
    khans, 38, 41; of Muscovites, 64, 66; of
    Muslims, 268; of Nicholas I, 158; in
    Ottoman Empire, 197, 199; of peasants,
    113, 206; persecution of, 32, 85; policies
    on, 129–34, 201; protection of, 138;
    regulation of, 208–10; in Rus, 54–55; in
    Russia, 169–70; in Siberia, 70; of
    Slavophiles, 162; in Time of Troubles,
    58; war of, 261; of Zasulich, 217
Remezov, Semyon Ulianovich, 70, 80, *81;*
    illustration by, *71*
Republic of Tatarstan, treaty with,
    371–72
republics; Communist Parties in, 293–94;
    declaration of, 266; as national, 297;
    of USSR, 355
revolution, 396–97. *See also* specific
    revolutions; of Stalin, 295
revolutionary divide; class across, 266–75;
    nationality across, 266–75
revolutionary movement; Bloody Sunday
    for, 243; clashes in, 244; energy of, 243;

in judicial system, 216; Marx, K., for,
    221; persecution in, 218
Rice, Condoleezza, 386–87
Riga, Liliana, 226
Right Socialist Revolutionaries, 276
Riurik (prince), 18–19
Riurikid dynasty, 52, 57
Rodzianko, Mikhail, 255–56
Rogger, Hans, 119
Roman Empire, 2–3, 87
Romanov, Michael (Tsar Mikhail
    Alekseevich), 59, 91
Romanov dynasty, 8, 59
Romantic Age, 82
Romanticism, 119
Roosevelt, Franklin Delano, 314
Roosevelt, Priscilla, 114
Roosevelt, Theodore, 240
Rose Revolution, 376
Rossiiskaia imperiia. See Russian Empire
Rostovtsev, Iakov, 188
royalty. *See also* grand prince; of Moscow,
    39; women in, 103
RSDRP. *See* Russian Social Democratic
    Workers' Party
RSFSR. *See* Russian Soviet Federal
    Socialist Republic
rulers; challenges for, 105–6; emperors as,
    2–3; empresses as, 103–4; legitimacy of,
    58n16; of Mongols, 62; mothers of,
    57–58; of Russia, 62; women as, 98–114
Rus. *See also* Russia; evolution of, 17–43;
    history of, 7; lands of, 17–20; map of, *21,
    31;* peoples of, 18–20, 21–23, 25–27;
    religion in, 54–55; Russian Orthodoxy
    in, 54–57; trades in, 17–20, 41
Russia. *See also* Imperial Russia; Moscow;
    Russian Empire; Soviet Union;
    ambitions of, 385; anti-Semitism in, 222;
    autocracy in, 192; Caucasus of, 178–79;
    censorship laws in, 215; challenges of, 8;
    civil rights in, 222; colonizers in,
    200–201; community of, 117; conquests
    for, 166–77; consciousness of, 116–17;
    culture of, 116–21; differentiation in,
    235; education in, 158, 200, 221; ego of,
    341, 398–99; elites in, 13; empires of, 1;
    enemies of, 184; evolution of, 4–8;
    expansion of, 66–67, 166–77, *171;*
    foreign policy of, 384; future of, 181; as

hegemony, 402; history of, 1, 12–13, 15–16, 90; identity of, 117; image of, 159, 161, 386, 394, 402; imperial formations of, 6–16; imperial power in, 1; internal colonization of, 14; language of, 9–10, 202–3; liberation in, 9; literature in, 180; modernity in, 238; as motherland, 256; national character of, 119; nation of, 177–81; as New Israel, 57; opera in, 160; Orthodox Slavs in, 62; patriotism in, 117–18; political parties in, 224–25; radical movement in, 87; rebellions in, 166–77; religion in, 169–70; rulers of, 62; sacrifices for, 217; social class in, 9–11; at war, *150*, 183–85

Russian Civil War, 261, *284;* battle lines of, 277; people of, 285

Russian Empire, 3; building of, 124; demise of, 254; ending of, 5; ethnic groups in, *195;* expansion of, *63*, 134–39; foreigners in, 121–34; geography of, 122; Germany in, 123–24; image of, 75, 87; Jews in, 129; map of, *232;* policies of, 125; population of, 134; social status in, 126–27

The Russian Empire: A Multi-Ethnic History (Kappeler), 13

Russian Federation, 365; as authoritarian, 373; weakness in, 367

Russian Left, 265

Russian Orthodoxy; religious unity of, 60; renewing of, 374; in Rus, 54–57

Russian Revolution, 272, 280

Russian Social Democratic Workers' Party (RSDRP), 221, 246. *See also* Social Democrats.

Russian Soviet Federal Socialist Republic (RSFSR), 298

Russian Soviet Federative Socialist Republic, *232*

Russian-Tatar, agreements of, 66

Russian-Turkish War, 173, *198*

Russia: People and Empire, 1552–1917 (Hosking), 13

Russification; culture of, 199–203; as forced, 290; policies in, 200n30

Russkaia Pravda, 30

Russo-Georgian War, *387*

Russo-Japanese War, *239*

Ruthenians. *See* East Slavic Orthodox

S

Saakashvili, Mikheil, 376, 387, 388, 401

St. Catherine of Alexandria, 98

Sakwa, Richard, 367–68, 377–78

salons, 104

SALT I. *See* Strategic Arms Limitation Treaty

Sanborn, Joshua A., 256–57, 259

satellites, 342

Saunders, David, 143

SDKPiL. *See* Social Democracy of the Kingdom of Poland and Lithuania

Second Great Patriotic War. *See* World War II

Second World War. *See* World War II

Secret Committee. *See* Main Committee

Seeley, John Robert, 264

Sentimentalism, 119

serfs. *See* peasants

Sevastopol Stories (Tolstoy), 184

Shafirov, Peter, 94

Shamil (anti-Russian leader), 172, *173*, 174

Shcherbakov, Aleksandr, 312

Shelest, Petro, 330

Shephard, Jonathan, 23, 29

Shevardnadze, Eduard, 331–32, 349–50, 376

Shishkov, Alexander, 149

Siberia; conquering of, 69–70; conversion of, 70; culture of, 166–67; exiles to, 67, 156–57, 206; industry in, 67–68; natural resources in, 67; protection of, 68; religion in, 70

Siberia and the Exile System (Kennan), 238

Siegelbaum, Lewis H., 230, 302, 304

Silver Age, 245

Simmel, Georg, 85

Singer Sewing Machine Company, *257*

Six-Day War of 1967, 334

Six Wonders of Soviet Life, 347

skifskaia strategiia (Scythian Strategy), 147

Slavic Congress, 196–97

Slavo-Greco-Latin Academy, 93, 104

Slavophiles, 162–63

Slezkine, Yuri, 56, 122, 318, 319

Slocum, John, 166–67

Slovtsov, Peter, 167

Smith, Alison, 126–27

Smith, S. A., 257–58

Smutnoe vremia (Time of Troubles), 52

Sneath, David, 29
Snyder, Timothy, 313
social class; divide of, 267; progress in,
    223; in Russia, 9–11
Social Democracy of the Kingdom of
    Poland and Lithuania (SDKPiL), 221
Social Democrats, 221, 222, 223, 224, 225,
    246, 247, 253, 255, 261, 265, 270, 273,
    276, 278, 287; Bolsheviks, 224, 225;
    Finnish, 221, 273; Georgian, 221, 278,
    287; Mensheviks, 225, 276, 278, 287;
    Georgian, 221, 278, 287; Polish, 221
socialism, 163, 223, 226; collapse of,
    260–61; democracy compared to,
    349–50, 364–65; Gorbachev on,
    349–50; subjectivity of, 326
Socialist Realism, 296
Socialist Revolutionary Party (SRs), 223,
    226, 270
social-political movements, 221–22
society; changes in, 345; contradictions
    of, 243–44; in USSR, 346
Soderstrom, Mark, 167
solar polity, Lieberman on, 29
Solidarity Union, 354
Solovev, Sergei, 177
Sophia Alekseevna (regent, Sovereign
    Lady), 93
Solzhenitsyn, Aleksandr, 339, 369
Sorge, Richard, *248*
soslovnost' (the estate system), 246
South Caucasus, 293. *See also*
    Transcaucasia.
sovetskii chelovek (Soviet person), 10
Sovetskii narod (Soviet People), 10,
    304, 363
Soviet Constitution, 352
Soviet intelligentsia, 161–66, 349
Sovietism, 31
Soviet Man, *305*
Soviet Marxism, 297
Soviet People. *See Sovetskii narod*
Soviet person. *See sovetskii chelovek*
Soviet Russia; allies of, 285; constitution
    of, 282; nationality policies of,
    280–88
Soviet Social System, 308n28
Soviet Union. *See also* Union of Soviet
    Socialist Republics; end of, 11; fall of, 4;
    passport from, *10*

Spasovich, Vladimir, 216–17
Speranskii, Mikhail, 142, 145, 166
Sputnik, 342
SRs. *See* Socialist Revolutionary Party
Stalin, Joseph, 9, 283, *323*; attacks on, 327;
    for consumerism, 318–19; death of, 319,
    322, 329; genocide by, 300; on Great
    Russian Chauvinism, 310; health of, 317;
    Khrushchev on, 339; migration under,
    302; platform of, 288; power of, 301–2;
    revolution of, 295; successors of, 342;
    threats to, 294; transformation by,
    295–96; in World War II, 313
Stalin era, 325–26
Stalinism, 301–2
state; as empire, 77–78; Kievan Rus as, 29,
    31; Muscovy as, 44–45, 47; of Muslims,
    62; for nation, 77; nation compared to,
    149; railroads for, 237; rebuilding of,
    368–76
state of nations, 301–9
Stoler, Anne, 4
Stolypin, Petr, 245, 251
Storch, Heinrich, 87
St. Petersburg, 90
Strategic Arms Limitation Treaty
    (SALT I), 343
Struve, Peter, 264
succession, 91–93; changes in, 36; of Peter
    I, 98–114
Sudebnik (law code), 47–48
Sultan-Galiev, Mirsaid, 293
Sunderland, Willard, 122–23, 237, 285, 336
Suny, Ronald, 12
Supreme Privy Council, 101
Supreme Soviet, 365
Suvorov, Aleksandr, 311
szlachta (nobility), 205

T

Table of Ranks, 91, 95–96
Tale of Bygone Years (The Primary
    Chronicle), 18
The Tale of Bygone Years (The Primary
    Chronicle), 18, 23
Taliban, 344
Tallemant, Paul, 104
Tambiah, S. J., 29

Tatars. *See* Mongols

Tatishchev, Vasilii, 123

taxes; assessment of, 53; for Ivan IV, 48; officials of, 48

Terebenev, Ivan, 150, 151

Tereshchenko, N., 305

Thatcher, Margaret, 348–49

Thyrêt, Isolde, 57

Tiflis, 204

Time of Troubles, 8, 91. *See also Smutnoe vremia;* debate of, 57; religion in, 58

Timofeev, Yermak, 69

Tiutchev, Fedor, 203

Tobolsk, 66

de Tolly, Barclay, 152

Tolstoy, Lev, 184–85, 194, 196

torture chamber, 103

totalitarian model, 323–24

trades; fur as, 19–20, 67–68; gas as, 67; oil as, 67; in Rus, 17–20, 41

tradition; of primogeniture, 22; of *zemskii sobor*, 49

Transcaucasia. *See also* South Caucasus; autonomy of, 278; map of, *278*

Treaty of Brest-Litovsk, *264*, 277

Treaty of Kuchuk-Kainardji, 138

Treaty of Portsmouth, 240

Treaty of San Stefano, 197, 199

Trediakovskii, Vasilii, 104

Trepov, Fedor, 216

Tretiakov, Pavel, 213

Trotsky, Leon, 243, 274–75

Trubetskoi, Ivan, 101

tsar. *See also* emperors; Ivan IV as, 50; Michael Romanov as, 59

tsaritsa, 57. *See also* empresses

Tsar of Kazan. *See* Ivan IV (Ivan the Terrible)

U

Ukraine "Little Russia," 73; and anti-Semitism, 207–209, 219, 222; and emancipation, 188; annexation of, 73; conflicts with, 388–92; cultural influence, 93; famine in, 300; flight to, 54; historical relation to Russia, 7, 20; independence of, 282; language of, 207; Lenin on, 282–83; map of, *391;* national identity, 164, 196, 200, 208, 246–7, 249–52, 261–3, 268–9; prejudice in, 207–8; presidents of, 376; Rada, 273

Ukrainian Brotherhood of Cyril and Methodius, 164

Ukrainian Social Democratic Union, 294

Ukrainian Socialist Revolutionists, 294

Ungern-Sternberg, Roman Feordorovich von, 285

Union of Sovereign States, 359

Union of Soviet Socialist Republics (USSR), 288; alcohol consumption in, 347; assimilation in, 297; breakup of, *360;* civil society in, 348; Cold War in, 317–23; collapse of, 360–61; crime in, 347; culture of, 334–36, 338–39; as defunct, 359–60; deportations and resettlements in, *303;* developments in, 342; empire of, 337–40; employment in, 347; filmmakers in, 336; foreign policy of, 340–44; ideology of, 290; industrialization of, 291; language of, 361–62; leaders of, *345;* living space in, 346; map of, *356, 360;* national identity of, 307; politics of, 324; Putin on, 369–70; Reagan on, 355; republics of, 355; society of, 346; stagnation in, 344–49; success of, 299; tensions in, 307; transformation of, 295–96; vision of, 290; voters of, 361; working class of, 347; in World War II, 296, 312–13

unions, 76

Unofficial Committee, of Alexander I, 141

USSR. *See* Union of Soviet Socialist Republics

Ustav (statute), 166

Ustrialov, Nikolai, 235–36

Uvarov, Sergei, 158

V

Valuev, Petr, 207

Varangians, 18–19. *See also* Rus

Vasilevich, Ivan. *See* Ivan III

Vasilii II (Grand Prince), 55–56

Vasilii III (Grand Prince), 55, 61

velikaia derzhava (Great Power), 11

Velikii kniaz' (Grand Prince), 20

Vereshchagin, Vasilii; art of, 213, *214,* 215; death of, 213, 215; patriotism of, 213

Vernadsky, George, 27–28, 375
Viazemskii, Petr, 179–80
Vietnam, 343
Vilnius (Wilno, Vilno), "White Russia," 73
violence, 52, 62
Vishniak, M. V., 270
Vladimir of Kiev (Grand Prince), 20, 22
Vorontsov, Mikhail, 203
vote; for Jews, 269; for women, 269
Le voyage de l'Isle d'amour (Tallemant), 104

W

Walicki, Andrzjei, 163
war; Alexander I at, 145, 147, 149; Armenia
    at, 277–78; in art, 151–52; Catherine II
    at, 135–37; Communist Party at, 277;
    within family, 32–33, 37; with Germany,
    256; Lenin on, 265–66; patriotism
    during, 149–50; peasants at, 277; Peter I,
    134–35; with Poland, 135–37; poster of,
    312; of religion, 261; Russia at, 150,
    183–85; in Vietnam, 343
war imagery, 239–40
Warsaw Pact, 315, 381
weapons, 342–43
Weber, Max, 17, 376
Weinrich, Max, 207
Western Europe, 15
White House, 366
White Terror, 280
Whittaker, Cynthia Hyla, 118
Wilson, Woodrow, 230
Winter War of 1939-1940, 302
Witte, Sergei, 236–37; of autocracy,
    249–50; memoirs of, 250
wives; of Decembrists, 157; abduction and
    purchasing of, 68; of Vladimir of Kiev, 22
women. See also empresses; mothers;
    tsaritsa; wives; specific women;
    challenges for, 105–6; duty of, 202;
    economy under, 103–4; in radical
    movement, 217; rebellions of, 258; reign
    of, 103–4; rights for, 296; rulers as,
    98–114; as soldiers, 311–12; vote for, 269

Women's Battalion of Death, 275
working class; of USSR, 347; victory of, 347
World War I, 230; causes of, 255; family
    during, 256; impact of, 260; losses of, 266
World War II (Second Great Patriotic
    War), 152; fatalities of, 302, 313;
    on imperialism, 315; sacrifices during,
    317; Stalin in, 313; USSR in, 296, 312–13
Wortman, Richard, 149, 159

X

xenophobia, 199–200, 320

Y

Yalta Conference, 314
Yanukovych, Viktor, 389
Yekelchyk, Serhy, 321, 327
Yeltsin, Boris, 72, 354, 397; intent of, 401;
    leadership of, 357, 357–58, 365–66; as
    president, 366–68; successor of, 369
Yermak (Cossack leader), 66
Yiddish; culture of, 294; language as, 294;
    promotion of, 294
Young Pioneers, 338
Yugoslav Communists, 345

Z

Zarobian, Iakov, 332–33
Zasulich, Vera, 216–17
Zedong, Mao, 342
Zelnik, Reginald, 321
zemlia (land/people), 80, 81
Zemshchina (the Land), 50
zemskii sobor (assembly of the land),
    48–49
zemstva (local councils), 192–94, 207–8,
    218–220, 243, 251, 269, 400
Zhdanov, Mikhail, 317
Zinoviev, Grigorii, 286
Zitser, Ernest, 96–97